Comparative Economic Systems

Comparative Economic Systems

Fourth Edition

Paul R. Gregory
University of Houston

Robert C. Stuart
Rutgers University

HOUGHTON MIFFLIN COMPANY   BOSTON   TORONTO
Dallas   Geneva, Illinois   Palo Alto   Princeton, New Jersey

DEDICATION

To Peter and Elizabeth Gregory
and Floyd and Gladys McCaig

Sponsoring Editor: Denise Clinton
Development Editor: Karla Paschkis
Project Editor: Susan Westendorf
Design Manager: Pat Mahtani
Art Editor: Caroline Ryan
Cover Designer: Mark Caleb
Manufacturing Coordinator: Priscilla J. Bailey
Marketing Manager: Michael Ginley

Cover photo:
JOHNS, Jasper.
Between the Clock and the Bed. (1981)
Encaustic on canvas, three panels, overall 6′⅛″ × 10′⅜″.
Gift of Agnes Gund.
Photograph © 1992 The Museum of Modern Art, New York.

Printed in the U.S.A.

Library of Congress Catalog Card Number 91-71991

ISBN: 0-395-47281-4

BCDEFGHIJ-D-98765432

Contents

Preface

THE FIRST EDITION OF THIS WORK was written in the mid 1970s, a period of stagflation, energy shocks, and general unease concerning the long-run future of market capitalism. Although planned socialist economies were experiencing their own troubles, the problems of capitalism appeared to be the most pressing. The second edition was written in the early 1980s, during the unexpectedly rapid reduction of the rate of inflation and the acceleration of economic growth in the West. The remarkable economic performance of Japan had become a topic of everyday conversation. These situations seemed to highlight the declining economic fortunes of parts of the East. Although talk of meaningful economic reform continued in the East, only the Chinese reform appeared to be yielding real benefits.

The third edition of this text was written in 1988. The mid to late 1980s was an era of conservative economic policy in the West. In virtually all major industrialized capitalist countries, conservative governments had come to power to pursue policies of privatization and to reduce the scope of government. Japan continued to be the envy of the West with its strong currency, rapid growth, low unemployment, and positive trade balances. The "four tigers" of Asia (Taiwan, Singapore, South Korea, and Hong Kong) gained strong footholds in world manufacturing and threatened to one day replace Japan. The major economic story of the late 1980s was the East's decision to attempt serious reform of planned socialism. It was much too early to know whether these attempts, spearheaded by the Soviet General Secretary Gorbachev, would lead to lasting change of the planned socialist economic systems. When we wrote the third edition we needed to wait for subsequent editions to answer this question.

Although much has happened since we prepared the third edition, in a real sense we must still await the outcome of ongoing changes in socialist economies.

The preparation of this fourth edition has been a challenge of major proportions. While all of the traditional problems of writing such a book in the field of comparative economic systems remained, the field itself was (and still is) undergoing change spurred in large part by sudden and dramatic adjustments in the socialist world. In light of these sweeping changes, our text has changed too: the combined descriptive and analytic approach that has been popular from the first edition has been refined and improved. We now divide the text into six parts. In Part I we set up the analytic framework that is applied throughout the text, including a new chapter on issues of transition and reform. In Parts II and III we focus on economic systems in theory and in practice, respectively. Part IV focuses on interrelationships and performance of economic systems. We analyze socialist economies in transition in Part V and in Part VI theorize on future prospects.

In a sense, comparative economic systems has never been as challenging or exciting as it is in this era of transformation. Changes in the socialist world have opened up whole new avenues of research as information that had been hidden became available; at the same time, the Pacific Rim and other areas of the world have gained economic prominence, further enriching the field. In response to these shifts, we have added five new chapters: Chapter 1, Economic Systems in an Era of Change, Chapter 4, Economic Reform: Capitalism and Socialism, Chapter 16, Perestroika: The Soviet Reform Experience, Chapter 17, China: Socialism, Planning, and Development, and Chapter 18, Eastern Europe: Socialism in Transition. And all existing material was extensively revised. We have preserved our analytic framework that helps students define, describe, and compare various economic systems, even during these times of rapid and significant change. We have also expanded the Instructor's Resource Manual, adding and updating chapter introductions, test questions, case studies, and references. We hope the new chapters and new material in this edition convey the scope and excitement of comparative economic systems today.

Throughout the various editions we have relied upon a number of colleagues for helpful comments. We especially wish to thank Frank Holzman of Tufts University, Fred Zapp and Irwin Collier of the University of Houston, Gertrude Schroeder-Greenslade of the University of Virginia, Marvin Jackson of Arizona State University, Roger Morefield of the University of St. Thomas, Jan Svejnar of the University of Pittsburgh, Ira Gang of Rutgers University, and Gary Beling of Princeton University.

In the preparation of the fourth edition, we have also received review comments from a number of referees. We want to thank Gordon Bergsten of Dickinson College, Giulio Gallarotti of Wesleyan University, Leonard Kloft of the Miami University of Ohio, Susan Linz of Michigan State University, Edward Merkel of Troy State University, Roger Morefield of the University of St. Thomas, Michael Murphy of Tufts University, Dominick Perello of the California Polytechnic State University, Richard Pomfret of Simon Fraser University, Ronald Soligo of Rice University, and David Wishart of Wittenberg University. Their efforts have been greatly appreciated. Finally, as the readers of this work will appreciate, it is difficult to write a definitive work as the subject at hand changes on a daily basis. The staff at Houghton Mifflin, and especially Sponsoring Editor Denise Clinton, Development Editor Karla Paschkis, and Project Editor Susan Westendorf, have been most understanding of these circumstances. While accepting responsibility for the outcome, we thank those who helped along the way.

P.R.G.
R.C.S.

Comparative Economic Systems

PART I

ECONOMIC SYSTEMS: ISSUES, DEFINITION, COMPARISONS

1 Economic Systems in an Era of Change

THE FIELD OF COMPARATIVE ECONOMIC SYSTEMS has traditionally focused on comparing various countries that rely on different economic systems or organizational arrangements for the allocation of resources. Interest has centered on how to isolate such systems from other forces that affect the use of resources in order to understand how differences among economic systems influence economic outcomes. The obvious implication has been that some systems or system components might be found to be "better" than others — that is, more effective for achieving such national economic objectives as economic growth and consumer well-being.

It has always been difficult to classify economic systems — and especially to relate the differences among them to variations in performance. However, it has been convenient to think of systems in terms of basic and important characteristics, such as ownership (private or other) and decision-making mechanisms (free market of central plan). Thus we usually visualize a spectrum of systems ranging from market capitalism to centrally planned socialism, with various types of mixed arrangements lying between. Such a characterization has been useful for comparing the Western industrialized market economies with the planned socialist systems of the Soviet Union and Eastern Europe. Although systems change over time, the socialist–capitalist framework of comparison has until recently proved able to accommodate the modest changes taking place in socialist systems. However, since the advent of major political changes in the Soviet Union in 1985, unprecedented systemic changes have been taking place in the USSR and in many of the formerly planned socialist systems of Eastern Europe.

ECONOMIC SYSTEMS IN A NEW ERA

Although the roots of the rapid changes now under way reach back to the 1980s and earlier, the 1990s ushered in a new world order. The dramatic and aston-

3

ishing events of 1990 and 1991 — the ending of the cold war, German reunification, the fall of the communist governments in Eastern Europe, and the failed coup attempt in the Soviet Union — caught most observers off guard. The 1990s promise to be a decade of uncertainty as the new world order unfolds and seeks a new equilibrium. For the analyst of different economic systems, traditional models and approaches must be questioned; they may not be appropriate for tracking change deeper and more rapid than could have been imagined just 10 years ago. Even so, a number of critical issues must be addressed and resolved during the decade of the 1990s. How these major issues are resolved will determine the shape of the next century and the way in which different economic systems contribute to the resolution of critical economic problems.

1. Will the Soviet Union and its former Eastern Europe satellites succeed in transforming themselves into viable economies based on market allocation and non-state ownership? Will the economic decline of this region be reversed and the peoples involved gain access to a standard of living consistent with the resource base?
2. Will the Soviet Union and Eastern Europe become full-fledged members of the world economic community, opening up new product and technology markets for themselves and for their Western partners?
3. Will the Chinese embark on renewed economic and political reforms to rejuvenate their economy after the setbacks to reform that occurred in the late 1980s?
4. Will Western Europe and North America continue to move toward unification of world markets at the expense of national sovereignty? How will the industrialized West accommodate the desire of Eastern Europe to become part of this unification process?
5. Will the developing economies of Latin America, Asia, and Africa begin to make economic progress relative to the more industrialized countries of the world so that prosperity will cease to be limited to a small fraction of the world's population?
6. To what degree and in what ways will the new political and economic arrangements generate economic progress in the face of critical constraints such as energy requirements and the need to curtail environmental decay?

THE COMMUNIST WORLD

The year 1985 marked the starting point for serious change in the communist bloc.[1] In this year, the newly selected general secretary of the Soviet Communist party, President Mikhail Gorbachev, announced his intention to initiate "radical" reform of the Soviet political structure, society, and economy. Up until this point, the Soviet Union had been the most important example of a centrally planned socialist economic system that was experiencing serious problems in economic performance but had limited interest in economic reform. Gorbachev's call for radical reform was initially greeted with considerable skepticism. After all, Gorbachev was an *apparatchik* — a person who rose through the party ranks and therefore could be expected to cling to past goals and methods. Few observers in 1985 could anticipate that five years later, Mikhail Gorbachev would receive the Nobel Peace Prize for his bold reforms, especially those related to Eastern Europe and the field of foreign policy.

As the new Soviet leadership introduced one reform after another, even the most skeptical of observers came to see that real changes were taking place. Thus, in spite of some discrepancies between the rhetoric of reform and the reforms actually instituted, the terms *glasnost, democratization,* and *perestroika* entered the Western vocabulary. They colorfully represent the radical reforms designed to change the economic systems and political arrangements of the Soviet Union and its Eastern European allies. Indeed, the pace of political and social change was rapid. Open criticism of the regime was tolerated; curbs on freedom of speech and of the press were significantly reduced; national and republican parliaments, city councils, and even factory managers were elected. Mass emigration of disaffected Soviet minorities was allowed, foreign travel became easier, religious activities were encouraged, and Marxist–Leninist ideology was disavowed. Most significant from a political and potentially economic perspective, the constitutionally guaranteed "leading role" of the Communist party became the subject of open discussion and debate. Indeed political dominance of the Soviet Union by the Communist party would end in the summer of 1991.

The immediate international consequences of liberalization in the Soviet Union were far-reaching. The lack of Soviet sympathy for conservative communist regimes in Eastern Europe became apparent. Soviet tanks would no longer be used to prop up unpopular dictatorships. Caught in the pincers of liberal reform in the Soviet Union and the attraction of consumer affluence in Western Europe, former communist dictatorships tumbled one after the other. As neighboring communist regimes granted access through their territories, East German citizens fled to West Germany, threatening to depopulate the former German Democratic Republic. The Berlin Wall was opened in November of 1989 and subsequently dismantled. The émigrés' "voting with their feet" became so pronounced that the unpopular regime of Erich Honecker fell in November of 1989, to be replaced by that of Lothar De Maiziere, the last leader of East Germany before full reunification in 1990.

The overthrow of the East German communist regime was followed by a series of mostly bloodless revolutions in Eastern and central Europe. By the end of 1989, the Communist political structure in Czechoslovakia (the Czech and Slovak Federal Republic) was toppled, as Vaclav Havel was elected president and Alexander Dubcek speaker of the parliament. Free popular elections held in 1990 sustained the mandate of Havel and his Civic Reform party. In Bulgaria, the Communist leader Todor Zhivkov was replaced in November of 1989. Finally, in the spring and summer of 1990, elections left a majority of communists in the Bulgarian parliament but resulted in the naming of a new president, Zhelyu Zhelev, a non-communist. In Hungary similar events unfolded. In the fall of 1989, agreement was reached on the creation of a multi-party system and on free elections to be held in 1990. In the spring of 1990, after elections were held, The United Democratic Front (a party in opposition to the reconstituted former Communist party) won, and Jozef Antall became prime minister. Events in Poland had generally anticipated those elsewhere. With the rise of Solidarity to political power in the summer of 1989, Tadeusz Mazowiecki became prime minister and General Wojciech Jaruzelski president. These arrangements were, short-lived, however. In September of 1989, General Jaruzelski announced that he would step down, a move that led to the election of Lech Walesa, who replaced Tadeusz Mazowiecki as the Polish leader. Finally, the despotic dictator of Romania, Nicolae Ceausescu, was executed in a bloody uprising. By the summer of 1990, elections placed Ion Ilies in the position of president, though unrest continues.

The process of political change in Eastern Europe typically followed a two-step pattern. First, the unpopular totalitarian communist regime was replaced by reform-minded communists, who formed coalition governments with non-communists. In this phase, the Communist party's monopoly on political power was broken. In the second stage, a non-communist coalition government was elected on a platform of closer alliance with the West and the establishment of a market economy. *Economic disarray resulting in popular discontent and the withdrawal of Soviet backing were two major forces that led to these developments.*

Events in China were equally dramatic, but they had quite different results. In the early 1980s, the aging Chinese communist leadership seemed determined to open the country to the West and to reform the Chinese planned economic system. The reintroduction of private incentives in agriculture and the initial influx of foreign investment boosted economic growth and brought about substantial improvements in living standards. However, liberalization quickly spilled over into political and social life. When, in the spring of 1989, opposition groups began to demand fundamental changes — an end to the Communist party monopoly, free speech, and democratic elections — the communist regime decided to crack down on the reform movement. This decision culminated in the May 1989 Tiananmen Square massacre, the arrest of leading dissidents, and the introduction of sanctions by Western governments against the Chinese regime.

The Chinese retreat to conservatism was in stark contrast to developments in the Soviet Union and Eastern Europe. Although the process of effecting economic reform in the Soviet Union has proved difficult, in Eastern Europe there was general acceptance of the long-term goals of reform: establishment of a market economy, multi-party elections, and free speech. In China there was instead a marked retrenchment in favor of traditional communist ideals: a slowing of economic reform and a return to dogmatic one-party rule. Little of substance had changed in the China of 1990, and many suggested that only the demise of an aged leadership could revive the prospects for political reform and the resumption of real economic changes.

By the start of the 1990s, conservative communist regimes were to be found only in China, Cuba, and Albania. And in 1990, the Albanian president Ramiz Alia responded to demonstrations with some concessions. Also, the Asian communist countries, Vietnam and North Korea, took preliminary steps toward reform and reconciliation with their archenemies in the West (the United States and South Korea).

From our brief survey of recent events in the formerly socialist world, it is evident that economic change must follow political reform. However, the reforms that have taken place in the Soviet Union and in Eastern Europe have already demonstrated that political and social reform are easier to achieve than fundamental economic reform — that is, moving from a socialist command economy to a market economy. The communist world does not yet know how to dismantle the command economic system, which in many quarters is now derisively labeled the "administrative-command economy." Moreover, although consensus exists that market allocation based on private ownership should be one of the long-term goals of general economic reform, no one appears to know the formula for a successful transition from the administrative-command economy to the market economy. As we have noted, analysts of differing economic systems have tended to think in terms of system models such as market capitalism and centrally planned socialism. Real-world variants and issues of systemic change have been widely discussed, but much less attention has been paid to *transition* from one system to another, and especially to the sorts of policies that might be useful in a period of transition. These are critical issues for the contemporary analyst of different economic systems, because for the most part, political change has already taken place in the countries of Eastern Europe, and economic change (in varying stages) is still in progress. As we shall see, Poland, Hungary, and Czechoslovakia are leading the way in systemic change, and the eastern part of Germany is another fascinating, rather special case. In the Soviet case, fundamental political change has been recent (1991) leaving radical economic reform to be explored at the republic level under new decentralized arrangements.

THE INDUSTRIALIZED WEST

In the past, we have been accustomed to thinking of economic reform or change in socialist systems as center-directed and sporadic, and of change in market systems as decentralized and ongoing. Although change was less dramatic in the industrialized West, change did occur in the 1980s, and remarkable events are slated for the 1990s as well.

With few exceptions, the 1980s witnessed voter repudiation of the more extreme forms of social democracy. The 1980s were dominated by Reaganism in the United States and by Thatcherism in England — both movements designed, at least in theory, to replace the ills of "big government" with the benefits of the market. In Germany, the conservative Christian Democratic party strengthened its hold over German politics at the expense of the waning Social Democratic and Environmentalist (Greens) parties. Western conservatism put into motion policies designed to reduce the role of government in the economy and to shift existing government functions from federal to state and local levels. Tax reductions were used to improve incentives, welfare programs were cut, and privatization was encouraged in Great Britain, Germany, and France. Even Sweden, long a symbol of welfare statism, experienced a voter backlash against excessive social expenditures and high tax rates.

The conservative economic policies that characterized the industrialized West spread into Latin America, Africa, and Asia in the 1980s. In Latin America, programs were initiated to reestablish private enterprise, and experiments with planned socialism were largely aborted. In Asia, the remarkable rise of the "Four Tigers" (Singapore, South Korea, Taiwan, and Hong Kong) demonstrated that formerly poor Asian countries could industrialize rapidly and compete in world manufacturing markets by employing laissez-faire economic policies. The strong economic performance of the Four Tigers contrasted sharply with the continued stagnation of India and Pakistan, countries that continued to pursue economic policies of state interventionism and protection.

The 1980s also revealed the limits to conservative economic policies. United States political experience clearly showed public unwillingness to alter fundamentally the social security system put in place in the 1930s. Moreover, U.S. voters refused to accept pro-growth tax reforms that appeared to benefit the wealthy. And the British experience under Thatcher revealed a general unwillingness to abandon the national health service or to support growth-oriented tax reform that appeared to favor upper-income groups.

The 1980s saw a strong expansion of economic internationalism in the industrialized West. The West European governments agreed to a united European economy that is to become effective in 1992. The United States and Canada agreed to establish a barrier-free North American market. This decisive move toward economic integration has raised the issue of multinationalism versus national sovereignty — a divisive issue that must be resolved in the 1990s. Multinationalism threatens national identity and weakens sovereign control over economic destiny. How much autonomy should supranational European economic organizations enjoy? Should a European central bank be granted the authority to administer a common monetary policy and to issue a common European currency?

The highly publicized political movement toward economic multinationalism has been accompanied by a deeper and more gradual trend, the increased integration of the world economies. The major industrial firms of the West are no longer constrained by national boundaries. In fact, they are no longer national companies; rather, they have become multinational corporations. The IBMs, Siemens, and Sonys of the world are now equally at home in New York, Mexico City, Montreal, London, and Singapore. An oil venture in Indonesia may be carried out by a consortium of British Petroleum, Royal Dutch Shell, and Exxon and may be financed by funds from the Bank of Tokyo and the Deutsche Bank. A slight change in U.S. interest rates can cause billions of dollars to flow from Hong Kong, Zurich, and Toronto to New York. Transactions between Venezuela and Austria are conducted in U.S. dollars. Financial news services in the United States start the day with closing quotes from the Tokyo stock exchange.

THE THIRD WORLD

The fields of comparative economic systems and economic development traditionally share some common ground, although the former overlaps the latter only when both low levels of economic development and differences between systems are encountered in the same case, as presently, for example, in China. When we examine China, our interest focuses primarily on the nature of the system and its influence on resource allocation; we are less concerned with development issues and the well-being of the population per se. After all, even in its most rigid forms, socialism has never been presented as an engine of economic progress for less developed countries (LDCs).

One of the most striking features of the world economy of the 1990s is that prosperity remains limited to a small proportion of the world's population. More than three-quarters of the world's population continues to live in poverty. The average citizen of Asia, Africa, and Latin America remains largely untouched by the industrial–technological revolutions that have created enormous affluence in North America, Western Europe, Australia, and parts of Asia. The twentieth century offers only a few examples of countries that have made the transition from relative poverty to relative affluence: Japan in the 1950s and, in the 1980s, Hong Kong, Singapore, South Korea, and Taiwan.[2]

The challenge of the 1990s is to create — through aid, technical assistance, and enlightened government policy — conditions that will enable more countries to make the transition from relative poverty to relative affluence.

THE CHOICE OF ECONOMIC SYSTEMS

This book is about different economic systems — capitalism, socialism and a variety of mixed arrangements. The economic system under which we live has a profound impact on our daily lives. Under Western capitalism, we can own shares of stock, be private owners of land, start new businesses with minimal government interference, and purchase what we want as long as we can pay the price. We can see our jobs evaporate as business conditions worsen, but we are generally free to take business risks and to reap the rewards if taking these risks pays off. Under traditional Soviet-style socialism, we are not free to own property other than a house, a car, and personal belongings. We are not free to start a business. We work as employees of the state. Our jobs are guaranteed regardless of whether our employer is making the right or wrong business decisions, and regardless of how much effort we expend on the job. Even though we have money in our pockets, we are not able to buy many of the things we want. Unless we occupy a privileged position, we spend much of our time standing in lines, hoping to buy the few products available on the shelves of state stores.

The first full-fledged experiment with planned socialism began in the Soviet Union in the late 1920s, roughly a decade after the October revolution of 1917. After World War II, the Soviet experiment expanded into Eastern Europe,

China, North Korea, and North Vietnam. At the peak of this experiment, about one-third of the world's population lived in countries generally described as centrally planned socialist economic systems dominated by Marxist–Leninist orthodoxy.

The spread of Soviet-style communism stimulated a debate about which economic system, capitalism or socialism, is "better." Viewed in the contemporary context of the decline — and even the collapse — of socialist economic systems and their accompanying communist political systems, the answer to this question appears obvious. But the question of the relative superiority of different economic systems has not always been easy to answer. Moreover, it would be premature to suppose that all characteristics of a socialist economic system will (or should) necessarily disappear.

In the 1930s, the contrast between the depression-ridden West and the efforts of the Soviet Union at superindustrialization cast real doubt on the superiority of capitalism. At this time, the weaknesses of the capitalist system were all too evident, whereas the fundamental flaws of the Soviet economic system were hidden behind a veil of official secrecy and claims of extraordinary successes. The immediate postwar period of the 1950s saw the remarkable economic successes of West Germany and Japan, but the stagnant economic performance of the United States and Great Britain caused some to question the overall vitality of the capitalist system. In contrast, a confident Soviet Union launched the first manned space vehicle and declared its intention to "bury" the West. Few will forget the flamboyant performances of then Soviet leader Nikita Khrushchev as he boasted about Soviet economic performance. Many in the West argued that the question was not *whether* the Soviet Union would overtake the United States as an economic power, but *when* it would happen. The Soviet economy had experienced high rates of economic growth and was expecting them to continue. Yet even Khrushchev warned the Soviet people that in the face of the Soviet ability to build basic industrial capacity, the system might well have "steel blinders" and might lack the ability to adjust and diversify. The era of Leonid Brezhnev revealed to what degree the Soviet economy was, in fact, unable to adjust to change.

The decade of the 1970s was a time of trouble for both East and West. The West was staggered under two oil shocks and two major recessions. The East, on the other hand, sunk into a long-term economic decline. Growth rates of output and productivity slumped, and there was little prospect for a revival of the higher growth rates of the immediate postwar period.

The gap between the economic performance of East and West became more pronounced in the 1980s. The West experienced a sustained recovery from the oil shocks of the 1970s, and the major capitalist power, the United States, began its longest uninterrupted business expansion in 1981. The East, on the other hand, continued its secular decline. In the Soviet Union, this decline came to be called the period of stagnation as it grew evident that the traditional system was incapable of providing improved living standards for an impatient population. Promises that things would be better in the future lost their meaning to people who had made considerable sacrifices from the 1930s through World War II, and even thereafter, in spite of the "thaw" of the Khrushchev years.

Even more troubling, it became increasingly obvious that however one might assess the command economy as a mechanism for building industrial capacity in the early years of industrialization, the system was fundamentally incapable of generating significant growth in productivity. In the face of limits to the growth of inputs, the call for greater reliance on "hidden reserves" proved fruitless. The search for market efficiency became paramount.

The contrast between the economic growth and consumer affluence of the West and the secular stagnation and consumer poverty of the East set into motion the "radical" reform process that installed non-communist regimes in much of Eastern Europe. News publications in both East and West declared the final victory of capitalism over socialism and proclaimed Marxist–Leninist thought an historical dead end. Although these proclamations of victory may be premature, the failure of communism to deliver on its long-term promises has forced formerly communist regimes to explore alternatives both political (democratization) and economic (privatization). In some cases, for example the Soviet Union, political change may fundamentally alter the makeup of the country, as in this case republics have declared their sovereignty.

As we will discover throughout this book, the search for economic alternatives has proved to be a major challenge. The transition to a market economy represents the traversing of largely uncharted waters. Moreover, it represents the challenge of achieving economic efficiency and economic progress combined with an equitable distribution of rewards. There are no simple answers. As economic change occurs in the formerly socialist command economies, we can be sure that it will vary from case to case and that it will generally be slow and painful even where it succeeds.

PROBLEMS OF TRANSITION

The greatest challenge of the 1990s is to chart the successful transition from planned economy to market economy. To date, no planned economy has completed the transition. A consensus has emerged in the East concerning the long-term objectives of the transition: to install market allocation of resources in place of government allocation, to rely primarily on private initiative and profit incentives, and to replace state ownership with forms of private and collective ownership. Some, at least, also hope to preserve key "socialist" objectives in the process: a "fair" distribution of income, a strong social safety net, and low rates of unemployment and inflation. Unfortunately, however, there is little consensus on the appropriate mechanics of the transition — on how to move from planned economy to market economy. Moreover, there is even less consensus on the tolerance of the population for change as the new system is implemented and a new social contract defined.

The key ingredients of the transition are the creation of new property rights, the creation of market institutions, and a reduction in the state's role in allocating resources. How does one move to a market system from the current system, in which the productive assets of society are owned by the state (that is, by no one in particular), most prices are set by the state, and most decisions are made by state officials? Whereas the West went through a century-long evolutionary process in creating the legislative, social, and psychological foundations of a market economy, the East must complete these processes in a short period of time. And in addition to making the appropriate organizational arrangements, it must modernize or disband its inappropriate and in large part outmoded industrial capacity. The cost of such an adjustment will necessarily be high.

Agreement on the long-term goals of the transition does not spell agreement on the appropriate strategy. Should the transition be slow in order to cushion the triple blows of inflation, unemployment, and dislocation? Or would a slow transition make it impossible to break the strangle hold of vested interests, thereby dooming the reform process to failure? What should be done about regional differences, which in some cases, such as that of the Soviet Union, are significant? As this book will explain, both slow and rapid transitions are being tried in the East. To date, the Soviet Union has pursued a gradualist strategy, whereas Poland has tried an abrupt, "cold turkey" approach. Yet many would argue that the Polish case is unique: Its economic reform is to take place in a socioeconomic setting differing sharply from that in, say, the Soviet Union. However, events in the Soviet Union in August and September of 1991 may well speed up the process of economic reform. The failed coup, the end of Communist party dominance and the beginning of new governmental arrangements lends new meaning to declarations of sovereignty by Soviet republics. Economic reform in the Soviet Union will no longer be mainly center-directed, the inevitable result being substantial regional differences and new inter-regional trading arrangements.

Systemic change will also unfold in other important arenas. Hungary, a country with a relatively long history of economic reform, has embarked on serious reform through the abolition of planning, the introduction of macroeconomic stabilization for the transition period, and the beginning of privatization. A similar pattern is unfolding in Czechoslovakia, a country with only limited experience in reform.

Finally, we must not forget that the problems of transition affect the West as well as the East. The West stands to be a major beneficiary of a successful transition. The removal of ideological differences should speed the elimination of political differences. Inclusion of the economies of the East in the world economic community should spur world economic growth. The opening up of the Soviet economy will make the rich natural resources of the Soviet Union available to world technology and markets. What role should the West play in the transition now under way? Should it provide major financial assistance, such as the United States gave Western Europe in its postwar Marshall Plan? Or would our providing of assistance slow reform by reducing the pressure for fundamental change?

SUMMARY

Until the dramatic changes introduced in the Soviet Union in the mid-1980s, there had been limited systemic change in the planned socialist economic systems. Although the decade of the 1990s will witness continuing substantial changes in the formerly planned socialist systems, it will also test the ability of these newly created systems to resolve fundamental economic and social problems. From the perspective of the analyst of economic systems, the most important problem to be addressed in the 1990s is transition of the Soviet-style planned economies to market-oriented economies based on private property rights. The 1990s will also test the willingness of the industrialized economies of the West to sacrifice national economic autonomy in order to achieve multinational economic objectives. The West must also deal with integration of the Eastern economies — as they move from plan to market — into the prevailing world economic order and must decide how best to support the transition process.

As these changes take place, the relative poverty of the Third World remains a problem that defies simple solution yet must be part of the worldwide revitalization of economic systems. Many less developed countries looked to macroeconomic planning as a mechanism of economic growth and development. Now, in a world where such arrangements are being replaced by open-economy market systems, what role the LDCs will play in the new world order is an issue that cannot be ignored.

NOTES

1. The reader should note that countries functioning under a single dominant communist party are, from a political perspective, generally described as communist countries. However, although there is disagreement on how different economic systems ought to be classified, these countries are generally described as having planned socialist systems.
2. Another exception is the oil-rich countries of the Middle East. Their rise to affluence was based on ownership of oil-rich land.

RECOMMENDED READINGS

The World Bank, *World Development Report 1990* (New York: Oxford University Press, 1990).

Robert W. Campbell, *The Socialist Economies in Transition: A Primer on Semi-Reformed Systems* (Bloomington: Indiana University Press, 1991).

Moshe Lewin, *The Gorbachev Phenomenon* (Berkeley: University of California Press, 1991).

Warren Shaw and David Pryce, *World Almanac of the Soviet Union: From 1905 to the Present* (New York: Pharos Books, 1990).

Richard F. Staar, ed., *Yearbook of International Communist Affairs* (Stanford, Calif.: Hoover Institution Press, 1991).

2 | Definition and Classification

THE FIELD OF COMPARATIVE ECONOMIC SYSTEMS is more difficult to characterize than other fields of economics. It has been described as "a field in search of a definition."[1]

Comparative economics is the study of economic problems across comparable economic settings. Comparative economists might, for example, compare the growth rates of industrialized countries or labor force participation rates in developing countries. In either case, the forces influencing the variables are studied in a transnational setting. **Comparative economic systems** is the study of economic outcomes in different economic settings. In comparing economic problems across economic settings, the comparative economist must isolate and measure the impact of the economic system on the observed outcomes. The economic system is an important input to the economic process, along with the conventional inputs — land, labor, and capital. The economic system is assumed to matter in observable and understandable ways.

How might the economic system affect economic outcomes? Economic outcomes are influenced by social, economic, geographic, political, and random forces. The comparative economist must develop methods to understand and control (hold constant) all relevant variables in order to understand the role of the economic system.[2] For example, we know that level of economic development is an important factor in explaining many economic outcomes.[3] We expect an economy with a low per capita income to have a relatively large share of its labor force in agriculture; we expect just the reverse for an economy with a high per capita income. Level of development is a characteristic that can be measured, albeit imperfectly, and its impact on economic outcomes can be determined. But what about less readily measurable factors such as ideology, institutional arrangements, and social, cultural, and historical forces? Although they are not traditional economic inputs, they can be important in accounting for economic outcomes.[4]

Comparative economic systems must deal in a systematic manner with the totality of economic and noneconomic factors, including the economic system, that affect economic outcomes.

ECONOMIC SYSTEMS: DEFINITION

Countries have institutional arrangements termed economic systems, which are used to allocate resources to achieve economic objectives. To the extent to which outcomes differ as economic systems differ, we must isolate the economic system from its setting in any particular country and from other variables that may influence outcomes. Further, we must measure the system's impact, so that observed differences in outcomes can be related to differences in systems. Before we can do either, however, we must have a working definition of an economic system.

Traditional and Modern Approaches to Definition

People seem to know what an economic system is, but there is little agreement about how to describe one in objective terms. The traditional approach devoted little attention to problems of definition and measurement, dealing instead with a number of stylized economic systems — fascism, socialism, capitalism, feudalism. Either the "isms" are not defined at all, or they are defined in terms of one or two key characteristics. For example, socialism is defined in terms of the social ownership of the means of production.

The modern approach defines economic systems in terms of a broad series of characteristics — property ownership, processing and utilization of information, decision-making processes, and behavior rules. The modern approach rejects the notion that an economic system is either "capitalist" or "socialist." Instead, the economic system is determined by a number of characteristics. And these characteristics can be blended, so there is a large variety of possible economic systems, depending on how the characteristics are mixed.

There are two drawbacks to the modern approach. The first is that developing consensus on definitions or descriptions of the characteristics of economic systems is extremely difficult. The second drawback is that people have been brought up on the "isms." After all, the contemporary world has been divided into economic and political blocs known as capitalist, socialist, and communist systems. What ultimately interests people is how well capitalist and socialist economic systems solve the problem of resource allocation. Any approach that relies exclusively on technical characteristics to define economic systems and avoids the communism–capitalism dichotomy is likely to disappoint the student. Moreover, a technical approach tends to neglect the issue of change in economic systems. As J. M. Montias writes,

> Capitalism, communism, socialism, and kindred terms, whatever system traits they may in actuality represent, have a life of their own. They live as symbols or clusters of symbols in the minds of participants in all modern systems . . . , and they may have a profound influence on the way actual systems change or on the reasons why they fail to change.[5]

A Compromise Solution

As Frederic Pryor has noted, "the concept of an 'economic system' is almost impossible to define exactly."[6] However, definition is essential for measurement and comparison. We compromise by dealing with three stylized economic systems — capitalism, market socialism, and centrally planned socialism. Each system is defined within the multidimensional framework of the modern approach. We limit our definitions to modern economic systems. We shall not deal with slave, feudal, and traditional societies or with theoretical variants such as utopian socialism. The emphasis is on the focal point of modern comparative economic systems: capitalism and socialism.

Definition of the Economic System

We adopt the definition of an economic system proposed by Assar Lindbeck.[7] This definition emphasizes the multidimensional nature of an economic system, and it represents a reasonable consensus of current thinking.

Definition An **economic system** is a set of mechanisms and institutions for decision making and for the implementation of decisions concerning production, income, and consumption within a given geographic area.

Broadly speaking, the economic system consists of mechanisms, organizational arrangements, and rules for making and executing decisions about the allocation of scarce resources. An economic system can vary in any of its dimensions, particularly in its structure, its operation, and its adaptability to change through time. As Pryor has written, it "includes all those institutions, organizations, laws and rules, traditions, beliefs, attitudes, values, taboos, and the resulting behavior patterns which directly or indirectly affect economic behavior and outcomes."[8]

Economic systems are **multidimensional,** a feature that can be conveniently formalized in the following manner:

$$ES = f(A_1, A_2, \ldots, A_n) \tag{2.1}$$

As equation 2.1 indicates, an economic system (ES) is defined by its attributes (A_i) or characteristics, where there are n such attributes. An economic system cannot be defined fully in terms of a single characteristic such as property ownership; rather, the full set of characteristics must be known before ES is specified. We shall focus on four general (and often overlapping) attributes $(n = 4)$ that are critical in differentiating economic systems:

1. Organization of decision-making arrangements
2. Mechanisms for the provision of information and for coordination: market and plan
3. Property rights: control and income
4. Mechanisms for setting goals and for inducing people to act: incentives

These four characteristics have been chosen because we expect economic systems to differ within them. They have also been chosen because they affect economic outcomes. We do not list features that are relatively uniform across systems — for example, the organization of production in factory units.

FOUR CHARACTERISTICS OF ECONOMIC SYSTEMS

We shall now examine each of the four characteristics and explain why economic outcomes differ with respect to them. Initially, the characteristics appear to have little in common with ordinary characterizations of economic systems as capitalist or socialist. However, later in this chapter we shall bring together the traditional and modern approaches to formulate working definitions of capitalism and socialism.

The Organization of Decision-Making Arrangements

Nobel laureate Herbert Simon writes that "organization refers to the complex pattern of communications and other relations in a group of human beings."[9] According to Montias, "an organization consists of a set of participants (members) regularly interacting in the process of carrying on one or more activities. . . ."[10] The organization must be allowed to have some turnover in its membership and must be able to change the activities it pursues. It is generally accepted that organized behavior has certain advantages over unorganized behavior. In an organization, goals exist, information is created, and assumptions and attitudes are formed, all of which play a part in the making of decisions.

Organizations typically exhibit a hierarchy in which some individuals issue commands or orders to other members of the organization, who must comply with the orders. One reason for this arrangement is suggested by Armen Alchian and Harold Demsetz.[11] Technology requires members of the organization (say, a firm) to work together in "team production." Because output is produced as a team effort, it is difficult to assess each individual's contribution. There may be a tendency to slacken effort in such a work environment unless someone (a boss) monitors work effort and determines the rewards of individual members.

An economic system is the most complex organization of social science. Economic systems must make decisions concerning the allocation of resources. One way to describe an economic system is in terms of the level at which resource-allocation decisions are made. Economic systems are **decentralized** if decisions are made primarily at low levels in the organization; they are **centralized** if decisions are made primarily at upper levels.[12]

The agents who operate in an economic system are grouped into subunits, or smaller organizations. An enterprise may be a branch of a company that is owned by a conglomerate corporation. A government enterprise may be subordinated to a branch department, which is subordinated to a ministry. The actual allocation of resources takes place in the enterprise, yet the decisions that determine resource allocation may be made either at the enterprise level or above. The resource-allocation decision could be made at the lowest level (at the enterprise), at an intermediate level (the company or the branch department), or at a high level (the conglomerate corporation or the ministry).

Two factors determine at what level resource-allocation decisions are made: the manner in which authority is distributed within the hierarchy and the manner in which the hierarchy utilizes information.

In a perfectly centralized economy, the authority to make decisions rests in a single central command, which issues orders to lower units in the organization. The perfectly decentralized case would be a structure where all decision-making authority rests with the lowest subunits (households and individual firms), independent of superior authorities. Economic systems are characterized as centralized or decentralized on the basis of where the authority to make decisions lies. In the real world, authority is typically spread through various levels in the hierarchy.

The level of decision making also depends on the handling of information. According to Leonid Hurwicz, perfect centralization of information means that a single decision maker possesses all information about all participants, their actions, and their environment.[13] In this context, decentralization implies that such a decision maker possesses less than complete information. In simplest terms, an "informationally decentralized" system is one that generates, processes, and utilizes information at the lowest level in the organization without exchanging information with higher levels in the organization. In a decentralized system, for example, information on prices is exchanged only among the lowest units. Conversely, an "informationally centralized" system involves the generation, processing, and utilization of information by superior agencies and the subsequent transmission of only limited pieces of information to lower subunits.

Identifying levels of decision making in terms of a formal organization chart can be misleading. Figure 2.1 shows why. In column A, there are three levels in the hierarchy. In column B, there are two — resulting, say, from eliminating the intermediate level or from combining the lower and intermediate levels. At first glance, the change from A to B appears to be a move toward the centralization of decision making. The removal of the intermediate organization seems to concentrate decision-making authority at the center. But elimination of the intermediate organization *might* cause authority to devolve to the subunits. Formal organizational changes do not necessarily affect the distribution of authority and the utilization of information. And organization charts may not describe the de facto organization of an economic system.

Market and Plan

The **market** and the **plan** are the two major mechanisms for providing information and for coordinating decisions in economic systems. It is common to identify centralization with plan and decentralization with market, but there is no simple relationship between the level of decision making and the use of market or plan as a coordinating mechanism. In market economies, it is possible to combine considerable concentration of decision-making authority and information in a few large corporations with substantial state involvement, and yet to have no system of planning as such.[14] On the other hand, economies that are characterized as planned can vary substantially: Witness the centralized planning in the Soviet Union, the "indicative" planning system of France, and the combinations of plan and market that exist in other countries. To identify an economy as planned does not necessarily reveal the prevalent coordinating mechanism or, for that matter, the degree of centralization in decision making. Both depend on the *type* of planning mechanism.

The many ways in which the term *planning* is used contribute to the confusion over market and planning as coordinating mechanisms. A **planned economy** is one wherein subunits are coordinated by specific instructions or directives formulated by a superior agency (a planning board) and disseminated through a plan document. The participants are induced to carry out the directives via appropriate incentives or threats, which are designed by the planning authorities. The specifics differ from one case to another. The basic point, however, is that in a planned economy, economic activity is guided by instructions or directives devised by higher units and subsequently transmitted to lower units. Rewards depend on the achievement of plan directives. A planned economy

Figure 2.1 Levels of Decision Making in an Economic System

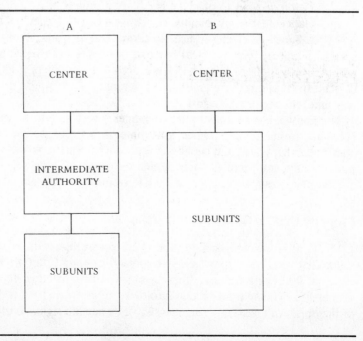

(defined in this sense) and a market economy are mutually exclusive: in the former, resources are allocated in accordance with the instructions of planners, who thereby usurp the role of the market as an allocator of resources.

Indicative planning is a second form of national economic planning. Here the market serves as the principal instrument for resource allocation, but a plan is prepared to guide decision making. An indicative plan is one in which planners seek to project aggregate or sectoral trends and to provide information beyond that normally supplied by the market. An indicative plan is *not* broken down into directives or instructions for individual production units; enterprises are free to apply the information in the indicative plan as they see fit, though indirect means are often used to influence economic activity.

In the case of a market economy, the market — through the forces of supply and demand — provides signals that trigger organizations to make decisions on resource utilization. The market thereby coordinates the activities of decision-making units. Households earn income by providing land, labor, and capital, and with this income they buy the goods that firms supply. Firms and households respond to the market. Other mechanisms for information or coordination are not necessary, and decision-making authority is vested at the lowest level of the economic system.

The ultimate decision makers are different in planned and market economies. In a market economy, the consumer can "vote" in the marketplace and exercise **consumer sovereignty**. If consumer sovereignty prevails, then the basic decision of what to produce is dominated by consumers in the marketplace. In a planned economy, on the other hand, decisions are made by the planners, and hence **planners' preferences** prevail. Where planners' preferences dominate, the basic decision of what to produce is made by planners.

In a planned economy, planners must base their instructions to production units on some social preference function (that is, some known ordering of society's desires). For political reasons or to promote incentives, however, planners may well have to take into account consumers' preferences. It is difficult to envision a pure planners' preference system, where the wishes of the consumer are totally disregarded.

Neither would one expect pure consumer sovereignty to prevail in a market economy. In market economies, governments can exercise considerable influence over what goods and services are produced. Furthermore, factors such as public goods, externalities, and the market power of large concentrated firms abridge the consumer's ability to dictate resource allocation.

Property Rights: Control and Income

J. M. Montias has written that "the word **ownership** refers to an amalgam of rights that individuals may have over objects or claims on objects or services" and that "these rights may affect an object's disposition or its utilization."[15] Ownership rights may be divided into three broad types. First is the **disposition** of the object in question — the transfer of ownership rights to others, as in the selling of a privately owned automobile. Second, ownership may include the right to **utilization**, whereby the owner can use the object in question in a manner deemed appropriate. Third, ownership may imply the **right to use the products and/or services** generated by the object in question.

Ownership rights may be temporary or permanent, and they may well rest with different individuals at any time. The individual who rents an automobile has the right (within regulated limits) to the *utilization* of that automobile, but not to its *disposition*. The owners of a private firm have a claim over the profits of the firm, even though the operation may be significantly circumscribed by government rules and regulations. De jure ownership rights may differ significantly from de facto rights. For example, although members of Soviet collective farms (*kolkhoz*) "own" the assets of the farm in the form of kolkhoz-cooperative property, departing members cannot sell their share of these assets.

Broadly speaking, there are three forms of property ownership — **private, public**, and **collective** (cooperative). Under private ownership, each of the three ownership rights belongs to individuals, whereas under public ownership, these rights belong to the state.

How do differences in ownership rights affect economic outcomes? Consider an economic system in which all three ownership rights belong to individuals. As the owners seek to maximize their lifetime incomes, capital will be disbursed so as to yield the highest rate of return commensurate with the risk involved. If capital is owned by the state, the rules of capital allocation may be different. Greater attention may be paid to long-term social rates of return. Moreover, time preferences may differ according to whether individuals or the state owns the capital. The distribution of income will differ according to state or private ownership: Property income will accrue to private owners in the one case, to the state in the other. Finally, because the allocation of capital ultimately determines the direction of economic activity, the ownership of capital will determine whether allocation is done by private individuals or by the state.

It is clear why property rights are used to characterize economic systems. Traditionally, the classification of economic systems has been in terms of "isms" (capitalism, socialism, feudalism), where the nature of the property rights distinguishes each system. In the Marxian schema (discussed in Chapter 6), changes in the economic system are signaled by changes in ownership of the means of production. Indeed, property ownership patterns are more readily measurable than the other system characteristics, although the impact of the ideology of property rights on economic outcomes is less certain than one might expect.[16]

Incentives

An economic system can also be characterized in terms of the incentives that motivate people. As Frederic Pryor has written, "Goals and incentives are . . . vital links in understanding the transformation of property rights and informational inputs into effective actions."[17]

An incentive mechanism should induce participants at lower levels to fulfill the directives of participants at higher levels. As Montias notes, an effective mechanism must fulfill three conditions.[18] First, the person who is to receive the reward must be able to influence the outcomes for which the reward will be given. Second, the superior (principal) must be able to check on the subordinate (agent) to see whether tasks have been executed properly. Third, the potential rewards must matter to the agent.

In a hierarchy in which superiors issue binding directives to their subordinates, incentives would not be necessary if the principal had perfect information. Armed with perfect information, the principal would automatically know whether the agent was carrying out designated tasks properly. In complex organizations, however, principals typically lack such perfect information. The subordinate knows much more about local circumstances than the superior, and the superior cannot issue perfectly detailed instructions to the subordinate. Because of the imperfect information of the principal, the agent gains local decision-making authority in a number of realms. The principal needs to devise an incentive system that will induce the agent to act in the interests of the superior when the subordinate makes such local decisions. If the principal's incentive system is flawed, the agent will not act in the interest of the superior.

The superior can devise and use either material or moral incentives to motivate the subordinate. Material incentives have typically been dominant in modern economic systems, yet some systems have attempted to emphasize moral rewards. **Material incentives** promote desirable behavior by giving the recipient a greater claim over material goods. **Moral incentives** reward desirable behavior by appealing to the recipient's responsibility to society (or the company) and accordingly raising the recipient's social stature within the community. Moral incentives do not give recipients greater command over material goods. In simpler terms, the difference between material and moral incentives is the difference between giving an outstanding performer a cash bonus and bestowing a medal.

Different justifications for material rewards have been advanced. According to the neoclassical theory of distribution, those who provide inputs to the system (private owners in a market system) are rewarded according to their productivity. Material incentives are a reward for higher productivity. The Marxian explanation of income differentials in a capitalist society is discussed in Chapter 6. A case for material incentives can be made even when capital is not privately owned. Marx argues that material rewards are necessary for socialist societies to progress. When ownership of the means of production becomes public and socialism is attained, differential material rewards should persist, but moral incentives (to build socialism for future generations) will become more important. Eventually, when a stage of material abundance is reached, distribution can be based on the notion "from each according to his ability, to each according to his needs." In the Marxian framework, one would expect material rewards to be gradually replaced by moral incentives.

Comparing Economic Systems:
A Mode of Classification

We have examined the attributes that characterize economic systems. Figure 2.2 summarizes the alternative options available for each attribute. We have selected four criteria for distinguishing among economic systems. Although additional criteria could have been introduced, these four are especially useful. They result in a three-fold classification of economic systems: *capitalism*, *market socialism*, and *planned socialism*. As Figure 2.3 shows, each system is characterized multidimensionally in terms of the four criteria we have established.

- **Capitalism** is characterized by private ownership of the factors of production. Decision making is decentralized and rests with the owners of the factors of production. Their decision making is coordinated by the market mechanism, which provides the necessary information. Material incentives are used to motivate participants.
- **Market socialism** is characterized by public ownership of the factors of production. Decision making is decentralized and is coordinated by the market mechanism. Both material and moral incentives are used to motivate participants.

Figure 2.2 Attributes of Economic Systems

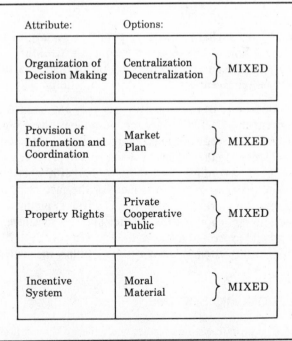

Figure 2.3 The Classification of Economic Systems

	CAPITALISM	MARKET SOCIALISM	PLANNED SOCIALISM
Decision-making Structure	Primarily Decentralized	Primarily Decentralized	Primarily Centralized
Mechanisms for Information and Coordination	Primarily Market	Primarily Market	Primarily Plan
Property Rights	Primarily Private Ownership	State and/or Collective Ownership	Primarily State Ownership
Incentives	Primarily Material	Material and Moral	Material and Moral

- **Planned socialism** is characterized by public ownership of the factors of production. Decision making is centralized and is coordinated by a central plan, which issues binding directives to the system's participants. Both material and moral incentives are used to motivate participants.

These definitions raise as many questions as they answer. They merely state the most important characteristics of economic systems; they do not tell us how and how well each system solves the economic problem of resource allocation. Under capitalism, how do the owners of the factors of production actually allocate their resources, according to what rules, and with what results? Under market socialism, how can public ownership of the factors of production be made compatible with market coordination? In fact, is public ownership ever compatible with market coordination? Under planned socialism, how is information gathered and processed to allocate resources effectively? How is it possible to ensure that the system's participants will follow the center's directives?

SUMMARY: ECONOMIC SYSTEMS

1. Comparative economic systems studies the effect of the economic system on economic outcomes.

2. An economic system makes and implements decisions about production, income, and consumption.
3. Economic systems are multidimensional. The four main characteristics of an economic system are how decision-making arrangements are organized, whether coordination is determined by market or plan, how property rights are organized, and what the incentive system is.
4. Economic systems can be broadly classified as exhibiting capitalism, planned socialism, or market socialism.

NOTES

1. Alexander Eckstein, "Introduction," in Alexander Eckstein, ed., *Comparison of Economic Systems: Theoretical and Methodological Approaches* (Berkeley: University of California Press, 1971), p. 1. On defining the field of comparative economic systems, the reader is also referred to Morris Bornstein, "An Integration," ibid., pp. 339–355; and John Michael Montias, *The Structure of Economic Systems* (New Haven: Yale University Press, 1976).
2. The objectives of an economic system may be formulated in different ways – for example, by a single person (dictator) or on the basis of some democratic process. On the question of social choice, the classic work is Kenneth Arrow, *Social Choice and Individual Values*, 2nd ed. (New York: Wiley, 1963). See also G. M. Heal, *The Theory of Economic Planning* (New York: North Holland, 1973), Ch. 2.
3. For a study that attempts to analyze differences in outcomes in terms of differing levels of economic development, see Hollis Chenery and Moises Syrquin, *Patterns of Development, 1950-1970* (New York: Oxford University Press, 1975).
4. Neoclassical economic theory focuses on land, labor, and capital as the traditional inputs to the production process. Although nontraditional inputs such as organization and management are thought to be important, economists have largely been unsuccessful in measuring their impact. For a discussion of these issues in the context of economic development, see Charles P. Kindleberger and Bruce Herrick, *Economic Development*, 3rd ed. (New York: McGraw-Hill, 1977).
5. Montias, *The Structure of Economic Systems*, p. 8.
6. Frederic Pryor, *Property and Industrial Organization in Communist and Capitalist Nations* (Bloomington: Indiana University Press, 1973), p. 337.
7. See Assar Lindbeck, *The Political Economy of the New Left: An Outsider's View*, 2nd ed. (New York: Harper & Row, 1977), p. 214.
8. Pryor, *Property and Industrial Organization*, p. 337, adapted from T. C. Koopmans and J. M. Montias, "On the Description and Comparison of Economic Systems," in Eckstein, *Comparison of Economic Systems*, pp. 27–78.
9. Herbert A. Simon, *Administrative Behavior*, 2nd ed. (New York: Free Press, 1966), p. xvi.
10. Montias, *The Structure of Economic Systems*, p. 8. For a discussion of the relationship between organization and comparative economics, see Benjamin Ward, "Organization and Comparative Economics: Some Approaches," in Eckstein, *Comparison of Economic Systems*, pp. 103–133.
11. A. A. Alchian and H. Demsetz, "Production, Information, Costs and Economic Organizations," *American Economic Review*, 62 (December 1972), 777–795. For a survey of organizations, see Marcus Alexis and Charles Z. Wilson, *Organizational Decision Making* (Englewood Cliffs, N.J.: Prentice-Hall, 1967), Ch. 1. For a discussion of organizational principles, see Simon, *Administrative Behavior*.
12. This section relies heavily on the pioneering work of Leonid Hurwicz, Thomas Marschak, and others. See, for example, Leonid Hurwicz, "Centralization and Decentralization in Economic Processes," in Eckstein, *Comparison of Economic Systems*, pp. 79–102; Leonid Hurwicz, "Conditions for Economic Efficiency of Centralized and Decentralized Structures," in Gregory Grossman, ed., *Value and Plan* (Berkeley: University of California Press, 1960), pp. 162–183;

and Thomas Marschak, "Centralization and Decentralization in Economic Organizations," *Econometrica*, 27 (1959), 399–430.

13. Hurwicz, "Centralization and Decentralization in Economic Processes," p. 96. For a discussion of various meanings of the concepts of centralization and decentralization, see Pryor, *Property and Industrial Organization*, Ch. 8.

14. A classic case is John Kenneth Galbraith's view of the contemporary American economy. See John Kenneth Galbraith, *Economics and the Public Purpose* (Boston: Houghton Mifflin, 1973).

15. Montias, *The Structure of Economic Systems*, p. 116. For a useful survey of recent literature on the subject of property rights, see Eirik Furubotn and Svetozar Pejovich, "Property Rights and Economic Theory: A Survey of Recent Literature," *Journal of Economic Literature*, 10 (December 1972), 1137–1162. For a discussion of these issues in a comparative context, see Pryor, *Property and Industrial Organization*.

16. For a discussion of ideology as a system determinant, see Alexander Gerschenkron, "Ideology as a System Determinant," and the discussion thereafter in Eckstein, *Comparison of Economic Systems*, pp. 269–299.

17. Pryor, *Property and Industrial Organization*, p. 338.

18. Montias, *The Structure of Economic Systems*, Ch. 13.

RECOMMENDED READINGS

Alexander Eckstein, ed., *Comparison of Economic Systems: Theoretical and Methodological Approaches* (Berkeley: University of California Press, 1971).

H. Stephen Gardner, *Comparative Economic Systems* (New York: Dryden, 1988).

Gregory Grossman, *Economic Systems* (Englewood Cliffs, N.J.: Prentice-Hall, 1967), Chs. 2–3.

Vaclav Holesovsky, *Economic Systems: Analysis and Comparison* (New York: McGraw-Hill, 1977), Ch. 2.

Heinz Kohler, *Comparative Economic Systems* (Glenview, Ill.: Scott, Foresman, 1989).

John Michael Montias, *The Structure of Economic Systems* (New Haven: Yale University Press, 1976).

Egon Neuberger, "Classifying Economic Systems," in Morris Bornstein, ed., *Comparative Economic Systems: Models and Cases*, 4th ed. (Homewood, Ill.: Irwin, 1978).

Egon Neuberger and William J. Duffy, *Comparative Economic Systems: A Decision-Making Approach* (Boston: Allyn and Bacon, 1976).

Svetozar Pejovich, *The Economics of Property Rights: Towards a Theory of Comparative Systems* (Norwell, Mass.: Kluwer Academic Publishers, 1990).

Gary M. Pickersgill and Joyce E. Pickersgill, *Contemporary Economic Systems*, 2nd ed. (New York: West, 1985).

Frederic Pryor, *Property and Industrial Organization in Communist and Capitalist Nations* (Bloomington: Indiana University Press, 1973).

——, *A Guidebook to the Comparative Study of Economic Systems* (Englewood Cliffs, N.J.: Prentice-Hall, 1985).

Martin Schnitzer, *Comparative Economic Systems*, 5th ed. (Cincinnati: South-Western, 1991).

P. J. D. Wiles, *Economic Institutions Compared* (New York: Halsted, 1977).

Andrew Zimbalist and Howard Sherman, *Comparing Economic Systems: A Political–Economic Approach* (New York: Academic, 1984).

"What Is Comparative Economics?" *Comparative Economic Studies*, 31 (Fall 1989), 1–32.

3 Evaluation of Economic Outcomes

CHAPTER 2 CONSIDERED THE NATURE OF AN ECONOMIC SYSTEM and presented several possible definitions. Four major characteristics were used to identify an economic system — the decision-making structure (levels of decision making), mechanisms for information and coordination (market versus plan), property rights (private versus public), and incentives (material versus moral). Finally, a classification scheme was presented whereby economic systems are divided into the categories of capitalism, market socialism, or centrally planned socialism.

This chapter considers how observed economic outcomes, or economic performance, can be systematically related to the economic system. This, after all, is what the comparison of economic systems is all about. We consider methods of comparison; what we mean by economic outcomes or economic performance; and, finally, how we might control for variables apart from the economic system when relating outcomes among systems differences.

METHODS OF COMPARISON: MODELS VERSUS REALITY

Most people have little interest in theoretical models of economic systems. They are, however, interested in the relative economic performance of economic systems. Nevertheless, if we wish to associate economic performance with the economic system, we must understand how the economic system and other factors affect outcomes. For example, suppose we analyze unemployment rates in socialist and capitalist economic systems and discover that unemployment rates are lower in socialist systems. Are we then justified in concluding that the socialist economic system is the main force driving this observed outcome? Clearly, without our knowing the many forces that influence employment patterns, such a conclusion would be premature.

The field of comparative economic systems tends to be structured on two levels: **models** and **reality**.[1] Models, though highly abstract, are useful. They make it possible to compare the theoretical differences among systems, they supply a common terminology, and they provide a "norm" against which actual performance can be judged. But even though theories or models may provide useful predictions about outcomes, which can then be compared with actual results, most observers are more interested in finding out how well a particular system performs in the real world.[2] Our major interest, then, is to compare one real-world system with another. Because no single set of criteria will satisfy all observers, we study the performance of economic systems in terms of a variety of criteria, such as growth, consumer well-being, and inflation.

THE FORCES INFLUENCING ECONOMIC OUTCOMES

Real-world economies do not fit the neat theoretical molds of the pure models. Instead, the real world is populated by **mixed economies**, which combine elements of market and plan, public and private ownership, and material and moral incentives. Furthermore, economic outcomes are also the result of forces beyond the economic system per se — for example, the level of economic development and resource endowment.

The measurement of how closely a particular economy conforms to the theoretical ideal is a complex and, in most cases, insoluble problem. Moreover, in empirical applications it is very difficult, if not impossible, to provide a quantitative measure of the economic system. Thus to study the impact of the economic system on outcomes in empirical applications, we must deal with generalized groupings of capitalist, planned socialist, and market socialist countries.

Another fundamental aspect of the measurement issue must be raised. Let us assume that we are somehow able to measure the system component in an adequate manner, and let us refer to this measure as ES. We are interested in how ES affects economic outcomes, which we denote as O. Yet economic outcomes depend on factors other than the economic system — natural resource endowments, the level of economic development, the size of the economy, labor and capital inputs, random events, and so on. These are termed **environmental factors**[3] and denoted as ENV. Finally, economic outcomes depend on the **policies** that the policy makers in economic systems choose to follow, which we denote as POL. In notational form, we have

$$O = f(\text{ES}, \text{ENV}, \text{POL}) \qquad (3.1)$$

where

> O denotes economic outcomes
> ES denotes the economic system
> ENV denotes environmental factors
> POL denotes policies pursued by the economic system

Equation 3.1 and Figure 3.1 highlight the methodological problem of determining the impact of ES on O — the *ceteris paribus* ("other things being equal") problem. Insofar as outcomes depend on factors in addition to the economic system, one cannot isolate the impact of ES without first controlling for (holding constant) ENV and POL. Let us illustrate this problem with some examples.

Labor productivity (the "outcome") in the Soviet Union has been low relative to that of the United States and industrialized Western Europe.[4] Is this low productivity a consequence of the system of planned socialism, environmental and policy factors, or some combination thereof? This question cannot be easily answered, primarily because the level of economic development of the Soviet Union (as measured, say, by per capita income) lags behind that of the United States and Western Europe, and productivity is positively associated with level of development. Can the Soviet productivity gap be accounted for entirely by environmental factors, or is the economic system itself partially or fully to blame? These issues are central to the problem of evaluating the performance of economic systems.

What do we mean by policy factors, and what is their relationship to the economic system? Let us consider two examples, which illustrate the complexity of the relationship. The tendency of the planned socialist economies to pursue rapid economic growth as a top priority is well known. This choice affects economic outcomes, for the planned socialist economies have adopted a pattern of resource allocation designed to achieve the growth objective. Yet is the priority of growth a policy, or is it inherent to planned socialism? A second example is the tendency of the planned socialist economies to underutilize foreign trade potential (trade aversion). Trade aversion affects economic outcomes through its impact on industrial structure, relative prices, and economic efficiency in general. Again, one must ask whether trade aversion is a policy or is inherent in the planned socialist model?

Figure 3.1 Forces Influencing Economic Outcomes

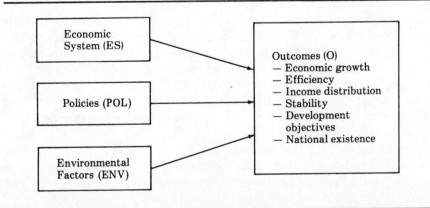

A factor may be appropriately classified as policy if it could be significantly changed without changing the underlying economic system. It must be classified as a direct attribute of the economic system if it cannot conceivably be altered without an alteration of the economic system. Such an approach provides us with some conception of how policy influences and system influences might differ.

Policies tend to be closely intertwined with the economic system. They are nonetheless important to the evaluation of economic systems. In most instances, trade aversion leads to a lower standard of living than would have prevailed had there been international specialization. The standard of living is often used as a performance indicator. Should this weakness be attributed to the economic system or to policies pursued by the economic system?

To understand the impact of the economic system on economic outcomes, one must understand the impacts of all other significant environmental and policy factors. In other fields of economics, the economic system is taken as "given," and one can more easily isolate the effect of changes in particular variable on economic outcomes. The comparative economist must determine the impact both of economic systems and of other factors on economic outcomes. Appendix 3A, at the end of this chapter, discusses the statistical methods for analyzing the effect of the economic system on economic outcomes.

THE EVALUATION OF OUTCOMES: THE SUCCESS CRITERIA PROBLEM

When the outcomes of differing economic systems are compared, we wish to determine which economic system performs "best" in achieving its goals. How are we to evaluate the differing outcomes in order to decide which is "best"? Two crucial problems arise.

First, to evaluate the outcomes of differing economic systems, we must select a set of performance criteria. Because people typically do not agree on the appropriate criteria, the selection tends to be subjective.

Second, even if agreement could be reached on a list of criteria for evaluating outcomes, how will the criteria be added together if (as is quite likely) economic systems yield different results? In such instances, one must somehow add the disparate results together by assigning **weights** for aggregation. This produces a single index of achievement, which can then be compared across systems. Clearly, the weights selected will determine the value of the index of achievement, but they are themselves subjective and depend on the values held by the particular observer.[5]

It is logical to think that the economic system should have as its objective the achievement of a maximal value of the economic outcome (O), subject to the constraints imposed by the economic system (ES), policies (POL), and environmental factors (ENV), which include technology and resource constraints. In notational form, the objective is to

$$\text{Maximize: O}$$
$$\text{Subject to (ES, ENV, POL)} \qquad (3.2)$$

From this, it would seem that evaluating the performance of economic systems would be (theoretically at least) a rather simple matter. After adjusting for differences in environment and policy, one would have only to determine which system achieved the highest economic outcome. If there were agreement on the measurement of outcomes, it would work this way. Instead, the economic outcome (O) is a function of a series of performance indicators:

$$O = \sum_{j=i}^{k} a_j o_j \qquad (3.3)$$

where

o_j = desirable (or undesirable if negative) economic outcomes
a_j = the relative importance of the various outcomes

Consider the following example, in which economic systems designated A and B both generate two outcomes designated 5 and 9. If system A assigns weights of 0.2 and 0.8 to the outcomes 5 and 9, respectively, the weighted sum of the outcomes in this system will be 8.2. At the same time, if system B assigns weights of 0.7 and 0.3 to the outcomes 5 and 9, respectively, then the weighted sum of the outcomes in system B will be 6.2. Although the outcomes are identical, the use of different weights reveals that system A is superior to system B. Thus the selection of weights is crucial.

Just as individuals assign different weights (a_j) to different economic goals, so one would expect economic systems to assign different weights to those goals.[6] Moreover, the evaluation of these goals changes over time. One need only note the changing priority of economic goals in the United States or the fact that capitalist societies attach different weights to the items on a rather similar list of economic goals or objectives.

Equation 3.3 summarizes the crux of the problem. Because different societies assign different subjective weights (a_j) to economic outcomes (o_j), the measurement of economic performance depends not only on o_j but also on a_j, which must remain subjective. For example, one economic system may assign priority to economic growth and allocate resources accordingly. In so doing, it attaches relatively low weights to the other goals. Another economic system may attach a dominant weight to price stability and allocate its resources accordingly. It is likely, in this scenario, that the first system will perform better in terms of the growth objective and that the second system will perform better in terms of price stability. Which system has outperformed the other? The answer depends on one's personal judgment of which goal is more important.

THE DETERMINATION OF SYSTEM PRIORITIES

How are national priorities determined in practice? The involvement of substantial subjective elements does not mean that priorities are not in fact established, although they do change over time partly as a function of change in the economic system itself.[7]

The determination of national priorities differs from system to system. In societies where political power is largely centralized, the prevailing political authority exercises decisive control over the formation of national goals. In the Soviet Union, for example, the Communist partly has historically played a dominant role in goal formation.[8] This does not mean that other forces have no influence, but their roles have been relatively limited. (In socialist societies, where political power is substantially concentrated, the process of modernization itself leads to some pluralization of the society and to the formation of influential interest groups.)[9]

In democratic capitalist societies, establishing priorities is more complicated. This complexity is reflected in the various arrangements through which individuals can express preferences by voting. The vote may indicate a preference among political candidates with differing positions on major national issues, or it may be a "vote" cast in the marketplace indicating what goods and services are desired. However, pressure groups such as trade unions, manufacturers' associations, and professional associations can and do exert substantial influence. Even though majority voting prevails, legislation that advances minority interests may be passed.[10] Also, even in a pluralistic democratic society, as power becomes concentrated (whether in the hands of individuals in the form of wealth or in the hands of lobby groups or corporations), there is a tendency for the goal formation process to change.[11] In a democratic society, the change may take place slowly. In a society where power is centralized, change may be more sudden, though not necessarily revolutionary.

Before we consider the goals that an economic system might pursue, another matter must be raised. If various goals are laudable, why not pursue all of them? Unfortunately, specific goals can often be achieved only by sacrificing other, less important goals. The necessity of choosing to pursue some goals at the expense of others is a consequence of the fundamental scarcity of resources, which prevents every economic system from producing unlimited quantities of goods and services. Instead, choices must be made among goals.

The nature of the tradeoffs is not always clearly defined. Can unemployment in the United States be lowered without increasing inflation? Is sustained economic growth compatible with a cleaner environment? Can the Soviet Union sustain rapid growth of both GNP and military power? The existence of tradeoffs is important in at least two dimensions. First, we cannot assess the performance of economic systems without some insight into the nature of the tradeoff among alternatives that has been made. Second, when one goal must in some degree be sacrificed to achieve another, we should not criticize a system for not achieving a goal that it has, in effect, decided not to pursue.

PERFORMANCE CRITERIA

We have selected a set of performance criteria that can be generally applied to assess economic outcomes. We realize that any such list will omit some criteria (military power, for instance, or environmental quality) that are important to some observers. We shall use the following criteria to evaluate economic outcomes:

1. Economic growth
2. Efficiency
3. Income distribution
4. Stability (cyclical stability, inflation, unemployment)
5. Development objectives
6. Viability of the economic system

In utilizing these six performance criteria, we shall proceed with a three-stage order of development. First, we shall examine each criterion and attempt to assess interrelationships and tradeoffs among them. Second, as we build our stylized models of capitalism and socialism, we shall generate hypotheses about how we expect each system to perform with regard to each criterion. Third, as we later look at real-world economic systems in action, we shall compare their performance in terms of these criteria.

Economic Growth

Probably the most widely used indicator of economic performance is economic growth. **Economic growth** refers to increases in the volume of output that an economy generates over time or to increases in output per capita.[12] We are interested in economic output and its growth because, for a particular economic system at a particular time, the material well-being or welfare of its population can be approximated by the volume of goods and services per capita at its disposal.[13] Changes in the volume of output per capita over time normally bring about changes in the welfare of the population in the same direction. Using this interpretation, we can compare levels of well-being of different systems at any time, or over time, to evaluate the rate at which economic progress is being made.

Because economic growth is so widely employed as a performance indicator, it is useful to spell out some complications. First, severe measurement problems arise in assessing economic growth, especially when different economic systems are compared. These sorts of problems have been discussed at length in specialized literature on economic growth.[14] Second, it is difficult to untangle the causes of differences in economic growth. Such differences may be a consequence of the economic system, but they may also result from environmental and policy factors. The process of economic growth is so complex that it defies easy description; therefore, we can never be sure of the system's impact on growth. For example, economic growth is related to level of development.[15] If one compares the growth of two economic systems over time, when each system begins with a different base, one may expect, *ceteris paribus*, differences in growth performance.

Third, the uncertain link between the growth of output and increases in quality of life should be emphasized. Economic growth is enhanced by capital formation, but to expand the capital stock, saving (refraining from current consumption) is required. It may well be that the savings of the present generation will bear fruit in the form of living standard improvements only for later generations. The decision to postpone present consumption in favor of future consumption must be confronted in any economic system, whether the choice is made primarily by consumer or by planner. The outcome of this decision has an impact on growth performance and on current living standards.

It has been argued that capitalist systems consistently underrate the merits of future consumption and hence save too little to make adequate provision for the future.[16] Thus we anticipate higher savings ratios in socialist systems and, accordingly, a more rapid rate of growth of the capital stock and, *ceteris paribus*, a higher rate of growth of output.

Efficiency

A second measure of system performance is economic efficiency. The concept of **efficiency** refers to the effectiveness with which a system utilizes its available resources (including knowledge) at a particular time (**static efficiency**) or through time (**dynamic efficiency**).[17] Static and dynamic efficiency are interrelated in a complex manner, but both are multidimensional in the sense that they depend on a wide variety of factors.

The concept of efficiency can be conveniently illustrated by the production possibilities schedule shown in Figure 3.2. The initial production possibilities schedule (*AB*) illustrates all feasible combinations of producer and consumer goods that a particular economic system is capable of producing at a particular time by using all available resources at maximal efficiency. The production possibilities schedule shows that, given its existing resources, the system has a menu of production choices open to it. Economic systems must choose where to locate on the schedule. In capitalist societies, the consumer–voter dominates this choice. In planned socialist societies, planners make the decision.

It is worth emphasizing that the labels we have attached to the axes in Figure 3.2 are arbitrary. We could have chosen other goals and could have examined a number of possible tradeoffs among goals. However, the *shape* of the production possibilities frontier is not accidental. The fact that it is a curve convex from the origin illustrates a basic fact of economic life: As one attempts to produce increasing amounts of, say, consumer goods, one has to give up ever larger amounts of producer goods to obtain identical increases in consumer goods. In more technical terms, there is a diminishing marginal rate of technical substitution between the production of consumer goods and the production of producer goods.

The production possibilities schedule is a useful device for illustrating the concept of efficiency. We have already indicated that *AB* represents the capacity of a particular economic system at a particular time. Static efficiency requires an economic system to be operating on its production possibilities frontier — for example, at point *p*. Output combinations beyond *AB* are impossible at that time; combinations inside *AB* are feasible but inefficient. An economic system that has the capacity *AB* but is producing at point *p'* is statically inefficient, because it could move to point *p* and produce *more of both* goods with no increase in available resources.

Dynamic efficiency refers to the ability of an economic system to enhance its capacity to produce goods and services over time without an increase in capital and labor inputs. Dynamic efficiency is indicated by movement of the frontier outward from *AB* to *CD* (without an underlying increase in resources); the distance of this movement indicates the change in efficiency.

Like other indicators of system performance, static and dynamic efficiency are subject to complex measurement problems. The basic approach to measuring static efficiency is to make productivity calculations, as measured by the ratio of the output of an economic system to the inputs available. Dynamic efficiency is measured by changes in this ratio over time.

Figure 3.2 The Production Possibilities Schedule

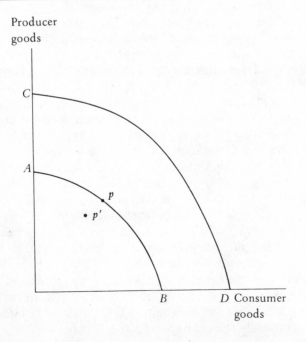

Economic growth and dynamic efficiency are not the same. The output of a system may grow by increasing efficiency (finding better ways of doing things with the same resources) or by expanding the amount of, say, labor but using that labor at a constant rate of effectiveness. The former is often termed **intensive growth**, the latter **extensive growth**.

Income Distribution

How well an economic system distributes income among the participants in the system is the third criterion for assessing economic performance. Technically, income distribution is measured by the well-known Lorenz curve or Gini coefficient, as shown in Figure 3.3. Our ability to measure income distributions does not, however, answer the question of what constitutes good distribution. There may be substantial agreement on the definition of bad income distributions (for example, where 1 percent of the population receives 95 percent of all income); judgments about intermediate cases are more difficult to make.

What constitutes an equitable distribution of income?[18] Equity involves fairness, though what is considered fair differs from case to case and over time. One criterion of fairness might involve reward according to contribution to the production process. In a capitalist society, personal income is determined by the human and physical capital one owns and by their prices as determined by factor markets. Income differences reflect differences in effort (provision of labor services), differences in frugality (provision of capital), inheritance of physical and human capital, luck, and so on. The market distribution of income may be modified by the tax system and the provision of social services. The extent to which government redistributive action is justified on equity grounds is a matter of continuing controversy in capitalist societies. Under socialism, the factors of production are, with the exception of labor, publicly owned. Thus even if Marxian ideology did not dictate that labor be the only productive input, the distribution of incomes would differ under socialism and capitalism. Capital and land are both socially owned in a socialist society; hence, their remuneration belongs to the state, not directly to individuals.

What is the relationship between the efficiency of an economic system and its distribution of income? In particular, to what degree is it possible to lessen income inequality in a capitalist (or even socialist) system without retarding effort, capital inputs, and risk taking? Do steeply progressive taxes (capitalism) or state-dictated wage equality (socialism) limit personal incentives and motivations? This matter is of more than theoretical interest. First, we have already noted that system goals may conflict and that choices must be made. Can social goals — for example, the elimination of poverty — be pursued without impairing efficiency? Second, analyzing different economic systems may provide us with important evidence on the equity–efficiency tradeoff, evidence that is difficult to accumulate from one system alone.

Stability

The fourth criterion by which to assess the performance of economic systems is economic stability. By **stability** we mean the absence of significant fluctuations in growth rates, the maintenance of acceptable rates of unemployment, and the avoidance of excessive inflation. Economic stability is a desirable objective for two reasons. The first is that various segments of the population are damaged by instability. Individuals on fixed incomes are hurt by unanticipated inflation; the poorly trained are hurt by unemployment. Second, cyclical instability can lead to losses of potential output, making the economic system operate inside its production possibilities schedule.

Figure 3.3 Measuring Income Inequality: The Lorenz Curve

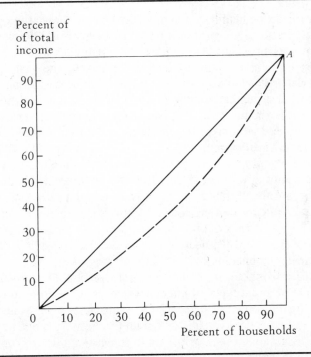

Explanation: Percent of households is measured on the horizontal axis, percent of income on the vertical axis. Perfect equality would be, for example, where 10 percent of households received 10 percent of all income. This would be illustrated by a 45-degree line between the origin (O) and point *A*. Inequality can be illustrated by the dashed line. The further the dashed line bows away from the 45-degree line, the more unequal the distribution of income. In the diagram, for example, the bottom 20 percent of households receive 10 percent of income. A comprehensive measure, known as the *Gini coefficient*, is typically used to measure income inequality. The Gini coefficient is the area between the 45-degree line and the dashed line divided by the entire area under the 45-degree line.

Capitalist economies have historically been subject to fluctuations in the level of economic activity — in other words, to business cycles.[19] In planned socialist economies, aggregate economic activity (including investment) has been more subject to the control of planners. Although cyclical activity could arise in a planned socialist society — for example, through planning errors or transmission through the foreign sector — the economic growth of a socialist society is less likely to suffer cyclical fluctuations than that of a capitalist society (we will elaborate on this hypothesis in Chapter 7).

The matter of stability in economic growth is of practical importance. Potential lost at any particular time is lost forever. A system that, because of cyclical instability, does not reach its potential at various times cannot be expected to achieve its potential rate of growth through time. Thus the matter of cyclical instability, the length and the severity of cycles, and the forms in which they find expression are important indicators of the relative success of economic systems.

Inflation, a second manifestation of instability, may appear in open form as a general rise in the price level, or it may occur in repressed form as lengthening lines for goods and services, regional and sectoral shortages, and the like. In capitalist economies, inflation typically occurs in the first form; in the planned socialist economies (where planners set prices), it has historically manifested itself in repressed form. In any event, excessive inflation is viewed as an undesirable phenomenon; it can distort economic calculation (where relative prices are used as sources of information), cause increased use of barter, and alter the income distribution.

Excessive unemployment is also undesirable. It implies, along with the personal hardships of those unemployed, less than full utilization of a system's resources. It is difficult, however, to measure causal factors and to compare unemployment rates across economic systems, because the planned socialist economies for many years did not maintain records on unemployment (which was said to have been "liquidated"). Moreover, the standard definition of unemployment (the unemployed are those seeking employment but unable to find jobs) leaves room for differences in interpretation. Economists recognize that there are different types of unemployment, ranging from unemployment associated with the normal changing of jobs to chronic, hard-core unemployment.

These definitions, however, fail to account for the more subtle but important concept of **underemployment,** or the employment of individuals on a full-time basis at work in which they utilize their skills at less than their full potential. Underemployment (which may be common in the planned socialist economies) is less visible than unemployment, but it can have a similarly adverse effect on capacity utilization. It typically takes the form of overstaffing, a situation in which ten people are employed for a job that could be accomplished just as well by five.

At first glance, stability appears to be one performance criterion that is unambiguously good because desirable goals need not be sacrificed to attain it. Closer inspection, however, reveals possible tradeoffs. Consider an economy that guarantees employment (underemployment?) to all. What effect will this have on incentives and job performance? Moreover, in such a system, the temptation would exist to keep inefficient firms in operation for the sake of stable employment, and this would have a negative impact on efficiency.

Development Objectives

The performance criteria we have been discussing are familiar to most and uncontroversial to many. Few would argue that economic growth, efficiency, stability, and a "good" distribution of income are unimportant, despite disagreement on the weights that should be assigned to each. But what about development objectives? What are they, and why should they be included as a separate performance criterion?

Most of the world's people live in poverty, and their primary concern is economic development. Although the industrialized nations have tended to assign a rather small weight to the problems of the less developed countries (LDCs), those countries would be most interested in comparing economic systems in a development context. What can be learned from the development paths of capitalist and socialist economic systems that might help LDCs? Does one economic system offer a means to rapid economic development that others do not?

It could be argued that it is redundant to evaluate economic systems according to their success in achieving development objectives: Economic systems that achieve the first four objectives (particularly rapid growth) also achieve development goals. It could also be maintained that the industrialized capitalist systems developed early without conscious development objectives. The planned socialist economies, on the other hand, historically maintained a set of priorities that emphasized rapid economic development ("building socialism") above other goals. It is in this light that one can understand Soviet emphasis on the growth objective. Thus, to some extent, we are up against the success criterion problem, for the planned socialist economies have placed greater emphasis on development goals than their capitalist counterparts.

The planned socialist economies would probably argue that there is a distinction between growth objectives and development objectives, for they have viewed economic development as the growth of particular branches and particular structural changes. This view is shared by some Western economists, who also view development as a combination of economic growth and structural change. The question is: Can one economic system perform "better" in producing the structural changes required for economic development?

Although there is controversy over what causes economic development, statistically the pattern that emerges from nations that have been developing, or are developing, shows a remarkable degree of consistency.[20] The sectoral patterns of development are familiar: The product and labor force shares of industry increase while those of agriculture decline; the urban sector grows proportionally while the rural sector declines proportionally; and so on. When these structural features are examined across systems at a particular time and over time, they reveal a good deal about the development paths followed by a particular economic system. Western authorities have identified a "socialist path" of development in which at given levels of economic development, investment shares are high relative to what one might observe in capitalist systems. There is also a tendency to favor industry over agriculture in investment shares, to promote heavy industry over light industry, to keep agriculture relatively labor-intensive and industry relatively capital-intensive, and to minimize the size (and costs) of the urban sector.[21]

In a planned economy, it has been argued, concentration of power in the hands of the planner facilitates rapid adjustments in the structural features of the economy. In the capitalist economy, on the other hand, those sorts of structural change take place relatively slowly in response to changing market forces. We shall compare systems, therefore, not only in terms of their structural features at given levels of development, but also in terms of the speed with which these features change. In particular, we shall examine the possibility that eventually there will be structural convergence so that, quite apart from structural differences at a certain time (controlling for level of development), structural features will become increasingly similar at increasingly high levels of economic development.

Viability of the Economic System

The ultimate test of an economic system is its long-term viability. The basic premise of Marxian economics is that over the course of history, "superior" economic systems replace "inferior" ones. In the Marxian scheme, capitalism replaces feudalism and then socialism replaces capitalism. Inferior systems are beset by internal contradictions that make it impossible for them to survive over the long term. Marx depicted capitalism as an unstable system suffering from a number of insurmountable internal contradictions. These internal contradictions, he believed, ensured the eventual demise of capitalism and its replacement by the "superior" system of socialism.

Since the beginning of the Soviet experiment with planned socialism (and its eventual expansion to one-third of the world's population), there has been little discussion of the long-term viability of the planned socialist variant. Rather, discussion has focused on the *relative* economic performance of planned socialism. Most experts felt that planned socialism, though inefficient, would be able to muddle along — to survive, but at relatively low levels of efficiency and consumer welfare.

Events of the late 1980s have again highlighted the issue of the long-term viability of planned socialism. Significantly, the goal of the reform movements in the Soviet Union and Eastern Europe is transforming the planned economic system into a market economic system. The rejection of the planned socialist system by the political leadership casts serious doubt on this economic system's ability to deliver an economic performance strong enough to ensure its continued existence.

Among the other performance criteria — economic growth, efficiency, income distribution, stability, and development objectives — the long-term viability of the economic system itself stands out as the dominant test of performance. If an economic system cannot survive, it has clearly proven itself inferior to those systems that can.

It may, however, be premature to declare the demise of the planned socialist system. The move away from planned socialism in the Soviet Union and Eastern Europe may yet be reversed. And planned socialism continues to have appeal in China and in parts of Africa.

SUMMARY: EVALUATION OF ECONOMIC OUTCOMES

1. Many forces in addition to the economic system influence economic outcomes. It is difficult to relate differences in observed outcomes to differences in the economic system as opposed to other factors, such as the resource base.
2. The economic system is an organizational arrangement that influences resource allocation. Comparative economics relates differences in economic systems to observed differences in outcomes.
3. Both the economic system and other factors affect observed outcomes. The other factors are policies and environmental factors. The latter is a catchall term for a variety of influences; one is endowment in natural resources.
4. Two major problems arise in comparing the performance of economic systems: first, how to select the criteria that will be used to make the comparison; second, once the criteria have been selected, how to add them together (select appropriate weights) to come to an unequivocal conclusion about the relative performance of economic systems. The criteria, and the importance attached to them, are subjective, so there are bound to be differences of opinion when system performance is assessed.
5. Five criteria — economic growth, efficiency, income distribution, stability, and development objectives — can be used to measure economic performance. Each performance indicator provides a different perspective on the performance of economic systems. Not all goals can be achieved simultaneously, so it is necessary to make tradeoffs among objectives. Tradeoffs make the evaluation of economic performance difficult, because different economic systems have emphasized different objectives. A sixth criterion is the long-term viability of the economic system.

NOTES

1. For a survey of these issues, see, for example, Morris Bornstein, ed., *Comparative Economic Systems: Models and Cases*, 3rd ed. (Homewood, Ill.: Irwin, 1974), Ch. 1.

2. The use of deductive models is criticized in a recent work by Trevor Buck. Buck argues that the *predictions* derived from utopian models (in particular those of perfect capitalism, central planning, and self-management) are identical. Further, he argues that "empirical evidence cannot test utopian models." For elaboration, see Trevor Buck, *Comparative Industrial Systems* (New York: St. Martin's, 1982), Ch. 1.

3. Here we are following the approach suggested in Tjalling C. Koopmans and John Michael Montias, "On the Description and Comparison of Economic Systems," in Alexander Eckstein, ed., *Comparison of Economic Systems: Theoretical and Methodological Approaches* (Berkeley: University of California Press, 1971), Ch. 2.

4. The reader is referred to Abram Bergson's studies of comparative Soviet-United States factor productivity: Abram Bergson, *The Economics of Soviet Planning* (New Haven: Yale University Press, 1964), Ch. 14; Abram Bergson, *Planning and Productivity Under Soviet Socialism* (New York: Columbia University Press, 1968); and Abram Bergson, "Comparative Productivity," *American Economic Review*, 77 (June 1987), 342–357.

5. For a recent attempt to develop a framework in which to analyze outcomes, see Koopmans and Montias, "On the Description and Comparison of Economic Systems," pp. 27–78; for an earlier survey of the problem, see Bela Balassa, "Success Criteria for Economic Systems," in Morris Bornstein, ed., *Comparative Economic Systems: Models and Cases*, rev. ed. (Homewood, Ill.: Irwin, 1969), pp. 2–18.

6. There is a considerable body of literature on system goals. See, for example, John Michael Montias, *The Structure of Economic Systems* (New Haven: Yale University Press, 1976), Ch. 3; Kenneth Arrow, *Social Choice and Individual Values*, 2nd ed. (New York: Wiley, 1963); G. M. Heal, *The Theory of Economic Planning* (New York: North Holland, 1973), Ch. 2.

7. One of the difficult aspects of goal formation in economic systems is the fact that goals and system structure are not independent of each other. For a discussion of this point see Montias, *The Structure of Economic Systems*.

8. For a detailed treatment, see Leonard Shapiro, *The Communist Party of the Soviet Union* (New York: Random House, 1971); for a brief treatment of the Communist party in relation to the formation of economic policy, see Paul R. Gregory and Robert C. Stuart, *Soviet Economic Structure and Performance*, 4th ed. (New York: HarperCollins, 1990), Ch. 7.

9. The standard work on this question is H. Gordon Skilling and Franklyn Griffiths, eds., *Interest Groups in Soviet Politics* (Princeton, N.J.: Princeton University Press, 1971); for the case argued with regard to industrial managers, see Jeremy R. Azrael, *Managerial Power and Soviet Politics* (Cambridge, Mass.: Harvard University Press, 1966).

10. The literature of modern public choice has reached some disturbing conclusions about the rationality of majority-rule voting procedures in single- and multi-issue settings. See James Buchanan and Gordon Tullock, *The Calculus of Consent* (Ann Arbor: University of Michigan Press, 1962).

11. This is a fairly standard critique of capitalism – namely, that the impact of the consumer is quite limited and, in fact, is replaced over time by the views of powerful lobby groups, large corporations, and so on. This view has been expressed by a number of authors, among them John Kenneth Galbraith, *The New Industrial State* (Boston: Houghton Mifflin, 1967); Assar Lindbeck, *The Political Economy of the New Left: An Outsider's View*, 2nd ed. (New York: Harper & Row, 1977); and Samuel Bowles, David M. Gordon, and Thomas E. Weisskopf, *Beyond the Waste Land: A Democratic Alternative to Economic Decline* (New York: Anchor Press/Doubleday, 1983).

12. For a discussion of economic growth, see, for example, Charles P. Kindleberger and Bruce Herrick, *Economic Development*, 3rd ed. (New York: McGraw-Hill, 1977), Ch. 3; and Philip A. Neher, *Economic Growth and Development: A Mathematical Introduction* (New York: Wiley, 1971).

13. On the technical aspects of measurement, see Abram Bergson, *The Real National Income of Soviet Russia Since 1928* (Cambridge, Mass.: Harvard University Press, 1961), Ch. 3; on the general question of how to measure the well-being of a nation, see Kindleberger and Herrick, *Economic Development*, Ch. 1.

14. The question of cross-country comparisons has been discussed in great detail, especially for the tricky though interesting case of comparisons between the Soviet Union and the United States. For a discussion of some of the major issues, see Robert W. Campbell, N. Mark Earle, Jr., Herbert S. Levine, and Francis W. Dresch, "Methodological Problems Comparing the U.S. and U.S.S.R. Economies," in U.S. Congress, Joint Economic Committee, *Soviet Economic Prospects for the Seventies* (Washington, D.C.: Government Printing Office, 1973), pp. 122–146.

15. For an analysis of growth patterns, see Hollis Chenery and Moises Syrquin, *Patterns of Development, 1950–1970* (London: Oxford University Press, 1975).

16. This is a standard socialist critique of capitalism. See, for example, A. C. Pigou, *Socialism Versus Capitalism* (London: Macmillan, 1960), Ch. 8; for a summary statement of this view, see Heinz Kohler, *Welfare and Planning: An Analysis of Capitalism Versus Socialism* (New York: Wiley, 1966), Ch. 5; for an in-depth treatment, see Maurice Dobb, *Welfare Economics and the Economics of Socialism* (Cambridge, England: Cambridge University Press, 1969).

17. For a discussion of these concepts in the comparative context, see Bergson, *Planning and Productivity Under Soviet Socialism*.

18. For an introductory discussion of income inequality, see Roy Ruffin and Paul Gregory, *Economics* (Glenview, Ill.: Scott, Foresman, 1983), Ch. 22; see also Paul Taubman, *Income Distribution and Redistribution* (Reading, Mass.: Addison-Wesley, 1978).

19. There is a large body of literature pertaining to stability. For an introduction, see Rudigor Dornbusch and Stanley Fischer, *Macroeconomics*, 4th ed. (New York: McGraw-Hill, 1987).

20. See Chenery and Syrquin, *Patterns of Development*.

21. Much of the analysis of socialist development has been from the examples of the Soviet Union and the East European countries. For a summary of this position, see Gregory and Stuart, *Soviet Economic Structure and Performance*, Ch. 12.

RECOMMENDED READINGS

Kenneth Arrow, *Social Change and Individual Values*, 2nd ed. (New York: Wiley, 1963).

Bela Balassa, "Success Criteria for Economic Systems," in Morris Bornstein, ed., *Comparative Economic Systems: Models and Cases*, rev. ed. (Homewood, Ill.: Irwin, 1964).

Trevor Buck, *Comparative Industrial Systems* (New York: St. Martin's, 1982).

Etienne Kirschen and Lucian Morissens, "The Objectives and Instruments of Economic Policy," in Morris Bornstein, ed., *Comparative Economic Systems: Models and Cases*, 4th ed. (Homewood, Ill.: Irwin, 1978).

Assar Lindbeck, *The Political Economy of the New Left: An Outsider's View*, 2nd ed. (New York: Harper & Row, 1977).

John Michael Montias, *The Structure of Economic Systems* (New Haven: Yale University Press, 1976).

APPENDIX 3A: MEASUREMENT OF THE SYSTEM IMPACT

Comparative economics is interested in measuring the impact of the economic system on economic outcomes. In the process, it must sort out the effects of the system from policy and environmental factors. A number of outcomes in the Soviet (socialist) case are said to result from the influence of particular Soviet resource allocation arrangements, such as the downplaying of foreign trade and the lack of consumer goods. However, let us consider for the moment the matter of urbanization. We have chosen urbanization in order to show how to measure the system effect, though, in fact, urbanization patterns in various economic systems are a matter of considerable interest in their own right.

Comparative Urbanization Patterns: System Influences

Analysis of historical data provides a model of the relationship between economic development, as measured by per capita gross national product (GNP) and the proportion of a country's population living in urban areas (URB). This relationship is depicted diagrammatically in Figure 3.4.

Suppose we wish to consider whether urbanization patterns differ systematically between socialist and capitalist systems. The reader might well ask how urbanized the Soviet Union is and how its level of urbanization compares, say, to that of the United States? Data for the late 1980s reveal that, according to existing definitions, about 65 percent of the Soviet population lives in urban centers, whereas the equivalent figure for the United States is about 75 percent. Aside from the critical issue of differences in definition, can we conclude that the Soviet Union is less urbanized than the United States? Such a conclusion may be warranted, yet from Figure 3.4 we know that lower Soviet urbanization should be expected, because the Soviet Union is at a lower level of economic development than the United States. Clearly there are two possible explanations for the patterns we observe. Each is developed in Figure 3.5.

Panel A of Figure 3.5 provides one possible explanation of the observed urbanization pattern: Urbanization patterns are similar in socialist and capitalist economic systems, and differences are accounted for by the simple fact that urbanization *levels* are related to levels of economic development. Because the Soviet Union is at a lower level of economic development than the United

Figure 3.4 Urbanization and Economic Development

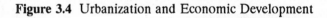

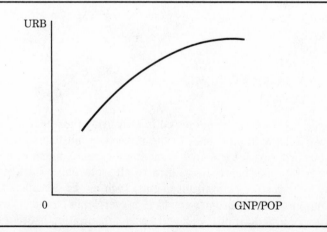

States, the Soviet level of urbanization is also lower. Were the Soviet Union suddenly to achieve the same level of development, the two countries would have the same urbanization rate.

Panel B suggests a different interpretation: Socialist and capitalist urbanization patterns are systematically different. Even when we control for the level of economic development, socialist systems are less urbanized, suggesting that there are characteristic features of socialism — possibly aspects of the economic system or policies — that systematically influence urbanization. To resolve this issue, we need to examine empirical evidence relating to the forces within each system that influence the observed outcomes. Let us consider this question in greater detail.

In Chapter 2, we outlined an approach to the study of differing economic systems. This approach is based on the desirability of isolating the impact of the economic system and assessing that impact (both its direction and its magnitude) on observed outcomes. In notational form, the following approach was suggested:

$$O = f(\text{ES}, \text{ENV}, \text{POL}) \qquad (3\text{A}.1)$$

We argued that outcomes (O) are a function of the economic system (ES), the environment in which the economic system functions (ENV), and, finally, the policy (POL). Can we, in practice, empirically estimate the foregoing relationship for real-world economic systems? Within certain limitations we can in fact estimate this relationship and thus give empirical content to the comparison of economic systems. In this particular case, the outcome (O) is the level of urbanization, measured by the percentage of population living in urban areas; the environmental or controlling factor (ENV) is the level of economic development, measured by per capita gross national product; the economic system (ES) is considered explicitly — in our case it is capitalist or socialist.

Figure 3.5 Urbanization in Different Economic Systems

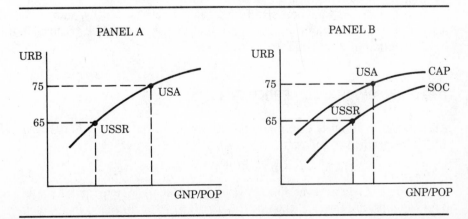

Thus we argue that proxies can be developed for the variables in equation 3A.1 and that the following explicit functional relationship can be posited:

$$URB_i = a + b(GNP/POP)_i + u_i \tag{3A.2}$$

This relationship, which is assumed to have the usual characteristics (a positive relationship between per capita income and urbanization), enables us to examine statistical regularities or irregularities across a number of systems. In practice, there are several ways to estimate equation 3A.2 to give explicit consideration to the economic system. Statistically, our task is to observe a particular relationship (in this case, urbanization) in samples drawn from two populations (capitalist and socialist) and to consider, on the basis of the available statistical evidence, whether the results that we obtain can be assumed to have come from two different populations.

THE FORECASTING APPROACH

Equation 3A.2 can be estimated from data drawn from a sample of capitalist or market systems. Having derived estimates for the parameters of the equation (the constant a and the coefficient b), we then have a simple model from which predictions can be made. Specifically, using sample data on per capita gross national product from capitalist systems, we would use the predictive equation to forecast values for URB_i in socialist systems. The forecast values tell us the expected level of urbanization of each socialist country, assuming that they follow the "normal" capitalist relationship between income and urbanization. We can then compare the actual socialist values of URB_i with those predicted by our equation. Assuming that our predictive equation captures the "normal" capitalist relationship, differences between predicted and actual values of URB_i would tell us whether socialist countries are, relative to capitalist countries, underurbanized, overurbanized, or about the same.

This approach has the distinct advantage of indicating how particular socialist countries behave relative to "normal" patterns. As it stands, however, we have no test of the statistical significance of our results. Finally, should we observe that the deviations are not uniformly positive or negative, some additional criterion of evaluation would be necessary.

THE DUMMY VARIABLE APPROACH

An alternate method is to use dummy variables.[1] In this approach, equation 3A.2 is respecified as follows:

$$URB_i = a + b(GNP/POP)_i + cDUM + u_i \tag{3A.3}$$

We assign the dummy variable the value 1 for socialist systems and the value 0 for capitalist systems, and then we estimate it by using an aggregated sample of socialist and capitalist countries. The statistical importance of the economic system in influencing urbanization levels is assessed by determining the significance and magnitude of the coefficient attached to the dummy variable.

A variant of the dummy variable approach is used to isolate differences in *both* the intercept and the slope, thus providing a better explanation of why the socialist and capitalist patterns differ. Were we to use this variant in our present example, the dummy variable would be defined as before: 1 for socialist systems and 0 for capitalist systems. A second dummy variable would be defined as follows:

$$DUMG = (DUM) (GNP/POP)$$

In this variant, the equation to be tested would be

$$URB_i = a + b(GNP/POP)_i + cDUM + dDUMG + u_i \qquad (3A.4)$$

As before, we would make this estimate by using data from capitalist and socialist systems, and the results would be assessed by examining the magnitude and significance of the coefficients. The c coefficient captures differences between intercepts, and the d coefficient differences between slopes, in the urbanization–income relationship.

THE CHOW TEST

A third method for examining system differences in a relationship such as equation 3A.2 is the Chow test.[2] In this approach, equation 3A.2 is estimated separately, once using capitalist and once socialist sample data. Two sets of parameter estimates exist, one for the socialist, the other for the capitalist sample. The Chow test is used to determine whether the coefficients (for example, the coefficient b in equation 3A.2) are in fact statistically different in the sense that they can be said to come from different populations. If the Chow test shows the parameters to be statistically different, the conclusion is that the economic system acts to render the relationship between per capita income and urbanization different.[3] The empirical evidence on urbanization patterns seems to support the outcome postulated in Panel B of Figure 3A.2.[4] However, although we place considerable emphasis on this sort of analysis in our characterization of different outcomes across economic systems, the analysis presents a number of problems. The modeling of the relationship between systems and outcomes remains simplistic. Moreover, econometric issues such as appropriate specification, along with the usual problems of data availability in the international context, complicate our attempts to analyze these relationships.

NOTES

1. For a discussion of dummy variables, see, for example, Gregory C. Chow, *Econometrics* (New York: McGraw-Hill, 1983), Ch. 2.

2. For a discussion of the Chow test, see Edward J. Kane, *An Introduction to Statistics and Econometrics* (New York: Harper & Row, 1968), p. 341.
3. For a useful comparison of various approaches, see Edward A. Hewett, "Alternative Econometric Approaches for Studying the Link Between Economic Systems and Economic Outcomes," *Journal of Comparative Economics*, 4 (September 1980), 274–294. Also see John Michael Montias, *The Structure of Economic Systems* (New Haven: Yale University Press, 1976), Ch. 5.
4. See Gur Ofer, "Economizing on Urbanization in Socialist Countries: Historical Necessity or Socialist Strategy?" in Alan A. Brown and Egon Neuberger, eds., *Internal Migration: A Comparative Perspective* (New York: Academic, 1977), Ch. 16. For a broader discussion, see Henry W. Morton and Robert C. Stuart, *The Contemporary Soviet City* (Armonk, N.Y.: M. E. Sharpe, 1984).

4 Economic Reform: Capitalism and Socialism

IN CHAPTERS 2 AND 3, WE NOTED THAT ECONOMIC OUTCOMES are broadly influenced by three main forces: the economic system, the environment in which the economic system functions, and economic policies. We also characterized the economic system, or set of mechanisms guiding resource allocation, on four important dimensions: the decision-making structure (centralized versus decentralized decision making), information and coordination mechanisms (market versus plan), property rights (private versus state or collective), and incentives (material versus moral). However, economic systems and their characteristics are not cast in stone. Any or all of the four major system characteristics can be changed. Economic reform offers the opportunity to change one or more of the system characteristics in a minor or a major way. For example, a slight increase in the share of public ownership might be considered a minor change, whereas the movement from plan to market would certainly constitute a major change.

REFORM OF ECONOMIC SYSTEMS

Although economic reform can be observed in both capitalist and socialist economic systems, there has been a tendency to view change in the different economic systems in different ways. In this chapter, as we examine change in both capitalist and socialist systems, the different perspectives will be apparent. Economic reform in capitalist systems is generally **evolutionary** in nature; it is gradual and is to a significant degree introduced on a decentralized basis. Economic reform in socialist systems, however, has typically been **revolutionary** in nature; it is abrupt and is introduced by a central authority (such as a communist party). Although exceptions to this simple classification exist, it is nevertheless useful in examining and understanding economic reform.

Economic systems have experienced economic reforms that have changed their fundamental character. The introduction of command planning and collective agriculture into the Soviet Union in the late 1920s and the subsequent introduction of such arrangements into Eastern Europe and China after World War II are examples of fundamental and rapid changes in economic systems. In these cases, decision-making arrangements were centralized, the market was replaced by the plan, state ownership supplanted the private ownership of property, and moral incentives became increasingly important. The replacement of command planning by worker-managed socialism in Yugoslavia in the 1950s is another important case where fundamental change occurred in an economic system. Finally, in recent times we have the important examples of Eastern Europe and the Soviet Union, where varying degrees of systemic change are still under way. Specifically, an attempt is being made to shift from plan to market allocation, changing all system characteristics in important respects.

If past economic reforms in socialist economic systems can generally be identified as "packages" of change introduced by a central authority, the reforms of capitalist systems are more difficult to characterize. The economic systems of contemporary industrialized countries are clearly different from those that prevailed in these countries, say, 100 years ago. And there have been truly fundamental changes, such as those that took place in the movement from feudalism to capitalism. Yet these changes occurred rather gradually, and the lack of clear milestones makes it difficult to attach specific dates to the transition. When resources are allocated through markets, changes in allocation procedures are less visible than they are when a central authority makes sweeping changes by fiat. At the same time, contemporary economic history provides us with examples where specific changes have been envisioned in capitalist economic systems. Examples include privatization during the Thatcher years in Great Britain and, in the United States, the Full Employment Act of 1946 and major programs associated with particular U.S. presidents, such as the Great Society of Lyndon Johnson.

Thus far we have identified economic reform as change in the identifying characteristics of an economic system and have noted that it occurs, though in varying ways, in both capitalist and socialist economic systems. Unfortunately, it is overly simplistic to assume that a reform program, once developed, will in fact be implemented. How is the implementation of economic reform to be assessed and measured?

Measuring the implementation of economic reform is a complex task. For one thing, economic reform is generally introduced in an effort to alter economic outcomes through changes in system characteristics. Should we judge the implementation of reform by looking at outcomes, or should we look directly at the changes made in the characteristics of the system? If neither outcomes nor characteristics change, do we consider the reform to have been a failure, or do we consider it to have been something less than a full-blown economic reform?

Furthermore, how are basic measurement problems to be handled? For example, if a reform program is intended to change several system components but in fact does not do so, how do we weigh the components and the changes made in them to assess the extent of fulfillment achieved?

The problems of measuring the implementation of reform are not unique to any particular economic system. Many would argue that Soviet economic reforms of the pre-Gorbachev era (for example, the Kosygin reforms of the 1960s) failed. Most changes in capitalist economic systems evoke controversy, and it is often difficult to assess the effectiveness of changes implemented in the name of reform. Moreover, reforms may fail for a variety of reasons. Let us look more closely at these issues.

First, we have already noted that isolating changes in system characteristics from changes in economic outcomes is difficult. Moreover, if we look at changes in outcomes (clearly a desired impact of economic reforms), how can we be sure that the new outcomes were not in fact a result of forces other than systemic changes? Soviet authors typically argued that the Kosygin reforms of 1965 *were* in fact being implemented, because Soviet surveys of enterprise managers indicated changes in managerial decision-making rules. However (and over and above the problem of inadequate empirical evidence on reform implementation), Western observers generally argued that the reforms were *not* being implemented. In addition, Soviet economic performance showed no improvement into the 1970s.

Second, some reforms fail because they were ill-conceived or were only partially implemented. For example, one of the objectives of privatization in Eastern Europe is the decentralization of decision making from planners to the enterprise level. But economists frequently note that with a high degree of industrial concentration, the outcomes of privatization may be rather different from those the reformers anticipated. Thus, although reformers seek the benefits of a competitive market mechanism, in fact the basic industrial structure may result in monopoly and in all the ills associated with it. To take another example, if prices are to replace plan rules for decision-making purposes, these prices must be meaningful in the sense of reflecting relative scarcities. Price reform must accompany changes in decision-making procedures.

Third, as we emphasized earlier, it is often difficult in practice to isolate policy changes from system changes. Yet it is likely that the nonharmonious development and implementation of reform measures and policy changes may lead to the failure of reform. Thus a policy change may be implemented, but the necessary systemic changes may not be implemented, resulting in an ineffective policy change.

Finally, as we examine the progress of economic reform, it will become evident that how we should assess the extent of change depends to a great extent on the nature of the reform we are observing and on whether, in fact, the changes are systemic or simply policy adjustments. For instance, as we examine developments in the countries of Eastern Europe, we will observe that it is easier to follow the results of changes in macroeconomic policies (for example, stabilization policies and exchange rate policies) than to assess the impact of systemic or organizational changes implemented to boost enterprise efficiency. It is easier to examine the progress of inflation than to examine changes in efficiency. The former is conceptually simpler than the latter, and reasonable data are more likely to be available. Moreover, the time frame of change may well be different. We might expect minimal lags in the implementation of a policy change designed to curb inflation, but much greater lags in the implementation of a systemic change designed to increase efficiency.

Having examined the general context of economic reform, we shall now consider reform in capitalist and socialist economic systems, respectively. This approach reflects our conviction that the development, implementation, and measurement of reform differ in these differing economic systems.

CHANGE IN CAPITALIST ECONOMIES

Many scholars have tried to create a framework useful in characterizing the nature of change in capitalist economic systems. Possibly the most famous attempt was that made by Karl Marx (see Chapter 6). From a contemporary perspective, however, Marxian principles may be inappropriate to the task at hand. Although a large body of literature has been generated in numerous efforts to assess the accuracy of Marx's predictions about economic systems, scholars do not agree on how accurate his major predictions have been. Moreover, the dominant theme of Marx's work was not modifications designed to change the nature of capitalist systems, but rather more general issues of system transition — in particular, the movement from capitalism to socialism.

In the absence of a general theory of system change, we shall examine important real-world attempts at reform but shall avoid discussing the details of changes in specific countries. We proceed by examining changes in the four basic system components outlined in Chapters 2 and 3.

Property Rights: Private versus Public

The ownership of property is a fundamental distinguishing characteristic of different economic systems, and it is a characteristic that can be measured, albeit imperfectly. Significant changes in the shares of public and private ownership of property can fundamentally alter the nature of a capitalist economic system. Indeed, if the state owned a major share of existing property, we would no longer classify the system as capitalist.

Real-world capitalist systems are mixed, some having higher shares of public ownership than others. Privatization occurs when property that had previously been publicly owned is sold to private owners. Public ownership increases when property that had previously been privately owned becomes publicly owned, or **nationalized**. The shares of public and private ownership can be changed either by government spending programs that create new government-owned capital (such as the U.S. federal government's Tennessee Valley Authority project initiated during the Great Depression) or by direct government buying or selling of existing facilities. By selling its shares of British Air, for example, the British government increased the share of private ownership in the United Kingdom.

And by buying a failing steel company, the British government increases the share of public ownership.

Public sentiment in favor of public ownership was highest in the United States during the Great Depression. In the United Kingdom, the election of labor governments in the 1940s and 1950s showed political support for nationalization, whereas the lengthy tenure of a conservative government from the late 1970s to the early 1990s showed support for privatization. Alternating socialist and conservative governments in France also reflect rising and falling sentiment for privatization and nationalization. In West Germany, both socialist and conservative governments have consistently favored privatization since the end of the Second World War. The German government has sold its shares of major corporations to private owners throughout the postwar era.

The figures cited in Chapter 9 for the United States show that government shares of structures and land have not changed noticeably since the early 1930s, nor has the share of output produced by government enterprises. After a rise in public ownership in the early 1930s, the share of government ownership has remained fairly stable, despite a substantial increase in output shares consumed by government.

Table 4.1 shows the government shares of fixed capital in 1955, 1980, and 1987 in seven industrialized capitalist countries (including Greece). It should be emphasized that the wide differences in ownership shares are partially the result of different accounting procedures, but even so, substantial changes in government ownership shares within each country cannot be observed from these figures. In some countries, government ownership shares have fallen (Canada and Greece). In others, they have risen (United Kingdom and Sweden). In the majority of countries, government shares of capital have been stable over

Table 4.1 Share of Government Ownership of Fixed Capital, Capitalist Countries (percentages of total)

	1955	1980	1987
Canada	22	24	23
Finland	–	16	16
France	16	17	–
Greece	3	1	–
Sweden	4	7	–
United Kingdom	11	14	–
West Germany	7	8	8
Unweighted average	11.2	9.9	–

Source: OECD, *Flows and Stocks of Fixed Capital, 1955–1980* (Paris: OECD, 1983); OECD, *Flows and Stocks of Fixed Capital, 1962–1987* (Paris, OECD, 1989).

the 25-year period. In France, West Germany, and Finland, government ownership shares either were unchanged or changed only slightly.

Table 4.1 reveals that overall there has been little change in private and
public ownership shares in capitalist countries, suggesting that these countries
have reached a basic consensus on the distribution of public and private ownership. Changes in governments over the years have not notably altered this
consensus, although the reader should be aware that measuring the importance
of government ownership is difficult in any economy.

The conservative governments elected in the United States and Western
Europe in the 1980s brought a rising tide of privatization. It is difficult to tell
whether this trend will continue long enough to fundamentally change the
shares of private and public ownership in the industrialized capitalist countries,
but in view of the long-term stability of ownership shares, this outcome seems
unlikely.

Decision-Making Arrangements:
Trends in Competition

Changes in the extent of competition alter the nature and operation of a capitalist economy, but they do not result in the system's ceasing to be capitalist.
A capitalist economy in which monopoly is the prevalent form may operate
inefficiently and may cause consumers to pay high prices, but it is still a capitalist economy.

The degree of competitiveness in a capitalist economy is affected by antitrust
laws, regulations, trade policies, and court interpretations of antitrust policy.
it is extremely difficult to generalize about trends in state policy toward competition. The best-documented trend is the postwar relaxation of international
trade barriers. The industrialized capitalist countries have created international
arrangements for dismantling the restrictive trade barriers that were put in
place during the Great Depression, and there is little doubt that the degree of
international competition has expanded at a rapid rate throughout the postwar
period. Trade barriers have been lowered in both product markets and factor
markets (see Figure 4.1). In the 1990s, one can speak of a world capital market
in which financial capital flows freely and quickly among Europe, North America, and the industrialized Asian countries.

The amount of deregulation is another visible indicator of state policy
toward competition. When a potentially competitive industry is regulated by the
state (which often results in anticompetitive behavior), the degree of competition is reduced. The trend toward deregulation started in the United States in
the late 1970s, and it spread from North America to Western Europe and
Japan in the 1980s. Deregulation has been most prominent in transportation,
communications, and banking, but it remains to be seen whether other capitalist countries will deregulate to the extent of the United States and whether the
deregulation experiment will continue in the United States through the 1990s.

The least visible aspect of state competition policy — and the most difficult
to characterize — is antitrust policy and the mechanisms designed to implement

these policies. Most industrialized capitalist countries allow more exemptions from antitrust laws than does the United States, which exempts primarily farming operations and labor unions; however, antitrust laws that prevent abuse of monopoly power exist in nearly every advanced capitalist country. Unlike the U.S. laws, which declare all formal price-fixing agreements illegal, other industrialized capitalist countries judge price-fixing arrangements on the basis of whether they result in reasonable prices. If they do, they are not illegal per se.

In the United States, there have been few major changes in antitrust legislation since the 1930s. The changes that have occurred have taken place in the courts. Initially, the courts interpreted the antitrust laws as outlawing anticompetitive behavior, but in the early 1950s, antitrust laws were interpreted as outlawing monopoly power per se, whether this power was abused or not. The 1970s and 1980s have seen a move toward a more liberal interpretation of antitrust laws, stemming from the recognition that businesses must compete in international markets against close substitutes and that antitrust laws should not be used to penalize competitive successes.

Growing international competition and deregulation should increase the degree of competition in capitalist countries. Moreover, rapid technological progress produces a wider variety of competitive products and promotes com-

Figure 4.1 Average U.S. Import Duties, 1900–1990

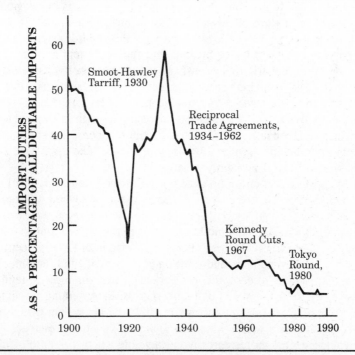

Sources: *Historical Statistics of the United States; Statistical Abstract of the United States.*

petition. William Shepherd has attempted to measure the changing degree of competition in the U.S. economy. He concludes that the American economy became more competitive after 1960 as a consequence of growing international competition and deregulation.[1] According to Shepherd, the share of the U.S. economy that was effectively competitive remained fairly stable at 52–54 percent between 1939 and 1958 but rose to 77 percent by 1980. Similar studies have not been conducted for the other industrialized capitalist countries, so we do not know whether the American experience is representative. However, because virtually all industrialized capitalist countries have been subject to growing international competition, and because, according to Shepherd, growing international competition has stimulated increased competition in the U.S. economy, the impact of this development may be equally strong in other capitalist countries.

Incentives:
Income Redistribution Under Capitalism

Capitalism uses material incentives to motivate economic behavior, and a move away from material incentives would signal a fundamental change in the capitalist economic system. If a capitalist state altered the distribution of income earned in factor markets, participants' earnings in factor markets would become less decisive in determining their command over resources. For example, if the tax system equalized the distribution of income after taxes, material rewards would cease to guide economic decision making. Changes in tax policy can indeed change the nature of the capitalist economic system.

For a tax system to have a large impact on the reward system, taxes must make up a large share of factor income, and the tax system must redistribute income. Income is redistributed via either a **progressive tax** (which redistributes proportionally away from high-income earners) or a **regressive tax** (which redistributes proportionally away from low-income earners). In other words, in a progressive tax system, the tax's share of income rises with income; in a regressive system, that share falls. In order to redistribute income in a substantial way away from high-income earners, the tax system must take up a large share of factor income and must be highly progressive.

Table 4.2 gives information on changes in the tax system's shares of income in 1960 and 1985 and in the shares of income taken by several different taxes. The table shows that in all the capitalist countries surveyed, taxes rose as a percentage of GNP. The most modest rise was in the United States — from 27 to 29 percent; the largest rise was in Sweden — from 28 to 49 percent.

The shares of income taxes and taxes on goods provide indirect information on the redistributive role of the tax system. Taxes on income tend to be progressive, whereas taxes on goods are regressive. Assuming no significant changes in income tax rates by income bracket, the tax system would become more progressive as a whole when the share of income taxes rose. The tax system would become more regressive as a whole when the share of taxes on

Table 4.2 Changes in the Capitalist Tax System

	Taxes as a Percentage of GNP			Share of Total Taxes						Social Security Transfers as Percentage of GDP		
				Income Taxes[b]			Taxes on Goods					
	1960	1980[a]	1987[a]	1970	1985	1987	1970	1985	1987	1960	1981	1988
United States	27	29	30	48	42	44	19	18	17	5.0	11.1	10.6
Canada	24	32	34	45	43	47	32	33	29	7.9	9.9	12.0
France	32	42	45	18	18	18	38	29	29	13.5	20.3	21.7
Italy	27	30	36	17	36	36	38	26	26	9.8	5.7	17.3
Japan	20	25	30	41	46	47	22	15	13	3.8	10.6	11.8
Sweden	28	49	57	54	42	41	29	25	24	8.0	18.2	15.1[c]
United Kingdom	28	35	37	40	38	37	29	31	31	6.8	12.9	16.0
West Germany	30	38	38	32	33	34	32	27	25	12.0	17.2	–

[a] percentage of GDP
[b] individual and corporate
[c] 1987

Sources: *Statistical Abstract of the United States* (international comparisons); OECD, *Historical Statistics* (Paris: OECD, 1990).

goods rose. Table 4.2 reveals a mixed picture. In five of the countries, the income tax share of total taxes remained stable or fell. In the other three countries, the income tax share rose. In only two countries (Italy's rising share and Sweden's falling share) were the changes substantial. The table also shows a generally declining reliance on taxes on goods. The share of taxes on goods fell substantially in France, Italy, and Japan. Only Canada and the United Kingdom recorded small increases in the share of taxes on goods.

Not having readily available information on income tax rates, we can draw only cautious conclusions about these data in Table 4.2. There has been a substantial increase in the share of taxes of factor income in the industrialized capitalist countries, but there has not been a substantial shift in the form of taxation. Although there has been a slight drift away from taxes on goods and toward taxes on income (which should increase the progressivity of the tax system), these changes have been relatively minor, except in Italy. The overall conclusion is that the redistributive role of the tax system has not changed much in capitalist economies, even though the share of taxes has been rising.

What have capitalist governments done with the increasing tax share of GNP? The last columns show the dramatic rises in the shares of social security transfers as a percentage of GNP. The effect of social security transfers on economic rewards depends on how these transfers are distributed. If they are distributed according to contributions, they do not alter the factor distribution of income. If they are distributed in a manner unrelated to contributions (such as in poverty programs), they do alter the distribution of income.

The evidence that has been collected for the United States shows that, although the tax system does not materially alter the distribution of income, the distribution of transfers does.[2] The major instrument of state income redistribution in the United States is the distribution of transfer payments to low-income recipients. The growing GNP share of social security transfers suggests that a significant alteration in material rewards may have occurred in capitalist economic systems through the distribution of social security transfers to the less advantaged.

Profit Sharing and Worker Participation   A basic characteristic of capitalism is that the owners of capital (individual proprietors, partners, or corporate shareholders) are rewarded out of profits. Workers are paid wages that do not vary directly with profits. Capitalism can change its character by sharing profits with workers. Such a change would require new incentive arrangements.

Because profits fluctuate more than wage income, the owners of capital are, in effect, making a deal with workers that as long as the business remains solvent, workers will receive their contracted wages. Owners of capital, who bear risk in the form of fluctuating returns on capital, earn a return to reward them for risk taking. The worker accepts a nonfluctuating wage and, in return, is prepared to follow the directions of management.

The fundamental nature of the relationship between worker and owner of capital can be altered by profit sharing. If rewards to workers depend in part on the profits of the business, the worker becomes a partial capitalist and bears a part of the risk of fluctuating profits. If workers' incomes depend entirely on the profits of the enterprise, then they basically become capitalists.

The advantages of a profit-sharing economy are that workers are more materially interested in the profitability of the enterprise. They will be more inclined to work in the interests of the enterprise than before, and they will be less inclined to shirk work. A profit-sharing economy has another advantage: If workers' pay rises and falls with profits, the economy becomes more flexible. Recessions cause wages to drop, and falling wages stimulate employment.

The notion of profit sharing is not new, but it has gained increasing attention in capitalist economies because of the large-scale use of profit sharing in postwar Japan.[3] In Japan, worker bonuses average about one-quarter of annual earnings, and they are paid out of profits. Although the relationship between profits and worker bonuses is not clear-cut, Japanese workers certainly benefit from higher profits in the form of higher year-end bonuses.

Information Mechanisms: Market Versus Plan

A major characteristic of capitalist economic systems is their reliance on the market mechanism to provide information for decision makers. At the same time, there is much debate over the extent to which various failures of the market mechanism might be reduced or eliminated by state intervention in market capitalist economic systems. This intervention can take a variety of forms and, for each form, can vary in intensity.

An important change in the policy sphere has been widespread acceptance of the notion that government is responsible for macroeconomic stability. This change — that is, the general implementation of Keynesian economic thinking — has taken place in the period since World War II, especially in the 1960s and thereafter. Capitalist governments use different tools in both fiscal and monetary spheres to pursue stabilization, but most do perceive stabilization as a critical function of the state. Moreover, it is important to emphasize that even though stabilization is in significant part a matter of policy, such policies frequently require important systemic changes. Most capitalist systems have put in place a variety of monetary and fiscal mechanisms designed to implement stabilization policies. Although the role of the state in macroeconomic stabilization remains a subject of discussion and controversy, capitalist countries have generally experienced greater macroeconomic stability in the second half of the twentieth century (despite major energy shocks in the 1970s) than in the first half of the twentieth century or in the nineteenth century. Business cycles have become less severe.

A rather different sort of change in capitalist systems is represented by the introduction of some sort of planning mechanism — and thus a reduction in reliance on the market mechanism. In this dimension, there are important differences among real-world capitalist systems, though the magnitude of these differences is often hard to measure.

For example, as we look at specific capitalist systems later in this book, interesting contrasts will emerge. Great Britain, a country known for the important role government plays in its market economy, has had very limited practical experience with national economic planning. France, on the other hand, is well known for its application of **indicative planning**, an approach to planning designed to achieve certain benefits (better decision making based on more and better information) without being vulnerable to what is widely perceived as one of the costs of planning, the possibility of authoritarian control in an otherwise democratic system. Unfortunately, as we shall see, it has been difficult to discover the extent to which indicative planning in France has had an impact on economic outcomes.

Japan is yet another interesting case of a market capitalist economy where the state plays an important role. But, as in Great Britain, the state's role is really exercised by means other than planning per se. And these patterns of state influence do not seem to have changed significantly in recent years.

There are of course cases where market capitalist systems have developed some form of planning to supplement and/or modify market outcomes. The Scandinavian countries are cases in point, though extended discussions of incorporating some planning in the United States have produced little change over the years. In the United States, there is no planning in the sense of utilizing a national economic planning mechanism, though one could argue that a great deal of planning does in fact occur through large government branches, powerful corporate entities, and the like. Recent discussion has focused on the perceived need for an **industrial policy**, or system mechanisms to develop and implement policies designed to promote the health of the capitalist economy — for example, through technological change.

Although the nature and degree of state intervention differ considerably from one capitalist system to another, the major industrialized capitalist systems do not rely significantly on plan mechanisms for allocating resources.

CHANGE IN SOCIALIST ECONOMIES

At the beginning of this chapter, we emphasized the basic theme that economic systems can be changed — that is, that one or more of the four basic system components can be changed — a process we term economic reform. We also noted that although economic reform occurs in both capitalist and socialist economic systems, reform in the latter has been viewed as revolutionary in character and has usually been regime-directed. There are also other differences.

In our examination of the impact of economic reform, we stressed that measurement is difficult. With some difficulty, one can observe changes in system components, but the effectiveness of reform is most likely to be judged by its ultimate impact on economic outcomes. Though there has been a great deal of interest in economic reform in planned socialist systems, observers have tended to view such reform as quite modest in character and as having limited impact on economic outcomes. Again we might cite the Kosygin reforms of the mid-1960s, in which the Soviet Union's objective was to change the rules that guided enterprises in the hope of increasing efficiency in the economy. It is not clear that rules in fact did change, and the result was a reform that failed, whether it is judged directly in terms of its impact on system characteristics or indirectly in terms of its impact on economic outcomes.

In light of the apparently limited effectiveness of past economic reform in planned socialist economic systems, some have characterized these reform attempts as simple experimentation. There is a tendency to view contemporary socialist economic reforms as *radical* in character, thus distinguishing it from earlier, less meaningful reform attempts, even though most socialist economic reform is driven by poor economic performance. In any case, and however we might characterize socialist economic reforms over time, the nature of recent reform programs has sharply increased interest in such reforms from both a theoretical and a practical point of view.

In this section, we focus on four main issues pertaining to socialist economic reform: What have been the major economic forces driving the process of economic reform in socialist economic systems? What reform alternatives or models are available for changing system components in those countries seeking change? To the extent that contemporary socialist economic reform may be termed radical in character, how shall we analyze the implementation of economic reform? And, where most or all system components are changed to significant degrees, can we generalize about system transition and especially about the nature of policies necessary to guide the transition process? The background provided by this analysis will enable us to understand both the nature of Perestroika in the Soviet Union and the more general process of economic reform and change in Eastern Europe and the Soviet Union.

Why Socialist Reform?

Although economic reform is of great theoretical interest, contemporary socialist reform programs have been driven by much more pragmatic issues. The predominant force promoting economic reform in the Soviet Union and Eastern Europe has been concern about economic performance. Most indicators of economic performance reveal that the Soviet and East European systems slipped significantly over the past two decades. Specifically, rates of growth of output declined steadily between the late 1950s and the mid-1980s. For countries whose hallmark was once rapid economic growth, such a trend has important implications. Without improvements in productivity, the growth of consumer well-being must lag. And even in less developed socialist systems such as China, reform motivated by poor performance has been important.

Many reasons have been advanced to explain the general slackening of economic performance, but the fact remains that the planned socialist economies have found the transformation from extensive to intensive growth very difficult. The basic Stalinist model, though draconian and costly, nevertheless served to bring idle and underused resources into the production process. However, the luxury of idle resources is, for many socialist systems, over. Economic growth and the expansion of consumer well-being must come from improved productivity, or what socialist systems have in the past described as **intensification.**

We do not know exactly why intensification in socialist systems has proved difficult. Clearly there are consumer pressures in these systems, and clearly they have grown more complex over time. In this sense, advances in planning methods have not kept pace with the demands on the planning system. But most important, the diffusion of technology in these systems has been inadequate. These systems are not demand-driven, and enterprise rules generally do not stimulate growth in productivity and cost reduction. Efficiency has simply not been a hallmark of the classic Stalinist command economy. Moreover, in contrast to the cyclical nature of productivity problems in market systems, socialist systems seemed to experience a long, steady decline of productivity growth through the 1980s.

Interest in socialist reform began in the 1960s and grew in the 1980s and 1990s. By the mid-1980s, performance in most socialist systems had slipped to the point where demand could not be met. With inadequate incentives, there appeared to be little hope for improved productivity. Moreover, most socialist countries have not been able to compete well enough in export markets to afford significant imports of consumer products. Seen in this perspective, the imperative of reform is evident, although the sudden spread of radical economic reform in the late 1980s is an issue yet to be fully explored.

Socialist Economic Systems: Reform Models

We have said that the reform of planned socialist economic systems has always focused on changes in some or all of the basic system components. However, we also noted that prior to the dramatic changes of the late 1980s and 1990s, most reform in socialist systems was judged to be very modest and was characterized as an attempt, by means of very limited systemic changes, to make the existing system work better. Recent reforms, however, which we have characterized as radical, are generally described as having the potential to change *all* system components and to change them significantly. Thus, as we will see when we discuss contemporary economic reform in Eastern Europe, many of the reform programs envisioned propose the elimination of central planning and its replacement by market forces.

Much of the literature on socialist economic reform, then, has focused on reform models that differ in the intensity of the reform program. We follow this pattern by characterizing socialist reform in terms of three basic variants: attempts to make planning work better, changes in organizational arrangements, and decentralization of decision making. All three models focus on changes in the four major system components.

Most observers of socialist economic reform have characterized the first two reform models as approaches of very limited intensity, designed primarily to sustain the basic components of the traditional planned socialist economic system while making some systemic modifications intended to improve economic performance. On the other hand our third model, decentralization, has come to be associated with radical economic reform that generally implies major systemic change.

There is a further sense in which our conception of socialist economic reform has been altered by recent events. In the past, because socialist reform was generally viewed as very modest, relatively little attention was paid to the implementation process itself. However, in light of the intensity of radical economic reform, a great deal of attention is now being paid to the implementation process itself, or to what is termed the transition from one system to another. We turn now to an examination of the three basic reform models.

Improving the Planning Mechanism Many Western observers consider improving planning to be a weak alternative — one that signals unwillingness to make serious changes in the economic system. The arguments in support of this alternative are that problems of economic performance arise largely because planning has not been perfected and that basic planning can be improved through the application of more sophisticated computer technology. For example, to the extent that enterprise managers make bad decisions because they lack information, ready access to accurate information through an advanced computer network would alleviate the problem. Devising better planning methods, installing better information channels, and paying more attention to incentive compatibility, it is believed, can perfect the planning system and improve economic performance. The 1970s were devoted to a number of attempts to improve planning both in the Soviet Union and in Eastern Europe.

Organizational Reform Changing the organizational arrangements of the existing plan structure represents a second reform alternative. A typical organizational reform is the introduction of intermediate organizations into the organizational hierarchy. Ministries, it has been argued, are too distant from the enterprises they supervise. Moreover, each ministry supervises enterprises that produce too diverse an array of products. Ministries cannot keep in touch with enterprise behavior and do not truly understand the problems peculiar to the enterprises they oversee. Thus as intermediate agency or association should be placed between the ministries and groups of enterprises that produce similar products. The intermediate association, it is argued, could understand and manage a particular group of firms more successfully.

Another way to implement organizational reform would be to shift the emphasis from sectoral to regional planning. An economy planned on a sectoral basis may place the interests of the branch over national interests. A shift to regional planning might loosen the grip of an entrenched bureaucracy and encourage a better flow of information among units in the economy. It was this type of reform that Nikita Khrushchev tried, without success, in the Soviet Union in the late 1950s and early 1960s. Most — though not all — past reform attempts in socialist systems have been organizational in nature.

Decentralization   Decentralization, our third broad category of socialist economic reform, is difficult to characterize precisely. In general terms, decentralization is a shifting of decision-making authority and responsibility from upper to lower levels. Decentralization is often viewed as "real" reform that can fundamentally change the nature of economic systems and, especially, reduce the role of central planning.

Decentralization implies that decisions about resource allocation will be shifted downward in the economic hierarchy. Most important, in a decentralized economy, decision are not made by planners but are reached at lower levels by means of what are frequently termed **economic levers** — prices, costs, profits, rates of return, and the like. Decentralization of decision making in an economic system entails both the devolution of decision-making authority and responsibility *and* the use of different decision-making tools in the process. To put it another way, although some form of planning may still exist, decentralization implies that local decision makers (for example, enterprise managers) pay less (if any) attention to planners and more attention to market signals.

This type of economic reform has frequently been characterized as **real reform** or **significant reform** to distinguish it from mere organizational change. In contemporary terms, it is likely to be called **radical reform**. Its existence raises new and difficult questions about the development of markets — and thus market signals — in systems previously dominated by planners, by state-ownership of property, and by an absence of market signals.

Finally, we should note that although classifying reform into models in this manner can be useful, few real-world efforts at reform can be simply characterized in single dimensions. Indeed, the reform issue is growing more complex rather than less. For example, the contrast between past Soviet reform efforts and contemporary reform efforts in Eastern Europe is striking. The former were largely organizational in character and had little impact. The latter seem intended to dismantle the planned socialist systems and replace them with market systems. This intensity of reform demands that we pay attention to the implementation of reform, and especially to the nature of economic policies appropriate to the transition process. We turn, then, to a further examination of radical reform.

Radical Reform Programs: Design and Development

We are in an era when most reforms under way in the formerly planned socialist systems are considered radical in character. As we noted in Chapter 1, political structures have changed. And however present reform programs differ, most seek to move significantly away from the plan toward the market and to change all system components in major ways. Moreover, although past reforms might well be viewed as center-directed, there is a fundamental sense in which present reforms are being driven from below and thus require basic changes in the social contract. Thus the mechanics of transition to the market are difficult and, indeed, are made more difficult by a lack of vision of the desired outcome. For this reason, it would be premature to predict the demise of socialism and of socialist policies in areas such as income distribution, public goods, and the like.

Both the design of a reform program and its implementation are influenced by a variety of important forces that can differ in important ways from one country to another. We find it convenient to isolate these forces for purposes of discussion, but they are interrelated in complicated ways in the real world.

1. Change in any system is generally resisted in whole or at least in part by some of the system participants. Thus the nature of the political system and the evolution of that system through time (and especially during the process of reform implementation) both facilitate and constrain the success of economic reform. For example, in systems that have been relatively centralized and dominated by a single political party over many years, participants have achieved success largely working *within* the system. Thus one can expect managers, administrators, bureaucrats, and those segments of the population whose economic position will be affected to resist such change. Even in cases where political power has remained relatively centralized, participants have vigorously resisted change when it was not in their own interest to be supportive. The long-standing but largely unsuccessful reform efforts in the Soviet Union in the past offer a good example. In sharp contrast, the failed Soviet coup in August 1991, the demise of Communist party power, and the declaration of independence by Soviet republics are all forces sharply reducing participant resistance to change. However, having stressed the importance of political factors in the development and implementation of economic reform, it is important also to appreciate that economic reform is a difficult process. The political system itself should not automatically be blamed for problems that arise in the design or implementation of reform.
2. Environmental factors, which we have argued affect economic outcomes, are also important determinants of the success of reform. Such factors are many and varied. For example, the size of the country, its resource endowment, and the nature of regional development patterns are key issues. It is not unreasonable to assume that systemic change is facilitated in systems that are not lacking in basic resources and do not suffer from extreme regional economic disparities.
3. The nature of the economic system and its past policies are important. For example, one could argue that a system that has been relatively centralized, trade-averse, and biased in investment patterns will have created and sustained organizational arrangements that are very difficult to change. Its

industrial structure will be biased toward heavy industry and away from consumer needs, and the lack of impact of foreign market influences will have created a structure that cannot readily adapt to new market forces. To take quite a different example, centralized systems dominated by plan arrangements have typically not developed the infrastructure necessary for decentralized decision making. Banking arrangements in such systems do not facilitate the development of markets, and monetary policy is not a mechanism for guiding the system. Thus the development of reform varies with the past economic experience of the country, and we should not be surprised that such experiences differ widely in such cases as Poland, Yugoslavia, and Albania. It is not really the *level* of economic development that has been achieved that is important here, but rather the *nature* of that development in terms of the mechanisms used, the policies followed, the length of time involved and the economy that has resulted.

Reform Programs: Implementation

The process of actually implementing economic reforms has received a great deal of attention lately. This is because recent reforms, especially those in Eastern Europe and potentially those in the Soviet Union, envision fundamental change: the development of a market economy through privatization and the development of a market infrastructure and policies typically used for the guidance of market systems. Under these rather dramatic circumstances, it is necessary to consider not only the basic design of reform programs, but also the conditions under which they are implemented and, especially, the nature of the **transition process**. During this period, elements of both old and new coexist, policy mechanisms capable of guiding both must be available, and a variety of new and important issues emerge.

First, the issue of sequencing is important. Sequencing can be characterized in different ways, though in the past, the focus has been on the **sectoral** ordering of economic reform. As we examine the reform process in different cases, it becomes clear that China has chosen to emphasize change in the rural economy first and adjustment in other sectors thereafter. One could argue that this strategy makes sense in a poor country with a large population predominantly engaged in agricultural pursuits. The Soviet experience provides an interesting contrast. As we examine Perestroika, it becomes apparent that it has not been an "agriculture first" strategy. Though the Soviet emphasis on industry can be defended for a country at a higher level of development than China, the inadequacies of Soviet agriculture inflict serious daily problems on Soviet citizens. Some effort to resolve these problems (for example, through better distribution arrangements) might yield substantial short-run benefits, could encourage the population to support the overall reform, and should cost little.

Although sequencing has traditionally been viewed as a rather broad issue of reform strategy, there is a much more pressing interpretation. Consider the case of an enterprise manager in a planned economy that is shifting to a market basis for resource allocation. If prices are to be used in the decision-making process, the mechanism for setting and changing prices (the market) must be developed. We have already noted that if prices are to replace plan rules for decision making, prices must change to reflect relative scarcities. Does one attempt to develop the market, then change the enterprise "rules," and then eliminate the planner? The ordering of reform "components" is further complicated by the fact that they all take significantly different amounts of time to implement. Thus, at any stage in the reform process, there are likely to be major imbalances of implementation.

In addition to issues related to sequencing, the speed of reform implementation is a matter of much debate. A **gradualist approach** envisions the slow and careful implementation of reform in successive stages, and the reformed system is expected to be in place and fully functioning only after several years. A different approach is that of "shock therapy." Here changes in policies and mechanisms (for example, taxes and prices) are made quickly and implemented in a short period of time. The speed possible is generally viewed as inversely related to the magnitude of intensity of the adjustment anticipated. For example, the application of "shock therapy" in the Polish case was widely viewed as feasible because the intensity of adjustment needed in the Polish economy (for example, the magnitude of difference between actual retail prices and equilibrium retail prices) was not inordinately large. Moreover, democratic support for reform was stronger in the Polish case than in many others. It has also been argued that more rapid change tends to reduce the likelihood and the degree of resistance. In practice, however, most socialist reform has not tended to be rapid, though the speed of reform in such systems in the 1990s is different in every case.

A third critical element of reform implementation is the actual development of new system components designed to replace socialist components. Although one can usually point to the need for an infrastructure that generally did not exist under socialist arrangements, the most notable component that must be developed is the market and related price-setting mechanisms. In this sense, it is easy to understand why the process of economic reform in Eastern Europe is often termed simply privatization.

If decisions (both household and enterprise) are to be made with the assistance of market signals (prices), then the existing prices must be changed where they are inappropriate (that is, where they do not reflect relative scarcities), and, most important, a mechanism of price formation (the market) must be put in place and activated. Market mechanisms are easily defined in theory, but in practice the issue is much more complex. Moreover, new system components can be rejected, which is in part a problem of sequencing.

Privatization   In almost all contemporary socialist reform programs, **privatization** is a major issue. The assumption underlying this initiative is the belief that private property is essential to the development of markets — a view not universally popular among socialist thinkers. However, as we will see later in this book, there are significant differences among cases. In some East European countries, a strong drive toward privatization has been slowed not by ideology but rather by the practical difficulties of privatization. In other cases (for example, the Soviet Union), the matter of ownership is under intense and continuing debate.

Property rights in socialist systems are inherently political. Moreover, changes in these rights imply important changes in the loci of economic powers and the manner in which these powers are used. To whom will ownership be conveyed, how will it be conveyed, and to what degree will the resulting arrangements establish a competitive environment? In most cases, there is a sense that ownership rights ought to be conveyed broadly, and there is much discussion about formulating some sort of share arrangements and a market in which such shares can be traded. It is difficult, however, to evaluate the work of enterprises in these systems, let alone to establish a mechanism through which the purchase of shares can be financed. Usually these mechanisms simply do not exist. Sometimes, partial state ownership of some sort of transitional arrangements can be envisioned. Moreover, in almost all cases, there are a wide variety of enterprises. Some are efficient, attractive, and easily privatized. Others are losing money, are inefficient, and are unattractive to almost any potential buyer.

Beyond the issue of actually implementing privatization in a technical sense, it is not always clear what sort of market will result. It is generally argued that once firms are privatized and central supply mechanisms are eliminated, interfirm transactions will serve to adjust prices. But often, especially where a country is small, the industrial structure is inherently noncompetitive, necessitating the development and implementation of antitrust procedures — another element missing from the existing infrastructure.

Sectoral Problems   Much of our discussion of reform has been general in nature, and we have looked at problems that have arisen, to one degree or another, in all radical socialist reform efforts. It is important to note that, over and above these general issues, individual sectors have problems peculiar to those sectors. In agriculture, for example, the issues that emerge include the privatization of land, the development of markets for driving production, and the elimination of agricultural subsidies. The problems may be general, but frequently the solutions must be specific to the sector.

Consider another critical area, that of foreign trade. As we will see, reform of foreign trade has for a variety of reasons been a critical component of the overall reform process. Yet again, special problems arise. In most cases, the reform of foreign trade arrangements has begun with decentralizing the trade decision-making structure from a monopolistic ministry into the individual enterprises, changing the rules used to make decisions, and (finally) altering the financial arrangements for conducting trade. Whereas ownership patterns tend to be adjusted initially through the development of joint ventures and other such cooperative arrangements, the critical reform issue remains the adjustment of the domestic currency to realistic values so that convertibility can be attained. Again, the process frequently unfolds in a sequential pattern that start with limited access to foreign exchange, domestic currency auctions, and the like. Market forces are gradually introduced, beginning with limited internal convertibility; full convertibility is effected later.

Transition Policies   So far we have focused mainly on the complex issues of changing the economic system (typically, replacing plan with market). In addition to changes in the system, changes in policies must occur — changes appropriate for an awkward period of transition. Indeed, as we have emphasized, the distinction between policy and system is not always clear. Where privatization proceeds reasonably smoothly, one can envision corresponding policy adjustments, such as the installation of enterprise investment policies. A more difficult issue is the development of macroeconomic policies, especially appropriate fiscal and monetary policies. At the macro level, it is essential to develop policies capable of sustaining a stable economy and *at the same time* promoting growth within the context of reform. The goal is macroeconomic stability *and* microeconomic efficiency. This is a task of major proportions.

We will see, as we study different systems, that planned socialist systems have typically employed direct state access to resources as a mechanism for controlling their use. Thus, although such systems have large and important budgets, expenditures are directly controlled by the state, and revenues are accumulated directly through producing enterprises. Moreover, these are quantity-driven systems wherein money and monetary policy traditionally play only a limited role. However, as the state apparatus and the planning system are dismantled, new patterns of expenditure emerge, and new sources of revenue (in particular, taxes) must be developed. At the same time tight state control over monetary matters is relaxed appropriate monetary control mechanisms and institutions must be created.

During the transition period, it is tempting for the government to offset revenue loss by printing money. To the extent that new market mechanisms are not in place, production does not increase, and inflation is an inevitable result. Moreover, to the extent that enterprise decision making is decentralized and begins to respond to market signals, traditional overstaffing policies of an earlier socialist era are abandoned, and unemployment is introduced. Traditional mechanisms such as unemployment benefits and retraining programs must be developed.

Even with a reasonably clear reform program and an accurate vision of the outcome, the transition period poses unique challenges. Practice often leads theory as these challenges are addressed. There are no simple blueprints for the transition process, nor is it ever the same in any two different countries.

THE REFORM ERA

It is evident from our discussion in Chapter 1, and from our introduction to economic reform in this chapter, that the 1990s is a dynamic decade in the field of comparative economic systems. In the past, reasonable stability of economic systems prevailed, and any reform was modest and conservative. Since the advent of Perestroika in the Soviet Union, what we have termed radical reform has been the more common reform pattern. This pattern of reform implies the reduction or elimination of planning as we know it, the introduction of market mechanisms, and the expansion of foreign trade through market mechanisms. The design and introduction of these market mechanisms, the changes that they promote, and the population's response represent a major challenge of the transition era. Moreover, as the social contract is redefined and the well-known ills of capitalism (inflation and unemployment) are introduced, some people call for the resurrection of socialist principles. Thus the basic issue of market efficiency versus socialist equity is still actively debated.

As we discuss real-world examples of radical economic reform in subsequent chapters, many of the issues introduced in this chapter will be examined in greater detail. These major cases of economic reform will provide us a context in which to compare theory and practice.

SUMMARY

In Chapter 2, we noted that economic systems can be characterized in terms of four important dimensions: levels of decision making, information mechanisms, property rights, and incentives. In this chapter, we focused on *change*, or economic reform, in both capitalist and socialist economic systems. We emphasized that economic reform also implies changes in system components. Reform in capitalist systems is frequently viewed as evolutionary in nature, resulting in large part from the decentralized operation of market mechanisms. Reform in socialist systems has been characterized as revolutionary, or centralized and regime-directed.

Historically, most reforms in both capitalist and socialist economic systems have been rather modest. However, as we will see when we examine contemporary economic reform in the Soviet Union and in the countries of Eastern Europe, socialist reform in contemporary times is frequently characterized as radical: Major changes occur in most if not all system components. This change in the nature of reform has sparked renewed interest in economic reform — and especially in the impact of radical reform and in the transitional arrangements necessary to implement it.

NOTES

1. William G. Shepherd, "Causes of Increased Competition in the U.S. Economy, 1939–1980," *Review of Economics and Statistics* (November 1982), 613–626.
2. Edgar K. Browning, "The Trend Toward Equality in the Distribution of Net Income," *Southern Economic Journal*, 43 (July 1976), 914.
3. The theoretical foundation of a profit-sharing capitalist economy is provided by Martin L. Weitzman, *The Share Economy* (Cambridge, Mass.: Harvard University Press, 1984) and Martin L. Weitzman, "The Simple Macroeconomics of Profit Sharing," *American Economic Review*, 75 (December 1985), 937–953.

4. For an analysis of Japanese profit sharing, see Merton J. Peck, "Is Japan Really a Share Economy?" *Journal of Comparative Economics*, 10 (December 1986), 427–432.
5. Most of the contemporary literature on socialist economic reform focuses on country-specific cases. We will cite this literature as we look at specific cases in subsequent chapters of the book. A useful summary of the traditional views on socialist reform can be found in Paul Hare, "Economic Reform in Eastern Europe," *Journal of Economic Surveys*, 1 (1987), 25–58. For a provocative discussion, see W. Brus and K. Laski, *From Marx to the Market* (Oxford, England: Clarendon Press, 1989), and Janos Kornai, *The Road to a Free Economy* (New York: Norton, 1990).
6. For a general discussion, see Barbara Lee and John Nellis, "Enterprise Reform and Privatization in Socialist Economies" (Washington, D.C.: World Bank Discussion Papers, no. 104, 1990).

RECOMMENDED READINGS

Edvardo Borensztein and Manmohan S. Kumar, "Proposals for Privatization in Eastern Europe" (Washington, D.C.: IMF working paper, April 1991).

W. Brus and K. Laski, *From Marx to the Market* (Oxford, England: Clarendon Press, 1989).

David Cameron and Peter Hauslohner, eds., *Political Control of the Soviet Economy* (Cambridge, England: Cambridge University Press, forthcoming).

Robert W. Campbell, *The Socialist Economies in Transition: A Primer on Semi-Reformed Systems* (Bloomington: Indiana University Press, 1991).

"Eastern Europe: Coming Around the First Turn" (Washington, D.C.: CIA, May 1991).

Sabastian Edwards, "The Sequencing of Economic Reform: Analytical Issues and Lessons from the Latin American Experience," *World Economy*, 1 (1990).

Janos Kornai, *The Road to a Free Economy* (New York: Norton, 1990).

Oliver Letwin, *Privatizing the World* (London: Cassell, 1988).

Barbara Lee and John Nellis, "Enterprise Reform and Privatization in Socialist Economies" (Washington, D.C.: World Bank Discussion Paper no. 104, 1990).

Peter Murrell, " 'Big Bang' Versus Evolution: East European Economic Reforms in the Light of Recent Economic History," *PlanEcon* (July 26, 1990).

———, "Public Choice and the Transformation of Socialism," *Journal of Comparative Economics*, 14 (June 1991), 203–210.

Richard Portes, "Introduction to Economic Transformation in Hungary and Poland," *European Economy*, 43 (March 1990).

J. Tedstrom, ed., *Socialism and Perestroika's Dilemmas of Soviet Economic Reform* (Boulder, Colo.: Westview Press, 1990).

PART II

ECONOMIC SYSTEMS IN THEORY

5 | Theory of Capitalism

THERE IS NO SINGLE THEORETICAL MODEL OF CAPITALISM, and no two capitalist economies are exactly alike. Controversy exists over the role of the state, the role of market imperfections (externalities, monopoly, public goods), and the inherent cyclical instability of capitalism.

This chapter is about the theory of capitalism. Subsequent chapters discuss capitalism in practice. This chapter asks: How well should capitalist market economies *in theory* resolve the problem of allocating scarce resources among competing ends? This issue is important for two reasons. The first is that the theories of capitalism and socialism yield hypotheses concerning expected differences in performance among systems, and those hypotheses can be tested against the experiences of capitalist and socialist nations. The second is that one may be most interested in the theoretical models themselves and in what they suggest about the performance of economic systems under **ideal conditions**. Because actual economies diverge from the ideal, it could be argued that their performance cannot be used as a test of the system's "true" performance and that the performance issue must be resolved at the theoretical level.[1]

HOW MARKETS WORK

The theory of capitalism focuses on how a market economy works. It examines the role of prices in harmonizing the wishes of consumers and producers.

Equilibrium and the "Invisible Hand"

The pioneering analysis of market capitalism is Adam Smith's *The Wealth of Nations*, published in 1776.[2] Speaking against the mercantilist position that free trade could lead to a country's ruin, Adam Smith argued that a highly efficient and harmonious economic system would emerge if competitive markets were left to function freely without government intervention and if government acted to protect property rights.

Smith's underlying notion was that if individuals were given free rein to pursue their own selfish interests, an "invisible hand" (that is, the competitive market) would cause them to behave in a socially responsible manner. Products desired by consumers would be produced in the appropriate assortments and quantities, and the most efficient means of production would be used. No government or social action would be required to bring this about, for individuals acting in their own interests could be counted on to do the right thing. In fact, government action would probably interfere with this natural process, so government should be limited to providing essential public services — national defense, a legal system to protect private property, and highways — that private enterprise could not produce on its own. An equilibrium of consumers and producers would be created spontaneously in the competitive marketplace, for if the actions of consumers and producers were not in harmony, the market price would adjust to bring the two groups into equilibrium.

Smith's notion of a natural tendency toward an efficient economic equilibrium was the foundation for the liberal economic thought of the nineteenth century. In the words of one authority, Smith's most important triumph was that "he put into the center of economics the systematic analysis of the behavior of individuals pursuing their self-interest under conditions of competition," and this remains "the foundation of the theory of resource allocation."[3] Most of the later theorizing aimed at a further elaboration of Smith's vision of market capitalism. This theorizing became known as neo-classical economics.

Partial Equilibrium

Adam Smith's description of markets was incomplete, and it was left to his successors to provide more formal analyses of the price system. The partial-equilibrium approach initiated by Alfred Marshall and developed more fully by J. R. Hicks and Paul Samuelson suggests a more formal way to describe the "invisible hand."[4]

It is assumed that two motivating forces drive market capitalism: the desire of producers to maximize profits and the desire of consumers to maximize their own welfare (utility) subject to the constraint of limited income. Under competitive conditions, producers will be prepared to supply larger quantities at higher prices, combining inputs to minimize costs. Consumers, seeking to maximize their welfare, will purchase less at higher prices. The producer and consumer meet in the marketplace, where their conflicting objectives are brought into equilibrium. If the quantity demanded exceeds the quantity supplied at the prevailing price, the price automatically rises, squeezing out some demand and evoking a larger supply until all those willing to buy and all those willing to sell at the prevailing price can do so. At this point, an equilibrium price is established, the market clears, and there is no tendency to depart from the equilibrium unless it is disrupted by some exogenous change (see Figure 5.1).

This description underscores how market resource allocation works under competitive conditions. All other things being equal, an increase in consumer demand for a particular product disrupts the established equilibrium, and the price starts to rise. As the price rises, producers find it in their interest to supply a larger quantity of the product. If larger profits can be obtained at the new price, additional producers enter the market. On the demand side, the rise in the price causes substitution (substitution of now less expensive commodities) and income effects (the effect of lower real income), thereby reducing the quantity demanded (see Figure 5.2). In sum, the increase in demand causes resources to be shifted automatically to the product in greater demand, and the wants of the consuming public are met without intervention from outside forces. Consumers are said to be **sovereign** because the economy responds to changes in their demand.

General Equilibrium

Partial-equilibrium analysis of competitive markets suggests that markets for individual products can function smoothly in isolation from the remainder of the economy. However, economies consist of thousands or even millions of distinct but interrelated markets in a constant state of change. It remains to be established whether disequilibrium forces will disrupt the neat harmony of the

Figure 5.1 Market Equilibrium in a Competitive Economy

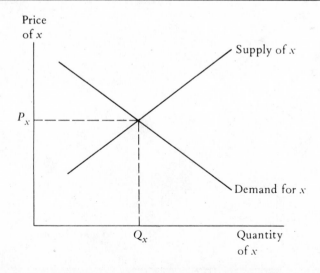

Explanation: In a competitive market economy, the price at which x sells will be P_x. If the price were *below* this level, the quantity demanded would exceed the quantity supplied. The *shortage* of x would cause the price of x to rise. If the price were *above* P_x, the quantity supplied would exceed the quantity demanded. The surplus of x would then cause the price of x to fall. Only at P_x is the quantity supplied equal to the quantity demanded (Q_x).

partial-equilibrium model. A French economist, Leon Walras, was one of the first theorists to address this question. He arrived at the sanguine conclusion that in theory, at least, competitive capitalism would be able to generate a set of general-equilibrium prices that could clear all markets simultaneously.[5] Walras's theory demonstrates that despite the enormous complexity of market interactions, a general equilibrium can be obtained. This **general equilibrium** means that the divergent interests of consumers and producers can be harmonized not only for single markets, but for all markets simultaneously.

Subsequent research in general-equilibrium economics has built on and elaborated the Walrasian system with similar but less general results, none denying the possibility of a general equilibrium under conditions of competitive capitalism.[6]

Optimality of Competitive Capitalism (Pareto)

Demonstrating that a general equilibrium can exist does not prove that it will be desirable or optimal. The Italian economist Vilfredo Pareto formulated a set

Figure 5.2 Consumer Sovereignty in a Competitive Economy

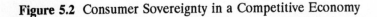

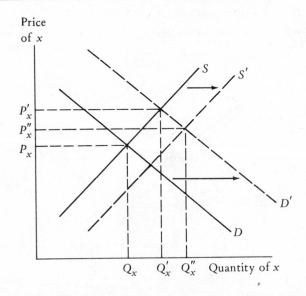

Explanation: We begin with the market for x in equilibrium at price P_x and quantity Q_x. *There is an increase in consumer demand from D to D'*. As a consequence, the price of x rises to P'_x and the equilibrium quantity *rises* to Q'_x. If economic profits are being made at this new price, new firms will enter the market and the supply curve will eventually shift to S'. Now a new long-run equilibrium is established at price P''_x and quantity Q''_x. An increase in consumer demand *automatically* leads to an increase in the quantity produced. The long-run effect on market prices depends on the entry of new firms at the higher price.

of conditions, now called **Pareto optimality**.[7] A "Pareto-optimal" allocation of resources exists when "production and distribution cannot be reorganized to increase the utility of one or more individuals without decreasing the utility of others."[8]

The direct approach of defining optimality as maximization of the total satisfaction of all members of society would require a subjective evaluation of the importance of one individual's satisfaction vis-à-vis another's (interpersonal utility comparisons). Should resources be allocated from the rich to the poor because the increase in the satisfaction of the poor would be greater than the decrease in the satisfaction of the rich? We have no objective method for answering such questions. What we have is Pareto's indirect definition. Under a Pareto-optimal allocation of resources, a maximal output is being produced from available resources.

Pareto optimality forms the core of modern welfare economic theory, which seeks to evaluate the desirability of various economic states. The issue of special interest here — whether market capitalism can be expected to yield optimal resource allocations — is also central to the study of welfare economics. The answer is that under certain conditions — perfect competition in production and consumption, equality of private and social costs (or benefits), and taxation systems that do not alter competitive decisions — capitalist resource allocation will indeed be Pareto-optimal.[9]

In simplest terms, this can be demonstrated by noting that, under perfect competition, the price P (reflecting the marginal utility of consumption) of each commodity will be equated with its marginal cost of production, MC. The equality of P and MC is a necessary condition for welfare maximization. MC reflects society's opportunity cost of producing the last unit of production, and P reflects its marginal benefit. If costs and benefits are not equal at the margin, welfare can be increased by a redistribution of resources.

Pareto optimality does not serve as a clear guide to determining the single "best" allocation of resources. In fact, an almost infinite number of resource allocations may be compatible with Pareto optimality, some of them calling for highly unequal distributions of income. Moreover, the "optimal" distribution of income is not even considered. In some manner, then, society must select, from all possible allocations of resources, that allocation (and underlying income distribution) that it judges to be "best."[10]

Capitalism under conditions of monopoly and other forms of imperfect competition violates Pareto optimality. Figure 5.3 compares competitive and monopolistic price and output determination. A capitalist economy that includes imperfectly competitive industries where price is greater than marginal cost will be suboptimal. *How* suboptimal would seem to depend on the strength of monopolistic forces in the economy, but it is difficult to provide a rigorous proof of this intuitive logic. "Second-best" solutions cannot be proved without exception to represent an unambiguous improvement over more monopolistic arrangements. For example, it cannot be demonstrated that in *all* cases an economy that is, say, 90 percent competitive is "better" than one that is 80 percent competitive. Nevertheless, under certain likely conditions, it can be demonstrated that a change to more competition does make an economy more nearly "optimal."

A perfectly competitive economy violates Pareto optimality in the case of market failures caused by the presence of public goods and externalities of production and consumption. (These issues will be discussed later.)

Figure 5.3 The Competitive and Monopolistic Models

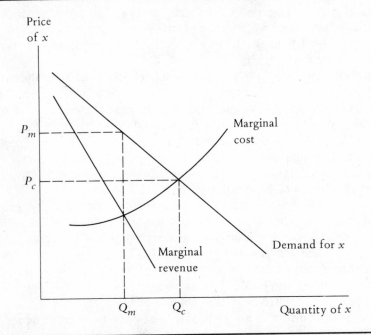

Explanation: This diagram presents the models of price and output determination under conditions of perfect competition and monopoly.

Let us suppose that industry X could be organized either as a monopoly (with a single producer) or as a competitive industry (with a large number of producers). The marginal costs are the same whether the industry is a monopoly or is perfectly competitive. The industry demand schedule and the industry marginal-cost schedule are given in the diagram. The latter is the marginal-cost schedule of the monopolist (in the case of the monopolistic industry) or the sum of the individual marginal-cost schedules of producers (in the case of the competitive industry).

Because the demand schedule is negatively sloped, the monopolist's marginal revenue is less than the product price. To maximize profits, the monopolist produces that output (Q_m) at which marginal cost and marginal revenue are equated and sells this output at the price dictated by the market (P_m). Competitive producers produce output levels at which the product price and marginal costs are equal; therefore, the supply schedule of the competitive industry is the industry marginal-cost schedule. The competitively organized industry produces Q_c, and the product sells for P_c.

The monopoly produces less than the competitive industry and charges a higher price. The monopolist charges a price greater than the marginal costs of production, whereas the competitive industry equates price and marginal cost. Because price and marginal revenue are not equal, an economy made up of monopolies is not Pareto-optimal.

The Efficiency of Capitalism: Hayek and Mises

The noted Austrian economists, Friedrich Hayek and Ludwig von Mises have written about the *relative* superiority of market economies over planned socialist economies.[11] Their arguments rest on the efficient manner in which market economies mobilize and utilize information, in contrast to the inefficient use of information in planned socialist and market socialist economies. Hayek writes that the principal economic problem is not how to allocate given resources (the problem posed by Pareto), but "how to secure the best use of resources known to any member of society, for ends whose relative importance only these individuals know. Or, to put it briefly, it is a problem of the utilization of knowledge not given to anyone in its totality." Economic agents (consumers and producers) specialize in information about prices, products, and location that is relevant to them in their daily lives. Economic agents need not know all prices, products, and locations to behave efficiently in the marketplace. According to Hayek and Mises, the fact that market economies efficiently generate information in the form of market prices, which enable producers and consumers to plan their actions in a rational manner, is the principal advantage of capitalism and will ensure its relative superiority over planned socialism. This is their argument for the theoretical and practical superiority of market capitalism. They feel that the planned socialist economies would prove too difficult to manage because of the complexity of information and incentive problems.

The picture of capitalism that we have developed is one of a harmonious resource allocation system, strongly inclined toward equilibrium in production (especially under competitive conditions), and proceeding at a high degree of efficiency. This harmony occurs without the benefit of government intervention and control. Critics of the harmonious model point to the need for state intervention to deal with monopoly power, externalities, public goods, and income distribution problems. They also stress the inherent cyclical instability of capitalism and the problems of making rational public choices.

REASONS FOR STATE INTERVENTION

The appropriate level of state intervention into the affairs of private enterprise is one of the most vigorously disputed issues in the theory of capitalism. The neoclassical position, descended directly from Adam Smith, is that in the absence of monopoly and other forms of imperfect competition, and in the absence of external effects, the economic role of the state should be strictly limited. In particular, the state should supply only those public goods — such as national defense, public roads, a legal system, and foreign policy — that private enterprise on its own would not be able to provide in optimal proportions. The theory of public goods, first articulated formally by Nobel laureate Paul Samuelson, explains why laissez-faire capitalism will underproduce such goods.[12] The question we wish to consider here is in what instances state intervention is called for to correct deficiencies in the activity of private enterprise.

Monopoly and Imperfect Competition

The nonoptimality of monopoly has been emphasized by economists since, and even before, publication of *The Wealth of Nations*. Formally analyzed by Alfred Marshall around the turn of the century, the theory of monopoly is a standard feature of introductory economics courses.[13] The crux of the monopoly problem is the monopolist's inclination to restrict output below the level that would be reached in a competitive situation. Because competitive outputs and prices are Pareto-optimal, the existence of monopoly necessarily means a suboptimal allocation of resources. Monopolists underproduce and overcharge relative to competitive producers. Monopoly causes a deadweight loss, in that the gains of the monopolist are less than the losses to consumers. Figure 5.3 demonstrated that monopolies produce less and charge higher prices than competitive markets.

Monopoly behavior is not explained by extraordinary greed on the part of the monopolist, who is simply attempting to maximize profits. By definition, the monopolist is the sole producer in a particular market. Therefore, to sell a large volume of output, the monopolist must lower the price. The perfectly competitive producer, as a price taker, can sell all he or she desires at the price established by the market. Monopolists fail to expand their output to the point where the marginal cost (which measures the marginal cost of output in terms of society's resources) equals price (which measures the marginal benefit of output to society). Rather, monopolists who wish to maximize profits must restrict their output.

Economists such as Edward Chamberlin and Joan Robinson have evaluated market arrangements that fall between perfect competition and monopoly.[14] The two intermediate market forms are oligopoly and monopolistic competition.[15] It is beyond the scope of this work to describe them in detail. All we shall say is that both oligopoly and monopolistic competition (like monopoly) violate the criteria of Pareto optimality, although they probably deviate less from optimality than pure monopoly. Because of the greater degree of competition facing monopolistic competitive firms, the degree of monopoly power at their disposal (as measured by the gap between P and MC) is likely to be small. They may represent a reasonable approximation of perfect competition. In the case of oligopoly, it is difficult to draw general conclusions because the outcome depends on the manner in which a small number of large, interdependent firms behave. In some instances (collusive oligopoly, for example), the degree of monopoly power may be great; in other cases (price-warring oligopolists), the degree of monopoly power may be small.

Social Control of Monopoly Power

Economic theory suggests four approaches to the control of monopoly, three of which require collective intervention. The first is to use the state's authority to *tax and subsidize* to correct the underutilization of resources by monopolistic producers. The basic idea, proposed by A. C. Pigou and Arnold Harberger, is to combine subsidization with consumer and producer taxation to induce the monopolist to expand output to the competitive level, while at the same time producing a social tax dividend for society. A graphical description of this approach is provided in the accompanying note.[16]

The obvious difficulty is that tax authorities must make quite sophisticated calculations in order to implement it. The use of subsidies and taxes to obtain an optimal allocation of resources from a monopolist does not seem too practical, although the theory of how to do so is clear.

The second form of state intervention is *direct regulation* of monopoly. Theoretically, state regulatory authorities could dictate that the regulated natural monopoly produce the efficient quantity of output at which P equals MC and force the monopolist to charge a regulated price equal to marginal costs. In this manner, the regulators could dictate directly an efficient allocation of resources. There are two practical difficulties with this approach, however. How are regulators to know market demand and monopoly marginal costs? The monopoly might be tempted to inflate its costs by lax management or other means in order to obtain a higher regulated price. The second difficulty is that marginal-cost pricing would probably force the monopolist to operate at a loss (if marginal costs were sill declining at the output where P equals MC). The existence of regulated losses would require a system of subsidization, which would tend to disrupt the optimal allocation of resources.

The third approach is that recommended by Milton Friedman — to *leave natural monopolies alone* because regulation would be poorly managed and would encourage monopolists to be inefficient.[17] The unregulated monopoly, prompted by the desire to maximize profits and keep potential competitors out of the market, would supply a larger quantity at a lower price than that charged by a regulated monopoly. Moreover, even monopolists must face some form of competition in the long run and cannot get by indefinitely with an inefficient use of resources.

The final collective approach applies to cases where competitive production is also possible. The state, through enforcement of antitrust and anticartel legislation and through the removal of legal obstacles to competition could serve to *transform the industry from monopolistic to competitive.*

Modern theory has pondered whether there are natural limitations on monopoly power. Unless freedom of entry were highly restricted, monopolists would avoid charging monopoly prices for fear of attracting competitors in the long run.

External Effects and Collective Action

The notion of **external effects** was pioneered by the English economist A. C. Pigou.[18] It refers to situations where the actions of one producer (or consumer) directly affect the costs (utility) of a second producer (or consumer). By direct effects, we mean effects that take place outside of the price system. These external effects may be harmful, in which case they are called an **external diseconomy,** or they may be salutary, in which case they are known as an **external economy.** An example of an external diseconomy of production is the dumping of wastes into a river by one producer, requiring a producer downstream to increase costs by installing water purification equipment.

When external effects are present, the allocation of resources is not optimal, even if the economy is perfectly competitive. Producers of the external effect are not required to take the external impact of their actions into account when making decisions. Rather they seek to maximize their private profit on the basis of the private costs of production, not on the basis of social costs. The producer of an external harmful effect therefore produces an output level in excess of the optimum, for a private producer tends to underestimate the true social costs of production (Figure 5.4).

Corrective Action in the Case of Externalities

Economic theory suggests remedies to correct for misallocations caused by external effects. One is the internalization of such effects — for example, by merging both the enterprises producing and those being affected by external effects. Consider the example of the waste-dumping factory. If it merged with the downstream factory, the water purification costs would become private costs for the combined enterprise, and waste dumping would be limited as a natural consequence of profit maximization.

In the absence of opportunities for internalization, remedies may require state action, such as taxation and subsidies to equate private and social costs. If an excise tax equal to the external diseconomy could be levied on the producer, private costs would equal social costs. To maximize private profits, the producer would be forced to limit output to the level at which price and marginal *social* costs are equal — the condition required for an efficient allocation of resources.

When appropriate taxes and subsidies cannot be levied, one alternative is state regulation. Government regulators determine the optimal allocation of resources and administratively decree that producers supply the optimal output mix. The major drawback is that enforcement and policing costs may be quite high, for it is not clear how one would obtain compliance with regulations. Moreover, there is the enormous problem of calculating private and social marginal costs — the data required for effective regulation.

A third approach to the externality problem is voluntary agreements among the parties involved. This notion was first suggested by Ronald Coase.[19] He contends that under certain conditions, the creator and recipient of the external effect can come to a mutually satisfactory agreement that restores an optimal allocation of resources. Whenever harmful externalities exist, the affected parties have opportunities for gains from trade by striking deals. In the absence of legal obstacles, the amount of shared gains from an agreement must exceed the costs of transacting the agreement. Coase's novel conclusion, therefore, is that if the transaction costs of reaching an agreement are small, private agreements can correct the misallocation of resources caused by external effects. If mutually acceptable bargains are not reached in the presence of small transaction costs, the divergence between private and social costs is probably inconsequential. As E. J. Mishan, another pioneer in the theory of externalities, comments: "Rationalizing the *status quo* in this way brings the economist perilously close to defending it."[20]

The most important drawback to voluntary agreements is exactly the problem of transaction costs and other impediments to agreement, especially when the number of parties involved is large. When a small number of parties are involved, then voluntary agreements do seem feasible. When a large number of parties must participate in the agreement, some of whom have relatively small stakes in the matter, the probability of reaching a mutually acceptable agreement is small.

Figure 5.4 The Inefficiency of External Costs

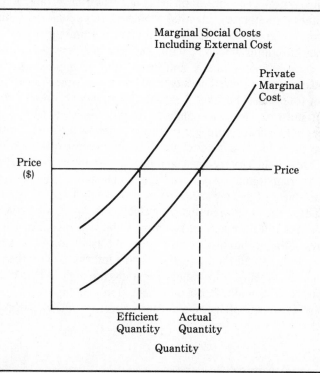

Explanation: When externalities are present, enterprises base their decisions on private marginal costs. This perfectly competitive firm produces where P = private marginal cost, not where P = full marginal cost. Thus externalities cause competitive firms to produce more than the optimal quantity.

PROBLEMS OF PUBLIC CHOICE

Theorists of capitalism agree that in some instances government must supply certain goods and services. Public goods — national defense, police protection and a legal system, dams, flood control projects, and the like — will not be supplied in efficient quantities by the private economy for two principal reasons: Nonpayers (called free riders) cannot be prevented from enjoying the benefits of the public good; and one person's use of the good does not generally prevent others from using it. Both of these features make it difficult for the private sector to produce public goods.

How efficiently will government supply such public goods? How rational is public choice? Public-choice theorists, such as James Buchanan, Gordon Tullock, and Kenneth Arrow, have concluded that certain factors prevent public choices in a democratic (majority-rule) society from being made in an efficient manner.[21]

Efficiency in the case of a public good requires, at a minimum, that the marginal benefits enjoyed by users of the good equal or exceed the marginal costs of supplying the good. Will this necessarily be the case in a society in which public-choice decisions are made by majority-rule voting? Public-choice theory outlines a number of potential problems: First, majority voting fails to take into consideration the intensity of preferences among voters. A number of voters may have intense feeling about a specific public-expenditure decision, whereas others may be virtually indifferent. Yet each person's vote counts equally, and changes in preferences typically do not change the voting outcome (the median voter rule). Second, there may be a tendency toward vote trading when voters must decide on a number of public-choice issues. A group that wishes one public-expenditure program may offer its support for the public-expenditure program of a second group if that group will form a majority coalition. Through such logrolling techniques, public-expenditure programs may be enacted where marginal costs exceed marginal benefits. Moreover, politicians are in the business of getting reelected and are likely to serve special-interest groups that are instrumental in financing election campaigns. The voter, on the other hand, does not have a great incentive to be well informed about public-choice issues. The individual voter is aware that his or her vote is unlikely to change any outcome, and the costs of gathering information on the large number of technically detailed government programs are high. It is therefore in the rational voter's economic interest to remain "rationally ignorant." Logrolling, vote trading, and rational ignorance cause governments to authorize public programs that are not economically efficient.

INCOME DISTRIBUTION

In a capitalist economy, people who own resources that command a high price have higher incomes than those who own resources that command low prices.

How equally or unequally should income be distributed? To what extent should the state redistribute income?

The marginal productivity theory of income distribution follows from the fact that the private owners of labor, land, and capital are paid the marginal revenue product of their factor. If the factor market is perfectly competitive, the owner receives the actual value of the marginal product of the factor. Thus, argue some economists, the resulting distribution of income is "just" because factor owners receive a reward that is equal to the factor's marginal contribution to society's output. Bestowing rewards according to marginal productivity encourages the owners of the factors of production to raise the productivity of their factors. If the state were to alter this distribution scheme markedly, there would be less incentive to raise the marginal productivity of one's own factors. There would be less investment in human capital and less risk taking, and (accordingly) society's output would be less.

Critics of this "natural justice" view point out that the marginal productivity of any factor depends on the presence of cooperating factors. An American coal miner may work with millions of dollars of capital equipment, whereas the Indian coal miner who works just as hard works with only a pick and shovel. The marginal productivity of the American coal miner is therefore many times that of the Indian coal miner. Moreover, marginal productivity is affected by human capital investment, and not everyone has equal access to education.

There are a number of arguments in favor of a redistributive role for the state. First, people are not indifferent to the welfare of others, and their own welfare is diminished by poverty around them. Yet despite altruistic motives, there are strong incentives against charitable contributions. Any one person's contribution can have only a negligible effect on poverty. The insignificance of any one donor creates a substantial free-rider problem, which means that it is unlikely for voluntary contributions to have a significant impact on the distribution of income. Government income redistribution programs eliminate the free-rider problem. Only the state is in a position to alter the distribution of income.

The philosopher John Rawls has advanced another argument in favor of state intervention.[22] Rawls argues that an unequal distribution of income persists because those who benefit from income inequality are unwilling to accept changes that favor the poor. People are unwilling to agree to redistribution because those who will be rich know fairly early in life their chances of being rich. For this reason, a social consensus can never be formed whereby the rich agree to redistribute income to the poor.

Rawls asks: How would people behave if they did not know in advance their lifetime endowment of resources? How would they react if they operated behind a "veil of ignorance"? Rawls maintains that under this condition, people would naturally act to minimize the risks of being poor and would therefore reach a social consensus in favor of a fairly equal distribution of income. If people, operating behind a veil of ignorance, would naturally favor an equal distribution of income, then society should have an equal distribution of income.

Insofar as voluntary charitable giving will not effect this result, the state is justified in redistributing income from the rich to the poor.

MACROECONOMIC INSTABILITY

A major challenge to the neoclassical vision of self-regulating capitalism was mounted by John Maynard Keynes in *The General Theory of Employment, Interest, and Money*, published in 1936 against the backdrop of the world depression.[23] The depression seemed to deny neoclassical notions of an automatic tendency toward equilibrium over time. Keynes's assertion that positive government action was required to stabilize capitalist economics represents his major contribution to capitalist thought.

Keynes

Keynes focused on the mainstay of classical equilibrium theory, Say's Law.[24] According to **Say's Law**, there can be no lasting deficiency of aggregate demand because the act of producing a given value of output creates an equivalent amount of income. If that income were not spent directly on consumer goods, it would be saved. The savings would end up being spent as well, for interest rates would adjust to equate *ex ante* savings and *ex ante* investment. Accordingly, depressions could not be caused by deficiencies in aggregate demand. If one were only patient, eventually prices and wages would adjust to bring about an equilibrium at full employment. If unemployment did exist, it would be because workers were unwilling to accept the lower real wages required for labor market equilibrium. As long as prices and wages are flexible, there will be an automatic adjustment mechanism to restore full employment.

Keynes argued that there is no assurance that equilibrium will occur at full employment or that the automatic adjustment mechanism will work with reasonable speed. Thus — and this is the foundation of the Keynesian revolution — it is the responsibility of government to ensure full employment of the nation's resources.

Keynes disputed the conclusions of the neoclassical school in the following manner. First, he argued that wages and prices are not nearly so flexible (especially downward) as the neoclassical economists believed. He pointed to the fact that despite considerable unemployment, money wages were not falling in England in the 1920s and 1930s. Second, he argued that aggregate saving is not significantly affected by the interest rate; rather, it is principally dependent on the level of income. According to Keynes, the investment–savings relationship would be especially troublesome because of the cyclical instability of investment expenditures; only by chance would enough investment be forthcoming to guarantee full employment.

Keynes saw no reason why macroequilibrium should occur at a rate of output sufficient to ensure full employment. Therefore, it is the responsibility of government, by appropriately raising or lowering its spending and taxes (fiscal policy) or by controlling investment spending (through monetary policy), to ensure that equilibrium occurs near full employment. Because investment spending is quite unstable, government must be prepared to counteract investment fluctuations with compensatory actions.

After the Second World War, Keynes's advocacy of discretionary monetary and fiscal policy came to be widely accepted by economists and public officials, who felt justified in abandoning the traditional hands-off policies favored by the neoclassical school. Federal budgets could be openly in deficit in order to stimulate the economy. In the United States, for example, tax cuts and tax increases were imposed for the express purpose of manipulating aggregate demand. The practice of demand management became standard procedure in Western Europe, Japan, and Canada. Monetary policy also became an instrument of macroeconomic regulation. In the height of optimism in the mid-1960s there was talk of being able to "fine-tune" the economy, and the business cycle was declared dead. The general acceptance of these notions was called the **Keynesian revolution**.

Self-Correcting Capitalism: Monetarism and Rational Expectations

Keynes and his contemporary followers questioned the cyclical stability of capitalism. Without government intervention to moderate business cycles, there will be a significant loss of output and employment. Keynesian economics advocates **policy activism** — the discretionary use of monetary and fiscal policy to try to prevent or ameliorate the business cycle. Activist monetary and fiscal policy is required to keep the economy on an even keel.

The monetarists, under the intellectual leadership of Milton Friedman, and rational expectations economists, led by Robert Lucas, argue against the use of activist macroeconomic policy to combat capitalism's cyclical instability.[25] They argue that capitalism is considerably more stable than Keynes had thought. In fact, the Great Depression was an aberration caused in large part by blunders in economic policy. The capitalist economy has a built-in self-correcting mechanism that will restore it to full employment or to the natural rate of unemployment. If the economy is operating at an unemployment rate above the natural rate, a slowing down of the inflation rate (or even deflation in extreme cases) will restore the economy to full employment. Lower prices raise aggregate supply, and aggregate employment rises until the natural rate is reached.

The monetarists argue against the use of activist policy. Because fiscal policy is decided primarily by politics rather than economics, monetary policy has been the most flexible tool of activist policy. Monetarists maintain that activist monetary policy is as likely to do harm as good. Lengthy and indeterminate lags separate the recognition of a macroeconomic problem, the taking of necessary monetary action, and realization of the effect of that action on the economy.

An anti-inflationary policy adopted during a period of rising prices may begin to affect the economy at the very time an expansionary monetary policy is required. Rather than running the risk of policy mistakes, the monetarists favor a fixed-monetary-growth rule, which would bind monetary authorities to expand the money supply by a fixed rate each year (roughly equal to the real growth of the economy) regardless of the state of the economy.

Advocates of the **rational expectations theory** also argue against activist policy. They maintain that activist policy will have the desired effect on the economy only if the policy catches people off guard. If taxes are lowered for the purpose of stimulating employment, and people know from experience that lower taxes raise inflation, people will take actions to defeat the policy. If monetary authorities expand the money supply to raise employment, and workers and employees know that more monetary growth means more inflation, the higher wages and prices will not raise employment or real output.

The basic message of the monetarists and rational expectations economists is that capitalism is much more stable than Keynes had thought and that activist policies are likely to harm the economy. It is better to rely on the self-correcting forces of the capitalist economy to restore it to equilibrium than to count on government policy makers to do so.

THE PERFORMANCE OF CAPITALIST ECONOMIC SYSTEMS: HYPOTHESES

Chapter 3 discussed criteria by which to judge the performance of economic systems: economic growth, efficiency, income distribution, and stability. What hypotheses, if any, follow from the theory of capitalism in each of these areas? First, let us say that it is difficult to formulate hypotheses at this point, because our principal concern is the efficiency of capitalism vis-à-vis other economic systems; these hypotheses would best be stated in relative terms. (See Table 5.1.)

Efficiency

Capitalism should provide a high level of efficiency, especially in the static case. The more competitive the economy, the more efficient the economy. The producer's desire to maximize profits and the consumer's desire to maximize utility lead to a maximal output from available resources under conditions of perfect competition. Imperfect competition and external effects reduce this efficiency. Another point promoting static efficiency is capitalism's apparent ability to process and utilize information more effectively than an economic system in which the market is lacking. Probably the most important point is that profit maximization, under all market arrangements, strongly encourages the efficient (least-cost) combination of resources to produce output.

Stability

Stability is the ability of an economic system to grow without undue fluctuations in the rate of growth and without excessive inflation and unemployment. Of course, it is a subjective judgment what "undue" and "excessive" mean in such a context. Keynes argued that capitalist economies are not stable, at least in terms of short-run automatic equilibrating forces. Monetarists and rational expectations theorists believe that capitalist economies are (or could be) inherently more stable if left to their own devices; so there is considerable disagreement on this point. However, capitalism continues to suffer periodic bouts of inflation, unemployment, and growth fluctuations, which the general public regards as troubling.

Income Distribution

The theory of capitalism cannot make definitive judgments about equity and how resources should be divided among the members of capitalist societies. Only value judgments can provide answers. We lack a consensus about "fairness," and without an agreed-upon definition it is difficult to arrive at hypotheses. Instead, we can only consider empirical measures of income distribution and make statements like the following: Income is distributed more equally in society X than in society Y. It is difficult to proceed further and say income is distributed "better" ("more fairly") in X or in Y.

The theory of capitalism, however, does suggest the likelihood of significant inequalities in the distribution of income. The factors of production are owned predominantly by private individuals, and the relative value of these factors is determined by the market. Insofar as human and physical capital and natural ability are not likely to be evenly distributed, especially when such things can be passed from one generation to another, private ownership of the factors of production raises the likelihood of an uneven distribution of income and wealth among the members of capitalist societies. Exactly how unevenly income and

Table 5.1 Hypothesis on the Performance of Capitalist Economic Systems

Criterion	Performance
Efficiency	Good
Stability	Potentially poor; debate over government role
Income distribution	Unequal in the absence of state action
Economic growth	No clear *a priori* hypothesis: greater efficiency versus potentially lower capital formation

wealth are distributed will depend on the distribution of human and physical capital and also on the redistributive role of the state.

Economic Growth

One of the supposed advantages of planned socialist economies is their ability to direct resources to specific goals, such as economic growth and military power. To a greater extent than capitalist economies, they can marshal resources for economic growth, if they so desire, by controlling the investment rate and the growth rate of the labor force. Although capitalist governments can and do affect the investment rate, the amount saved is largely a matter of individual choice, and it is likely that individual choice will result in lower savings rates than a planned socialist economy. Thus if the growth of factor inputs is left to individuals, one would hypothesize a slower rate of growth of factor inputs and hence of economic growth, *ceteris paribus*, under capitalism.

A counterbalancing factor must be considered: the hypothesized efficiency of capitalist economies. Static efficiency means that a maximal output is produced from available resources and (with a given saving rate) a greater volume of savings is available relative to less efficient production methods. Moreover, there is the unresolved matter of the dynamic efficiency of capitalist economic systems. Up to this point, capitalist theory has had relatively little to say about dynamic efficiency. It is conceivable that the greater static and dynamic efficiency of capitalism can compensate for the lesser control over the growth of productive resources.

Viability of the Capitalist System

The viability of capitalism has been demonstrated by both theory and historical experience. Capitalist theory points to its inherent tendencies toward equilibrium. And historical experience shows that capitalism has survived several centuries and that there are no signs of impending collapse.

SUMMARY: THEORY OF CAPITALISM

1. This chapter discusses how well capitalism solves the problem of resource allocation and what economic role the state should play in the capitalist system. The mainstream approach maintains that if one is prepared to accept the underlying distribution of income, resource allocation will be optimal if the economy is perfectly competitive. Optimality is defined as an allocation of resources that cannot be changed to make at least one person "better off" without making at least one other person "worse off" (Pareto optimality). If the economy is reasonably competitive, capitalism will be self-regulating and will yield "good" allocation of resources, ignoring any problems of "unfair" distributions of income. The policy prescription is that the role of

government should be strictly limited and that government should maintain a hands-off policy toward business.

2. Critics of this model of self-regulating capitalism have focused on several perceived weaknesses. Keynes attempted to demonstrate that the economy could establish a stable macroequilibrium at less than (or greater than) full employment. It was, therefore, the government's responsibility to bring about an appropriate macroequilibrium. Critics have also emphasized that with imperfect competition, resource allocation could not be optimal and the government would therefore have to step in to correct the abuses of monopoly power through regulation and taxation. Moreover, other economists have demonstrated that resources will be misallocated whenever externalities are present; government must therefore ensure that social as well as private costs and benefits are considered in private economic decisions.

3. The notion of self-regulating capitalism has its contemporary defenders as well as its critics. The monetarists, under the leadership of Friedman, have mounted an important counterattack on the Keynesian revolution. Some have even argued that capitalism will automatically take care of its monopoly and externality problems without government intervention.

4. Capitalism should perform well in the efficiency area but tends to be unstable. The distribution of income is less equitable than under social ownership (although the state can redistribute income). No firm hypothesis can be put forward concerning economic growth.

NOTES

1. Examples of how the latter approach has been applied are found in Abram Bergson, *The Economics of Soviet Planning* (New Haven: Yale University Press, 1964); Jaroslav Vanek, *The Participatory Economy* (Ithaca, N.Y.: Cornell University Press, 1971), Chs. 2–3; and Benjamin Ward, *The Socialist Economy* (New York: Random House, 1967), Chs. 8–9. We also refer the reader to our discussion of the socialist controversy in Chapter 7.

2. Adam Smith, *The Wealth of Nations*, ed. Edwin Cannan (New York: Modern Library, 1937).

3. George Stigler, "The Successes and Failures of Professor Smith," *Journal of Political Economy*, 84 (December 1976), 1199–1214.

4. It is difficult to single out a few individuals and claim that they are the major contributors to partial-equilibrium analysis, but these three would appear on most lists: Alfred Marshall, *Principles of Economics*, 8th ed. (New York: Macmillan, 1948); J. R. Hicks, *Value and Capital*, 2nd ed. (Oxford, England: Oxford University Press, 1946); and Paul Samuelson, *Foundations of Economic Analysis* (Cambridge, Mass.: Harvard University Press, 1948).

5. Leon Walras, *Elements of Pure Economics*, Jaffe translation (London: Unwin-Hyman, 1954). Walras demonstrated this proposition by noting that in a general-equilibrium framework, the demand and supply schedules in each market (let us assume m such markets) are functions of their own price and the prices of all other commodities in the economy. This follows from the fact that when all markets are allowed to interact simultaneously, changes in commodity prices can affect demands and supplies in other markets because of the existence of substitute and complementary relationships. As formulated by Walras, the general-equilibrium system consists of m equations and m unknowns — a seemingly desirable state of affairs, mathematically speak-

ing, for it suggests the existence of an equilibrium set of prices (under certain conditions, it was later demonstrated), which will cause all markets to clear simultaneously.

At this point, Walras introduced and then resolved an important indeterminacy in the model, and this resolution is his major contribution to general-equilibrium analysis. Because the value of purchases in the economy must *identically* equal the value of sales (Walras's identity), the general-equilibrium system actually consists of only $m - 1$ independent equations, a concession that at first appears to leave the solution for the set of equilibrium prices indeterminate. Walras's resolution of this problem was to demonstrate that, in actuality, the number of unknown prices is also $m - 1$, for only *relative* prices affect supply and demand. Accordingly, one commodity must be singled out as a numeraire, and the system can then be solved for a consistent set of *relative*-equilibrium prices.

6. Subsequent research on general equilibrium has addressed the issues of existence and stability. The *existence* literature addresses the point that the mere equality of equations and unknowns does not ensure the existence of a set of equilibrium prices, for existence will depend on functional forms of utility and production functions, and realistic values (zero or positive prices and quantities) are required for an acceptable general-equilibrium solution. The research of Kenneth Arrow and Gerard Debreu reveals that a general equilibrium does exist under certain conditions associated with perfect competition and orderly utility and production functions. The *stability* literature addresses the issue of the stability of the general equilibrium — that is, whether there is an automatic tendency for the economy to return to a general equilibrium after this equilibrium has been disrupted.

7. For a detailed treatment of Pareto's economics and philosophy, see Vincent Tarascio, *Pareto's Methodological Approach to Economics: A Study in the History of Some Scientific Aspects of Economic Thought* (Chapel Hill: University of North Carolina Press, 1968).

8. James Henderson and Richard Quandt, *Microeconomic Theory: A Mathematical Approach*, 2nd ed. (New York: McGraw-Hill, 1971), Ch. 7.

9. For a simple presentation of the conditions of Pareto optimality, see F. M. Bator, "The Simple Analytics of Welfare Maximization," *American Economic Review*, 47 (March 1957), 22–59. For more sophisticated treatments, see Henderson and Quandt, *Microeconomic Theory*, Ch. 7.

10. The standard reference on the second-best hypothesis is R. G. Lipsey and Kelvin Lancaster, "The General Theory of the Second Best," *Review of Economic Studies*, 24 (1956–1957), 11–32.

11. Friedrich Hayek, "The Price System as a Mechanism for Using Knowledge," *American Economic Review*, 35 (September 1945), 519–530; and Ludwig von Mises, *Socialism: An Economic and Sociological Analysis* (New Haven: Yale University Press, 1951).

12. Paul Samuelson, "The Pure Theory of Public Expenditure," *Review of Economics and Statistics*, 36 (November 1954), 26–30.

13. For a brief but lucid discussion of monopoly theory, see George Stigler, *The Theory of Price*, rev. ed. (New York: Macmillan, 1952), pp. 204–222.

14. Joan Robinson, *The Economics of Imperfect Competition* (London: Macmillan, 1933); Edward Chamberlin, *The Theory of Monopolistic Competition*, 6th ed. (Cambridge, Mass.: Harvard University Press, 1948).

15. *Oligopoly* is defined as a market comprising a few sellers, interdependent in their output and pricing decisions, producing either a homogeneous or a differentiated product. *Monopolistic competition* is defined as a market consisting of a large number of producers, producing a slightly differentiated product, with limited barriers to entry.

16. Figure 5.5 (shown on p. 95) is adapted from Henderson and Quandt, *Microeconomic Theory*, pp. 277–279. The figure assumes (for purposes of simplification) constant marginal costs (MC) equal to average total costs (ATC).

In order to induce the monopolist to increase output to Q_c, he or she must be paid a unit subsidy equal to EC, the total subsidy being the area of the rectangle $FECP_c$. The monopolist's increase in costs from going from Q_m to Q_c is Q_mBQ_cC, whereas the increase in revenues is the area under the MR curve, or Q_mBEQ_c. Therefore, the monopolist's profits decline by the difference between the increase in revenues and the increase in costs, or the area BCE, which should equal the original profits P_mABP_c, because we have constructed the example so that the monopolist is now making zero profits at Q_c. The monopolist will be just as well off at Q_c as at Q_m if the state charges a lump-sum tax equal to P_cBEF, for that will leave the original profits, the BCE triangle, intact.

Consumers have been made better off as a consequence of the expansion of output from Q_m to Q_c and the decline in price from P_m to P_c. Assuming zero income elasticities (to avoid shifts in the demand schedule as prices change), the increase in consumer surplus is measured by the area under the demand schedule between Q_m and Q_c, or the area Q_mACQ_c. However, consumers pay only the area under the MR curve, or Q_mBEQ_c, to the producer, leaving them with a surplus of $AEBC$. The state can therefore tax this surplus away without reducing consumers' satisfaction below its original level at A, and the state is required only to make to the producer a net payment equal to BCE to keep the producer at the original level of profit. Therefore, the state has generated a surplus equal to the triangle ABC as a consequence of moving the producer from Q_m to Q_c, the Pareto-optimal output and price level.

17. Milton Friedman, "Monopoly and Social Responsibility of Business and Labor," in Edwin Mansfield, ed., *Monopoly Power and Economic Performance*, 3rd ed. (New York: Norton, 1974), pp. 57–68; and George J. Stigler, "The Government of the Economy," in Paul Samuelson, ed., *Readings in Economics*, 7th ed. (New York: McGraw-Hill, 1973), pp. 73–77.

18. The discussion of externalities is based on the following sources: E. J. Mishan, "The Postwar Literature on Externalities: An Interpretive Essay," *Journal of Economic Literature*, 9 (March 1971), 1–28; George Daly, "The Coase Theorem: Assumptions, Applications, and Ambiguities," *Economic Inquiry*, 12 (June 1974), 203–213; and Eirik Furobotin and Svetozar Pejovich, "Property Rights and Economic Theory: A Survey of Recent Literature," *Journal of Economic Literature*, 12 (December 1972), 1137–1162.

19. R. H. Coase, "The Problem of Social Costs," *Journal of Law and Economics*, 3 (October 1960), 1–44.

20. Mishan, "The Postwar Literature on Externalities," p. 17.

21. James Buchanan and Gordon Tullock, *The Calculus of Consent* (Ann Arbor: University of Michigan Press, 1974); Kenneth Arrow, *Social Choice and Individual Values* (New Haven: Yale University Press, 1976).

Figure 5.5 The Social Control of Monopoly

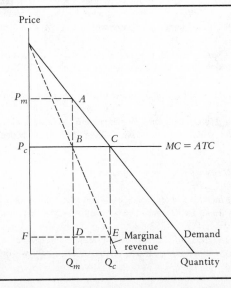

22. John Rawls, *Theory of Justice* (Oxford, England: Clarendon Press, 1976).
23. John Maynard Keynes, *The General Theory of Employment, Interest, and Money* (New York: Harcourt, 1936). The most important early work to interpret Keynes's general theory for non-specialists was Alvin Hansen, *A Guide to Keynes* (New York: McGraw-Hill, 1953).
24. There is considerable controversy over what Keynes actually meant to say in *General Theory*, and some authorities argue that the more popular interpretations of Keynes are incorrect. For discussion of this controversy, see Don Patinkin, *Money, Interest, and Prices*, 2nd ed. (New York: Harper & Row, 1965); Axel Leijonhufvud, *On Keynesian Economics and the Economics of Keynes* (New York: Oxford University Press, 1968); Herschel Grossman, "Was Keynes a 'Keynesian'? A Review Article," *Journal of Economic Literature*, 10 (March 1972), 26–30; and Alan Coddington, "Keynesian Economics: The Search for First Principles," *Journal of Economic Literature*, 14 (December 1976), 1258–1338. For a historical perspective on the Keynesian revolution, see Alan Sweezy *et al.*, "The Keynesian Revolution and Its Pioneers," *American Economic Review, Papers and Proceedings*, 62 (May 1972), 116–141.
25. The discussion of the monetarist school is based on the following sources: Milton Friedman, ed., *Studies in the Quantity Theory of Money* (Chicago: University of Chicago Press, 1956); Milton Friedman and A. J. Schwartz, *A Monetary History of the United States* (Princeton, N.J.: Princeton University Press, 1963); Milton Friedman, *Dollars and Deficits* (Englewood Cliffs, N.J.: Prentice-Hall, 1968); Franco Modigliani, "The Monetarist Controversy, or, Should We Forsake Stabilization Policies?" *American Economic Review*, 67 (March 1977), 13; Edmund Phelps, *Microeconomic Foundations of Employment and Inflation Theory* (London: Macmillan, 1974); and Milton Friedman, "Inflation and Unemployment," *Journal of Political Economy*, 85 (June 1977), 451–472.

RECOMMENDED READINGS

The Neoclassical Model

F. M. Bator, "The Simple Analytics of Welfare Maximization," *American Economic Review*, 47 (March 1957), 22–59.

Abram Bergson, "A Reformulation of Certain Aspects of Welfare Economics," *Quarterly Journal of Economics*, 52 (February 1938), 310–334; reprinted in R. V. Clemence, ed., *Readings in Economic Analysis* (Reading, Mass.: Addison Wesley, 1950), Vol. I, pp. 61–85.

J. de V. Graaff, *Theoretical Welfare Economics* (London: Cambridge University Press, 1957).

James Henderson and Richard Quandt, *Microeconomic Theory: A Mathematical Approach*, 2nd ed. (New York: McGraw-Hill, 1971), Chs. 5–7.

J. R. Hicks, *Value and Capital*, 2nd ed. (Oxford, England: Oxford University Press, 1946).

David M. Krebs, *A Course in Microeconomic Theory* (Princeton, N.J.: Princeton University Press, 1990).

Paul Samuelson, *Foundations of Economic Analysis* (Cambridge, Mass.: Harvard University Press, 1948).

Tibor Scitovsky, *Welfare and Competition*, rev. ed. (Homewood, Ill.: Irwin, 1971), Chs. 20–21.

Adam Smith, *The Wealth of Nations*, ed. Edwin Cannan (New York: Modern Library, 1937).

Macroeconomic Theory

Martin Bailey, *National Income and the Price Level*, 2nd ed. (New York: McGraw-Hill, 1971).

Alan Coddington, "Keynesian Economics: The Search for First Principles," *Journal of Economic Literature*, 14 (December 1976), 1258–1338.

Paul Davidson, *Money and the Real World* (London: Macmillan, 1972).

Rudiger Dornbusch and Stanley Fischer, *Macroeconomics*, 4th ed. (New York: McGraw-Hill, 1987).

A. S. Eicher and J. A. Kregel, "An Essay on Post-Keynesian Theory: A New Paradigm in Economics," *Journal of Economic Literature*, 13 (December 1975), 1293–1314.

Milton Friedman, *Dollars and Deficits* (Englewood Cliffs, N.J.: Prentice-Hall, 1968).

———, ed., *Studies in the Quantity Theory of Money* (Chicago: University of Chicago Press, 1956).

Robert J. Gordon, "What Is New Keynesian Economics?" *Journal of Economic Literature*, 28 (September 1990), 15–71.

———, *Macroeconomics*, 5th ed. (Glenview, Ill.: Scott, Foresman, 1990).

Herschel Grossman, "Was Keynes a 'Keynesian'? A Review Article," *Journal of Economic Literature*, 10 (March 1972), 26–30.

John Maynard Keynes, *The General Theory of Employment, Interest, and Money* (New York: Harcourt, 1936).

Axel Leijonhufvud, *On Keynesian Economics and the Economics of Keynes* (New York: Oxford University Press, 1968).

N. Gregory Markew, "A Quick Refresher Course in Macroeconomics," *Journal of Economic Literature*, 28 (December 1990), 1645–60.

Franco Modigliani, "The Monetarist Controversy, or, Should We Forsake Stabilization Policies?" *American Economic Review*, 67 (March 1977), 1–19.

Market Failures: Imperfect Competition, Income Distribution, Externalities, and Public Choice

James Buchanan and Robert Tollison, eds., *Theory of Public Choice: Political Applications of Economics* (Ann Arbor: University of Michigan Press, 1972).

James Buchanan and Gordon Tullock, *The Calculus of Consent* (Ann Arbor: University of Michigan Press, 1974).

Edward Chamberlin, *The Theory of Monopolistic Competition*, 6th ed. (Cambridge, Mass.: Harvard University Press, 1948).

R. H. Coase, "The Problem of Social Costs," *Journal of Law and Economics*, 3 (October 1960), 1–44.

E. J. Mishan, "The Postwar Literature on Externalities: An Interpretive Essay," *Journal of Economic Literature*, 9 (March 1971), 1–28.

A. C. Pigou, *The Economics of Welfare*, 4th ed. (London: Macmillan, 1946).

John Rawls, *Theory of Justice* (Oxford, England: Clarendon Press, 1976).

Joan Robinson, *The Economics of Imperfect Competition* (London: Macmillan, 1959).

Paul Samuelson, "The Pure Theory of Public Expenditure," *Review of Economics and Statistics*, 36 (November 1954), 26–30.

F. M. Sherer and David Ross, *Industrial Market Structure and Economic Performance*, 3rd ed. (Boston: Houghton Mifflin, 1990).

6 Marxism–Leninism

ONE COMMON THEME UNITES ALL THEORISTS OF CAPITALISM: Capitalism, either on its own or through revisions that do not alter its basic character, can resolve the economic problem of resource allocation. The Marxist–Leninist tradition, on the other hand, argues that capitalism is subject to basic internal contradictions that cannot be remedied through reform of the system. Marx wrote that the capitalist system would eventually succumb to these contradictions and be replaced by a new (superior) socialist order.

THE ECONOMICS OF MARX

Although Marxist–Leninist thought is currently in disarray, at one time approximately one-third of the world's population lived in nations vowing allegiance to its ideals. Its appeal has been strong, particularly in poor countries. Whether Marxist–Leninist thought remains in disrepute will depend on the success of economic reforms now under way in the Soviet Union and Eastern Europe. Figure 6.1 represents a schematic diagram of the major developments of Marxist–Leninist thought.

Dialectical Materialism

Karl Marx (1818–1883) and his collaborator, Friedrich Engels (1820–1895), mounted the most serious challenge to capitalism in Marx's three-volume *Capital* (*Das Kapital* in German).[1] Much of *Capital* was published posthumously under the editorship of Engels.[2] *Capital* concludes that capitalism is an unstable economic organization, the lifespan of which is inevitably limited.

Marx's theory of capitalism is based on his materialist conception of history,[3] which involves a belief that economic forces (called **productive forces**) determine how production relations, markets, and most generally society itself (the **superstructure**) are organized. Weak productive forces (underdeveloped human and physical capital resources) result in one arrangement for producing goods

Figure 6.1 Schematic Development of Marxist Thought

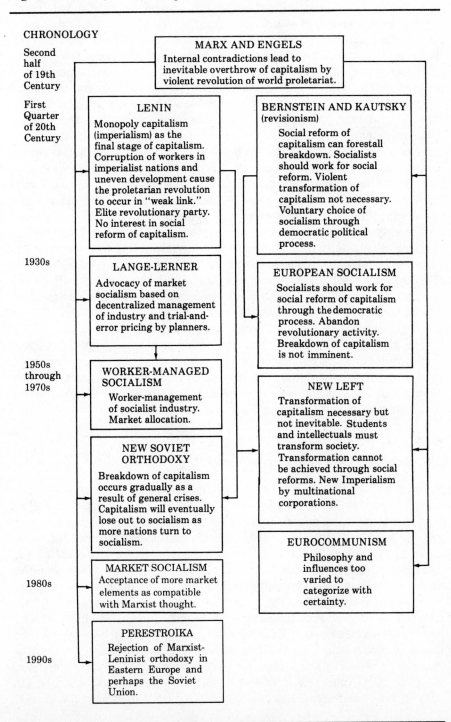

CHRONOLOGY

Second half of 19th Century

First Quarter of 20th Century

1930s

1950s through 1970s

1980s

1990s

MARX AND ENGELS
Internal contradictions lead to inevitable overthrow of capitalism by violent revolution of world proletariat.

LENIN
Monopoly capitalism (imperialism) as the final stage of capitalism. Corruption of workers in imperialist nations and uneven development cause the proletarian revolution to occur in "weak link." Elite revolutionary party. No interest in social reform of capitalism.

BERNSTEIN AND KAUTSKY (revisionism)
Social reform of capitalism can forestall breakdown. Socialists should work for social reform. Violent transformation of capitalism not necessary. Voluntary choice of socialism through democratic political process.

LANGE-LERNER
Advocacy of market socialism based on decentralized management of industry and trial-and-error pricing by planners.

EUROPEAN SOCIALISM
Socialists should work for social reform of capitalism through the democratic process. Abandon revolutionary activity. Breakdown of capitalism is not imminent.

WORKER-MANAGED SOCIALISM
Worker-management of socialist industry. Market allocation.

NEW SOVIET ORTHODOXY
Breakdown of capitalism occurs gradually as a result of general crises. Capitalism will eventually lose out to socialism as more nations turn to socialism.

NEW LEFT
Transformation of capitalism necessary but not inevitable. Students and intellectuals must transform society. Transformation cannot be achieved through social reforms. New Imperialism by multinational corporations.

MARKET SOCIALISM
Acceptance of more market elements as compatible with Marxist thought.

EUROCOMMUNISM
Philosophy and influences too varied to categorize with certainty.

PERESTROIKA
Rejection of Marxist-Leninist orthodoxy in Eastern Europe and perhaps the Soviet Union.

and services (**production relations**), and strong productive forces lead to different, more advanced production arrangements. Thus, a society with underdeveloped economic resources would be expected to have similarly underdeveloped production relations and superstructure (manifested in barter exchange, serf labor, a rigid social hierarchy, and religious biases against commerce). As the productive forces improve, new economic and social relationships emerge (such as hired rather than serf labor and monetary rather than natural exchange). These new arrangements are not compatible with the old set of economic, cultural, and social relationships. When they come into contact, tensions and conflicts mount.

Eventually, the incompatibilities become so great that a qualitative change (usually the result of violent revolution or war) occurs. New production relations and a new superstructure, compatible with the new productive forces, replace the old order. These **qualitative changes** are inevitable because societies are destined to evolve from a lower to a higher order.

The engine of change is the conflict between old and new, primarily in the form of class antagonisms (the emerging capitalist class versus the landed gentry in feudal societies, the worker versus the capitalist in capitalist societies). The process of evolutionary and inevitable qualitative change through the competition of opposing forces (**thesis versus antithesis**) is the foundation of Marx's theory of **dialectical materialism**, which is based on the teachings of the German philosophers Georg Wilhelm Hegel and Ludwig Feuerbach.

The upshot of Marx's materialist conception of history was his contention that societies evolve according to an inevitable pattern of social and economic change in which lower systems are replaced by more advanced systems. In this manner, feudalism is bound to replace slavery, capitalism inevitably displaces feudalism, and socialism eventually replaces capitalism.

The Class Struggle and Surplus Value

According to the dialectic, the victory of capitalism over feudalism represents a qualitative step forward for society. A highly efficient productive machine (capitalism) replaces an inefficient one (feudalism) based on semiservile labor and governed by traditional landed interests. Two landmarks signal the emergence of capitalism. The first is the initial accumulation of capital by the emerging capitalist class (the bourgeoisie) — a process Marx called **primitive capitalist accumulation**. The second indicator is the formation of a "free" labor force at the disposal of capitalist employers. Laborers are separated from control over the factors of production (land, tools, livestock) and are left with only their own labor to sell. At this point the capitalist, who now controls the means of production, hires this free labor, and capitalist factories are established to serve as the new vehicle for commodity production. In this manner, the basic class conflict of capitalism is created — the conflict between the working class and the capitalist, who "owns" the labor services of the worker.

A new superstructure emerges in which all social, political, and religious institutions serve the interests of the new ruling class, the bourgeoisie.

Marx's **labor theory of value** and **theory of surplus value** are key to explaining the long-run dynamics of capitalism. Marx maintained that value (true price) is determined by the amount of labor embodied directly and indirectly in the commodity, plus profit. Marx did not deny that in the short run, commodity prices are determined by supply and demand and could therefore diverge from their underlying labor values. Moreover, even in the long run, the prices of individual commodities may deviate systematically from their labor values because of differing capital intensities of production (the transformation problem).[4] Despite these reservations, two basic points remain: Value is generally equal to labor inputs, and only direct labor can produce profits (surplus value).

Marx's labor theory of value states that the value of a commodity (C) equals the sum of direct labor costs (v), indirect labor costs (c), and surplus value (s), Marx's term for profits.[5]

$$C = c + v + s \qquad (6.1)$$

Marx's definitions of fixed capital or indirect labor costs (c) and variable capital or direct labor costs (v) differ somewhat from the modern use of the terms. Fixed capital (c) refers to outlays for the services of plant, equipment, inventories, and expenditures for materials, the common feature of which is that they embody past labor, which has already been exploited. In modern terminology, c represents the non-labor costs of production (depreciation, material costs, insurance charges, and others). By v Marx means the direct labor costs of production — that is, wage costs.

The feature that distinguishes labor from the other factors of production (land, capital, and materials) is that the employer can compel workers to produce a value that exceeds the value of the labor the workers must "sell" to maintain themselves. Yet the employer is not required to pay workers the full value of their production — only enough to allow them to subsist. A particular worker may have to perform 8 hours of work to produce a value sufficient to meet subsistence needs; yet the employer can force the worker to create a surplus (s), which will accrue to capitalists, by working 12 hours — 4 hours more than are required to satisfy subsistence needs. Marx was unclear about how **subsistence needs** were to be defined; it is not clear whether he meant physical subsistence or some socially accepted consumption norm. Other factors of production (c), though essential to the production process, cannot create surplus value, for the surplus value created in their production has already been appropriated by the capitalist class. Direct labor is the sole source of surplus value (s). Workers are exploited because they produce the surplus but it accrues to the capitalist class.[6] Surplus value plays a central role in Marxian theory, for the capitalist's desire to maximize profits is the driving engine of capitalism.

Whether workers receive a share of the surplus value depends on whether they are paid subsistence wages or above-subsistence wages.[7] Marx maintained that wages would tend toward subsistence in the long run, because capitalism creates a large number of unemployed workers (called the **reserve army of the unemployed**) whose existence ensures that wages will not rise for long periods above subsistence.

Three relationships illustrate Marx's view of the dynamics of capitalism. The first is the **rate of exploitation**, s', which is

$$s' = \frac{s}{v} \qquad (6.2)$$

The rate of exploitation equals profits divided by the wage bill. If a worker is required to work 12 hours per day, of which only 8 hours are needed to meet subsistence requirements, surplus value is 4 and the rate of exploitation is 4/8 or 0.5. The worker will receive a wage equal to subsistence requirements (8 hours or production), and the employer will receive a profit of 4 hours of production.

The second relationship is called the **organic composition of capital** (q), which Marx defines as the ratio of fixed capital to total (fixed plus variable) capital:

$$q = \frac{c}{c + v} \qquad (6.3)$$

The third relationship is the **profit rate** (p), which Marx defines as the ratio of surplus value to total capital:

$$p = \frac{s}{c + v} \qquad (6.4)$$

or, substituting from equation 6.3,

$$p = s' \, (1 - q) \qquad (6.5)$$

As equation 6.5 indicates, the profit rate is the product of the rate of exploitation times $(1 - q)$. Thus, the higher s', the higher p; and the higher q (the greater the share of fixed capital), the lower p. If there were no variable capital ($v = 0$), there would be no profits (an expected result because only direct labor creates surplus value). The trend in the long-run profit rate depends, according to Marx's definitions, directly on s' and inversely on q.

The Law of the Falling Rate of Profit, Exploitation, and Crises

Marx pictured capitalism, at least in its early stages, as a world of cut-throat competition. He believed that the capitalist was driven to maximize profits (surplus value) and to accumulate more capital out of profits.

The forces of competition compel capitalists to increase the organic composition of capital (q), causing the profit rate to fall. Capitalists, operating in intensely competitive markets, are forced to introduce cost-saving innovations, lest their competitors do so before them and drive them out of business.[8] Capitalist A introduces a new labor-saving technology, attracts competitors' customers through lower prices, and experiences a temporary increase in profits above "normal" levels. The profits are short-lived, however, because competitors respond by introducing the same cost-saving techniques, and new competitors enter the market in response to windfall profits. Excess industry profits are eliminated, and no capitalist ends up better off. But fixed capital has been substituted for labor (q rises), and unless something happens to offset the rise in q, the profit rate will decline. There is an inherent tendency to substitute fixed for variable capital throughout the economy, even though variable capital (labor), is the sole source of surplus value. Marx predicted the profit rate would fall, with disastrous consequences for capitalism.

The proposition of the declining profit rate depends on a strong *ceteris paribus* condition that casts doubt on its inevitability.[9] For now, let us continue Marx's line of reasoning.

As the profit rate falls, internal contradictions and weaknesses in the system become apparent. In an effort to halt the decline in p, capitalists attempt to increase the exploitation of their workers (to raise s'), and alienation and exploitation intensify. Moreover, the declining profit rate leads to the failure of marginal businesses, and bankrupt capitalists now swell the ranks of the unemployed. The misery of the proletariat worsens. Those fortunate enough to be employed are exploited and alienated; the unemployed are in even worse shape.

A more ominous phenomenon is the tendency toward overproduction and disproportions.[10] Workers are kept at subsistence wages by high unemployment; capitalists, driven by the desire to accumulate capital, are not willing to increase their spending on luxury goods. Moreover, the ranks of the capitalists are thinning, as monopolies drive smaller capitalists out of business. Yet all the while, the productive capacity of the economy is growing because of the growing capital-intensity of industry. Aggregate demand falls chronically short of aggregate supply; recessions and then depressions occur, and worldwide crises become commonplace. The declining profit rate leads to declines in investment spending and to further shortfalls in aggregate demand. Disproportions in individual branches, such as steel and energy, can further intensify crises.

Marx described only generally the final stages of the **capitalist breakdown**. Overproduction, underconsumption, disproportions, and the exploitation and alienation of workers combine to create the conditions necessary for the violent overthrow of capitalism.[11] The proletariat unites against the weakened capitalist class and, through a violent *world* revolution, establishes a new socialist order. Marx and Engels had little to say about this new order. Implicit in Marx's writings on the final stage of capitalism is the point that the contradictions will be most intense in the most advanced capitalist countries; the proletarian revolution will be initiated there.

LENIN: MONOPOLY CAPITALISM
AND IMPERIALISM

Vladimir Ilich Lenin (1870–1924), the father of the Russian Revolution, wrote primarily about the politics of revolution (prior to 1917) and the practical problems of governing the first socialist state. His most important economic works, *The Development of Capitalism in Russia* and *Imperialism, the Highest Stage of Capitalism*, were both researched and written from exile.[12]

Better known for his theory of revolutionary strategy (the concept of an elite revolutionary party),[13] Lenin studied the final stage of capitalism, which he called **monopoly capitalism** or, equivalently, **imperialism**. Lenin's writings on imperialism are best understood in terms of his ambition to lead a Russian Marxist revolution. Marx and Engels were counting on the German proletariat to initiate the revolution. Lenin, as a Russian revolutionary, had to demonstrate why the revolution began in Russia instead. After it was apparent that the Russian Revolution would not turn into a world revolution, Lenin had to explain why the proletarian revolution was confined to the Russian borders (**socialism in one country** versus **world revolution**).

Monopoly Capitalism

According to Lenin, Marx and Engels, writing during the intermediate stages of capitalism, did not have the opportunity to observe the mature stages of capitalism. Lenin concentrated his efforts on the final stage of capitalism, which he called **monopoly capitalism**. Lenin felt that mature capitalism will be different from the competitive system that characterizes early and intermediate capitalism. A monopoly capitalist system will be dominated by giant trusts, cartels, and monopolies, many operating on an international basis. In spite of their power, monopolies will not totally eliminate competitive producers; rather a **dual economy** of coexisting monopolistic giants and competitive industries will emerge. Friction between them will be considerable as the former gradually wear down the latter.

The emergence of monopoly as the dominant economic organization signals the final stage of capitalism. Lenin listed five characteristics of monopoly capitalism:

1. The concentration of production in the hands of fewer and fewer industrial giants
2. The merger of financial and industrial capital, as the banks and financiers come to exercise greater control over the allocation of capital resources
3. The emergence of capital (rather than commodity) exports as the major form of international exchange
4. The division of the world into economic spheres of influence and control by monopoly capitalists

5. The subdivision of the world into corresponding political spheres of influence by the governments of mature capitalist countries.[14]

Lenin's picture of maturing capitalism is not much different from that of
Marx, though it is more sharply defined. The Marxian contradictions are still
present: the declining rate of profits, the class struggle between capitalist and
worker, and the worsening condition of the proletariat. But there are crucial
differences between Marx's and Lenin's visions, and they are related to Lenin's
justification of a proletarian revolution in backward Russia.

According to Lenin, the class struggle would continue in the mature imperialistic countries. In one sense, it would be worsened by the merger of financial
and industrial capitalism. Financial capitalists would come to control capital,
and the ownership and management of industrial enterprises would be separated. Instead of the earlier system of owners, professional managers would
run industries, while an idle class of rentiers would reap the benefits of the
efforts of labor. On the other hand, in the mature countries the class struggle
would be softened by the use of trade unions to bribe the working class with
a share of surplus value. This bargain would be necessary because the wealth
of the advanced imperialist economies would be dependent on exploitation of
the weak colonial countries. In this manner, the proletariat is corrupted; the
exploitation of the working class is exported to weaker countries; and foreign
workers are exploited to benefit the capitalists and privileged workers in the
rich countries.

The Theory of Uneven Development

The **theory of uneven development** is the cornerstone of Lenin's analysis of the
locus of the proletarian revolution.[15] According to Lenin, monopoly capitalism
will experience uneven development both within economic branches and among
capitalist countries. Growth will be uneven because of the friction between
monopolistic and competitive branches, because the decline of competition will
force the state to rescue failing monopolistic industries, and because monopolists will restrain production. On the international level, latecomers (such as the
United States) will be growing rapidly, while the more mature (and decaying)
capitalist countries (such as France) will be in decline. However, because the
underdeveloped world has already been partitioned by the monopoly capitalists,
latecomers must acquire a foreign dominion by taking it away from a declining
power. The law of uneven development ensures global competition and conflict
among the imperialist powers as they vie for the control of foreign resources
and markets.[16]

These military conflicts and wars leave the imperialist powers weakened,
especially the relatively backward countries. This weakness provides the working class with the opportunity to rise up against their capitalist oppressors.
Because the workers in the advanced imperialist countries have already been

bought off, the revolution is not likely to break out there. Rather it is likely to occur in the **weakest link** of the capitalist chain, for there the contradictions and class conflict are most intense. The proletarian revolution, then, should begin not in Germany or England, but in Russia, the weak link in the capitalist chain.

Russia as the Weak Link and the Problems of Transition

According to Lenin, Russia was a peculiar mix of mature and less-advanced capitalism. Lenin underscored the dual nature of the Russian economy. On the one hand, Russian heavy industry was highly concentrated and monopolistic. The Russian industrial worker had already experienced the alienation and exploitation required for the formation of a revolutionary outlook. The Russian state played a prominent role in supporting heavy industry and protecting vested monopoly interests. In fact, the Russian industrial proletariat was exploited both by the monopolistic employers and by the state.[17] Moreover, Russia itself acted as an imperialist power in central Asia, China, and Manchuria. Lenin, however, stressed that there were backward features of Russia as well. Russian industry depended on foreign capital and technology and was in a semicolonial position. Second, handicraft industry continued to dominate the production of consumer goods, in contrast to the control of heavy industry by monopolies. Finally, Russian agriculture was plagued by the vestiges of feudalism and still employed backward cultivation techniques.

From this, Lenin concluded that Russia was indeed the weakest link in the capitalist chain. Its advanced features had served to create a revolutionary industrial proletariat, which, if guided by a **revolutionary elite** (the Bolshevik party), would be ripe for the overthrow of capitalism. Russia's backward features would ensure an inability to compete effectively in the imperialistic struggle, leaving Russian monopoly capitalism in a vulnerable position.

Because Russia was admittedly a less-advanced capitalist country, would it be necessary to pass through a transition period (a **bourgeois revolution**) to set the stage for the final proletarian revolution? This ideological issue split the leadership of the Bolshevik party. Leon Trotsky argued in favor of a **permanent revolution**. The Russian proletariat should carry the revolution throughout the world from the bourgeois to the socialist stage in one uninterrupted sequence.[18] Lenin argued against Trotsky by noting that a transition period between the fall of capitalism and the introduction of socialism would be required. In fact, allowing **state capitalism** to develop in Russia would promote the eventual socialist victory.[19]

Lenin reasoned as follows. The monopolization of industry in the hands of finance capital would mean socialization of the production process. Market forces would virtually disappear, to be replaced by a centralized structure directed by economic administrators. State capitalism could exploit the working classes only so long as the capitalists remained in control If a proletarian dictatorship could take control of this monopoly structure (seize the "commanding heights" of the economy), the enormous productive capacity of monopoly capitalism could be turned to benefit the working classes. If the old order were to be "smashed," as the Bolshevik theoretician Nikolai Bukharin urged,[20] this would represent a step backward, for the socialization process would have to be started again from the beginning.

Subsequent events, most important among them the Russian civil war, rendered this controversy among Lenin, Bukharin, and Trotsky moot; the wartime emergency made a transitional alliance between the new and old orders impossible.[21]

REVISIONISM

Marxist thought after Marx, Engels, and Lenin went in different directions. In the Soviet Union, Marxism–Leninism ossified into dogma until the late 1980s.[22] Important Marxist theorists and leaders such as Leon Trotsky and Nikolai Bukharin — older Russian revolutionaries who had fallen from favor with the Bolshevik establishment — were ignored or disparaged. Other socialist writers — Bernstein, Tugan-Baranovsky, Kautsky, Luxemburg — were written off as "revisionists" or "deviationists." Serious development of Marxist thought ended in the Soviet Union with the ascendancy of Stalin in the late 1920s. The Soviet establishment was content to issue periodic political economy "textbooks" on Marxism–Leninism, which served to articulate the latest party orthodoxy. The *Glasnost* of the late 1980s and early 1990s represents the first effort to reopen serious discussion of policy in the Soviet Union since the twenties.

Soviet Orthodoxy: The General Crisis of Capitalism

Soviet ideological textbooks of the 1960s and 1970s had to adapt Marxism–Leninism to capitalism's failure to break down and to the rising prosperity of capitalist workers.[23] The **theory of the general crisis of capitalism**[24] sought to explain how the transition from capitalism to world socialism was to take place despite rising prosperity in the industrialized capitalist world.

The general crisis theory argued that there would be a general and gradual deterioration of the monopoly capitalist countries as a consequence of internal and external weaknesses. The process would be accelerated by the existence of an advancing socialist world (the Soviet Union, China, Eastern Europe, and others), which would demonstrate to developing countries the superiority of the Marxist alternative. The world's population would gradually shift from capitalism to socialism; the expansion of the communist world after the Russian Revolution was cited as the empirical proof of this thesis. On a political level, the general crisis theory provided the basis for **peaceful coexistence** between capitalism and socialism, put forward in the 1960s, a concept that appears to be a significant "revision" of Marxist thought. With peaceful coexistence, the capitalist world be unable to compete with communism and, in the long run, would lose out to its superior competitor.

What forces were expected to cause the gradual deterioration of capitalism? They were the traditional crisis factors emphasized by Marx, combined with more recent historical developments: loss of colonial territories after World War II, wars of national liberation, continuing internal antagonisms between capitalist and worker, and uneven growth of mature capitalist countries. Over the long run, capitalism would disappear, but without the benefit of a violent proletarian world revolution.

The *perestroika* reforms of the late 1980s and early 1990s called into question the relevance of Marxist–Leninist principles. To a great extent, Marxism–Leninism has ceased to be an official ideology in the Soviet Union and Eastern Europe. This de-ideologization has eliminated the need to reconcile historical developments with Marxist–Leninist predictions.

Revisionist Thought After Marx

Socialist thought after Marx and Engels focused on two themes. The first theme was the possibility of efficient resource allocation in a **market socialist** economy. The second theme was the possibility of changing capitalism to make proletarian revolution unnecessary. We classify as "revisionists" those who denied the necessity of the collapse of capitalism and its violent overthrow.

The revisionist movement began in Germany after the death of Engels in 1895.[25] Its aim was to revise Marx in light of ongoing experience. The major question addressed was whether capitalism could be changed in a positive manner to avoid the need for proletarian revolution. The revisionists were involved in the trade union movement in Europe and felt that social reform and the promotion of democracy were more reasonable social goals than the revolutionary politics of Lenin. The revisionists believed that the breakdown of capitalism was not imminent and perhaps would never come to pass.

Eduard Bernstein (1850–1932) was a close colleague of Engels and a member of the German social democratic movement. His revision of Marxism at the turn of the century was regarded as an important event in the history of Marxism–Leninism. Bernstein argued that the breakdown of capitalism was no longer inevitable because of recent meliorative trends in capitalist development. The severity of economic crises had lessened, and the class struggle was no longer so sharply defined. In this new, milder environment, the necessity of an immediate, violent, socialist revolution was no longer apparent. The evils of capitalism would gradually be eliminated as the public became more educated and enlightened. In the long run, these meliorative tendencies would become so strong that the civilized public would be allowed voluntarily to select socialism as the established economic order without the benefit of violence.

Mikhail Tugan-Baranovsky (1865–1919), an eminent Russian economist and "Legal" (moderate) Marxist, was also prominent in the revisionist movement.

Tugan-Baranovsky argued that Marx's theories of the crisis and breakdown of capitalism were incorrect, primarily because there is no inherent tendency for the profit rate to fall and because underconsumption (overproduction) will not be a problem in the advanced capitalist countries. Capitalism could continue to expand indefinitely. According to Tugan-Baranovsky, humankind "will never achieve socialism as a gift of blind elementary economic forces."[26] Instead, people must work slowly and gradually in an enlightened manner for the eventual adoption of socialism without violent revolution.

Karl Kautsky (1854–1938), another prominent representative of social democracy in Germany, was at one time regarded as the most authoritative spokesman for orthodox Marxism. It was Kautsky who made the initial counter-attack against Bernstein's revisionism. In 1902 he formulated the view that chronic depression would drive workers to select the socialist alternative and that social reforms would not ease class antagonisms. However, by the mid-1920s, Kautsky had joined the revisionists by challenging the inevitability of the breakdown of the capitalist system. According to Lenin, Kautsky exhibited revisionist tendencies much earlier by asserting that the working class might be able to achieve a balance of power with its class opponents through the growth of democracy.[27]

THE NEW LEFT

The New Left, which became prominent in the United States and Western Europe in the mid-1960s, represented an unusual blend of orthodox Marxism-Leninism with new radical thought.[28] This movement was influenced by numerous and disparate writers, ranging from the founders of orthodox Marxism (Marx, Engels, and Lenin) to older critics of capitalism (Paul Baran, Paul Sweezy, Maurice Dobb, Ernest Mandel, Andre Gorz, and Joan Robinson) and non-Marxist writers such as John K. Galbraith, Herbert Marcuse, and C. Wright Mills. Revolutionary leaders such as Mao, Ho Chi Minh, Fidel Castro, and Che Guevara were also prominent in New Left thinking, as were the anarchist philosophers Bakunin and Kropotkin. The New Left was more than a simple Marxist revival and, in fact, differed in important respects from orthodox Marxism.[29]

Agreement and Disagreements

The New Left and orthodox Marxists agreed that capitalist society is disharmonious and must be transformed into a new socialist society. Capitalist society is inherently corrupt and cannot be salvaged by means of social reform. The New Left shared the Leninist lack of interest in social reforms and there parted company with the revisionists, who felt that social reform would obviate the need for revolution.

The basic disagreement with orthodox Marxism concerned the inevitability of socialism. The New Left agreed with the revisionist claim that the breakdown of capitalism was neither inevitable nor imminent. The working class in the industrialized capitalist countries had been integrated into capitalist society and could no longer be counted on to force the radical transformation of capitalist society. A new revolutionary elite composed of students and intellectuals must assume this function. Revolutionary senses had been dulled by rising affluence, and those directly excluded from this prosperity — the blacks and browns, women, and the elderly — were too weak to serve as an effective revolutionary core. The radical transformation of capitalist society was not only not inevitable, as Marx and Lenin had claimed, it was highly unlikely.[30]

New Left Criticism of Contemporary Capitalism

The New Left criticism of modern capitalism accepted much of the traditional Marxist critique. The unequal distribution of economic and political power under capitalism particularly provoked New Left writers. Specifically, the New Left argued that there is an intimate relationship between private economic status and political power; if income is distributed unequally, political power will be distributed unequally as well. The class conflict should be viewed as a conflict over the distribution of political power. The capitalists — the monopolists, the multinational corporations, the Rockefellers — exercise undue political power. Although public officials are ostensibly subject to the dictates of the majority, capitalist democracy does not actually operate on the "one man, one vote" rule; rather, those with economic power control political processes.

The control of political power by monopoly capitalists has important consequences for the world economy. The prosperity of the rich countries depends on militarism and on the exploitation of poor countries. Without rising military expenditures, aggregate demand would be insufficient to maintain real incomes at their present levels; and without exploitation of the resources and workers of the underdeveloped world, the wealth of the affluent capitalist countries could not be maintained. The powerful can ensure the continued expansion of military outlays and the continued suppression of the resource-rich but economically poor countries. The New Left theory of imperialism agreed with Lenin that the prosperity of the rich depends on exploitation of the poor in other countries and that the working class in the rich countries becomes corrupted. One new twist was that this "new imperialism" was assumed to be engineered by multinational corporations, which transcend national boundaries, rather than by the state. In this manner, corporate imperialism replaces state imperialism.[31]

Alienation and the Quality of Life

Despite its relative affluence, the working class in the advanced capitalist countries remains alienated. The root source of this alienation is that the labor market deprives workers of control over their labor services and transfers it to those who control capital and technology. Workers are isolated from decision making, forced into a depersonalized work atmosphere, and subjected to the anonymity of the assembly line. Capitalist production serves as a strong instrument of social control. Moreover, freedom of choice in the capitalist labor market is strictly limited by social stratification. Women are excluded from high-paying and rewarding occupations, minorities are excluded from craft trade unions, and so on. Most important, entry into rewarding occupations — management, the professions, banking — depends on the wealth of one's family because of the expense of higher education and the importance of family contacts. Wealth and inequality tend to be passed from one generation to another.

CAPITALISM'S CRITICS

Orthodox Marxism obviously underestimated the long-run viability of capitalism. Capitalist economic crises have not worsened. There is no evidence of a secular decline in profit rates or of a runaway increase in unemployment. Workers in the advanced capitalist countries have experienced a rising real standard of living, taking them above anything that could conceivably be defined as subsistence level. Capitalism continues to experience business cycles, but their amplitudes appear to be lessening. The proletarian revolution failed to spread beyond the boundaries of the Soviet Union, and the introduction of socialism into Eastern Europe after World War II by the Soviet army did not follow the orthodox Marxist model despite Soviet efforts to cast it in this mold. The establishment of Marxist regimes in China and Yugoslavia at the end of World War II took place without the protection of the Red Army, but these were scarcely the mature capitalist countries of which Marx and Engels spoke.

The revisionists, who early came to doubt the inevitability of the capitalist breakdown, were more on track. It may be relevant to ask whether capitalism spared itself from the fate predicted by Marx by reforming itself (Keynesian macroregulation, the introduction of social reforms) or whether Marx was just plain wrong. In any event, capitalism's failure to show signs of imminent collapse required substantive "revisions" of Marxism–Leninism. The major revision has been denial of the need for a radical transformation of capitalism into socialism by a violent world proletarian revolution — a revision forced by the continued strength of the capitalist world.

The rejection of Marxism–Leninism in much of the Soviet Union and Eastern Europe has dealt a serious, perhaps fatal blow. The failure of the socialist planned economy to produce growth and prosperity has necessitated a pragmatic, nonideological approach to economic policy.

That Marx did not correctly predict the future of world capitalism does not alter his position as a giant in the history of economic thought. Marx's prognostications have proved to be no further off the mark than those of Ricardo and Malthus, who predicted that capitalism would reach a stationary state because of rapid population growth and diminishing returns.[32] No one denies the importance of their contributions to the history of economic thought.

Finally, one could assess the radical challenge in terms of the economic organization that it proposes in place of capitalism.[33] It is easy to emphasize the weaknesses of the established order of capitalism, but one must consider whether socialism, either of the planned or of the market socialist variety, can do a better job. On this point, the challengers of capitalism are remarkably silent. Marx and Engels had very little so say about the new socialist order that would take the place of capitalism after its breakdown. The Soviet system of resource allocation through central planning evolved after the death of Lenin and has exhibited severe weaknesses. The New Left did not provide a clear blueprint of its ideal society; it offered, instead, some general references to decentralization and reliance on moral rather than economic incentives.

At the end of Chapter 5 we presented certain hypotheses concerning the expected performance of capitalism. Capitalist theory hypothesizes great productive efficiency but, on the negative side, warns against macroeconomic instability. Marxian thought agrees with this assessment. Marx and Lenin were impressed with the productive efficiency and production potential of capitalism. Lenin even suggested taking advantage of this strength during the transition period to lay the foundations for the coming socialist society. Marxism–Leninism also agrees with capitalist theory about the inherent instability of capitalism, only in a more lethal form. In fact, it was a tenet of orthodox Marxism that the instabilities would be so severe as to cause the eventual collapse of capitalist society. Well-intentioned reforms would not prove sufficient to prevent this collapse.

SUMMARY: MARXISM–LENINISM

1. Karl Marx pictured capitalism as an unstable economic system, doomed to be replaced in a violent manner by a superior socialist order. Labor alone creates surplus value, yet the capitalist system would be inevitably driven to replace labor with capital, causing the profit rate to fall. As the profit rate fell, the capitalist would increase the exploitation and alienation of the worker, unemployment would rise, and crises of overproduction and disproportions would occur. In the end, the capitalist system would break down, and the proletariat would establish a new socialist order.

2. V. I. Lenin analyzed the final stage of capitalism, which he called monopoly capitalism or imperialism. Monopoly capitalism would be dominated by trusts, cartels, and monopolies operating on an international basis. Its distinguishing features would be the concentration of production, the merger of financial and industrial capital, the dominance of capital exports, and division of the underdeveloped world into spheres of economic and political influence. The class struggle would continue, but capitalists in the advanced capitalist countries would seek to buy off the proletariat. This, combined

with the uneven development of the capitalist world, would cause the revolution to break out in the weakest link in the capitalist chain.

3. In the Soviet Union, the first Marxist state, there was little effort to expand Marxian thought. Instead, Soviet theorists had to update Marx to account for the failure of capitalism to succumb to its inherent contradictions. The theory of the general crisis of capitalism maintained that the transition from capitalism to world socialism would take the form of a gradual victory of socialism over capitalism.

4. The revisionist movement began after the death of Engels and was largely associated with the social democratic movement in Germany. The characteristic feature of revisionism was its acceptance of the fact that the overthrow of capitalism is not imminent and that one should work for reform of the capitalist system.

5. The New Left movement represented a blend of Marxism–Leninism and revisionism. The New Leftists agreed with orthodox Marxism that capitalism cannot be salvaged by means of social reform. Instead, it must be transformed into a new socialist society. The working class, however, has been integrated into capitalist society and will not be prepared, unless reeducated, to be an effective revolutionary force. Intellectuals must unite those disenchanted with capitalist society to transform society, but the probability of this occurring is low.

6. The failure of the planned economies of the Soviet Union and Eastern Europe in the late 1980s has caused widespread rejection there of Marxism–Leninism and a movement away from ideology.

NOTES

1. Two works that seek to describe the basics of Marx's economics in the language of conventional economic theory are Oskar Lange, "Marxian Economics and Modern Economic Theory," *Review of Economic Studies*, Vol. II (June 1935); and Murray Wolfson, *A Reappraisal of Marxian Economics* (New York: Columbia University Press, 1966).

2. Karl Marx, *Capital* (Chicago: Charles Kerr and Company), Vol. I, 1906; Vols. II and III, 1909. For an annotated (East) German edition, see Karl Marx, *Das Kapital*, Band 1–3 (Berlin: Dietz Verlag, 1962).

3. Our discussion of the economic theories of Marx and Engels is based primarily on the following sources: Paul Sweezy, *The Theory of Capitalist Development* (New York: Monthly Review Press, 1968); Wolfson, *A Reappraisal of Marxian Economics*; Alexander Balinky, *Marx's Economics: Origin and Development* (Lexington, Mass.: Heath, 1970); John Gurley, *Challengers to Capitalism: Marx, Lenin, Mao* (San Francisco: San Francisco Book Company, 1976); William Baumol, Paul Samuelson, and Michio Morishima, "On Marx, the Transformation Problem, and Opacity – A Colloquium," *Journal of Economic Literature*, 12 (March 1974), 51–77; *Grundlagen des Marxismus–Leninismus: Lehrbuch*, German translation of the 4th Russian edition (Berlin: Dietz Verlag, 1964); Karl Marx and Friedrich Engels, *The Communist Manifesto*, in Arthur Mendel, ed., *Essential Works of Marxism* (New York: Bantam Books, 1965), pp. 13–44; Paul Samuelson, "Understanding the Marxian Notion of Exploitation: A Summary of the So-called Transformation Problem Between Marxian Values and Competitive Prices," *Journal of Economic Literature*, 9 (June 1971), 399–431; and Leon Smolinsky, "Karl Marx and Mathematical Economics," *Journal of Political Economy*, 81 (September–October 1973), 1189–1204.

4. See Sweezy's discussion of the transformation problem in Sweezy, *The Theory of Capitalist Development*, pp. 109–130. For a mathematical discussion of the transformation problem in terms of modern economic theory, see Samuelson, "Understanding the Marxian Notion of Exploitation," pp. 399–431; and Baumol, Samuelson, and Morishima, "On Marx, the Transformation Problem, and Opacity," pp. 51–77.

5. Marx's labor theory of value is a theory of long-run values. Marx was interested in long-term, deep, underlying price determinants and felt that labor inputs would determine values in the long run. In the short run, prices would be subject to shifts in supply and demand and could diverge from values. For a discussion of this, see Wassily Leontief, *Essays in Economics, Theories and Theorizing* (New York: Oxford University Press, 1966), pp. 72–83.

6. Other socialist economists have sought to demonstrate the existence of exploitation by using the conventional marginal productivity theory of income distribution in place of the labor theory of value. Oskar Lange, for example, argues that the receipt of the marginal products of capital and land by individual owners of capital and land resources is equivalent to the exploitation of labor. This is true because the owners of capital do not necessarily deserve to obtain the returns to capital and land that more rightly belong to labor. On this, see Oskar Lange and Fred M. Taylor, *On the Economic Theory of Socialism*, ed. Benjamin Lippincott (New York: McGraw-Hill, 1964), pp. 99–102. Another tack has been to demonstrate, using marginal productivity theory, that under conditions of imperfect competition in either the product or labor market, workers will receive less than the value of the marginal product they produce. The gap between the value they produce and the wage they receive is regarded as exploitation. For the classic discussion of this point, see Joan Robinson, *The Economics of Imperfect Competition* (London: Macmillan, 1959).

7. There is considerable controversy over whether, when he wrote of "subsistence wages," Marx had in mind the notion of biological subsistence or the satisfaction of necessary wants as determined by society. According to Wolfson, *A Reappraisal of Marxian Economics*, pp. 11–94, Marx definitely had the latter interpretation in mind.

8. Another possible explanation for capital–labor substitution is given by Sweezy, *The Theory of Capitalist Development*, Ch. 9. A burst of investment activity can cause a temporary reduction in the reserve army of the unemployed and a rise in wages above subsistence. The increase in the relative price of labor therefore induces capitalists to substitute capital for labor.

9. The basic problem is that an increase in the organic composition of capital is likely to lead to an increase in the rate of exploitation s'. As q goes up, labor productivity increases, and the amount of labor required to meet the subsistence needs of the worker is reduced. One cannot therefore predict what will happen to the profit rate, for these two forces tend to offset one another. Even such a devoted admirer of Marx as Sweezy concludes that "it is not possible to demonstrate a falling tendency of the rate of profit by beginning the analysis with the rising organic composition of capital" (ibid., p. 105). He concludes that other factors causing the rate of profit to fall must be considered.

10. For the analyses of Marx's theory of crises, see Sweezy, *The Theory of Capitalist Development*, Chs. 8–10; and Wolfson, *A Reappraisal of Marxian Economics*, Pt. IV.

11. According to Sweezy, *The Theory of Capitalist Development*, Ch. 11, the Marx–Engels description of the end of capitalism and the coming of socialism was scattered and sketchy. Their failure to deal more thoroughly with the breakdown of capitalism led to the **breakdown controversy** among socialist writers — Eduard Bernstein, M. Tugan-Baranovsky, Karl Kautsky, Rosa Luxemburg, and others. The central issue of this controversy was whether a violent overthrow of capitalism was obviated by reform of the capitalist system and the capitalist government. For Lenin's view of Kautsky and "revisionism," see V. I. Lenin, *State and Revolution*, in Mendel, *Essential Works of Marxism*, pp. 103–198; and V. I. Lenin, *Izbrannye proizvedeniia*; Tom I (Moscow: Gospolitizdat, 1960), pp. 56–63 ("Marxism and Revisionism").

12. V. I. Lenin, *The Development of Capitalism in Russia* (Moscow: Foreign Languages Publishing House, 1956); V. I. Lenin, *Imperialism, the Highest Stage of Capitalism* (London: Martin Lawrence, 1933).

13. Lenin's revolutionary strategy is given in V. I. Lenin, "What Is to Be Done?" in Robert Tucker, ed., *The Lenin Anthology* (New York: North, 1975), pp. 12–114.
14. Lenin, *Imperialism* p. 81.
15. *Grundlagen des Marxismus–Leninismus*, pp. 305–306.
16. The role of war in promoting radical revolutions was an integral part of Nikolai Bukharin's revolutionary theory. For a discussion of Bukharin's theories, see Stephen Cohen, "Bukharin, Lenin, and the Theoretical Foundations of Bolshevism," *Soviet Studies*, 21 (April 1970), 436–457; and Stephen Cohen, *Bukharin and the Bolshevik Revolution: A Political Biography, 1888-1938* (New York: Knopf, 1973).
17. Lenin, *State and Revolution*, pp. 103–198.
18. Lenin's view of the state as an instrument of capitalist exploitation is related in ibid., pp. 123–198. In *State and Revolution*, Lenin justifies the necessity of a strong state apparatus after the proletariat revolution, contrary to Engels's position (expressed in his famous anti-Dühring paper) that the state should "wither away." Lenin's main justification is that a state apparatus is necessary to oppress the previous oppressors, the capitalists. Only when the former oppressors have been eliminated will the need for a state apparatus disappear. Bukharin disagreed, arguing that a strong state could conceivably eliminate the crises and contradictions of advanced capitalism and eliminate revolutionary opposition. Thus the first order of business of the socialist revolution was to smash the existing state apparatus. For Bukharin's views, see Cohen, "Bukharin, Lenin, and the Theoretical Foundations of Bolshevism"; Cohen, *Bukharin and the Bolshevik Revolution*; and H. Ray Buchanan, "Lenin and Bukharin on the Transition from Capitalism to Socialism: The Meshchersky Controversy, 1918," *Soviet Studies*, 28 (January 1976), 66–82.
19. Maureen Perrie, "The Socialist Revolutionaries on 'Permanent Revolution,' " *Soviet Studies*, 24 (January 1973), 411–413.
20. This discussion is based primarily on Buchanan, "Lenin and Bukharin," pp. 66–82.
21. For our discussion of this period of Soviet economic history, see Paul Gregory and Robert C. Stuart, *Soviet Economic Structure and Performance*, 3rd ed. (New York: Harper & Row, 1986), Ch. 2. For a contrasting interpretation of Lenin's role during this period, see Paul C. Roberts, *Alienation and the Soviet Economy* (Albuquerque: University of New Mexico Press, 1971), Ch. 2.
22. Apparently, basic intellectual research on Marxism persisted in other countries of Eastern Europe, despite the example of the Soviet Union. For a study of the Polish case, see Domenico Nuti, "The Political Economy of Socialism – Orthodoxy and Change in Polish Texts," *Soviet Studies*, 25 (October 1973), 244–270.
23. E. Varga's book *Changes in the Economy of Capitalism Resulting from the Second World War* was the first in a series of more realistic analyses of modern capitalism. For a discussion of Varga's work and its orthodox Stalinist critics, see Richard Nordahl, "Stalinist Ideology: The Case of the Stalinist Interpretation of Monopoly Capitalist Politics," *Soviet Studies*, 26 (April 1974), 239–260.
24. See *Grundlagen des Marxismus–Leninismus*. One can also look at the series *Political Economy: A Textbook*, published by the Academy of Sciences of the Soviet Union, Department of Political Economy.
25. Our discussion of revisionism is based primarily on Sweezy, *The Theory of Capitalist Development*, Chs. 11–12; and Wolfson, *A Reappraisal of Marxian Economics*, Ch. 5. Of the two authors, Wolfson provides a more impartial analysis; Sweezy makes a more emotional attack on the revisionists.
26. Sweezy, *The Theory of Capitalist Development*, p. 195.
27. Lenin, *State and Revolution*, pp. 103–128.
28. The discussion of the economics of the New Left is based on these sources: Assar Lindbeck, *The Political Economy of the New Left: An Outsider's View*, 2nd ed. (New York: Harper & Row, 1977); Robert Heilbroner, "Radical Economics: A Review Essay." *American Political Science Review*, 66 (September 1972), 1017–1020; Harry Magdoff, "Militarism and Imperialism,"

American Economic Review, Papers and Proceedings, 60 (May 1970), 237–242; Stephen Hymer, "Discussion of Economics of Imperialism," *American Economic Review, Papers and Proceedings*, 60 (May 1970), 243–246; Thomas Weisskopf, "Theories of American Imperialism: A Critical Evaluation," *Review of Radical Political Economics*, 6 (Fall 1974), 41–57; Martin Bronfenbrenner, "Radical Economics in America, 1970," *Journal of Economic Literature*, 8 (September 1970), 747–766; John Gurley, "The State of Political Economics," *American Economic Review, Papers and Proceedings*, 61 (May 1971), 53–62; Raymond Franklin and William Tabb, "The Challenge of Radical Political Economics," *Journal of Economic Issues*, 7 (March 1974), 128–140; Paul Sweezy, "Toward a Critique of Economics," *Review of Radical Political Economics*, 2 (Spring 1970), 1–8; Paul Baran and Paul Sweezy, *Monopoly Capitalism* (New York: Monthly Review Press, 1968); and Bruce McFarlane, "The Political Economy of the New Right," *Review of Radical Political Economics*, 4 (Summer 1972), 85–89. Although most conventional economists view Lindbeck as a sympathetic observer of the New Left, the New Left is dissatisfied with his treatment of their views. McFarlane even refers to Lindbeck's critique as the "New Right" counterattack.

29. The New Left's critique of neoclassical economics is discussed in Lindbeck, *The Political Economy of the New Left*, Pt. 1.
30. Paul Baran and Paul Sweezy abandoned Marx's faith in the proletariat to produce the revolutionary overthrow of capitalism. Yet the disenchanted (the old, the poor, the unemployed) are too scattered to constitute a real force in capitalist society. Thus Baran and Sweezy predict mass neurosis in place of revolution. On this, see Bronfenbrenner, "Radical Economics in America, 1970," p. 763.
31. For the New Left's theory of imperialism, consult Magdoff, "Militarism and Imperialism," pp. 227–242; Hymer, "Discussion of Economics of Imperialism," pp. 243–246; and Weisskopf, "Theories of American Imperialism," pp. 41–57.
32. For an analysis of the differences between Marx's and Ricardo's theories of declining profit rates, see Kazimierz Laski, "Zur Marxischen Theorie des tendenziellen Falles der Profitrate," *Wirschaft und Gessellschaft*, 3 (1976), 27–42.
33. This, Lindbeck's strongest criticism of the New Left, is echoed in Paul Samuelson's foreword to Lindbeck's book *The Political Economy of the New Left*.

RECOMMENDED READINGS

Marxism

Alexander Balinky, *Marx's Economics: Origin and Development* (Lexington, Mass.: Heath, 1970).

John Gurley, *Challengers to Capitalism: Marx, Lenin, Mao* (San Francisco: San Francisco Book Company, 1976).

Karl Marx, *Capital*, trans. Samuel Moore and Edward Aveling (New York: Modern Library, 1906).

Karl Marx and Friedrich Engels, *The Communist Manifesto*, in Arthur Mendel, ed., *Essential Works of Marxism* (New York: Bantam Books, 1965), pp. 13–44.

Arthur Mendel, ed., *Essential Works of Marxism* (New York: Bantam Books, 1965).

Paul Sweezy, *The Theory of Capitalist Development* (New York: Monthly Review Press, 1968).

Murray Wolfson, *A Reappraisal of Marxian Economics* (New York: Columbia University Press, 1966).

Leninism

Paul Baran and Paul Sweezy, *Monopoly Capitalism* (New York: Monthly Review Press, 1968).

Stephen Cohen, "Bukharin, Lenin, and the Theoretical Foundations of Bolshevism," *Soviet Studies*, 21 (April 1970), 436–457.

V. I. Lenin, *The Development of Capitalism in Russia* (Moscow: Foreign Languages Publishing House, 1956).

——, *Imperialism, the Highest Stage of Capitalism* (London: Martin Lawrence, 1933).

——, *State and Revolution*, in Mendel, *Essential Works of Marxist*, pp. 123–198.

New Left

Martin Bronfenbrenner, "Radical Economics in America, 1970," *Journal of Economic Literature*, 8 (September 1970), 747–766.

Raymond Franklin and William Tabb, "The Challenge of Radical Political Economics," *Journal of Economic Issues*, 7 (March 1974), 128–140; reprinted in David Mermelstein, ed., *Economics: Mainstream Readings and Radical Critiques*, 3rd ed. (New York: Random House, 1976), pp. 30–41.

John Gurley, "The State of Political Economics," *American Economic Review, Papers and Proceedings*, 61 (May 1971), 53–62.

Robert Heilbroner, "Radical Economics: A Review Essay," *American Political Science Review*, 66 (September 1972), 1017–1020; reprinted in Assar Lindbeck, *The Political Economy of the New Left: An Outsider's View*, 2nd ed. (New York: Harper & Row, 1977), pp. 174–183.

Assar Lindbeck, *The Political Economy of the New Left: An Outsider's View*, 2nd ed. (New York: Harper & Row, 1977) (with polemics by George Bach, Stephen Hymer and Frank Roosevelt, Paul Sweezy, and Assar Lindbeck).

Bruce McFarlane, "The Political Economy of the New Right," *Review of Radical Political Economics*, 4 (Summer 1972), 85–89; reprinted in Lindbeck, *The Political Economy of the New Left*, pp. 184–207.

Harry Magdoff, "Militarism and Imperialism," *American Economic Review, Papers and Proceedings*, 60 (May 1970), 237–242; reprinted in Lindbeck, *The Political Economy of the New Left*, pp. 184–207.

Paul Sweezy, "Toward a Critique of Economics," *Review of Radical Political Economics*, 2 (Spring 1970), 1–8.

Thomas Weisskopf, "Theories of American Imperialism: A Critical Evaluation," *Review of Radical Political Economics*, 6 (Fall 1975), 41–57; reprinted in Mermelstein, *Economics*, pp. 210–225.

7 Theory of Planned Socialism

MARX ANALYZED CAPITALISM. He had little to say about socialism. Marx did not address the issue of how a socialist society would deal with the resource allocation problem. Indeed, the question of rational resource allocation under socialism did not arise formally until the early 1900s. At that time the role of the state in the economic system stirred a debate known as the socialist controversy. There is no socialist economic paradigm[1] equivalent to the model of perfectly competitive capitalism. This fact explains why so little attention has been devoted to socialist economics in standard works on the history of economic thought.[2]

Chapter 2 identified two models of socialism: planned socialism and market socialism. This chapter focuses on the planned socialist variant that emerged from the Soviet experience. The next chapter discusses the market socialist variant.

THE MARXIST–LENINIST VIEW OF SOCIALISM

Although Marx did not analyze socialist working arrangements, he did develop a framework for predicting the triumph of socialism over capitalism. For Marx, the historical evolution from primitive societies to communism was inevitable.[3] Capitalism, because of its exploitation of workers and internal contradictions, would be replaced by socialism. Capitalism would be an engine of economic progress, the results of which would be more evenly shared under socialism.

Socialism itself would be an intermediate step, a system ultimately to be replaced by communism. **Communism**, the highest stage of social and economic development, would be characterized by the absence of markets and money, distribution according to need, material plenty, and the withering away of the state. In the meantime, under socialism, vestiges of capitalism would continue and some familiar institutions would remain. The most important institution would be the state, which under socialism would be transformed into a **dictatorship of the proletariat**. Marx emphasized a strong role for the state, a role that was subsequently strengthened by Lenin.[4] Under socialism, though, the state would be representative of the masses and therefore noncoercive. The state would own the means of production as well as rights to surplus value. Under socialism, each individual would be expected to contribute to the system according to capability, and rewards would be distributed according to that contribution. Subsequently, under communism, the basis of reward would be need. However, need would presumably have a meaning rather different from the one assigned to it under capitalism, where wants are continually expanding.

Many changes and additions have been made to the Marxian model originally developed in the nineteenth century. Lenin wrote extensively on the role of the state under socialism, especially on the tactics of revolution. Stalin contributed mainly to the discussion of **socialism in one country**, the question of whether socialism could be built successfully in a single country or whether world revolution was essential for the victory of socialism.

Lenin emphasized that inequalities and capitalist vestiges would still exist under socialism and that, accordingly, coercive actions by the state would be necessary.[5] Lenin promoted (and applied under war communism in the Soviet Union) a peculiar view of the state in which the task of administering the economy's affairs was viewed as simple, capable of being handled by all.[6] There was no need, Lenin argued, for specialists, because the tasks of management were regarded as quite routine. These views were subsequently modified, although they form the basis of later Soviet thinking on management.

Marx, Engels, and Lenin wrote about the role of the state and income distribution under socialism. They did not deal with the more fundamental issue of how scarce resources were to be allocated during the socialist phase.

THE SOCIALIST CONTROVERSY: THE FEASIBILITY OF SOCIALISM

There is no single socialist economic paradigm. Socialist economics must be assembled partly from theory and partly from historical experience.

Resource allocation under socialism has been widely discussed over the past 75 years, a discussion loosely termed the **socialist controversy**. The prevailing view is that workable resource allocation under socialism is certainly possible. Present-day discussion focuses more on the comparative economic efficiency of socialism.

Socialist economic theory must explain how resources are to be allocated under socialism. If the socialist economy is planned, how will planners make rational decisions about the use of scarce resources? Is private ownership necessary for the proper functioning of markets?

Barone: A Theoretical Framework

The first consistent theoretical framework of resource allocation under socialism was developed by the Italian economist Enrico Barone. In 1907, Barone published "The Ministry of Production in the Collectivist State."[7] Here he argued, though in a limited and purely theoretical way, that prices, understood as **relative valuations**, are not bound to the market. A central planning board (hereafter designated CPB) could establish prices, or "ratios of equivalence" among commodities.

Barone's model consisted of a vast array of simultaneous equations relating inputs and outputs to the ratios of equivalence. When solved (Barone admitted that a real-world solution would be impractical), the equations could provide the appropriate relative valuations of resources required to balance demand and supply. A CPB armed with perfect computation techniques would require perfect knowledge of all relevant variables, specifically (1) individual demand schedules, (2) enterprise production functions, and (3) existing stocks of both producer and consumer goods. Barone's principal conclusion was that the CPB's computed resource allocation would be remarkably similar to that of competitive capitalism. In fact, he saw no reason for substantial differences.

One could question the practicality of this approach, both at the time Barone was writing and even in the present state of improved computer technology. Nevertheless, it demonstrated that the relative valuations of resources essential for rational resource allocation could be discovered by imputation (solving equations) rather than through the particular institutional arrangements of the market.

The Challenge of Ludwig von Mises

The discussion of this matter went little further until the 1920s and 1930s, when three important developments took place. First, Ludwig von Mises mounted a formidable and now famous attack against the case for rational resource allocation under socialism.[8] Second, a number of Soviet authors made important contributions to the theory of planning, then in its formative stages. Third, the noted Polish economist Oskar Lange set forth his now famous model of market socialism (to be discussed in the next chapter).[9]

Mises's challenge was directed toward the problem of allocating producer goods in a socialist economic system, a task presumably in the hands of the state (with the allocation of consumer goods left to the market). Mises argued that for a state to direct available resources rationally toward the achievement of given ends (even if resource availabilities and ends are known), a knowledge of relative valuations (prices) would be essential. Mises maintained that the only way to establish these valuations would be through the market mechanism, absent in a socialist state where producer goods are owned and allocated by the state. If prices are the vehicle by which relative scarcities are reflected, why not artificially simulate prices via a system of equations as proposed by Barone? Mises argued that it would be difficult if not impossible to separate the allocation function from the workings of the market. Both, he suggested, are tied together through the profit motive and the existence of private property.

Much has been written about the profit motive and private property.[10] Mises argued that individuals are motivated by the urge for material self-betterment, which translates into utility and profit maximization. Second, individuals and enterprises are motivated to produce goods and services as efficiently (rationally) as possible so as to increase profits. Third, the drive for achievement cannot be socialized; that is, the urge for betterment cannot be translated from the individual to the group. Furthermore, if resources are owned by the state, profits accrue to the state, not to individuals. Thus, Mises argued, the motivation for utilizing available resources in the best (most efficient) way is lost.

The responses to Mises's original position have varied. There have been two main interpretations. The first is that Mises was saying that socialism could not "work" in the sense that resource allocation would be impossible in the absence of a market mechanism. The second and more common interpretation of Mises is that socialism cannot work *efficiently*. In fact, the debate over the relative merits of socialism and capitalism has focused on the question of relative efficiency.[11]

Kornai: Socialism and Shortage

Hayek and Mises emphasized the complexity and incentive problems of socialism. The Hungarian economist Janos Kornai has focused on the inherent tendency of socialist economies to operate under conditions of shortage. Kornai's major work, *The Economics of Shortage*, was published in 1980. In this and other works, Kornai provided a theoretical explanation for the inability of socialist economies to avoid shortages.

Kornai argues that the planned socialist economic system is a system of **shortage**, where shortage is a systemic, perpetual, and self-reproducing condition.[12] Others have argued that persistent shortages or excess demand in the socialist systems is a function of readily identifiable, though not necessarily easily corrected, forces. Consumer goods are simply not a high priority but rather are supplanted by producer goods and military production. Furthermore, errors in planning, inadequate incentives, and other system characteristics lead to continuing shortages.

From a very different perspective, Kornai argues that the economy of shortages arises from the nature of the enterprise in the planned socialist system.[13] The socialist enterprise operates under fundamentally different rules from the capitalist enterprise. The capitalist enterprise is motivated to maximize profits. It makes its input and output decisions on the basis of prices established in markets. As a profit maximizer, the capitalist enterprise has little incentive to overdemand resources. If it employs more resources than technology requires, its profits suffer. The capitalist enterprise experiences a **hard budget constraint**. Faced with input prices and output prices, the capitalist enterprise must cover its costs while earning an acceptable rate of return on invested capital. If it fails to meet its budget constraint, the capitalist firm will fail in the long run. The capitalist firm must live within its means. The hard budget constraint polices capitalist enterprise activities and effectively eliminates shortage (in the sense of excess demand for inputs).

The socialist firm operates in a supply-constrained economy. Socialist planners have as their objective the rapid expansion of outputs, and they tend to judge the performance of socialist enterprises on the basis of rates of output expansion. The manner in which socialist enterprises select inputs to meet their output objectives is of less importance than the output targets themselves. Although socialist enterprises face prices for inputs and outputs, their resource allocation decisions are aimed at meeting output targets. Relative prices play only a minor role.

The capitalist enterprise that fails to live within its means is punished by bankruptcy. The socialist enterprise that fails to cover costs plus a rate of return on the state's invested capital does not suffer the same consequences. Socialist planners value enterprises for their outputs; socialist enterprises that make losses remain in business by virtue of state subsidies. Accordingly, socialist enterprises face a **soft budget constraint**. Socialist enterprises can live beyond their means, if necessary, over the long run.

The hard budget constraint forces capitalist enterprises to limit their demands for inputs. The soft budget constraint on socialist enterprises fails to reward them for restricting their input demands. Hence the socialist system generates continuous excess demands for inputs. The supply of inputs falls chronically short of the demand for inputs, and persistent shortages or imbalances result.

Economic systems must allocate resources in an orderly fashion. Persistent imbalances and chronic shortages detract from the orderly allocation of resources. With imbalances, those who obtain resources may be those who will not put them to their best and highest use. Kornai's analysis of socialism is related to the complexity and motivation issues raised by Mises and Hayek. Kornai's conclusion is that the socialist motivation system and inattention to relative prices disrupt the orderly allocation of resources under socialism.

RESOURCE ALLOCATION UNDER PLANNED SOCIALISM

The socialist controversy raised the key issues of resource allocation under conditions of socialism. On the one hand, it raised the complexity issue for planned socialism. Barone showed that the CPB would, in theory, have to gather data and solve simultaneous equations for millions of products. Such a task would be beyond the capabilities of any real-world CPB. On the other hand, the socialist controversy raised the motivation issue for both planned and market socialism. If the means of production are owned by society at large, how are managers to be motivated to combine resources efficiently and to take innovative risks?

The discussion that follows pursues these questions for planned socialism. We begin with the origins of the theory of planned socialism in its first real-world experiment, the Soviet Union in the 1930s, and then we proceed to the theory of planning.

Origins: The Soviet Union in the 1920s

The 1920s have been described as "the golden age of Soviet mathematical economics."[14] There was relatively open discussion in the Soviet Union, including an important discussion about the appropriate path and mechanisms for economic growth under socialism.[15] The emphasis was on formulating a socialist path of development, guided by Marxist–Leninist ideological principles. Pioneers in mathematical economics, a key area for the subsequent development of the theory of economic planning, were very active. Under these conditions, it is not surprising that prior to the Stalinist crackdown of the late 1920s, Soviet planners and theoreticians pursued the theory of planning under conditions of social ownership. Possibly the most important practical work of this period was the development of **balances of the national economy**, forerunners of the input–output analysis of Wassily Leontief, and of **material balances**, the planning system used in contemporary planned socialist economies. The development of the material balance approach remains a major (though simple) contribution of considerable practical importance.[16]

The material balances formulated by Soviet economists focused on the need to determine aggregate demands and supplies for basic industrial commodities and to bring them in balance without relying on market forces. More specifically, the theoretical underpinning of the material balance approach (input–output analysis) demonstrated that the productive relations of an economic system could be approximated by a system of simultaneous equations along the lines suggested by Barone.

A significant omission in the Soviet discussion of the 1920s was the matter of how enterprises might be guided at the micro level. Some Soviet economists even argued that the whole discussion of relative values (prices) under socialism was irrelevant because the **law of value** would not exist under socialism.

Although there is no necessary inconsistency between Marxian economics and mathematical economics, Stalin thought otherwise. This view ended open discussion in the Soviet Union, a situation that did not change until after Stalin's death in the early 1950s.

Economic Planning: A Paradigm for Planned Socialism

It is not surprising that the Soviet discussions of the 1920s focused on **national economic planning**. If market-resource allocation is to be eliminated, some alternative arrangement must be used in its place.

There has been a tendency to associate national economic planning with socialism in both a political and an economic context. Actually, planning is consistent with a wide variety of organizational and ideological arrangements. Nevertheless, the idea that an economic system could be centrally planned stems in large part from the Soviet experience. Even in the countries where most national planning is done — for example, the Soviet Union — the theory of planning is really only a set of pragmatic principles; there is not "theory" comparable to the paradigm of the market economy. In this sense, most real-world national planning is a pragmatic exercise.

Planning is a term with widely differing connotations. Different authors have used different definitions, but there are basic elements in common. Gerald Sirkin writes, "Planning is an attempt, by centralizing the management of the allocation of resources sufficiently, to take into account social costs and social benefits which would be irrelevant to the calculus of the decentralized decision maker."[17] The emphasis here is the appropriate *level* of decision making and the social versus the private element in the decisions taken.

Abdul Qayum defines planning as "a systematic and integrated program covering a definite period of time, approved or sponsored by the state to bring about a rationalization of resources to achieve certain national targets using direct and indirect means with or without state ownership of resources."[18] Here we have a broader and more inclusive definition, which nonetheless includes elements of the previous definition — notably, the implication of centralization in the decision-making process.

Michael Todaro, writing in the context of development planning, defines planning as follows: "Economic planning may be described as the conscious effort of a central organization to influence, direct, and, in some cases even control changes in the principal economic variables (e.g., GDP, consumption, investment, savings, etc.) of a certain country or region over the course of time in accordance with a predetermined set of objectives."[19] Todaro further emphasizes that the key concepts are influence, direction, and control, and he defines an economic plan "as a specific sets of quantitative targets to be reached in a given period of time."

The concept of plan formulation has been described succinctly by G. M. Heal, who writes that it can be viewed as "solving a constrained maximization problem."[20] Plan formulation involves doing the best one can to achieve objectives, albeit with limitations on available resources.

In contrast to the increasing specificity of these definitions, it is interesting to consider the following Soviet definition:

> Socialist planning is based upon strict scientific foundations; it demands the continuous generalization of the practical experience of the construction of Communism as well as the utilization of the accomplishments of science and technology. To operate the economy according to plan means to foresee. Scientific foresight rests on the reconciliation of the objective economic laws of socialism. Plans carry in socialism the character of objectives. The planned direction of the economy requires that priorities be established and the main priorities of the economic plan are the branches of heavy industry, for they determine the development of all industrial branches as well as the economy as a whole.[21]

Although some of the elements of this definition (for example, the "objective economic laws of socialism") may be difficult to interpret, the definition contains some familiar concepts, such as the ability to foresee and the existence of objectives.

These definitions, though differing in specifics, differ relatively little in terms of substance. A **national economic plan** is a mechanism to guide the activity of an economy through time toward the achievement of specified goals or objectives. The notion of *control* is fundamental to the concept of planning. Planning is more than forecasting. Although forecasting involves projections of future economic activity, planning is substantively different: The planner attempts to *alter* the economy's direction of movement and hence to change economic outcomes. It is convenient to categorize planning as either indicative or directive. In the case of **indicative planning**, targets are set in the hope of affecting economic outcomes by providing information external to the market; typically, individual firms receive no directives from planners. In the case of **directive planning**, however, targets are set by planners with the expectation of directly altering outcomes, because plan targets are legally binding on enterprises. A popular expression in the Soviet Union was that "the plan is law." Indicative planning will be discussed in more detail in a later chapter.

If the economic activity of a country is to be planned, three basic steps are required. First, a plan has to be constructed that specifies the goals or objectives to be achieved and the means for achieving those goals. A time frame must also be specified. Second, there must be an organizational mechanism for executing the plan and, in particular, a means to guarantee that the participants in the economic system will in fact attempt to achieve plan goals. In short, there must be an incentive system to harmonize the behavior of participants with goal achievement. Finally, there must be a means to evaluate outcomes and, where they differ from targets, to ensure appropriate feedback to adjust the direction of future economic activity.

The literature on national economic planning can be conveniently divided into two categories. First, there is the literature devoted to the planning methods actually utilized in the planned socialist economic systems. This literature describes material balance planning, the Soviet origins of which have already been discussed. Second, there is the literature devoted to national economic planning models, which usually employ some optimizing (mathematical) procedure. Although the basic principles of planning are common to both lines of thought, the planned socialist economies have utilized the material balance approach.

Material Balance Planning

The material balance approach to national economic planning has been widely used in the planned socialist economic systems. The central planning board specifies a list of goods and services that are to be produced in the plan period. Once the CPB determines the inputs (land, labor, capital, and intermediate products) needed to produce one unit of output (generally on the basis of historical input–output relationships), it can draw up a list of input requirements necessary for meeting the specified output objectives. Obviously the CPB would like to produce as much output as possible, but the availability of inputs limits how much can be produced given available technology.

The CPB must ensure a balance between outputs and inputs. For each factor input and intermediate good, the amount needed to produce output (the demand) must be equated with the amount available (the supply). If a balance between the two sides does not exist, then administrative steps must be taken to reduce demand and/or expand supply. A balance must exist for each item, and there must also be an aggregate balance of demand and supply.

On the supply side, there are three main sources of inputs: production, stocks on hand, and imports. On the demand side, there are two main elements: interindustry demand, where the output of one industry (for example, coal) is used as the input for another industry (for example, steel); and final demand, consisting of output that will be invested, consumed by households, or exported. Thus adjustment is possible on both the demand and supply sides, and it is through administrative adjustment that demand and supply are balanced. This procedure is in basic contrast to the operation of the market in market economies, where prices adjust to eliminate imbalances.

For a modern economic system, maintaining an appropriate balance between the supplies and demands for all products would be an enormous task, a point emphasized by Hayek and Mises. In fact, the planned economies that use the material balance approach plan only the most important inputs and outputs, handling others on a more decentralized basis. Although this means that only a portion of total output is within the control of central planners, it is nevertheless sufficient to exert a major degree of influence over the economic outcomes.

Even in this more limited context, Barone's question — how to solve the equations — remains a problem. The problem of balancing supply and demand can be conveniently formalized in the following manner:

$$
\begin{array}{cc}
\text{Sources} & \text{Uses} \\
X_1 + V_1 + M_1 = X_{11} + X_{12} + \cdots + X_{1n} + Y_1 \\
X_2 + V_2 + M_2 = X_{21} + X_{22} + \cdots + X_{2n} + Y_2 \\
\vdots \\
X_n + V_n + M_n = X_{n1} + X_{n2} + \cdots + X_{nn} + Y_n
\end{array}
$$

where n items are included in the balance, and

X_i = planned output of commodity i
V_i = existing stocks of commodity i
M_i = planned imports of commodity i
X_{ij} = interindustry demand; that is, the amount of commodity i required to produce the planned amount of commodity j
Y_i = the final demand for commodity i; that is, for investment, household consumption, or export

Table 7.1 depicts a simplified material balance. Note that for each commodity a balance exists. In the case of steel, there are three sources on the supply side: production of 2,000 tons, no stocks on hand, and imports of 20 tons, for a total supply of 2,020 tons. On the demand side, there are six users of steel: the coal industry using 200 tons, the steel industry using 400 tons, the machinery industry using 1,000 tons, the consumer goods industry using 300 tons, exports of 100 tons, and domestic use of 20 tons, for a total demand of 2,020 tons. In this example, supply and demand are balanced at 2,020 tons.

Computational, administrative, and data-gathering limitations set an upper limit on the number of items that can be handled by material balance planning. Which items will be planned and which unplanned? Typically, the items that are of major significance to the achievement of state objectives are included in the plan. Items not included in the plan are planned at a lower level in the hierarchy. Plan authorities have discovered that the economy can be effectively controlled by manipulating a relatively small number of important inputs.

How does the CPB know how much of each input ($X_{ij}s$) will be necessary to produce a unit of output? The coefficient relating input to output is typically derived from the previous year's planning experience and adjusted somewhat (usually upward) to allow for investment and productivity improvements. Moreover, these coefficients are normally assumed to be constant over varying ranges of output — an assumption that causes problems when an industry is expanding and experiencing increasing (or decreasing) returns to scale. Gathering the information necessary to keep the coefficients up to date is a real problem. Most planned socialist systems rely on communications with enterprises, a process that is time-consuming and not necessarily reliable.

Material balance planning must deal with the interrelatedness of economic sectors. Suppose, for example, that during the process of plan formulation or execution, a need arises to expand the output of a particular commodity or a previously unknown input shortage is discovered. If more steel is needed, so also will more coals be needed for the production of the steel. But to produce more coal, more electricity is needed, and on, and on, and on. These so-called second-round effects reverberate throughout the economic system, making it very difficult to obtain a balance. To what degree can planners take second-round effects into account? In theory, a number of reformulations of the plan would be necessary. In practice, most planners allow for the initial or most serious repercussions, leaving the remainder to be absorbed as shocks by the system.

The balancing of demands with supplies is the essence of material balance planning. But what about optimality? Optimality implies selecting the *best* plan of all those with which it would be possible to achieve a balance. The best plan is the one that maximizes the planners' objectives. Although it is mathematically possible to elaborate the criteria for selecting an optimal plan from among a number of feasible variants, most planned socialist economies are able to prepare two or three variants at best, and there is no reason for the selected variants to be optimal.

When we examine Soviet planning in practice, we shall have a chance to consider further aspects of material balance planning. At this juncture, let us simply observe that material balance planning is a mechanism that works, albeit

Table 7.1 Sample Material Balance

	Sources			Intermediate Inputs Required by				Final Uses	
	Output	Stocks	Imports	Coal Industry	Steel Industry	Machinery Industry	Consumer Goods Industry	Exports	Domestic Uses
Coal (tons)	1,000	10	0	100	500	50	50	100	210
Steel (tons)	2,000	0	20	200	400	1,000	300	100	20
Machinery (units)	100	5	5	20	40	10	20	10	10
Consumer goods (units)	400	10	20	0	0	0	100	100	230

Demonstration that a balance exists:

Sources of coal: 1,010 tons   = uses of coal: 1,010 tons
Sources of steel: 2,020 tons   = uses of steel: 2,020 tons
Sources of machinery: 110 units   = uses of machinery: 110 units
Sources of consumer goods: 430 units = uses of consumer goods: 430 units

Source: Paul R. Gregory and Robert C. Stuart, *Soviet Economic Structure and Performance* (New York: Harper & Row, 1986), p. 169. Reprinted by permission of Harper & Row. Copyright © 1974 by Paul R. Gregory and Robert C. Stuart.

at a low level of efficiency. Furthermore, it enables the planners to select key areas on which pressure can be applied to seek rapid expansion, regional economic growth, or whatever. On the other hand, it is cumbersome, and achieving a balance frequently requires the existence of buffer or low-priority sectors (typically consumer goods) that can absorb planning mistakes.

Raymond Powell examined how economies that operate through material balance planning have been able to survive and generate growth.[22] Powell points out that material balance planning does not prevent participants in the economy (managers, ministers, and planners) from responding to nonprice scarcity indicators. Because there will inevitably be planning errors (imbalances between output targets and the inputs allocated to produce these targets), managers and planners will be confronted with various indicators of scarcity. Managers will recognize that some materials are harder to acquire than others or that some materials held by the enterprise are scarcer than others. Ministries will receive warnings from their enterprises concerning production shortfalls and material shortages and will have to assess the reliability of this information. On the basis of this nonprice information, resources will be reallocated within the firm according to perceived indicators of relative scarcity. Managers may allocate internal resources (personnel and trucks) to seek out and transport scarce materials. Ministries and central planners will reallocate materials to enterprises that, according to the scarcity indicators they receive, have relatively high marginal products. According to Powell, these natural responses to scarcity indicators introduce into material balance planning the rationality that allows it to function and survive.

The Input–Output Model[23]

The input–output model offers an alternative approach to administrative material balance planning. In theory, it gives planners an opportunity to determine balances quickly (through high-speed computers) and hence to explore alternative resource allocations.

An input–output table is a graphical presentation of the national accounts of an economy and illustrates the flows among the various sectors. The economy is divided into **sectors** of which there are two broad types — those that produce output (final output for consumption or intermediate output) and those that use final output (either as an intermediate input to further production or as a final consumption item). Sectors may correspond to industries, the number of which depends on the degree of disaggregation. Naturally, the greater the number of sectors, the more accurately the table reflects real economic interrelationships. At the same time, data and computational problems normally place severe limits on size. A simple input–output table is presented in Figure 7.1.

The sum total of goods and services produced (gross national product) is equal to the sum total of factor incomes (gross national income) used to produce this output. This concept is illustrated in the input–output table. The sum of all inputs used in, say, agriculture (sum of entries in the second column) is numerically equal to the total output of the agricultural sector (sum of entries in the second row). Each column in the input–output table illustrates both the source and the amount of input that will be used from each source in producing output. The inputs are of two types, **primary inputs** (labor, capital, and land) and **intermediate inputs** (steel, agricultural products). At the same time, each row shows how the output of the particular sector (agriculture in this case) is distributed among the various users (of agricultural products). In this table, there are two types of users: industries that use agricultural products as intermediate inputs for manufacturing, and final consumers who use agriculture products directly without further processing.

The input–output table is a simple yet highly useful picture of resource flows in an economic system. We should emphasize, however, that input–output economics relies on several crucial and limiting assumptions.

1. *Aggregation:* Obviously, the fewer the sectors, the easier it is to manipulate the table. The larger the number of branches, the more realistic the table, but the more difficult it is to compile and manipulate. On the other hand,

Figure 7.1 Schematic Input–Output Table

USING SECTOR / PRODUCING SECTOR	INTERMEDIATE USE			FINAL USE			TOTAL OUTPUTS
	Steel	Agriculture	Other branches	Consumption	Exports	Other branches	
Steel							
Agriculture							
Other branches	INTERINDUSTRY, QUADRANT I			FINAL USE, QUADRANT II			
Land							
Labor	VALUE ADDED, QUADRANT III			DIRECT FACTOR PURCHASE, QUADRANT IV			
Capital							
TOTAL INPUTS							

generalized branches such as "agriculture" and "manufacturing" tell us little about the real working arrangements of an economy.

2. *Time frame:* The simple model presented here is *static* and does not, therefore, allow for change through time. The amount of labor required to produce a unit of steel is assumed not to change over time.

3. *Returns to scale:* We are assuming constant returns to scale. That is, the input–output ratios are the same, regardless of the *volume* of output being produced.

Our interest focuses largely on Quadrant I, for here are the **technical coefficients** relating inputs to outputs. Specifically, this quadrant tells us how much of a particular input is required to produce a unit of a particular output. Clearly this technical relationship is crucial for specifying what will be produced and what inputs will be available for this production activity. How are these coefficients determined?

If there are i rows and j columns in the input–output matrix, then any cell can be described as a_{ij}, which represents the amount of i that is used to produce a unit of j as a proportion of the total output of j. These technical coefficients are defined in the following manner:

$$a_{ij} = \frac{x_{ij}}{X_j}$$

where:

x_{ij} = the amount of input i used in industry j
X_j = the total output of industry j

What is the relationship between the input–output framework and material balance planning? First, knowledge of the matrix of technical coefficients is crucial to the development of a plan, whether that plan is constructed by a simple material balance technique or by more sophisticated methods. For example, if a plan is to be feasible, input availabilities must be sufficient to produce desired outputs. Clearly, knowledge of the technical coefficients can assist in making such a determination.

Second, if one knows the relationship between inputs and outputs, then with a given feasible objective, one in effect knows the relative worth (value) of different inputs in the production process. Thus a set of **relative prices** can be determined from the input–output model.

Third, the basic input–output model, even with a fair degree of aggregation, provides the planner with important information about the relationship between inputs and outputs.

Suppose the technical coefficients (a_{ij}) are known. How can the planner determine whether a particular objective is possible with available inputs? The input–output model says that for n sectors, the total production of each sector is the sum of intermediate demand and final demand. In notational form, this relationship can be expressed as follows:

$$\sum_{j=1}^{n} x_{ij} + Y_i = X_i \qquad (7.1)$$

But we know something about the amount of i needed to produce a unit of j. Specifically, this relationship is as follows:

$$x_{ij} = a_{ij}X_j \qquad (7.2)$$

Substituting equation 7.2 into equation 7.1, we derive the following relationship:

$$\sum_{j=1}^{n} a_{ij}X_j + Y_i = X_i \qquad (7.3)$$

Rearranging terms, we get

$$Y_i = X_i - \sum_{j=1}^{n} a_{ij}X_j \qquad (7.4)$$

Equation 7.4 expresses the basic relationship among final demand, interindustry demand, and total production. This basic relationship can be more conveniently expressed in matrix notation as follows:

$$X = AX + Y \qquad (7.5)$$

or by rearranging terms

$$Y = (I - A)X \qquad (7.6)$$

where:

I = identity matrix
X = a vector of planned outputs
A = the matrix of technical coefficients
Y = a vector of final outputs

If the matrix of technical coefficients (A) is known to the planner, then the feasibility of a given vector of plan targets (X) can be readily determined by the matrix multiplication. Clearly, even if the focus of the planner should change, knowing any two of the three components of this relationship makes it easier to determine the third component.

How useful is this model in practice? Although aggregation reduces the realism and the practical applicability of the model, it nevertheless remains useful as a method of checking the feasibility of alternative scenarios. The input–output model performs a number of functions: it provides a mathematical formulation of material balances, and it shows how supply–demand balances can be achieved mathematically via computers. Although problems that arise in the real-world, collection and manipulation of data, limits its applicability, the input–output model supplies the theoretical underpinnings of material balance planning.

Optimization and Economic Planning

Soviet material balance planning is the actual planning method used by the Soviets to allocate resources. As we have noted, Soviet material balance planning is a pragmatic method for planning an economy by administrative means. Its objective is to provide a rough balance between supplies and demands of a relatively limited number of key industrial commodities. Because of its administrative complexity, Soviet material balance planning aims at achieving a balance; it does not aim at achieving the optimal balance.

The theory of economic planning focuses on the problem of achieving an *optimal* balance. It shows how, in theory, planners can plan for the economy to produce the optimal combinations of outputs, subject to the constraint of limited land, labor, and capital resources. No present-day economy actually allocates resources by using administrative planning techniques that select detailed optimal combinations of outputs. Although the solution to such a planning problem is evident in theory, in practice it is elusive.

The planning problem can be expressed in the following manner:

$$\text{Maximize } U = U(X_1, X_2, \ldots, X_n) \qquad i = 1, \ldots, n \qquad (7.7)$$

Here X_i are products that are produced subject to existing technology:

$$X_i = f(u_1, u_2, \ldots, u_m) \qquad (7.8)$$

where u_j are resources (land, labor, materials, and others) and are subject to

$$u_j \leq b_j \qquad j = 1, \ldots, m \qquad (7.9)$$

where b_j represents resource availabilities, and u_j represents the total amount of resource j used by all producers. Moreover, resources are employed at zero or positive levels:

$$u_j \geq 0 \qquad (7.10)$$

The goal of planning is to achieve the maximal value of equation 7.7, which is termed the **objective function**. The objective function summarizes the planners' economic objectives and provides a precise relationship between the utility derived by society (U) and the output of goods and services (X_i) from which that social utility, or satisfaction, is derived. In turn, the magnitude of goods and services available is a function of resource availabilities (u_j) with given technology. Resources cannot be used beyond their available supplies (b_j), either in the aggregate or for any individual resource.

The critics of the Barone model explained why such optimal planning is virtually impossible in practice. First, an economy produces millions of distinct products and factor inputs. Even with powerful computers, it is not possible to solve the millions of simultaneous equations for the optimal combinations of inputs and outputs. To reduce the computational problem to manageable proportions, planners would have to work with *aggregations* of distinct commodities (such as tons of steel or square meters of textiles). Real-world economies do not operate with aggregated commodities. Factories require steel goods of specific grades and qualities. To go from a planning solution based on aggregate inputs or outputs to real production and distribution processes is an extremely complicated problem. Second, even if planners could gather the necessary information and make the complicated calculations, it is still not clear how to get enterprises actually to produce the planned commodities by using optimal combinations of inputs. This is the problem of creating an incentive scheme that encourages firms to implement the optimal production and distribution computed by planners. A related problem is the generation and processing of data. The information burden on planners is already excessive even if there is accurate and unbiased reporting by the enterprises. However, planners might find it difficult to elicit accurate information from enterprises, because their success or failure might hinge on these statistical reports.

A final problem with optimal planning is obtaining agreement on the objective function of society. How are planners to know what goods and services are more important than others? Presumably, planners would have some insights on this issue, but the more complex the economy becomes, the more difficult it might be to determine the relative social valuations of different goods and services. In a complex economy, planners must know whether industrial plastics are more important than stainless steel or ceramics, all of which might serve similar functions as substitutes. Appendix 7A explores the computation problems of planning.

Coordination: How Much Market? How Much Plan?

In our discussion of planning, two themes emerge. First, there is the matter of how much control the central planning board is to exercise over economic outcomes. Should all decisions be made from above by planners, or should there be some decentralization to lower levels? Second, there is the matter of actually solving the plan to achieve both consistency and optimality. In most planned socialist systems, the practical approaches to these problems involve simplification through limitation of the formal planning procedures to important outputs and inputs, and a downgrading of the optimality criterion. Furthermore, mistakes are typically absorbed by low-priority (buffer) sectors. Also, most real-world systems utilize intermediate arrangements that combine plan and market. For sectors viewed by the planners as crucial to the achievement of state objectives (for example, steel), the CPB plays an important role; for sectors viewed as substantially less important (for example, light industrial goods), the CPB may play a minor role. Most approach planning as only a partial means for the allocation of resources. The "priority principle" (that is, focusing on important sectors such as steel and chemicals) serves to limit the range of inputs and outputs planned at the center. Plan techniques are of the material balance type; they are substantially distant from the more sophisticated and theoretically elegant optimization models that we have described.

Critics of the planned socialist system argue that the complexities of the real world make it impossible for the CPB to handle its tasks, let alone to expect the individual firm to follow its directives. The supporters of planned socialism, on the other hand, have argued that choices in production and consumption are generally much simpler than neoclassical economic theory implies. These sorts of issues remain at the center of the debate over the relative merits of the plan versus the market.

The theory of planning stresses the *formulation* of a plan, consisting of a set of objectives and the means for achieving the objectives. However, plans are of little value unless they are implemented. Implementation calls for incentives that induce economic agents to achieve the goals planners have set. The record of the Soviet Union and other planned socialist economic systems shows that ensuring appropriate motivation is a serious problem. Managers frequently work with plan objectives that are poorly specified, if not contradictory. When managers are asked to execute plans with limited information under such conditions, a large element of informal (and often dysfunctional) decision making takes over where plan directives were intended to be dominant.

THE PERFORMANCE OF PLANNED SOCIALISM: HYPOTHESES

In Chapter 5, we put forth several hypotheses concerning the expected performance of capitalist economic systems in terms of the performance criteria of economic growth, efficiency, and income distribution. We shall now attempt to do the same for socialist economic systems.

Because we have no paradigm of socialist economic systems, the formulation of hypotheses is especially difficult. Moreover, it is difficult to formulate hypotheses independently of the performance of real-world socialism. We now know a great deal about the efficiency problems of planned socialism in practice. Although it does not constitute a scientific approach to hypotheses formulation, real-world experience is hard to ignore.

Income Distribution

The first hypothesis is obvious. Income should be more equally distributed under planned socialism than under capitalism. The state (society) owns capital and land, and the returns on these assets go to the state. It is conceivable, but not likely, that the state will distribute this nonlabor income *less* equitably than capitalist societies. Presumably, authorities in planned socialist economies attach considerable importance to the "fair" distribution of income. We therefore expect income to be distributed relatively equally in a planned socialist economy.

Efficiency

The critics of planned socialism believe that planned socialist economies have difficulty in efficiently allocating resources. Planners, they feel, would have great difficulty in processing information, constructing a plan, and motivating participants. Moreover, the planned socialist economy would not automatically generate relative prices that would enable participants to make good use of resources. These theoretical difficulties suggest the hypothesis that planned socialist economies operate at relatively low levels of efficiency. Planning techniques that aim at optimality still have limited real-world applicability, and planned socialist economies have had to use material balance planning procedures that are unlikely to place them on their production possibilities schedules (see Figure 3.2). In fact, the aim of material balance planning is consistency, not optimality. Thus the hypothesis that the planned socialist economies do not perform well in terms of both dynamic and static efficiency appears to be a fairly safe one.

Economic Growth

In planned socialism, the state is able to exercise greater control over the investment and savings rates than under capitalism. This is true because virtually all nonlabor income accrues to the state. One would therefore expect a higher savings rate under both forms of socialism, because the socialist state is likely to adopt rapid growth as a priority objective (the building of socialism).

In the planned socialist economies, rapid growth is promoted both by the high savings rate and by the direction of resources by planners into growth-maximizing pursuits. At first glance, therefore, it would appear that one should hypothesize a higher growth rate for the planned socialist economies. The complicating factor, however, is the hypothesized lower efficiency of the planned socialist economies. Thus we must again refrain from stating a strong hypothesis about the relative growth of planned socialism, which must be left as an empirical issue.

Stability

We hypothesize that the planned socialist economies will be more stable than their capitalist counterparts. In making this statement, we do not deny the fact that significant concealed instabilities (repressed inflation, underemployment) will be present in the planned socialist economies. We base our hypothesis of greater stability on the following considerations. First, investment spending will be subject to the control of planners and will probably be maintained at a fairly stable rate. Thus fluctuations in investment spending (a major source of instability in capitalist economies) will probably be small. Second, material balance planning will lead to an approximate balance of labor supplies and demands. Third, supplies and demands for consumer goods will be subject to a great deal of state control (planners set industrial wages and determine the output of consumer goods). Moreover, the state will be less subject to popular pressures to pursue inflationary monetary policies. Fourth, firms operating under pressure to meet output targets will provide workers with guaranteed jobs.

Development Objectives

We refrained from suggesting a hypothesis concerning capitalism's ability to achieve development objectives, because this can be done only in a comparative setting. Despite the arguments raised by Vanek, we fail to see any particular advantages of market socialism over market capitalism. The possible exception is the greater control, in the former, over the savings and investment rates.

The planned socialist economies appear to have one advantage: their ability to concentrate available resources on developmental objectives. The ability to direct resources to specific aims could result in more rapid structural changes and higher growth, which would lead to an acceleration in the pace of economic development above what it would have been under market capitalism. Again, countervailing forces render the verdict uncertain. Can the hypothesized higher efficiency of market capitalism outweigh these advantages? This is one of the major questions in the field of comparative economic systems, and we obviously cannot provide any unequivocal answers at this point.

SUMMARY: THEORY OF PLANNED SOCIALISM

1. Marx and Lenin had little to say about how resource allocation would proceed under socialism. Barone showed the theoretical feasibility of socialist resource allocation but failed to provide a workable scheme. The critics of socialism (Mises and Hayek) argued that socialism would be inefficient, if not unworkable, because of computation, evaluation, and incentive problems. Kornai emphasized the natural tendency of planned socialism toward shortage.
2. There is no paradigm of planned socialism. At a practical level, resources are allocated by the administrative material balance method, which, in theory at least, could be augmented by input–output procedures. The material balance method originated in the Soviet Union as an outgrowth of the practical experience of Soviet planning.
3. The theory of economic planning could serve as a model for the planned socialist economy. The theory of planning emphasizes the choice of optimal plan variants subject to resource constraints. The theory of planning has had limited real-world application because of aggregation and computation problems.
4. The planned socialist economy must use some market allocation. Procedures have to be adopted that limit the administrative burden on the center and give some discretion to local organizations.

NOTES

1. See A. C. Pigou, *Socialism Versus Capitalism* (New York: St. Martin's, 1960), Ch. 1. For a brief definition, see Benjamin N. Ward, *The Socialist Economy* (New York: Random House, 1967), Ch. 1; for a broader definition, see J. Wilczynski, *The Economics of Socialism* (London: Unwin Hyman, 1970), Ch. 1.
2. See E. Ray Canterbery, *The Making of Economics* (Belmont, Calif.: Wadsworth, 1976); or Robert Lekachman, *A History of Economic Ideas* (New York: McGraw-Hill, 1976). For a treatment in the context of the history of economic thought, see Edmund Whittaker, *Schools and Streams of Economic Thought* (Chicago: Rand McNally, 1966), Chs. 10–11; for a collection of original sources, see Alec Nove and D. N. Nuti, eds., *Socialist Economics* (Harmondsworth, England: Penguin Books, 1972).
3. In the Marxian schema, capitalism is the engine that was to create the developed and industrialized economy; socialism would be concerned with providing an "equitable" distribution of the productive capacity developed under capitalism. Although socialism was not intended to be the mechanism for economic development, this is precisely the role in which it has been cast.
4. For a survey, see R. N. Carew Hunt, *The Theory and Practice of Communism* (Harmondsworth, England: Penguin Books, 1963), Chs. 6, 15.
5. Lenin's views on this matter are elaborated in his *State and Revolution*, published in 1917.
6. This view, though largely discredited during the period of war communism in the Soviet Union, has remained influential in present-day Soviet attitudes toward industrial and agricultural management. This attitude is used to support the argument for technical rather than managerial training in large enterprises.
7. The important articles on this debate can be found in F. A. Hayek, ed., *Collectivist Economic Planning*, 6th ed. (London: Routledge and Kegan Paul, 1963).
8. See Ludwig von Mises, "Economic Calculation in Socialism," in Morris Bornstein, ed., *Comparative Economic Systems*, rev. ed. (Homewood, Ill.: Irwin, 1969), pp. 61–68.
9. The best source for the original article by Oskar Lange and related discussion is Benjamin Lippincott, ed., *On the Economic Theory of Socialism* (Minneapolis: University of Minnesota Press, 1938), reprinted by McGraw-Hill in 1964.
10. Pigou, *Socialism Versus Capitalism*, Ch. 1.
11. Abram Bergson, *Essays in Normative Economics* (Cambridge, Mass.: Harvard University Press, 1966), Ch. 9; also see Abram Bergson, "Market Socialism Revisited," *Journal of Political Economy*, 75 (October 1967), 663–675.
12. See Janos Kornai, *Economics of Shortage* Vols. A and B (New York: North-Holland, 1980). For a discussion of some of the issues raised by Kornai, see Paul G. Hare, "Economics of Shortage and Non-Price Control," *Journal of Comparative Economics*, 6 (1982), 406–425. An excellent summary is Kornai, "Resource Constrained Versus Demand Constrained Systems," *Econometrica*, 47 (July 1979), 801–819.
13. See Janos Kornai, *Anti-Equilibrium: On Economic Systems Theory and the Tasks of Research* (Amsterdam: North-Holland, 1971); and Janos Kornai, *Rush Versus Harmonic Growth* (Amsterdam: North-Holland, 1972); *Overcentralization in Economic Administration* (London: Oxford University Press, 1959); and *Growth, Shortage, and Efficiency: A Macrodynamic Model of the Socialist Economy* (Berkeley: University of California Press, 1983).
14. See Leon Smolinski, "The Origins of Soviet Mathematical Economics," in Franz-Lothar Altmann, ed., *Jahrbuch der Wirtschaft Osteuropas* [Yearbook of East European Economics], Band 2 (Munich: Gunter Olzog Verlag, 1971), pp. 137–154.
15. The most famous Soviet growth model is by P. A. Feldman and is discussed in Evsey Domar, *Essays in the Theory of Economic Growth* (New York: Oxford University Press, 1957), pp. 233–261. The classic work on the Soviet industrialization debate is Alexander Erlich, *The Soviet Industrialization Debate, 1924–1928* (Cambridge, Mass.: Harvard University Press, 1962).
16. R. W. Davies and S. G. Wheatcroft, eds., *Materials for a Balance of the National Economy 1928/29* (Cambridge, England: Cambridge University Press, 1985).

17. Gerald Sirkin, *The Visible Hand: The Fundamentals of Economic Planning* (New York: McGraw-Hill, 1968), p. 45.
18. Abdul Qayum, *Techniques of National Economic Planning* (Bloomington: Indiana University Press, 1975), p. 4.
19. Michael P. Todaro, *Development Planning: Models and Methods* (Nairobi: Oxford University Press, 1971), p. 1.
20. G. M. Heal, *The Theory of Economic Planning* (New York: American Elsevier, 1973), p. 5.
21. *Political Economy: A Textbook*, 4th ed. (Berlin: Deitz, 1964), pp. 496, 499.
22. Raymond Powell, "Plan Execution and the Workability of Soviet Planning," *Journal of Comparative Economics*, 1 (March 1977), 51–76.
23. H. B. Chenery and P. G. Clark, *Interindustry Economics* (New York: Wiley, 1959); R. Dorfman, P. Samuelson, and R. Solow, *Linear Programming and Economic Analysis* (New York: McGraw-Hill, 1958); W. W. Leontief, *Input–Output Economics* (New York: Oxford University Press, 1966); Michael P. Todaro, *Development Planning: Models and Methods* (Nairobi: Oxford University Press, 1971); and Vladimir Treml, "Input–Output Analysis and Soviet Planning," in John Hardt *et al.*, eds., *Mathematics and Computers in Soviet Planning* (New Haven: Yale University Press, 1967).

RECOMMENDED READINGS

Socialism in Historical Perspective

G. D. H. Cole, *Socialist Economics* (London: Gollancz, 1950).
R. N. Carew Hunt, *The Theory and Practice of Communism* (Harmondsworth, England: Penguin Books, 1963).

The Socialist Controversy

F. A. Hayek, ed., *Collectivist Economic Planning*, 6th ed. (London: Routledge and Kegan Paul, 1963).
Benjamin N. Ward, *The Socialist Economy* (New York: Random House, 1967).

Economic Planning

John Bennett, *The Economic Theory of Central Planning* (Cambridge, Mass.: Blackwell, 1989).
Morris Bornstein, ed., *Economic Planning, East and West* (Cambridge, Mass.: Ballinger, 1975).
Roger A. Bowles and David K. Whynes, *Macroeconomic Planning* (London: Unwin Hyman, 1979).
Phillip J. Bryson, *Scarcity and Control in Socialism* (Lexington, Mass.: Heath, 1976).
Parkash Chander and Ashok Pavikh, "Theory and Practice of Decentralized Planning Procedures," *Journal of Economic Surveys*, 4 (1990), 19–58.
G. M. Heal, *The Theory of Economic Planning* (New York: American Elsevier, 1973).
Zoltan Kenessey, *The Process of Economic Planning* (New York: Columbia University Press, 1978).
Don Lavoie, *National Economic Planning: What Is Left* (Cambridge, Mass.: Ballinger, 1985).
Abdul Qayum, *Techniques of National Economic Planning* (Bloomington: Indiana University Press, 1975).
Gerald Sirkin, *The Visible Hand: The Fundamentals of Economic Planning* (New York: McGraw-Hill, 1968).
Nicolas Spulber and Ira Horowitz, *Quantitative Economic Policy and Planning* (New York: Norton, 1976).
Michael P. Todaro, *Development Planning: Models and Methods* (Nairobi: Oxford University Press, 1971).

General Works

Andrew Levine, *Arguing for Socialism: Theoretical Considerations* (London: Routledge and Kegan Paul, 1984).
Bernard Crick, *Socialism* (Minneapolis: University of Minnesota Press, 1987).
Alec Nove, *The Economics of Feasible Socialism* (Winchester, Mass.: Unwin Hyman, 1983).
J. Wilczynski, *The Economics of Socialism,* 4th ed. (London: Unwin Hyman, 1982).
Jerzy Obiatynski, *Michael Kalecki on a Socialist Economy* (Basingstoke: MacMillan, 1988).
S. Pejovich, *Socialism: Institutional, Philosophical, and Economic Issues* (Norwell, Mass.: Kluwer Academic Publishers, 1987).

APPENDIX 7A: THE PLANNING PROBLEM

We have emphasized that the competitive market model, though a theoretical construct, nevertheless serves as a useful basis for analyzing both the structure and the function of the capitalist market economy. In recent years, there have been increasingly sophisticated attempts to construct a similar paradigm for the planned economy. Although the theory of planning is beyond the scope of this book, we shall present here a brief outline of the direction in which this analysis is proceeding.

Chapter 7 showed that an economic plan is simply an application of maximization under constraints. It also pointed out the difficulty of actually solving for an optimal plan. This appendix discusses price and nonprice solutions to an optimal plan problem.

The planning problem, then, is conceptually quite straightforward. With given objectives and constraints, how is the objective function to be maximized? The plan, as we have outlined it thus far, tells us what we would like to do and what means are available for the achievement of these objectives. It does not, however, tell us what to do to achieve these goals. At this juncture, a solution for the planning problem must be found. A variety of methods, known as **planning routines**, are available.

Planning Routines

The planning problem is similar to a maximization model for a single firm and can be solved by well-known procedures. However, the matter of aggregation and the large number of inputs and outputs introduce a degree of complexity that makes it necessary to look for different solution routines. Much of the literature on planning is devoted to a discussion of these routines, their various positive and negative features, and different models of application. Most planning routines are one of three basic types: price-guided, nonprice-guided, or some mixture of the two. Before we turn to an examination of these different routines, some general observations are necessary.

Because the task of determining the solution to a national economic plan is so large, it is usually approached in a number of steps known as **iterations**. A simple example of an iterative approach is an auction. When the auctioneer holds up an item to be sold, he or she does not know who will purchase the item or what the price will be. Both pieces of information (the solution in this case) are obtained by a series of sequential steps in which the auctioneer hears bids from various potential buyers. The auctioneer (and the seller of the item) would like to obtain the highest possible price and to do so with the least possible expenditure of time. The iterative approach to solving a planning problem is similar, and analogous criteria can be used for evaluating the effectiveness of planning routines: Which planning routine achieves the "best" solution in the least amount of time (or, in this case, the smallest number of iterations)? These are important questions when one is dealing with a national economic plan for which vast amounts of computational inputs are required. The material balance approach solves this problem by accounting for only the most serious reverberations resulting from imbalance.

As planners move through a series of iterations to approach a final solution, how do they know that the initially nonoptimal values of the choice variables will improve as they are adjusted? The ability of a planning routine to move closer and closer to the maximal value of the objective function is known as **convergence**. A matter of substantial theoretical complexity, convergence is also of great practical importance. In the case of an auction, if there is excess demand for a particular producer good, the auctioneer will raise the price. Will this adjustment necessarily (under all conditions) reduce the excess demand? As the auctioneer appeals to additional bidders in sequence, will the selling price necessarily increase at each stage? Reaching the "best" value of an objective function in the most efficient manner possible is at the heart of selecting the planning routine most appropriate for a particular application. Procedures for optimization are the subject of a vast body of literature in economics and related disciplines, generally described as mathematical programming.

In addition to obtaining the maximal value of the objective function, the plan must be **feasible**. A plan that is feasible is one the objectives of which can be realized with the available inputs, technology, and so on. The concept of feasibility seems simple enough. The feasibility conditions are given in equations 7.8 to 7.10 in Chapter 7 proper. In fact, as we have seen, feasibility is the most important criterion of good plan formulation in material balance planning. There are, however, two important complications. First, plan objectives are necessarily based on data that are probabilistic, so it is necessary to choose methods that can handle errors appropriately. Second, there is the element of uncertainty when plan objectives are established for some future time period (as they usually are). It is not clear that the methods viewed as appropriate for handling existing data will also be appropriate for handling projections into the future.

There are a wide variety of planning routines. The most fundamental distinctions among them, however, are in the nature of the *information* that will be derived from the exercise and the manner in which the information will be utilized. *Prices* are the most familiar information mechanism in the market economy. A planning routine may be designed to give the planners prices, which can be used in varying ways to allocate resources in the system. An alternative model solves only for physical quantities of inputs and outputs, information that would then be conveyed to producing units in the system for action. Obviously, it is possible to combine the price and nonprice approaches.

The distinction between price and nonprice planning can also be illustrated using equations 7.7 and 7.10. In theory, both should yield the same result: an allocation of resources that maximizes the objective function. Nonprice planning requires planners to solve directly for the X's and the u's and then order producers to produce this mix of outputs (X's) with the prescribed mix of inputs (u's). Price planning requires the planners to solve for the set of factor prices that will induce producers to supply the same mix of outputs by using the same mix of inputs. Let us now examine the main variants of price-guided and nonprice-guided planning routines.

Planning with Prices

We have already examined resource allocation in the market economy, and we need not emphasize further the important role of prices. Prices are similarly important in the market socialism model. Indeed, much of the discussion of market socialism revolves around the basic issues of how prices are to be formed and, once formed, how they will be used to manipulate economic outcomes. Under centrally planned socialism, price-guided planning models seek to find a set of scarcity (equilibrium) prices to which enterprises are allowed to respond or that help planners establish resource allocation directives.

The most famous price-guided planning routine is the Lange model, which will be examined in the next chapter. From a theoretical point of view, the crucial question in the Lange model is the procedure for finding equilibrium prices. Specifically, if the initial prices quoted to firms turn out to be wrong (result in excess demand or supply), will the price adjustment procedure followed by the CPB necessarily eliminate the imbalance? To use planning language, one is interested in whether there exists an equilibrium solution and, in addition, whether the adjustment procedure being used (trial and error) will lead to convergence. Although the technical literature on this matter is beyond the scope of our present discussion, the Lange trial-and-error algorithm is likely to lead to an equilibrium solution.

The Lange model is only one variant for determining equilibrium prices in a price-guided model. However, it is not necessary (at least in theory) to simulate the market process to form prices. This brings us to a fundamental point in our discussion of price-guided planning: the possibility of generating equilibrium prices directly from the planning process without the use of a market mechanism. How can prices be formed in this way? To maximize an objective function, there are two problems, which economists describe as finding the **primal solution** and finding the **dual solution**. The primal solution is the set of

X's (and the distribution of the u's to produce them) that yields the maximal value of the objective function. The dual solution is the set of resource prices that will induce producers (following, say, the Lange rules) to produce the optimal set of X's.

Let us cast the relationship between the primal and dual solutions in a framework familiar to every student of microeconomic theory. Consider the case of a single firm. The maximization of output implies the minimization of inputs for a given output. If such a firm were not using the minimal amount of inputs for a given output, then clearly it could rearrange its inputs and expand the volume of output. In a formal sense, then, the objective of the firm can be specified as achieving a given output with minimal inputs or, alternatively, as maximizing output with a given amount of inputs. What is the importance of this duality to planning?

If output is maximized under given technology, then under these circumstances the ratios in which the inputs are being used at the margin represent their relative values as determined by their availability and their usefulness in the productive process. From this, relative scarcities can be established, which is what prices are intended to reflect. These relative scarcities can be established as the result of a mathematical exercise and quite apart from any particular set of institutional or organizational arrangements. The most important implication is that the *market is not necessary* for the formulation of rational prices.

When a constrained maximization problem of the sort we have been discussing is solved, there will be both a primal and a dual solution. The latter provides a set of shadow prices, which, under appropriate conditions, have the same meaning as prices generated under a perfectly competitive market economic system. What exactly is a shadow price? A **shadow price** represents the increase in the maximal value of the objective function generated by a one-unit increase in the particular factor. Thus if a one-unit increase in factor b_j (*ceteris paribus*) fails to increase the value of the objective function, then the shadow price of the factor is zero. On the other hand, if a one-unit increase in b_j increases the value of the objective function, then b_j has a positive shadow price. Thus the marginal product of the factor b_j is positive.

The logic of the procedure for calculating shadow prices is straightforward. However, when it is applied to an entire economic system, a number of problems must be confronted.

First, for the model to be computationally feasible, a considerable amount of aggregation is necessary. Having added together a number of products and factors and treated them as though they were homogeneous, one then finds it difficult to draw inferences about the valuation and use of specific products and factors from a model in which they no longer have individual identities.

Second, there are always problems pertaining to data. In particular, a great many data are needed — data that are not only of the right type but are also updated through time as underlying conditions change. Hayek and Mises argued that the task of gathering such data would overwhelm any planning agency.

Third, the complexity of the interrelationships in a modern economic system tends to grow as the economy grows in size and maturity, creating massive computational problems. Even if data could be gathered in sufficient detail, it is questionable whether existing computational techniques could supply solutions. Although it is theoretically possible to break up (decompose) a model consisting of systems of equations, decomposition techniques are complex and have had limited real-world applicability.

Thus far we have considered two price-guided approaches to solving the planning problem. Both are extremes. The Lange model indirectly utilizes the market mechanism; the computation of shadow prices utilizes an abstract mathematical model and is not tied to the market or to other particular organizational arrangements. Instead, the solution of mathematical equations, presumably by computer, fully substitutes for the functioning of the market.

Nonprice Planning

The alternative approach to price planning is nonprice planning. Nonprice planning can be interpreted in two ways. The first interpretation is that nonprice planning involves the primal solution for the optimal set of inputs and outputs. Planners accordingly send directives concerning these physical inputs and outputs to producing enterprises. Throughout the process, planning is conducted without reference to prices, although, as we have seen, underlying resource valuations are implicit in this exercise.

A second interpretation of nonprice planning is quantity planning, where prices are irrelevant. The most notable example of this is quantity planning using a static input–output model, where prices are irrelevant because factor proportions are presumed rigidly fixed by existing technology. The strict relationship between inputs and outputs does not change when input prices change. The input–output model is described in the body of Chapter 7. We have already noted the close resemblance between input–output planning and the material balance approach.

The foundation of input–output planning is the **technology matrix**, a matrix of technological coefficients such that all inputs can be related to all outputs, necessarily with a fairly high degree of aggregation for an entire economy. Assuming that this sort of information is available, how does one solve the planning problem? The CPB must first specify the objectives it wishes to achieve. Then, with the aid of the appropriate technological coefficients, the inputs required to meet the stated objectives can be established. Firms are then assigned (directly) input and output targets. For those familiar with the algebra of input–output economics, these points can be illustrated succinctly. Gross output (X) is utilized either as intermediate inputs AX (where A is the technology matrix) or for final uses (Y). That is,

$$X = AX + Y$$

Final uses, however, are related to gross outputs as follows:

$$Y = (I - A)X$$

where I is an identity matrix. Thus once planners have specified the desired final output mix (Y), they can calculate the gross outputs (X) necessary for every branch to produce the final outputs. The availability of primary resources constrains the choice of final outputs. For more on this, see the section of this chapter entitled "The Input–Output Model."

Nonprice planning differs substantially from the price-guided procedures. In the nonprice variant, firms have little freedom of decision making. There are, in the extreme, no prices. Firms are told in detail what to produce and what inputs to use. This is, in effect, the basis of the material balance approach. With the appropriate amounts of information, it is theoretically possible to achieve a balance of supplies and demands in this framework.

As with other plan algorithms, the crucial question here is the nature of the adjustment process through time. The CPB would be involved in the gathering and processing of vast amounts of information, a procedure with practical limitations. Computation techniques would dictate a fairly high degree of aggregation with all the attendant problems that aggregation implies. Finally, as with the Lange model, it is a strong but necessary assumption that firms will follow instructions and thus always exhibit function (goal-oriented) behavior.

REFERENCES

G. M. Heal, *The Theory of Economic Planning*, Ch. 2. See also Roger A. Bowles and David K. Whynes, *Macroeconomic Planning* (London: Unwin Hyman, 1979), Ch. 3; John Bennett, *The Economic Theory of Central Planning* (Cambridge, Mass.: Blackwell, 1989).

G. B. Dantzig and P. Wolfe, "A Decomposition Principle for Linear Programs," *Operations Research*, 8 (January–February 1961), 101–111; for a summary, see Nicolas Spulber and Ira Horowitz, *Quantitative Economic Policy and Planning* (New York: Norton, 1976).

8 Theory of Market Socialism

MARKET SOCIALISM is, as the term suggests, a hybrid of market and plan. It is an economic system that combines social ownership of capital with market allocation. As such, it offers the potential of combining the "fairness" of socialism with the efficiency associated with market allocation. The state owns the means of production, and returns to capital accrue to society at large. Because resources are allocated primarily by markets, many of the problems of planned socialism — the administrative and computational burdens and the problem of valuing resources — appear to be avoided.

This chapter presents the theory of market socialism. Unlike the perfectly competitive model of capitalism, there is no single paradigm of market socialism. Instead, there are alternative visions of market socialism, one characterized by state ownership of the means of production, the other by worker ownership. Both visions rely on markets (or at least artificial markets) to do the job of resource allocation.

Whereas it has been possible to study the actual workings of both market capitalism and planned socialism, the world has little experience with market socialism. This lack of real-world practice makes the theory of market socialism even more important. We must rely heavily on theory to understand the properties of this type of economic system. As this chapter will show, market socialism has both advantages and drawbacks. The major problems appear to be how to motivate participants to use resources efficiently and how to make markets work when capital is not owned by private individuals.

The appeal of market socialism is obvious. The widespread rejection of planned socialism in the late 1980s and early 1990s has elevated market socialism to the status of the major alternative to capitalism. The reform leadership of the Soviet Union and Eastern Europe may find market socialism a more palatable solution than market capitalism insofar as it promises to avoid the more negative features of market capitalism. Put another way, the demise of communism in Eastern Europe does not mean the demise of socialist thought and especially democratic variants of socialism. The latter will sustain, especially in poor countries striving to achieve improved levels of living.

146

MARKET SOCIALISM: THEORETICAL FOUNDATIONS

The problems of optimal planning — computational difficulty and motivation — make market socialism appealing. Permitting the market to direct a number of resource allocation decisions reduces the burden on the central planning board (CPB). Also, by allowing individual participants to respond to market incentives, market socialism may offer greater inducements to combine resources efficiently at the local level.

Advocates of market socialism have had to answer two questions raised by Hayek and Mises (see Chapter 7). If the means of production are owned by society, what assurances are there that capital will be used efficiently? And will the social ownership of capital distort incentives or lead to perverse economic behavior?

THE LANGE MODEL

The most famous theoretical model of market socialism is the trial-and-error model proposed by the Polish economist Oskar Lange.[1] This model focuses on the use of a general equilibrium framework (emphasized in the writings of Barone, Pareto, and Walras), approaching a "solution" through a number of sequential stages (emphasized by Walras).

A number of economists (most notably H. D. Dickinson and Abba Lerner) contributed to the Lange model, and a number of variants of the model exist.[2] Furthermore, the **Lange model** of market socialism differs from our definition of market socialism in that Lange envisioned only some indirect usage of the market.

What are the essential features of the Lange-type market socialist model? The model posits three levels of decision making (see Figure 8.1). At the lowest level are firms and households, at the intermediate level industrial authorities, and at the highest level a CPB. The means of production, with the exception of labor, are state-owned. Consumer goods are allocated by the market.

The CPB would set the prices of producer goods. Producing firms would be informed of these prices and would be instructed to produce in accordance with two rules: Produce the level of output at which price is equal to marginal cost, and minimize the cost of production at that output. Households would be left alone to make their own decisions about how much labor to supply.

Because the initial prices of producer goods would be arbitrarily set by the CPB, there is no reason to believe that as firms followed the rules (assuming that they did in fact follow the rules), the "right" amount of goods and services would be produced and supplies and demands would be in balance. What would the planners do if there were an imbalance?

If there were an excess supply of a particular good, its price would be lowered by the CPB. If there were excess demand, its price would be raised by the

CPB. Thus, in a sequential process, the CPB would adjust prices until they were at the "right" levels — that is, where supply and demand were balanced.

In addition to setting prices, the central planning board would also allocate the social dividend (rents and profits) earned from the use of productive resources owned by the state. This dividend could be distributed in the form of public services or investment, the latter decision made in conjunction with the intermediate industrial authorities. The state would have a substantial degree of power because it could determine both the magnitude and the direction of investment, though Lange argued that investment funds should be generally allocated to equalize marginal rates of return in different applications. Considerable central control over the economic system would be maintained by the CPB. At the same time, prices would be used for decision making to relieve the CPB of a substantial administrative task.

Let us examine some of the proposed advantages of the Lange model. Lange envisioned that with the means of production owned by the state, both the *rate* and the *direction* of economic activity would in large part be determined by the state. Thus the returns from and the influence of private ownership would be removed. Accordingly, the distribution of income would be substantially more even than under capitalism. Furthermore, the mix of output would be different, and insofar as the investment ratio would be a major determinant of the rate

Figure 8.1 The Organization of Market Socialism in the Lange Framework

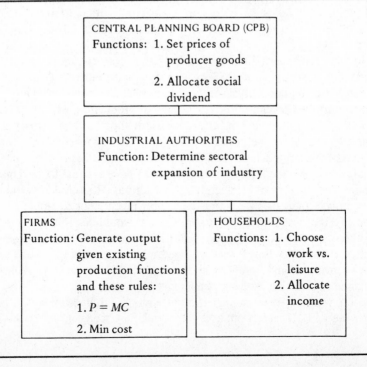

of economic growth, this rate too would be largely state-determined. Both these features of the Lange model (a more even distribution of income and state control over investment) are presumed advantages.

Lange argued that externalities could be better accounted for because the state could manipulate resource prices. Other economists — for example, Jan Tinbergen and Maurice Dobb — have argued that, in general, decisions made at higher levels rather than lower levels are likely to be "better" in terms of preventing undesirable environmental effects.[3] Lange further presumed that state control over savings and investment would reduce cyclical instability, a mainstay in the socialism critique of capitalism.

Real-world market systems depart from the perfectly competitive model. Simulation of the market, argued Lange, would utilize the positive aspects of the market while eliminating its negative characteristics. In this context, it is ironic that Lange said little about the problems that would arise when difficulties of entry, economies of scale, or changes in technology were present. These forces are crucial in determining the degree of competition in a capitalist economic system. Might not some of these problems arise in the real-world operation of a Lange-type model?

Critics of the Lange Model

The Lange model captured the fancy of many observers over the years, but it has not been without critics. Lange himself recognized that the many tasks assigned to the CPB could lead to a large bureaucracy, long considered a negative feature of socialism. The most outspoken critic on this score has been the Nobel laureate F. A. Hayek. Hayek has suggested that although the task set for the CPB might be manageable in theory, it would probably be unmanageable in practice.[4]

Abram Bergson and others have pointed to a key problem in the Lange model: that of ensuring appropriate managerial motivation.[5] How would the intermediate authorities, and especially enterprise managers, be motivated to follow Lange's rules of conduct even if they knew marginal costs? The problem of establishing a workable incentive structure has been a major theme in modern socialist economic systems.

Bergson also emphasized the possibility of monopolistic behavior in the Lange framework — if not at the enterprise level, then at the intermediate level. This problem and the matter of relating one level to another are substantially neglected in the original formulation of the Lange model.

Although the Lange model uses features of capitalism, it is also characterized by many elements normally associated with socialism. The scholarly literature, therefore, has tended to focus on whether the Lange model can operate in reality and, if so, how effectively. The Lange model has also sparked great interest because most existing socialist systems use a crude form of trial and error for the setting of prices, at least for consumer goods. Real-world reliance on the trial-and-error methods is important, for mathematical models of planning (and price formulation) have been of limited practical use in spite of their theoretical elegance.[6]

MARKET SOCIALISM: THE COOPERATIVE VARIANT

A second variant of market socialism is the cooperative economy, or labor-managed economy. The interest in worker participation stems from both the theory of cooperative economic behavior elaborated in this section and the systems of worker management used in Yugoslavia, Western Europe, and now Eastern Europe.

The cooperative model of market socialism stems from the notion that people should participate in making the decisions that affect their well-being. Jaroslav Vanek, a major advocate of the "participatory economy," emphasizes this theme:

> The quest of men to participate in the determination and decision-making of the activities in which they are personally and directly involved is one of the most important sociopolitical phenomena of our times. It is very likely to be the dominant force of social evolution in the last third of the twentieth century.[7]

Vanek uses five characteristics to identify the participatory economy:

1. Firms will be managed in participatory fashion by the people working in them.
2. Income sharing will prevail and is to be equitable — that is, "equal for labor of equal intensity and quality, and governed by a democratically agreed-upon income-distribution schedule assigning to each job its relative claim on total net income."[8]
3. Although the workers may enjoy the fruits of the operation, they do not own, and must therefore pay for, the use of productive resources.
4. The economy must always be a market economy. Economic planning may be used through indirect mechanisms, but "never through a direct order to a firm or group of firms."[9]
5. There is freedom of choice in employment.

In essence, resources are state-owned but are managed by the workers in the enterprises, whose objective is to create a maximum dividend per worker. Cooperative socialism belongs to the more general category of market socialism, because there is state ownership of the means of production but also an exchange of goods and services in the market without intervention by central planners. Producer goods would use market prices, as opposed to prices manipulated by the CPB in the Lange framework. The cooperative form of socialism has been viewed as an important and path-breaking addition to socialist thinking, especially by those who would identify with democratic socialism as a political system.

Theoretical analysis of the cooperative model dates from an article by Benjamin Ward published in 1958 and the subsequent elaboration of the participatory economy by Vanek.[10] Resources (with the exception of labor) are owned by the state and will be used by each firm, for which a fee will be paid to the state. Prices for both producer goods and consumer goods will be determined by supply and demand in the market. Enterprises will be managed by the workers (who may hire a professional manager responsible to them), who will attempt to maximize the dividend per worker (net income per worker) in the enterprise. With this objective, management must decide on input and output combinations.

In addition to levying a charge for the use of capital assets and for land, the state will administer the public sector of the economy and may levy taxes to finance cultural and industrial development. In this environment, how will the cooperative firm behave? Let us examine two cases: first, the short run, where there is a variable supply of labor but capital is fixed; second, the long run, where both labor and capital are variable.

The cooperative model assumes that the enterprise manager wishes to maximize net earnings per worker (Y/L), and that output (Q) is solely a function of the labor input (L) in the short run. The output can be sold on the market at a price (P) dictated by *market* forces. The firm must pay a fixed tax (T) on its capital. In the short-run variant, capital is fixed; so is the tax. Under these conditions, the firm will seek to maximize the following expression:

Maximize
$$Y/L = \frac{PQ - T}{L} \tag{8.1}$$

where

$$Y/L = \text{net income per worker}$$
$$P = \text{price of the product}$$
$$Q = \text{quantity produced}$$
$$T = \text{fixed tax levied on capital}$$
$$L = \text{labor input}$$

Maximum net income per worker in equation 8.1 will be achieved when the amount of labor hired (L) is such that the value of the marginal product of the last worker hired is the same as average net earnings per worker, or, in terms of the notation of equation 8.1, when the following balance is achieved:

$$P \cdot MP_L = \frac{(PQ - T)}{L} \tag{8.2}$$

where

$$MP_L = \text{marginal product of labor}$$

The logic of this solution is quite simple. If the enterprise can increase average net revenue by hiring another worker — that is, if the marginal product of the last worker hired is greater than average net revenue — then the worker should be hired and average net revenue can be increased. The addition of workers should continue until the value of the marginal product of the last person hired and the average net revenue are the same. If the manager were to hire, at the margin, a worker the value of whose marginal product were less than the average net revenue per worker, then the net income of remaining workers would fall.

In the *long run*, the cooperative must select its optimal capital stock (K), on which it will pay a rental charge (r) per unit of capital used. The firm now seeks to maximize its average net revenue as given by the following expression:

Maximize $$Y/L = \frac{PQ - rK}{L} \qquad (8.3)$$

where

$$K = \text{amount of capital}$$
$$r = \text{the charge per unit of capital}$$

The maximum value of this expression (average net revenue per worker) will be achieved in a manner similar to that of the short-run case. As long as the value of the marginal product of capital ($P \cdot MP_K$) is greater than the rental rate (r) paid on capital, more capital should be hired and utilized until the return and the cost are equalized ($P \cdot MP_K = r$). This rule applies to the perfectly competitive capitalist firm and the Lange-type firm as well. The same rule as equation 8.2 would apply for the hiring of labor, except that the charge for variable capital would have to be deducted as follows:

$$P \cdot MP_L = \frac{PQ - rK}{L} \qquad (8.4)$$

These two cases, the short run and the long run, are both simple variants of the cooperative model. The short-run case is elaborated diagrammatically in Figure 8.2. Note that the model assumes that both product and factor markets are perfectly competitive and that there is no interference by the state.

The cooperative model works through product and factor markets. Households supply labor services as a consequence of maximizing household utility in the choice of work versus leisure. In this way labor supply schedules are determined, as are demand schedules for consumer goods. Firms maximize net revenue per worker and in so doing are prepared to supply goods and services at various prices and at the same time purchase inputs at various prices.

There is a close relationship between the cooperative model and the competitive capitalist and Lange models. In essence, the cooperative model captures the efficiency features of both. In the Lange model, the firm follows two rules, equating price and marginal cost and minimizing average cost of production. In the cooperative model, these two rules are replaced by a single rule (in the short run represented by equation 8.2). In the case of the capitalist market economy, the firm follows the rule of equating marginal cost and marginal revenue, which in the case of perfect competition reduces to the Lange rule; so here too, the cooperative variant simply replaces this rule with equation 8.2.

There is now a considerable body of literature on the cooperative model and its variants. Many pertinent issues have been raised by the model's critics as well as by its admirers.

Criticism of the Cooperative Model

The cooperative model has been analyzed in detail by Benjamin Ward. Ward notes that the two key features of the model are "individual material self-interest as the dominant human motivation" and "the resort to markets as the means of allocating resources."[11] Ward devoted considerable attention to analyzing the response of the cooperative to various changes in capital charges, taxes, input prices, and product prices.[12] For the capitalist and the Lange-type firm, an increase in price will induce an increase in output (that is, a positively sloped supply curve). Ward demonstrated that the cooperative supply curve may well be negatively sloped (that is, an increase in price generates a *decrease* in output), especially in the short run.[13] If true, this would certainly be a per-

Figure 8.2 The Cooperative Model

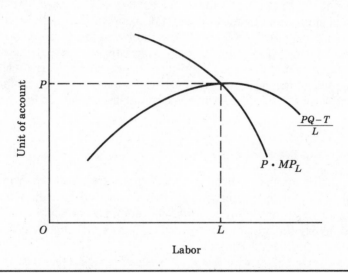

Labor

Explanation:

$$\frac{PQ - T}{L} = net \text{ receipts per worker}$$

$$P \cdot MP_L = \text{marginal value product of labor}$$

If the cooperative wishes to maximize the value of net receipts per worker, it should hire labor until the value of the marginal product of the last worker hired is the same as the net receipts per worker. In the diagram, the cooperative would hire OL labor, and each worker would receive OP.

verse and undesirable result, especially in an economy where resources are allocated by the market. Such a result might (though it would not necessarily) threaten both the existence and the stability of equilibrium in product markets.

Ward also argued that if two cooperatives producing an identical product use different technologies, there will be a misallocation of labor and capital that would not occur if the two were capitalist firms.[14] In the case of the capitalist firms, both would hire labor until the wage was equal to the value of the marginal product ($W = P \cdot MP_L$), for both would face the same market-determined wage (W) and hence would generate the same value of marginal product. In the case of the cooperative, however, unless the production functions are identical, the average net revenue per worker will differ between the two cooperatives. Although each cooperative equates average net revenue per worker with the marginal product of the last worker hired, overall output could be increased by moving workers to the cooperatives where the value of the marginal product is higher.

Ward also argued that the cooperative might be undesirable if it existed in a noncompetitive environment.[15] Specifically, he contends that the monopolistic cooperative would be less efficient than either its competitive cooperative twin or its monopolistic capitalist twin. The monopolistic cooperative would hire less labor, produce less output, and charge a higher price than either the competitive cooperative or the monopolistic capitalist firm.

Critics of the Lange model raised the issue of how to ensure appropriate managerial motivation. To the extent that the cooperative utilizes hired professional management, the problem of how to motivate and regulate managers will exist. Ward noted that in some cases the cooperative will have the incentive to expand, although in the absence of private property holding, it is not clear who the entrepreneur will be.[16] It is possible that the state would play an important role here because it would control some of the investment funds.

Advantages of the Cooperative Model

Strong support for the cooperative model comes from Jaroslav Vanek, who argues that the participatory economy is an element of social evolution that will be especially important in future years.[17] In addition to prescribing the participatory economy for present-day economies, Vanek also argues that it is the best alternative for developing economies.

Vanek does not agree with Ward's criticisms. He argues that if two cooperative firms have access to identical technology, and if there is free entry and exit, the input–output decisions of the cooperatives will be identical to those of two capitalist firms operating under the same condition.[18] Moreover, Vanek argues, the result will be much more desirable socially, because in the capitalist case the workers are rewarded according to the value of the marginal products, whereas under the cooperative case, workers are rewarded according to the decision of the collective, which they themselves control.

Vanek also maintains that under certain likely cases, the supply curve of the cooperative firm will not be negatively sloped as Ward suggests. If the cooperative is a multiproduct firm, or if it faces an external constraint (for example, a limited supply of labor), Vanek shows that the firm's supply curve will be positively sloped.

Vanek argues that the imperfectly competitive cooperative firm will be superior to the imperfectly competitive capitalist firm because it will have no incentive to grow extremely large and hence to dominate a particular market. Further, the cooperative will have no incentive to act in a socially wasteful manner — to create artificial demand for a product through advertising. Finally, Vanek maintains that both the demand for investment and the supply of savings will tend to be greater in the cooperative than in the competitive capitalist environment.

Many of the issues surrounding the comparative performance of cooperative and capitalist firms seem highly abstract and theoretical. They are, however, of basic importance to the efficiency of each system. The response of the cooperative firm to market signals determines the extent to which it can meet consumer goals and, in the long run, the extent to which an appropriate industrial structure is established in line with long-term development goals and aspirations.

Many of the supporters of the cooperative model, especially Vanek, argue that beyond these specific performance characteristics, the crucial features of the cooperative are its "special dimensions." Among the most important would be the elimination of the capitalist dichotomy between management and labor. It is also argued that there would be greater social justice in the distribution of rewards.[19]

Over the years, there has been a great deal of interest in various forms of what might be broadly termed market socialism. In part, the appeal of market socialism rests on the appeal of socialism per se: greater equality in the distribution of income, more attention to the public sector, and more worker control. In another dimension, however, its appeal rests on the perception that these features of socialism can be combined with a useful resource allocation mechanism — namely the market — and that this can be done with personal freedom and participation.

HYPOTHESES CONCERNING MARKET SOCIALISM

Yugoslavia, a small country beset by a wide range of problems, has experimented with worker-managed socialism. But for the most part, we lack real-world experience with market socialism either of the Lange or of the worker-managed type. Consequently, we do not have the advantage of long historical experience to test hypotheses concerning the economic performance of market socialism. The following paragraphs represent our best analytical — though somewhat speculative — efforts.

Income Distribution

The easiest hypothesis to formulate concerns the distribution of income under market socialism. Inasmuch as capital continues to belong to society, we would expect income to be distributed more nearly equally under market socialism than under capitalism. Even in the case of worker-managed enterprises, the state must be paid a fee for the use of capital, and presumably, the state would divide such income among the population on a fairly equal basis. Some reservations must be expressed, however. As critics have pointed out, prosperous worker-managed firms might protect extraordinarily high earnings by excluding outsiders. This type of behavior could lead to significant inequality in wage income.

Economic Growth

Proponents of market socialism claim that market socialism would yield relatively high rates of growth, primarily because society would plow earnings from capital back into the economy. This conclusion, however, assumes that the socialist state would not be pressured into putting the "social dividend" into current consumption in the form of subsidies and social services. Such pressure would be particularly strong in the case of democratically elected socialist governments. For these reasons, we believe it risky to presume that market socialism will yield higher investment rates — and hence higher rates of growth — than the capitalist model. The outcome is far from certain.

Efficiency

The theory of market socialism does not yield strong propositions concerning economic efficiency. Arguing that market socialism can indeed be more efficient than capitalism, its advocates cite the lack of monopoly, the greater attention to externalities, and individual participation in decision making. Its critics, however, mount equally convincing arguments about the inefficiency of market socialism: motivation problems, perverse supply curves, and the difficulty of finding equilibrium prices. Accordingly, we cannot venture any hypotheses about the relative efficiency of market socialism.

Stability

Advocates of market socialism make the following case for greater economic stability: The state will have greater control over the investment rate, so sharp fluctuations in investment can be avoided. Counterarguments exist, however. If market socialist economies (we are using the Lange model) have trouble adjusting prices to equilibrium, macroeconomic instabilities associated with nonequilibrium prices might be experienced. Moreover, democratically elected officials will be under strong pressure to pursue "popular" economic policies (the political business cycle), while feeling less pressure from market forces to tighten the reins on economic policy. Again, we cannot propose any strong hypotheses concerning the relative stability of market socialism.

SUMMARY: THEORIES OF MARKET SOCIALISM

1. Market socialism holds considerable appeal because it promises to combine the better features of capitalism (efficiency) and of socialism (equal distribution of income).
2. Lange's model of market socialism proposes trial-and-error pricing to achieve equilibrium. Socialist managers react to these prices by producing where price and marginal cost are equal and by minimizing costs. Lange argued that this model would be fair, offer the efficiency associated with perfect competition, deal better with externalities, promote growth, and be cyclically stable.
3. The critics of the Lange model argue that an economic system patterned after it would be computationally inefficient, lack proper managerial motivation, and possibly suffer from monopoly.
4. The cooperative model uses worker management in enterprise decision making. Workers share profits and pay a rental charge for productive assets that continue to belong to society at large. Advocates of the cooperative model argue that such a system would be fair, efficient, and stable and would offer the population certain other advantages.
5. Critics of the cooperative model maintain that an economic system operated in accordance with it would be unstable, would be relatively inefficient, and would experience problems with managerial motivation.

NOTES

1. Benjamin Lippincott, ed., *On the Economic Theory of Socialism* (Minneapolis: University of Minnesota Press, 1938).
2. See, for example, F. M. Taylor, "The Guidance of Production in a Socialist State," *American Economic Review*, 19 (March 1929); reprinted in Lippincott, *On the Economic Theory of Socialism*, pp. 39–54; H. D. Dickinson, *Economics of Socialism* (London: Oxford University Press, 1939); and Abba P. Lerner, *The Economics of Control* (New York: Macmillan, 1944).
3. See the discussion in Maurice Dobb, *The Welfare Economics and the Economics of Socialism* (Cambridge, England: Cambridge University Press, 1969), p. 133 and footnotes thereto.
4. F. A. Hayek, "Socialist Calculation: The Competitive Solution," *Economica*, n.s. 7 (May 1940), 125–149; reprinted in Bornstein, *Comparative Economic Systems*, pp. 77–97.
5. Abram Bergson, *Essays in Normative Economics* (Cambridge, Mass.: Harvard University Press, 1966), Ch. 9.
6. The sophisticated works of Soviet mathematical economists have been brought to Western readers by Zauberman, Ellman, and others. See, for example, Alfred Zauberman, *The Mathematical Revolution in Soviet Economics* (London: Oxford University Press, 1975); Michael Ellman, *Soviet Planning Today* (Cambridge, England: Cambridge University Press, 1971); Martin Cave, Alastair McAuley, and Judith Thornton, eds., *New Terms in Soviet Economics* (Armonk, N.Y.: M. E. Sharpe, 1982).
7. Jaroslav Vanek, *The Participatory Economy* (Ithaca, N.Y.: Cornell University Press, 1971), p. 1.

8. Ibid., p. 9.
9. Ibid., p. 11.
10. For Ward's original contribution, see Benjamin Ward, "The Firm in Illyria: Market Syndical-ism," *American Economic Review*, 48 (September 1958), 566–589. See also E. Domar, "The Soviet Collective Farm as a Producer Cooperative," *American Economic Review*, 56 (September 1966), 734–757; and Walter Y. Oi and Elizabeth M. Clayton, "A Peasant's View of a Soviet Collective Farm," *American Economic Review*, 58 (March 1968), 37–59. For a general treat-ment of Vanek's argument, see Vanek, *The Participatory Economy*; and for a detailed analysis, see Jaroslav Vanek, *The General Theory of Labor-Managed Market Economies* (Ithaca, N.Y.: Cornell University Press, 1970). For a more recent collection, see Jaroslav Vanek, *The Labor-Managed Economy: Essays* (Ithaca, N.Y.: Cornell University Press, 1977).
11. Ward, *The Socialist Economy*, p. 183.
12. Ibid., Chs. 8–10.
13. Ibid., pp. 191–192.
14. Ibid., pp. 184 ff.
15. Ibid., pp. 201 ff.
16. Ibid., Ch. 9.
17. For the general treatment, see Vanek, *The Participatory Economy*.
18. See Vanek, *The General Theory*.
19. For background on participatory socialism, see, for example, Ellen Turkish Comisso, *Worker's Control Under Plan and Market* (New Haven: Yale University Press, 1979), Chs. 1–2; Hans Dieter Seibel and Ukandi G. Damachi, *Self-Management in Yugoslavia and the Third World* (New York: St. Martin's, 1982); Howard M. Wachtel, *Workers' Management and Workers' Wages in Yugoslavia* (Ithaca, N.Y.: Cornell University Press, 1973), Ch. 2.

RECOMMENDED READINGS

Market Socialism: Traditional Views and Counterthoughts

Avner Ben-Ner and Egon Neuberger, "The Feasibility of Planned Market Systems: The Yugoslav Visible Hand and Negotiated Planning," *Journal of Comparative Economics*, 24 (December 1990), 768–790.

Abram Bergson, "Market Socialism Revisited." *Journal of Political Economy*, 75 (October 1967), 663–675.

H. D. Dickinson, *Economics of Socialism* (London: Oxford University Press, 1939).

Don Lavoie, *Rivalry and Central Planning: The Socialistic Calculation Debate Reconsidered* (New York: Cambridge University Press, 1985).

Abba P. Lerner, *The Economics of Control* (New York: Macmillan, 1944).

Benjamin Lippincott, ed., *On the Economic Theory of Socialism* (New York: McGraw-Hill, 1964).

Peter Murrell, "Did the Theory of Market Socialism Answer the Challenge of Ludwig von Mises? A Reinterpretation of the Socialist Controversy," *History of Political Economy* 15, 1 (1983), 92–105.

Gabriel Temkin, "On Economic Reforms in Socialist Countries: The Debate on Economic Calcula-tion Under Socialism Revisited," *Communist Economies*, 1, 1 (1989).

James A. Yunker, "The Equity-Efficiency Tradeoff Under Capitalism and Socialism," *Eastern Economic Journal*, 17 (January–March 1991), 31–44.

Market Socialism: The Labor-Managed Variant

Katrina V. Berman, "An Empirical Test of the Theory of the Labor-Managed Firm," *Journal of Comparative Economics*, 13 (June 1989), 281–300.

Norman J. Ireland and Peter J. Law, "Management Design Under Labor Management," *Journal of Comparative Economics*, 12 (March 1988), 1–23.

Derek C. Jones and Jan Svenjar, eds., *Advances in the Economic Analysis of Participatory and Labor Managed Firms*, Vols. 1–4 (Greenwich: JAI Press, various years).

Kathryn Nantz, "The Labor-Managed Firm Under Imperfect Monitoring: Employment and Work Effort Responses," *Journal of Comparative Economics*, 14 (March 1990), 33–50.

Hugh Neary, "The Comparative Statics of the Ward–Domar Labor-Managed Firm: A Profit-Function Approach," *Journal of Comparative Economics*, 12 (June 1988), 159–181.

V. Rus and R. Russell, eds., *International Handbook of Participation in Organization* (New York: Oxford University Press, 1989).

Fernando B. Saldanha, "Fixprice Analysis of Labor-Managed Economies," *Journal of Comparative Economics*, 13 (June 1989), 227–253.

Jaroslav Vanek, *The General Theory of Labor-Managed Market Economies* (Ithaca, N.Y.: Cornell University Press, 1970).

———, *The Labor-Managed Economy* (Ithaca, N.Y.: Cornell University Press, 1977).

———, *The Participatory Economy* (Ithaca, N.Y.: Cornell University Press, 1971).

Benjamin N. Ward, *The Socialist Economy* (New York: Random House, 1967).

PART  III

ECONOMIC SYSTEMS IN PRACTICE

9 The American Economy: Market Capitalism

Having outlined the theories of capitalism, planned socialism, and market socialism, we are now ready to see how each works in practice. The theories of capitalism and socialism provide the foundations for our discussion of real-world capitalist and socialist economies.

Chapters 9 and 12 examine the American and Soviet economies. In terms of size and of economic and political power, the United States and the Soviet Union traditionally have been the most important representatives of their respective systems. Certainly, both economies provide a reasonable laboratory for evaluating their respective systems. They possess rich natural resources, military power, and large domestic markets.

The United States is one of the world's most advanced industrial nations. The Soviet Union is an ailing industrial giant. The United States has been a relatively advanced country for more than a century; the Soviet Union became an industrialized country only in the 1930s. Moreover, there are striking differences in climate, culture, and nationality, and such differences must be "held constant" before one can begin to evaluate the relative merits of economic systems.

We present American and traditional Soviet resource allocation arrangements on as parallel a basis as possible. For each economy, we discuss how materials, labor, and capital are allocated. Then, in the American case, we turn to the role of the state in economic affairs. In the Soviet case, we turn to the role of the market. Surprisingly, it is much more difficult to describe resource allocation in the American economy, because it is largely accomplished through markets without the outside influence of a hierarchy of authorities. The Soviet case is easier to describe; there, resource allocation worked on the basis of concrete institutional and bureaucratic procedures. In our initial comparison, we describe the Soviet economy as it worked prior to the economic reforms of the late 1980s and early 1990s. We do so in order to understand the economic bases underlying relations among the superpowers since World War II. Thereafter, in Chapter 16, we turn to an examination of a very different Soviet Union in the era of Perestroika.

RESOURCE ALLOCATION IN THE PRIVATE SECTOR

The role of government is more limited in the United States than it is in other countries. Government ownership has been limited even in the case of natural monopolies and transportation, which in most other countries are government-owned or -operated. The United States has no apparatus for economic planning, and the market makes the overwhelming majority of resource allocation decisions.

The term **private sector** refers to the business sector, where private ownership prevails and government regulation is not pervasive. According to Milton Friedman's calculations for 1939, some one-fourth of economic activity in the United States was government-operated or -supervised, leaving a residual of three-fourths for the private sector.[1] This breakdown appears to be representative for the 1980s as well.[2]

Business Organization

Business enterprises in the United States (and in capitalist countries in general) are divided into three categories on the basis of legal organization: sole proprietorships, partnerships, and corporations.

The **sole proprietorship** is owned by one individual, who makes all the business decisions and absorbs the profits (or losses) that the business earns. A **partnership** is owned by two or more partners, who make all the business decisions and share in the profits and losses of the business. The major advantages of these forms of business organization are their relative simplicity (the proprietorship is simpler than the partnership) and the fact that, under existing tax law, their profits are taxed only once. They have two major disadvantages: (1) the owners are personally liable for the debts of the business, and (2) the ability to raise capital is limited, dependent as it is on the owners' ability to borrow against personal assets.

The third form of business organization, the **corporation**, is owned by its stockholders and has authorization to act as a single person. A board of directors, elected by the stockholders, appoints a professional management team to run the corporation. The advantages of the corporation are (1) that its owners (the stockholders) are not personally liable for the debts of the corporation (limited liability), (2) that its management team can be changed if necessary, and (3) that it has more options for raising capital (through the sale of bonds and additional stock). A major disadvantage of the corporation is that its income is taxed a second time when corporate earnings are distributed to stockholders as dividends. Double taxation gives American corporations an incentive to reinvest earnings rather than pay out dividends.

These three forms of business organization are supplemented in the United States by innovative legal arrangements (such as limited liability partnerships) designed to circumvent a variety of weaknesses, yet the threefold classification remains valid. Figure 9.1 and Table 9.1 show the distribution of U.S. enterprises according to legal form of business organization. Although sole proprietorships account for the bulk of American businesses (70 percent), they account for only 6 percent of business revenues. Corporations, though few in number (about 20 percent of the total), account for 90 percent of business revenues. The larger size of the corporation is explained by limited liability and the greater ability of the corporation to raise capital. The sole proprietorship is important in agriculture, retail trade, and services; the partnership is important in finance, insurance, real estate, and services; the corporation is the dominant form in other sectors.

The Product Market

Resource-allocation arrangements depend on the degree of **market power** in different product markets. There is no accurate measure of market power, but the most frequently used measure is the **concentration ratio**. The concentration ratio gives the percentage of industry sales accounted for by the largest 4, 8, or 20 firms. For example, a 4-firm concentration ratio of 80 percent means that the 4 largest firms account for 80 percent of industry sales. An industry with a very low concentration ratio is generally a "competitive" industry; one with a very high concentration ratio is an "oligopoly" or near-monopoly. (The comparison is not exact for various reasons: the difficulties of defining industry boundaries; the availability of competitive substitutes; the fact that some firms operated in regional and local markets, others in national and international markets; and so on.)

Figure 9.1 Proprietorships, Partnerships, and Corporations, 1988

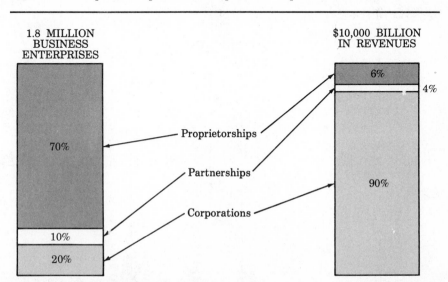

Source: *Statistical Abstract of the United States.*

Table 9.1 Proprietorships, Partnerships, and Corporations, by Industry, 1986

Industry	Number (in thousands)			Business Revenues (in billions of dollars)		
	Proprietorships	Active Partnerships	Active Corporations	Proprietorships	Active Partnerships	Active Corporations
Total	12,394	1,703	3,428	559.4	378.7	8,281.9
Agriculture, forestry, and fishing	324	147	106	11.6	6.0	71.8
Mining	160	53	41	7.2	14.7	86.9
Construction	1,577	60	341	87.5	26.8	399.4
Manufacturing	329	28	285	19.6	22.2	2,614.5
Transportation, public utilities	576	21	139	27.4	12.6	717.9
Wholesale and retail trade	2,190	173	940	192.5	68.5	2,472.5
Finance, Insurance, Real Estate	56	853	537	36.2	112.6	1,365.0
Services	1,238	326	1,011	168.9	111.7	550.6

Source: *Statistical Abstract of the United States.*

The degree of competition in the U.S. economy is a hard thing to measure. Most concentration studies focus on manufacturing, which, although it is the most visible branch of U.S. industry, it accounts for only one-fourth of national income. Many industries that produce raw materials, such as agriculture, forest products, and coal, are organized competitively. Yet government price-support programs in agriculture have affected the behavior of agricultural producers, and the owners of coal mines often band together in associations. Retail stores and most services operate in local markets and operated largely in a competitive environment, although there are exceptions.

Estimates of the overall level of competitiveness (including agriculture, manufacturing, trade, and services) are few and far between. Milton Friedman's estimates for the year 1939 indicate that the private sector was then between 15 and 25 percent "monopolistic" and between 75 and 85 percent "competitive."[3] A recent study finds that the degree of competition has increased for the U.S. economy as a whole since the 1960s.[4] See Table 9.2.

Competitive Industries   Competitive producers are **price takers**. They cannot influence prices, so they maximize profits by expanding their output to the

Table 9.2 Trends in Competition in the U.S. Economy, 1939–1980

Sectors of the Economy	Share of Each Sector That Was Effectively Competitive (percent)		
	1939	*1958*	*1980*
Agriculture, forestry, and fisheries	91.6	85.0	86.4
Mining	87.1	92.2	95.8
Construction	27.9	55.9	80.2
Manufacturing	51.5	55.9	69.0
Transportation and public utilities	8.7	26.1	39.1
Wholesale and retail trade	57.8	60.5	93.4
Finance, insurance, and real estate	61.5	63.8	94.1
Services	53.9	54.3	77.9
Total	52.4	56.4	76.7

Note: In this table, an effectively competitive industry is one in which the 4-firm concentration ratio was below 40 percent, entry barriers were low, market shares were unstable, and prices were flexible. The extent of oligopoly in the economy is the measure of the combined shares of dominant-firm and tight-oligopoly industries.

Source: William G. Shepherd, "Causes of Increased Competition in the U.S. Economy, 1939–1980," *Review of Economics and Statistics*, November 1982, 613–626. Used by permission of Elsevier Science Publishers, Amsterdam.

point where marginal cost is equal to the product price. If for some reason (say, an unexpected shift in demand) above-normal profits are made, excess profits disappear as new firms enter the market.

Prices are formed in competitive industries by supply and demand. Take the case of basic agricultural products (wheat, pork bellies, soy beans, frozen orange juice), which are traded on commodity markets. These markets are called **perfect markets** because at any time, all buyers pay the same price. All potential buyers and sellers are participants in the market, and information concerning prices is available almost instantaneously. All participants know, for example, the price of a bushel of wheat at any time.

Producers and users of commodities, however, are not the only participants in the market. Commodity speculators buy and sell in the hope of buying at a low price and then selling high. Commodity markets establish not only prices of commodities for immediate delivery, but also prices (called **futures prices**) for deliveries at some specified date in the future. Thus an American wheat farmer can contract, even before the crop has been planted, to sell next year's harvest at a specified price in the commodity market.

In the real world of the U.S. economy, most competitive industries are not perfectly competitive because they sell slightly differentiated products. Most of the rules just described, however, apply in general terms. Even though a product is differentiated, producers have little control over price. In each market, prices are established by supply and demand, and **arbitrage** (buying in the cheap market and reselling in the expensive market) prevents large price disparities between markets. Although these markets are not perfectly competitive, they closely approximate perfect competition.

Imperfectly Competitive Industries   Competitive markets work in a fairly invisible and low-key manner. Highly concentrated, noncompetitive industries follow a wide variety of behavior patterns.

The surprising feature of U.S. manufacturing is that the degree of concentration appears to have scarcely changed since the turn of the century (see Table 9.3). According to G. Warren Nutter's famous study, in 1900 roughly one-third of manufacturing net output came from industries wherein the four largest firms accounted for one-half or more of industry output. In 1963 and 1982, the figure was still one-third. Morris Adelman reports similar findings for the period 1947–1958, when the average concentration ratio of the four largest firms in each industry rose only from 35 to 37 percent. Between 1931 and 1960, the share of the 117 largest manufacturing firms in total manufacturing assets remained stable at 45 percent.[5]

Economic theory suggests that concentrated industries with a great deal of market power will enjoy larger profit rates. Joe S. Bain and H. Michael Mann have shown that profit rates in the 1930s and 1950s tended to rise with concentration and with barriers to entry, although this effect was more pronounced in the 1950s.[6] More recent studies find that at concentration ratios above 70 percent, concentration is strongly related to profit rates. Barriers to entry appear to have an even stronger positive effect on profit rates. At lower rates of concentration, the relationship among profits, concentration, and entry barriers appears weak or even nonexistent.[7]

Another gauge of the degree of competition in the U.S. economy is how much output would increase if monopoly were eliminated. Researchers — notably Arnold Harberger and David Schwartzman — have calculated such "monopoly welfare losses."[8] They conclude that if monopoly were to disappear, national income would increase by less than 1 percent. These calculations do not deny that the distribution of income between the monopolist and the consumer is seriously distorted by monopoly. Rather, what is calculated is the "deadweight loss" of monopoly — that is, the loss of output due to monopoly.

Critics of monopoly such as Gordon Tullock and Anne Krueger have pointed out that monopoly rent-seeking raises society's losses above deadweight losses.[9] Examples of monopoly rent-seeking include bribing public officials to gain monopoly franchises and lobbying to gain protection from foreign imports. Because substantial profit gains accrue to the monopolist, people are prepared to expend substantial resources to turn a competitive industry into a monopoly. Harvey Leibenstein has emphasized the "organizational slack" or "X-inefficiency" of monopoly. Because monopolists are faced with less competition, they are under less pressure to minimize costs of production. The competitive firm that fails to minimize costs may be forced out of business, but

Table 9.3 Trends in Concentration in American Manufacturing: Two Measures

Year	Percentage of Output by Firms with 4-Firm Concentration Ratio of 50 percent or Above (1)	Percentage of Output of 100 Largest Firms (2)
1895–1904	33	n.a.
1947	24	23
1954	30	30
1958	30	32
1972	29	33
1977	28	33
1982	24	33

Sources: G. Warren Nutter, *The Extent of Enterprise Monopoly in the United States, 1899–1939* (Chicago: University of Chicago Press, 1951); pp. 35–48, 112–140; F. M. Scherer, *Industrial Market Structure and Economic Performance* (Boston: Houghton Mifflin, 1980), pp. 68–69; *Concentration Ratios in Manufacturing, 1977 Census of Manufacturing*, MC77-SR-9; *1982 Census of Manufacturers*, MC82-S-7.

the monopoly can relax. If one takes monopoly rent-seeking and X-inefficiency into account, society's losses from monopoly may be considerable.

Harold Demsetz argues in a different vein that the higher profits of large enterprises result from their superior cost performance.[10] If prices are set competitively so that each firm acts like a price taker, then economic profits accrue to those firms that have lower costs of production. The higher profit rates found in highly concentrated industries are the result of the superior efficiency of large firms.

The Labor Market[11]

Labor is allocated largely through labor markets in the United States. In competitive labor markets, employers demand larger quantities of labor at low wages. The supply of labor is a positive function of the wage rate offered, and a wage rate equating the supply and demand for labor is established automatically in the marketplace.

There are no measures to indicate how competitive the U.S. labor market is. Obvious examples of highly competitive labor markets include markets for domestic help, farm labor, most white-collar occupations, and banking employees. Labor market analysis focuses on the causes of deviations from the competitive model: union power, government intervention, and discrimination.

Unions   Only 20 percent of the U.S. labor force belongs to a labor union. In the 1930s, union members accounted for 6 to 7 percent of the labor force. Union membership rose in the 1940s and peaked at 25 percent in the mid-1950s. Since then the percentage has declined — despite the notable increase in union membership among public employees — largely because of the rapid growth of white-collar employment. The American trade union movement is more decentralized than its counterparts in Europe. More authority rests with local unions, and the movement has failed to produce its own political party. The American union movement consists of loose federations of local unions banded into national unions. With notable exceptions, bargaining over wages proceeds on a company-by-company basis. In recent years, however, the trend has been toward collective bargaining at the national level and bargaining over local issues at the local level.

Most American unions are associated with the AFL–CIO (American Federation of Labor–Congress of Industrial Organizations). The AFL–CIO accounts for almost 80 percent of all union members.

American workers were slower to organize than their European counterparts, because unfavorable legislation existed until the early 1930s: The Sherman Antitrust Act of 1890 was initially applied against "monopolistic" labor unions, court orders prohibited union activity, and "yellow dog" contracts required employees to agree not to join a union. The Norris–LaGuardia Act of 1932 and the Wagner Act of 1935 laid the legislative foundation for the growth of unionism.

How much have unions altered the process of labor allocation? There are wide differences of opinion. Some (Milton Friedman, for example) argue that unions have had only a minimal impact on employment and wages. Unions act as highly visible **intermediaries** between the forces of supply and demand, and the pattern of wages and employment is virtually identical to that which would have prevailed without unions. Collective bargaining cannot negate the forces of demand over the long term, because too high wages would result in a substitution of other factors for labor.

Most studies show that unions raise wages in unionized industries. Unions control wages through their power to strike and to control the supply of (and in some case, through work rules, the demand for) labor. Unions raised wages in the unionized sector some 25 percent during the mid-1930s, 5 percent during the late 1940s, and some 10 to 15 percent during the 1950s. The most recent studies show that union wages are 15 to 18 percent higher than they would have been in the absence of unions. For the entire economy, the impact of unionization is probably small. Union wages are emulated in the nonunionized sector, and higher union wages reduce employment in the unionized branches and hence place downward pressure on wages in nonunionized branches.

What has been the effect of unions on productivity? Economists have traditionally believed that unions have a negative effect on productivity. Unions were thought to limit output per worker through disruptive strikes, featherbedding practices that kept employers from using labor efficiently, and distortion of union–nonunion wages. Some economists have questioned this view. Albert Hirschman, Richard Freeman, and James Medoff maintain that unions actually raise productivity by giving union members a collective voice. Without union representation, the only voice workers have against bad employers is to exit — that is, to leave the enterprise. With unions, workers can gain effective representation and can work from within to improve conditions. Unions can have a positive effect on productivity in three ways: Unions reduce worker turnover and thus limit hiring and training costs. In the union setting, senior workers are more likely to provide informal training and assistance. And the union provides for an improved information flow between workers and managers.

Government Intervention in the Labor Market   A second extramarket force in the labor market is government. Government affects wages through licensing and other procedures that regulate the supply of labor in particular occupations. It also affects the supply of labor in the long run through its policies toward public education and job training. Moreover, antidiscrimination legislation, hiring quotas, and the like also affect employment practices. Probably the most disputed role of government is minimum wage legislation. Its opponents argue that minimum wages disrupt the market process and create unemployment among the poor workers the legislation seeks to assist. Supporters argue that minimum wages are unlikely to have a significant effect on employment and are necessary to protect weak workers, who are at a disadvantage in the bargaining process.

Discrimination The third extramarket force in the labor market is discrimination by race and gender, which excludes particular races and sexes from particular occupations (such as specific craft unions) and channels them into overpopulated occupations. An example is the channeling of women into public school teaching. A great deal of research has attempted to estimate the effect of discrimination on earnings of African Americans, Mexican-Americans, and women. The general consensus is that discrimination does exist, once other factors such as background and education are held constant, but that its overall effect on wages in the United States has been limited. Within specific occupations, the discrimination effect on the observed minority wage differential is small. The most significant impact of race and sex discrimination results from the exclusion of minorities from specific occupations.

The Capital Market

The **capital market** brings together suppliers and users of credit. Businesses undertake investment projects as long as the anticipated rate of return exceeds the cost of acquiring capital funds. At the margin, projects are undertaken wherein the rate of return just equals the cost of borrowing. Accordingly, the lower the cost of acquiring investment funds, the higher the demand for investment will be.

The supply of investment funds to the capital market depends on the savings of individuals, government surpluses or deficits, retained profits, and depreciation. In the U.S. capital market, the supply of investment funds is seldom channeled directly from the saver to the investor. Such transactions are normally handled by **financial intermediaries**, such as commercial banks, savings banks, and insurance companies. In the corporate sector (which accounts for some three-fourths of business borrowing), there are three sources of investment finance. The corporation can raise capital by issuing debt, by issuing additional stock, or by using retained earnings. The supply of investment funds varies positively with the interest rate.

A striking feature of American capital markets (and capital markets in general in industrialized capitalist countries) is the prevalence of financial intermediation. Financial intermediaries borrow funds from one set of economic agents (people or companies with savings) and lend to other economic agents. Financial intermediaries serve a useful purpose by making it unnecessary for borrowers and lenders to seek each other out. A commercial bank, for example, borrows from its depositors (by accepting checking and savings account deposits) and then lends to a corporation building a new plant. If borrowers and lenders had sought each other out, the lender would have received a higher rate of interest and the borrower would have paid a lower rate of interest. The fact that lenders and borrowers pay for financial intermediation suggests that the service performed is a valuable one. Of the private domestic funds advanced for private investment in the early 1980s, 88 percent was supplied through financial intermediaries.

The U.S. capital market is a well-organized market in the sense that national securities markets (the New York and American Stock Exchanges, markets for federal funds, and others) bring together all potential borrowers and suppliers of investment funds, and information concerning investment alternatives is readily and almost instantaneously available to all participants. It is misleading to speak of a U.S. capital market, for there is an *international* capital market. The huge amount of international data in the financial section of the daily newspaper demonstrates this fact. The net result is an approximate equalization of rates of return on all investments **at the margin** once they are adjusted for risk.

This equalization of rates of return at the margin is considered to be an important positive feature of capital markets, because it leads to an efficient allocation of capital resources. If rates of return were not equal at the margin, then capital funds could be redistributed from projects with a low rate of return to those with higher rates, and output could be increased without an increase in capital resources.

THE ROLE OF GOVERNMENT IN THE AMERICAN ECONOMY

Just as it is fitting to consider the role that the market plays in the planned socialist economy, so is it fitting to consider the role of nonmarket forces, primarily the public allocation of resources, in predominantly market-oriented economies. The scope of government activity has been more limited in the United States than in most advanced capitalist countries. In fact, the American experience may suggest the minimal functions of government compatible with modern industrial capitalism.

There is little dispute that government must provide **public goods**, commodities that are consumed jointly and that nonpayers (free riders) cannot be excluded from enjoying. There is more debate about the other functions of government.[12] How far the government should go in fulfilling them is a matter of dispute.[13]

The Scope of the Public Sector

The data presented in Figure 9.2 shed light on the role of government in the American economy. The government's claim on labor and capital resources indicates how productive resources are divided between government and business uses. Government (federal, state, and local) employs approximately 16 percent of the American labor force and owns approximately 18 percent of the stock of structures, one-eighth of all land, and one-twentieth of all inventories. Government owned approximately 15 percent of the national wealth and accounted for some 7 percent of total labor, capital, and land inputs in the late 1950s.

Government's share of productive resources has increased steadily over the last hundred years. At the turn of the century, government accounted for some 4 percent of employment and owned 6 percent of the stock of structures and 13 percent of the stock of land. By 1939, the government's share had increased substantially (to 18 percent of structures and 19 percent of land), while its share of the labor force rose to about 10 percent. Since the late 1930s, government's share of employment has increased by 80 percent, but its share of national wealth has risen only slightly. The United States appears to have reached a national consensus on the distribution of wealth, which has remained fairly stable for about 50 years. There is now little serious talk of large-scale nationalizations, and most of the major decisions in this area (broadcasting, communication satellites, atomic energy) have come down on the side of private ownership.

Government produces about 15 percent of national income, of which the overwhelming portion is produced not by government enterprises but by "general government." The business sector accounts for over 80 percent of national income; the remainder is accounted for by government and nonprofit institutions. The encroachment of government enterprises on private business has been minimal. Government enterprises account for less than 2 percent of the national income. Rather than government enterprises supplanting private

Figure 9.2 Indicators of Government Participation in Economic Activity and Wealth in the United States, 1900–1990

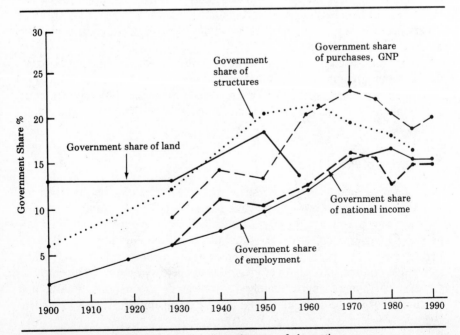

Source: Tables 9.2 and 9.3. The dots (·) indicate the years of observations.

enterprises, it has been the expansion of general government activities that has accounted for rising government output.

The government's share of national income has been rising steadily over the last hundred years (4 percent in 1869 to 8.5 percent in 1919 to 15 percent in 1985). Since the 1930s, the increase in the federal government's share has been more substantial than that of state and local government. Since 1929, business's share of national income has fallen from 91 percent to 81 percent at the expense of the rise in general government and nonprofit institutions.

Government purchases account for about one-fifth of the total. Interestingly, most of the historical increase in the share of government purchases has been due to rising state and local government spending and federal defense spending.

It is important to put these U.S. developments in perspective. An examination of other industrialized capitalist countries (Figure 9.3) shows that the scope of the public sector in the United States is average or even below average if one considers that most countries do not bear a substantial defense burden. If one looks only at nondefense spending, the U.S. government's share of total

Figure 9.3 The Relative Size of Government in the United States and Other Countries, 1960 and 1987

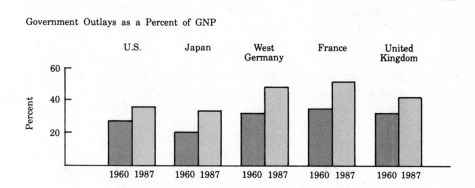

Government Outlays as a Percent of GNP

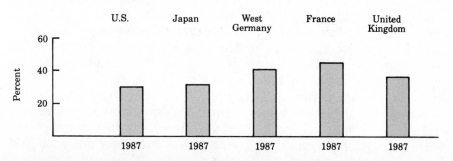

Taxes as a Percent of GNP

Source: *Handbook of Economic Statistics 1990*, CPAS 90–10001, September 1990, pp. 17–18.

spending appears relatively small by international standards. The rising share of government output and expenditures is also unexceptional; it has characterized the economic growth of capitalism for over a century. The U.S. tax burden is also relatively modest.

Some people view the rising share of government with alarm; others consider it too small. All one can say for sure is that in the United States, the allocation of resources between the public and private sectors is basically a matter of public choice.

THE PROVISION OF PUBLIC GOODS: THE CASE OF NATIONAL DEFENSE

Government in the United States bears the principal responsibility for providing public goods, although it must be noted that in the real world there are few "pure" public goods. The activity that dominates the so-called public goods market in the United States is national defense, which is also the best theoretical example of a public good; we shall therefore use it to illustrate how the U.S. government deals with public goods.

Two issues must be considered. The first is how decisions are reached concerning national defense's share of total public resources. The second issue is the market structure under which defense goods are produced.

Resource Allocation by the Defense Industry   The share and product mix of national defense are decided by the political process. The connection between the government and the large manufacturers of military hardware has been called the **military–industrial complex**. Three explanations of weapons procurement have been offered: the strategic, the bureaucratic, and the economic.[14]

The strategic explanation is that defense planners determine weapons procurement on the basis of rational calculations about the foreign military threat. The bureaucratic explanation is that defense spending is the product of a disorganized tug of war among the various interests that make up the military-industrial complex, not of any rationally calculated plan of national security. One branch of the military exerts pressure to obtain the weapons system it favors, while a rival branch applies similar pressure in favor of its project. Or one system manufacturer exerts, through strategic members of Congress or lobbyists, pressure in favor of its design for a major new weapons system. According to the bureaucratic explanation, the overall distribution of resources depends on the outcome of this struggle of vested interests.

Economics provides the final explanation. According to this view, defense spending is based on its impact on the overall economy. In the view of the New Left, an expanding defense budget is necessary to preserve full employment and economic stability. According to another view, contracts for major weapons systems will be granted, not on the basis of which company will produce the most effective system, but in order to preserve established contractors located in politically important states.[15]

A related consideration is the extent to which the private defense contractors themselves are able to determine, or at least influence, defense spending. According to some, the economic and political power of the major defense contractors is sufficient to exert significant control over the allocation of defense resources.[16] Although these observers have probably overrated the power of defense contractors, there is evidence that their view is at least partially true.[17]

The Market Structure of the Defense Industry   Defense contracting procedures have been the subject of intense scrutiny. Most observers agree that these procedures violate the principle that national defense should be provided at a minimum cost of society's resources. Some authorities, in fact, argue that the current system leads to excessive cost and subsidies. The market structure of the U.S. military–industrial complex consists of the U.S. government, as a monopsonistic buyer, purchasing from a small number of defense contractors. The government purchases a weapons system from a single supplier, who is granted a monopoly to develop the system. Often there is no serious negotiation with potential competitors. Defense contracts are typically let on a cost-plus basis, whereby the manufacturer agrees to supply a particular weapons system at a negotiated cost plus an agreed-upon profit margin. Because there is little competition among producers, and because the manufacture of a new weapons system is surrounded by technological uncertainty, the government is in a poor position to judge whether the manufacturer is operating efficiently.

Most suggestions for reform of the military procurement system center on either the nationalization of the defense industry or the introduction of more competition into the existing system.[18] The major disadvantage of nationalization is that the monopoly over new weapons systems would then reside directly with the U.S. government; pressure to seek out cost-effective techniques would still be lacking. The second approach does not appear to be politically feasible, because strong vested interests favor the existing system of protecting and subsidizing established defense contractors.

Personnel and National Defense   Until 1973, the personnel needs of the armed forces were met by a national draft operated by the Selective Service System. Conscription was employed to fill the gap between the number of volunteers joining the military at established wage rates (the supply) and the quotas established by the armed services (the demand). The costs of maintaining the armed forces therefore consisted of payments to armed service personnel *plus* the loss of income incurred by those draftees who had to forgo higher incomes outside the military. To some extent, however, individuals with higher earning capacities were excluded from the draft by educational and occupational exemptions.

Military personnel prior to 1973 were handled largely outside of the labor market. With the winding down of the Vietnam War, the U.S. government turned to a voluntary army in 1973. Military personnel needs were to be met by raising military pay and benefits to the level required to bring the supply of and demand for military personnel into approximate balance. This use of the market represents a return to the practice of using hired troops. It has the advantage of relying on freedom of choice of occupation and avoiding the economic inefficiency of conscripting individuals with high earning capacities. Its disadvantages are that the armed forces are made up primarily of the disadvantaged, for whom military pay scales are attractive, and that the whole notion of national service is circumvented.

Health, Education, and Welfare

U.S. government public assistance has been limited to public education, some low-cost health care for the poor, and social security insurance for retirement, disability, and unemployment. Such services are typically supplied on a mixed private enterprise–public service basis with the user paying a portion of the cost.

The mix of private versus public support has been shifting toward public provision, and it reflects a changing public attitude toward government responsibility. Over the last half-century, this change has been most dramatic in the areas of health expenditures, social welfare expenditures, and social insurance (Table 9.4), which had been regarded as private or charitable obligations. Prior to the 1930s, almost all retirement, health, and unemployment insurance was purchased on a voluntary private basis; in 1929 only 10 percent of personal health expenditures were funded by governmental agencies. Public elementary and secondary education has dominated the American education system for quite a while, but the government share of support for higher education has increased substantially over the last 50 years. During that time, public universities have supplanted private universities as the dominant institutions in higher education.

Two general rules have governed public assistance. The first is that, if feasible, goods should be provided on an "in-kind" basis (for example, subsidized school lunches and food stamps) rather than as income payments. This suggests an unwillingness to rely on freedom of choice and a feeling that the poor are not to be trusted to allocate their incomes wisely. The second general rule is that families should not have the power to shop around for education or public health, despite arguments that making such choice possible would force suppliers to be more efficient and responsive to the consumer.

U.S. GOVERNMENT POLICY TOWARD MONOPOLY

In the United States, government monopoly policy has been neither uniform nor consistent. In some instances, government policy restricts competition (tariffs, licensing, agricultural price supports); in others, it seeks to restrain monopoly power and to promote competitive behavior.

Government Ownership

Several options are open to government with regard to natural monopolies, which for a variety of reasons must serve as the sole suppliers of a product. The government can nationalize them in the "public interest." It can also tax them in order to transfer monopoly profits to the state and to guarantee an output/ price combination more consistent with competitive standards. A third alternative is government regulation. A fourth is for the government to auction exclusive franchises to operate natural monopolies. This option would transfer much of the monopoly return to the state.[19]

In the United States, all of these approaches have been employed, though discriminatory monopoly taxation and franchise auctions are rare. Public ownership of natural monopolies is common at the local and state levels but rare at the federal level. Municipal services such as local transportation, garbage collection, water, electricity, gas, public wharves, and state transit authorities are often owned and operated by state and municipal government. Over 20 percent of all electrical energy is generated by government or cooperative arrangements, and 10 percent of all utility payments go to government enterprises. In only 2 of the 10 largest cities is the municipal transit system privately owned. Approximately 3 percent of all residential housing construction has been undertaken by public authorities.[20]

Table 9.4 Expenditures on Public Assistance in the United States, 1890–1987

Year	Public Social Welfare Expenditures as a Percent of GNP[a]	Public Social Insurance Expenditures as a Percent of GNP	Health Care Expenditures as a Percent of Total	Public Higher Education Expenditures as a Percent of Total
1987	18.4	10.8	–	–
1985	18.9	10.1	36	65.0
1980	18.5	8.0	39	66.3
1970	15.3	5.7	35	67.5
1955	8.6	2.6	26	64.0
1929	3.9	.2	10	41.0
1920	–	–	–	38
1900	–	–	–	–
1890	2.4	–	–	–

[a] Social welfare expenditures include social insurance and public aid, education, veterans' programs, child nutrition, and rehabilitation programs.

Source: U.S., Department of Commerce, *Historical Statistics of the United States: Colonial Times to 1970* (Washington, D.C.: Government Printing Office, 1975), Series B236-247, H1–31, H412–432, H716–727; *Statistical Abstract of the United States*.

Government enterprise operated by the federal government is more limited: operating the postal services (now a semigovernmental operation), administering public lands (the Forest Service), lending and guaranteeing loans (the FHA and VA programs), providing insurance against various risks (social security), generating electricity (the Tennessee Valley Authority) and engaging in limited manufacturing activities (Redstone Arsenal, the U.S. Government Printing Office).[21]

Local, state, and federal government enterprises account for less than 2 percent of national income. The public's decision to leave natural monopolies in the hands of private owners has been in marked contrast to the European pattern, where the state owns and operates most natural monopolies — and even enterprises that are not natural monopolies (such as automobile manufacturing, national airlines, and railroads).

Despite their small scope, it is nevertheless important to consider how well U.S. public enterprises perform. In public enterprises, the incentive to restrict output and raise prices should not be so strong as under private ownership. On the other hand, the pressures to reduce costs and to innovate are generally weaker. Moreover, red tape and civil service restrictions may impede efficiency in the public enterprise. At the empirical level, the evidence is mixed. One authority concludes (after reviewing the European experience as well) that "the evidence is presently insufficient to support a sharp choice between the alternatives on straightforward economic performance grounds."[22]

In industries where public and private enterprises coexist, the former represent a potential yardstick for evaluating the private sector. The prime example is the Tennessee Valley Authority (TVA), the largest electrical utility in the United States. The exceptionally low costs of the TVA have been used to challenge the rates of private utilities. Yet TVA's lower costs do not unambiguously establish the greater efficiency of public ownership, for, as the private utilities point out, the TVA enjoys certain privileges not accorded the private companies.

Public enterprise could conceivably improve resource allocation by forcing private producers to behave more competitively and efficiently. Strategies available to the public enterprise include price undercutting and the threat to expand capacity. According to one authority, these strategies have rarely been used because of the opposition of private enterprises and the reluctance of managers of public enterprises to compete with private industry.

Regulation

The overwhelming political choice has been to regulate industries that possess monopoly power rather than to use public ownership.[23] **Regulation** has been exercised by a wide variety of local, state, and federal agencies. Other kinds of regulation — control by the courts or by the terms of franchises, charters, and city ordinances — have proved ineffective in the United States, and the public has turned instead to administrative regulation, either by an official of executive government or by semi-independent commissions operating under general legislative authority.[24]

Regulation at the state and local level is principally directed at natural monopolies — specifically, the electric, gas, and telephone companies. At the national level, federal commissions have regulated both monopolistic industries (such as local telephone service) and those with a potentially significant degree of competition (such as trucking and airlines). The stated rationale for federal regulation has been to ensure quality of service and to guarantee the public "reasonable" prices without unfair discrimination among users. A degree of monopoly power, however, is generally a necessary but insufficient condition for regulation. Buyers have to be at a disadvantage in bargaining by virtue of the fact that the service is an essential, nonpostponable one for which there are few good substitutes. Although the American automobile industry is more concentrated than the natural gas or rail industry, the latter two have been regulated, whereas the other has remained free from direct regulation. There are historical reasons for regulation as well. The railroads were placed under the supervision of the Interstate Commerce Commission at a time when they possessed considerable monopoly power. Motor and air transport lessened this power, yet the commission could not continue to regulate railroads without extending federal regulation to other forms of transport.

Generally, the regulatory commissions have controlled entry into the industry by granting franchises and licenses — for a new airline route, say, or a new interstate natural gas pipeline. Rarely are these licenses or franchises actually sold (for the purpose of diverting the ensuing profits to the public). Rather, it is assumed that regulation will prevent excessive profits.

It is the responsibility of the regulators to set "reasonable" rates for the services of regulated producers. In this, the regulatory commissions have been guided by the principle, guaranteed by the Fifth and Fourteenth Amendments protecting private property, that rates should be sufficient to cover operating costs plus a "proper" rate of return on invested capital. A second principle is that the rate structure should not discriminate among buyers, except when such discrimination is justified by cost differences.

Before this pricing formula can be applied, several important matters must be resolved: How are operating costs to be defined? What is an appropriate rate of return on invested capital? How is the rate base (the value of tangible and intangible assets of the company) to be measured? The regulated price is essentially a cost-plus price, and additions to cost will, in time, be passed on to the user. This may well reduce the incentive to seek out cost economies. Moreover, there is the problem of dealing with illegitimate or padded costs, such as buying materials from an unregulated affiliate at inflated prices in order to increase that company's profits.

Determining an appropriate rate of return to regulated firms has been another area of controversy. The rate of return should be high enough to attract new capital; hence, the interest rate on recently floated debt has often been used as the rate of return. According to one authority, however, the rates of return that regulatory commissions and the courts have historically allowed have been "conventional or arbitrary, bearing no apparent relation to any statement of principles . . . usually based upon expert testimony with little pretense of economic analysis."[25] The rates allowed have varied from state to state and from time to time, ranging between 5½ percent in the 1940s and 11 percent and higher during the 1970s and 1980s.

An Assessment of Regulation

Most authorities give regulation relatively poor marks, especially in industries that are not natural monopolies.[26] Regulation of natural monopolies has had a remarkably small effect on the prices charged consumers. Opponents of regulation argue that operating costs will fall when potentially competitive industries are freed from regulation (deregulated).

Why have the regulatory commissions not had a more beneficial impact on the industries they regulate? There are several possible explanations. The first is that the balance of power between the regulators and the regulated is uneven. The regulated industries have well-paid staffs, whereas the regulatory commissions (the state commissions particularly) are understaffed and underpaid. Regulated industries appear to be able to circumvent regulations if necessary. Moreover, the commissioners themselves tend to be in close contact with the industries they regulate, not with the consumers they are supposed to represent. The very *methodology* of regulation also remains a problem. A commission has no way of knowing what operating costs would be if the most efficient production techniques were used. Even if it did know, it would lack the authority to mandate use of these techniques. Instead, it must simply accept the actual operating costs of the utilities as given, except in obvious cases of corruption or gross mismanagement.

To show that regulation has been less than optimal does not establish that a superior alternative exists, especially in the case of natural monopolies. Because they cannot be organized on a competitive bases, they will possess significant monopoly power. Despite its weaknesses, direct regulation may be the best alternative.

Deregulation[27]

The Airline Deregulation Act was signed in October 1978. Under this act the airlines, rather than the Civil Aeronautics Board, set their own fares and chose their own routes (subject to the important availability of landing slots). The Civil Aeronautics Board went out of existence at the end of 1984. This first major deregulation act was followed in 1980 by the Motor Carrier Act (which curbed the Interstate Commerce Commission's control over interstate trucking), the Staggers Rail Act (which gave the railroads more choice in setting rates and selecting routes), and the Depository Institutions Deregulation and Monetary

Control Act (which eliminated government-set ceilings on interest rates and reduced differences between commercial banks and thrift institutions).

The **deregulation** movement was designed to remove the government from the business of regulating potentially competitive businesses such as the airlines, trucking, and banking. In all cases, opponents of deregulation warned that deregulation would lead to deteriorating service, pricing wars, and an unstable industry.

U.S. experience has shown that deregulation leads to lower prices for most — but not all — consumers. Consumers in small markets characterized by high costs are no longer protected and now have to pay prices closer to costs. Deregulation has increased the diversity of services offered and has given consumers more freedom of choice. Firms that had been protected by regulation have lowered their costs substantially, and these lower costs are being passed on to their customers. Deregulation has also had its losers. Firms that could not meet competitive pressures have gone out of business or have been acquired by more successful firms. Employees have seen their earnings fall as firms have sought ways to lower their costs.

In the airline industry, the problems of high fuel prices, terrorism, and high debt resulted in the concentration of the industry in the hands of a few giant airlines. In banking, a number of problems (such as corruption and the inflation of the 1970s and early 1980s) led to massive failures both in the savings and loan industry and in commercial banking. These negative experiences have caused some to question the wisdom of deregulation.

Antitrust Legislation

The major alternative to direct regulation of monopoly is legislation to control market structure and market conduct.[28] The most important piece of federal **antitrust legislation**, the Sherman Antitrust Act of 1890, confronts these issues. The Sherman Act was the government's reaction to public hostility toward the trust movement of the late nineteenth century in the transportation, steel, tobacco, and oil industries. The Sherman Act contains two sections. Section 1 declares "every contract, combination . . . or conspiracy" in restraint of interstate commerce illegal. Section 2 makes the attempt to monopolize interstate commerce a federal offense. Section 1 prohibits a particular type of market *conduct* (conspiring to restrain trade), whereas Section 2 enjoins a particular market *structure* (monopoly). The language of Section 2 is vague, and this imprecision has led to varying court interpretations over the years. According to the language of Section 2, **monopolization** is prohibited, not **monopolies**. The Sherman Act clearly bans the act of creating a monopoly but is ambiguous on the legality of existing monopolies.

The Sherman Antitrust Act of 1890 forms the foundation of American antitrust legislation. The Clayton and Federal Trade Commission acts of 1913 established a commission to investigate "unfair" business practices (the Federal Trade Commission) and prohibited specific illegal business practices. The

Wheeler–Lea Act of 1938 gave the Clayton Act more teeth by declaring unfair or deceptive business practices illegal. The Celler–Kefauver Act of 1950 tightened up the antimerger provisions of the Clayton Act. (See Table 9.5).

American antitrust policy is made by Congress and by the courts, for it is in the courts that actual antimonopoly policy has been set. The basic issue confronting the courts was whether certain forms of market conduct were prohibited or whether the monopoly market structure was illegal per se. If so, it was then up to the courts to decide what constituted a monopoly. In the early court rulings (the American Tobacco and Standard Oil cases of 1911 and the U.S. Steel case of 1920), the courts interpreted the Sherman Act as enjoining anticompetitive market conduct (price cutting to eliminate competition, mergers, price fixing) but not the existence of monopoly per se. This became known as the "rule of reason."[29]

The rule of reason appeared to be reversed when the courts ruled in 1945 that Alcoa was in violation of the Sherman Act because it controlled over 90 percent of U.S. aluminum output. Although Alcoa had not used its monopoly power to restrain trade unfairly, the courts ruled that size alone was a violation of antitrust statutes. Thus an important inconsistency appeared to be removed. The rule of reason had implied that companies engaging in practices that would ultimately lead to monopoly were in violation of the Sherman Act but that existing monopolies, if they behaved well, were not in violation.

The Alcoa ruling was gradually eroded by court decisions of the 1970s and 1980s. The basic problem with the Alcoa decision was that it appeared to punish all monopolies, even those that became monopolies by means of superior innovation and management. The Eastman Kodak case of 1972 and the FTC ruling in favor of DuPont in 1978 established that monopolies created through superior management and innovation were not in violation of the Sherman Act. The Alcoa decision was also weakened when the Justice Department dropped its thirteen-year-old suit against IBM in 1982.

Table 9.5 An Overview of U.S. Antitrust Legislation

Act	Date	Provisions
Sherman Act	1890	Section 1: restraint of interstate commerce illegal
		Section 2: attempt to monopolize illegal
Clayton Act	1914	Declared specific business practices illegal
Federal Trade Commission Act	1914	Established the FTC to secure compliance with Clayton Act
Wheeler–Lea Act	1938	Banned deceptive business practices
Celler–Kefauver Act	1950	Broadened ban on mergers

Price Fixing and Mergers

In the United States, the courts have generally found price-fixing agreements among producers and mergers of large companies engaged in the same line of business to be in violation of the antitrust laws.[30] Formal arrangements for fixing prices have consistently been ruled illegal restraints of trade. The United States stands virtually alone among the industrialized capitalist countries in holding that formal arrangements for price fixing are illegal per se, even if the resulting prices are "reasonable." The courts have thus avoided the difficult issue of distinguishing "reasonable" from "unreasonable" price fixing.

The more difficult enforcement issue, however, has been collusion without outright agreement on pricing policy. Prior to 1948, the courts held that informal price coordination was illegal even if a formal price conspiracy could not be shown. After 1948, in order to demonstrate an illegal conspiracy, it had to be shown that the pattern of pricing could not conceivably have occurred if each firm had acted independently in its own self-interest.

The basic legislation against mergers is found in the Clayton Act of 1914 and in the Celler–Kefauver Act of 1950. Especially since 1950, the courts have adopted a virtual prohibition of mergers between firms with substantial market shares. The only exceptions appear to be (1) mergers wherein one firm takes over another that is on the verge of bankruptcy and (2) conglomerate mergers wherein one firm takes over another that is in a different line of business. In various rulings, the courts have decided that mergers involving combined market shares of 20 percent and even lower constitute an undue lessening of competition.

In its strict interpretation of antimerger statutes, the United States stands alone among the industrialized capitalist countries, most of which encourage mergers that serve to increase the scale of production. In Western Europe, for example, the burden of proof is on the government to establish that the social costs of a proposed merger exceed its benefits. In the United States the burden of proof lies with the merging firms, and if significant market shares are involved, the merger will be declared illegal per se.

An Evaluation of Antitrust Policy

The most relevant criterion for evaluating government policy toward monopoly is its effect on U.S. economic structure and performance. Since the antitrust laws have been in effect, there has not been a significant increase in the concentration of American industry, whereas the second half of the nineteenth century witnessed a substantial increase in concentration. (The government's inability to prevent the conglomerate mergers of the 1960s and 1970s, however, has probably led to an increased concentration of ownership.) Many have speculated on the manner in which the antitrust laws contributed to the stability of concentration in the twentieth century. According to one authority, antitrust legislation made three important contributions to the maintenance of workable competition: It prevented European-type cartelization of American industry, it prevented consolidations that would have led to dominant industries, and it helped to preserve freedom of entry and equality of opportunity.[31]

Although it does appear that government policy has contributed to the maintenance of workable competition in the U.S. economy, not all such policy has been consistent. In fact, a great many government activities have been designed to *reduce* the competitiveness of the American economy: protective tariffs for selected industries, price supports for agricultural products, the patent system, licensing, and so on.

GOVERNMENT AND MACROECONOMIC STABILITY

Planning for macroeconomic stability on the United States is limited to use of the indirect tools of monetary and fiscal policy. No national economic plan is drafted by government. In this, the United States deviates significantly from other industrialized capitalist countries, most of which have some form of national economic planning. (Our case studies of capitalist variants in Chapter 10 focus on national economic planning in France and Britain.) Congressional proposals to introduce a rather mild form of economic planning have generated considerable controversy.[32]

Prior to the Great Depression, the prevailing notion in government circles was that monetary and fiscal policy should be as neutral as possible. "Neutral" meant interfering as little as possible with private economic activity. After the Great Depression and the acceptance of Keynesian economics, this view changed; by the 1960s both major political parties came to accept the view that discretionary monetary and fiscal policy should be used to counter cyclical unemployment and inflation. Although some American monetarists and rational-expectations theorists have spoken out in favor of a return to the traditional neutralist view, monetary and fiscal planners continue to engage in countercyclical policy.

The Federal Reserve System (the Fed) is in charge of formulating monetary policy. Established in 1913, the Federal Reserve System consists of twelve Federal Reserve district banks coordinated by the board of governors in Washington, D.C. In the United States the "central bank" is more decentralized along regional lines than is common for central banks, but it nonetheless performs the functions of a central bank — regulating the money supply through open market operations, managing the discount rate, setting reserve requirements, and so on.

Authority over fiscal policy is diffused among the various executive and legislative bodies in charge of government spending and taxation, and the balance of authority has tended to shift over time. It is therefore difficult to describe briefly how important fiscal decisions are made. The president can propose budgets, but only Congress can approve them. The Treasury Department can propose changes in the tax structure, but it is the Congress that amends and approves such executive suggestions.

One point emerges clearly when we compare the existing machinery for conducting monetary and fiscal policy: The conduct of monetary policy is more divorced from the business of day-to-day politics than is that of fiscal policy. Members of the Board of Governors of the Fed are appointed for fourteen-year terms and, although they owe their ultimate responsibility to the Congress, a tradition of independence for the Fed has evolved. Recurring proposals call for greater congressional control of the Fed, and there is evidence that the Fed does seek to pursue a monetary policy consistent with that of the current administration. The conduct of fiscal policy is very much a matter of politics, so it has proved difficult to conduct countercyclical fiscal policy. This is especially true during periods of inflation, when politically unpopular budget cuts and tax increases are shunned.

The postwar period has witnessed a battle between monetarists and Keynesians over the conduct of monetary policy. The Keynesians argue that the Fed should aim at controlling interest rates, whereas the monetarists argue that the Fed should control the rate of growth of the money supply. In a historic decision, the Fed decided in 1979 that it would reverse its policy of controlling interest rates and turn to controlling the money supply — a clear-cut victory for the monetarist position. In the 1980s, the Fed returned to a more pragmatic policy of interest rate targets *and* monetary-growth targets.

On the whole, the distinctive feature of economic planning in the United States is its virtual absence. Price and wage controls have been applied during periods of inflation, in the form of either voluntary guidelines or mandatory wage and price limitations. The most dramatic examples of this were the price freezes of 1971–1973, after which the economy returned to measures that were more voluntary.

Government Activity and Externalities

In an economic system using price signals for resource allocation decisions, incorrect signals (signals that do not recognize both public and private costs and benefits) can lead to incorrect decisions in the sense of not recognizing external costs and benefits. Thus, externalities, like pollution, are permitted because their full cost is not always recognized. Benefits are lost because their value is not recognized. Government can play a role in lessening these imbalances. No comprehensive program for dealing with externalities exists at the federal level, and the responsibility for environmental protection is diffused among a wide variety of federal, state, and local agencies. Some of these agencies have an exceptional record of environmental protection; an example is the U.S. Soil Conservation Service. Others, such as the U.S. Environmental Protection Agency, lack sufficient authority to correct serious cases of misallocation.

Three themes should be stressed in assessing the role of the state in dealing with the externality problem. The first is that the division of authority and responsibility among local, state, and national agencies (control of air pollution, for example) has made it difficult to devise effective programs. In many cases, external effects transcend local political boundaries; dealing with them requires some form of national or regional coordination. The second theme has been the general reluctance to use market forces (such as taxes on polluters). Fines, prohibitions, and other administrative orders have been the principal means of enforcement. The third theme is the general unwillingness to consider "optimal" levels of environmental disruption — that is, the level of pollution reduction one should aim for, given the fact that it can be attained only at the expense of society's resources.[33]

The record of environmental protection varies by locality and region. In some areas, heavy emphasis has been placed on environmental protection, and enforcement of meaningful pollution regulations is strict. Examples include the efforts to prohibit development of additional refining capacity and offshore drilling in the Northeast and the furor over the generation of nuclear power in different parts of the country.

Government Policies and the Distribution of Income

To what extent does government in the United States redistribute income through taxation and the distribution of social services? The distribution of income is measured by the Lorenz curve (defined in Chapter 3), which compares family income by rank (say, the lowest to the highest fifth of all families) with percentage share of income either before or after taxes. Some studies "tailor" the Lorenz curve by adjusting for age differences, for differences in family size, and for the distribution of government services.[34]

As measured by the Lorenz curve before taxes and any other adjustments, the U.S. distribution of income seems to have changed little since 1950. In 1950, the lowest and the highest fifth of families accounted for 5 and for 45 percent of all income, respectively. By 1982, those figures were 5 and 42 percent. The change since 1929 has been more substantial: The share of the highest fifth of U.S. families declined from 54 percent to 43.5 percent in all income between 1929 and 1985.[35] It has been argued that if one adjusts these figures for differences in age and family size, then the trend toward greater equality is even more evident.[36]

The traditional view is that government has not played a significant role in redistributing income from upper-income to lower-income groups. Although the federal tax system is progressive (upper-income families pay a higher percentage of their income in taxes than do lower-income families), state and local taxes are regressive (upper-income families pay a lower percentage of income). On balance, therefore, the total tax system is roughly proportional (each income group pays the same percentage of its income in taxes), and the after-tax distribution of income is little different from the before-tax distribution.

Remember, though, that all such calculations are inexact because of the difficulty of determining what proportion of business and property taxes are passed on to the consumer in the form of higher prices. Joseph Pechman and Benjamin Okner have found that if one assumes such taxes are almost entirely passed on to the consumer, then the tax system is proportional. If one assumes they are borne by the producer, however, Pechman and Okner found that the tax system becomes progressive, but only at the very top and very bottom of the income distribution.[37]

According to some, the state plays a greater redistributive role than is commonly thought.[38] The basis for such claims is that lower-income groups receive larger shares of government in-kind benefits (food stamps, welfare, public education) than their shares of money income. If one includes the value of these benefits in income and then subtracts income and payroll taxes, the distribution of disposable income is much more nearly equal than the unadjusted figures suggest. Figure 9.4 shows calculations from a study by Edgar Browning to illustrate this position. The redistributive role of government in the United States is probably much less significant than in other industrialized capitalist countries. Thus, relatively speaking, the government plays a modest role in the redistribution of income in the United States.

Figure 9.4 Lorenz Curves: U.S. Income Distribution Before and After Income and Transfer Payments, 1972

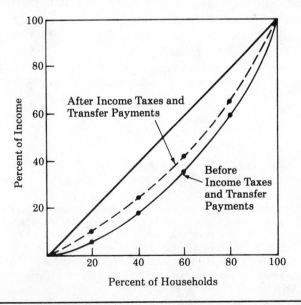

Source: Based on Edgar K. Browning, "The Trend Toward Equality in the Distribution of Net Income," *Southern Economic Journal*, 43 (July 1976), 914.

SUMMARY: RESOURCE ALLOCATION IN THE AMERICAN ECONOMY

1. Resource allocation is determined primarily by market forces in the United States; that process conforms well both to our definition of market capitalism and to the theoretical description of capitalist resource allocation. Exceptions to the rule of competitive resource allocation are monopoly, trade unions, and government intervention. The forces of supply and demand are the principal determinants of resource allocation in the American economy.

2. Government plays a significant role in the resource allocation process. Major government activities are the regulation and control of industries that possess some degree of market power. Government enterprises, unlike those of many other advanced industrialized countries, constitute an insignificant share of economic activity. Some 25 percent of economic activity is directly affected by government activities (that is, government spending and government-regulated industries). The remaining economic activity is conducted by the "private sector."

3. Government affects economic activity in the United States principally by regulation and by antitrust policy. The amount of government ownership in the United States is less than in other industrialized capitalist countries. The impact of regulation on the prices of regulated monopolies has been limited, and potentially competitive industries have been deregulated. The Sherman Antitrust Act is the major antitrust act of the United States, and it has been subject to differing court interpretations over time. In the United States, the government's effect on the distribution of income has been limited. Government redistribution works primarily through the unequal distribution of in-kind services rather than through the tax system. In Chapter 12, we shall turn to resource-allocation arrangements in the Soviet economy, and we shall see that Soviet arrangements differ radically from those of the United States.

NOTES

1. Milton Friedman, "Monopoly and Social Responsibility of Business and Labor," in Edwin Mansfield, ed., *Monopoly Power and Economic Performance*, 3rd ed. (New York: Norton, 1974), pp. 57–68.
2. According to Frederic Scherer, *Industrial Structure and Economic Performance*, 2nd ed. (Boston: Houghton Mifflin, 1980), p. 519, the government-regulated sector accounted for 11 percent of GNP in 1965. The government sector accounted for another 12 percent, yielding a total of 23 percent in 1965, a figure close to the 25 percent figure for 1939.
3. Friedman, "Monopoly and Social Responsibility of Business and Labor," pp. 57–68.
4. William G. Shepherd, "Causes of Increased Competition in the U.S. Economy, 1939–1980," *Review of Economics and Statistics* (November 1982), 613–626.
5. See Scherer, *Industrial Market Structure*, pp. 68–70; James V. Koch, *Industrial Organization and Prices*, 2nd ed. (Englewood Cliffs, N.J.: Prentice-Hall, 1980), p. 181; and Morris Adelman,

"Changes in Industrial Concentration," in Mansfield, *Monopoly Power and Economic Performance*, pp. 83–88.

6. Joe S. Bain, *Barriers to New Competition*, pp. 192–200; H. Michael Mann, "Seller Concentration, Barriers to Entry, and Rates of Return in Thirty Industries," *Review of Economics and Statistics*, 58 (August 1966), 296–307.

7. Leonard W. Weiss, "Quantitative Studies of Industrial Organization," in Michael D. Intrilligator, ed., *Frontiers of Quantitative Economics* (Amsterdam: North Holland, 1971); Leonard Weiss, "Concentration-Profits Relationship and Antitrust," in Goldschmidt et al., eds., *Industrial Concentration: The New Learning* (Boston: Little, Brown, 1974), pp. 184–233.

8. The Harberger results can be found in Arnold Harberger, "Monopoly and Resource Allocation," *American Economic Review*, 44 (May 1954), 77–87.

9. Anne Krueger, "The Political Economy of the Rent-Seeking Society," *American Economic Review*, 64 (June 1974), 291–303; Gordon Tullock, "The Welfare Cost of Tariffs, Monopolies, and Theft," *Western Economic Journal*, 5 (June 1967), 224–232; Harvey Leibenstein, "Allocative Efficiency vs. X-Inefficiency," *American Economic Review*, 56 (June 1966), 392–415.

10. Harold Demsetz, "Industry Structure, Market Rivalry, and Public Policy," *Journal of Law and Economics*, 16 (April 1973), 1–10.

11. Our discussion of the U.S. labor market and the figures cited are from the following sources: William Bowen and Orley Ashenfelter, eds., *Labor and the National Economy*, rev. ed. (New York: Norton, 1975); H. Gregg Lewis, *Unions and Relative Wages in the United States* (Chicago: University of Chicago Press, 1963); Stanley Masters, *Black–White Income Differentials* (New York: Academic, 1975); Cynthia Lloyd, ed., *Sex, Discrimination and the Division of Labor* (New York: Columbia University Press, 1975); Michael Boskin, "Unions and Relative Real Wages," *American Economic Review*, 62 (June 1972), 466–472; George Johnson, "Economic Analysis of Trade Unionism," *American Economic Review, Papers and Proceedings*, 65 (May 1975), 23–28; Albert Rees, *The Economics of Trade Unions* (Chicago: University of Chicago Press, 1963); C. J. Paisley, "Labor Union Effects on Wage Gains: A Survey of Recent Literature," *Journal of Economic Literature*, 18 (March 1980), 1–31; and Richard Freeman and James Medoff, "The Two Faces of Unionism," *The Public Interest*, 57 (Fall 1979), 73–80; and Ronald G. Ehrenberg and Robert S. Smith, *Modern Labor Economics*, 3rd ed. (Glenview, Ill.: Scott, Foresman, 1988).

12. The original statement of the merit goods (wants) concept is found in Richard Musgrave, *The Theory of Public Finance* (New York: McGraw-Hill, 1959).

13. For a classic debate over the proper scope of government and "nongovernment," see Paul Samuelson, "The Economic Role of Private Activity," *A Dialogue on the Proper Economic Role of the State*, in Paul Samuelson, ed., *Readings in Economics*, 7th ed. (New York: McGraw-Hill, 1973), pp. 78–84; and George J. Stigler, "The Government of the Economy," *A Dialogue on the Proper Economic Role of the State*, ibid., 73–77.

14. For more on the various explanations of the U.S. weapons procurement system, see James Kurth, "The Political Economy of Weapons Procurement: The Follow-On Imperative," *American Economic Review, Papers and Proceedings*, 62 (May 1972), 304–311.

15. Seymour Melman, *Pentagon Capitalism* (New York: McGraw-Hill, 1970); and Kurth, "The Political Economy of Weapons Procurement," pp. 304–311.

16. For Galbraith's view, see John Kenneth Galbraith, "Power and the Useful Economist," *American Economic Review*, 63 (March 1973), 1–11.

17. For a more moderate view of the power of the military–industrial complex, see Adam Yarmolinsky, "The Industrial–Military Complex: II," in Edwin Mansfield, ed., *Defense, Science, and Public Policy* (New York: Norton, 1968), pp. 42–43.

18. For suggestions on how to improve the current procurement system, see Carl Kaysen, "Improving the Efficiency of Military Research and Development" with comments by Paul Cherington, in Mansfield, *Defense, Science, and Public Policy*, pp. 114–131.

19. For arguments in favor of the fourth approach, see Friedman, "Monopoly and Social Responsibility of Business and Labor," pp. 57–68; and George Stigler and Claire Friedland, "What Can

Regulators Regulate? The Case of Electricity," in Paul MacAvoy, ed., *The Crisis of the Regulatory Commissions* (New York: Norton, 1970), pp. 39–52.

20. These statistics are from Department of Commerce, *Historical Statistics of the United States: Colonial Times to 1970* (Washington, D.C.: Government Printing Office, 1975), Series N15–29, S86–94, 6416–469, Y505–521; and Clair Wilcox, *Public Policies Toward Business*, 3rd ed. (Homewood, Ill.: Irwin, 1966).

21. Wilcox, *Public Policies Toward Business*, Ch. 20.

22. Scherer, *Industrial Structure and Economic Performance*, p. 421.

23. The following discussion of regulation is based on these sources: Wilcox, *Public Policies Toward Business*, part III; Scherer, *Industrial Structure and Economic Performance*, Ch. 18; and Paul MacAvoy, "The Rationale for Regulation of Field Prices of Natural Gas," in MacAvoy, *The Crisis of the Regulatory Commissions*, pp. 152–168; Robert E. Litan and William D. Nordhaus, *Reforming Federal Regulation* (New Haven: Yale University Press, 1983); and Lawrence J. White, *Reforming Regulation* (Englewood Cliffs, N.J.: Prentice-Hall, 1981).

24. The first of these commissions was established in New England before the Civil War, with authority over the railroads, and in the Midwest in the 1870s. Commissions for the regulation of public utilities were set up only in the early twentieth century (1907); in some instances, public utility supervision was entrusted to the already established railroad commissions. Federal regulation was initiated first in 1887 with the Interstate Commerce Commission, the first major federal regulatory commission.

    State commissions in almost all states have jurisdiction over railroads, motor carriers, water, electricity, gas, and telephones, and about one-half have the authority to regulate urban transit, taxicabs, and gas pipelines. Commissioners are either elected or appointed by the governor of the state. The staffs of the commissions are generally small and are generally poorly funded compared to the legal staffs of the industries they regulate.

    There are five federal commissions. The Interstate Commerce Commission (established in 1887) regulates railroads, interstate oil pipelines, and interstate motor and water carriers. The Federal Power Commission (established in 1920) has jurisdiction over power projects and the interstate transmission of electricity and natural gas. The Federal Communications Commission (established in 1933) regulates interstate telephone and telegraph and broadcasting. The Securities and Exchange Commission (established in 1934) regulates securities markets. The Civil Aeronautics Board (established in 1938) supervises domestic and international aviation. These federal commissions are staffed by commissioners appointed by the U.S. president for terms of five to seven years, and their staffs range from 1000 to 2000 employees. In general, the professional staffs on the federal commissions are better paid and better qualified than their state counterparts, but their salaries are not competitive with those paid by the regulated industries.

25. Wilcox, *Public Policies Toward Business*, p. 326.

26. See, for example, the selections by Merton Peck (on transportation), Richard Caves (on air transport), and Paul MacAvoy and E. W. Kitch (on natural gas) in MacAvoy, *The Crisis of the Regulatory Commissions*, pp. 72–93, 131–151, 152–186.

27. This discussion is based on Roy J. Ruffin and Paul R. Gregory, *Principles of Microeconomics*, 3rd ed. (Glenview, Ill.: Scott, Foresman, 1988), Ch. 14; Elizabeth E. Bailey, "Price and Productivity Change Following Deregulation: The U.S. Experience," *The Economic Journal*, 96 (March 1986), 1–17. See also C. Winston, "Conceptual Developments in the Economics of Transportation," *Journal of Economic Literature*, 23 (1985), 57–94; T. Keeler, *Railroads, Freight, and Public Policy* (Washington, D.C.: Brookings, 1983); A. F. Friedlander and R. H. Spady, *Freight Transport Regulation* (Cambridge, Mass.: M.I.T. Press, 1981).

28. This discussion is based on Scherer, *Industrial Structure and Economic Performance*, Ch. 19 and pp. 469–494; A. D. Neale, *The Antitrust Laws of the United States of America* (Cambridge, England: The University Press, 1962), pp. 2–5; Eugene Singer, *Antitrust Economics* (Englewood Cliffs, N.J.: Prentice-Hall, 1968), Ch. 2; Marshall C. Howard, *Antitrust and Trade Regulation* (Englewood Cliffs, N.J.: Prentice-Hall, 1983); Oliver Williamson, *Markets and Hierarchies:*

Analysis and Antitrust Implications (New York: The Free Press, 1975); and Howard, *Antitrust and Trade Regulation.*

29. The landmark cases were the Standard Oil and American Tobacco cases of 1911. In both instances, the courts ruled that these companies, both accounting for some 90 percent of industry output, should be dissolved into smaller companies. The courts' reasoning, however, was that Standard Oil and American Tobacco were in violation of the Sherman Act not because they accounted for such a large share of industry output (that is, not because they were monopolies), but because they had engaged in "unreasonable" restraints of trade. The implication of this ruling was that if these companies had behaved better toward their competitors, they would not have been held in violation of the Sherman Act. This so-called rule of reason was the prevailing interpretation of the Sherman Act until 1945. The rule of reason was upheld in 1920 with the U.S. Steel case. The company controlled over half of industry output yet had not treated its competitors unfairly or sought to control steel prices. In this case, the courts upheld the rule of reason, stating that the law does not make mere size or the existence of unexerted power an offense.

30. This discussion is based on material in Wilcox, *Public Policies Toward Business,* Ch. 11; and Mansfield, *Monopoly Power and Economic Performance,* pt. II.

31. These conclusions are from Simon Whitney, *Antitrust Policies,* Vol. II (New York: Twentieth Century Fund, 1958), p. 429; summarized in Wilcox, *Public Policies Toward Business,* p. 281.

32. Richard Musgrave, "National Economic Planning: The U.S. Case," *American Economic Review, Papers and Proceedings,* 67 (February 1977), 50–54.

33. Edwin Mills, "Economic Incentives in Air-Pollution Control," in Marshall Goldman, ed., *Controlling Pollution: The Economics of a Cleaner America* (Englewood Cliffs, N.J.: Prentice-Hall, 1967), pp. 100–108.

34. See, for example, Morton Paglin, "The Measurement and Trend of Inequality: A Basic Revision," *American Economic Review,* 65 (September 1975), 598–609; and Edgar Browning, "The Trend Toward Equality in the Distribution of Income," *Southern Economic Journal,* 43 (July 1976), 912–923.

35. These figures are from Department of Commerce, *Historical Statistics of the United States,* series G; and *Statistical Abstract of the U.S.*

36. Paglin, "The Measurement and Trend of Inequality," pp. 598–609.

37. Joseph Pechman and Benjamin Okner, *Who Bears the Tax Burden?* (Washington, D.C.: Brookings, 1974).

38. Browning, "The Trend Toward Equality," pp. 912–923. Also see Edgar Browning and William R. Johnson, *The Distribution of the Tax Burden* (Washington, D.C.: American Enterprise Institute, 1979).

RECOMMENDED READINGS

William Bowen and Orley Ashenfelter, eds., *Labor and the National Economy,* rev. ed. (New York: Norton, 1975).

Edgar Browning and William R. Johnson, *The Distribution of the Tax Burden* (Washington, D.C.: American Enterprise Institute, 1979).

Richard Caves, *American Industry: Structure, Conduct, and Performance,* 4th ed. (Englewood Cliffs, N.J.: Prentice-Hall, 1977).

Lance Davis et al., *American Economic Growth, An Economist's History of the United States* (New York: Harper & Row, 1972).

Ronald Ehrenberg and Robert Smith, *Modern Labor Economics,* 3rd ed. (Glenview, Ill.: Scott, Foresman, 1988).

Richard Freeman and James Medoff, "The Two Faces of Unionism," *The Public Interest,* 57 (Fall 1979).

W. G. Friedman and J. F. Gardner, eds., *Government Enterprise, A Comparative Study* (New York: Columbia University Press, 1970), Ch. 11.

James V. Koch, *Industrial Organization and Prices*, 2nd ed. (Englewood Cliffs, N.J.: Prentice-Hall, 1980).

H. G. Lewis, *Unionism and Relative Wages in the United States* (Chicago: University of Chicago Press, 1963).

Paul MacAvoy, ed., *The Crisis of Regulatory Commissions* (New York: Norton, 1970).

Edwin Mansfield, ed., *Monopoly Power and Economic Performance*, 3rd ed. (New York: Norton, 1974).

Joseph Pechman, *Who Paid the Taxes, 1966–85?* (Washington, D.C.: Brookings, 1985).

Joseph Pechman and Benjamin Okner, *Who Bears the Tax Burden?* (Washington, D.C.: Brookings, 1974).

F. M. Scherer and David Ross, *Industrial Market Structure and Economic Performance*, 3rd ed. (Boston: Houghton Mifflin, 1990).

Eugene Singer, *Antitrust Economics* (Englewood Cliffs, N.J.: Prentice-Hall, 1968).

Don E. Waldman, ed., *The Economics of Antitrust* (Boston: Little, Brown, 1986).

Leonard Weiss and Michael Klass, eds., *Regulatory Reform: What Actually Happened* (Boston: Little, Brown, 1986).

10 Variants of Capitalism: Mature Economies

WE HAVE EXAMINED THE THEORIES OF CAPITALISM and the capitalist economy of the United States. In this chapter, we look at five major variants of the market capitalist model — France, Great Britain, Germany, Japan, and Sweden. These countries have been chosen because of certain distinguishing features that make each country especially interesting to comparative economists. We discuss these features and present background material about each country so that the special characteristics can be placed in proper historical and analytical context. The structural features of these countries are presented in Table 10.1.

All of these countries can be classified as market capitalist systems in which the market is the primary mechanism for resource allocation, private ownership is the dominant form of property holding, and material incentives are used to motivate people. Moreover, all are mature capitalist economies, and the state plays important but varying roles.

If the economies of these countries are broadly similar, what are their distinguishing characteristics? France in a market capitalist system in which a national economic plan has been used to influence resource allocation. The French plan has been of particular interest as a form of noncoercive or **indicative planning**, although it is difficult to decide whether the improved French economic performance after World War II was achieved because of the plan or in spite of it. French indicative planning is an attempt to combine market and plan in a capitalist economic system.

Great Britain is an example of **mature capitalism**. The industrial revolution began in Great Britain in the eighteenth century, so the nation has had almost 200 years of experience as an industrialized capitalist country. Great Britain has experimented with state ownership of basic industries, with redistribution of income through the tax system, with the provision of public services by the state, and with the use of incomes policies to stabilize the economy. British politics is characterized by strong differences in economic policy between the two dominant political parties that have held power alternately over recent decades. Labour Party governments have favored public ownership and an

Table 10.1 Selected Structural Features of Developed Capitalist Variants

Feature	France	Great Britain	West Germany	Japan	Sweden	U.S.A.
Per capita GNP, 1988, in U.S. $	16,090	12,810	18,480	21,020	19,300	19,840
Percent of population urban, 1988	74	92	86	77	84	74
Percent of GDP derived from industry, 1988	37	42	51	41	43	33
Government expenditure as a percent of GNP, 1988	43.1	37.6	29.9	17	40.8	22.9
Gross domestic investment as a percent of GDP, 1988	21	21	21	31	19	15
Average annual rate of inflation, 1980–88	7.1	5.7	2.8	1.3	7.5	4.0
Defense expenditure as a percent of total central government expenditure, 1988	–	12.6	8.9	–	6.8	24.8

Sources: All data are from World Bank, *World Development Report 1990* (New York: Oxford University Press, 1990), Tables 1–32.

aggressive government role in income redistribution. Conservative governments have favored privatization, deregulation, and a less aggressive state role in redistributing income.

Germany, which describes itself as a **social market economy**, is of interest because of its attempts to combine market allocation with worker participation and government intervention to achieve social goals. The strong performance of the postwar German economy makes the social market economy model especially interesting. Moreover, the merger of the former East and West Germanys presents important new challenges to the united Germany.

The Japanese economy has achieved the highest growth rate among the major industrialized capitalist countries. This was accomplished through high rates of capital formation and rapid technological progress. Japan's strong economic performance has made it one of the most important industrialized economies in the world. In considering the sources of Japanese economic success, we look at the role of Japanese lifetime-employment policy, state industrial policy in promoting new industries, and government capital formation programs.

The Swedish economy is a prominent example of what is generally termed the **welfare state**. Sweden is a country and an economic system that has managed to combine efficiency generated through the market mechanism with an egalitarian distribution of income and benefits more typical of socialist ideology. Although world problems such as the energy crisis have had their impact on Sweden, the system has nevertheless proved surprisingly resilient. Although waning support for the social democrats and possible membership in the European Community could result in major changes in the Swedish economic system and its policies, past Swedish economic experience remains important.

In each of these countries, we examine the features that have been of interest to Western observers. Because these features differ considerably, so too will our methods of examination. For example, we focus on the nature of planning in France but on the broad pattern of development in Japan. We do not attempt to force the cases into a unifying mold as we examine their distinguishing features.

Furthermore, our examination is for the most part divorced from the economic problems occupying current headlines. For example, French indicative planning was less important in the 1980s than it was in the early postwar era, yet it is the experiment with indicative planning and its success or failure that fascinate comparative economists. Moreover, the Conservative government that Great Britain has had from the mid-1970s into the 1990s has introduced economic policies that could change the basic nature of British capitalism.

FRANCE: INDICATIVE PLANNING IN A MARKET ECONOMY

The post-World War II French economic system is viewed as a significant test of whether national economic planning and a democratic capitalist society can be effectively and harmoniously combined.[1] For those who believe that some or all of the ills of capitalism require some form of state intervention, the French example has been cited on both practical and theoretical grounds.[2] French planning uses noncoercive intervention while preserving the market economy. Moreover, the French planning mechanism has remained modest in size, an important issue raised by Hayek and others in the socialist controversy.

It is ironic that our primary interest in the French economy centers on its indicative planning, for there has been a significant decline in French involvement in planning since the late 1960s. Nevertheless, in the period when the French planning system was being structured and restructured (1949–1969), the economy grew at an average annual rate of 4.7 percent, a very good performance by international standards.[3] Did the French economy achieve this substantial economic progress after the war because of or in spite of national economic planning? To pursue this question, let us examine the background of the French case, the planning mechanism, and its impact on economic outcomes.

France: The Setting

Countries, as representatives of economic systems, possess unique features such as location, size, and cultural and historical characteristics, all of which influence the economic system. Although such features of economic development frequently cannot be isolated and measured, they may be of great importance in molding the course of events. France, a country whose history and traditions bore heavily on its acceptance of national economic planning, is certainly a case in point.

France is a major world power with a long, rich, and varied history. It has a population of roughly 55 million people residing predominantly in urban areas and a total land area just over twice the size of the state of Colorado. Although France enjoys excellent agricultural conditions, agriculture represents a relatively small proportion of gross domestic product (as is the case in most developed countries). By international standards, France is a developed country with a high standard of living and a contemporary record of good economic growth.

To understand the French economic system, one must understand the French political system. France is a republic whose president is elected to serve for a term of seven years. The president in turn appoints the prime minister. The National Assembly or Parliament is elected.

Although one might look to earlier times to discover the roots of French thought on the appropriate economic role of the state, it is worth emphasizing that during the Fifth Republic, under the leadership of Charles De Gaulle (1958–1969), the power of the French presidency was substantially enhanced.[4] This power has been retained during the post-De Gaulle era, though its impact on the economy has varied over time.

During the 1970s, with growing concern for inflation, unemployment, and balance-of-payments problems, austerity was imposed under the leadership of

Georges Pompidou and Valéry Giscard d'Estaing. This was a period of declining interest in planning as a mechanism to guide recovery. In short, France became less and less interesting as a case of indicative planning.[5]

In the spring of 1981 François Mitterrand, a socialist, was elected to the French presidency, and a socialist majority was sent to the French National Assembly. Mitterrand was reelected in 1988. Although one might have expected a socialist government to be more sympathetic to planning, it is not clear that this has been the case, as we shall show. Nevertheless, planning is still evident in France, the tenth plan terminating in 1992, the year of unification for the European market.

France and Indicative Planning: The Background

France has a long history of a strong state and, more important, acceptance of a strong role for the state in management of the nation's economic affairs.[6] This historical experience contrasts sharply with that of the United States, Canada, and Great Britain, where it is an article of faith, at least in most business circles, that the least government is the best government.[7] French history was an important element in the widespread postwar acceptance of planning by many segments of the French population. Indeed, the early development of the plan by M. Jean Monnet (the founder of the European Common Market) was predicated on acceptance of the plan mechanism by influential business leaders.

The French have tended to view their economy in a rather long-term perspective, emphasizing the primary importance of balanced economic growth and development.[8] Faith in the ability of the unfettered market mechanism to produce economic harmony is not strong. Even within the framework of national economic planning, the French have been willing to utilize mechanisms that are often viewed with skepticism in other countries. For example, the mixed enterprise in which the state and the private sector combine their entrepreneurship and managerial skills has a long history in France. The pattern of interchanging executives between the public and the private sector has facilitated a better understanding of the problems in each sector.[9] For example, the recruitment of top executives for the public sector from the upper echelons of management creates a managerial style very different from that found in Britain.[10]

Although these characteristics of the French economy may have facilitated the introduction and operation of a planning mechanism, such a step represents both practical and theoretical problems for the market economy. Witness, for example, the widespread discussion generated by proposals to introduce mild forms of planning in the United States.[11] Although the U.S. case may be exceptional, the path to national economic planning in capitalist economic systems has generally been slow and unsure. Moreover, it has proved difficult to test the extent to which planning has in fact influenced economic outcomes.

The basic case for indicative planning — the theoretical underpinning of the French system — rests on the manner in which information guides the economic system in the face of uncertainty.[12] Specifically, it is argued that decision making can be improved if some agency (a "planning" agency) collects, processes, and disseminates information to any and all decision makers in the economy. The mechanisms for plan implementation are also important. Indicative planning is nonauthoritarian in the sense that no directive targets are issued and economic agents are encouraged to pursue plan objectives via indirect incentives. The nonauthoritarian nature of indicative planning has been viewed as a major positive feature of this mechanism.

French planning began immediately after World War II, when countries such as England and West Germany were dismantling the controls and planning of the war years. As in other countries that began to experiment with planning at that time, the planning experiment in France subsequently underwent significant change, especially as the economy moved away from the immediate postwar problems toward a period of more "normal" operation. The first plan, begun in 1946 and subsequently extended to 1952, was essentially a transitional plan and was closely associated with the name of Jean Monnet.[13] Monnet headed the General Planning Commissariat, working closely with the Marshall Plan, and utilized direct controls to manipulate economic activity.

French planning has changed significantly over the years, largely in response to the changing needs of the French economy. The changes, however, have been mostly in terms of *goals* and the *means* to achieve these goals rather than in the administrative machinery of the plan. In effect, each plan on a five-year horizon has had a theme. The first plan focused on the development of key sectors: transportation, agricultural machinery, steel, electricity, coal, and cement. The second five-year plan emphasized the improvement of productivity. The third was devoted to economic growth and the foreign sector. The plans thereafter departed from the traditional sectoral emphasis and focused instead on improved economic performance in general. They also placed strong emphasis on social goals: lessening income differentials, redressing regional economic imbalances, and so on.

Vera Lutz argues that one should really distinguish between the Monnet and the post-Monnet plans. The former, she argues, were expedient at the time and were based on direct controls. The latter, on the other hand, relied on the indirect mechanisms for implementation that ultimately became the hallmark of French planning.[14]

The Plan Mechanism

The organizational arrangements of French planning remained relatively unchanged from after World War II until the early 1980s, at which time substantial modifications were made. Because the pre-1980s arrangements are important to any assessment of the planning system, we shall discuss them before noting recent changes.

Historically, French planning relied on an unpretentious institutional structure to force a social consensus among various interest groups, such as business, trade unions, regions, and so on. The main planning organ was the

General Planning Commissariat, a small and relatively modest operation. Under the General Planning Commissariat, some thirty "vertical" and "horizontal" modernization commissions were responsible for sectoral projections. The "vertical" commissions dealt with various sectors of the economy, whereas the "horizontal" commissions dealt with economy-wide matters such as finance. Consultation, a major feature of the French system, was achieved through the work of the Economic and Social Council.

The plan itself was based on a series of alternative projected growth paths for the French economy, including major state priorities, which were formulated by the Planning Commissariat. Subsequent elaboration was developed by the modernization commissions with help from various state agencies. In essence, then, the French plan consisted of rather broad sectoral growth targets related to input, output, investment, productivity, and so on. These targets were derived from macroeconomic projections for the aggregate economy and included state objectives, but they also recognized important constraints, such as the foreign sector.

Basically, despite the changes made in the 1980s, French planning continues to rely on many traditional features. It is, however, a simpler mechanism with an important new task, integrating the French economy into the European Community (1992).

Characteristics of Indicative Planning

The traditional French plan, unlike its Soviet counterpart, does not order firms to do things. The plan is indicative; it offers suggested targets at a fairly high level of aggregation. The plan projections are a source of information that firms can use, along with traditional market signals, to make decisions. Why would a firm bother to look further at the French plan if it is not compulsory? The mechanisms for plan implementation, both direct and indirect, are another distinctive feature of French planning, a feature that outside observers have discussed with praise and scorn.[15]

The state has two major vehicles for influencing economic outcomes: the budget and public ownership. Not all forms of investment that flow through the state are governed by the national economic plan. Furthermore, the degree of control the plan agencies exert over state investment differs substantially, depending on the particular case.[16] Plan control over investment in large public enterprises is considerable, but such control is limited in the case of local government investments.

It is difficult to untangle the budgetary process to measure the impact of the state on investment, especially in light of various changes as plan emphases have shifted over the years.[17] Investment by the state (not including public enterprises) has averaged roughly 12 percent of aggregate investment (compared to 20–23 percent in Great Britain). French public investment, moreover, has been concentrated in key sectors such as housing.

Like state investments, public ownership in France is concentrated in key sectors such as banking, coal, gas and electricity, transportation, and auto and aircraft production. As a producer, consumer, and financier, the state sector of the French economy is in a position to influence economic activity in both the public sector and the private sector. These mechanisms have varied over time, but the state has influenced the availability and terms for credit, the availability of crucial inputs such as electricity, the regional distribution of resources, and tax incentives.

Plan fulfillment depends on whether firms tend to follow the plan. The logic of the plan suggests that the plan is designed to achieve the best possible French economic performance that is consistent with intersectoral harmony. Thus a firm, especially a large firm, operating in harmony with plan directives should be able to do *its* best and to avoid unpredictable constraints. This, if true, is an attractive feature of French planning: the creation of a predictable and harmonious business environment.[18] Evidence suggests that French firms have in fact paid attention to the plans, especially firms important enough to know that the plan may influence their operation.

Monnet argued that a plan is likely to be carried out if those who will be implementing it have a voice in its creation.[19] This aspect of the French system is exemplified by the administrative structure of the plan mechanism, especially the modernization commissions, where traditionally diverse interests (particularly labor, the state, and business) come together to discuss differences and to forge a consensus. The relationship between business and the state in France is said to foster an interchange of ideas and understanding where there would otherwise be antagonism — in Great Britain and the United States, for instance.

Events of the 1970s (especially external shocks to the economy) resulted in a loss of interest in the planning mechanism. Then the election of a socialist president in 1981 presented an opportunity for renewed planning activity. Although domestic economic problems and external events continued to keep planning on a back burner throughout the 1980s, some signs of interest in planning appeared.[20]

In the early 1980s, a special commission was set up to assess the French planning system. While this assessment was in progress, external economic conditions resulted in termination of the eighth five-year plan (1981–1985) and its replacement with an interim plan (1982–1983). (Ultimately there was a new, ninth, five-year plan for the years 1984 to 1988.) Although the interim plan reflected the socialist government's policy of expanding the role of the public sector, conditions created by the worldwide recession took priority. French economic policies, therefore, were designed primarily to address the realities of weak foreign markets, inflation, and unemployment. These issues, along with the matter of European integration, have remained important in the tenth plan (1988–1992).

The socialist government created a Ministry for Economic Planning and Regional Policy in 1981. Next, a National Planning Commission was established to bring together, in addition to the Minister of Planning, interest groups such as trade unions, regions, and employers for the purpose of spelling out plan priorities and methods of plan fulfillment. Along with these organizational changes, procedural changes were introduced. The new planning process distinguishes between identification of plan objectives and designation of the methods by which plan objectives will be achieved. The first phase places new emphasis on realistic macroeconomic projections; the second is concerned with such mechanisms as regional development, technological advancement, and so forth.

Another change of the 1980s is that regional plans are developed and incorporated into the national plan. In addition, contracts have become an important mechanism for achieving plan fulfillment. One might argue that the recent changes are more an attempt to revitalize planning than to change its basic nature. However, the organizational *framework* of French planning clearly *has* undergone change. The notion of achieving objectives that are spelled out in a national consensus is given new force through the use of contractual arrangements. Moreover, in addition to emphasizing better planning in a number of dimensions, the arrangements of the 1980s harmonize regional and national objectives.

By the standards of contemporary and past planned socialist economic systems, the French planning system is modest and relatively simple. What has been the impact of this system on the French economic experience?

Has French Planning Worked?

The features that have made the French planning system attractive to many, especially its apparent consistency with the values of a Western pluralistic society, would be of little value if the plan did not work. Most observers of the post–World War II French economy would argue that in spite of some problems, the French economic record has generally been very good. Has indicative planning, albeit in a limited form, contributed to that performance?

There are many reasons why it is difficult to assess the impact of the French planning system on economic performance. However, three major issues stand out.

First, the planning system has changed in many ways. For example, in the 1950s planners were concerned with rather specific sectoral goals in what was almost a developmental context. During the 1960s the plan grew more sophisticated and plan objectives broadened. By the 1970s, especially under conservative leadership, interest in planning waned. During that period traditional economic difficulties such as inflation, unemployment, and trade deficits were countered largely via traditional monetary and fiscal policy.[21] Market allocation was strengthened through the reduction of controls, less emphasis on the public sector, and more attention to the development of efficient capital markets. In a very real sense, it was an era of reduced state intervention in the economy and of movement toward an "industrial policy."

Although considerable attention was paid to changing the planning arrangements in the 1980s, the need to resolve macroeconomic problems overshadowed improvement of the planning system.

A second and closely related issue is the effectiveness of the plan mechanism over time. Some observers argue that French planning has been of limited importance, especially in recent years, because planning is poorly done.[22] Only limited amounts of information are used to generate the plan, and plan objectives (consisting of single projections) are much too simplistic. Furthermore, it has been argued that this sort of information has been of little value to industrial firms, even state-owned firms, operating independently of state control. Finally, the 1970s witnessed declining coordination in the business sector, further reducing the potential usefulness of the plan to decision makers.

The 1980s saw renewed emphasis on plan execution. Procedures were established to monitor plan performance. In addition, both public and private sectors became more involved in monitoring plan performance and received more information. Even so, available evidence suggests that these changes have done little to enhance the importance of planning.

Third, in a mixed economy like that of France, what indicators can we use to judge the effectiveness of the plan? When specific results are examined — for example, sectoral growth targets in the 1950s — there tends to be considerable difference between plan and actual achievement. On this basis, plan performance is rather poor. Other observers, however, focus on more general outcomes, such as the rate of growth of output. There is a tendency to argue that the plan must have had something to do with improved growth.

One way to look at the impact of the plan is to ask business firms, both public and private, to what extent their decision making has been influenced by plan directives. Hans Schollhammer found that, on balance, French firms did consider the plan important, especially in providing useful information and creating a dynamic business environment.[23] The firms that paid attention to the plan were for the most part large, capital-intensive, and domestically owned. One could argue that this evidence, in combination with good economic performance in the postwar years, presents a circumstantial case in favor of the French planning system.

Another test is to examine the record of plan fulfillment. Have the mechanisms of plan implementation been so strong and the targets so realistic that plan fulfillment has generally been achieved?

In a study of plan fulfillment, Vera Lutz, a critic of French planning, argues that, on balance, the achievement record of French planning has been dismal.[24] In fact, Lutz argues, the French system of planning is not central planning at all. It is little more than "collective forecasting." Lutz's examination of the plan target and achievement data suggests that the degree to which targets were achieved has varied widely from one target to another and, overall, has probably not improved over time.

In another major study of French planning, John J. McArthur and Bruce R. Scott argue that "the national planning process did have some influence on the *general* measures and macroeconomic programs used by the state to shape the economic environment in which companies and industries worked."[25] McArthur and Scott contend that the plan mechanism has influenced economic outcomes through its *indirect* use of state influence. They suggest that the plan has had very little direct influence on corporate decision making, nor, they claim, has it had indirect influence through the state's manipulation of selective means of control. They argue that this lack of influence can be explained at least in part by the inability of the planning mechanism to adapt to the changing needs and circumstances of the French economy.

A survey by J. R. Hough suggests that the planning system may have been a factor creating a favorable climate for the good economic growth that France has achieved, at least prior to the energy crisis of the 1970s.[26]

In a survey of the literature on indicative planning and its relationship to the French experience, Saul Estrin and Peter Holmes argue that in spite of its theoretical basis, planning in France "lost practically all practical relevance after 1965."[27] Thus Estrin and Holmes emphasize the growing lack of interest in planning, poor planning, and inadequate mechanisms to implement plans.

A useful consensus on the French experience is provided in a study by Stephen S. Cohen.[28] Cohen points out that when economic progress is rapid, it is easy to be generous in interpreting the economic impact of planning. Although we have stressed improved French economic performance, that record changed for the worse in the 1970s. It may be that the plan mechanism did not adapt from its original objective of postwar recovery to the needs of what Cohen describes as "general resource allocation planning." With adverse macroeconomic conditions, the French government turned to traditional techniques for manipulating economic activity. Failure of those economic policies, combined with growing lack of interest in planning, resulted in a virtual halt in plan adaptation.[29]

Have the reforms of the 1980s changed the importance of planning in the French economy? Martin Cave suggests that pessimism is appropriate.[30] Cave notes that many of the reforms of the 1980s (for example, the National Planning Commission) have simply not worked. Moreover, the Mitterrand government, preferring traditional macroeconomic tools, has not placed confidence in the plan. There is very little evidence to suggest that planning has regained a position of importance in the French economy. However, the debate continues with regard to both the extent of planning and its possible impact on the French economy.

The French Economy: Approaching the 1990s

The 1980s was a period of change in the French economy, and yet it would seem that planning has yet to play a major role, even under a socialist government. One might suggest that in the face of continuing economic difficulties, Mitterrand has pursued austerity (or *riguer*) along with change in a socialist context. The latter has involved expansion of the state role through further nationalization and a new social policy.

Although there were some signs of improvement in the French economy by 1983, trends of the 1970s and the early 1980s under the impact of world recession and the domestic energy crisis were viewed as unacceptable. The growth of gross domestic product slowed from an average annual rate of 5.6 percent in the period 1967–1973 to an average annual rate of 2.8 percent in the period 1973–1980.[31] For the period 1980–1985, gross domestic production grew at an average annual rate of 1.1 percent. Unemployment rose from 2.8 percent in 1974 to 8.6 percent in 1982.[32] Inflation increased from an average annual rate of 8.0 percent (1965–1980) to 9.5 percent (1980–1985). For the same two periods, the rate of growth of both exports and imports declined sharply. For the period 1985–1989, French real GNP grew at an average annual rate of just over 2.6 percent, with a rate well over 3 percent in 1988 and 1989. For the latter half of the 1980s, consumer prices increased at an average annual rate of just over 3.5 percent, while unemployment remained at just over 10 percent.

In the interim plan (1982–1983), the Socialist regime moved to raise taxes, restrict consumption, and reduce balance-of-payments deficits, the latter by concentrating on import reduction, export expansion (especially to under-developed nations), and devaluations.

The initial years of the Mitterrand government witnessed a substantial increase in the role of government in the French economy. Beginning in late 1981 and early 1982, a policy of nationalization was announced, especially in relation to the large industrial trusts where state involvement was already substantial. Substantial nationalization took place in the banking sector as well.[33]

In a study of the early years of the Mitterrand government, Bela Balassa notes that the public sector share "has risen from zero to 71 percent in iron ore, from 1 to 79 percent in iron and steel, from 16 to 66 percent in other metals, from 16 to 52 percent in basic chemicals, and from zero to 75 percent in synthetic fibers."[34] This certainly constitutes a trend toward greater government involvement in the French economy, evident even in the 1970s. For example, total government expenditure as a proportion of gross domestic product grew from 36.7 percent in 1960–1962 to 45.6 percent in 1977–1979. This growth in government share is comparable to that experienced by Great Britain over the same period but is well below that of the United States, where the government share grew from 28.5 percent to 33.9 percent. During the period from 1960–1962 to 1977–1970, real public expenditure in France grew at an average annual rate of 6.22 percent.[35]

Although it is quite clear that the socialist government of François Mitterrand has moved on a course different from that of his immediate predecessors, there is little agreement on whether these changes are fundamental and far-reaching or are of rather minor importance. Throughout the 1980s, France has been faced with the need to address basic and traditional economic problems. Revisions in French economic policies and organizational changes in the planning system have not fundamentally altered the operation of the French economy, though the focus on European integration presents new challenges.

GREAT BRITAIN: MATURITY, INSTABILITY, AND INCOME POLICY

Whether rightly or wrongly, the postwar French economy carries an image of success through indicative planning. In contrast, Britain has projected an image of poor economic performance, which is blamed on so-called socialism and, to a lesser degree, on the rise of economic planning and control. In fact, Great Britain has had experience with national economic planning only since the early 1960s. Britain's popular classification as a socialist economy derives from general acceptance of the public provision of services such as medical care, the use of highly progressive taxes, and the nationalization of important sectors of the British economy.[36] Postwar British economic performance was generally poor until the 1980s, and the economy has suffered from cyclical instability, imbalance in the foreign sector, and substantial inflation and unemployment.[37]

The 1970s was a difficult decade for Great Britain. There was evidence of stagnation and a continuing search for its causes. Some observers were concerned about the growing role of the state in the economy.

The election of a Conservative government under the leadership of Margaret Thatcher in 1979 was a pivotal point in contemporary British economic history. British economic performance improved in the 1980s under a package of Conservative economic reforms focusing on deregulation, privatization, incentives, and a redefined role for trade unions. It is difficult at this early stage to separate the effects of these policies from those of other events, such as the discovery and exploitation of North Sea oil and gas. In the early 1990s, it is unclear whether the replacement of Margaret Thatcher by John Major will lead to significant changes in "Thatcherism."

Britain is neither a planned economy nor a socialist system, according to our definition. The role of the state is significant but not exceptional by European standards (see Table 10.1). Britain is, however, a mature economy in the sense that it was the first to experience industrialization in the eighteenth century. In addition, it remains at a high level of development in terms of the structure of production, urbanization ratios, and demographic characteristics.[38] Other economies in Western Europe and North America, however, have surpassed Great Britain in terms of some conventional development indicators. Thus by *maturity* we mean, in the British case, longer experience with economic development.

Comparative analysts who look at the British economy often do so for the wrong reasons — for example, to study nationalization, public services, and sharply progressive taxes. These features are important components of the British economy, but they are not unique. Other more successful economies resemble Britain in terms of nationalization, public services, and progressive taxes. We consider a broader question: In the long run, are maturity and stagnation an inevitable combination? What we want to know is whether a particular combination of economic and political forces can account for Britain's apparent inability to deal with maturity (although a full assessment of the 1980s may eventually change this focus on stagnation).

Great Britain: The Setting

Great Britain is an island economy; its land area is slightly greater than that of the state of Minnesota. Britain's history of achievement and its rise to world power have not been matched by good economic performance in contemporary times. Much of the modern literature on the British economy focuses on the reasons for this modest performance — indeed relative decline — in an era of advancement for many West European countries.

Great Britain has a population of just over 57 million persons, roughly 75 percent of whom live in urban areas. Although Great Britain was the home of the Industrial Revolution and the source of much innovative industrial activity, the resource base of the economy is quite limited. Thus it is not surprising that in modern times, the fate of the British economy is very closely tied to performance in the foreign sector. As in other developed countries, the British economy is dominated by the service and industrial sectors. The agricultural sector contributes only a very small fraction of gross domestic product.

Great Britain has limited amounts of good agricultural land, and given its relatively large population, intensive land use is essential. Although Great Britain has substantial deposits of coal and iron ore, these deposits have been heavily exploited and are not of high quality. From the 1960s through the 1990s, attention has focused on the discovery of substantial reserves of oil and natural gas in the North Sea and on the extent to which these reserves can be utilized to sustain and improve British economic performance.

Background of the British Economy

Great Britain is an open economy, particularly vulnerable to external shifts over which it has no control. Problems in the foreign sector have been a key theme of the postwar period. As a rough indicator of the importance of the foreign sector to the British economy, note that in 1985, the sum of merchandise imports and exports represented 46 percent of British gross domestic product, whereas the comparable figure for the United States was 15 percent.

The British concept of an appropriate role for the state in economic affairs is very different from that prevailing, for example, in France.[39] France had experienced economic difficulties in the prewar years and was acutely aware of the need for economic recovery. Whatever the motivating force, the state would play an important role in the direction of the French economy, and planning was viewed as the appropriate mechanism. In Britain, however, in spite of substantial war damage, the immediate postwar emphasis was on preserving the independence of small business and on interfering with the economy only through fiscal and monetary policy. The Keynesian revolution convinced the British of the superiority of "demand management" over central economic planning. Though impossible to quantify, this attitude about the role of the state has been an important factor in the divergent economic paths taken by France and Britain.

Britain has suffered from rather significant regional inequalities.[40] Certainly, regional inequalities have always existed. Modernization has fostered urbanization and the increased mobility of labor and has brought the problems of regional differences to the attention of policy makers and the public. The regional question has been at the forefront of British economic policy.

The British political structure is based on strong conservative and labor parties, both of which have a role in the parliamentary structure, thus providing a testing ground for the capitalist *and* socialist ideologies. Labor policy is said to be basically socialist, particularly on questions of nationalization and income distribution. But there is an erroneous tendency in the West to associate socialism with planning, and this is completely contrary to the British socialist tradition. As Andrew Schonfield points out, "By 1948, the basic elements of modern planning were present in Britain as in no other major Western country."[41] But there it ended until the limited introduction of planing in the 1960s. The basic elements of planning to which Schonfield refers are the Development Councils set up in the late 1940s to exert state control over the private sector, the nationalized sectors, state ownership of the Bank of England, and the wartime experience with planning.[42] All could have been important elements in a comprehensive planning system, but with the advent of a Conservative government in 1951, national economic planning was not seriously discussed for more than a decade.

Probably the most important reason for this delay was the British Labour Party's view of socialism, which was based on old-style ideological convictions that had no connection to modern economic planning. Furthermore, wartime planning was short-term crisis planning that had little to do with long-term planning of the entire economy. After the war, the wartime controls were phased out, though the nationalized industries (in varying degrees) remained. However, nationalization does not mean planning unless there is a mechanism to coordinate economic activity. In postwar Britain the mechanism was to be predominantly the market.

War damage in Britain (as in France, Germany, and Japan) was extensive. The war years called for special means to direct British economic activity toward the single purpose of military victory. During the transition to peace, wartime controls were largely replaced by the market mechanism, but there was growing concern for the health of the economy. In the middle and late 1950s, this concern became an obsession with poor economic performance.[43]

The British experience is, like that of France, a special case. It is a case for which the theoretical underpinning — the economics of maturity — is limited.[44] It is, however, interesting because it is a case that may ultimately be relevant for other mature economic systems.

The British Economy: The Early Postwar Era

When a market economy has been operating for some time under controls, release from those controls can create adjustment difficulties. Such was the case in the immediate postwar British economy. Although British economic performance was relatively good in the late 1940s and early 1950s, the roots of subsequent inadequate economic performance were evident even in these early years. Policy measures taken to offset the subsequent malaise were at best useless and at worst harmful.[45] What were the roots and the dimensions of the impending economic problems?

British economic problems of the 1950s and 1960s are now familiar. The most visible was a growing balance-of-payments deficit produced in large part by Britain's declining ability to compete in export markets and by its over-extended aid program. This problem was combined with growing home demand for imports, a slackening though respectable rate of economic growth, and increasing regional inequalities surfacing through inadequate mobility of labor and growing unemployment. Rather than treat underlying causes, the British government chose to stimulate and stabilize economic growth through the traditional macroeconomic policy of demand management. Subsequent evidence suggests that the experience was destabilizing — and sufficiently so for it to be described as a period of "stop-go" policies.[46] In a sense, however, it was a continuation of the immediate postwar concern for the short run and a neglect of long-run policy remedies.

There have been many explanations of the poor performance of the British economy in the first decade and a half after the war. The main explanations put forward were inadequate (inflexible) supplies of labor, inadequate investment, poor distribution of investment in non–growth-producing areas, inability of the British economy to move ahead technologically, the burden of progressive taxation, and a heavy defense burden. In addition, demand management was inept and contributed to poor performance. Attention has focused on the foreign sector, notably the growing pressure of imports, worsened by the role of sterling as a key world currency and the apparent inability of Britain to maintain a strong competitive position in world export markets.

Many would consider these features symptoms rather than causes. True, the inability of exports to keep up with the growth of imports was obviously a factor in the balance-of-payments problems, but why this backsliding in the growth of exports? Above all, why was the British economy in the early postwar years unable to adapt to change? The British managerial structure in industry and the civil service power structure are both molded by tradition, which has for years served in place of expertise. Trade unions, on balance, have probably tended to be skeptical of technological change, seeing it as leading to unemployment. In short, the British economy proved incapable of adapting to its new role in the world economic community and to the new role of the British consumer, whose expectations were high in the 1950s.

The British Economy: Planning in the 1960s

Although the main elements of national economic planning were present in the immediately postwar British economy, the subject received no attention after the election of a Conservative government in 1951 and languished until 1961, when the Conservative government itself introduced a measure of planning into the British economy. Alarm over economic difficulties caused this policy shift, though the instigation of planning meant very little under Conservative guidance and continued to mean little under subsequent Labour leadership.

In a period of generally poor economic performance, a balance-of-payments crisis in 1961, and concern for the shape of future relations with the emerging European Economic Community, the Conservative government in 1962 established the National Economic Development Council.[47] Both labor and industry generally supported the idea of planning, though each had a different concept of what shape planning might assume. Both also shared a rather peculiar view that there must be an "arm's-length" relationship between the state and the plan. In addition to creation of the main plan organization (the NEDC), a professional staff was organized in the newly created National Economic Development Office. Economic development committees (initially about 30) were created as well to serve as a forum for planning discussions by leaders of labor, business, and government.

There were really two economic plans prepared for the 1960s. One, begun in 1962, was to govern the growth of the economy through 1966. The second plan, introduced in 1965 and abandoned in 1966, was to govern the growth of the economy through 1970. Both plans were essentially a sectoral elaboration of a projected aggregate growth rate. According to observers, both were based on inadequate information and had no means of implementation. Both failed.

As Werner Z. Hirsch observes, the years that followed were not really years of economic planning. They were, at least until the mid-1970s, merely a continuation of the British government's effort to develop macroeconomic forecasting and use it to manipulate economic outcomes.[48] The culmination of this exercise was the passage, under the Labour government, of the Industry Act of 1975, which created the National Enterprise Board and Planning Agreements. The National Enterprise Board was provided with funds to assist private industry and also to extend the scope of the public sector. The Planning Agreements were designed to increase collaboration between the private sector and government and to coordinate government assistance.

In most respects, the British experience with national economic planning was a failure. It did not alter economic outcomes in desired ways. However, as Hirsch points out, it might be more appropriate to consider the experience as one designed to improve communication, information flows, and hence decision making, not as an exercise in planning per se. What were some of the more general problems of this experience?

First, any planning system must have accurate and up-to-date information. Furthermore, the planners must be privy to state decision making and especially to the state budget, which is a crucial element in both plan formulation and execution in a pluralistic society. During the early years of planning, there was no close relationship between NEDC and those who were making the important decisions in government, especially the treasury. Planners were not even informed of government financial and budgetary decisions.

Second, there was a continuous struggle over how various interest groups — notably unions, corporations, and the state — would be represented. Even if one is skeptical about French claims of harmony, the contrast between the British and the French experience is striking. In Britain, instead of a state plan formulated with the inputs of interest groups and with built-in incentives for fulfillment, the planning structure proved to be a bargaining arrangement with an arm's-length relationship between the state and the planners. Schonfield notes that "the crucial issue in modern capitalist planning, which is the relationship between public power and private enterprise, remains open and undecided in the British case."[49]

Third, powerful tools used for plan implementation in France — bank control over investment, tax incentives, and others — were not brought to bear in Britain. In the British case, the state did have a substantial degree of control over state spending and over the rate and pattern of investment, but both were directed within a traditional framework of monetary and fiscal policy, and neither had much to do with the plan.

Fourth, organizational change, surely a destabilizing element, was frequent, especially with the shifts between Labour and Conservative governments. Throughout the 1960s traditional policy measures continued to be used. Discussion focused more on the necessity for formulating an incomes policy. Personal income rose much more rapidly than gross domestic product.[50] To bring the two in line and to stabilize economic activity, fiscal and monetary policy were used, along with efforts to reach agreements with labor and management concerning wage and price increases. Such policies were described as "stop-go" policies in the 1950s, as "income policies" in the 1960s, and as "demand management" thereafter.

The "British Disease"

Observers of the British economy have identified a number of specific problem areas — investment levels and patterns, a noncompetitive position in export markets, a high burden of taxation, problems in the allocation of labor, and the defense burden — as manifestations or causes of Britain's economic difficulties of the postwar era.

Investment as a proportion of gross domestic product was between 16 and 20 percent, rising somewhat during the 1950s and 1960s. This ratio was well below that of France and West Germany. Furthermore, although government and public enterprises accounted for over 40 percent of domestic capital formation, there is little evidence that the government played any useful role in directing investment activity toward growth-producing sectors or regions. Moreover, the British capital stock (per worker) has been unusually small compared with that of the other countries.[51]

The British tax system has also been singled out as a cause of economic problems. Is the tax burden of the British economy unusually high? The answer to this question is probably yes. The progressive tax on personal income has been higher in Great Britain than in the United States, but it has been significantly lower in Britain than in the United States for corporation. Furthermore, the disparity between the British personal and corporate tax widened between the 1950s and the 1960s, a change that depressed personal incentives. The loss of skilled professionals (physicians, engineers, and so forth) to other countries during this period is certainly consistent with this interpretation. The outcome of steeply progressive taxation — namely, a lessening of income differentials – can be seen in the British case. Data for the mid-1960s suggest that the income distribution in Britain was narrower than that in West Germany, France, or even Yugoslavia.[52]

Compared to countries such as France, Germany, and Italy, the British economy did not do well in obtaining economic growth from increases in the quality and quantity of the labor force. At the same time, the process of collective bargaining in Britain contributed to low industrial productivity. Contrary to the popular concept that Britain is plagued by strikes, for the period 1955–1964 many fewer days (as a proportion of employment in key sectors) were lost to strikes in Britain than in France, West Germany, Italy, or the United States.[53] However, this statistic may simply indicate a greater willingness on the part of private and public management to accede to wage and work-rule demands.

Finally, turning to the question of defense burden, the share of gross domestic product devoted to defense in Great Britain has been smaller than that in the United States but considerably larger than that in West Germany, France, or Italy. Although defense spending shifts resources away from other potential uses, it is not clear that this process has depressed Britain's economic growth.

Nationalization and the Market

To assess British economic performance, it is useful to return to our basic classification of economic systems in terms of the decision-making structure, the mechanisms for information and coordination, property rights, and the incentive system. How might we describe the postwar British economy in terms of these characteristics?

Britain is frequently described as a socialist, if not a planned socialist, economic system.[54] This identification is based on the perception of the state's playing a substantial role through the budgetary process, nationalized firms in key sectors, and (to a lesser degree) the existence of national economic planning. Although there is no single indicator of the state's role in an economic system, most available evidence supports the view that the role of the state in the British economy has been smaller than generally perceived and does not justify classification of the system as socialist.

A study by Frank Gould of public expenditure patterns in a number of Western industrialized countries sheds light on the growth of government spending.[55] General government spending as a proportion of gross domestic product in 1960–1962 was 37 percent for France, 33 percent for the United Kingdom, and 28.5 percent for the United States. By the years 1977–1979, these shares had risen to 46 percent, 45 percent, and 34 percent, respectively. During this period, real general government expenditures grew at an average annual rate of 6 percent in France, 4 percent in the United Kingdom, and almost 5 percent in the United States. Gould concludes that although state and local government spending has assumed greater importance, the major explanation for the rise in general government spending can be found in the growth of government transfers. As a proportion of general government spending, government transfers in 1977–1979 represented 60 percent in France, 47 percent in the United Kingdom, and 41 percent in the United States. Public expenditure patterns in the United Kingdom do not appear to be difference from those of other industrialized countries at the aggregate level.

The public sector in Britain has played a substantial role in both savings and investment. Public saving as a proportion of aggregate saving in the economy fluctuated from a low of 21 percent (1960) to a high of 46 percent (1950) over the period 1950–1966. For the same years, public investment as a proportion of total investment fluctuated from a low of 31 percent (1950) to a high of 56 percent (1952) and in recent years has been just over 40 percent. Over these years, public savings has averaged 31 percent of total savings, while public investment has averaged 42 percent of total investment. Judged by the experience of other industrialized countries, these ratios are average or, at best, slightly above average.[56] Thus while the public sector is important in the British economy, the system remains essentially a decentralized market-type economy.

Although public enterprise is highly visible in some sectors of the British economy, its overall contribution is really not large.[57] Although the share of public corporations in the capital formation of the public sector has grown (largely at the expense of capital formation by the central government), the contribution of public enterprises to output remains small. In 1950, for example, the net output of the public enterprise sector in Britain accounted for just over 8 percent of British gross domestic product; the equivalent figure for 1967 was just over 7 percent.[58]

. It is difficult to judge the overall success of the nationalization experience, because in most cases nationalization came about as a result of problems in the particular sectors involved. However, in spite of a continuing conflict among objectives — that is, between financial health and some interpretation of public service or benefit — the former has generally prevailed, and it is not clear that the nationalized industries have been especially important in carrying out government economic policies. Finally, the role of the state in incentive arrangements is larger in Great Britain than, for example, in the United States in areas such as public goods. At the same time market arrangements predominate in the allocation of labor and these arrangements differ sharply from those found in socialist systems.

The British Economy in the 1970s and 1980s: An End to Stagnation?

Our discussion so far has rated British performance as rather poor. Indeed this has been the prevalent view. Some have argued that the problems plaguing the

British economy are unique to that system, representing the "British disease."[59] Others have argued that the British economy is in a phase of deindustrialization brought on by a decline in importance of manufacturing.[60]

The negative picture might be summed up in the following way: In spite of a persistent effort to manipulate aggregate demand, economic performance has been inadequate relative to that of other industrialized European economies. This performance gap, it has been argued, stems from a poor labor–management system, poor work attitudes, and a management system incapable of growth and change. These forces, which are deeply ingrained in the British system, resulted in low growth of productivity in manufacturing, an inability to compete in export markets, a growing domestic demand for imports, and the like.

To some degree, the assessment of British economic performance depends on the standards chosen for judgment. For example, the rate of growth of output in Britain in the 1960s was modest when compared to that of other Western industrialized economies. However, the same can be said for the United States. What seems to be distinctive is the British pattern of change in the 1970s. While most economies experienced problems in the 1970s, British performance was inferior relative to that of other industrialized countries, in particular those of the OECD group.[61]

Real gross domestic product per person grew by 2.4 percent per annum in Britain in the 1960s and by 1.9 percent in the 1970s. Comparable figures for the United States were 2.9 percent and 1.8 percent; for Japan they were 15.9 and 4.8 percent, respectively.[62] In the 1970s Britain lost ground. For example, in 1967, per capita gross domestic product of Great Britain was 86 percent of the OECD average; by 1978, the comparable figure was 72 percent.[63]

Most countries experienced rapid inflation in the 1970s. However, the British rate of inflation generally exceeded that of other Western industrialized economies. Indeed, for most years from the late 1960s through the late 1970s, the rate of inflation in Britain exceeded the average in all OECD countries.

Turning to the question of labor market performance, unemployment increased substantially in the 1970s, though not always to levels experienced in other countries. At the same time, wages increased without concomitant rises in labor productivity. The increasing unit labor costs made British exports less competitive abroad. This latter trend was partially offset by the declining value of the pound sterling. For example, between 1966 and 1977, the average annual increase in unit labor costs in Britain was 11.5 percent, while the comparable figures for Japan, France, and the United States were 8.1 percent, 7.7 percent, and 4.4 percent, respectively.[64] Britain's share in the world export of manufactures declined between 1951–1955 and 1973–1977 by 11.4 percent. While the United States experienced a comparable decline of 7 percent, West Germany's share grew by 8 percent, Japan's by 9.8 percent, and France's by 0.3 percent.[65]

The analysis of such numbers can proceed indefinitely. What are we to conclude from this exercise? In a study of British economic performance in the 1970s, W. B. Reddaway concluded that the "disease" view is one-sided, saying that while other economies had done better, "Even in the less satisfactory

1970s the economy made faster progress, in real terms, than in any pre-war decade, and the two previous decades might be regarded as a golden age."[66] At the same time, a Brookings study argued that in the decade between 1967 and 1978, Britain lost ground among OECD countries, markedly so after 1973. The authors conclude: "Britain's economic malaise stems largely from its productivity problem, whose origins lie deep in the social system."[67]

Despite a wide variety of views on the health of the British economy, most agree that British economic performance in the 1970s was poor. The discovery of North Sea oil in the late 1970s and early 1980s was an important factor limiting the bad economic news for Britain. This positive input has a finite life span, however, and continuing improvement must rest on more fundamental changes in the British economy.[68]

As we look at the British economy of the 1980s, much of what we have said before might be viewed as an exercise in economic history. If so, is it a useful exercise? Many would think so, for although the Thatcher programs of the 1980s brought important changes to the performance of the British economy, there is still a nagging feeling that it is, after all, a troubled economy temporarily strengthened by North Sea oil.

British economic policies of the 1980s clearly represented a significant departure from those of earlier years. Such a departure is difficult to evaluate in the short run, although the volume of literature on the subject is already large.[69]

It is not surprising that the conservative focus of the Thatcher government placed much of the blame for past failures in performance squarely on past economic policies, especially the ambitious role of the government in the British economy. Accordingly, economic polices in the 1980s were designed to reduce the role of government — and to do so in four important areas.[70]

First, to improve market stability, a monetary policy designed to reduce the rate of inflation was instituted. A reduction in the rate of growth of the money supply was combined with less public sector borrowing and less use of fiscal policy. This aspect of the Thatcher economic policy became known as a monetarist macroeconomic policy and has understandably been compared to policies of the Reagan administration in the United States. It came to be known officially as the "Medium Term Financial Strategy."

Second, to reinstitute a competitive market economy, government controls and regulations were reduced. This policy, designed to stimulate private market initiative, applied to both the domestic and the international economy.

A third area of focus, related to the issue of a competitive market economy, involved "privatization," or the return of the public sector (especially nationalized industries) to private ownership and operation.

Finally, steps were taken to reduce the powers of trade unions and make them more responsive to their members.

The implementation of these policy measures in the 1980s generated a discussion of great importance. Obviously, the Thatcher government found implementation difficult. At the same time, British economic performance improved, though critics suggest that the improvement will be short-lived.[71]

Some success has been achieved in control of inflation: The average annual rate of inflation in Great Britain was 11.1 percent for the period 1965–1980; for the period 1980–1988, the rate was reduced to 5.7 percent.[72] However, critics charge that this reduction was achieved only at a significant price. First, manufacturing output fell sharply in the early 1980s, although it recovered in the mid- and late 1980s. The average annual rate of growth of industrial output was −0.5 percent for the period 1965–1980 and 1.9 percent for the period 1980–1988.[73] Second, unemployment increased steadily through the mid-1980s, from single-digit numbers in the 1970s to double-digit numbers in the 1980s (it declined significantly thereafter).

Have deregulation and the privatization of the British economy succeeded? To the extent that the British effort to deregulate can be described as an industrial policy, it has been selective and difficult to evaluate. As one author has noted, British policy is based in large part on the notion that private ownership is in itself sufficient to generate efficient markets; at the same time, however, selective government support has increased.[74] For example, the British government has attempted to invigorate regional policy, stimulate industries where advanced technology is important, and boost the quality of investment. There has also been substantial privatization of firms, ranging from British Petroleum in the early 1980s to British Airports, British Airways, and automobile producers in the mid- and late 1980s. The impact of privatization remains unclear. The British government has in effect divested itself of a variety of assets, but it is uncertain whether this transition in ownership will effect major changes in the management of these assets in the future.

Finally, with respect to trade unions, the government has instituted a number of changes in union rules in order to limit unions' power in the economy. In addition, certain social policy reforms aimed at stimulating individual effort have been implemented. These include a reduced tax burden and a strengthened social security net for specific groups, such as the unemployed. It is difficult to assess the effectiveness of these changes, because they are still underway. Although there has probably been a reduction of trade union power, critics suggest that this outcome is the result of the economic downturns rather than of any specific changes made by the government.[75] Nevertheless, the government can point with pride to a reasonably good rate of economic growth in the 1980s, along with significant gains in productivity.

As we assess the prospects for the future, a number of considerations seem relevant. First, for the economist interested in different economic systems, Britain in the 1980s clearly made a significant departure from the past. Although stagnation and the "British disease" were dominant themes of the 1970s, a shift to the right has introduced new organizational arrangements, new policies, and an underlying faith in the free market economy as a mechanism to stimulate British economic performance. Clearly this experiment bears watching. Many have argued that the gains that have been made are inherently short-run, and will not be able to stand the test of time. Critics suggest that gains — the reduction of inflation and the enhancement of productivity — have been made at the expense of other objectives that the government considers less important, such as full employment. Moreover, changing patterns of international trade, especially development of the European Community, present new challenges for the 1990s.[76]

GERMANY: THE SOCIAL MARKET ECONOMY[77]

The economy of West Germany, the Federal Republic of Germany, belongs in a discussion of the variants of capitalism for three reasons. The first is that the economic performance of the West German economy is generally perceived to be the strongest of the major European countries throughout the postwar era. West Germany emerged as the economic leader of Europe. The second reason is West Germany's combination of free market forces with significant state intervention to achieve desired social goals. The Germans label this combination the **social market economy** (soziale Marktwirtschaft) of the Federal Republic.[78] The combination of good economic performance with some of the ideals of a welfare state make Germany an interesting case study. Finally, unification of the former German Democratic Republic with West Germany provides a unique historical example of integration.

Background

The Federal Republic of Germany (Bundesrepublik Deutschland) came into existence as a federal republic in the late 1940s as the three allied occupation forces (the United States, England, and France) converted their occupation zones into a unified economic area (Vereinigtes Wirtschaftsgebiet) in 1947. A 1948 currency reform established the three occupation zones as a single currency area; Soviet authorities kept the Soviet occupation zone out of this currency union. This event signaled the splitting of Germany into two Germanys. The Basic Law for the Federal Republic of Germany was passed on June 23, 1949. It established West Germany as a federal republic consisting of a federal government (with two legislative houses and a federal bureaucracy of ministries), the states (Länder), and the local governments (Gemeinden). The Federal Republic was a democracy with two major parties, the Christian Democratic Union (CDU) and the Socialist party (SPD), that have dominated the political scene throughout the postwar era. Along with governmental bodies and agencies, a number of quasi-state organizations such as labor unions, employer organizations, and chambers of commerce are active in economic affairs.

The integration of the former German Democratic Republic into the Federal Republic of Germany has created a large nation by European standards. These formerly distinct nations now occupy a land area of approximately 350,000 square kilometers and had, in 1990, a total population of 78 million. This means that Germany now has a land area roughly two-thirds that of France and a population some 22 million greater.

From an ethnic perspective, the population is almost entirely German; religious affiliation is split between Roman Catholic and Protestant.

We turn now to a discussion of the development of the former West German economy. After that, we shall treat the issue of unification.

Origins of the Social Market Economy

The social market economy originated in the immediate postwar years. Its intellectual heritage can be traced to the so-called Freiburg school of neoliberalism, the most important representatives of which were Walter Eucken and Alfred Muller-Armack.[79] The Freiburg school believed that the state should play an active role in ensuring the workability of the competitive market system and that the market system should serve as the major instrument for allocating resources. The state should be prepared to intervene, however, to achieve important social goals. Intervention should be compatible with the underlying market order; thus policies that disrupt the working of the market (direct orders, price freezes, and so on) should be avoided.

The political background of the social market economy can be traced to the immediate postwar years of Allied occupation. The initial Allied policy was to continue the wartime controls. Until 1947 the objective of allied policy was to enforce payment of reparations and to destroy the German military industry potential. When the emphasis turned to long-term rehabilitation and recovery, direct controls were dismantled and the running of the country's economy was gradually returned to German hands. Ludwig Erhard, the minister of economics during the Adenauer years, was a strong proponent of the teachings of the Freiburg school. He strongly favored decontrol, deregulation, and the turning of economic decisions over to the impersonal hands of the market.[80] The choice of market versus plan was heatedly debated, with the social democrats coming out in favor of strong state planning. Memories of the chaos of the inflationary 1920s and the depression of the 1930s had convinced many German politicians of the dangers of a market economy. Two major political events signaled the return to market resource allocation: the Currency Reform and Price Reform of June 1948 and the passage of the Basic Law (Grundgesetz) of the Federal Republic in May 1949, the latter serving as the German constitution. Those events established the principle of the sanctity of private property, which was to serve as the foundation of economic policy in the postwar era.

Unlike the United States, where national economic goals (with the exception of full employment) are unwritten, the economic goals of the Federal Republic have been written into law. These goals are price stability (a stable currency) and full employment, balance-of-payments equilibrium, and stable economic growth. Three social goals, closely associated with the notion of the social market economy, are also identified in German law: social equity, social security, and social progress. The social goals provided much of the basis for state intervention in economic affairs in the Federal Republic.[81]

Characteristics of the Social Market Economy

The principal features of the social market economy have evolved over the years. The first principle remains the sanctity of private property. The second is that resource allocation should follow the dictates of the market unless there is a serious conflict with national social objectives. There is no significant planning apparatus in Germany, and the macroplanning that does exist works through traditional monetary and fiscal policy, with principal emphasis on monetary policy as carried out by the Bundesbank (the central bank).[82] German fiscal policy coordinates the budgets of the different levels of government (federal, state, and local). Unlike the United States, where fiscal policy is the responsibility of the federal government, the German "stability law" sets up a Business Cycle Commission (Konjunkturrat) and Finance Planning Commission (Finanzplanungsrat) to coordinate the federal, state, and local budgets for fiscal policy goals. In the area of monetary policy, German policy makers were never strongly caught up in the Keynesian revolution. The Bundesbank is more politically independent than the American Federal Reserve, and a country that has experienced hyperinflation is more likely to see inflation as a monetary phenomenon. Monetarism has been a long-run feature of German macropolicy. The economic forecasting of macroeconomic variables is a relatively recent phenomenon and is done by semi-independent research institutes, which serve as consultants for the federal government. In fact, a striking characteristic of the German economic apparatus is the virtual absence of planning machinery at the federal level.

In view of the emphasis the Freiburg school placed on the state's responsibility to ensure the workability of competition, it is informative to see what procompetition arrangements have emerged. Government policies in favor of competition are based on the anticartel law of 1957.

It is interesting to contrast the Law Against Limitations on Competition (Gesetz gegen Wettbewerbsbeschränkungen) with American antitrust legislation. First, the German law is quite specific, and the courts have played a relatively minor role in interpreting the law. Second, the German law singles out labor unions as a clear exception to the anticartel rule. Labor is recognized as being unlike other commodities, and labor's right to form unions is clearly affirmed. Third, the German law uses both the Verbotsprinzip (outright prohibition) and the option to correct market abuses. Horizontal cartel contracts and agreements are illegal outright, whereas firms that occupy market-dominating positions are merely subject to the control and scrutiny of the cartel authorities. The law provides detailed definitions of "market-dominating" firms based on market shares (33 percent single-firm concentration ratio), financial power, and barriers to entry. Cartel authorities are supposed to disallow mergers if the merger produces a market-dominating firm.

The Law Against Limitations on Competition allows exceptions and exemptions that appear to contradict the basic principles of the social market economy. Agricultural, credit, insurance, transportation, rebate, "structural crisis," and "rationalization" cartels are exempted from the cartel laws. A "structural crisis" cartel, for example, is permitted when there has been a long-term decline in demand that requires the creation of a cartel to salvage an industry. A "rationalization" cartel can be formed when a cartel is deemed necessary to introduce new technologies into the industry. Critics point out that cartel authorities are placed in the position of having to judge whether a structural crisis exists or whether a new technology will be introduced only if a cartel is formed. This practice tends to lessen competition during economic downturns.[83]

The state actively limits competition in a number of areas based on its social responsibilities to the public. Examples of such interventions are strict state regulation of business hours, state support of minimum price legislation for brand-name articles, rent controls, laws that give renters virtual property rights, and government rules on the firing of employees, none of which is very unusual by European standards.

One type of state activity should be singled out — the extensive role played by state (Länder) governments in managing the occupational training of young workers. The chambers of commerce allocate young people into apprenticeships in industry and establish rules whereby local industries are responsible for the training of young workers, at the expense of these industries.

Social Correctives of the Market Economy

In the Federal Republic, social correctives of market resource allocations are actively pursued in cases of conflict between private economic decision making and national social objectives. Such social correctives occur in five major areas: (1) the security of employment, (2) the protection of employees, (3) insurance against the risks of workers, (4) improvement of the distribution of income, and (5) other measures that have a significant impact on social policy.

The first three instances are typical of most industrialized capitalist countries and involve programs of employment services; protection against dangerous employment conditions and protection of teen-age workers; unemployment, hospitalization, and accident insurance; and so on. The unusual aspects of the German case are that such programs were instituted so early (under Bismarck in 1881) and that they are so comprehensive in contemporary terms.

The German welfare state is highly developed and rapidly expanding. State expenditures as a share of GNP rose from 32.5 percent in 1960 to about 50 percent in the late 1980s. The share of social expenditures of GNP rose in the same time period from 21 percent to 30 percent. Between 1960 and the mid-1980s, expenditures for the state health insurance system rose by a factor of 10. Critics of the rising share of government expenditures point to the inefficiencies that such government programs eventually produce.

Correctives aimed at improving the distribution of income are more unusual. In Germany, progressive income taxes are not the principal vehicle for making the market-determined distribution of income more equal. Rather, the objective has been to use other instruments — the promotion of asset formation among lower-income groups, direct transfer payments (examples are child allowances and subsidization of rental payments), and direct state intervention (government funding of public housing and obligatory health insurance). Finally, the state has supported programs to allow workers to share in the profits of their enterprises as well as to have a say in the conduct of enterprise affairs (codetermination), all of which may affect the real distribution of income.

Let us first consider state policies to promote capital formation in general and savings of lower-income groups in particular. In some instances, the state supplements the savings of low-income families through a schedule of premiums, especially for savings, that cannot be withdrawn for seven or more years. Savings for home purchases receive similar treatment, and employer contributions to employee life insurance or other savings programs receive favorable tax treatment. These two features, in addition to government programs to ensure workers' access to the distribution of enterprise profits, seek to render even the lower-paid workers less dependent on their wage income. Earnings from assets should serve as income supplements. A side benefit of such pro-capital-accumulation (and anticonsumption) policies is to encourage a high domestic savings rate and a higher domestic growth rate.

In addition to these policies to promote capital formation even among working families, the income distribution is made more nearly equal by direct government interventions. A prime example is the fact that most apartment construction in contemporary Germany is funded (or sponsored) by state organizations for the purpose of making low-cost housing available to lower-income groups.

Codetermination and Labor Unions

An important aspect of government social policy is codetermination (Mitbestimmung). Codetermination means having worker representatives on the boards of directors of corporations. The objective of this policy is "industrial democracy," or forcing management to take workers' interests into consideration when making policy. Initially applied only to selected industries, codetermination has applied to almost all industry since German law was revised in 1976.[84] Firms with two thousand or more employees fall under the codetermination legislation. A separate codetermination law applies to the coal, iron, and steel industries.

According to the law, stockholders and workers should have an equal number of representatives on the board of directors. For example, if the board consists of twelve members, six should represent the stockholders and six the employees. Of the latter, two must be representatives of the labor union, and at least one must be a "leading employee" (such as a foreman). The codetermination law requires the election of a chairman (Vorsitzender) of the board of directors. In the absence of a majority, the chairman is elected by the representatives of the stockholders. In this way, the codetermination law seeks to avoid a stalemate by giving the chairman the deciding vote in the case of an evenly split board. Although labor and stockholders appear to have parity on the board of directors, the stockholders actually have the advantage because of the way the chairman is selected and because "leading employees" often side with the stockholders.

The 1976 regulations are still being tested in the German courts. Because codetermination rules call for a nearly equal labor voice, they call into question the protection of private property guaranteed in the German constitution. Another objection raised to the codetermination legislation is that it puts labor representatives on both sides of the collective bargaining table and thus gives labor an unfair advantage. In steel industry negotiations, however, labor representatives on the management boards have sided with management against the steel workers' demand for a 35-hour workweek. It is not obvious, therefore, how labor representatives will behave when they in fact join management.

The codetermination law gives labor a voice in major policy decisions, but the board of directors rarely deals with shop-level issues. The Enterprise Constitution Law (Betriebsverfassungsgesetz, or BVG) of 1972 gives labor a voice in shop-floor decisions. The BVG requires the election of an enterprise council in enterprises employing five or more workers; "leading employees" are not eligible for election to that council. The enterprise council has codetermination responsibilities in the following areas: wages, length of the working day, firings, and layoffs. The influence of the enterprise council is strongest in personnel areas; every termination requires the approval of the enterprise council.

The BVG law of 1972, on paper at least, substantially constrains management in the area of personnel decisions. How the law works in practice remains to be fully researched. It is not yet known whether most enterprises actually follow the letter of the BVG law. Also, its effect on productivity remains to be measured. On the positive side, worker participation may raise worker loyalty and enthusiasm and reduce turnover; on the negative side, worker participation may prevent management from making necessary personnel changes.

Labor and Collective Bargaining

The right of workers to join together to form trade unions is recognized in the German constitution and the cartel laws. Workers have the freedom to contract with management or management organizations through collective bargaining. The "closed shop" (wherein all workers must belong to the union) is not allowed in Germany. The percentage of the labor force belonging to unions in Germany is approximately 41 percent, much higher than the current American ratio of less than one in five. German unions are organized on an industry basis to prevent competition among individual unions for members. German unions are grouped into federations, the most important being the German Federation of Unions (Deutscher Gewerkschaftsbund), which accounts for 84 percent of all union membership.

Collective bargaining between unions and management generally proceeds at a relatively high level. Unions have the right to strike, and management has the right to lock workers out (Aussperrungen), or close down firms in which workers are striking. The volume of strikes is relatively low in Germany (58 days per 1000 workers per year for the period 1970 to 1979), but it is noteworthy that management has been willing to respond to strikes with lock-outs. For example, 1971 and 1978 were years of relatively high strike activity in Germany. In both years, the number of workdays lost through lock-outs was about two-thirds of the number of workdays lost through strikes. German labor laws do not require compulsory arbitration, but this device is commonly used to settle stalemates. Once unions and management agree to arbitration, they must hold their peace. Arbitration proposals are not binding, but they impose strong psychological pressure on the parties to agree.

The low frequency of strikes in Germany and the relatively low nominal wage increases agreed to by unions in the postwar period point to comparatively successful labor-management relations in postwar Germany. Many factors could contribute to this success: the codetermination laws, the role of the enterprise council, and the traditional German fear of inflation.

An interesting feature of German social policy is the notion that problems of income distribution should not be solved by collective bargaining for higher nominal wages by unions and management. Although German workers are organized into powerful unions and the German social democratic party is strongly influenced by organized labor, collective bargaining in Germany has been more quiescent than in other European countries. Whether the government's social policies can be credited for this fact or whether fear of inflation is at the root, we cannot determine; but the failure of German unions to be more demanding has probably been an important factor in the lower rates of inflation in Germany.

Public Enterprise

The role of public enterprise is greater in Germany than in the United States. Not only do state enterprises dominate transportation and communication and the construction of apartment dwellings, but there is significant state participation in mining and metallurgy.[85] In some cases, government participation is indirect (as in the recent case of the Krupp industries); in others it is carried out through holding companies. Nevertheless, one cannot cite government enterprises as a unique feature of the German social and market economy, for it is quite typical of Europe in general.

In fact, the German experience with nationalization has been the reverse of the British experience, at least prior to the 1980s. In Germany, the emphasis has been on denationalization (Privatisierung). The Federal Treasury Ministry (Bundesschatzministerium) was established in 1957 to deal with public enterprises. It was set up not as an instrument of central management but rather to lay the foundations for denationalization. The management of public enterprises has typically been decentralized to the enterprise itself. Two methods of denationalization have been used: (1) the sale of formerly public enterprises to private persons or private groups and (2) social denationalization, which is achieved by establishing a new type of equity, the so-called popular share, to be sold to low-income citizens on a preferential basis. The main denationalizations were those carried out at Volkswagen and Veba.

Union-owned and -organized enterprises represent a mix of public and private enterprise. For example, the union-owned Gruppe Neue Heimat was once the largest European apartment construction firm, the Bank fur Gemeinwirtschaft is the fourth-largest German interregional bank, and the Coop-Unternehmen forms the second-largest retail trade organization in Germany. Officially, these firms were founded to serve the common good, not to maximize profits.

Performance

The annual growth rate of the West German economy averaged 4.5 percent between 1950 and 1987. Its most rapid growth came in the immediate postwar era, with a 1950–1960 growth rate of 8.5 percent. The West German investment rate has remained consistently around 25 percent of GNP — one of the highest among industrialized countries. A relatively low unemployment rate accompanied this rapid growth. In the 1950s and 1960s, unemployment rates at or below 1 percent were common. The German unemployment rate (like that in other Western countries) has increased since the mid-1970s, reaching the 7 percent range in 1987. Consumer prices increased at remarkably low rates for such rapid growth and low unemployment. In the 1950s consumer prices increased at a 2.6 percent rate. In the inflationary 1970s, the German inflation rate was a relatively low 5 percent per annum. In the 1980s, German inflation was under 1 percent per annum. Relative price stability led to a stable and generally rising exchange rate and a positive trade balance. The outstanding performance of the West German economy, especially during the late 1940s and 1950s, has caused analysts to speak of the German "economic miracle" (Wirtschaftswunder).

Unquestionably, the postwar performance of the German economy has been good. To what extent this performance is related to the economic system is, as always, difficult to know. However, certain aspects of the German system have arguably been important in influencing economic outcomes.

One unusual feature of the German system has been the rather intense effort on the part of state policy to promote capital formation, even among lower-income groups, while avoiding a steeply progressive income tax. Germany today has (along with Japan) one of the highest national savings rates of the industrialized countries, and this is at least a partial consequence of state policy. The concerted effort to promote investment while restraining consumption seems to have paid off in terms of economic growth and price stability, two of the hallmarks of the German Wirtschaftswunder.

Moreover, German state policy has sought to prevent discord between worker and employer, principally by ensuring the social security of the German worker. Contemporary developments in the area of codetermination can be viewed as a continuation of social reforms begun in the Bismarck era. These policies, combined with the traditional German fear of hyperinflation, have perhaps served to limit the wage demands of German unions, despite their enormous economic and political power.

If interest has long focused on Germany's social market economy, interest in the 1990s centers on the integration of the former East and West Germanys into a single nation and on the ability of this nation to sustain economic progress in spite of the costs of unification in a rapidly changing European economic setting. We turn next to a discussion of unification.

Germany: Unification

As we noted in Chapter 1, the unification of what was formerly the German Democratic Republic (GDR) with the Federal Republic of Germany (FRG) took place in 1990 and was an event of major political and economic significance. Prior to unification, examinations of the two countries focused on the GDR as a centrally planned socialist economic system and on the FRG as a market capitalist economic system. Although understanding these earlier arrangements is important from an historical perspective, contemporary interest centers on the political and economic reality of a new German economy, an economy formed through the unification of what were two very different economic systems. However, to understand the problems of unification, it is necessary to look at the arrangements that existed before it took place.[86]

In this section, we examine three important themes. We offer a brief analysis of the systemic arrangements of the former GDR. We discuss the state of the two economies on the eve of unification. And we examine the process of unification and the problems of integrating the former GDR into the market economic system of the FRG.

The GDR as a Planned Socialist Economic System   The economies of the FRG and the GDR prior to unification presented economists and others with an interesting case study for the analysis of differences between capitalism and socialism. This was especially fruitful because the two countries were similar in many dimensions *except* the economic system and economic policies. Though not all other things were equal, the *ceteris paribus* assumption was viewed justified for a variety of reasons.

1. Although there were notable differences in population dynamics in the period following World War II, the two economies could be viewed as having had, at the end of the war, a very similar stock of human capital and an essentially homogeneous population.

2. A second, closely related, issue was the presence of shared traditions, culture, and tastes. These characteristics' being common to both the FRG and the GDR argues in support of treating their nonsystem characteristics (the environmental factors) as similar on the eve of the introduction of a very different economic system into the GDR.
3. At the outbreak of World War II, Germany was among the most modern industrial economies. The FRG and the GDR were roughly equivalent in per capita income and per capita industrial output. Moreover, the structures of the capital stocks was similar, and foreign trade could be characterized, in both cases, as typical of a more advanced economy.

If there were similarities that facilitate comparison of the former Germanys, there were also differences, some of which must have affected economic outcomes in the postwar period.

1. The GDR was a much smaller economy (the population of the GDR was roughly 25 percent that of the FRG) at the end of the war. And this proportion was to decline further, in part because of different population policies in the GDR and in part because of the "republic flight" (the ongoing loss of population from the GDR to the FRG between 1945 and 1961, which varied annually from 144,000 to 365,000).
2. It has generally been argued that the resource base of the GDR was inferior to that of the FRG. Nevertheless, lignite coal was relatively abundant for fuel and for generation of electricity. Moreover, one could argue that with a smaller population, the GDR had a more favorable ratio of population to land.
3. The war and its aftermath treated the GDR and the FRG differently. It has been estimated that 50 percent of the GDR's industrial capacity had been destroyed by the end of the war, compared to 25 percent of the FRG's. And whereas the GDR was making reparation payments in the early postwar period, the FRG benefited from assistance under the Marshall Plan. (At the same time, the FRG eventually paid out some 33 billion marks in Wiedergutmaching payments, a sum double the amount of Marshall Plan aid.)

Thus both similarities and differences existed in nonsystem characteristics, but the economic systems themselves certainly were different in the postwar years. The Soviet model was introduced into the GDR after the war, and by the end of the 1940s, virtually all industry, banking, and transportation had been nationalized and were functioning under a system of central planning. The process of collectivization in agriculture began seriously in the early 1950s and was completed by the end of the decade. The only private ownership was to be found in some retail trade and in handicrafts.

The model of planning and management introduced into the GDR after the war was basically the same as the Soviet administrative command model, which we examine in detail in Chapter 12. The Communist party dictated priorities to a state planning commission, which, in conjunction with ministries, established binding plans to govern enterprise operations. As in the Soviet Union, the system of balances was used for planning.

In addition to the similarities in system arrangements between the Soviet Union and the GDR, there was also similarities in the reform of these systems. Beginning in the early 1960s, the GDR introduced the **New Economic System**, modifications to existing arrangements designed to maintain central planning but to decentralize some decision making to groups of state enterprises (formally Unions of State Enterprises or VVBs). As with early Soviet reform attempts, which we discuss in detail in Chapter 16, the objective was to improve lagging economic performance through limited devolution of planning authority, the latter to be coordinated through a system of semi-decentralized contracts among economic units. This system would, in effect, be a major component of the material balance system.

The New Economic System was apparently abandoned in the early 1970s. In large part, this was a result of the recentralization of decision making and the continued use of gross output targeting, which were typical of these systems. The drive for improved efficiency to sustain rapid economic growth was channeled, in the 1970s and 1980s, in a different direction. The thrust was the creation of new intermediate planning organizations known as combines (*Kombinat*) that differed from the earlier VVBs but were similar to those in the Soviet Union (*obedinenie*). The combines were formed to exploit economies of scale, to establish more effective supply relationships, and to provide better investment allocation. In effect, this system was designed to replace the three-level system (enterprise, intermediate authority, central authority) with a two-level system (combine, central authority). The combine would manage and coordinate its member enterprises. What powers the central authority was to have over the combine was a major and largely unresolved issue of this reform.

The economic system we have described closely resembled the Soviet administrative command model, and important policy positions were also very similar. The emphasis was on economic growth (especially increases in gross output) through high investment in industry. Moreover, policies in agriculture were similar to those in the Soviet Union, and the mechanisms and directions of foreign trade came to resemble those of the Soviet Union as the GDR was integrated into the COMECON system (discussed in Chapter 14). Incentive arrangements were typical of the planned socialist system: reduction of income differentials, reliance on public goods, and the moral suasion of the socialist model.

If the economic system of the GDR closely mirrored the Soviet administrative command model, so too did its economic outcomes. These outcomes are especially important because they bear on both the costs and the benefits of unification. What was the state of the economy of the GDR on the eve of unification, and how did this economy compare to that of the FRG?

The FRG and the GDR on the Eve of Unification   It is important to emphasize that the political changes of the late 1980s will undoubtedly permit — and even necessitate — significant reassessment of economic performance of the GDR. We must therefore interpret traditional views with some caution. In Table 10.2

we present a summary statistical picture of the FRG and the GDR on the eve of unification.

The FRG outperformed the GDR in growth, but not by large amounts and not in per capita terms. At the same time, and unlike other planned socialist economic systems, much of the increases in output in the GDR were attributable to intensive growth. After the 1960s, however, the GDR was unable to sustain its rate of economic growth, and most notably, a growing gap in living standards between the GDR and the FRG emerged. This gap played a part in promoting the various reform attempts we have described. Moreover, given that these two similar societies existed side by side, it was difficult for the GDR to tolerate a growing differential in living standards.

In terms of other criteria developed in Chapter 3, the performance record of the GDR was mixed. Although the GDR seems to have enjoyed greater stability and a more even distribution of income than the FRG in the 1970s and into the 1980s, performance problems and a worsening of the relative position of the GDR were seen as signs of trouble in that economy.

Unification and the Era of Transition   As we will see when we discuss the general transition process, political change generally precedes transition as socialist economic systems shift from plan to market. The transition is often slow and difficult; new institutions must be defined, developed, and put in place. In addition to systemic change, policy changes are critical both for maintaining stability during the transition and for encouraging economic growth.

In the German case, West German laws were transferred east by treaty, and in 1990, the Deutschmark replaced the East German Ostmark, prices were freed, and trading arrangements were relaxed. In addition, the *Treuhnadanstalt* (Federal Privatizing Trust) held all the shares of East German firms (which were converted into joint-stock companies) and became the major mechanism through which privatization would take place. Much of the transition process in the former GDR has necessarily focused on the issue of privatization.

The "Truehand" has been much more than simply a mechanism to hold the shares of the formerly state-owned firms in the GDR. The Truehand was set up to be responsible for assembling the talent necessary to value and to liquidate these firms. As has been the case elsewhere, valuation has been very difficult. The most attractive firms found immediate buyers, but less attractive firms were faced with either liquidation or the need for interim support — another function of the Truehand. There were cases where financial discipline simply could not be imposed. And revenue problems, combined with the fact that wages in the former GDR had been sustained at inappropriately high levels (by state policy), led to a surge in unemployment. Unemployment grew from roughly 1.6 percent in June of 1990 to almost 9 percent by February of 1991, a major cost to be borne by the new unified German economy.[87]

Although a number of firms in the GDR were attractive to potential buyers, the technological level of the GDR, once viewed as the leading economy in the

Table 10.2 The Federal Republic of Germany and the German Democratic Republic: Selected Social and Economic Indicators, 1988

	Federal Republic of Germany	German Democratic Republic
Area and population		
Area (*in 1,000 square kilometers*)	249	108
Population (*millions*)	61.4	16.7
(*in percent of population*)		
Of working age	67.0[a]	65.0
Pensioners	18.5[a]	16.0
Employment		
Total employed (*in millions*)	27.4	9.0
(*in percent of population*)	44.5	53.9
Female employment (*in percent of total employment*)	38.1[a]	48.6
Employment by sector (*in percent of total*)		
Agriculture and forestry	4.0	10.8
Mining, manufacturing, and construction	39.8	47.1
Other sectors	56.2	42.1
Household income, consumption, and saving		
Average monthly gross earnings (*DM/M*)	3,850	1,270
Household saving (*in percent of disposable income*)	12.8	7.1
Households with: (*in percent of total*)		
Automobiles	97	52
Color television	94	52
Telephone	98	7[b]
Production, investment, and prices		
(*Annual real growth rate, 1980–88*)		
GNP/NMP	1.7	4.2
Gross fixed investment	0.7	2.0
Of which: Machinery and equipment	2.4	5.0
Consumer prices (*annual percent rate of change, 1980–88*)	2.9	–
External trade in goods		
(*in percent of total exports*)		
Exports to state-trading countries	4.4	69.5
Imports from state-trading countries	4.7	68.7
Trade balance (*in percent of GNP/NMP*)	6.0	1.0
Of which: State-trading countries	0.2	1.0
Monetary accounts of households		
Household financial assets[c] (*billions DM/M*)	1,196.6	167.2
Velocity of money[d]	1.11	0.97

[a] 1987.
[b] 1985.
[c] Currency and bank deposits. Year-end for the FRG and year average for the GDR.
[d] Private disposable income divided by household financial assets.

Sources: Statistisches Bundesamt, *Statistisches Jahrbuch der Bundesrepublik Deutschland, 1989*; Staatliche Zentralverwaltung für Statistik der DDR, *Statistisches Jahrbuch der DDR, 1989*; and Deutsche Bundesbank.

COMECON bloc, has turned out to be very low, necessitating fundamental change in the industrial base. Such changes will focus on several key issues.

1. To the extent that the privatization process includes the issue of *claims* derived, for example, from past confiscation of property, the privatization process is slower and substantially more complex. As we shall see later, this has been a problem in almost all cases of socialist transition, though different countries have responded to the problem in different ways.
2. If productivity levels in industry are to reach or even approach world-class levels, major new investments will be necessary. But in addition to investment per se, the appropriate management skills will be required to modernize outmoded industrial capacity. Indeed, as we have emphasized, the technological state of industry in the former GDR (and in other East European countries) has generally proved to be far lower than anticipated. By the middle of 1991, a number of firms had in fact been liquidated.
3. As in all cases of socialist transition, the definition of the market that is to prevail after the transition is quite unclear. The issue of industrial concentration is important. In the former GDR, there was substantial concentration in the existing industrial structure. Moreover, to the extent that it is the larger firms that are attractive and are bought by large Western firms, the level of industrial concentration is maintained if not actually increased. Such has indeed been the case, the major Western purchasers being companies such as Volkswagen, Daimler-Benz, and IBM Germany.
4. The social costs of privatization have risen and are bound to continue to rise. In addition to the need for direct financial support of the transition, the issues of unemployment, retraining, inflation, and the like will make defining a new social contract difficult. These immediate problems demand attention before other, long-term problems of infrastructure and, for example, housing.

The German Economy in the 1990s   German unification will succeed, though the length of the economic transition, the costs involved, and the contours of the future German economy remain to be determined. For obvious reasons, most observers of the socialist transition process view the German case as unique. The prospect of a former socialist neighbor integrating with a powerful economy such as the FRG has always led observers to suggest that the unification process occurring between the FRG and former GDR would be much simpler than that occurring in other cases, for example the integration of Hungary and Poland into the world economy.

At the same time, it is interesting that in spite of the ability of the FRG to transfer laws, institutional mechanisms, talent, and the like directly to the former GDR, many of the difficult problems associated with privatization elsewhere have arisen here as well. These problems, along with fundamental changes in the contours of trading arrangements in Europe (scheduled for 1992), will be a major challenge to the German economy. Privatization will be slow and costly, despite the unique setting in which it is taking place in Germany.

JAPAN: GROWTH THROUGH THE MARKET

Japan is a capitalist economy with a record of exceptional economic perform-ance. Japan's postwar rate of economic growth is the highest among the major industrialized countries. For the admirer of high rates of economic growth, thought to be a hallmark of the early years of planned socialist systems, Japan is cited as a capitalist alternative to the Soviet model for the developing nations. However, in Japan as in other countries, growth rates have slowed. In the 1980s attention focused on how, and how well, the Japanese economy can adjust to external shocks from the world economy.

Our discussion of Japan stresses three areas: the historical traditions and special circumstances of Japan, its economic performance, and various observers' explanations of Japan's impressive growth record.

Background of the Japanese Economy

Japan is a small country with adequate labor but generally limited supplies of natural resources and land. Prior to the Meiji restoration, which began in 1868, Japan was "a fossilized and closed society."[88] Therefore, interest in Japanese economic performance centers on the period since 1868, though the roots of modern development may be found in the Tokugawa period prior to the Meiji restoration.[89]

Japan, like Great Britain, is an island economy. With a population of approximately 123 million, 75 percent of whom live in urban areas, and a land area slightly smaller than that of the state of California, Japan is densely populated. Japan is a developed economy dominated by the service sector, the industrial sector, and a small agricultural sector.

Japan has a long, varied, and controversial history. Since its defeat in World War II, Japan has been governed under a democratic political system established by the Allied occupation forces. The Japanese parliament (Diet) is elected by the people; it chooses the prime minister, who is the leader of the country.

The Japanese have achieved rapid growth in a country whose natural resource base is minimal. Japan is not well endowed with minerals or fertile agricultural land. Thus Japanese performance must be explained by its economic system, its organizational arrangements, and the people who operate within this system.[90] Between the late 1860s and the early 1900s, Japan developed policy measures for economic growth based on special features of the Japanese system.

First of all, there was (and still is) among the Japanese population a unity of purpose fostered by the state and facilitated by Japanese cultural traditions and history. There are a discipline and devotion to work on the part of the laborers and a degree of paternalism on the part of employers seldom seen in other countries. Although it is difficult to pinpoint the sources of this unity, one observer has suggested that a long period of development of the labor market, based on the discipline of the home production process, and the generation of information for an efficient market combined to create an effi-cient and disciplined worker.[91]

Second, the state has performed important functions. The figures in Table 10.1 (with the possible exception of those on state ownership) suggest a rather modest role for the state in the Japanese economy. Such statistics may understate the role of the state in postwar Japan. For example, in the crucial area of capital formation, the government has played a key role, not only in promoting savings and investment, but also in encouraging the influx of foreign capital, which was important in the early years of Japanese development.

Although the rate of capital formation in postwar Japan has been much higher than in other capitalist economies, the *direct* state role has been smaller than in other nations. Government purchases have also been smaller proportionally than in any of these countries. The state's role, then, has been to stimulate *private* investment through strong incentives such as low tax rates, proinvestment state financial policy, and the limited provision of social services.

The role of the Japanese state as a purchaser was important in earlier times, especially in its capacity as an entrepreneur — a role that carries over to present-day Japan. This state function has been important not only in getting industry started but also in focusing investment in growth sectors, at the best scale of operation, and utilizing the best available technology.

Third, historical experience is crucial to understanding modern economic growth in Japan. During the Meiji restoration, the Japanese economy was opened up to Western technology. Enrollment in formal educational programs increased rapidly, as did participation in the labor force, and a "dual economy" developed. The dual economy consisted of a large, increasingly modern industrial sector requiring skilled labor, existing alongside relatively primitive industrial operations where labor with minimal skills was utilized.

Agricultural development accelerated during this period, and technological progress and the expansion of conventional inputs (labor and fertilizer) were important to creating an agricultural surplus. Agriculture's role in Japanese development — in particular, the use of high taxation to extract the surplus — remains a matter of controversy.[92]

Fourth, military activity has been an important factor. The rapid pace of development after the 1860s through World War I was fostered in part by military spending. Thereafter, at least until 1946, war was a dominant theme. World War II warped the structure of production and led to an economy governed by controls and, later, manipulated by the American occupation forces. American occupation policies were primary land reform (large holdings were broken up), deconcentration of industrial ownership, the introduction of trade unionism, and an end to the military commitment.[93] All had important implications for Japan's development in the postwar period. No simple set of features can explain Japanese growth.

Japanese Economic Growth

Japanese economic growth is compared to that of other countries in Chapter 15. However, because rapid growth is a salient feature of the Japanese case, we shall consider its underlying features here.

Although the Japanese economy has been growing rapidly for a long time, the interesting facet of this record, as Kazushi Ohkawa and Henry Rosovsky emphasize, is the accelerating trend of economic growth at a particularly high level. The rate of growth of output of the Japanese economy in the postwar years has been exceptionally high by international standards, averaging close to 10 percent annually. This rate meets or exceeds even those of such rapidly growing countries as Germany and the Soviet Union. Growth rates through the 1980s have been much slower, though they are certainly respectable by international standards.

The Japanese economy is a capitalist market economy, in which national economic planning has played only a marginal role. One cannot look to extra-market mechanisms, such as planning, to explain Japanese growth. What, then, has led to this impressive economic performance? It is very difficult to isolate the key features that have influenced any economic system's performance. However, the path-breaking work of Ohkawa and Rosovsky identifies two general influences: those that are narrowly economic and those of a broader nature.[94] Let us examine each in turn.

The economic explanations for postwar (and earlier) Japanese economic development, according to Ohkawa and Rosovsky, were a technology gap, a high rate of capital formation, and the availability of appropriate labor supplies. Being a closed economy, Japan had a technology gap and thus could benefit in a major way from the absorption of Western technology. Technology assimilation was facilitated by sharp increases in the size of the capital stock (through imports of capital, a high propensity to save, and the state's promotion of capital formation) and by elastic supplies of labor. Furthermore, the dual labor market permitted the shift of labor from the primitive to the modern sector at a rate dictated by the needs of the advanced sector, and wage increases lagged behind advances in productivity.[95]

At the same time, the Japanese economy was able to promote a growing role in foreign markets. During the early stages of development, while modern industry was growing, exports were derived primarily from traditional industries such as textiles. As modern technology was assimilated, Japanese exports shifted away from the traditional products toward the high-technology products that Japan, owing to its productive but relatively inexpensive labor, could produce with comparative advantage. In part, industrial development at home was enhanced by the state's policy of starting import-competing industries. These factors, combined with reparations from China and an aggressive external posture, made the foreign sector an important contributor to Japan's growth.

The factors emphasized by Ohkawa and Rosovsky are familiar — technology, capital creation, development of the labor force. The difference may be Japan's ability to assemble these features in a harmonious way. Ohkawa and Rosovsky place great emphasis on the noneconomic or special features of the Japanese nation. What are the important noneconomic features of the Japanese development experience?

First, we must again emphasize the important and multidimensional role of the state. The state gave impetus and direction to the drive for economic growth. The state intervened selectively and has been an important catalyst for ensuring not only a high rate of investment but also its proper distribution. For example, beyond the approval of general economic policies by the Diet, government is also more directly involved in business. Government offices (genkyoku) supervise individual industries, and ministries supervise sectors of the economy. Also, there are ministries (such as the Ministry of Finance) the interests of which cross specific industrial borders. Finally, the government is directly involved in a wide range of economic matters: the encouragement of designated industrial projects through low-interest loans from the Japan Development Bank, regulation of antitrust matters by the Fair Trade Commission, and so on.[96]

The role of the state in the Japanese economy is difficult to classify. It remains one of the intriguing aspects of the Japanese economic system. In terms of readily quantifiable indicators of state economic activity such as revenue and expenditure, the role of the state is small relative to most other industrialized capitalist systems. At the same time, the state has been very important as a facilitator of the market process, as the creator of a harmonious business environment, and as an entrepreneur and overseer of the development process.

Second, what Ohkawa and Rosovsky describe as the "human element" has been a very important factor in the Japanese story. In Japan, labor has a peculiar and growth-conducive attitude toward industry — the "permanent employment" system and the submissive attitude of labor toward the industrial establishment.[97] In addition, rising family incomes have produced unusually high levels of savings, most appropriate for rapid growth but hard to explain on other than traditional and cultural grounds.

Prior to World War II, the government suppressed the growth of the trade union movement, although it did grow to some degree along with the development of government regulations concerning the labor market. Having gained recognition in the postwar period, trade unions have a voice in wages, supplemental benefits, and working conditions. They are constrained, however, in that they are enterprise unions, enrolling long-term employees. Their primary strength is in the largest industrial enterprises.[98]

Third, one could cite a number of other factors — some narrowly economic, others less so — that have been important: favorable population growth and hence labor supplies, the end to military expenditure, and the limiting of low-growth sectors (such as housing).

Industrial Organization

An economy's industrial organization can affect its performance, and most capitalist theories associate competition with "good" economic performance. The Japanese economy presents a test case, for it appears to have combined an industrial structure dominated by giant vertical and horizontal trusts with rapid economic growth.

Prior to World War II, Japanese industry was dominated by giant holding companies called *zaibatsu*, which represented a complex maze of interlocking directorships, banking relationships, and family ties.[99] At the end of the war, this concentration of ownership had proceeded to the point where fewer than four thousand zaibatsu-connected families owned almost 50 percent of total outstanding shares. The American occupation forces sought to eliminate zaibatsu dominance by outlawing holding companies, breaking up monopolies, and making mutual shareholdings among zaibatsu firms illegal.

In the postwar era, shareholding in industry and banking has become more evenly distributed among the population. New industrial groupings called *kieretsu* have replaced the old zaibatsu organizations. Kieretsu can be either vertical or horizontal, either a large firm in charge of smaller ("children") firms or a horizontal association of interest groups. These new groups are less powerful than the old zaibatsu, and it is possible for a firm within a grouping to place its own interests above those of the group, an action inconceivable before the war.

One enduring feature of the large Japanese company is its emphasis on industrial paternalism. Established employees of large companies are, in effect, guaranteed lifetime employment. They are taught to think of the company as their family, and they believe that if they work hard for the company, the company will take care of them. John M. Montias singled out this characteristic of the Japanese enterprise for study and found that this "permanent employment" constraint on Japanese management is likely to alter resource allocation patterns, at least in theory.[100]

Clearly, arrangements for the allocation of labor in the Japanese economy differ from those familiar to Western students. Indeed, the Japanese economy has been characterized as a **share economy**, based on a framework suggested by Martin Weitzman.[101] The evidence for this characterization — the bonus system in Japan — is not strong, though differences in the allocation system make Japanese labor markets of great interest to the comparative analyst.[102]

The concepts of industrial paternalism and lifetime employment have received a great deal of attention, in large part because the system seems so different from other capitalist countries. How can labor be allocated in a rapidly changing environment if it is not mobile?

The answer to this question lies largely in the difference between appearance and substance. In fact, a number of forces at work in the Japanese economy limit the impact of guaranteed employment.[103] First, not all members of the Japanese labor force are covered by guaranteed employment. One study suggests that roughly 30 percent of the industrial labor force is covered by some form of guaranteed employment.[104] Second, Japanese firms have ways to create flexibility in employment. For example, a temporary labor force can be utilized, and the payment system, where bonuses can be important, serves as an inducement for employees to work hard. Third, Japanese firms can rely on subcontracting for industrial parts, thus lessening the need to hire the labor force necessary to produce these parts on a sustained basis. Finally, guaranteed employment does not mean that inefficient firms are in some way maintained. On the contrary, both the pressures of the market and the role played by government agencies encourage the productive sectors and discourage the unproductive sectors. All these factors substantially mitigate what would otherwise appear to be a starkly different system of labor–management relations.

Japanese Planning

Economic planning has not been an important element in the Japanese economy. Japan has had a planning agency since the late 1940s and has assembled numerous plans. Japanese plans have been highly pragmatic, with frequently shifting goals. They have been highly aggregative and are based on a simple extension of the national accounts. The plan targets (in addition to being highly aggregative) have been projected only to terminal years of the five-year planning period, making them of minimal value to private firms even when those firms want to be integrated into the plan projections.

One measure of the value of a plan is how closely it is fulfilled. Japanese economic performance has typically been better than that called for by the plan. Plan targets have typically been exceeded, sometimes by very large amounts. This sort of inaccuracy renders the plan targets of little use for purposes of coordination and leads to skepticism about the plan and the necessity for continued corrections by individual firms.

Although the discipline of Japanese firms and their management would make them look at and consider the plan, the real force of intervention in the life of the economy has been the state, not the planning agency.[105] Although we have emphasized this fact, it is worth noting again that discussion of intervention in the Japanese economy focuses not on the Economic Planning Agency but on the Ministry of International Trade and Industry, where the real power lies. In this sense, the state, its agencies, and its budget are the focus of attention. Thus whether we describe the mechanisms of the Japanese economy as planning or as something less, the state arguably plays an important role in directing the path of Japanese economic growth and development.

Japan: Industrial Policy?

Thus far we have traced the development of the Japanese economy by focusing on features that are thought to have contributed to rapid economic growth. It has been difficult, if not impossible, to render any substantive judgment on the role of government in the Japanese economy. Let us examine this question further.

First, Japanese social structure differs markedly from that in the United States. Above all, Japan is a country dominated by both vertical and horizontal organization, where group allegiance, formal and informal, is very important. Japanese society might be likened to a family, where the role of each member contrasts markedly with the sort of individualism familiar to us in the United States.

Second, government does play an important role in the Japanese economy, yet its role is difficult to measure.[106] The Japanese ministerial structure has a substantial impact on the economy, not only through direct participation in key aspects of economic life, but also through its indirect influence. For example, the Ministry of Finance, along with the Bank of Japan, is responsible for the traditional functions of monetary control. In the outside world, however, it is the Ministry of International Trade and Industry (MITI) that receives most attention.[107]

MITI has an impressive formal role, being responsible for international trade, domestic production, and domestic industrial structure. Whether formal or informal, though, MITI is frequently viewed as the purveyor of an "industrial policy" geared to promoting rapid economic growth.[108] MITI is responsible for guiding and influencing economic decisions by promoting key sectors of the economy and carefully phasing out other, low-productivity sectors. MITI uses public funds for research and development and provides assistance for organizational change, such as mergers. Although MITI is an important vehicle for transmitting information in the Japanese economy, few describe this function as planning.

Beyond the ministerial system, there is considerable government involvement in the economy. This activity ranges from the traditional provision of "public goods" to activities in less traditional areas. For example, special financial institutions provide supplementary services to the private industrial sector.

Traditional measures of government involvement in an economic system probably don't capture the essence of the Japanese system. In the absence of a major formal role for government and planning, the government is nevertheless able to influence both short- and long-term decision making. Rather than formal and powerful involvement in a few traditional and noticeable areas, the government exerts its influence through a myriad of arrangements that guide economic growth. Enthusiasts of an industrial policy cite the Japanese experience.

During the 1970s, American admiration for the Japanese economic system grew. In a time of general economic turmoil, the Japanese were perceived to have found the keys to sustained economic growth. Many writers attempted to discover the precise identity of the growth forces — whether industrial policy, a special role for the government, the managerial system, the labor–management arrangements, or the nature of Japanese society and the Japanese work force. This admiration has been limited only by our apparent inability to transplant these growth forces and by continuing friction in Japanese–American trade relations.

The 1970s, however, were not a tranquil decade for the Japanese economy. The early 1970s brought Japan two major shocks. The first was the move by the Nixon administration to end the long-fixed exchange rate between the American dollar and the Japanese yen and move toward a flexible exchange rate.[109] The second event was the initial impact of the energy crisis in 1973. The average annual rate of growth of real GNP declined from above 10 percent in the late 1960s to generally lower rates in the mid 1970s. The average annual rate of inflation reached almost 25 percent in 1974. Other performance indicators showed similar trends. Productivity (output per man-hour) in manufacturing declined, and manufacturing unit costs increased dramatically.

The late 1970s brought on a second, less severe energy crisis and (possibly more important) a sharply increasing positive balance on the current account. Once again, the problem of balancing Japanese–American trade became a major issue.

Nevertheless, the condition of the Japanese economy was generally positive: Although the rate of economic growth declined in the 1980s, performance was still impressive. Between 1965 and 1980, gross domestic product grew at an average annual rate of 6.3 percent, and from 1980 to 1987, 3.7 percent. For the same periods, the average annual rate of inflation declined from 7.5 to 1.5 percent.[110] Policies of restraint, intended to bring inflation under control and to restore economic growth and balance-of-payments equilibrium, were largely successful. The economic performance of the Japanese economy remained strong through the end of the 1980s.

For the student of comparative economic systems, interest in the Japanese economic system and its economic policies has shifted. Through the 1960s and into the 1970s, interest centered on the impressive growth of the Japanese economy and its relationship to Japanese institutions and policies. Through the 1970s and 1980s, however, students tried instead to understand how the Japanese economy had been able to handle the shock of oil price increases while maintaining economic growth with low rates of inflation and unemployment.[111] Therefore, current discussion of the Japanese economy focuses on adjustment and, in particular, on adjustment to the new international economic conditions of the late 1980s and 1990s.

SWEDEN: THE WELFARE STATE IN A
MARKET CAPITALIST SETTING

The Swedish economic system and its performance are of interest to many for a single but vitally important reason. Sweden is viewed as a system that has been able, over an extended period of time, to sustain economic progress through the efficiency of the market while at the same time implementing an egalitarian distribution of income more typical of a welfare state. Although the decade of the 1970s was a challenge to Sweden, nevertheless the Swedish system is admired by many and has become a centerpiece of attention as a "middle way" to economic reform and change. This focus remains important, though in recent years, some have questioned the long-term viability of Swedish arrangements.

As with other system variants, it is useful to examine the nature of economic outcomes in the Swedish case and the forces influencing these outcomes, specifically the environmental setting, the systemic or organizational arrangements of the Swedish economy, and Swedish economic policies.[112]

Sweden: The Setting

Sweden is a relatively small but highly industrialized country. It has a total area of roughly 450,000 square kilometers (somewhat larger than the state of California), and it had a population of just over 8.5 million in 1990. As of 1988, Sweden had a per capita gross national product of almost $20,000 measured in U.S. dollars, the third highest in the world (behind Switzerland and Japan).[113] The bulk of this income is derived from industry and services; agriculture plays a very small role.

Since World War II, Sweden has experienced a long period of economic progress based on the development of its resources (timber, hydroelectric energy, and iron ore) with major reliance on a market economy and participation in foreign trade. During the 1960s, the growth of real gross domestic product in Sweden was over 4 percent annually. Although this rate was cut in half in the decade to follow, Sweden nevertheless sustained reasonable real growth rates of over 2 percent annually in the 1980s. Foreign trade is of vital importance to Sweden. In recent years, foreign trade turnover (exports plus imports) has accounted for more than 70 percent of gross national product, a very high proportion by international standards. As we examine the Swedish record and the difficulties Sweden had in coping with the decade of the 1970s, these facts will be of major importance.

Sweden is the prototype of a developed industrial society that has a significant involvement in foreign trade and a high standard of living based on an educated labor force functioning largely in an urban, industrial setting. It is a system, however, that has combined market efficiency with an egalitarian distribution of income in a democratic political setting. These arrangements are of major interest to comparative economists.

Sweden: The Welfare State?

Thus far we have emphasized that the Swedish economy has achieved a high level of output based on a good growth record. This type of economic performance facilitated the growth of consumption. However, although productivity growth was substantial in the 1960s, the decade of the 1970s brought this rapid growth in productivity to an end and presented a challenge to be faced in the 1980s. This challenge was serious: A system with declining economic performance simply could not support the pace at which the standard of living had been growing. Moreover, many began to question whether Sweden had really achieved compatibility between efficiency and equity.

Although the role of the state in influencing distribution can be measured in a variety of ways, a few basic numbers will serve to illustrate the Swedish case. The Swedish economy is predominantly a private enterprise economy in production, but a very different picture emerges when we examine the distribution of the product. For example, in the late 1980s fully 26 percent of aggregate demand was that of government, compared to 20 percent in the United States and 9 percent in Japan. For the same year, total government expenditure in Sweden accounted for 40.8 percent of gross national product; the comparable figure for the United States was 22.9 percent.[114]

Who receives the benefits of Swedish government spending? Not surprisingly, housing, amenities, social security, and welfare accounted for fully 54.2 percent of government spending in 1988 — more than 20 percentage points greater than the proportion allotted to the equivalent sort of spending in the United States. Education also commands a much greater share of government spending in Sweden than in the United States, though of course the Swedish share of defense spending is much lower. Surprisingly, health accounted for a modest 1.1 percent of central government spending in 1988, compared to 12.5 percent in the United States.

As one might expect, major government programs in Sweden are financed by major taxes. In 1988, total central government revenue in Sweden accounted for 42.9 percent of gross national product; the comparable figure for the United States was 19.7 percent, and for the United Kingdom 36.4 percent. In addition to this much larger role for the state in Sweden, the sources of government revenue also differ significantly. In 1988, taxes on income, profits, and capital gains accounted for only 17.8 percent of Swedish central government revenue; the comparable figure for the United States was a whopping 51.5 percent. Social security contributions claim a high and similar share in both countries, but Sweden relies heavily on taxes on goods and services. This category accounts for 29.0 percent of central government revenue in Sweden, compared to a paltry 3.6 percent in the United States.

Possibly the ultimate test of state policies designed to redistribute income is examination of actual distribution outcomes. Unfortunately, many problems plague the measurement of income distribution, and estimates must be interpreted with some skepticism. However, the impact of the welfare state does show up in the Swedish case. For example, on the basis of household income for the mid-1980s, the lowest-earning 20 percent of households in Sweden received 8 percent of all household income, whereas the top-earning 20 percent of households received 26.9 percent of income. Comparable figures for the United States are 4.7 and 41.9 percent, respectively.[115]

Sweden: The Economic System

So far we have characterized the Swedish economy as a market economy based largely on private ownership but wherein the state plays a major role as an agent of income redistribution. The nature of the Swedish economic system is more complex and deserves additional attention.

1. From an environmental perspective, the nature of Sweden dictates to a large measure the sorts of outcomes that one expects to observe. For example, it

is obvious that Sweden, as a small country that needs to import fossil fuels, will be a major player in world markets and will be influenced by those markets in turn. Moreover, with a highly educated labor force, one would expect a production structure and economic policies appropriate to the available factor mix.

2. The essence of the Swedish model is the setting of social democracy, a system where, as one observer put it, a complementary rather than a competitive relationship exists between the competitive and the cooperative aspects of social existence.[116] Thus in terms of goals and the means through which goals will be achieved, the views of the population are articulated through participation in a variety of groups such as unions, clubs, and the like.

3. Within the framework of social democracy, important market information is shared in such a way that the process is viewed as contributing to social gain for most if not all of the population. Thus in the sphere of labor allocation, the Swedish economy is viewed as having a very active labor market in which labor mobility is critical to the effective allocation of labor. At the same time, the existence of industry-wide collective agreements preserves a measure of control over wage increases that is designed to promote both economic growth and stability.

4. Employees can participate in enterprise management, at least on an advisory basis, through worker councils. In addition, workers can participate in ownership through employee investment funds — a mechanism to, in effect, convert profits into employee ownership. Employee ownership is controversial, but its basic thrust is to create harmony between the interests of worker and enterprise.

5. The Swedish state is an active participant in the economy through the use of traditional tools of monetary and fiscal policy, which is especially important in an open economy. As we shall see, the state's role in this sphere has been controversial.

6. Sweden maintains an egalitarian distribution of income largely through transfers of various types, providing generous benefits for retirement, medical care, education, and the like. These programs, and Sweden's continuing commitment to full employment, create an environment of substantial economic security.

Performance: The Health of the Swedish Model

A key theme in this book has been how various systems responded to the economic challenges of the 1970s and early 1980s — and in particular to the energy crisis of the earlier decade. We have emphasized that most systems experienced difficulty during these troubled times.

The Swedish economy was no exception. Indeed, the problems of the 1970s and 1980s led many to ask whether the Swedish model had outlived its usefulness. Simply put, the energy shocks of the 1970s increased domestic costs, which, along with poor productivity performance, led to an erosion of the

Swedish position in external markets. But the government followed a policy of expanding the deficit, which in turn stimulated inflation. Although it was more complex than this simple description suggests, the situation appeared to mainly a case where planners failed to find the appropriate policy mix, rather than evidence of any fundamental problems in the Swedish system. Some, however, argued that more basic changes were at work.

In a major survey of the Swedish model published in 1985, Erik Lundberg noted that in addition to failures of stabilization policies, support for the social democrats became more fragmented, and policy objectives were contradictory.[117] A theme noted by Lundberg and other observers was the conflict between existing wage-setting arrangements and the continued drive for an egalitarian distribution of income — a conflict that squeezed profits and limited the attractiveness of investment, while at the same time generating low levels of unemployment in largely artificial and noncompetitive ways. Finally, Lundberg emphasized the changing nature of the international economy, a setting where Sweden faced increasingly limited policy options and a greater need to conform to policies of other major countries. In essence, the problems were more than simply policy mistakes incorporating basic elements of the Swedish system. Indeed, these issues are of great moment in the 1990s, as Sweden takes steps to join the European Community.

In a major study of the Swedish economy conducted by the Brookings Institution and published in 1987, the authors concluded that there is "no evidence that Sweden cannot sustain domestic growth and international competitiveness if the economy is managed well."[118]

Sweden: A Model for Socialist Systems?

It is not difficult to understand why the Swedish arrangement might be viewed as an attractive model for those systems in transition toward the market. This model seems to combine the efficiency of the market mechanism with a distribution of rewards that is appealing to socialists. However, as attractive as some of the elements of the Swedish model may be, implementing it in formerly planned socialist systems would be fraught with complications.

First, however we might judge the success of the contemporary Swedish model, we must remember that it functions in an economy that is operating at a sharply higher level of economic development than is typical of the formerly socialist systems. The problems facing the socialist systems are different from those facing the Swedish model in the 1990s.

Second, the debate over the long-term viability of the Swedish model has not been resolved. Swedish economic performance in the latter part of the 1980s has been modest: increases in per capita product of less than 2 percent and inflation above 7 percent. Moreover, whether the market mechanism is compatible with large-scale redistribution or transfers remains a point of contention.[119] Declining popularity of the social democrats reflects growing discontent with Swedish economic outcomes.

Third, quite apart from the merits of the economic model, the Swedish environment in which this model has functioned is very different from that found in most other cases. The political and social arrangements in Sweden are widely viewed as fundamental to harmonious operation of the Swedish economy. It has proved difficult to sustain this environment in Sweden, let alone to consider transplanting it to another setting.

Finally, providing substantial social benefits necessitates high levels of taxation. In recent years, there has been growing resistance to such taxation, which may be the ultimate test of tolerance, even under Swedish political and social arrangements, if these arrangements are sustained through the 1990s.

SUMMARY:
VARIANTS OF CAPITALISM: MATURE ECONOMIES

This chapter examines capitalist systems that were selected because their differing systemic arrangements are of interest to the comparative economist. There are significant variations in the contemporary economic performance of these systems, but it is important to emphasize one underlying fact. For most systems, the 1950s and 1960s were relatively tranquil decades, and thus they were years in which basic system characteristics could be studied. On the other hand, the 1970s and 1980s have been anything but tranquil, as energy shocks and recession have had worldwide repercussions. In these decades, most systems have had to develop a response to world market forces. These responses have differed from case to case, as have the outcomes. On balance, strength seems to have prevailed, especially for countries such as Germany, Sweden, France, and (notably) the newly industrialized countries of Asia, which we discuss in Chapter 11. All seem to have been able to sustain progress into the 1990s as new patterns of world trade emerged.

1. France used indicative planning in the 1950s and 1960s to promote economic growth. French indicative planning issues nonbinding plans based on a social consensus. Indirect means are used to promote plan fulfillment. Recent years have seen a move away from indicative planning and toward traditional monetary and fiscal policy, though indicative planning mechanisms remain of interest to economists.
2. Traditionally the economic role of government has been important in Great Britain, not so much because of its planning activities, but rather through the budgetary process and public ownership. Until recently, Britain was viewed as a case of economic stagnation, but the Conservative government of Margaret Thatcher significantly improved the nation's economic performance in the past decade. The Thatcher approach was based on the use of monetary policy, stimulation of incentives and competitive markets, and privatization. Debate over this record centers first on its costs, such as those that unemployment entails. Second, critics question the economy's potential

61. Poor performance after 1973 is emphasized in Caves and Krause, *Britain's Economic Performance*.

62. Reddaway, "Problems and Prospects for the U.K. Economy," table 1.

63. Computed from Caves and Krause, *Britain's Economic Performance*, table 2, p. 3.

64. Pollard, *The Wasting of the British Economy*, table 3.3, p. 53.

65. Ibid., table 1.2, p. 12.

66. Reddaway, "Problems and Prospects for the U.K. Economy," p. 225.

67. Caves and Krause, *Britain's Economic Performance*, p. 19.

68. For interesting background, see Bernard N. Nossiter, *Britain — A Future That Works* (Boston: Houghton Mifflin, 1978).

69. Useful sources include David S. Bell, ed., *The Conservative Government, 1979-84: An Interim Report* (London: Croom Helm, 1985); Paul Hare, *Planning the British Economy* (London: Macmillan, 1985); Grahame Thompson, *The Conservatives' Economic Policy* (London: Croom Helm, 1986); Alan Walters, *Britain's Economic Renaissance* (New York: Oxford University Press, 1986); and "Planning in Britain," *Journal of Comparative Economics* 19, 3 (1985).

70. Alan Walters, *Britain's Economic Renaissance*, pp. 4-5.

71. For a critical view, see David S. Bell, *The Conservative Government*.

72. World Bank, *World Development Report 1987* (New York: Oxford University Press, 1987), p. 203.

73. Ibid., p. 205.

74. Grahame Thompson, *The Conservatives' Economic Policy*, Ch. 7.

75. David S. Bell, *The Conservative Government*, Ch. 3.

76. World Bank, *World Development Report 1987*, p. 223.

Germany

77. Our discussion is based on the following sources: Heinz Lampert, *Volkswirtschaftliche Institutionen* (Munich: Verlag Franz Vahlen, 1980); G. Gutman, W. Klein, S. Paraskewopolous, and H. Winter, *Die Wirtschafts-Verfassung der Bundesrepublik Deutschland*, 2nd ed. (Stuttgart: Fischer, 1979); Hannelore Hamel, ed., *Bundesrepublik Deutschland-DDR, Die Wirtschaftssysteme*, 4th ed. (Munich: C. H. Beck, 1983); and Gerhard Brinkman, *Okonomik der Arbeit*, Vol. I (Stuttgart: Ernst Klett Verlag, 1981).

78. This label is credited to A. Muller-Armack, "Soziale Marktwirtschaft," in *Handwörterbuch der Sozialwissenschaften*, Band IX (Stuttgart: Fischer, 1956), p. 390.

79. H. Jorg Thieme, *Soziale Marktwirtschaft: Konzeption und wirtschaftspolitische Gestaltung in der BRD* (Hanover: Berenberg, 1973), pp. 12-28; and Wolfram Engels, *Soziale Martwirtschaft: Verschmähte Zukunft* (Stuttgart: Seewald, 1973), pp. 40-45.

80. L. Erhard and A. Muller-Armack, *Soziale Marktwirtschaft* (Frankfurt am Main: Ullstein, 1972).

81. See Gutman, et al., *Wirtschaftsverfassung*, Ch. 8.

82. Thieme, *Soziale Marktwirtschaft*, pp. 83-87.

83. Lampert, *Institutionen*, pp. 31-49.

84. Martin Schnitzer and James Nordyke, *Comparative Economic Systems*, 2nd ed. (Cincinnati, Ohio: Southwestern, 1977), p. 328.

85. J. H. Kaiser, "Public Enterprise in Germany," in W. G. Friedman and J. F. Garner, *Government Enterprise: A Comparative Study* (New York: Columbia University Press, 1970).

86. For a discussion of the GDR and comparisons to the FRG, see Paul R. Gregory and Gert Leptin, "Similar Societies Under Differing Economic Systems: The Case of the Two Germanys," *Soviet Studies* 29 (October 1977), 519-541.

87. For recent comparative data, see Paul R. Gregory and Robert C. Stuart, *Comparative Economic Systems*, 3rd ed. (Boston: Houghton Mifflin, 1989), Ch. 13. Unemployment data are from George A. Akerlof, Andrew K. Rose, and Janet L. Yellen, "East Germany in from the Cold: The Economic Aftermath of Currency Union," paper presented at the Conference of the Brookings Panel on Economic Activity, Washington, D.C., April 4, 1991, p. 92.

Japan

88. Angus Maddison, *Economic Growth in Japan and the USSR* (London: Allen and Unwin, 1969), Ch. 1.
89. For an excellent survey of the early years of Japanese economic development, see Kazushi Ohkawa and Henry Rosovsky, *Japanese Economic Growth* (Stanford, Calif.: Stanford University Press, 1973).
90. For an examination of the Japanese growth experience, see Lawrence Klein and Kazushi Ohkawa, eds., *Economic Growth: The Japanese Experience Since the Meiji Era* (Homewood, Ill.: Irwin, 1968); Japan Economic Research Center, *Economic Growth: The Japanese Experience Since the Meiji Era*, Vols. I and II (Tokyo: Japan Economic Research Center, 1973); and Hugh Patrick and Henry Rosovsky, eds., *Asia's New Giant: How the Japanese Economy Works* (Washington, D.C.: Brookings, 1976). For a discussion of Japanese economic planning, see Shuntaro Shishido, "Japanese Experience with Long-Term Economic Planning," and Tsunshiko Watanabe, "National Planning and Economic Growth in Japan," both in Bert G. Hickman, ed., *Quantitative Planning of Economic Policy* (Washington, D.C.: Brookings, 1965); and William Lockwood, ed., *The State and Economic Enterprise in Japan* (Princeton, N.J.: Princeton University Press, 1965). For an analysis of Japanese labor markets, see Koji Taira, *Economic Development and the Labor Market in Japan* (New York: Columbia University Press, 1970). For a discussion of Japanese multinationals, see Ozawa Terutomo, *Multinationalism Japanese Style* (Princeton, N.J.: Princeton University Press, 1979); Yoshi Tsurumi, *The Japanese Are Coming: A Multinational Interaction of Firms and Politics* (Cambridge, Mass.: Ballinger, 1976); and M. Y. Yoshino, *Japan's Multinational Enterprises* (Cambridge, Mass.: Harvard University Press, 1976). For a general discussion of the Japanese economic system, especially its organizational features, see G. C. Allen, *The Japanese Economy* (London: Weidenfeld and Nicolson, 1981).
91. Taira, *Economic Development*.
92. For a brief discussion, see Allen, *The Japanese Economy*, Ch. 5; for background, see I. J. Nakamura, *Agricultural Production and the Economic Development of Japan, 1873–1922* (Princeton, N.J.: Princeton University Press, 1966).
93. Maddison, *Economic Growth in Japan and the USSR*, Ch. 4.
94. For a survey of Japanese economic growth, see Ohkawa and Rosovsky, *Japanese Economic Growth*, Ch. 2.
95. Various aspects of the Japanese labor market are discussed in Allen, *The Japanese Economy*, Ch. 9; and Taira, *Economic Development*.
96. For a useful survey of organizational features of the Japanese economic system, see Kanji Haitani, *The Japanese Economic System* (Lexington, Mass.: Heath, 1976).
97. Ohkawa and Rosovsky, *Japanese Economic Growth*, Ch. 5.
98. In addition to Taira, *Economic Development*, see Robert E. Cole, *Japanese Blue-Collar: The Changing Tradition* (Berkeley: University of California Press, 1971); for a summary, see Robert E. Cole, "Industrial Relations in Japan" in Morris Bornstein, ed., *Comparative Economic Systems, Models and Cases*, 3rd ed. (Homewood, Ill.: Irwin, 1974), pp. 93–116.
99. Kozo Yamamura, "Entrepreneurship, Ownership and Management in Japan," in M. M. Postan et al., *Cambridge Economic History of Europe*, Vol. VII, pt. 2 (Cambridge, England: Cambridge University Press, 1978), pp. 215–264. See also Eleanor M. Hadley, *Antitrust in Japan* (Princeton, N.J.: Princeton University Press, 1970); Richard E. Caves and Masu Uekusa, *Industrial Organizations in Japan* (Washington, D.C.: Brookings, 1976); and Haitani, *The Japanese Economic System*.
100. John M. Montias, *The Structure of Economic Systems* (New Haven: Yale University Press, 1976), pt. 5.
101. Martin Weitzman, *The Share Economy* (Cambridge, Mass.: Harvard University Press, 1984).
102. Merton J. Peck, "Is Japan Really a Share Economy?" *Journal of Comparative Economics* 10 (1986), 427–432.

103. For a recent discussion, see Gregory B. Christainsen and Jan S. Hagendorn, "Japanese Productivity: Adapting to Changing Comparative Advantage in the Face of Lifetime Employment Commitments," *Quarterly Review of Business and Economics*, 23 (Summer 1983), 23–39. For a discussion of the labor–management issue in a growth context, see Harry Oshima, "Reinterpreting Japan's Postwar Growth," *Economic Development and Cultural Change*, 31 (October 1982), 1–43.

104. Christainsen and Hagendorn, "Japanese Productivity," p. 30.

105. The classic work on the Japanese factory is J. G. Abegglen, *The Japanese Factory* (Glencoe, Ill.: Free Press, 1958).

106. Assessing the role of government in the importance of the "public" sector in the Japanese economy is difficult for definitional reasons. For a discussion, see Chalmers Johnson, *Japan's Public Policy Companies* (Washington, D.C.: American Enterprise Institute, 1978).

107. Much has been written about MITI. For basics, see Haitani, *The Japanese Economic System*; for more detail, see Chalmers Johnson, *MITI and the Japanese Miracle* (Stanford, Calif.: Stanford University Press, 1982); and Christainsen and Hagendorn, "Japanese Productivity."

108. For a more restrained view of the role of MITI in the 1970s, see Kozo Yamamura, "Success That Soured: Administrative Guidance and Cartels in Japan," in Kozo Yamamura, ed., *Policy and Trade Issues of the Japanese Economy* (Seattle: University of Washington Press, 1982), pp. 77–112. On the role of the state in supporting key sectors, see also Gary R. Saxonhouse, "What Is All This About 'Industrial Targeting' in Japan?" *The World Economy*, 6 (September 1983), 253–273.

109. The movement from fixed to flexible exchange rates was, of course, much more an issue than U.S.–Japanese trade. See Patrick and Rosovsky, *Asia's New Giant*, Ch. 6. See also Takafusa Nakamura, *The Postwar Japanese Economy* (Tokyo: University of Tokyo Press, 1981), pt. 3; for specific references to the impact of oil shortages, see Yoichi Shinkai, "Oil Crises and Stagflation in Japan," in Yamamura, *Policy and Trade Issues of the Japanese Economy*, pp. 173–193.

110. Data are from World Bank, *World Development Report 1987* (New York: Oxford University Press, 1987), pp. 202–205.

111. Useful sources for analyzing contemporary adjustment policies include Ronald Dore, *Flexible Rigidities* (London: The Athlone Press, 1986); Chikara Higashi and G. Peter Lauter, *The Internationalization of the Japanese Economy* (Boston: Kluwer Academic Publishers, 1987); Edward J. Lincoln, *Japan: Facing Economic Maturity* (Washington, D.C.: Brookings, 1988); and Yoshio Suzuki, *Money, Finance, and Macroeconomic Performance in Japan* (New Haven: Yale University Press, 1986).

Sweden

112. For a discussion of the Swedish Model, see Henry Milner, *Sweden: Social Democracy in Action* (New York: Oxford University Press, 1989); for background and a critique of the contemporary system, see Erik Lundberg, "The Rise and Fall of the Swedish Model," *Journal of Economic Literature* 23 (March 1985), 1–36; for an American assessment, see Barry P. Bosworth and Alice M. Rivlin, eds., *The Swedish Economy* (Washington, D.C.: Brookings, 1987).

113. World Bank, *World Development Report 1990* (New York: Oxford University Press, 1990).

114. *World Development Report 1990*.

115. *World Development Report 1990*.

116. See Henry Milner, *Sweden: Social Democracy in Action*.

117. Erik Lundberg, "The Rise and Fall of the Swedish Model."

118. Bosworth and Rivlin, *The Swedish Economy*, p. 19.

119. For a discussion of this point, see Assar Lindbeck, "Is The Welfare State in Trouble?" *Eastern Economic Journal* 13 (October–December 1987), 345–351.

RECOMMENDED READINGS

France

Bela Balassa, *The First Year of Socialist Government in France* (Washington, D.C.: American Enterprise Institute, 1982).

Bernard Cazes, "Indicative Planning in France," *Journal of Comparative Economics* 14 (December 1990), 607–619.

J.-J. Carre, P. Dubois, and E. Malinvaud, *French Economic Growth* (Stanford, Calif.: Stanford University Press, 1975).

Stephen S. Cohen, *Modern Capitalist Planning: The French Model* (Berkeley: University of California Press, 1977).

———, *Recent Developments in French Planning: Some Lessons for the United States* (Washington, D.C.: Government Printing Office, 1977).

Stephen S. Cohen and Peter A. Gourevitch, eds., *France in a Troubled World Economy* (Boston: Butterworth, 1982).

Saul Estrin and Peter Holmes, *French Planning in Theory and Practice* (Boston: Allen and Unwin, 1983).

John and Anne Marie Hackett, *Economic Planning in France* (Cambridge, Mass.: Harvard University Press, 1963).

Stanley Hottman and William Andrews, eds., *The Fifth Republic at Twenty* (New York: State University of New York Press, 1980).

J. R. Hough, *The French Economy* (New York: Holmes & Meier, 1982).

Richard F. Kuisel, *Capitalism and the State in Modern France* (New York: Cambridge University Press, 1981).

Vera Lutz, *Central Planning for the Market Economy: An Analysis of the French Theory and Experience* (London: Longmans Green, 1969).

John H. McArthur and Bruce R. Scott, *Industrial Planning in France* (Boston: Graduate School of Business Administration, Harvard University, 1969).

John Sheahan, *An Introduction to the French Economy* (Columbus, Ohio: Merrill, 1969).

W. Allen Spivey, *Economic Policies in France 1976–1981* (Ann Arbor: University of Michigan Graduate School of Business Administration, 1983).

Great Britain

David S. Bell, ed., *The Conservative Government, 1979–84: An Interim Report* (London: Croom Helm, 1985).

Frank Blackaby, ed., *De-industrialisation* (London: Heinemann Educational Books, 1979).

Richard E. Caves and Associates, *Britain's Economic Prospects* (Washington, D.C.: Brookings, 1968).

Richard E. Caves and Lawrence B. Krause, eds., *Britain's Economic Performance* (Washington, D.C.: Brookings, 1980).

Carlo M. Cipolla, ed., *The Economic Decline of Empires* (London: Methuen, 1970).

B. E. Coates and E. M. Rawstron, *Regional Variations in Britain* (London: Batsford, 1971).

Charles Feinstein, ed., *The Managed Economy* (Oxford, England: Oxford University Press, 1983).

John and Anne Marie Hackett, *The British Economy: Problems and Prospects* (London: Allen and Unwin, 1967).

Paul Hare, *Planning the British Economy* (London: Macmillan, 1985).

Werner Z. Hirsch, *Recent Experience with National Economic Planning in Great Britain* (Washington, D.C.: Government Printing Office, 1977).

R. Kelf-Cohen, *British Nationalization, 1945–1973* (New York: St. Martin's, 1973).

W. P. J. Maunder, ed., *The British Economy in the 1970's* (London: Heinemann Educational Books, 1980).

F. V. Meyer, D. C. Corner, and J. E. S. Parker, *Problems of a Mature Economy* (London: Macmillan, 1970).

National Institute of Economic and Social Research, *The United Kingdom Economy* (London: Heinemann Educational Books, 1976).

Sidney Pollard, *The Wasting of the British Economy* (New York: St. Martin's, 1982).

Grahame Thompson, *The Conservatives' Economic Policy* (London: Croom Helm, 1986).

Alan Walters, *Britain's Economic Renaissance* (New York: Oxford University Press, 1986).

Germany

George A. Akerlof, Andrew K. Rose, and Janet L. Yellen, "East Germany in from the Cold: The Economic Aftermath of Currency Union," paper presented at the Conference of the Brookings Panel on Economic Activity, Washington, D.C., April 4, 1991.

Gary R. Beling, "Selling Off the Family Silver? The Privatization of State Enterprises: The East German Case," unpublished paper, Princeton University, May 17, 1991.

Eduardo Borensztein and Manmohan S. Kumar, "Proposals for Privatization in Eastern Europe," Washington, D.C.: IMF Working Paper, April 1991.

Doris Cornelsen, "GDR: Current Issues," in NATO, *The Central and East European Economies in the 1990s: Perspectives and Constraints* (Brussels: NATO, 1990).

Irwin Collier, "The Estimation of Gross Domestic Product and Its Growth Rate for the German Democratic Republic" (Washington, D.C.: World Bank Staff Working Papers, #773, 1985).

Paul Gregory and Gert Leptin, "Similar Societies Under Differing Economic Systems: The Case of the Two Germanys," *Soviet Studies* 29, 4 (October 1977), 519–544.

Lutz Hoffmann, "Integrating the East German States into the German Economy: Opportunities, Burdens, and Options," paper presented at the American Institute for Contemporary German Studies, The Johns Hopkins University, Washington, D.C., November 13, 1990.

Barry W. Ickes, "What to Do Before the Capital Markets Arrive: The Transition Problem in Reforming Socialist Economies," paper presented at the Conference on the East European Transformation, Princeton University, May 3, 1991.

Henning Klodt, "Government Support for Restructuring the East German Economy," paper presented at the American Institute for Contemporary German Studies, The Johns Hopkins University, Washington, D.C., November 14, 1990.

Jack K. Knott, *Managing the German Economy* (Lexington, Mass.: Heath, 1981).

Oliver Letwin, *Privatizing the World* (London: Cassell, 1988).

Leslie Lipschitz and Donough McDonald, *German Unification: Economic Issues*, Washington, D.C., IMF, Occasional Paper #75, December 1990.

Claus Schnabel, "Structural Adjustment and Privatization of the East German Economy," paper presented at the American Institute of Contemporary German Studies, The Johns Hopkins University, Washington, D.C., December 1990.

Martin Schnitzer, *East and West Germany: A Comparative Economic Analysis* (New York: Praeger, 1990).

———, *Income Distribution: A Comparative Study of the United States, Sweden, West Germany, East Germany, the United Kingdom, and Japan* (New York: Praeger, 1974).

Wolfgang Stolper, *The Structure of the East German Economy* (Cambridge, Mass.: Harvard University Press, 1960).

Norbert Walter, "Beyond German Unification," *The International Economy*, (October/November, 1990).

Japan

J. G. Abegglen, *The Japanese Factory* (Glencoe, Ill.: Free Press, 1958).

G. C. Allen, *The Japanese Economy* (London: Weidenfeld and Nicolson, 1981).

Edward F. Denison and William K. Chung, *How Japan's Economy Grew So Fast: The Sources of Postwar Expansion* (Washington, D.C.: Brookings, 1976).

Ronald Dore, *Flexible Rigidities* (London: The Athlone Press, 1986).

Kanji Haitani, *The Japanese Economic System* (Lexington, Mass.: Heath, 1976).

Japanese Economic Research Center, *Economic Growth: The Japanese Experience Since the Meiji Era*, Vols. I and II (Tokyo: Japanese Economic Research Center, 1973).

Chalmers Johnson, *Japan's Public Policy Companies* (Washington, D.C.: American Enterprise Institute, 1978).

——, *MITI and the Japanese Miracle* (Stanford, Calif.: Stanford University Press, 1982).

Lawrence Klein and Kazushi Ohkawa, eds., *Economic Growth: The Japanese Experience Since the Meiji Era* (Homewood, Ill.: Irwin, 1968).

Edward J. Lincoln, *Japan: Facing Economic Maturity* (Washington, D.C.: Brookings, 1988).

William Lockwood, ed., *The State and Economic Enterprise in Japan* (Princeton, N.J.: Princeton University Press, 1965).

Angus Maddison, *Economic Growth in Japan and the USSR* (London: Allen and Unwin, 1969).

Ryōshin Minami, *The Economic Development of Japan* (London: Macmillan, 1986).

Takafusa Nakamura, *The Postwar Japanese Economy* (Tokyo: University of Tokyo Press, 1981).

Meiko Nishimizu and Charles R. Hulten, "The Sources of Japanese Economic Growth, 1955–71," *Review of Economics and Statistics*, 60 (August 1978), 351–361.

Kazushi Ohkawa and Henry Rosovsky, *Japanese Economic Growth* (Stanford, Calif.: Stanford University Press, 1973).

Kazushi Ohkawa and Hirohisa Kohama, *Lectures on Developing Economies: Japan's Experience and Its Relevance* (Tokyo: University of Tokyo Press, 1989).

Hugh Patrick and Henry Rosovsky, eds., *Asia's New Giant: How the Japanese Economy Works* (Washington, D.C.: Brookings, 1976).

M. M. Postan et el., eds., *Cambridge Economic History of Europe*, Vol. VII, pt. 2 (Cambridge, England: Cambridge University Press, 1978), Chs. 3–5 on Japan.

Ozawa Terutomo, *Multinationalism Japanese Style* (Princeton, N.J.: Princeton University Pres, 1979).

Yoshio Suzuki, *Money, Finance, and Macroeconomic Performance in Japan* (New Haven: Yale University Press, 1986).

Yosho Tsurumi, *The Japanese Are Coming: A Multinational Interaction of Firms and Politics* (Cambridge, Mass.: Ballinger, 1976).

Kozo Yamamura, ed., *Policy and Trade Issues of the Japanese Economy* (Seattle: University of Washington Press, 1982).

M. Y. Yoshino, *Japan's Multinational Enterprises* (Cambridge, Mass.: Harvard University Press, 1976).

Sweden

Barry P. Bosworth and Alice M. Rivlin, eds., *The Swedish Economy* (Washington, D.C.: Brookings, 1987).

Peter Lawrence and Tony Spybey, *Management and Society in Sweden* (London: Routledge and Kegan Paul, 1986).

Erik Lundberg, "The Rise and Fall of the Swedish Model," *Journal of Economic Literature* 23 (March 1985), 1–36.

Michael Maccoby, ed., *Sweden at the Edge* (Philadelphia: University of Pennsylvania Press, 1991).

Per-Martin Meyerson, *The Welfare State in Crisis — The Case of Sweden* (Stockholm: The Federation of Swedish Industries, 1982).

Henry Milner, *Sweden: Social Democracy in Action* (New York: Oxford University Press, 1989).

Bengt Ryden and Villy Bergstrom, eds., *Sweden: Choices for Economic and Social Policy in the 1980s* (London: Allen and Unwin, 1982).

11 | Variants of Capitalism: Developing Nations

IN CHAPTER 10 WE EXAMINED A VARIETY OF CAPITALIST SYSTEMS, all of which use the market mechanism and private ownership but wherein policy variants lead to rather different outcomes — for example, with respect to the distribution of income. All of those systems were developed, or mature, economies. In this chapter we turn to capitalist variants of a different nature — those involved in the process of economic development. Again, we choose countries that enable us to examine capitalism but that represent interesting and important variations.

India is an important example of capitalism in a large and poor country. Unlike China, India has chosen an economic system that is basically capitalist in character, but it combines this system with a significant degree of state influence, the latter implemented through various types of controls and a state planning system. Economic growth and economic development are important goals of Indian economic policy. Thus, because we seek examples of the early stages of economic growth and economic development in large and relatively poor countries, it makes more sense to compare India and China than, for example, China and the United States.

Next we examine the "Four Tigers": South Korea, Singapore, Taiwan, and Hong Kong. These countries have all experienced rapid economic growth and significant though uneven advances in the level of economic development. Most important for our discussion here, all are relatively small countries that utilize the market mechanism and a strategy of export-led industrialization.

This chapter, then, focuses on capitalism and on the policy combinations appropriate for promoting economic growth and economic development in different natural settings.

INDIA: THE QUEST FOR ECONOMIC DEVELOPMENT

Early in this book we posed a question: Does any one economic system appear better suited than others to solving the development problems of low-income countries? It is therefore incumbent on us to include a low-income country among our capitalist variants. There are more poor countries than affluent ones. In fact, affluence is limited to a very small proportion of the world's population. The difficulty is that there is more diversity among the less-developed countries (the LDCs) than among the industrialized economies. Some LDCs are only a step removed from the economic arrangements they have exhibited for centuries; others appear to be on their way to transforming themselves into developed countries. Moreover, the LDCs have diverse political and social institutions. In some, tribal or traditional authority still prevails; other LDCs have adopted Western democratic political institutions; and still others are controlled by dictatorships of one kind or another.

What common features can be extracted from this diversity? LDCs possess the characteristics generally associated with low levels of income: the dominant role of agriculture, high fertility and mortality rates, limited use of advanced technology, and lower saving rates. In addition to these features, LDCs share other characteristics: concentration of the ownership of wealth, reliance on indirect taxes, extensive government control of international transactions, poorly developed capital markets, and monopoly power in the limited industrial sector.[1]

It is also important, from a systems perspective, to appreciate the fact that poor countries have generally admired what has been viewed as the rapid economic progress of planned socialist systems. This admiration is reflected in such features as cooperative arrangements in agriculture and a major role for the state in economic development, not to mention the appeal of policies to influence the distribution of income. Will recent developments in the Soviet Union and Eastern Europe alter these views, and if so, what will be the results?

Rather than attempt to deal with the LDCs as a group, we have selected one, India. We believe that the Indian economy is reasonably representative of the operation of the capitalist economic system at low levels of economic development. Moreover, this populous and strategically important country is the closest capitalist counterpart to China, the planned socialist LDC discussed in Chapter 17.[2]

Basic Characteristics[3]

Table 11.1 shows summary statistics for India, with appropriate comparisons to China and the United States. India is the world's second most populous country (almost 850 million in 1990), with approximately 15 percent of the world's population. On the other hand, India accounts for under 2 percent of world GNP. These two facts highlight India's very low per capita income (roughly $300–$400 in U.S. dollars). Approximately 31 percent of India's GNP originates in agriculture, and only 1 in 4 persons lives in urban areas. Some 70 percent of the labor force works in agriculture. Population has tended to grow at a rate of over 2 percent per annum (compared to about 0.5 percent in the industrialized countries), and life expectancy is under 50 years. Only 1 in every 3 adults is literate.

Although India is a large country, natural conditions are less than ideal both from a climatic perspective and in terms of environmental decay, for example, resulting from industrial pollution and land use arrangements. India has substantial mineral deposits and large reserves of coal.

India has been called the world's largest democracy. Its government is patterned on the English parliamentary system, and over the years Indian politics has been dominated by the Congress Party. India comprises a multiplicity of ethnic groups, who speak different languages, and has suffered over the years from ethnic and regional strife. Indeed, this strife remains important in the 1990s.

The Indian Economy: Historical Background[4]

The Indian economy prior to independence from Britain in 1947 makes an ideal case study of a traditional society with a long history of colonial domination. Prior to British rule (first under the British East India Company and then under the Crown), the Indian moghul economy (so called because a Moslem minority was the ruling elite) operated according to long-standing traditional rules. Society was divided into castes: the religious leaders, warlords, and their retainers were at the top, and the small peasant and untouchable castes were at the bottom. In this hierarchical system, one's place in society, as well as one's occupation, was determined at birth. Occupations were not distributed according to the skills, qualifications, and wishes of individuals or according to the needs of society. Moreover, work was considered beneath the dignity of the upper castes; physical labor could be engaged in only by the lower castes.

Table 11.1 Selected Structural Features of Less-Developed Capitalist Variants

Feature	India	China	U.S.A.
Per capita GNP, 1988, in U.S. $	340	330	19840
Percent of population urban, 1988	27	50	74
Percent of GDP derived from industry, 1988	30	46	33
Government expenditure as a percent of GNP, 1988	17.8	n.a.	22.9
Gross domestic investment as a percent of GDP, 1988	24	38	15
Average annual rate of inflation, 1980–88	7.4	4.9	5.0
Defense expenditures as a percent of total central government expenditure, 1988	19.3	n.a.	24.8

Sources: All data are from World Bank, *World Development Report 1990* (New York: Oxford University Press, 1990), Tables 1–32.

In contrast to other feudal societies, the ruling class itself generally did not own the means of agricultural production and was not involved in its management. Instead, the actual land cultivators paid taxes (tribute, often 50 percent of the harvest) to the ruling classes according to custom and in return for protection, which was necessary in an area torn by regional factionalism, warlordism, and civil strife. Agricultural taxes were levied not only to meet the needs of general government but also to support the high living standards of the upper castes. In the village community, the ruling class controlled the land, but because property rights were poorly defined, the farm family (and the landlords) had little incentive to undertake land improvements. In the farm family, an extended family system prevailed whereby income was shared among brothers, cousins, uncles, and so on.

The wealthy classes were not motivated to make productive investments; instead, their savings were devoted to acquiring precious metals, and little social overhead investment (such as irrigation) was undertaken. Foreign trade was conducted primarily by foreigners, who traded Indian spices and handicrafts for gold and silver. The limited education that did exist was purely religious in character, and the education of women was proscribed.

Economic progress under the moghul economy was limited. Population did not increase for two thousand years. It is likely that in the sixteenth century, per capita income in India was on a par with that of Western Europe, and contemporary European visitors even felt that average living standards were higher in India than at home. By the time of British rule, however, per capita income in India was very low compared to that of Western Europe. Thus during the era when Europe was preparing for its initial industrialization and population expansion, the Indian moghul economy was becoming relatively backward. The reasons for this declining economic position are not hard to identify: the rigid caste system, religious restrictions, uncertain property rights, barriers against productive investment, and civil strife. It was this last, particularly the enmity between the majority Hindu population and their Moslem rules (as well as regional factionalism), that allowed the British to turn India easily into a colonial dominion.

The Indian economy under British rule was not dramatically different, but the British did remove the old moghul warlord aristocracy, replacing it with a new indigenous ruling elite (supportive of the British) and a professional British bureaucracy, both designed to preserve law and order. Britain's objective was not to promote the economic development of India but to use India as a guaranteed market for British products. Tariff barriers were erected against Indian textiles abroad, and the removal of the moghul princes reduced the demand in India for the traditional luxury products of Indian handicraft. The British accepted and even intensified the caste system by establishing themselves as a separate ruling class. After 1930, native Indians gradually infiltrated the bureaucracy. This native bureaucracy became a wellspring of nationalism and was instrumental in achieving independence for India in 1947.

During British rule, the population of India began to grow for the first time over an extended period, and the economy grew along with it. Nevertheless, per capita income failed to increase perceptibly. Although British colonial rule did establish conditions for the growth of output and population, it did not allow output growth to exceed population growth. The positive economic features of the colonial period were the creation of a professional bureaucracy, the introduction of a secular education system to replace the system of religious education, a reduction of the tax burden on agriculture, and the creation of some property rights in agriculture (for the new ruling class). Under British rule, the proportion of national income going to the nonvillage economy declined somewhat with elimination of the moghul elite, and a lower proportion of national income went to the new ruling elite (British officials, native princes, and their retainers). However, the share of income received by those at the bottom of the ladder did not increase.

The Modern "Socialist" Indian Economy

The modern Indian economy is the creation of the Congress party and its leaders, Mahatma Gandhi and Jawaharlal Nehru, who referred to India as a "socialist" economy, though they differed on the appropriate course of Indian socialism. Gandhi extolled the traditional village community as the ideal economic organization and downgraded industrialization and the profit motive. Nehru favored industrialization and emphasized heavy industry as the appropriate path for Indian socialism. According to our definition, *socialism* is largely a misnomer in the case of India, except for government ownership in industry and commerce. Indian leadership has not pursued a socialist distribution of income. India is still primarily an agricultural country, and the distribution of income depends mainly on the distribution of agricultural property. Since independence, only limited progress has been made in land reform. Although there have been some efforts to distribute land to the poor peasants, land remains unequally distributed, and there is no evidence that the range of income inequality has been reduced.[5] It is true that the pensioning off of the native princes and limitations on landholdings have reduced the number of enormous estates, but the land-limiting legislation has been circumvented, and many Indian states have not been able (or willing) to push land reform because of the strength of vested landed interests. The tax system continues to be regressive, direct taxes are rarely levied on land, and the nominally high urban income taxes are ameliorated by evasion and through numerous exemptions.

The pretax income distribution figures sum up the failure to establish a more equitable distribution of income. In 1960, the bottom 10 percent of families accounted for less than 1 percent of all income, while the top 10 percent accounted for over one-third. This income distribution is less equitable than in the industrialized capitalist countries (a less equitable distribution is characteristic of less-developed countries).[6] The after-tax distribution is not significantly different from this pretax distribution because of the predominance of regressive indirect taxes. A native Indian elite of civil servants, the military, and capitalists has replaced the British and the native princes at the top of the income distribution. Landless agricultural laborers, small landholders, and the urban poor remain at the bottom.

Rather than seeking to achieve "socialist" objectives through income redistribution, the architects of the modern Indian economy emphasized state ownership in industry. The feeling was that socialism could be achieved through state control of industry, which would serve as a surrogate for social change. State promotion of heavy industry (through ownership and government controls) was to lead to economic development and limit the concentration of wealth in private hands, and it was assumed that economic development would inevitably bring about necessary social change. In the early postwar period, the Indians adopted one basic feature of the Soviet development model (discussed in Chapter 12): the priority of heavy industry over light industry and agriculture. It was argued that the creation of a domestic heavy-industry base would lead to more rapid development, would promote domestic savings, and would make India less dependent on the outside world (freeing India to pursue an independent political course).[7]

India's heavy-industry strategy was reflected in the public ownership of heavy industries and banking. Steel, heavy machinery, chemicals, power, fuel, communication, transportation, and life insurance were nationalized in the early 1950s. In the 1970s the state moved to enlarge the public sector by nationalizing the large banks, the copper industry, the wholesale grain and jute trade, and a number of coal mines and textile mills. In some instances, the Indians followed the British pattern of nationalization to rescue failing private companies. In others (such as the wholesale grain trade), nationalization was undertaken to expand state control over the private economy. Nationalization was usually accomplished by compensation of previous owners (rather than expropriation), and an increasing "Indianization" of industrial ownership has evolved as foreign owners have been displaced.

Despite substantial nationalization, the scope of the public sector remains limited. Private enterprise still accounts for some 90 percent of industrial output.[8] The public sector (general government and public enterprises) accounts for approximately 15 percent of national output.[9] The government's share of savings is 13 percent.[10] These figures indicate that the role of the public sector in India is below average or small compared to that in the industrialized countries.[11] Thus the strategy of pursuing socialism through public ownership has had only a limited effect on the aggregate economy. However, one must bear in mind that the Indian economy is still highly underdeveloped and that most of the labor force remains concentrated in agriculture and personal services. This means that the share of the heavy-industry sector (the focal point of nationalization) must necessarily be limited. Moreover, the impact of public policy on economic affairs may be greater than the figures indicate because of a pervasive system of indirect controls and planning.

The organization of the private industrial sector is quite concentrated in India, and the objective of limiting industrial wealth holdings has not been achieved. At the end of the 1950s, the twenty largest industrial groups owned one-third of the share capital of the private corporate sector.[12] Although measures have been introduced since then to reduce this concentration of private wealth and power (the most significant being the nationalization of large banking interests), large private interests are probably promoted by the existing system of economic control. In addition, major industrialists are key figures in the Congress party.

Economic Planning in India[13]

Economic planning in India has attracted considerable attention because India is one of the few LDCs to have well-organized and sophisticated planning machinery. The planning apparatus in a typical LDC is as underdeveloped as the economy, so the Indian example serves as a useful test case of the potential contribution of the planning in an LDC.

According to the definitions developed in Chapters 7 and 8, Indian planning would be classified as indicative, even though its heritage is the Soviet experience. It is a noncompulsory form of planning, in keeping with the Indian philosophy that the use of force is contrary to Indian democracy. This is not to suggest that Indian plan directives have not been implemented. In the industrial sector a wide range of enforcement mechanisms have been available. Much heavy industry is directly owned by the state and can be expected to follow plan guidelines; industrial credit is largely state-controlled; import licenses are also granted by the state. The fact that the Indian economy has developed a relatively large heavy-industry sector for an LDC demonstrates better than anything else that planning has mattered. Nevertheless, India continues to be an agricultural country, and agriculture, which cannot be planned in any effective way, remains largely out of the control of planners.

India has concentrated on long-term plans, typically of five years' duration. Attempts to devise annual operational plans have not been successful. Planning goals and planning methods have changed over the years, although the general objectives (raising the rate of economic growth and the investment ratio, reducing inequalities, and stimulating employment) are familiar to observers of national economic planning. The first plan was based on simple Keynesian growth models. The second plan (1956–1961) emphasized the priority of heavy industry. Later plans have concentrated on multisectoral balances and have to some extent moved away from the emphasis on heavy industry.

Balances for the major industrial sectors have been constructed (via either rudimentary methods or input–output tables) to determine the consistency of the plan. A crucial component of the plan is the investment subplan, which indicates the growth rates of investment in the public and private sectors. The investment plan, which determines the basic direction of the economy, is most amenable to enforcement because of the state's control of public enterprises, raw-material allocations, investment credit, and imports.

Economic planning in India is carried out on an aggregated level; specific output directives are not normally issued to the private industrial sector. In the public sector, an industry often consists of a small number of publicly owned enterprises, so the aggregate directives can be converted into actual production and investment targets. On the surface, it would appear that Indian planners are in a better position to influence the behavior of industry with the arsenal of controls at their disposal, but it is difficult to establish what degree of control they actually exercise over the private sector.

Economic Controls[14]

Governmental controls over resource allocation are more extensive in India than in the industrialized capitalist countries. In addition to the planning apparatus, a whole range of extramarket controls are utilized. The rationale for these controls is the widespread belief that the free market cannot be trusted to allocate resources in a low-income country.

The basic instrument for control of private industry was the Industries Act of 1951, which covered almost all manufacturing, mining, and power. It gave the government authority to grant licenses for expanding capacity and to control the allocation and prices of raw materials and, in some instances, the prices of finished products. The prices of basic agricultural products are controlled by the state, and a complex zonal pricing system exists to regulate the flow of agricultural products from regions of surplus to regions of deficit. Moreover, the state disburses food products received under foreign aid programs and in this way exerts further influence over agricultural prices.

A most important instrument of state control is state regulation of foreign exchange and imports. Since the mid-1950s, India has been on a strict import and exchange control system. Imported capital equipment, crucial to industrial expansion, has been regulated by industrial licensing, and input and raw-material licenses have regulated the disbursement of imported materials to industrial users. The import control system has operated on the principles of essentiality and indigenous nonavailability. In order to justify an import, the domestic user has to demonstrate that the commodity is essential and that it cannot be purchased at home. Import restrictions, when strictly applied, have given automatic protection to domestic industry and, according to many economists,[15] have reduced the efficiency of the Indian economy.

In the late 1960s, the Indian system of economic controls was reexamined, and an attempt was made to limit controls (except for agricultural pricing) to large firms. The retention of controls, despite the growing recognition of their inefficiency, can be attributed to three factors.[16] The first is that many large firms actually like controls because they reduce risk and guarantee profits. Second, controls enhance the power and positions of bureaucrats. Third, distrust of the market is ingrained in the Indian bureaucracy.

It is difficult to quantify the effect of government controls on Indian resource allocation because one cannot know to what extent they are circumvented. What one can say is that the system of state controls is more comprehensive than that in the advanced capitalist countries.

Growth Performance

The growth of the Indian economy after 1947 represents a marked improvement over its historical performance. As we have already noted, the moghul economy was stagnant for centuries, and per capita income failed to grow during British colonial rule; therefore any growth of per capita income is an improvement over historical standards. The difficulty in evaluating Indian growth performance is that the world economy experienced accelerated growth after World War II, and India would be expected to participate in this acceleration.

India's per capita GNP averaged a 1.7 percent growth for the period 1965–1985. According to Angus Maddison, the reasons for this per capita growth rate are the expansion of government services (education and credit assistance), a high investment rate, the increase in both public and private investment, foreign aid, and the importation of advanced technology. Although inflation averaged about 7 percent annually in the 1980s, growth in real output has been sustained largely as a result of growth in the industrial sector.

On the positive side of the ledger, one can point to the steady but unspectacular rise in per capita income despite substantial population pressures. In the crucial agricultural area, output has expanded slightly more rapidly than population (at a per capita rate of about one-half of 1 percent per year). India's dependence on imported grains has declined over the years, and now India is largely self-sufficient in basic food grains. On the negative side, India's per capita income growth has been slow relative to the performance of other developing countries (whose per capita growth tended to be around 2 to 3 percent per year). India's growth performance has been well below that of China, although China and India began their postcolonial development from an equivalent point. Because of lower growth, India's per capita income today is only three-quarters that of China.[17] Additional negative features include persistent high unemployment (and underemployment), rapid inflation, and susceptibility to external shocks (such as the oil price explosion of the 1970s).

Maddison and Malenbaum argue that Indian growth has been substandard for the LDCs in the postwar era, and Maddison calculates that the Indian growth rate has been 25 percent below its potential.[18] The reasons for this underutilization of growth potential are India's extremely low per capita income, its relatively small per capita receipts of foreign capital, its poor natural resources, the drain of a large military, the retention of institutional constraints (caste restrictions, maldistribution of agricultural land, taboo on slaughter of livestock), and the inefficiency of public enterprise, which has been operated at a loss throughout most of the postwar era.

Capitalism in India

Notwithstanding the large share of government ownership of heavy industry and finance, India is a capitalist economy. The public enterprise sector is a small part of the total economy, and private ownership prevails throughout the rest of the economy. The dominant sector, agriculture, is characterized by private ownership of land. There has been no significant change in the distribution of income, and the inequality of income distribution is greater in India than in the advanced capitalist countries, whether calculated on a pretax or a posttax basis. Economic planning is primarily indicative, although planning of the public enterprise sector may carry with it some compulsory elements. Nevertheless, noncoercion remains the foundation of Indian planning.

Government intervention in private economic decision making is probably more extensive in India than in the advanced capitalist countries, although the actual degree of compliance is difficult to establish. Government controls have been placed on prices, imports, foreign exchange, raw materials, and capacity expansion. One reason for these controls is a rather deep-seated distrust of market resource allocation. On the other hand, controls seem to be a characteristic feature of capitalism under conditions of underdevelopment, so in this sense, India conforms to the general pattern of underdevelopment.

Problems and Prospects

The basic challenge facing India over the coming decades is to improve the utilization of its abundant resource, labor. Endemically high rates of unemployment and underemployment attest to labor's underutilization, but the best means of correcting the situation remains a heatedly debated issue. Should there be more or less planning? Should government intervention and controls be increased or reduced? Can ways be found to remove the remaining vestiges of feudalism and the caste system? Can centuries-old regional and ethnic factionalism be removed? Can there be any narrowing in income inequality? In a sense, the biggest decision facing India appears to be whether to choose more market or more plan. Should resource allocation be more fully entrusted to the market, with government acting on the sidelines to protect property rights and promote competition? Or is it dangerous to trust market guidance in a developing country?

ASIAN SYSTEMS: SOUTH KOREA, SINGAPORE, TAIWAN, AND HONG KONG

The "Four Tigers" — South Korea, Singapore, Taiwan, and Hong Kong — are frequently characterized as the newly industrialized countries of Asia.[19] These countries are the object of considerable interest in a region of the world where contemporary economic progress has been great but uneven. Moreover, these are all systems that have achieved significant rates of economic growth, judged by world historical standards, and have made progress through the market mechanism and a strategy of export-led industrialization. Although there are important differences among these countries, it is their similarities, and their economic progress via similar mechanisms and policies, that stand out. These Asian success stories deserve our attention.

Background

The Four Tigers vary considerably in size and natural endowment. In terms of population, the smallest country is Singapore (6 million) and the largest is South Korea (43 million). None is particularly well endowed with natural resources. For example, Singapore is a wholly urban society with a strong manufacturing base, an active service sector, and virtually no agriculture. At the other end of the spectrum, South Korea is an industrialized country with a substantial agricultural sector, an urbanization level of roughly 70 percent at the end of the 1980s, and limited amounts of such resources as coal. Taiwan has an important agricultural sector, but its natural and climatic conditions are less than ideal and minerals are in short supply. Agriculture is relatively unimportant in Hong Kong.

Performance: System and Policy

The evidence presented in Table 11.2 summarizes, in a few simple numbers, an economic success story. All these countries have experienced very rapid economic growth and limited inflation, resulting in significant levels of per capita product. Moreover, with variations, foreign trade has been a dominant mechanism. And though this dimension is difficult to measure accurately, the Four Tigers seem to have achieved these gains with little if any increases in inequality. They are, therefore, systems generating both efficiency and equity.

Economic growth has been driven by export-led industrialization. Exports have been largely manufactured, but in recent years a somewhat more diversified export pattern has emerged (for example, financial services in the case of Singapore).[20] Growth has been achieved with a traditional mix of inputs. Although external capital played a role in earlier years, rates of domestic saving have increased rapidly, as have rates of investment, the latter largely supported by domestic sources.

For example, in the case of South Korea, gross domestic savings accounted for 8 percent of gross domestic product in 1965 and for 38 percent in 1988. Between the same two years, gross domestic investment as a share of gross domestic product increased from 15 percent to 30 percent.[21] Similar changes occurred in Singapore; in Hong Kong, the ratios were high for both years but fell somewhat in the latter period.

Most of these countries have had modest and declining rates of population growth, though the transformation of agriculture has resulted in substantial growth of the labor force to support the industrialization process, most notably in South Korea and Taiwan. Structural change has been typical and quite rapid.

The setting of economic activity is predominantly a market economy with private ownership, but the role of the government has been important in varying ways. Although the arrangements for labor–management negotiations differ from one case to another, certain generalizations are possible. Through a strong government role and social consensus about that role, wage increases have been constrained such that labor costs in the manufacturing sector have not risen rapidly, as they often do during a period of rapid industrialization. Measures of government spending as a proportion of total product can be both difficult to compute and misleading. However, the evidence suggests a strong and growing role for the government sector in Singapore and Hong Kong, though less so in South Korea.

These institutions and policies, in conjunction with traditional macroeconomic policies designed to stimulate economic growth, have produced striking examples of Asian success. However, it is important to bear in mind that this success is dependent on the existence of attractive world markets. What is in store for the future?

Asia: The Future

The Asian success stories are important not only for what they tell us about the sources of successful economic growth and development, but also as models for those countries in Asia and elsewhere in which economic progress has not been achieved. We have noted that in spite of considerable differences in natural endowment, the Four Tigers have promoted rapid industrialization through strikingly similar policies focusing on the export sectors. Can these achievements continue through the decade of the 1990s?

Table 11.2 Selected Characteristics of the Four Tigers

	South Korea	Singapore	Taiwan	Hong Kong
Population, 1990, in millions	43	2.7	20	6
Per capita GNP, 1988, U.S. $	3600	9070	6000[b]	9220[a]
Growth: PCGNP Average annual, 1965–88	6.8	7.2	6.6[c]	6.3
Industry: share of domestic production, 1988	43	38	n.a.	29
Exports + imports/GNP 1988, U.S. $	–	347	97	–

[a] GDP
[b] 1989
[c] 1970–1985

Sources: World Bank, *World Development Report 1990* (New York: Oxford University Press, 1990); and Miyohei Shinohara and Fu-chen Lo, *Global Adjustment and the Future of the Asian-Pacific Economy* (Tokyo and Kuala Lumpur: Institute of Developing Economies and Asian and Pacific Development Centre, 1989).

If the past is any guide, the answer is likely to be yes. These systems have been surprisingly resilient in the face of cyclical downturns. Although examination of year-to-year growth rates in the 1980s indicates some slowing, projections suggest slower but very substantial rates of economic growth through the end of the century.

These systems have also been resilient in the face of a need to adapt. For example, South Korea has developed its heavy-industrial capacity as a basic strength of the economy.

Finally, a great deal of uncertainty exists about the future economic prospects of Hong Kong, which reverts to the People's Republic of China in 1997.[22] Although the Chinese have indicated that they will leave the market economy of Hong Kong intact, sustaining two economic systems may be difficult, especially inasmuch as foreign participation in the domestic economy of Hong Kong remains important. Moreover, the departure of talented people from Hong Kong will present a serious labor problem similar to that which occurred in cases such as the former German Democratic Republic.

Another factor in Asian economic growth has been the presence of a strong entrepreneurial class (sometimes from abroad) working with a population and labor force said to have a strong work ethic. Though more difficult to quantify than, say, investment, these factors may have been very important.

SUMMARY:
VARIANTS OF CAPITALISM: DEVELOPING NATIONS

1. As a large and quite poor country, India has pursued economic growth and development largely through the market mechanism, but with a socialist overlay in a number of dimensions. India has managed to sustain reasonable rates of economic growth, but it has a long way to go along the development path. Since the 1970s, the traditional comparison of India with China has been of even greater interest in light of major changes within the Chinese economy.

2. The "Four Tigers" of Asia (South Korea, Singapore, Taiwan, and Hong Kong) capture our attention for both diversity and uniformity. Though quite different in size, resource endowment, and the like, all have experienced rapid and sustained economic growth through reliance on the growth of manufacturing exports. Apart from inherent interest in these countries and their economic systems, there is also much interest in the export-led industrialization that these countries exhibit and in the extent to which such a strategy can be effective in other cases.

3. For the poor nations of the world, economic progress remains an elusive goal. It is unlikely that the major systemic changes taking place in Eastern Europe will result in any immediate reexamination of systemic arrangements in the less developed nations. However, there is bound to be a new emphasis on the market and on applications of the market.

NOTES

India

1. The literature on the economic characteristics of LDCs is summarized in Marvin Miracle, "Comparative Market Structures in Developing Countries" (Association for Comparative Economics, Proceedings in Conjunction with the Midwest Economic Association, Detroit, April 1970). Also see John Due, *Indirect Taxes in Developing Countries* (Baltimore: The Johns Hopkins University Press, 1970).
2. Indian and Chinese economic growth are compared in Subramanian Swamy, "Economic Growth in China and India, 1952–1970: A Comparative Appraisal," *Economic Development and Cultural Change*, 21 (July 1973), 1–84; and Wilfred Malenbaum, "Modern Economic Growth in India and China: The Comparisons Revisited," *Economic Development and Cultural Change*, 3 (October 1982), 45–84.
3. Data here are compiled from World Bank, *World Development Report 1990* (New York: Oxford University Press, 1990), Tables 1–32.
4. This discussion is based principally in Angus Maddison, *Class Structure and Economic Growth: India and Pakistan Since the Moghuls* (New York: Norton, 1971), Chs. 2–4.
5. Raj Krishna and G. S. Raychaudhuri, "Trends in Rural Savings and Capital Formation in India, 1950–51 to 1973–74," *Economic Development and Cultural Change*, 30 (January 1982), 289–294.
6. Maddison, *Class Structure and Economic Growth*, Ch. 6.
7. For a discussion of the Indian controversy over planning priorities, see Jagdish Bhagwati and Sukhamoy Chakravaty, "Contributions to Indian Economic Analysis: A Survey," *American Economic Growth*, 59 (September 1969), 4–29; and V. V. Bhatt, "Development Problem, Strategy, and Technology of Choice: Sarvadaya and Socialist Approaches in India," *Economic Development and Cultural Change*, 21 (October 1982), 85–100.
8. Maddison, *Class Structure and Economic Growth*, p. 119.
9. Allan G. Gruchy, *Comparative Economic Systems*, 2nd ed. (Boston: Houghton Mifflin, 1977), p. 638.
10. World Bank, *World Tables, 1976*, p. 428.
11. Ibid., summary tables.
12. Maddison, *Class Structure and Economic Growth*, p. 127.
13. Our discussion of Indian planning is based on Gruchy, *Comparative Economic Systems*, pp. 639–653; and Bhagwati and Chakravaty, "Contributions to Indian Economic Analysis," pp. 2–73.
14. This discussion is based on Maddison, *Class Structure and Economic Growth* pp. 120–125.
15. Bhagwati and Chakravaty, "Contributions to Indian Economic Analysis," pp. 60–66.
16. Maddison, *Class Structure and Economic Growth*, pp. 122–124.
17. Malenbaum, "Modern Economic Growth in India and China," pp. 45–84; World Bank, *World Tables, 1980*, pp. 372–375.
18. Maddison, *Class Structure and Economic Growth*, p. 81.

South Korea, Singapore, Taiwan, Hong Kong

19. There is a large literature on these economies. See, for example, Edward K. Y. Chen, *Hyper-Growth in Asian Economies* (London and Basingstoke, England: The Macmillan Press Ltd., 1979); Eddy Lee, ed., *Export-Led Industrialization and Development* (Geneva: ILO, 1981); Roy A. Matthews, *Canada and the Little Dragons* (Montreal: The Institute for Research on Public Policy, 1983); Miron Mushkat, *The Economic Future of Hong Kong* (Boulder, Colo., and London, England: Hong Kong University Press, 1990); Miyohei Shinohara and Fu-chen Lo, *Global Adjustment and the Future of Asian-Pacific Economy* (Tokyo and Kuala Lumpur: Institute of Developing Economies and Asian and Pacific Development Centre, 1989); Julian

Weiss, *The Asian Century* (New York: Facts on File, 1989); and Jon Woronoff, *Asia's "Miracle" Economies* (Armonk, N.Y.: M. E. Sharpe, 1986).

20. Eddy Lee, ed., *Export-Led Industrialization and Development* (Geneva: ILO, 1981); Robert A. Scalapino, Seizaburo Sato, and Jusuf Wanandi, eds., *Asian Economic Development – Present and Future* (Berkeley: University of California Press, 1985).

21. World Bank, *World Development Bank 1990* (New York: Oxford University Press, 1990).

22. For a discussion of this issue, see Miron Mushkat, *The Economic Future of Hong Kong.*

RECOMMENDED READINGS

India

A. N. Agrawal, *Indian Economy*, 2nd ed. (New Delhi: Vikas Publishing House, 1976).

Jagdish Bhagwati and Sukhamoy Chakravaty, "Contributions to Indian Economic Analysis: A Survey," *American Economic Review*, 59 (September 1969), 4–29.

Pramit Chaudhuri, ed., *Aspects of Indian Economic Development* (London: Allen and Unwin, 1971).

Francine R. Frankel, *India's Green Revolution* (Princeton, N.J.: Princeton University Press, 1971).

———, *India's Political Economy, 1947–1977* (Princeton, N.J.: Princeton University Press, 1978).

Raj Krishna and G. S. Raychaudhuri, "Trends in Rural Savings and Capital Formation in India, 1950–1951 to 1973–1974," *Economic Development and Cultural Change*, 30 (January 1982), 271–298.

William A Long and K. K. Seo, *Management in Japan and India* (New York: Praeger, 1977).

Angus Maddison, *Class Structure and Economic Growth: India and Pakistan Since the Moghuls* (New York: Norton, 1971).

Wilfred Malenbaum, "Modern Economic Growth in India and China: The Comparison Revisited, 1950–1980," *Economic Development and Cultural Change*, 31 (October 1982), 45–84.

C. H. Shah and C. N. Vakil, eds., *Agricultural Development of India: Policy and Problems* (New Delhi: Orient Longman, 1979).

Subramanian Swamy, "Economic Growth in China and India, 1952–1970: A Comparative Appraisal," *Economic Development and Cultural Change*, 21 (July 1973), 1–84.

South Korea, Singapore, Taiwan, Hong Kong

Edward K. Y. Chen, *Hyper-Growth in Asian Economies* (London and Basingstoke, England: The Macmillan Press Ltd., 1979).

Shirley W. Y. Kao, Gustav Ranis, and John C. H. Fei, *The Taiwan Success Story: Rapid Growth with Improved Distribution in the Republic of China, 1952–1979* (Boulder, Colo.: Westview, 1981).

Eddy Lee, ed., *Export-Led Industrialization and Development* (Geneva: ILO, 1981).

Roy A. Matthews, *Canada and the Little Dragons* (Montreal: The Institute for Research on Public Policy, 1983).

Miron Mushkat, *The Economic Future of Hong Kong* (Boulder, Colo., and London, England: Hong Kong University Press, 1990).

Gavin Peebles, *Hong Kong's Economy: An Introductory Macroeconomic Analysis* (New York: Oxford University Press, 1988).

Robert A. Scalapino, Seizaburo Sato, and Jusuf Wanandi, eds., *Asian Economic Development – Present and Future* (Berkeley: University of California Press, 1985).

Miyohei Shinohara and Fu-chen Lo, *Global Adjustment and the Future of the Asian-Pacific Economy* (Tokyo and Kuala Lumpur: Institute of Developing Economies and Asian and Pacific Development Centre, 1989).

Julian Weiss, *The Asian Century* (New York: Facts on File, 1989).

Jon Woronoff, *Asia's "Miracle" Economies* (Armonk, N.Y.: M. E. Sharpe, 1986).

12 | The Soviet Economy: The Command Experience

THROUGHOUT THIS BOOK WE HAVE ATTEMPTED to understand real-world economic systems and to compare these systems to their theoretical underpinnings. Our discussion of American capitalism was cast in this framework, and so is our treatment of the Soviet economy.

Traditionally, the Soviet economy has been classified as a centrally planned socialist economic system. However, widespread state ownership and the dominance of a national economic plan governing resource allocation, which was begun seriously in 1928, came to be questioned under a program of radical economic reform instituted by Mikhail Gorbachev in 1985. The nature of this reform process, or *Perestroika*, will occupy our attention in a subsequent chapter, because it is directed at fundamental change in the working arrangements of the Soviet economy. These changes, as we shall see, raise questions about what theoretical model is most appropriate for analyzing the contemporary Soviet economy. *Perestroika* represents a fundamental departure from Soviet economic policies of the recent past and deserves separate treatment.

What has become known as the **administrative command model** was the dominant mechanism for resource allocation in the Soviet Union for a period of almost sixty years. From a theoretical point of view, the Soviet experience with centrally planned socialism remains the major attempt to remake that society and its economy and to forge an approach to economic development that is often admired in less-developed nations, such as India. Unquestionably, future research in the era of Glasnost will improve our understanding of the Soviet past. How and how well did this economic system function? Does the Soviet experience with planning, revealing as it does both strengths and weaknesses, suggest that a command economy is a thing of the past?

As we emphasize throughout this book, the reform experience in the formerly planned socialist economies is far from complete, and the paths being followed differ considerably from one economy to another. In the Soviet case, understanding the reform era would be impossible without a thorough understanding of the Soviet economy that prevailed before reform. We turn, therefore, to a discussion of the Soviet experience with the administrative command model.

Historical Perspectives

Our examination of American capitalism was not cast in historical perspective. The American economy is, after all, an open economy undergoing change all the time. The Soviet experience has been rather different. Just as the Gorbachev era represents a sharp break with the recent Soviet past, the Bolshevik revolution of 1917 represented a sharp break with the preceding czarist era.[1] Indeed, Soviet experimentation with systemic and policy differences between 1917 and 1928 provide important insights into the roots of the administrative command system and the contemporary difficulties that arise in reforming that system. Historical perspective is therefore essential.

At the time of the Bolshevik revolution in 1917, the era of the czars came to a close and the era of the Soviets began. Although the Soviet economic system as we know it today generally dates from 1928, analysis and assessment of the Soviet era must begin with the base from which it grew: the *level* and *rate* of economic development at the end of the czarist era.

Economic development as of 1917 was at a relatively low level, judged by indicators such as per capita gross national product. However, there had been considerable increase in rate of growth, especially industrial growth, during the last three decades of czarist rule, and the Soviets could therefore build on an attractive base (transportation, industrial capacity, minerals, and so forth).

At the end of the 1920s the Soviet leader, Joseph Stalin, made two important decisions. First, a comprehensive system of central economic planning based on compulsory state and party directives was established. An abrupt end to the prevailing system of market relations in industry ensued, and there was a sudden shift in industrial production away from consumer goods and toward producer goods. Second, the agricultural sector was collectivized. A vast network of collective farms (*kolkhozy*) was created, in which more than 90 percent of Soviet peasant households were living by the mid-1930s.[2] These two major decisions, though sudden at the time, did not arise out of a vacuum.

Two economic "experiments" were conducted in the period immediately following the revolution of 1917: war communism (1917–1920) and the New Economic Policy (1921–1928).[3] Both responded to the need to consolidate power and at the same time to marshal economic resources in a time of crisis.[4]

War communism, implemented by Lenin during the Russian Civil War, saw the introduction of substantial state ownership (nationalization), an attempt to eliminate market relationships in industry and trade, and the gathering of agricultural products from the peasants by forced requisitioning. In a sense, it seemed that Lenin was attempting to by-pass socialism and move directly from a capitalist to a communist system. Whatever the intent, the economic consequences were a disaster by the end of the civil war; the economy was in ruin.[5]

In an attempt to instill economic recovery, Lenin introduced the New Economic Policy (NEP) in 1921. NEP signaled a partial return to private ownership (the so-called commanding heights of industry remained nationalized), reintroduction of the market as a primary mechanism for resource allocation, and implementation of a more viable tax system on agriculture. By 1927, the Soviet economy had recovered from the losses of war communism and was at, and in some cases above, the prewar level.[6]

The period of Soviet history from 1917 to 1928 provided some important lessons — lessons that permeated Soviet thinking. First, it became apparent that if the market were to be eliminated, some mechanism for coordination had to take its place. During war communism Lenin nationalized industries and eliminated the market, but he did not replace the market with a plan or some other substitute mechanism. Second, as a result, at least in part, of inept state policies, the peasants came to be viewed as holding considerable power over the pace of industrialization.[7] After all, the economy was largely agricultural, so both product and labor force would have to come primarily from the rural sector. Third, the response to Lenin's attempt to introduce payment in kind and to downgrade the importance of money during war communism made it obvious that, whatever the system, material **incentives** would be crucial to motivate labor.

In addition to the experience of war communism and NEP, the 1920s witnessed open and important discussions, the "great industrialization debate" and the beginnings of the theory of planning (discussed in Chapter 6).[8] The debate on industrialization focused on modes of industrialization and, in particular, on differing roles for the agricultural and industrial sectors. All participants agreed that industrialization was essential and that the peasants would play a key role. The end result, however, was not readily foreseen by the debate's participants.

The economic system that Stalin put in place in the late 1920s and early 1930s was radically different from then-existing systems. Although the economic system evolved through time, and a variety of reform attempts were made beginning in the late 1950s, the system Mikhail Gorbachev inherited in the mid-1980s looked surprisingly similar to that of earlier years.

The Setting

Before we examine the Soviet command economy, we should briefly discuss the setting in which that system has functioned.

By almost any measure, the Soviet Union is a very large country, a fact important both to its past and to its present economic development. The Soviet Union occupies 8.6 million square miles, an area more than twice that of the United States. In terms of population, the Soviet Union entered the 1990s with approximately 290 million persons, some 15 percent more than the population of the United States. The majority of the Soviet population (roughly 65 percent) lives in urban areas, and approximately 80 percent of the labor force is in industry and related nonagricultural occupations. Urbanization has characterized the Soviet experience, along with the traditional shift of the labor force away from rural/agricultural pursuits.

Equally significant, the Soviet Union has been a very diverse nation consisting of 15 union republics. The largest of these, the Russian Republic, accounts for just over 50 percent of the aggregate Soviet population. The remainder of the population is made up (until 1990) of the Latvians, Lithuanians, and Estonians (the Baltic region); the Ukrainians; the peoples of Central Asia, including Uzbekistan, Kirgizstan, Tadzhikistan, and Turkmenistan; and those of the Caucasus, including Georgia, Azerbaidzhan, and Armenia. These and other peoples of the Soviet Union infuse it with vast ethnic, cultural, and historical diversity. As we will see when we discuss the contemporary Soviet reform experience, ethnic and regional differences may well lead to a redefined union quite different from the traditional socialist union of fifteen republics (the Union of Soviet Socialist Republics, or USSR).

Sharp differences also exist in the Soviet Union's natural environment. The climate, for example, ranges from the hot, dry areas of Central Asia to the cold expanses of Siberia and the cool, wet plains of the west. Needless to say, significant regional differences in climate dictate major variations in resource usage, especially in agriculture.

Finally, the Soviet Union has an extraordinarily rich resource base. In addition to being a major producer of fish and forest products, the Soviet Union is amply endowed with minerals and is the world's largest producer of petroleum, coal, and iron ore. Indeed, there are very few minerals for which the Soviet Union has inadequate domestic reserves. It is not the existence of wealth, but the exploitation of this wealth for national gain, that has become the center of controversy in the 1990s. Our examination of the Soviet past will illuminate the reasons for this controversy.

THE SOVIET ECONOMY: A FRAMEWORK FOR ANALYSIS

Differences in outcomes can be related to differences in economic systems. As we have noted before, system differences fall into four basic and important categories: decision-making *levels*, mechanisms of information (*market* and *plan*), property rights (*public* versus *private*), and the nature of incentives (*material* versus *moral*).

As we examine the Soviet command economy and, in particular, the organizational arrangements used to allocate resources, it is important to ask two questions: How does this system differ from the ideal of planned socialism? How can the actual command system be categorized according to our six criteria?

In terms of the decision-making structure, the Soviet economy has been organized in a vertical hierarchical fashion. The Soviet state, operating through government ministries, and the Communist party, operating through party groups and cells, share authority and responsibility. There are a number of decision-making layers, including the state and party structure at the top, the ministries and regional authorities (and sometimes trust organizations) in the middle, and the basic production units (enterprises and farms) at the local level.

The Soviet command system is clearly a **centralized economic system** from the perspective of resource allocation and how that allocation is determined.

Turning to the mechanisms of information, the Soviet command economy is a **planned economy** in the sense that, for most units in the system, whether ministry or factory, the national economic plan and its subcomponents supply information on the key issues of what to produce and how to produce. At the same time, market influences exist in some segments of the Soviet economy – for example, in the allocation of labor and in the second, or underground, economy. Planning is the predominant mechanism, but it is not universal.

The most striking difference between the Soviet economy and the capitalist market systems is in the area of property rights. The Soviet state has been the dominant owner of property in the Soviet Union, and thus the utilization of property, whether a machine in a factory or a piece of land, is determined by the state. Exceptions to state ownership and control, such as property held by Soviet collective farms, are not especially important from a practical point of view.

Finally, given the fact that income from property accrues exclusively to the state, it should not be surprising to learn that **wage income** is the dominant source of earnings for the Soviet worker. In addition to material incentives, however, the Communist party and other organizations place considerable emphasis on moral incentives, which are important in the Soviet system.

Organizational Features of the Command Model

Since the beginning of the plan era in 1928, organizational change has occurred frequently in the Soviet Union. At the same time, there has been continuity in the basic arrangements, a stylized picture of which is presented in Figure 12.1. Under these arrangements, the Soviet Union is nominally governed by an elected government, the operative organ of which consists of the Council of Ministers at the federal (all-Union) and republican levels. A parallel structure, the Communist Party of the Soviet Union (CPSU), is the principal organ of control and supervision. It operates through a complex centralized structure beginning at the national level and terminating with individual party cells in each industrial enterprise, farm, and organization.[9] Regional party organizations are important agents that control the allocation of resources at the local level.

In this system, the means of production are (with only limited exceptions) owned by the state; firms and other organizations operate under the control of the state and party apparatus.[10] The agricultural sector is organized into state farms, collective farms, and a private sector, the latter governed by strict regulations. Both vertical and horizontal integration characterize the contemporary agricultural scene, as farms and industrial processing are linked in the form of agro-industrial combines.

The major decisions about resource allocation are made by Gosplan, the state planning agency. Traditionally, it is the communist party that develops the general directives on resource allocation. Gosplan then converts these directives into a set of operative plan targets, with the aid of the ministerial structure and the individual enterprises. Finally, it is the responsibility of the individual enterprises to carry out the plan directives.

We have noted that over the years, the organizational arrangements and the policy directives of the Soviet economic system have changed, and yet there has been remarkable stability. The administrative command system is a hierarchical command system in which public ownership is combined with substantial material incentives aimed at encouraging the carrying out of state and party directives. In this system, information flows from top to bottom and vice versa, intra-enterprise activities are plan-coordinated, and money and markets as we know them play only a limited role.

From an economic standpoint, two properties of the command system deserve emphasis. First, the major organization around which the industrial activity of enterprises and the agricultural activities of farms are organized is the **ministry**. Ministries are hierarchically organized by type of production — steel, agriculture, and so on. The ministerial structure was shifted to organization on a *regional* basis in 1957 under the leadership of Nikita Khrushchev. The purpose, apparently, was to break down the tendency of ministries to become

Figure 12.1 The Organization of the Soviet Economy: The Command Model

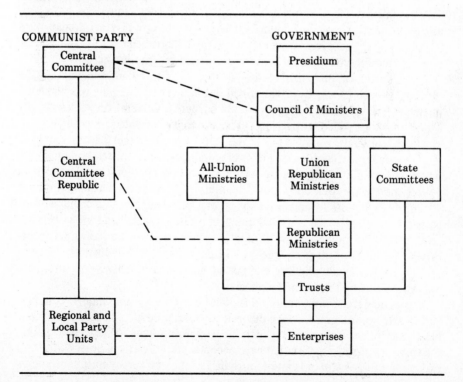

self-sufficient and to ignore interactions with other ministries. The reform did not work and was abandoned when Khrushchev fell from power in 1964. Ministries differ in importance, depending on their function. For example, the most important branches of industry are governed by all-union ministries. Important decisions concerning, for example, steel production facilities are made at the center. Union republican ministries disperse a measure of decision-making authority to the level of the republic (of which there were fifteen). The ministries, then, are the organizational superiors of the industrial and agricultural enterprises. Organizational reforms over the past decade have experimented with combining enterprises into trusts, which are intended to serve as an intermediary between the enterprise and the ministry.

Second, as we have said, planning is done by Gosplan, the state planning agency. Gosplan is the agency responsible for converting general directives of the Communist party into operative plans, with the help of the ministries and individual enterprises. Although planning, in the sense of making all economic decisions, is virtually impossible, we will see that in practice, the Soviet command system utilizes a variety of means to simplify the planning task.

PLANNING IN PRACTICE

Traditionally, the allocation of resources in the Soviet Union has been conducted primarily through the plan. There are short-term (1-year), longer-term (5- or 7-year), and even 20-year "perspective" plans. The 5-year and annual plans, which direct economic activity, are of central interest here.

The essence of plan formulation is the material balance technique, the theoretical basis of which was examined in Chapter 6.[11] The plan is formulated in the following manner (highly simplified here). General directives on the economy are provided by the CPSU and are converted into control figures by Gosplan. The control figures, or tentative production targets, are transmitted through the ministries down to the level of individual enterprises, comment and informational input being sought from each level in the hierarchy. The control figures then move back up through the hierarchy and at the Gosplan level are "balanced"; that is, for major items in the plan, supply and demand must balance. Once balance is achieved, the plan is disaggregated and the targets are once again disseminated down through the ministries to the individual enterprises. The final result is the **techpromfinplan** (technical–industrial–financial plan), which is legally binding and contains detailed directives for enterprise operations during the forthcoming year.

In practice, the formulation of this plan takes considerable time, is complex, and clearly cannot approach the theoretical ideals posed in Chapter 6. Our own brief description cannot do justice to the bargaining, haggling, interplay among the various units, and delays that have become integral parts of Soviet planning. Frequently the new plan is late in arriving, so the enterprise must continue to operate under the guidance of the old plan. The material balance system works in large part because it has built-in flexibility. The planning process does not start from scratch each year. This the plan for year t is, in effect, little more than a revision and update of the plan for year $t - 1$. This practice has been described as "planning from the achieved level." Although it simplifies the planning process, it builds in considerable inflexibility. In addition, Soviet planners do not plan all items produced by the economy; they plan at the center only a relatively small number of items. Major commodities such as steel and machinery are called **funded commodities** or **limited commodities** and are planned at the center. Their number has varied over time from a few hundred to a few thousand. Other commodities are planned at progressively lower and lower levels in the hierarchy, depending on their importance in the economy. This simplifies the planning process while leaving much to be done at the lower levels — for example, in the various republics.

In constructing balances for major materials, planners face a dilemma. On the one hand, they would like the balance to be achieved at the highest possible level; on the other hand, they know that the more *taut* the plan — that is, the closer the targets are to maximum capacity — the more likely it is that errors and supply imbalances will occur.[12] The approach is, in practice, to attempt to find a balance at a reasonably high level through adjusting input usage, manipulating final demand, adjusting stocks, and/or seeking foreign supplies. All these stratagems are devices for ensuring that the plan can be demanding yet at the same time in balance. Soviet planners do not employ sophisticated planning techniques to "balance" supplies and demands. In fact, ad hoc tallies of sources and material requirements are maintained, and past experience is the principal guide to what is justified. Accordingly, Soviet planners are usually satisfied if they are able to come up with a *consistent* plan, but they do not have the luxury of seeking out the *optimal* plan from among all possible consistent plans.

In addition to these formal mechanisms to adjust supply and demand, informal patterns of managerial response also serve to manipulate plan patterns, sometimes in undesirable directions. Buffer sectors, typically consumer goods, have also been used to absorb shortages as they arise.

Our picture of traditional Soviet planning is a distortion of reality, for it suggests an economy rigidly planned and controlled by central authorities. In relative terms this is correct. All economies combine some mix of market and plan, and the Soviet economy leans most heavily in the direction of planning by directive. Most facets of the Soviet economy are planned, and there is almost total public ownership of the means of production. But beneath the façade of rigid centralized planning, numerous informal and some quasi-market mechanisms affect resource allocation. We know relatively little about the scope and workings of these informal mechanisms, although we do have some hints about them.

We know that the formal plan is really only the initial blueprint for economic activity both at the economy-wide and at the enterprise level. The manner in

which the plan is revised in the course of plan fulfillment is probably as important as the initial plan itself. In fact, the changes and revisions that take place
after the plan is finalized are so great that some analysts question whether it
is appropriate to call the Soviet economy a planned economy. We also know
that a variety of unofficial markets (to be examined later in this chapter) exist
and are important, yet they have little to do with the formal planning process.[13]
Most products, in fact, are planned at regional or local levels or are not planned
at all. In some instances, indirect signals (for example, prices) play a role in
resource allocation, especially at the managerial level.

It is not possible to characterize precisely the balance between the formal
and informal forces that affect resource allocation in the Soviet Union. We
know that compared to market economies, the balance is strongly in favor of
centralized administrative allocation, but the role of informal forces has also
been recognized.[14]

Our earlier discussion of the theory of planning emphasized three important
stages in the planning process: plan development, implementation, and feedback.
Thus far, we have concentrated on organizational arrangements and on formulation of the plan. But plan implementation is in large part the responsibility
of the individual firm or agricultural enterprise. As we consider the role of the
individual production unit in this system, bear in mind a critical question: What
sort of rules are needed to ensure that each enterprise will in fact be motivated
to follow plan directives, will be able to do so, and thus will fulfill the wishes
of the central planners? What happens when mistakes in planning are made or
when allocation decisions are omitted from plan directives?

THE SOVIET ENTERPRISE

In the planned economy, all enterprises have a plan, which is usually specified
in annual terms but broken down into monthly (and even shorter) periods.
First, the plan is a comprehensive document covering many facets of the firm's
operations, and it carries the force of law. Second, the plan specifies both
inputs and outputs in physical and financial terms; it specifies the sources and
the distribution of funds for the firm; and so on. However, it would be erroneous to think that the Soviet manager is fully regimented, mechanically follows
instructions, and has little freedom of action. In fact, quite a lot of managerial
freedom exists. To understand Soviet management and plan fulfillment, one
must understand how managers respond in this environment and what impact
they have on the plan and its fulfillment.

Much of the traditional Soviet managerial milieu can be summed up as "the
managerial success indicator problem." In short, Soviet managers are offered
substantial rewards for achieving a number of planned (often conflicting)
objectives, but those objectives are fuzzy and often ill defined, leading at times
to peculiar and dysfunctional managerial behavior.[15]

Historically, **gross value of output** (in later years, gross sales) has been the most important target from the manager's viewpoint. The manager's performance has been judged on the basis of fulfillment of this target. But even if prices accurately reflected relative scarcities, it would be difficult for planners to specify output objectives unequivocally. For example, if managers are told to maximize the gross value of output, they will ignore items that make a small contribution (relative to their claim on scarce resources) to gross value and will overproduce items that make a large contribution. The *mix* of goods within the plan (assortment) will be ignored, if ignoring it is necessary to meet the gross output target. Within existing patterns of Soviet managerial bonuses, such behavior, though potentially disruptive to the system, is rewarding to the manager and the enterprise. The bonus system has typically paid little or nothing until the output plan is 100 percent fulfilled. Then rewards are paid for production over this level, resulting in an average managerial bonus of perhaps 25 or 35 percent of base salary.[16] Top managers receive bonuses in excess of 50 percent. Moreover, managerial perks and job tenure depend on fulfillment of the gross output target. Thus we find a combination of generally taut targets, uncertain supply (especially for "limited" goals), and substantial rewards for fulfillment of planned output targets. The result has been informal and frequently dysfunctional managerial behavior — a problem not anticipated by the socialist economic theorists, who assumed that managers would obey all rules handed down by superior authorities.

How do Soviet managers protect themselves and prosper in such an environment? First, managers can, during the plan formulation stage, attempt to secure "easy" targets — that is, targets that are relatively low vis-à-vis the actual capacity of the enterprise. This is a problem of any system in which participants can manipulate the objectives against which they will be measured. And it is why the reward system is so important in a planned economy.

Second, managers can emphasize what is important (in terms of their rewards) and neglect or ignore other areas. Thus cost-saving targets may be sacrificed, along with assortment targets, for the sake of ensuring fulfillment of gross output targets. This is a major explanation for the shortage of spare parts in the Soviet industrial sector: Their manufacture disrupts production lines and does not contribute sufficiently to rewards. Third, managers can seek "safety" in various other practices. For example, they can stockpile materials that are expected to be in short supply; they can avoid change, notably innovation; and they can establish unplanned (informal or "family") connections to ensure a supply of crucial inputs.

Many features of the informal Soviet managerial milieu are disruptive and shift the results of production away from those envisaged by the planners. Others are necessary to correct for errors made by planning authorities and for breakdowns in the supply system. Plan execution, therefore, is subject to a substantial measure of flexibility and variation not envisaged in the theoretical models: People simply do not do what they are told. But the state does not stand idle; it can and does exercise control over enterprise management.

Planners monitor enterprise performance, though this is not a simple task in an economy the size of the Soviet Union. The CPSU is an important institution for this purpose. Most organizations contain party cells, and enterprise managers are almost always party members. They are therefore aware of the priorities specified by the party. Nevertheless, at almost all levels of the Soviet economy there is a bias in favor of reporting successful results. If local enterprises perform well, the careers of local party officials are advanced, and so on up the hierarchy. Another very different but important monitoring device is the state bank (Gosbank).[17] Most Soviet enterprises are budget-financed, which means that funds both to and from enterprises flow through the state bank into and out of the state budget. The state budget is a major source of enterprise investment funds or, for an enterprise that loses money, of subsidy funds. Profits, too, are channeled through the state bank, and profit taxes are an important part of Soviet budgetary revenue. Each enterprise is required to hold accounts with the state bank where all transactions are recorded. Not only are the quantity and type of labor that a firm can use specified in the plan, but the fund used to pay for the labor must be held and monitored by the state bank.

Second, managerial behavior can be manipulated by the nature of rewards, both material and moral.[18] We have noted that Soviet managers can earn substantial monetary bonuses for meeting targets. There are also other rewards, such as housing, vacations, automobiles, and promotion. On the negative side, managers who do not perform can be dismissed, a sanction that was far more widely used in the early days of Soviet planning than it is today.[19]

Soviet plans exist in both physical and monetary variants. The financial plans are basically derived from the physical plans; Soviet domestic prices are used. Beginning in the reform era of the late 1950s, increasing attention has been paid to financial variables and hence to the nature and rationality of the Soviet price system. In market economic systems, prices are the primary mechanism for influencing resource allocation. The reality of the market seldom approaches the ideals of the market model, but there is nevertheless a need to ensure that relative prices reflect relative scarcities to the greatest extent possible. Indeed, as financial variables grew more important in the command economy, the issue of price formation also became crucial. In order to understand the transition from plan to market, it is essential that we understand the role of money and prices in the traditional command model.

PRICES AND THE ALLOCATION OF LAND, LABOR, AND CAPITAL IN THE COMMAND SYSTEM

Soviet Prices: General Features

With some exceptions, Soviet prices have been set by administrative authorities.[20] In the case of the collective farm markets, and in services provided by moonlighting workers, prices are the result of supply and demand forces. Soviet industrial prices are largely set to equal average cost by industrial branch plus a small profit markup. **Branch average cost** generally excludes rental and interest charges, and its use as a standard has result d in enterprises making both planned profits and planned losses within the same branch. Pricing authorities have sought, through periodic price "reforms," to raise prices enough to make enterprises profitable. This presumably means that when the price reform is introduced, enterprises at the margin will break even and others will make substantial profits. But the administrative difficulty of making frequent price reforms has meant that historically prices have been allowed to lag behind real cost increases, and at times the majority of enterprises in particular branches have made planned losses. During the last quarter-century, major price reforms have been rare. Wholesale prices established in 1955 remained generally in effect until 1966. The 1966–1967 price reform remained in effect until the general price reform of 1982.

As we will see when we discuss the abandonment of the administrative command model, prices have limited use in such a model, because they are simply unrelated to relative scarcities.

As far as inter-enterprise relations are concerned, wholesale prices play primarily an accounting role, for supplies and demands are administratively planned and are not functions of prices. However, when a product leaves the wholesale level to be sold at the retail level, the matter is not so simple. Figure 12.2 illustrates retail price formation.

The supply of consumer goods at the retail level is determined largely by the planners, although producers, if they have a choice in output mix, may choose to produce a product with a higher relative price. Thus we draw the supply curve (S) with a steep upward slope. The demand curve (D) is a function of relative prices, incomes, and tastes and cannot be controlled by the planners. How can the planners ensure that supply and demand will balance at the retail level? Typically, the retail price is established at or near market-clearing level by adding a tax (the **turnover** tax) or subsidy (if the wholesale price is above the clearing level). If the retail price were set at the wholesale (cost-based) price (P in Figure 12.2), there would be an excess demand of $Q'Q$, for OQ would be produced and OQ' demanded. Some form of rationing would have to be found.

In addition to administrative rationing and toleration of excess demand (as shown by long lines to purchase goods), Soviet authorities have relied heavily on the turnover tax to balance supply and demand. If the authorities choose to ration via price, the retail price is set at OP' and approximate equilibrium prevails. It is important to note that raising the retail price *does not* raise the quantity supplied above OQ, because the enterprise continues to receive the wholesale price OP for the product. The difference between the retail and wholesale prices (ignoring trade margins) is the turnover tax.

The turnover tax, in this case PP', is an important component of Soviet budgetary revenue. Unlike Western sales taxes, its proportion differs widely from one product to another, and it is included in the price rather than being added on at the time of sale. Its share of retail prices has declined slowly over time, as planners have increased supplies of consumer products and have raised the wholesale prices of farm products.

Although prices approach equilibrium at the retail level, it should be emphasized that this mechanism is very different from that prevailing in the capitalist market economy. What we see in the Soviet case as a tax would in effect be a profit accruing to the capitalist producer, which serves as a signal to existing producers to expand supply and to new producers to enter the market. There is no such signal in the Soviet case, because what would be profit in the capitalist context accrues as tax revenue to the state. The producer at the wholesale level is unaware of and largely uninterested in retail prices. Thus the link between consumer demand the producer is broken. Say demand increases from D to D'. As the producer continues to receive the wholesale price OP, the quantity produced remains at OQ. But at the old retail price OP', there is now an excess of demand over supply. The state reacts eventually by raising the turnover tax by $P'P''$.

It is fair to say that in the Soviet case, the value and the mix of consumer goods are determined by planners' preferences, not by consumer demand,

Figure 12.2 Soviet Turnover Tax

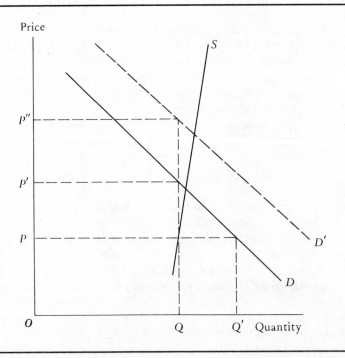

although in the long run, planners may well consider consumer signals when establishing plan targets. Thus it is argued that prices play only a very limited **allocative** role and are used primarily for functions such as measurement, control, and manipulation of the distribution of income.

Soviet price policy has always emphasized the desirability of pricing some goods and services relatively "low" and others relatively "high." This policy reflects a very different (socialist) attitude toward the appropriate ("equitable") distribution of income and toward determining what is a necessity and what a luxury. Thus the prices of books, housing, medical care, and transportation are very low, and the prices of automobiles and vodka are very high. Price policy affects the distribution of real incomes in accordance with state objectives.

The issues surrounding prices and pricing policies in the command economy are complex. In the pre-Gorbachev era, Soviet price reform was generally aimed at making prices more realistic in the sense of accurately reflecting production costs; thus they should promote greater efficiency in the use of inputs. However, many would argue that despite numerous reform attempts, Soviet prices have remained, throughout the plan era, largely ineffective in promoting the rational allocation of resources. Given the indispensable role of prices in a market system, one can readily appreciate the difficulty of replacing plan by market under these conditions.

Input Prices: Land and Labor

In the Soviet economy, the prices of inputs — land, labor, and capital — have reflected a peculiar combination of Marxian orthodoxy, pragmatism, and allocative necessity. There is, for the most part, no rental price for agricultural land. Land is allocated to collective and state farms administratively. Planners determine land utilization within the framework of the plan, taking into account the technical and local conditions of the agricultural enterprise. The absence of land charges makes farm accounting a questionable exercise, the result of which has been an endless debate over the role of land rent under socialism. Despite some interest in land valuation problems, the Soviet Union has not formalized a system of land valuation. Historically, however, Soviet planners have attempted to extract a rent from the Soviet countryside by using regionally differentiated procurement prices and differential charges for machine services provided by the state.

The allocation of labor in the Soviet Union is a very different case, for there is a price for labor in the form of a wage rate. How are wages set in the Soviet Union, and what role do wages have in allocating labor among that country's various occupations, uses, and regions?[21]

Historically, wage differentials have been one of several mechanisms utilized to allocate labor in the Soviet Union. The demand for labor is primarily plan-determined. Once output targets are established, labor requirements can be determined by applying technical coefficients that represent the amount of labor required per unit of output under existing technology. On the supply side, however, households are substantially free to make occupational choices and to decide between labor and leisure. The state has set wage differentials — for example, by occupation and by region — in an attempt to induce appropriate supplies to meet planned demands.

The basic wage-setting procedure is straightforward. For an industrial branch, a base rate is established. This rate determines the wage level for that branch relative to other branches. A schedule gives all rates above this level as a percentage of the base and establishes the pattern of wage differentials within the branch. Thus the level and differential can be adjusted by manipulating the base or the schedule. Soviet trade unions and individual workers play virtually no role in setting wages; wages are set by administrative authorities. But unlike many other areas in the Soviet economy, planners have been quite willing to *use* these differentials to manipulate labor supply. There is a substantial degree of market influence on the structure of Soviet wages.[22]

In addition to wage differentials, other devices are used to manipulate labor supply. Higher- and technical-education institutions are expanded in direct relation to the desired composition of the labor force, and this is a matter under state control. In addition, nonmonetary rewards, adulation in the press, social benefits, and other such inducements (moral incentives) have been used to affect the supply of labor. Organized recruitment by special organizations and the party has been important in the past but has declined in recent years, with the possibly important exception of the seasonal needs of agricultural production.[23] The Soviet system, therefore, combines both material and moral rewards, with the emphasis on the former.

Soviet labor policies, including the forced-labor campaigns of the 1930s, have ensured a very high rate of labor force participation to provide rapid economic development. In recent years, the participation rate, defined as the civilian labor force as a proportion of the able-bodied population, has generally exceeded 90 percent. On the other hand, structural problems have recently become more serious and will be a major test of the efficacy of central planning as a mechanism for allocating labor. For example, a very rapid (even if controlled) rate of urbanization has left shortages in some areas, surpluses in others. These imbalances are especially true for the regional distribution of labor, where Soviet authorities have not been able to meet the labor needs of Siberia and the Far North. In addition, the rather restrictive role of Soviet trade unions and the policy of "full employment" have resulted in underemployment — artificially high levels of staffing at the enterprise level. Under present conditions, it is quite difficult to lay off workers even if they are redundant. This problem has prompted the state to experiment with new programs to encourage the firing of unproductive workers. The Soviet economy has not solved the problem of microeconomic allocation of labor resources for a modern economy. The crucial question that arises is whether a full (or "overfull") employment policy can be maintained and at the same time ensure allocative efficiency. This is an important area for reform in Soviet planning methods.

Capital Allocation

We turn now to the matter of pricing capital, or determining an interest charge.[24] As we saw in Chapter 6, capital is not a value-creating input in the Marxian scheme. Why then should its use generate a reward in the form of a capital (interest) charge? Even if capital has no value-creating capacity, less is available than is demanded. Some means must be devised for its allocation. Furthermore, even if a "price" is used in this allocation function, it will perform *only* this function. Where all capital is owned by the state, the "income" from capital accrues directly to the state, not to individuals.

In the Soviet case, investment has been largely controlled by central planning authorities and the ministries. In drawing up the output plan, planners apply technical coefficients to determine the amounts of capital investment necessary to produce the planned output, and investment funds are authorized. Some funds are available from internal enterprise sources, but even these funds remain under control of the banking system. The aggregate supply of investment funds is largely under the control of planners. It is not surprising, therefore, that the ratio of saving to gross national product is very high in the Soviet Union — much higher, for example, than in the United States. Indeed, this illustrates a basic feature of planners' preferences. In a market capitalist economy, saving is influenced by government but is largely determined by individuals and businesses as they choose between consumption in the present and greater consumption in the future. In the Soviet context, the state controls the amount of saving (primarily by the state and by enterprises). In a capitalist economy, saving arises as undistributed profits in enterprises and an income that is not consumed in households. Both *types* of saving exist in the Soviet case, but because wages and prices are set by the state, the state can itself accumulate savings at whatever rate it chooses without recourse to the indirect method of taxation. This ability to control saving and investment is a powerful mechanism to promote a more rapid rate of capital accumulation than would probably be tolerated in an economy directed by consumer sovereignty.

Since the late 1960s, Soviet enterprises have paid an interest charge for the use of capital. This charge has typically been small (6 percent) and is designed to cover the administrative costs of making the capital funds available to the enterprise.

At the enterprise level, Soviet authorities have devised rules for choosing among investment projects. Suppose there is a directive to raise the capacity to generate a certain volume of electric power. Will the capacity be hydroelectric, nuclear, coal-fueled, or what? How can one compare the capital-intensive variant that has low operating costs to the variant that requires less capital initially but has high annual operating costs? Although quasi-market techniques for making this sort of decision were rejected by Stalin in the 1930s in favor of planners' wisdom, these methods surfaced again in the late 1950s and have been widely used in recent years.

Since 1958 planners have accepted the principle that the selection among competing projects should be based on cost-minimizing procedures. To illustrate, a general formula (the coefficient of relative effectiveness) to compare projects was in use after 1958:

$$C_i + E_n K_i = \text{Minimum}$$

where

C_i = current expenditures of the ith investment project
K_i = the capital cost of the ith investment project
E_n = the normative coefficient

This formula has been used to weigh the tradeoff between higher capital outlays (K_i) and lower operating costs (C_i). The notion underlying this formula is that that project variant should be selected that yields the minimum full cost, where an imputed capital charge is included in the cost of calculation. The capital cost (charge) is calculated by applying a "normative coefficient" (E_n) to the projected capital outlay.

For example, assume that a choice must be made between two projects, the first having an annual operating cost (C) of 10 million rubles and a capital cost (K) of 30 million rubles, the second having a C of 7 million rubles and a K of 50 million rubles. Applying a normative coefficient of, say, 10 percent yields a full cost of 13 million rubles for the first project and 12 million rubles for the second. The second project should be chosen, because it is the minimum-cost variant. However, suppose a normative coefficient of 20 percent is applied. In this case, the full cost of the first variant is 16 and that of the second variant is 17. In this case — and all that has changed is the normative coefficient — the first variant should be chosen.

An important feature of this formula should be noted. The higher the normative coefficient, the higher the imputed capital cost, and the *less* likely that capital-intensive variants will be selected. This is exactly what occurred between 1958 and 1969, when a system of differentiated normative coefficients was used. The pattern of differentiated norms followed the established principle of giving priority to heavy industry by applying low E_ns to heavy-industrial branches (thereby encouraging the selection of capital-intensive projects in these branches) and high E_ns to light industry. In 1969, a new *Standard Methodology*[25] replaced the earlier differentiated system with a standard normative coefficient of 12 percent. It was supposed to be applied equally to all branches of the economy.

The principle that capital should be allocated among projects on the basis of such rate-of-return calculations should not obscure the fact that the basic allocation of capital still proceeds through an administrative investment plan, which itself is a derivative of the output plan. The rate-of-return calculations are used only to select among projects that follow planners' preferences in the first place. Thus they are used to decide what type of plant should be used to generate electricity, not whether the investment should be in the generation of electricity or, for example, in steel production. In fact, the standardized coefficient introduced in 1969 has been watered down since then by numerous exceptions for particular branches of heavy industry and for various regions.

Financial Planning

As we have emphasized, the Soviet economy has been run by largely administrative rules and instructions. Although value categories (prices, costs, profits, and so on) have always existed, they have played only a limited role in allocating resources. Even in a centralized economy where few decisions are made at local levels, households make decisions about how much members will work and what they will buy. How can planners ensure that there will be a macroeconomic balance of consumer goods in the economy? Aggregate consumer demand and supply can be illustrated in the following framework:

$$D = WL - R \qquad\qquad (12.1)$$

$$S = P_1 Q_1 \qquad\qquad (12.2)$$

where

D = aggregate demand
S = aggregate supply
W = the average annual wage
L = the number of worker-years of labor used in the economy
R = the amount of income not spent on consumer goods
     (equal to the sum of direct taxes and savings)
Q_1 = the real quantity of consumer goods produced
P_1 = the price level of consumer goods

The problem here is conceptually quite simple. As the Soviet socialist economy developed rapidly in the early plan years, it paid labor increasingly large salaries to motivate higher participation and greater effort, but the state wanted that labor to produce producer goods, not consumer goods (Q_1). Thus the state permitted wages (W) to rise rapidly in order to encourage labor inputs (L) to rise. In the absence of sharp increases in Q_1, however, it was necessary to pursue alternative steps to achieve a balance between S and D — notably to let P_1 rise along with R (the latter rise engendered through forced bond purchases). However, prices were not allowed to rise fast enough to absorb the full increase in demand; an imbalance between aggregate supply and demand was allowed to develop. This technique, typical for any less developed economy during the early stages of development, is known as **repressed inflation** and has been used widely in the Soviet Union.[26]

During the years following World War II, the quantity of consumer goods increased, although simultaneous increases in purchasing power make it difficult to determine to what degree excess demand has been reduced. Indeed, as we noted earlier, Janos Kornai has developed a general model of the socialist economy suggesting that such systems can in fact be shortage-based systems, even when expansion in the production of consumer goods is taking place.

In recent years, the focus of this discussion for the Soviet Union and other formerly planned socialist systems has been the issue of repressed inflation.[27] Moreover, in a system where excess demand is unlikely to result in price increases, **disequilibrium analysis** (see Appendix 12A) proves to be an effective tool. Western research has focused on Soviet savings behavior as evidence of repressed inflation (people save because there is nothing to buy at prevailing prices). Moreover, much research effort has been focused on the direct modeling of consumer goods markets. Although this mode of analysis has stimulated a great deal of controversy, the evidence suggests that excess demand has been and remains a serious problem in the Soviet system. Indeed, as we look at the transition of the Soviet economy away from the command model, shortages seem to be much more prevalent than was earlier thought to be the case.

Market Forces in the Command Economy

The American economy is a market economy in which the state has come to play a growing and frequently controversial role. The Soviet economy, at least until the era of *Perestroika*, was a planned economy in which market forces were of only moderate and secondary importance. Thus, although the role of markets in the traditional Soviet economy is a matter of some controversy, their role in resource allocation has generally been viewed as an exception to the plan. The issue of markets in what we usually describe as a planned economy deserves additional attention.

In an economic system, ownership and control are closely related. The Soviet state, as the primary owner of the means of production, is assumed to exercise control over the direction of economic activity through the national economic plan. Our discussion of the Soviet economy has been cast in these terms, though the issue is not without controversy.

Paul Craig Roberts argues that the Soviet economy is a "polycentric" system in which control is diversified.[28] He maintains that the interaction of enterprises at the local level, their informal interrelationships, and the generation of local information flows, not the plan, are the main forces determining economic activity. Eugene Zaleski has concluded from his analysis of plan fulfillment that administrative adjustments made after the plan is finalized have a stronger bearing on resource allocation than do the plans themselves. Zaleski refers to the Soviet economy as an administratively managed (not a planned) economy.[29]

A number of other Western analysts have come to question whether the Soviet economy has been appropriately characterized as a "planned" economy. John H. Wilhelm argues that the original plan typically is not workable, is continuously changed in the course of plan fulfillment, and in the end is revised to correspond to expected fulfillment. Under these circumstances, Wilhelm argues, it is inappropriate to call the Soviet economy a planned economy.[30] Available evidence does not allow us to draw a firm conclusion on this question, but we would reject the argument that the plan is not a critical determinant of economic activity. Rather, the relevant issue is whether, and how much, additional forces affect economic outcomes.

Western economists have long argued that in some areas of the Soviet economy — for example, labor allocation — planners used market-type mechanisms to influence observed outcomes. Thus wage differentials have been used to influence the distribution of labor by region, by season, and by profession, and retail prices to allocate available consumer goods. The fact that wages and retail prices are set by planners does not rule out market forces. In such instances, planners are actually acting as market intermediaries.

A third role for market forces is the "second economy." The second economy has been analyzed extensively by Gregory Grossman, Dimitri Simes, Vladimir Treml, Michael V. Alexeev, Aron Katsenelinboigen, and others.[31] It consists of a number of market-type activities of varying importance and degrees of legality, all facilitating "unplanned" exchange among consumers and producers. According to Grossman, second-economy activities must meet at least one of the following two criteria: (1) the activity is engaged in for private gain; (2) the person engaging in the activity knowingly contravenes existing law.

Examples of second-economy activities abound. Indeed, since the advent of Glasnost, we have learned a good deal more about the second economy. A physician may treat private patients for higher fees. A salesperson may set aside quality merchandise for customers who offer large tips. The manager of a textile firm may reserve goods for sale in unofficial supply channels. A collective farmer may divert collective farm land and supplies to his private plot. Black marketeers in port cities may deal in contraband merchandise. Owners of private cars may transport second-economy merchandise. In some cases, official and second-economy transactions are intertwined. A manager may divert some production into second-economy transactions to raise cash to purchase unofficially supplies needed to meet the plan. The official activities of an enterprise may serve as a front for a prospering second-economy undertaking.

According to available accounts, second-economy activities are concentrated in collective farms and in the transportation network. Apparently, the supervision of collective farms is more lax; they therefore serve as better fronts for the second economy. Transportation enterprises are critical to the second economy, for its merchandise must somehow be moved. The increase in private ownership of automobiles has apparently enhanced the operation of the second economy.

How important is the second economy? Unfortunately, it is difficult to estimate accurately the magnitude of second-economy activity. In a survey of Soviet émigrés conducted by Gur Ofer and Aron Vinokur, earnings derived from activity other than that at the main place of employment were found to account for approximately 10 percent of earnings.[32] A study of Soviet alcohol production and consumption, conducted by Vladimir Treml in the mid-1980s, found that between 20 and 25 percent of transactions were illegal. However, it is important to emphasize that although the second economy was important in the overall command economy, there were substantial variations from one sector to another. It is not surprising for secondary activities to arise in an economic system characterized by rising incomes and limited resources devoted to the service sector. Moreover, the growth of a second economy might be viewed as in some ways helpful to those attempting to control the economy through planning arrangements.

The second economy has its advantages and disadvantages as far as the planners are concerned. It helps to preserve incentives, because higher wages and bonus payments can be spent in the second economy. Moreover, the second economy serves to reduce inflationary pressures on the official economy. On the negative side, the second economy diverts participants in the economy from planned tasks and loosens planners' control over the economy. Soviet authorities have long tolerated the second economy. Reforms of the late 1980s even moved to legalize a number of second-economy activities that do not involve the use of hired labor.

A fourth area of market influence is the private sector of Soviet agriculture. The farm family can, under certain restrictions, use a plot of land, hold animals, and raise crops. The resulting products are sold in markets (the kolkhoz market) tolerated by the authorities. Prices are freely established by supply and demand and provide a substantial portion of the farm family's income. It is not by accident that the private plots produce farm products that are poorly suited to planning, such as fruits, vegetables, and dairy products — all of which require much personal care and motivation.

The existence of second-economy activity in the administrative command economy is of more than passing interest. Although it is difficult to quantify this second economy with precision, it is nevertheless viewed as an important — if unevenly distributed — part of the overall economic system. It is of theoretical interest that such a mechanism arises in the command economy beyond the purview of the planners. Moreover, if we find that its magnitude increases over time, we may have discovered a crude indicator of the divergence between plan targets and achievements and consumer demands in the economy. Finally, as we shall see later, the second economy has become increasingly important as part of privatization in the Gorbachev era.

AGRICULTURE IN THE COMMAND ECONOMY

Our discussion of the American economic system did not include any specific treatment of agriculture. This omission reflects the fact that in an advanced economy such as the United States, agriculture plays a relatively much more modest role than it does in the developing Soviet economy. Even at the beginning of the Gorbachev era in the mid-1980s, agriculture accounted for 20 to 25 percent of Soviet gross national product and absorbed a great deal of the Soviet labor force. However, there is a second reason for looking more closely at Soviet agriculture: It exhibits unique organizational arrangements, and the results achieved have been modest in spite of continuing attention from Soviet policy makers.

As far back as the 1920s, the so-called peasant problem was viewed as central to any development effort in the Soviet Union. During war communism and the New Economic Policy, various forms of organization existed, but private peasant agriculture dominated.[33] The rural sector was seen as crucial to any Soviet development effort, because industrialization would depend on agricultural deliveries. Whether or not the perception of agriculture in the 1920s as the key to industrialization was correct, it was the rationale for Stalin's decision to collectivize in 1929.[34]

Two major institutions have been dominant in Soviet agriculture since the 1930s. The collective farms (**kolkhozy**) were to operate like cooperatives; the state farms (**sovkhozy**), in which the farmers would be paid like industrial workers, would be a "factory in the fields." The sovkhoz was and is a state enterprise with state-appointed management.[35] The kolkhoz was and is (in theory) a cooperative with elected management. Sovkhoz workers are state employees and therefore receive fixed wages like other state employees. Kolkhoz peasants, on the other hand, received a dividend instead of a wage. Because this unique payment system was the cornerstone of Stalin's attempt to extract a surplus from the countryside, dwelling on it for a moment is worthwhile, even though it was abandoned in 1966.[36]

Before 1966, payment for peasants in the kolkhoz was established in the following fashion. For a particular task assigned to a peasant by, say, a brigade leader, a certain number of labor days would be "paid" and recorded in the peasant's work book. The labor day was not necessarily a measure of time or effort, but rather an often arbitrary measure of work input. At the end of the year, the *value* of one labor day would be determined by the following formula:

Value of one labor day = farm income after required deliveries and
    other expenses ÷ total number of labor days
    for entire kolkhoz

The value of a labor day having been determined, it would then be possible to pay each individual a "dividend" by multiplying the number of labor days accumulated by the value of one labor day.

This system of payment was highly arbitrary. The work demanded for one labor day could and did vary regionally, seasonally, and from farm to farm. Furthermore, contrary to the principles of any good incentive system, the peasant had little idea in advance what she or he would earn per labor day. The labor day system was finally abandoned in 1966 and was replaced by a guaranteed wage.

Differences Between Collective Farms and States Farms

Most input and output determinations in the kolkhoz and the sovkhoz are planned in a fashion similar to that used in an industrial enterprise. There are, however, some noteworthy differences. First, the method of payment for labor in the kolkhoz was, until 1966, very different from that in the sovkhoz. Second, the manner in which capital investment has been provided is different: Kolkhoz investments have been largely self-financed; sovkhoz investment funds come directly from the state budget.[37] Third, until the late 1950s, machinery and equipment were maintained in the Machine Tractor Stations and were provided to the collective farms for a payment.[38] This mechanism served as an important external control over the management of the kolkhozy. Fourth, the method of distribution of output has been different. The sovkhoz, as a state enterprise, distributes the bulk of its output through the normal state trade channels, as an industrial enterprise might do. The kolkhoz, in contrast, has been required to make compulsory deliveries to the state, often at very low fixed prices; but the remainder of its output has been free for sale either to the state at higher prices or on the collective farm markets. This two-tier pricing arrangement has allowed the state to extract the product from the kolkhoz.

In both the kolkhoz and the sovkhoz, families are entitled to small plots of land (typically about half an acre) for their private use.[39] The produce from this land, which is very important in the case of some products (typically truck-garden products), can be consumed on the farm, sold to the state, or sold by the peasants in the collective farm markets. It is difficult to summarize the importance of the private sector in a few numbers. However, to give some idea of its impact, we note that in the 1960s, the private sector accounted for roughly 60 percent of total potato output, 70 percent of total vegetable output, and 30 percent of total milk output. In the postwar period, the private sector has accounted for approximately 40 percent of family income on collective farms. Peasants are also entitled to hold some animals, although the permitted number of each type has varied over time. For example, roughly 40 percent of all cows were owned privately in the 1960s.

Changes in Soviet Agriculture

Organizational arrangements in agriculture have changed substantially since the 1930s, although the kolkhoz, the sovkhoz, and the private sector remain at least in name to the present day. We note the main trends of change.[40]

First, since the 1940s, a program of merger and consolidation has sharply reduced the number and importance of kolkhozy; at the same time, the number of sovkhozy has increased, and their average size is greater. In 1940, there were 237,000 kolkhozy in the Soviet Union with an average sown area of 1235 acres. By the mid-1980s, the number of kolkhozy had been reduced to just over 26,000, and each kolkhoz had an average sown area of just over 8600 acres. As for sovkhozy, in 1940 there were 4200, averaging just over 6900 acres of sown area on each farm. By the mid-1980s, the number of sovkhozy had increased to almost 22,700, with an average sown area of almost 12,000 acres per farm.[41] In 1940, roughly 78 percent of all sown area was accounted for by kolkhozy; this was reduced to 44 percent by the mid-1980s.

Possibly the most important organizational change in contemporary Soviet agriculture has been the introduction of **agro-industrial integration** on a major scale.[42] Begun with renewed emphasis in the 1970s, agro-industrial integration has brought both kolkhozy and sovkhozy together with industrial-type activity (for example, processing) into integrated production units with centralized management. These changes, along with organizational changes on the regional level introduced with the Brezhnev "Food Program" of 1982, set the scene for further changes to occur with Perestroika under Gorbachev.

Second, there have been changes in planning and supervisory organs and in the farm managerial system. The Machine Tractor Stations were abolished in 1958, and their equipment was sold to the farms, a move that gave farm managers enhanced control over farm equipment. In addition, the quality of managerial personnel has improved dramatically in recent years.

Third, rural incomes have increased sharply since the 1950s, generally more rapidly than industrial incomes. In addition, a pension system introduced in the 1960s substantially improved the welfare of rural workers and peasants and reduced the rural–urban income differential.[43] However, expanded production costs at the farm level and unwillingness to raise retail food prices significantly have resulted in a very large subsidy to the agricultural sector.[44]

Fourth, after a period of extensive campaigns by Nikita Khrushchev in the 1950s (the Virgin Land Campaign, the corn program, and so on) designed to expand inputs, the emphasis in the 1960s and 1970s shifted to improvement of productivity, in part through significant increases in the volume of investment provided by the state.

Fifth, there has been an ongoing program to examine seriously the problems of agriculture in an urban industrial economy. For example, Soviet planners have devoted (though not always successfully) considerable attention to the problems of supplying large cities with vegetables. Also, efforts have been made to stem the continuing rapid flow of young males from the rural areas and hence to alleviate the problem of labor shortages and imbalances.

Soviet agriculture has always been of more than passing interest to Western observers. Catastrophic crop failures, minimal supplies of meat, and the virtual absence of produce in Soviet cities in winter are puzzling in a heavily industrialized nation. Many observers have laid the blame for uneven Soviet agricultural performance on unique Soviet organizational arrangements or on limited investment in agriculture.

We must ask whether the agricultural sector of the Soviet economy has been neglected in some sense and what sorts of policies were developed in the 1970s and early 1980s. The Brezhnev years saw important developments in Soviet agriculture, though change was implemented less flamboyantly than it had been under his predecessor. Capital investment increased from roughly 15 percent of aggregate investment to almost 27 percent — a substantial increment by any standard. At the same time, agricultural productivity remains a problem, imports are still very important, and Gorbachev criticizes agricultural performance. Clearly, productivity must be improved. But possibly more important, the infrastructure of Soviet agriculture must be improved, especially food processing, storage, and distribution arrangements.

In sum, it is difficult to study the Soviet development experience — and especially the implementation of the administrative command economy — without paying close attention to agriculture. As we have seen, agricultural policy was a focal point of controversy from the beginning, and it remained so in those East European nations where the Soviet model was imposed after World War II. During the postwar era, there was probably no sector in the Soviet economy to which so much attention was devoted. Even so, poor performance and sharply rising costs far exceeded what might reasonably be expected under less than ideal natural conditions. Agriculture remains a major challenge for the leaders of the "post-command" era.

INTERNATIONAL TRADE IN THE COMMAND ECONOMY

No discussion of the Soviet command model would be complete if it failed to address the role of international trade in this model.[45] Foreign trade has played a major role in the Soviet development experience. Moreover, the organizational arrangements used differ significantly from those generally found in market economic systems. Most observers would argue that both the policies and the systemic arrangements (and hence the outcomes) of foreign trade typical of the command model differ widely from those seen in a market context. Again, as we shall see when we discuss contemporary Soviet reforms, knowledge of the traditional arrangements is essential if we are to understand the difficulties of a transition from plan to market.

Because we devote a separate chapter (Chapter 19) to issues of international trade in different economic systems, and especially to the shift of those trade regimes toward the market, our discussion here is limited to specifics of the Soviet command model.

Decision making — in terms of what will be traded, with whom, and on what terms — is relatively centralized in three major areas: the Ministry of Foreign Trade (MFT), the *Vneshtorgbank* of Bank for Foreign Trade (BFT), and the various foreign trade organizations (FTOs). The formal organization of Soviet foreign trade is represented in Figure 12.3. The Ministry of Foreign Trade, like other Soviet ministries, is a relatively centralized body concerned with issues of foreign trade planning — the development of import/export plans, material supply plans, and balance-of-payments plans — all of which form an integral part of the Soviet material balance planning system.

Individual Soviet enterprises have generally not dealt with the external world, although reforms proposed by Gorbachev in the summer of 1987 would change this posture. Rather, for both imports and exports, enterprises have dealt with the FTOs in domestic currency at domestic prices, and the FTOs have dealt with the external world via financial arrangements handled by the Ministry of Foreign Trade and the BFT. In the Soviet case, a monopoly in the hands of the Soviet government conducts foreign trade. The domestic users or producers of goods entering the foreign market are substantially isolated from foreign markets by this foreign trade monopoly. As viewed by Western economists, Soviet foreign trade has operated according to formal rules: Export what is available to be exported to pay for necessary imports, and limit the overall volume of trade to control the influence of market forces on the Soviet economy.

Traditionally, most Soviet trade, even with other socialist countries, is bilateral — that is, directly negotiated for each trade deal with each trading partner. Bilateral trade means that Soviet exports and imports are handled largely on a barter basis. The well-known difficulties of operating according to offsetting barter deals have hampered Soviet trade turnover through the years. In part, bilateral trading arrangements arise from and contribute to the nonconvertibility of the Soviet ruble, which is not accepted as a medium of exchange in world financial markets.

Soviet organizational arrangements are not conducive to maintaining an expanding and competitive position in world markets, but Western economists have generally argued that the Soviet Union has followed a policy of deliberate "trade aversion."[46] What are the justifications for trade aversion? Dating from the late 1920s and early 1930s, Soviet trade ratios (that is, the ratio of imports and exports to gross national product) generally declined. For many years they

Figure 12.3 The Organization of Soviet Foreign Trade: The Command Model

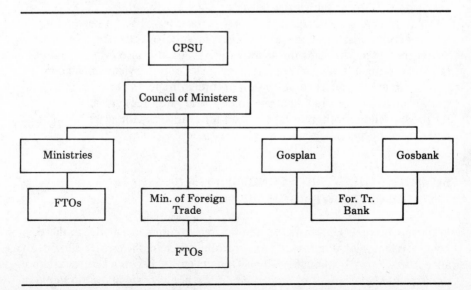

remained low by world standards. This pattern may have resulted from the Soviet Union's adverse position in world markets at that time, or it may have been in part a deliberate policy response. In any event, for the trade that *was* conducted, a very successful effort was made to redirect Soviet imports away from consumer goods and toward producer goods that contributed to the development effort.

Recent decades have witnessed changes in Soviet foreign trade. These changes may signal a changing trade posture, in particular a more aggressive posture in world markets.

First, Soviet trade ratios have been rising in recent years, signaling an increased participation in the world economy. The extent of this rise is difficult to estimate because of the peculiarities of Soviet foreign trade accounting,[47] but there is little doubt that Soviet participation in foreign trade in the 1980s is well above the rates of the 1950s and 1960s.

Second, the 1960s and 1970s saw important organizational changes. To take one major example, there has been continuing discussion in the Soviet Union about the need to make its enterprises more responsive to world markets and to streamline the FTOs as the mechanism through which enterprise contacts with world markets are channeled. These themes have become important components of reform in the Gorbachev era.

Third, there has been a revolution in Soviet attitudes toward foreign trade. There is renewed interest in Western, or neoclassical, trade theory and, most important, in the development and application of useful criteria on which to base trade decisions.

Fourth, the Soviet Union, though fundamentally conservative throughout the command era when compared to most of its East European neighbors, has nevertheless displayed increasing interest in participating in world trade arrangements and organizations. Thus Soviet attitudes toward the external world changed even before the Gorbachev era.

Most observers would agree that foreign trade has played a key role in the Soviet development experience. However, in spite of interesting changes in Soviet trading mechanisms through the mid-1980s, it is also evident that both the organizational arrangements and the policies of the Soviet command model have inhibited the effective utilization of foreign trade. In the face of dramatically changing world trading arrangements, and given the critical Soviet need for productivity growth, the stage was set for change as Gorbachev introduced Perestroika in the mid-1980s.

SUMMARY: THE SOVIET ECONOMY, 1928–1985:
THE ADMINISTRATIVE COMMAND MODEL

What has become known as the administrative command model is the economic system that dominated resource allocation in the Soviet Union for almost sixty years. Although Mikhail Gorbachev has begun a serious attempt to dismantle key features of this system, it is still a very significant example of economic development in a largely nonmarket context. The main features of this system are as follows:

1. The administrative command system was put in place in 1928 with nationalization of the means of production, a system of national economic planning, and the collectivization of agriculture. Although there have been numerous changes in this system over the years, its fundamental aspects have remained remarkably stable.
2. The Soviet system has been a relatively centralized economic system. The broad objectives of the Communist party have been implemented through the state planning agency (Gosplan), the ministries, and individual firms and agricultural units.
3. The essence of Soviet planning has been the material balance system, in which balances are developed to equate the demand and supply of key industrial commodities, labor inputs, and the like. The balance approach stresses consistency but not optimality, and there is only minimal reliance on money and prices for the allocation of resources.
4. Soviet enterprises are responsible for fulfilling plan targets, and managers are motivated within an incentive framework. In the absence of a price system reflecting relative scarcities and thus enabling managers to make rational decisions, dysfunctional behavior is a major problem.
5. Prices are cost-based, and the demand side has little or no influence. Prices serve primarily an accounting and control function. Retail markets and the allocation of labor are exceptions; here the allocative role of prices is greater. Although capital is allocated in accordance with rules that resemble rates of return, capital allocation is largely accomplished by administrative decree.
6. Market-type influence exists in the allocation of labor. At the same time, market forces are prevalent in the second economy, which, though it varies in importance from one sector to another, dominates in the service sector. Market mechanisms also play an important role in the private sector of Soviet agriculture.
7. Soviet agriculture has traditionally been dominated by the collective farms, the state farms, and the private sector. The latter is an important source of food products in spite of its relatively small size in terms of land area. In recent years, agro-industrial integration has become an important mechanism for combining farm activity with industrial processing.
8. Soviet foreign trade has been a state monopoly. Soviet domestic enterprises have been largely isolated from world markets the intermediary function of the Foreign Trade Organization and the nonconvertible ruble.

NOTES

1. For a general treatment of the Soviet economy and references to the specialized literature, see Paul R. Gregory and Robert C. Stuart, *Soviet Economic Structure and Performance*, 4th ed. (New York: HarperCollins, 1990); Alec Nove, *The Soviet Economic System*, 3rd ed. (New York: Unwin Hyman, 1986); and Michael Ellman, *Socialist Planning* (New York: Cambridge University Press, 1989). For useful background papers, see U.S. Congress, Joint Economic

Committee, *Soviet Economy in the 1980s: Problems and Prospects*, parts 1 and 2 (Washington, D.C.: Government Printing Office, 1982). For a briefer treatment of the Soviet economy, see Franklyn D. Holzman, *The Soviet Economy: Past, Present, and Future* (New York: Foreign Policy Association, 1982); and James R. Millar, *The ABC's of Soviet Socialism* (Urbana: University of Illinois Press, 1981).

2. For a discussion of these years, see M. Lewin, *Russian Peasants and Soviet Power* (London: Allen and Unwin, 1968); for a brief survey, see Gregory and Stuart, *Soviet Economic Structure and Performance*, Ch. 5.

3. A considerable amount has been written about the Soviet economy during these early years. See, for example, Alec Nove, *An Economic History of the U.S.S.R.*, rev. ed. (London: Penguin Books, 1982); Eugene Zaleski, *Planning for Economic Growth in the Soviet Union, 1928–1932* (Chapel Hill: University of North Carolina Press, 1971); Maurice Dobb, *Soviet Economic Development Since 1917*, 5th ed. (London: Routledge and Kegan Paul, 1960); E. H. Carr and R. W. Davies, *Foundations of a Planned Economy, 1926–1929*, Vol. I, pt. 2 (New York: Macmillan, 1969); Roger Munting, *The Economic Development of the USSR* (London: Croom Helm, 1982); R. W. Davies, *The Socialist Offensive, the Collectivization of Soviet Agriculture 1929–30* (London: Macmillan, 1980); and Thomas F. Remington, "Varga and the Foundation of Soviet Planning," *Soviet Studies*, 34 (October 1982), 585–600.

4. There is considerable debate about the *level* of economic development in the Soviet Union in 1917 and hence the readiness of that country, in the Marxian schema, for the introduction of socialism. For a discussion of this issue, see Gregory and Stuart, *Soviet Economic Structure and Performance*, Ch. 2; for more detail, see Paul R. Gregory, "Economic Growth and Structural Change in Tsarist Russia: A Case of Modern Economic Growth?" *Soviet Studies*, 23 (January 1972), 418–434; Paul R. Gregory, *Russian National Income 1885–1913* (New York: Cambridge University Press, 1983); and R. W. Davies, ed., *From Tsarism to the New Economic Policy* (Basingstoke, England: Macmillan, 1990).

5. By 1920 the index of industrial production (1913 = 100) had fallen to 20, the index of agricultural production had fallen to 64, and the index of transportation had fallen to 22. See Gregory and Stuart, *Soviet Economic Structure and Performance*, p. 58.

6. By 1928 the index of industrial production (1923 = 100) had risen to 102, the index of agricultural production had risen to 118, and the index of transportation had risen to 106. See ibid., p. 56.

7. For a discussion of the policy issues of this period, see Jerzy F. Karcz, "From Stalin to Brezhnev: Soviet Agricultural Policy in Historical Perspective," in James R. Millar, ed., *The Soviet Rural Community* (Urbana: University of Illinois Press, 1971), pp. 36–70; and Davies, *The Socialist Offensive*.

8. The classic work is Alexander Erlich, *The Soviet Industrialization Debate, 1924–1928* (Cambridge, Mass.: Harvard University Press, 1960). For a translation of original contributions to the debate, see Nicolas Spulber, *Foundations of Soviet Strategy for Economic Growth* (Bloomington: Indiana University Press, 1964).

9. There is, however, only a single candidate for each position, although Gorbachev has proposed changes. For a comprehensive discussion of the Soviet government and party-structure, see Jerry F. Hough and Merle Fainsod, *How the Soviet Union Is Governed* (Cambridge, Mass.: Harvard University Press, 1979). T. H. Rigby, *Political Elites in the USSR* (Brookfield, Vt.: Edward Elgar, 1990).

10. For a study of the Communist party of the Soviet Union, see Leonard Shapiro, *The Communist Party of the Soviet Union* (New York: Random House, 1971); and Hough and Fainsod, *How the Soviet Union Is Governed*. For a statistical survey of party membership, see T. H. Rigby, *Communist Party Membership in the U.S.S.R., 1917–1967* (Princeton, N.J.: Princeton University Press, 1968). For further evidence, see T. H. Rigby, "Soviet Communist Party Membership Under Brezhnev," *Soviet Studies*, 28 (July 1976), 317–337; and Jan Adams, *Citizen Inspectors in the Soviet Union: The People's Control Committee* (New York: Praeger, 1977).

11. The material balance technique has been analyzed in some detail. The classic article is J. M. Montias, "Planning with Material Balances in Soviet-Type Economies," *American Economic*

Review, 49 (December 1959), 963–985; for a summary, see Gregory and Stuart, *Soviet Economic Structure and Performance*, p. 163 ff. For a theoretical discussion, see Raymond P. Powell, "Plan Execution and the Workability of Soviet Planning," *Journal of Comparative Economics*, 1 (March 1979), 51–76.

12. This important point represents a sharp difference between the functioning of a planned economy and that of a market economy. In the market economy, the producing enterprise normally has supply contracts for required inputs. However, the firm can, with limitations, enter the market either to secure better contractual arrangements or to find a replacement if existing arrangements are interrupted for some reason. In the planned economy, the producing enterprise relies on an inter-enterprise delivery specified in the annual plan. If this delivery is interrupted for any reason, the producing enterprise has no market to which it may turn. In such cases production is typically interrupted. Unless formal or informal stopgap measures can be taken, the imbalances tend to accumulate throughout the economy.

13. See, for example, A. Katsenelinboigen, "Coloured Markets in the Soviet Union," *Soviet Studies*, 29 (January 1977), 62–85; Vladimir G. Treml, "Alcohol in the USSR: A Fiscal Dilemma," *Soviet Studies*, 27 (April 1975), 161–177; and Boris Rumer, "The 'Second' Agriculture in the USSR," *Soviet Studies*, 33 (October 1981), 560–572.

14. The role of the Soviet second economy has been the focus of a major research effort undertaken by Gregory Grossman and Vladimir Treml. The Grossman–Treml project involves interviews with recent Soviet émigrés concerning their personal experiences in the second economy. Gur Ofer and Aaron Vinokur have conducted studies of second-economy earnings among Soviet émigrés to Israel, and the Soviet Interview Project has studied second-economy earnings among recent Soviet emigrants to the United States. For results from these surveys, see J. R. Millar, ed., *Politics, Work, and Daily Life in the USSR* (New York: Cambridge University Press, 1987).

15. There is a substantial body of literature on the problems of Soviet enterprise management. See Joseph Berliner, *Factory and Manager in the USSR* (Cambridge, Mass.: Harvard University Press, 1957); David Granick, *The Red Executive* (New York: Doubleday, 1960); David Granick, *Managerial Comparisons of Four Developed Countries: France, Britain, United States and Russia* (Cambridge, Mass.: M.I.T. Press, 1972); William J. Conyngham, *The Modernization of Soviet Industrial Management* (New York: Cambridge University Press, 1982); and Jan Adams, "The Present Soviet Incentive System," *Soviet Studies*, 32 (July 1980), 360.

16. Gregory and Stuart, *Soviet Economic Structure and Performance*, pp. 215–216.

17. Unfortunately, relatively little research has been done on the structure and functions of the Soviet state bank. For a survey, see Paul Gekker, "The Banking System of the USSR," *Journal of the Institute of Bankers*, 84 (June 1963), 189–197; and Christine Netishen Wollan, "The Financial Policy of the Soviet State Bank, 1932–1970" (Ph.D. dissertation, University of Illinois, Urbana, 1972).

18. Incentives — how to make enterprises do what the center wants — have been the subject of a considerable amount of research. See David Conn, special ed., *The Theory of Incentives*, published as Vol. 3, no. 3, *Journal of Comparative Economics* (September 1979); and J. Michael Martin, "Economic Reform and Maximizing Behavior of the Soviet Firm," in Judith Thornton, ed., *Economic Analysis of the Soviet-Type System* (New York: Cambridge University Press, 1976).

19. In contemporary times, the rate of turnover of Soviet industrial managers has declined.

20. For a basic survey of Soviet price policy and citation of the important literature, see Gregory and Stuart, *Soviet Economic Structure and Performance*, Ch. 8. For an update, see Morris Bornstein, "Soviet Price Policy in the 1970s," in U.S. Congress, Joint Economic Committee, *Soviet Economy in a New Perspective* (Washington, D.C.: Government Printing Office, 1976), pp. 17–66; Morris Bornstein, "The Administration of the Soviet Price System," *Soviet Studies*, 30 (October 1978), 466–490; and Morris Bornstein, "Soviet Price Policies," *Soviet Economy*, 3, 2 (1987), 96–134.

21. For a discussion of Soviet wage-setting procedures, see Leonard J. Kirsch, *Soviet Wages: Changes in Structure and Administration Since 1956* (Cambridge, Mass.: M.I.T. Press, 1972); B. Arnot, *Controlling Soviet Labour* (London: Macmillan, 1988); D. Granick, *Job Rights in the*

Soviet Union: Their Consequences (New York: Cambridge University Press, 1987); and Silvana Malle, *Employment Planning in the Soviet Union* (Basingstoke, England: Macmillan, 1990).

22. See Abram Bergson, *The Economics of Soviet Planning* (New Haven: Yale University Press, 1964), Ch. 6.

23. The provision of appropriate manpower to the Soviet economy is a matter of both interest and complexity because it involves analysis of Soviet demographic trends. For a summary of statistical trends, see Murray Feshbach and Stephen Rapawy, "Soviet Population and Manpower Trends and Policies," in Joint Economic Committee, *Soviet Economy in a New Perspective*, 113–154. For the specific case of agriculture, see Karl-Eugen Wadekin, "Manpower in Soviet Agriculture — Some Post-Khrushchev Developments and Problems," *Soviet Studies*, 20 (January 1969), 281–305. Recent evidence is presented in Murray Feshbach, "Population and Labor Force," in Abram Bergson and Herbert S. Levine, eds., *The Soviet Economy: Towards the Year 2000* (Winchester, Mass.: Allen and Unwin, 1983), pp. 79–111; Jan Adams, ed., *Employment Policies in the Soviet Union and Eastern Europe*, 2nd ed. (New York: St. Martin's, 1987); and P. R. Gregory and I. L. Collier, "Unemployment in the Soviet Union: Evidence from the Soviet Interview Project," *The American Economic Review*, 78 (September 1988), 613–632.

24. For a brief summary of the socialist attitude toward an interest charge for capital, see A. C. Pigou, *Socialism Versus Capitalism* (London: Macmillan, 1937), Ch. 8. For a discussion of Soviet investment planning, see Gregory and Stuart, *Soviet Economic Structure and Performance*, Ch. 8. For details, see David A. Dyker, *The Process of Investment in the Soviet Union* (Cambridge, England: Cambridge University Press, 1983).

25. For a discussion of the rules, see Alan Abouchar, "The New Soviet Standard Methodology for Investment Allocation," *Soviet Studies*, 24 (January 1973), 402–410; P. Gregory, B. Fiedlitz, and T. Curtis, "The New Soviet Investment Rules: A Guide to Rational Investment Planning?" *Southern Economic Journal*, 41 (January 1974), 500–504; Frank A. Durgin, "The Soviet 1969 Standard Methodology for Investment Allocation Versus 'Universally Correct' Methods," *The ACES Bulletin*, 19 (Summer 1977), 29–53; Frank A. Durgin, Jr., "The Third Soviet Standard Methodology for Determining the Effectiveness of Capital Investment (SM-80, Provisional)," *The ACES Bulletin*, 24 (Fall 1982), 45–61; and Janice Giffen, "The Allocation of Investment in the Soviet Union: Criteria for the Efficiency of Investment," *Soviet Studies*, 33 (October 1981), 593–609. For a useful summary, see David Dyker, *The Process of Investment in the Soviet Union* (New York: Cambridge University Press, 1981).

26. Since the mid-1970s, there has been a debate over the extent of repressed inflation in the Soviet Union. See D. H. Howard, "The Disequilibrium Model in a Controlled Economy: An Empirical Test of The Barro-Grossman Model," *American Economic Review*, 66 (December 1976), 871–879; Richard Portes, "The Control of Inflation: Lessons from East European Experience," *Economics*, 44 (May 1977), 109–130; Richard Portes and David Winter, "A Planners' Supply Function for Consumption Goods in Centrally Planned Economies," *Journal of Comparative Economics*, 1 (December 1977), 351–365; and Richard Portes and David Winter, "The Demand for Money and for Consumption Goods in Centrally Planned Economies," *Review of Economics and Statistics*, 60 (February 1978), 8–18.

27. Joyce Pickersgill and Gur Ofer conducted early empirical studies of Soviet saving behavior and concluded that Soviet citizens appear to save for the same reasons as Westerners do. On this, see Gur Ofer and Joyce Pickersgill, "Soviet Household Saving: A Cross-Section Study of Soviet Emigrant Families," *Quarterly Journal of Economics*, 95 (August 1980), 121–144; and Joyce Pickersgill, "Soviet Household Saving Behavior," *Review of Economics and Statistics*, 58 (May 1976), 139–147. Other scholars see increases in excess demand as the cause of increases in saving. On this, see D. W. Bronson and Barbara S. Severin, "Recent Trends in Consumption and Disposable Money Income in the USSR," U.S. Congress, Joint Economic Committee, *New Directions in the Soviet Economy*, Part II-B (Washington, D.C.: Government Printing Office, 1966); and Igor Birman, *Secret Income and the Soviet State Budget* (Boston: Kluwer, 1981).

28. Paul Craig Roberts, "The Polycentric Soviet Economy," *Journal of Law and Economics*, 12 (April 1969), 163–181.

29. Eugene Zaleski, *Stalinist Planning for Economic Growth, 1932-1952* (Chapel Hill: University of North Carolina Press, 1980).

30. John Wilhelm, "Does the Soviet Union Have a Planned Economy?" *Soviet Studies*, 31 (April 1979), 268-274.

31. Gregory Grossman, "The 'Second Economy' of the USSR," *Problems of Communism*, 26 (September–October 1977), 25-40; Aron Katsenelinboigen, "Coloured Markets in the Soviet Union," *Soviet Studies*, 29 (January 1977), 62-85; Dimitri Simes, "The Soviet Parallel Market," *Survey*, 21 (Summer 1975), 42-52; and *Studies on the Soviet Second Economy* (Durham, N.C.: Berkeley-Duke Occasional Papers on the Second Economy in the USSR, December 1987).

32. Vladimir Treml, "Alcohol in the USSR: A Fiscal Dilemma," *Soviet Studies*, 41 (October 1973), 161-177; Dennis O'Hearn, "The Consumer Second Economy: Size and Effects," *Soviet Studies*, 32 (April 1980), 221; and Vladimir G. Treml, *Purchase of Food from Private Sources in Soviet Urban Areas* (Durham, N.C.: Berkeley-Duke Occasional Papers on the Second Economy in the USSR, September 1985).

33. For a discussion of the various forms of agricultural organization, see D. J. Male, *Russian Peasant Organization Before Collectivization* (Cambridge, England: Cambridge University Press, 1971); and Robert G. Wesson, *Soviet Communes* (New Brunswick, N.J.: Rutgers University Press, 1963).

34. For a survey of thinking on this issue, see Karcz, "From Stalin to Brezhnev."

35. Because the sovkhoz is a relatively straightforward state enterprise operating under the same general principles as the industrial enterprise, relatively little attention had been paid to its structure and operation. It is important to note, however, that whereas the sovkhoz is state-owned property, the kolkhoz is an ideologically inferior form of property holding known as kolkhoz-cooperative property. The future legal basis of the kolkhoz is uncertain. Many of the recent changes in the kolkhoz can be explained by the implementation of state policy designed to "improve" the kolkhoz and raise it to the same level as the sovkhoz. It is, however, a matter of speculation whether the kolkhoz will ultimately disappear. In a real sense, its original image has already disappeared.

36. For a detailed discussion of the kolkhoz and the labor day mechanism, see Robert C. Stuart, *The Collective Farm in Soviet Agriculture* (Lexington, Mass.: Heath, 1972) and R. W. Davies, *The Industrialization of Russia* Vols. 1 and 2 (Cambridge, Mass.: Harvard University Press, 1980). Recent research has supported the view that during the introduction of the collectives there was no increase in the net surplus generated by agriculture. For a discussion of this question, see James R. Millar, "Soviet Rapid Development and the Agricultural Surplus Hypothesis," *Soviet Studies*, 22 (July 1970), 77-93; and M. J. Ellman, "Did the Russian Agricultural Surplus Provide the Resources for the Increase in Investment in the USSR During the First Five-Year Plan?" *Economic Journal*, 85 (December 1975), 844-863. For a summary, see Gregory and Stuart, *Soviet Economic Structure and Performance*, Ch. 5. For a critical view, see David Morrison, "A Critical Examination of A. A. Barsov's Empirical Work on the Value of Balance Exchanges Between the Town and the Country," *Soviet Studies* 34 (October 1985), 570-584.

37. For a discussion of the financing of the kolkhozy, see James R. Millar, "Financing the Modernization of Kolkhozy," in Millar, *The Soviet Rural Economy*, pp. 276-303.

38. The standard work on the Machine Tractor Stations is Robert F. Miller, *One Hundred Thousand Tractors* (Cambridge, Mass.: Harvard University Press, 1970).

39. For an in-depth discussion of the private sector in Soviet agriculture, see Karl-Eugen Wadekin, *The Private Sector in Soviet Agriculture* (Berkeley: University of California Press, 1973); and A. Lane, "U.S.S.R.: Private Agriculture on Center Stage," in U.S. Congress, Joint Economic Committee, *Soviet Economy in the 1980s: Problems and Prospects*, pt. 2 (Washington, D.C.: U.S. Government Printing Office, 1982), pp. 23-40.

40. For a survey of postwar developments in Soviet agriculture and references to the specialized literature, see Gregory and Stuart, *Soviet Economic Structure and Performance*, Ch. 10.

41. Robert C. Stuart, "The Changing Role of the Collective Farm in Soviet Agriculture," *Canadian Slavonic Papers*, 26 (Summer 1974), 145-159.

42. For a survey, see K.-E. Wadekin, *Agrarian Policies in Communist Europe: An Introduction* (Totowa, N.J.: Allanheld and Osmun, 1982), Ch. 12.
43. Rural income levels are discussed in David W. Bronson and Constance B. Krueger, "The Revolution in Soviet Farm Household Income, 1953–1967," in Millar, *The Soviet Rural Economy*, pp. 214–257; and in more general terms in Gertrude E. Schroeder and Barbara S. Severin, "Soviet Consumption and Income Policies in Perspective," in Joint Economic Committee, *Soviet Economy in a New Perspective*, pp. 620–660.
44. For a discussion of subsidies, see W. G. Treml, "Subsidies in Soviet Agriculture: Record and Prospects," in U.S. Congress, Joint Economic Committee, *Soviet Economy in the 1980s: Problems and Prospects* (Washington, D.C.: U.S. Government Printing Office, 1982), pp. 171–186.
45. For a survey of Soviet foreign trade and references to the literature, see Gregory and Stuart, *Soviet Economic Structure and Performance*, Ch. 11.
46. For a different view, see Steven Rosefielde, "Comparative Advantage and the Evolving Pattern of Soviet International Commodity Specialization, 1950–1973," in Steven Rosefielde, ed., *Economic Welfare and the Economics of Soviet Socialism* (New York: Cambridge University Press, 1981), pp. 185–220.
47. See Vladimir Treml and Barry Kostinsky, *Domestic Value of Soviet Foreign Trade: Exports and Imports in the 1972 Input-Output Table*, Foreign Economic Report No. 20, U.S. Department of Commerce, October 1982.

RECOMMENDED READINGS

General Works

Robert W. Campbell, *The Soviet-Type Economies: Performance and Evolution*, 3rd ed. (Boston: Houghton Mifflin, 1981).
R. W. Davies, ed., *The Soviet Union* (Winchester, Mass.: Unwin Hyman, 1989).
Paul R. Gregory and Robert C. Stuart, *Soviet Economic Structure and Performance*, 4th ed. (New York: HarperCollins, 1990).
Franklyn D. Holzman, *The Soviet Economy: Past, Present, and Future* (New York: Foreign Policy Association, 1982).
James R. Millar, *The ABC's of Soviet Socialism* (Urbana: University of Illinois Press, 1981).
Alec Nove, *The Soviet Economic System*, 2nd ed. (London: Unwin Hyman, 1981).
United States Congress, Joint Economic Committee, *Gorbachev's Economic Plans*, Vols. I and II (Washington, D.C.: U.S. Government Printing Office, 1987).

Soviet Economic History

E. H. Carr and R. W. Davies, *Foundations of a Planned Economy, 1926–1929*, Vol. 1, pts. 1 and 2 (New York: Macmillan, 1969).
R. W. Davies, *The Industrialization of Soviet Russia*, Vols. I and II (Cambridge, Mass.: Harvard University Press, 1980).
Maurice Dobb, *Soviet Economic Development Since 1917*, 5th ed. (London: Routledge and Kegan Paul, 1960).
Alexander Erlich, *The Soviet Industrialization Debate, 1924–1928* (Cambridge, Mass.: Harvard University Press, 1969).
Paul R. Gregory, *Russian National Income, 1885–1913* (New York: Cambridge University Press, 1983).

Gregory Guroff and Fred V. Carstensen, *Entrepreneurship in Imperial Russia and the Soviet Union* (Princeton, N.J.: Princeton University Press, 1983).

Moshe Lewin, *Political Undercurrents in Soviet Economic Debates: From Bukharin to the Modern Reformers* (Princeton, N.J.: Princeton University Press, 1974).

Roger Munting, *The Economic Development of the USSR* (London: Croom Helm, 1982).

Alec Nove, *An Economic History of the U.S.S.R.*, rev. ed. (London: Penguin Books, 1982).

Nicolas Spulber, *Soviet Strategy for Economic Growth* (Bloomington: Indiana University Press, 1964).

The Communist Party and the Manager

Donald D. Barry and Carol Barner-Barry, *Contemporary Soviet Politics: An Introduction*, 2nd ed. (Englewood Cliffs, N.J.: Prentice-Hall, 1982).

William J. Conyngham, *The Modernization of Soviet Industrial Management* (New York: Cambridge University Press, 1982).

Andrew Freiis, *The Soviet Industrial Enterprise* (New York: St. Martin's Press, 1974).

David Granick, *Managerial Comparisons of Four Developed Countries: France, Britain, United States, and Russia* (Cambridge, Mass.: M.I.T. Press, 1972).

Leslie Holmes, *The Policy Process in Communist States* (Beverly Hills: Sage Publications, 1981).

Jerry F. Hough and Merle Fainsod, *How the Soviet Union Is Governed* (Cambridge, Mass.: Harvard University Press, 1979).

David Lane, *Politics and Society in the USSR*, 2nd ed. (London: Martin Robertson, 1978).

Nathan Leites, *Soviet Style in Management* (New York: Crane Russak, 1985).

Leonard Shapiro, *The Government and Politics of the Soviet Union*, 6th ed. (Essex, England: Hutchinson Publishing Group, 1978).

Selected Aspects of the Soviet Economy

R. Amann and J. M. Cooper, eds., *Industrial Innovation in the Soviet Union* (New Haven: Yale University Press, 1982).

Joseph S. Berliner, *The Innovation Decision in Soviet Industry* (Cambridge, England: Cambridge University Press, 1983).

Morris Bornstein, ed., *The Soviet Economy: Continuity and Change* (Boulder, Colo.: Westview Press, 1981).

Robert W. Campbell, *Soviet Energy Technologies* (Bloomington: Indiana University Press, 1980).

David A. Dyker, *The Process of Investment in the Soviet Union* (Cambridge, England: Cambridge University Press, 1983).

Franklyn D. Holzman, *International Trade Under Communism* (New York: Basic Books, 1976).

Alastair McAuley, *Women's Work and Wages in the Soviet Union* (London: Unwin Hyman, 1981).

Mervyn Matthews, *Education in the Soviet Union* (London: Allen and Unwin, 1982).

——, *Poverty in the Soviet Union* (New York: Cambridge University Press, 1987).

James R. Millar, *Politics, Work, and Daily Life in the USSR* (New York: Cambridge University Press, 1987).

Henry W. Morton and Robert C. Stuart, eds., *The Contemporary Soviet City* (Armonk, N.Y.: M. E. Sharpe, 1984).

Robert C. Stuart, ed., *The Soviet Rural Economy* (Totowa, N.J.: Roman and Allenheld, 1983).

Murray Yanowitch, *Social and Economic Inequality in the Soviet Union* (London: Martin Robertson, 1977).

Eugene Zaleski, *Planning Reforms in the Soviet Union, 1962–1966* (Chapel Hill: University of North Carolina Press, 1967).

For the Advanced Reader

Alan Abouchar, ed., *The Socialist Price Mechanism* (Durham, N.C.: Duke University Press, 1977).

Edward Ames, *Soviet Economic Processes* (Homewood, Ill.: Irwin, 1965).

Abram Bergson and Herbert S. Levine, eds., *The Soviet Economy: Towards the Year 2000* (London: Allen and Unwin, 1983).

Martin Cave, Alastair McAuley, and Judith Thornton, eds., *New Trends in Soviet Economics* (Armonk, N.Y.: M. E. Sharpe, 1982).

Michael Ellman, *Soviet Planning Today: Proposals for an Optimally Functioning Economic System* (Cambridge, England: Cambridge University Press, 1971).

David Granick, *Job Rights in the Soviet Union: Their Consequences* (New York: Cambridge University Press, 1987).

Kenneth R. Gray, ed., *Soviet Agriculture* (Ames: Iowa State University Press, 1990).

Donald W. Green and Christopher I. Higgins, *SOVMOD I: A Macroeconometric Model of the Soviet Economy* (New York: Academic, 1977).

Paul R. Gregory, *The Soviet Economic Bureaucracy* (Cambridge, England: Cambridge University Press, 1990).

John Hardt et al., *Mathematics and Computers in Soviet Planning* (New Haven: Yale University Press, 1977).

Peter Murrell, *The Nature of Socialist Economies: Lessons from Eastern European Foreign Trade* (Princeton, N.J.: Princeton University Press, 1990).

Steven Rosefielde, ed., *Economic Welfare and the Economics of Soviet Socialism* (New York: Cambridge University Press, 1981).

Robert C. Stuart, ed., *The Soviet Rural Economy* (Totowa, N.J.: Roman and Allenheld, 1983).

Judith Thornton, ed., *Economic Analysis of the Soviet-Type System* (New York: Cambridge University Press, 1976).

Alfred Zauberman, *Mathematical Theory in Soviet Planning* (Oxford, England: Oxford University Press, 1976).

APPENDIX 12A:
THE MEASUREMENT OF OUTCOMES IN THE
COMMAND ECONOMY

Throughout this book we have emphasized an important yet largely unresolved issue. As we analyze the functioning of the command economy, for example, to what extent are the traditional tools of neoclassical economic theory appropriate? In many cases, we wish to examine the outcomes in differing economic systems on the basis of Marxist–Leninist principles but to use tools of economic analysis that are familiar to the analyst of the market economy.

Suppose we wish to give empirical content to the familiar proposition that in the Soviet command experience, there has been persistent excess demand for consumer goods — that is, repressed inflation. One approach would be to use evidence typically described as anecdotal. Thus we might survey the Soviet media, seeking to learn about the complaints of consumers, the length of waiting lines, and so on. Such an approach, while sometimes inevitable in the absence of data, is not fully satisfactory. Indeed, sophisticated techniques are available for examining the nature of both demand and supply and for understanding whether excess demand exists in a particular case. These techniques, however, were developed for the market setting. Our task here is to examine these techniques in their simplest form and to consider extensions that have been proposed for analysis of the nonmarket experience. Although our immediate goal is understanding of an important phenomenon in the Soviet economic experience, rather broader methodological issues are involved.

The Market Context

If we wish to examine outcomes of the supply of and demand for, say, consumer goods in the market context, a familiar approach is to specify estimate demand and supply equations representing the particular market. Equations 12A.1 and 12A.2 illustrate the demand and supply equations, respectively.

$$Q_d = a + bP + cY + u \qquad\qquad (12A.1)$$

$$Q_s = d + eP + fC + u' \qquad\qquad (12A.2)$$

This model, designed only for illustrative purposes, would allow us to give empirical content to the demand and supply relationships, where demand is viewed as a function of prices (P) and incomes (Y), and supply is a function of prices (P) and some measure of production capacity (C). Familiar techniques are available for the estimation of this sort of model.[1]

This sort of model is generally not discussed in an introductory text in economics, but an important proposition underlying the model *is* generally discussed — namely, the identification problem. As most discussions of supply and demand emphasize, when we observe prices and quantities in the real world, let us say over time, we are in fact observing a series of equilibrium positions, or intersections of supply curves and demand curves. To take a simple case in which demand is unchanged but supply is increasing through time, the price–quantity combinations that we would observe are those represented by the letters A, B, and C in Figure 12.4.

Figure 12.4

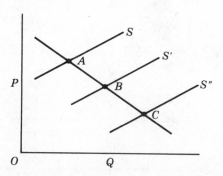

It is important to note that in this approach, the market clears; at each point in time, equilibrium prevails. Suppose, however, that the market does not clear. Let us consider the disequilibrium case.

The Disequilibrium Context

In recent theoretical and empirical work, it has been argued that the equilibrium approach may be inappropriate in the presence of persistent excess demand.[2] For example, if we consider a simple static case where the price is set by state authorities, the outcome could be represented by Figure 12.5, where the magnitude of excess demand is given by the distance Q_sQ_d, and the prevailing price is set by the state at OP'.

It is quite obvious that in this case we would not, in the real world, observe the intersection of the supply and demand curves when we examined combinations of price and quantity. Under the conditions specified in Figure 12.5, we would observe the state-set price of OP', some rationing device (about which we may or may not have information), and a resulting quantity actually sold, probably Q_s. If we move from this simple case to a more realistic case with persistent excess demand through time, it is clearly possible that the magnitude of the excess demand may change. Could we capture the increased complexity of this disequilibrium case in a formal model? One approach that has been suggested can be represented as follows:

$$Q_d = a + bP + cY + u \qquad (12A.3)$$

$$Q_s = d + eP + fC + u' \qquad (12A.4)$$

$$Q = \min(D,S) \qquad (12A.5)$$

Figure 12.5

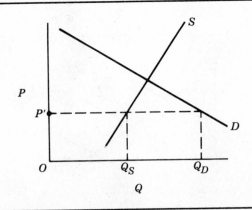

In this particular case, equation 12A.5 is introduced to provide a rule by which the suspected shortage will be handled. Once again, various methods of estimation are available, with price (P) assumed to be exogenous. In this approach, interest centers on the appropriate specification, on alternative methods of estimation, and, finally, on empirical verification of whether in fact a disequilibrium specification is appropriate.[3]

A more sophisticated variant would include the possibility that if there is excess demand in a particular market at a particular time, planners may (1) have some knowledge about this excess demand and (2) take some steps to lessen its magnitude through time. A number of attempts have been made to construct macroeconometric models of planned socialist economic systems. It is particularly appealing on a number of grounds to consider a model in which planners have available and utilize various policy controls for manipulation of the economic system through time. Although one can imagine a wide array of possible controls, let us, for the sake of illustration, consider a basic approach suggested by Richard Quandt.[4] Thus, to consider the response of planners over time, we specify a more complex model:

$$Q_t^d = a + bP_t + cY_t + u \tag{12A.6}$$

$$Q_t^s = d + eP_t + fC_t + u' \tag{12A.7}$$

$$Q_t = \min(D_t, S_t) \tag{12A.8}$$

$$P_t - P_{t-1} = g(D_t - S_t) + u'' \tag{12A.9}$$

In the model presented in equations 12A.6 through 12A.9, price (P) is again exogenous and is assumed to be the mechanism through which planners make adjustments. Specifically, planners vary price through time, depending on the magnitude of the excess demand. Other approaches could be considered, but this particular model captures the essence of the Lange adjustment and is thus of more than passing interest.

The disequilibrium approach is, of course, a competing hypothesis to the equilibrium approach and is not, therefore, necessarily limited to application in the case of the command economy. The approach is, however, relatively recent in origin. There is now a substantial literature applying this approach to the Soviet case, especially in the examination of consumer markets. The approach remains controversial, and methodological difficulties complicate both specification and estimation of the model.

NOTES

1. For a discussion of disequilibrium models that provides extensive references to the literature, see Richard E. Quandt, *The Econometrics of Disequilibrium* (New York: Basil Blackwell, 1988).
2. For example, Western interpretations of the Soviet consumer goods market have generally suggested that although there is excess demand, the turnover tax has been used to bring prices

close to the point of equilibrium. One could argue, however, that if prices are in fact "close" to equilibrium, planners would have sufficient knowledge and power to raise prices *to* equilibrium, thus eliminating the persistent complaints about shortages. The possibility of persistent excess demand deserves our attention, especially because it is a basic underpinning of the work of Kornai described in Chapter 7.

3. See, for example, Richard E. Quandt, "Tests of the Equilibrium vs. Disequilibrium Hypotheses," *International Economic Review*, 19 (June 1978), 435–452.

4. Ibid.

RECOMMENDED READINGS

R. J. Barro and H. I. Grossman, "A General Disequilibrium Model of Income and Employment," *American Economic Review*, 61 (March 1971), 82–93.

W. Charemza and M. Gronicki, *Plans and Disequilibria in Centrally Planned Economies* (Amsterdam: North-Holland, 1988).

Christopher M. Davis, "The Second Economy in Disequilibrium and Shortage Models of Centrally Planned Economies," *Berkeley-Duke Occasional Papers on The Second Economy In The USSR* (July 1988).

S. M. Goldfeld and R. E. Quandt, "Estimation in a Disequilibrium Model and the Value of Information," *Journal of Econometrics*, 3 (November 1975), 325–348.

———, "Single-Market Disequilibrium Models: Estimation and Testing," *The Economic Studies Quarterly*, 32 (April 1981), 12–28.

———, "Some Properties of the Simple Disequilibrium Model with Covariance," *Economics Letters*, 1, 4 (1978) 343–346.

David H. Howard, *The Disequilibrium Model in a Controlled Economy* (Lexington, Mass.: Lexington Books, 1979).

———, "The Disequilibrium Model in a Controlled Economy: An Empirical Test of The Barro-Grossman Model," *American Economic Review*, 66 (December 1976), 871–879.

Richard Portes and David Winter, "The Demand for Money and for Consumption Goods in Centrally Planned Economies," *Review of Economics and Statistics*, 60 (February 1978), 8–18.

———, "The Supply of Consumption Goods in Centrally Planned Economies," *Journal of Comparative Economics*, 1 (December 1977), 351–363.

Richard E. Quandt, *The Econometrics of Disequilibrium* (New York: Basil Blackwell, 1988).

———, "Tests of the Equilibrium vs. Disequilibrium Hypotheses," *International Economic Review*, 19 (June 1978), 435–452.

H. S. Rosen and R. E. Quandt, "Estimation of a Disequilibrium Aggregate Labor Market," *Review of Economics and Statistics*, 60 (1978), 371–379.

13 Yugoslavia: Worker Management and Market Socialism

MARKET SOCIALISM IS DISCUSSED IN CHAPTER 8. It is characterized by the combination of some socialist principles (public ownership of the means of production and an egalitarian distribution of income) with other, typically non-socialist elements (such as market allocation and decentralization of decision making).

The market socialist model has considerable appeal because it combines the best features of differing systems. Market socialism is seen as a means of avoiding the bureaucratization of economic life under socialism, while at the same time taking into account socialist concerns with income distribution, public goods, and externalities.

The reader might conclude that interest in a case such as Yugoslavia would decline with the apparent general collapse of socialist systems in recent years. This judgment would be premature. The discrediting of communist political systems does not necessarily mean the elimination of socialist economic systems, even if the latter do seem to lack economic efficiency. Indeed, to the extent that socialist ideals persist, it may be possible to combine socialist equity with market efficiency — precisely the central notion of market socialism.

If Yugoslavia has been viewed as *the* example of market socialism, it is much more than this. Yugoslavia is the major case study of **worker management**, a system in which some control — and hence authority and responsibility over enterprise decision making — rests with the workers or their direct representatives.[1] There is a great deal of interest in worker management, not only in its theoretical underpinnings, but also in its real-world operating characteristics. And here again, the Yugoslav experience is of great contemporary significance. As we shall see in our later discussion of the socialist economies in transition, varying forms of worker participation in management have received considerable attention and have been adopted in some cases as a basic component of democratization.

At least two other aspects of the Yugoslavian system merit attention. First, Yugoslavia is a relatively underdeveloped country. Yugoslavia ranks closest to Greece and Portugal in per capita income. As a middle-income developing country, Yugoslavia serves as a case study of economic development under market socialism. Second, Yugoslavia's size and regional diversity present a challenge both in its international economic arrangements and in its persistent attempts to reduce regional differences.

However we may come to judge the successes and failures of the Yugoslav experiment with market socialism, recent political events and instability may result in an end to the Yugoslav federation as we know it. If this occurs in the 1990s, the economic situation will change markedly. Before we consider contemporary events, however, it is necessary to examine the past Yugoslav economic experience.

HISTORICAL PRECEDENTS

The historical evolution of the Yugoslav economic and political system differs from that of other formerly socialist economic systems that we consider in this book. During World War II, the Nazi occupation of Yugoslavia brought with it substantial destruction and considerable population loss. The resistance movement was led by Josip Broz, better known in the West as Tito. Under Tito's leadership, the Yugoslavs liberated virtually all occupied territory themselves. He emerged as the postwar head of the Yugoslav Communist party — or the League of Communists of Yugoslavia (LCY), as the party would later be known. Unlike other rulers in Eastern Europe, Tito was not brought to power by Soviet force. His personal popularity and leadership during the war years were confirmed by a subsequent election. Tito remained Yugoslavia's leader until his death in 1980.

In spite of these facts, Yugoslavia at war's end began to put together an economic system very similar to that of the Soviet Union. The organizational structure was based on the ministerial system, and the Federal Planning Commission had wide powers to implement a national economic plan; the first was to begin in 1947. In 1948, without much public discussion, the Soviet Union and Yugoslavia severed relations, and Stalin expelled Yugoslavia from the Cominform (the Communist Information Bureau, precursor of the Warsaw Pact). From 1949 onward, Tito began to build a political and economic system that would one day be viewed as a different road to socialism.

As we examine the contemporary Yugoslav economic system, it is important to bear in mind several facets of its development in the 1950s and thereafter. First, in the absence of any clearly defined theoretical model of a worker-managed economic system, the Yugoslav economic system, like the Soviet system, was carved out largely through practical experience.[2] From its inception, organizational change and experimentation have been the rule rather than the exception. Second, though Yugoslavia has been a single-party state, it is very different from the Soviet Union. The precise role of the Communist party in the Yugoslav economic system has been and still is a matter of contention. Yugoslavia's leaders have demonstrated a willingness to change where necessary and to do so with some recognition of pluralistic interests. Regional diversity and strong ethnic differences have precluded the extreme centralization of the Communist party that is practiced in the Soviet Union and Eastern Europe.

The lack of centralization has been both an asset and a liability. It forced the leadership to experiment with market resource allocation. Ethnic and regional differences, on the other hand, prevented the creation of effective central instruments of taxation and monetary control.

Economic growth has been a major thrust of Yugoslav economic policy since the early 1950s. Western interest in Yugoslavia frequently centers on its system of worker management, but Yugoslavia is also a testing ground for whether this type of market socialism can generate economic growth and a high standard of living for its population. Although the Yugoslav federation may not survive in its present form, the Yugoslav economic experience remains important for understanding the more general process of transition in socialist economies elsewhere. Moreover, as we have emphasized, interest in worker management has remained strong.

The Setting

Yugoslavia's population of just over 23 million persons is divided equally between rural and urban residence. The land area of Yugoslavia is just over 255,000 square kilometers — approximately the size of Colorado. The terrain is generally mountainous, but there is a substantial coastline and many offshore islands. Tourism is an important industry and an important source of hard-currency earnings.

Yugoslavia is divided into six republics: Bosnia-Hercegovina, Croatia, Macedonia, Montenegro, Serbia, and Slovenia. In ethnic terms, the dominant population groupings are Serbian (36 percent), Croatian (20 percent), Muslim (9 percent), Slovenian (8 percent), Albanian (8 percent), Macedonian (6 percent), Yugoslav (5 percent), and several groups with lesser representation. In terms of religion, Eastern Orthodoxy and Catholicism are the dominant faiths. Yugoslavia has a long history of ethnic and regional enmity and jealousy. These issues, as we shall see, dominate political developments in the 1990s.

Yugoslavia is not well endowed with natural resources, although it does have coal, iron ore, and bauxite. Yugoslavia has a varied climate. Its land, only about one-quarter of which is arable, supports a diversified agricultural sector.

THE YUGOSLAV ECONOMY: ORGANIZATIONAL ARRANGEMENTS

Yugoslavia began its pursuit of worker management in the early 1950s. Since that time, change has been frequent (see Table 13.1), but the principle of self-management has endured. It is necessary to consider major shifts in economic policy to appreciate the evolution of the Yugoslav system.

As with most reform programs in socialist systems, changes in the Yugoslav economy have been identified with formal decrees, though associating changes with formal decrees is artificial. In practice, changes are usually introduced slowly and seldom follow formal decrees in their entirety.

Between 1952 and 1965, Yugoslavia pursued the development of the worker-managed enterprise. Controls were exercised by an essentially indicative planning system and by state and party mechanisms to promote plan implementation. Basic economic objectives were rapid economic growth, the reduction of regional differences, and the integration of Yugoslavia into the world economy.

The early years of worker management were characterized by a reluctance to decentralize decision making in such areas as investment allocation and the distribution of enterprise profits between worker compensation and retained earnings. In addition, state authorities were inclined to interfere in the price-setting process.

Prior to 1965 the state budget was the major dispenser of capital funds, which were acquired principally through taxes on industry and agriculture.

Table 13.1 Yugoslav Economic Reform

Period	Reform Measures
End of war to 1948	Rigid centralized planning; emphasis on collective agriculture; minimal use of market resource allocation.
1948–1965	Movement toward worker self-management; privatization of agriculture; indicative planning with extensive state and party interference in management appointments and in price, wage, and capital allocation decisions.
1965 to the mid-1970s	Increased reliance on market allocation; greater freedom for enterprises to make price, wage, and investment allocation decisions; less state and party interference; devolution of government activities to lower levels; continued use of indicative planning.
Mid-1970s	Creation of new enterprise arrangements and inter-enterprise arrangements; indicative planning from the ground up; further devolution of political authority; enlarged role of party and state in promotion of harmony of interests; social compacts and SMAs as instruments of social harmony.
1988	Announced reforms of the tax system, foreign debt rescheduling, and austerity programs in response to the economic crises of the mid-1980s.
1990	Privatization pursued in a setting of political and social tensions — basic differences between Serbia and other regions.

Investment funds were allocated largely on an administrative and political basis, often to promote regional equality. In fact, the investment decision was the last one to be decentralized and largely freed from strict government control, although state influence has remained strong in the investment area. Throughout the years, authorities feared that workers would allocate too large a portion of enterprise net income to themselves and too little to reinvestment in plant and equipment. There is theoretical support for this argument as well as empirical evidence that enterprise saving rates have fallen during periods of less strict government rules on the distribution of enterprise income.[3] Given the priority attached to the growth objective, one can understand official concern over enterprise saving decisions.

By 1965 the need for significant reform was apparent. Modifications of the existing system were inadequate to stem the mounting problems. In part, the problems were familiar: inflation, unemployment, and balance-of-payments problems. In another sense, however, the problems were less familiar. Ellen T. Comisso called the reforms of 1965 "more a decision by default than an act of positive policy."[4] Simply put, Yugoslav economic policies — particularly the system of controls and external constraints designed to achieve these policies — were not working effectively under changing conditions. Although the state had considerable power over the allocation of investment funds, it did not know how best to distribute these funds to lessen regional differentials. In addition to the ongoing debate on investment policy, there was lack of agreement on macroeconomic policy and on the types of controls that were appropriate to achieve policy objectives.

The economic reform of 1965 introduced two important changes in the Yugoslav economy. First, there was substantial devolution of decision-making authority to the enterprise level and increased reliance on the market as the coordinating mechanism. Second, the role of the state shifted significantly, again in the direction of lessening state control of the economy.

For example, although national economic plans continued to be prepared, they played no directive role in the economy. In addition, control of state funds was shifted downward in the political structure, and efforts were made to reduce the role of the state in enterprise decision making. The enterprise gained increased independence in the distribution of enterprise funds, and a new and more meaningful relationship with banks was established. Less reliance was placed on price controls. Finally, the 1965 reform called for a reformulation of the economic role of the Communist party in Yugoslav economic life.

The 1965 reform can be viewed as an effort to establish a truly decentralized model of worker self-management. Enterprises were to be allowed to make the most of their own decisions in a market context. The process of resource allocation was to be turned over to the "neutral" mechanism of the market. Some observers even date the real beginning of self-management to the 1965 reform, citing the strong external constraints on enterprises prior to that date.

The reforms of the 1970s were in part political and in part economic.[5] In the political sphere, reform arose largely out of the need to define an appropriate role for the Communist party in Yugoslav society. Its mission was to be rather different from that observed in other East European systems. The task of the party would be to harmonize widely divergent interests and to do so with a degree of pluralism — not an easy task.

With Tito's death in May of 1980, the political decentralization of Yugoslavia increased. Lacking a national leader who could overcome the strong regional enmities, the Yugoslavs turned to a collective presidency comprising representatives from six republics and two regions. This arrangement reflected the wish of the different regions not to be dominated by a strong central government. Each republic and region was given veto power over central government action.

It is not difficult to isolate the forces leading to economic reform. The 1970s and early 1980s were difficult periods for most economies, Yugoslavia's included. Many felt that the market was misapplied, and there was considerable dissatisfaction with the increased dependence on market forces introduced in 1965. Yugoslavia suffered from unemployment, inflation, energy shocks, growing internal inequality, and increasing difficulties in the international sphere.

Against this background, we examine the working arrangements of the Yugoslav economy, beginning with a description of the worker-management system prior to the changes of the 1970s. Then we examine the impact of recent changes on the system. Finally, we consider more broadly the Yugoslav economy of the 1970s and 1980s, how it has changed, and where it is going in the 1990s. The latter period is especially important, because the economic reversals of the 1980s raise questions about the workability of the system, especially in a politically unstable setting.

MICROECONOMIC ORGANIZATION

With the exception of agriculture and enterprises employing fewer than five persons, Yugoslav enterprises are organized as producer cooperatives with worker management as the operational system. Private ownership in retail trade is not allowed. Even government offices and communal and service organizations such as schools and the post office are worker-managed.

In the Yugoslav system, the workers do not own outright the assets of the enterprise; rather, they hold these assets in trust for society. The highest governing body of the Yugoslav enterprise is the workers' council, a committee of workers elected through secret ballot by the workers at large. In very large enterprises, the workers' council may elect a smaller management committee to handle routine operational matters.

Responsibilities of the workers' councils normally focus on long-range enterprise policy. Such policies include setting wage differentials, establishing smaller decision-making units within the enterprise, and allocating net income among personal incomes, incentive funds, and reinvestment (within limits allowed by law). In a sense, the functions of a workers' council are similar to those of the board of directors of a firm in a capitalist system. However, the members of the workers' council are elected by the workers, not by share-holders, and turnover is maintained by not permitting a member to serve more than two consecutive terms.

The enterprise director is chosen by the workers' council generally for a contract period of four years, though the director is usually reappointed.[6] Openings are supposed to be publicly advertised to invite competition for the available positions. However, government officials, the Communist party, and the trade unions have reportedly played an important role in the nominating process. In the early years, many managers were drawn from party ranks.

The enterprise director is charged with overseeing day-to-day operations and is typically empowered to manage production, integrate the work of different production units, make financial reports to the workers' council, and so on. Directors are apparently reappointed regardless of the enterprise's performance, and rarely is a director seeking reappointment subjected to serious competition for the job.

The influence of the enterprise director is generally greater than one might infer. From the point of view of the average worker (revealed in a survey of workers), the manager, his or her staff, and the skilled workers exercise considerably more influence over enterprise decisions than do rank-and-file workers. The director, however, has to contend with a number of outside forces, such as the party, the trade unions, and government and bank officials.

What is the prime objective of the Yugoslav enterprise? As we noted in Chapter 8, the theory of worker-managed economies assumes that the objective of worker-managed firms is to maximize an enterprise's net income per worker. According to Joel Dirlam and James Plummer, "There is no doubt that Yugoslav enterprises give heavy weight to the importance of maximizing their workers' incomes. . . . Nevertheless, a remarkably high proportion of enterprises appears to have emphasized growth and, at least since the 1965 reforms, modernization."[7] According to these authors, this is so because Yugoslav workers have had to be concerned with the long-term health of their enterprises, especially in a socialist country with a relatively high unemployment rate. This concern, coupled with official interest in enterprise reinvestment, explains adherence to the growth objective.

Continued losses usually mean the eventual bankruptcy of capitalist firms. In Yugoslavia there has been a strong tendency for local authorities and banks to bail out failing enterprises. The bail-out is typically accomplished by subsidies, tax exemptions, and low-interest loans. In 1968, for example, almost 1800 enterprises operated at a loss and were subsidized by the banks and government authorities.[8]

At the other end of the spectrum, a new enterprise can be formed by individuals or partnerships if total employment is less than five. As the enterprise grows, it must be converted into a socialized worker-managed firm, and the former owners are compensated. In other cases, municipal, regional, or national government bodies start up new enterprises and then turn them over to the workers for self-management.

Yugoslav antitrust (cartel) laws are lax. Not only are enterprises allowed to enter into business associations, but the structure of the Yugoslav economy does not promote competition among firms. Concentration ratios in Yugoslav manufacturing are probably above those of is West European neighbors, and the major competitive force is foreign imports,[9] which are subject to numerous restrictions and controls.

Although the system of worker management that we have described is fundamental to the Yugoslav economic system, the changes of the 1970s and 1980s have been important and far-reaching. Even though recent changes include a number of decrees the ultimate outcome of which is unknown, we must examine these reforms in some detail. We deal first with the long series of changes made in Yugoslav working arrangements. Then we discuss privatization within the context of socialist transition.

CHANGE IN CONTEMPORARY YUGOSLAVIA

The Yugoslav economy has been guided by three main acts. First, and possibly most important, a new constitution was promulgated in February 1974. The fourth constitution since World War II, this lengthy document provided for major organizational changes in the Yugoslav economic system. Second, the Associated Labor Law of November 1976 defined microeconomic organization. Finally, the Foreign Trade Act of 1978 attempted to regularize the conduct of foreign trade in a new framework. The reform proposals issued in 1988 sought to deal with the external and internal macroeconomic imbalances that emerged in the 1980s.

The 1974 constitution was important in two main dimensions. First, the overall emphasis was on decision making and resource allocation through **decentralization** at all levels. Powers and responsibilities formerly exercised at the federal level were to be shifted to the republican level, and those exercised at the republican level to the local level. In addition, new arrangements within the enterprise and other organizations attempted to shift decision making downward toward the work collective. Indeed, under the new arrangements the issue of defining the enterprise took on new importance. Second, in addition to shifting the focus of decision making to lower levels within the hierarchy, there was a new emphasis on information flows — specifically on horizontal consultation among subunits in the system. This emphasis, to be achieved through the creation of new organizational and consultative arrangements, was an important step toward local decision making.

The most important change within the enterprise and other organizations was the creation of a new labor organization at the most basic level. The BOAL, or *Basic Organization of Associated Labor*, is an association of workers in a factory.[10] Large enterprises may have more than one BOAL. As an example, separate BOALs might be created for the major divisions of an enterprise. The BOALs combine together contractually to form WOALs, or *Work Organi-*

zations of Associated Labor. Within the WOAL, however, each BOAL maintains its independence. The members of the constituent BOALs elect the workers' council, which in turn appoints executives. Workers must attend monthly and annual meetings of the BOALs. Rotation of worker council positions (a worker may serve only two consecutive terms) was designed to guarantee widespread participation over time.

The *Composite Organization of Associated Labor* (COAL) is a vertical or horizontal organization consisting of several WOALs.[11] This organization was designed to pursue commercial ventures in which vertical and/or horizontal integration is important. Once again, the autonomy of the participating units was to be maintained.

In addition to the organizational arrangements within and above the enterprise, all enterprises (and other organizations) belong to the Economic Chambers. These chambers exist at three levels above business associations. First, under federal law, there is the *Yugoslav Chamber of the Economy*; second, there are similar units at the republican and regional levels; and finally, there are chambers at the district and local level.

Broadly speaking, the economic chambers were intended to foster better economic performance. The economic chambers try to enhance productivity by holding discussions in delegate assemblies, the delegates being elected from the participating enterprises. Although the chambers do not have administrative authority or the power to coerce enterprises, it was assumed that contractual arrangements would arise. For example, enterprise plans for firms working in a similar sector of the economy may be harmonized by discussion of plan objectives in the appropriate economic chamber. Agreements of both a binding and a nonbinding nature may arise from these discussions, the intent of which is to guarantee plan fulfillment.

Decision making under these new organizational arrangements was designed to include substantial consultation, both horizontally and vertically. Discussion and consultation among government units, enterprises, social organizations, and other units were to be formalized in nonbinding agreements, or **social compacts**. These social compacts, while nonbinding, give formal expression to policy objectives and focus constituent action on these objectives.

A second and rather different expression of agreement is the SMA, or *Self-Management Agreement*. Unlike the social compacts, the SMAs were to be formal binding agreements, nonfulfillment of which could bring recourse in the courts. The SMAs cover agreements on basic and important questions. Within an enterprise, the BOAL would decide how to distribute enterprise income; that decision would be implemented through an SMA. This SMA would then become the guiding law on that particular question with the enterprise.

The basic goal of these reforms was apparent. In a country (and world) wracked by stagflation, oil shocks, and the external financial disturbances of the 1970s and 1980s, "social" controls over enterprise pricing decisions, profit distribution, and investment allocations appeared to be essential. Moreover, the increased decentralization of the late 1960s appeared to exacerbate the problem of regional inequality, and autonomous worker-managed enterprises revealed their inclination to favor the allocation of enterprise profits to wage increases rather than to investment. However, from the point of view of identifying the firm, these arrangements are complex.

The Yugoslav policy problem in the mid-1970s and early 1980s was not unlike that of the industrialized capitalist world: how to deal with rampant inflation, rising unemployment, and external disruptions without sacrificing market resource allocation. Like most of the capitalist countries, Yugoslavia settled on a form of **incomes policy**. The social compacts and SMAs, which call for consultation and negotiation between enterprises and governments, were an attempt to require economic agents to consider the social consequences of output, pricing, and investment decisions. The key to the Yugoslav experiment with incomes policy is its emphasis on the harmonization role played by the state and party and its reliance on voluntarism.

These changes can also be viewed as an effort to deal with a persistent problem of the Yugoslav self-management system: the tendency of workers to prefer wages over reinvestment of profits in the enterprise. Obligatory distribution formulas were abandoned in the 1960s, but initially nothing was put in their place. The SMA resolves this dilemma, because, unlike the nonbinding social compacts, the SMA is a formal binding agreement on the distribution of enterprise profits.

The formal thrust of these reforms was clearly decentralization of decision making, enhanced horizontal consultation, and harmonization of diverse interests through formal and informal agreements. But these reforms did not solve Yugoslavia's problems.[12] The main difficulties involved decision-making arrangements at the local and enterprise levels. The social compacts, for example, were slow and cumbersome and were unable to function smoothly in light of local differences and local powers. The process of negotiating social compacts and SMAs proved to be very time-consuming. Agreements were often concluded after the period under consideration had elapsed. Lack of speedy action was of particular concern where specific problems required timely action.

Problems also arose in other areas. For example, a major goal of Yugoslav economic policy has been to improve the capital allocation process. The role of the bank in enterprise financial decisions has been reduced, but it was not clear that the new arrangements dramatically improved capital allocation. Specifically, to the extent that capital outlays are substantially financed from within the enterprise, the state role in shifting capital funds from one enterprise, sector, or region to another was absent, and local mechanisms such as pooled financing are needed in the case of joint enterprise ventures.

Finally, it remains to be seen whether the price system can play an effective role in enterprise functions. The question of enterprise specialization, size, and structure rests heavily on inter-enterprise connections, especially the nature of price signals being received by the enterprise. If enterprise decisions are to result in the most effective use of available resources, transfer prices must reflect relative scarcities, a persistent problem in socialist economic systems.

The most interesting feature of the reforms discussed here has been the experimentation with building social consensus. Indeed, many economies have striven for this goal. One need only recall the consensus-building aspects of French indicative planning and of West German codetermination. Observers have noted a number of sources of friction that make social consensus difficult to achieve: Regional and local authorities want to keep their investment resources at home. Workers prefer to distribute enterprise profits as wages rather than to plow them back as investment. Rates of return may actually be higher in the more developed region, yet national policy calls for investment in the backward regions. In this environment, social consensus does not come easily, especially when the principle of voluntarism is observed.

Unfortunately, it is extremely difficult to build consensus in troubled economic times. When we turn to the performance issue, we see that Yugoslav economic performance was generally good in the 1970s but markedly less so in the 1980s. This fact, combined with the external search for balance between local institutions and the power of the Communist party, created an air of uncertainty in the 1980s. Uncertainty has increased significantly in the 1990s as political instability has been added to persistent economic difficulties.

Although our discussion of Yugoslav economic reform has included organizational change beyond the enterprise itself, the important changes external to the enterprise deserve further attention.

THE YUGOSLAV ENTERPRISE AND EXTERNAL FORCES

In most socialist economic systems, the national economic plan has been an important mechanism for allocating resources. The plan includes important directives for all units in the economy and provides authorities with the tools necessary to ensure movement toward plan objectives.

Yugoslav planning in the era of worker management had limited influence on resource allocation, and that influence declined over time. Traditionally, the Federal Planning Office has prepared a five-year and an annual national economic plan setting forth objectives (output, input, employment, prices, and so on) in major sectors of the economy disaggregated to the industry level. The function of this plan has been informational (indicative); it has not been the source of directives for influencing enterprise behavior.

In the 1970s, in addition to the development of competing forecasting arrangements, the planning process changed direction. In the past, plans had been prepared at the top and disseminated through the system. Now, the plan would be prepared as a consolidation of information flowing up from the bottom — but, as before, only for informational purposes. To the extent that local objectives were derived from local decision-making arrangements (for example, the SMAs), the accuracy and timeliness of plan information would rely heavily on the success of these local arrangements.

Most systems that use some form of indicative planning rely on fiscal, monetary and other controls to, at a minimum, influence enterprises to achieve plan directives. These sorts of controls have never been particularly strong in Yugoslavia, and their role has declined dramatically in recent years.

The case of monetary policy in general, and investment figures in particular, is instructive.[13] Prior to the 1960s, federal authorities had substantial control over investment in the Yugoslav economy through the General Investment Fund, which was derived in large part from taxation and enterprise profits. In the 1960s, power over the creation and distribution of investment funds was largely shifted to the banks, even though some federal controls were maintained until the late 1960s. Finally, in the 1970s, the thrust was toward reduction of bank influence over enterprises and expansion of the enterprise role in investment financing. The evidence on this issue is unclear, though there seems to have been little increase in the importance of investment financing at the enterprise level.

The usual instruments of monetary control have not been particularly important in the Yugoslav case. Monetary policy has been carried out by the National Bank of Yugoslavia at the federal level and by eight banks at the republican and provincial levels, but its increased control over credit expansion in the 1960s was not matched by control over enterprise credit expansion. As we have noted, the trend of the 1970s was to expand the enterprise role in this area.

Finally, most observers would agree that a major tool of monetary policy, interest rates, has not been important in Yugoslavia. Only in the late 1970s and early 1980s were interest rates raised as a means of controlling undesirable credit expansion. Low interest rates contributed to capital misallocations, another more general problem of socialist systems.

Fiscal policy in Yugoslavia has primarily aimed at achievement of long-term objectives, not control or elimination of short-run cyclical fluctuations. The reforms of the 1970s reduced significantly the fiscal role of government. Budgets below the federal level accounted for 80 percent of aggregate government spending in Yugoslavia.[14] Furthermore, lower levels of government are not permitted to run deficits, which limits their role in stabilization policy. Even funds devoted to promoting economic development in the less-developed regions were shifted from the federal to the republican level in the mid-1970s. The main source of budgetary revenue, the turnover tax, has also been shifted to the republican level.

Another major instrument of control in Yugoslav society is the Communist party, or LCY. Obviously party members, operating at all levels in the system, are in a position to be an important guiding force, yet the evidence on the nature of this role is mixed. More than any other East European nation during the socialist era, Yugoslavia attempted to harmonize relations between the regime and the population. How strong was the LCY in this scenario? Western views differ. Laura D'Andrea Tyson suggested a limited role for the LCY, arguing that in the past, where differences emerged, the LCY was not able to harmonize diverse interests.[15] John H. Moore, on the other hand, sees the LCY as a much more powerful coordinating mechanism and indeed views past Yugoslav economic growth much more as a policy of the state and the LCY than as a policy of the people.[16]

Clearly, the role of the LCY in Yugoslavia has been different from that of communist parties in the past socialist systems of Eastern Europe.

LABOR AND CAPITAL ALLOCATION

Capital

Our examination of the Soviet economy singled out labor and capital for discussion largely because of our interest in allocation procedures under central planning and in their impact on performance. Because Yugoslavia is fundamentally a market system, we would expect allocation procedures to be more akin to those with which we are familiar.[17] In part this is true, though some important and interesting distinctions warrant our attention.

Yugoslavia has generally maintained a very high investment rate more typical of centrally planned systems of Eastern Europe and the Soviet Union than of market systems.[18] For example, gross domestic investment as a proportion of gross domestic product increased from 30 percent in 1965 to 39 percent in 1985.[19] Between 1965 and 1980, gross domestic investment grew at an average annual rate of 6.5 percent, though this rate dropped to – 0.3 percent between 1980 and 1985.[20] As John H. Moore points out, measurement problems aside, it is evident that capital accumulation has been a major part of Yugoslav development strategy and a major contributor to Yugoslav economic growth.[21] We normally associate such high investment ratios with a fairly substantial degree of state and/or plan control over the economy (and in particular control over investment). It is interesting to speculate on the respective roles of the state, plan, and enterprise worker-management system in Yugoslav investment practice.

Some have argued that under a system of labor-managed enterprises, there may be a tendency to favor distributions to labor rather than capital accumulation. Is there any evidence on this question in the Yugoslav case?

Although there have been fluctuations, enterprise accumulation has been important over the years; it has generally accounted for about one-third of the funds invested in industry and mining. However, there is some evidence to suggest that in the absence of controls or regulations of some sort, wage increases tend to be favored over increases in accumulation.[22] In the Yugoslav case, however, evidence on this issue is clouded by the fact that there are substantial profitability variations by region, and by industry and enterprise, which largely result from wide performance differences.

The allocation of capital by region and by sector is invariably the focus of attention. In addition to maintaining a high rate of accumulation, a cornerstone of Yugoslav economic policy has always been the pursuit of economic growth and the reduction of regional income differentials through the promotion of economic growth and development in the poorer regions. Although this type of regional policy has tended to be controversial, a study by Tyson suggests that there has been considerable capital misallocation in Yugoslavia, most notably the tendency to concentrate further accumulation in sectors that are already capital-intensive.[23] This result, she argues, stems in part from enterprise regulations, but it can also be attributed to organizational arrangements that have limited the regional mobility of capital in spite of persistent bank power in the allocation process.

In keeping with the general reform program of the 1970s, the investment process has also been decentralized in anticipation of expanded horizontal consultation at the local level. In addition to decentralization in the control of funds channeled through the government sector, banks have raised interest rates and have put pressure on enterprises to finance larger portions of their capital investment programs.

One may wonder why Yugoslav authorities remain so concerned about capital allocation when the Yugoslav investment rate is one of the highest in the world. The answer is that the concern is not with the volume of investment, but rather with the enterprise's unwillingness to plow back profits and with the misallocation of investment funds. Regional authorities appear to be unwilling to invest their funds in other regions, preferring to keep investment funds within their own boundaries. Although Yugoslavia, as a developing country, is rich in labor, enterprises and political authorities appear to favor capital-intensive projects. Why? The Yugoslav system taxes enterprise labor usage heavily and capital lightly. In addition, capital-intensive projects serve to raise the incomes of workers who remain with the enterprise over the long run.

Labor

Labor allocation in Yugoslavia has been fundamentally a market process, though the mechanism of worker management and the peculiarities of Yugoslavia present some special problems.

In Yugoslavia, workers in self-managed enterprises are guaranteed a minimum annual wage. The remainder of the annual wage payment depends on enterprise performance. If the enterprise fails to earn enough net income to cover the guaranteed wages, the enterprise must cover them out of reserve funds or the state must subsidize the wage bill. It is the responsibility of the workers' council to establish the system of wage differentials in the enterprise (within limits set by law). This is supposed to be done, as far as possible, on the basis of the employee's contribution to the success of the enterprise (recall the socialist principle of "to each according to his contribution").

Some enterprises are more successful than others, sometimes because of factors having little to do with workers' performance; thus it has been common for workers who perform the same task but belong to different enterprises to receive different wages. This is especially true of enterprises that operate with high capital–labor ratios or occupy a dominant market position. However, according to a study by Howard Wachtel, wage differentials have been narrower in Yugoslavia than in most West European countries, so worker management does serve, to some extent, to level the distribution of wages among workers.[24] Evidence from the 1970s and 1980s suggest that Yugoslavia has a distribution of labor income very much like that of Eastern Europe.[25]

Reforms introduced in 1970 established the principles that wage differentials should capture present labor contributions and the proportion of *past* labor reinvested in the enterprise, but that differentials due to monopoly power should not be allowed.[26]

Although Yugoslav enterprises are worker-managed, this mechanism has not eliminated strikes, which are often called by specific groups of workers — say, unskilled workers — to protest the wage differentials established by the workers' council. These strikes are often undertaken for their political impact rather than to influence enterprise policy.

Rigidities in the Yugoslav labor market prevent it from being highly fluid. Some rigidities arise from the system of employee compensation. Positions in enterprises with high net income per worker are not freely available and are often rationed out to relatives and friends. Regional enmities prevent workers of one nationality from moving into a region populated by another nationality. On the positive side, as a result of its open-border policy, Yugoslavia is a part of the West European labor market, and this has acted as a pressure valve for young unemployed workers.

Yugoslavia is basically a labor surplus economy in the sense that labor is more abundant than capital. In spite of the export of Yugoslav workers to Western Europe, unemployment has been a persistent problem at home — a scenario rather different from that of other East European systems. Although the unemployment rate grew in the 1970s and 1980s and regional differentials worsened (suggesting some immobility of labor), there was considerable expansion in the number of jobs available and hence in the number of Yugoslavs employed in the domestic economy. In part this must have resulted from self-management agreements designed to enhance employment.

Although the supply of labor has typically exceeded the demand for labor in the aggregate, it is difficult to know to what extent market forces have influenced labor allocation in Yugoslavia. Sharp earnings and unemployment differentials by region and by sector on a continuing basis might suggest that market forces have not been strong.

As we have already noted, the distribution of enterprise earnings has increasingly come under the control of the individual enterprise. Thus the accumulation of revenues is associated with the BOAL, typically as a part of a WOAL. Although there is a minimum wage, and advances are generally based on anticipated enterprise earnings, adjustments to the advance are included in an overall self-management agreement covering the particulars of income distribution.

The extent to which wage increases beyond productivity gains have contributed to inflation in Yugoslavia is a matter of contention.[27] The distribution of enterprise income seems broadly to conform to the theory of the worker-managed enterprise, but pressure exists to expand wage payments rather than accumulation. Empirical evidence supports the view that much strike activity has been motivated by the desire for higher wages rather than by other social issues the trade unions handle.[28]

It has proved difficult to create employment and limit wage increases to productivity growth while making more effective use of labor resources. This was a major issue addressed by the reforms of the 1970s.

THE FOREIGN SECTOR

Foreign trade has been important to the Yugoslav economy. Like other small and relatively open systems, the Yugoslav economy faced a difficult period in the 1970s when world markets generally collapsed and energy prices soared. The scenario is familiar: In the face of slackening world markets, the Yugoslav economy faced increasingly tight export markets. At the same time, as a major importer of energy and manufactures, Yugoslavia saw its imports grow, resulting in persistent annual deficits and the accumulation of a large external debt, the bulk of which was in hard currency. To understand these developments and the Yugoslav response, we must look at the composition of Yugoslav foreign trade, the changing nature of Yugoslav trading arrangements, and the nature of trade policies.

Yugoslavia has generally experienced deficits in the merchandise trade balance. These deficits were lessened and sometimes eliminated by surpluses in services (particularly tourism) and remittances from Yugoslav workers abroad. The net result, however, was a growing external debt that reached approximately $20 billion by the end of 1985.[29] The bulk of the Yugoslav external debt was financed in world commercial markets, though the World Bank and the International Monetary Fund were also involved. What were the major forces underlying this unenviable trade posture?

First, the Yugoslav economy has not performed will in commodity trade. Although there were continuing fluctuations in the 1970s, there was a net slackening in the growth of commodity exports and no comparable slackening in the growth of imports.[30] Indeed, studies have emphasized the long-term dependence of the Yugoslav economy on imports — especially in key growth areas, such as intermediate goods for industrial production.[31] In addition, Yugoslavia has been heavily dependent on foreign energy sources (the USSR and Iraq) and has also been a major importer of capital goods.

The unattractive posture in merchandise trade led to and is reflected in important shifts in the regional distribution of Yugoslav trade. In the 1970s and 1980s, the centrally planned economies (and especially the Soviet Union) grew more important as trading partners of Yugoslavia for two reasons. First, Yugoslav exports of manufactures, not particularly competitive in Western markets (and especially noncompetitive in times of Western recession), found ready markets in the East, especially in the Soviet Union. Second, the traditional Western markets for Yugoslav exports weakened substantially. The net result was an expansion of trade between Yugoslavia and the Soviet Union, which is not attractive as a means of generating hard currency.

Although many would agree that this period has been peculiar in a number of dimensions clearly beyond the control of Yugoslav authorities, the more fundamental question is why Yugoslav exports are not more competitive in world markets. Is this simply a peculiarity of the time, or is it a more fundamental (and thus more troubling) feature of the Yugoslav and possibly other formerly socialist economies?

First, protectionist policies have contributed to difficulties in export markets. For example, even though Yugoslavia has a special agreement with the European Economic Community (EEC), limitations imposed by the EEC are a particular problem for Yugoslavia because its exports are predominantly those of a less-developed nation — that is, food products, raw materials, and the like.

Second, aspects of the domestic Yugoslav economy have hindered the development of competitive exports. Inflation in Yugoslavia during the 1970s substantially raised the cost of Yugoslav products for potential importers.

Third, Yugoslav authorities have not aggressively developed competitive export industries. The mechanisms for domestic capital allocation have favored domestic industries, and potential sources of comparative advantage (in labor-intensive industries, for example) have not been pursued.

Although specific steps were taken in the late 1970s and 1980s to stabilize the Yugoslav economy and to improve its debt position, the more interesting aspect of the 1970s was the reforms in the foreign trade arrangements and regulations. It is difficult if not impossible to judge the extent to which these changes may be effective in the future.

In keeping with the general trend toward decentralization arising from the new constitution of 1974 and subsequent decrees and laws, decentralization of foreign trade arrangements was also pursued. In 1977, Communities of Interest for Foreign Economic Relations (CIFERs) were established in the republics and regions (but not at the local level). The BOALs, as members of these CIFERs, would be responsible for planning foreign trade — that is, imports, exports, and the articulation of an overall foreign trade policy at the federal level. Indeed, an assumption of the Trade Act of 1978 was that any enterprise engaged in foreign trade should become a foreign trade organization with foreign earnings distributed through the CIFER mechanism. The CIFERs have considerable power over the conduct of foreign trade, including planning, import controls, the promotion of exports, distribution of foreign trade earnings, and supervision of self-management agreements in the trade sector. However, it was difficult for the CIFERs to harmonize successfully the diverse interests of the enterprises and other groups, to develop and articulate a consistent trade policy, and to carry out such a policy to the benefit of the Yugoslav economy.

Another major factor in Yugoslav foreign trade has been its exchange rate policy. The Yugoslav dinar is not a fully convertible currency, though convertibility has been a long-term objective. Yugoslav manipulation of the dinar has been dictated by market forces. For example, the dinar was devalued vis-à-vis the U.S. dollar in 1965, 1971, 1974, and 1980. The fact that the dinar was not pegged to the dollar resulted in an average annual depreciation of 1.7 percent. However, as Tyson and Eichler have pointed out, when the extent of inflation in Yugoslavia's principal trading partners is taken into account, the dinar turns out to have appreciated relative to the currencies of those countries.[32]

Yugoslavia is an associate in the Organization for Economic Cooperation and Development (OECD) and has a preferential trade agreement with the EEC. In addition, Yugoslavia has been an associate member of COMECON since 1964 and participates in a number of the latter's commissions and banking arrangements. Yugoslav trade policy and posture of the late 1970s and 1980s were aimed at handling an immediate problem: a mounting external hard-currency debt with associated debt-service charges. The foreign trade mechanism of the Yugoslav economy was altered significantly in the 1970s.

AGRICULTURE IN YUGOSLAVIA

During the years immediately following World War II, a reform program implementing producer cooperatives developed in Yugoslavia, though never at the pace exhibited by the Soviet Union during its earlier collectivization drive.[33] At the peak of this movement in 1950, roughly 36 percent of the agricultural land in Yugoslavia was part of a cooperative or a state farm (that is, socialized). However, a law passed in 1953 spelled out the conditions under which peasants could depart from cooperatives, and a steady decline in the number of cooperatives and their membership began. Small peasant farms have been replacing the cooperatives as the dominant form of ownership. Today, approximately 16 percent of agricultural land in Yugoslavia is socialized. The state sector, utilizing worker management, includes large-scale operations and agro-industrial complexes. Although the number of producer cooperatives is limited, Yugoslavia does have a number of general agricultural cooperatives the functions of which include providing technical advice, making marketing arrangements, and delivering inputs such as fertilizer.

Over time, agriculture's share in the Yugoslav economy has declined significantly, which is not unexpected during a period of economic development. For example, between 1965 and 1979, agriculture's share of the Yugoslav labor force declined from just under 50 percent to 34 percent, while agriculture's share of gross national product for the same period fell from just over 25 percent to 20 percent.[34] The average annual rate of growth of agricultural output in the 1970s was approximately 3.6 percent. There were substantial year-to-year fluctuations, however, and for the 1970s, per capita agricultural output grew at an average annual rate of slightly better than 2.5 percent.[35] Average annual growth for the 1980s was only 1.3 percent.

Although the overall output performance of Yugoslav agriculture has been reasonable in recent years, the agricultural sector suffers from a lack of modernization, and especially from a dichotomy between the socialized and private sectors. The basic statistics tell the story. For example, the share of gross fixed agricultural investment in aggregate investment has been just over 9 percent for the past 15 years. This is the lowest share of any country in Eastern Europe and is well below the product share of Yugoslav agriculture. It is not surprising that, for the same period, the level of agricultural output per capita has been the lowest in Eastern Europe. Furthermore, in the area of important inputs, (such as fertilizer and tractors), Yugoslavia generally falls well behind other East European countries. Although the rate of growth of these inputs to Yugoslav agriculture has been good, a lot remains to be done.

Through the years, considerable effort has been expended to stimulate Yugoslav agriculture, especially through improvement of prices, expansion of incentives, and so on. At the same time, Yugoslav agriculture has failed to move toward a modern footing in which it would have a smaller share in the economy and a higher level of economic development. This has been a central issue in discussions of the Federal Council for the Problems of Economic Stabilization, and it doubtless will be the basis of future agricultural policy. That policy, whatever specific form it may take, will surely focus on the modernization of Yugoslav agriculture, particularly modernization based on agro-industrial integration.

YUGOSLAV ECONOMIC PERFORMANCE

This chapter has focused on the economic objectives of the Yugoslav leadership. Rapid economic growth has been a consistent goal because of the underdeveloped nature (relative to Western Europe) of the Yugoslav economy. The maintenance of a "socialist" distribution of income has been another consistent goal, particularly in a socialist country in which much resource allocation is left to the market. A special Yugoslav goal, in light of the vast regional differences in this ethnically diverse nation, has been to reduce regional income differences. Added to these objectives are the common macroeconomic goals of full employment, reasonable price stability, and balance-of-payments equilibrium.

To what extent has Yugoslavia been able to achieve these objectives? Although we compare Yugoslav economic performance with that of other countries in Chapter 15, it is useful to note basic trends here. In doing so, we must emphasize that assessment of economic performance is always difficult because of the problems of measurement. In the Yugoslav case, there is also the serious problem of relating observed performance patterns to the periods when particular Yugoslav economic institutions of worker management existed.

From the 1950s through the 1970s, Yugoslav economic performance, judged in terms of the average annual growth of total and per capita gross national product, was very good. The pace of structural change was rapid, and Yugoslavia achieved a "socialist" distribution of income similar to that of other East European systems. Yugoslav economic performance in other areas was less satisfactory. Unemployment was a continuing problem, and the average annual rate of inflation accelerated into the double-digit range. Moreover, regional inequalities apparently sharpened in spite of policies intended to lessen them.

The decade of the 1980s was difficult for Yugoslavia. The negative trends noted above continued, and many of the positive trends were reversed — partly as a result of recession elsewhere in the world and continuing energy problems. For example, while gross domestic product grew at an average annual rate of 6.5 percent between 1965 and 1980, growth slipped to .8 percent for the period 1980 to 1985.[36] In the same two periods, the average rate of inflation increased from 15.2 percent to 45.1 percent. Moreover, export growth slowed in the 1980s, and import growth became negative. Yugoslavia's long-term debt increased dramatically — from 15 percent of gross national product in 1970 to 35.3 percent in 1985. In addition to new regulations pertaining to foreign exchange, foreign investment in Yugoslavia was made more attractive. The value of the dinar fell steadily against the dollar in the 1980s.[37] Domestic demand was constrained largely through investment. Gross domestic investment grew at an average annual rate of 6.5 percent between 1965 and 1980 but fell to a rate of – 0.3 percent between 1980 and 1985.

The reversals of the 1980s have once again called attention to the relationship among the economic system, reform of the system, and performance. This issue is particularly critical in the Yugoslav case, given the continuing search for a fully workable participatory market socialism.

The Reform Proposals of 1988

The 1965 reforms were aimed at strengthening the role of market resource allocation in Yugoslavia. The reforms of the 1970s were aimed at resolving the macroeconomic instabilities caused by the combination of worker-managed socialism, which were intensified by the worldwide inflations of the 1970s and early 1980s and by the stagflation of the same period. Tito's death in 1980 crippled Yugoslavia's ability to map out further economic reforms, because regional diversity and enmity reduced the role of the central government, and the Yugoslav communist party disintegrated into regional factionalism.

The 1980s saw rampant inflation, growing foreign debt, and actual declines in real per capita income; between 1988 and 1989, prices increased by a factor of 30. The unemployment rate averaged above 10 percent in the 1980s, and real personal income fell a whopping 39 percent between 1980 and 1986. Clearly, the goal of the 1970s reforms to achieve workable social compacts that would resolve the inflation and unemployment problems had not been realized. The root causes of the economic crisis of the 1980s were the tendency of Yugoslav firms to overexpand capacity (higher capital-intensity meant more net income per worker), the provision of credit by regional branches of the state bank at low interest rates and according to political needs, the inability of the divided regions to agree on demand-management fiscal policies, overvaluation of the dinar, and the lack of a strong central bank to control the growth of the money supply.[38]

The crises of the late 1970s and 1980s motivated the Yugoslav leadership to devise in 1988 a new set of economic reforms, designed specifically to deal with the macroeconomic imbalances of inflation, unemployment, and trade deficits. A price freeze was put into effect in early 1988. Yugoslavia entered into negotiations with the International Monetary Fund to achieve a rescheduling of Yugoslavia's soaring foreign debt in return for an austerity program that would put Yugoslavia's financial house in order.

The reforms put forward by the collective Yugoslav leadership in 1988 called for import restrictions, incentives to increase domestic savings, reductions in government expenditures on social services, higher interest rates and cost of capital, slower growth of the money supply, the restriction of "grey market" financial transactions, and a more progressive tax system. The Yugoslav national bank was to have greater autonomy and authority and the federal government was to play a larger role in coordinating the budgets of republican and regional governments.

Yugoslavia in the 1990s: Performance and Reform

The Yugoslav economic experience has been an interesting experiment — an attempt to combine the efficiency of the market mechanism with the social policies of socialism. Although the Yugoslav experience has been unique in a variety of ways, the outcome is important because the basic equity–efficiency tradeoff has been such a dominant theme in contemporary thinking about different economic systems.

Unfortunately, all the economic difficulties that plagued the Yugoslav economy in the 1980s worsened as the decade came to an end and a new decade began. Although there was movement toward privatization and the sale of enterprise shares to workers and employees, these efforts to change have encountered obstacles. Moreover, the approach has raised questions about the extent of competition in the markets of any privatized Yugoslav economy.

In spite of the moves toward privatization, the early 1990s have been a very difficult period. Inflation continued unabated, in large part because the lack of effective central economic policies contributed to wage increases. Output declined, unemployment increased, and the trade deficit widened. Since January 1991, all trade with the Soviet Union has been conducted in hard currencies. As we will see in Chapter 18 when we discuss more general issues of transition in Eastern Europe, this shift to hard currencies has resulted in major changes in trade patterns.

Possibly most important, social tensions in Yugoslavia have increased significantly since 1990, and differences between Serbia and the remainder of the country threaten to result in dissolution of the federation in its present form. In light of these events, it seems likely that severe measures of economic stabilization will have to precede or at least coincide with privatization. Political instability will make it difficult for either stabilization or privatization to succeed. Moreover, it may be difficult to sustain even a loose federation. Efforts in the spring of 1990 to define a new *Yugoslav Community* focused on the development of a Yugoslav common market designed to liberalize trade internally and (ultimately) externally. But republic moves toward independence in the summer of 1991 worsened both the political and the economic situation.

SUMMARY

Yugoslavia has traditionally been characterized as a market socialist economy that uses a system of worker management at the enterprise level. These sorts of arrangements are of great theoretical interest, but it has proved difficult to analyze their impact on economic outcomes in the Yugoslav case. Moreover, though market forces have been dominant in the operation of the Yugoslav economic system, the role of the Communist party, both as a mechanism to develop and sustain national unity and as a force in resource allocation, has been less than clear. In a sense, therefore, our analysis of the Yugoslav economic system neither provides conclusive evidence on the costs and benefits of market socialism nor fully illuminates the controversial issues of worker management or participatory socialism in general. In recent years, our attention has focused on Yugoslav macroeconomic performance, and especially on the problems of political instability in an era of reform. For Yugoslavia, stability and reform are key issues of the 1990s.

NOTES

1. Worker participation can take many forms. The system we have in mind is one in which workers have a voice in decision making within the enterprise but do not own the assets of that enterprise. Though certain types of guarantees and minimums may prevail, the worker is, fundamentally, a residual claimant (after expenses and taxes) to enterprise income.
2. For a discussion of earlier arrangements, see Joel B. Dirlam and James L. Plummer, *An Introduction to the Yugoslav Economy* (Columbus, Ohio: Merrill, 1973); Deborah Milenkovitch, *Plan and Market in Yugoslav Economic Thought* (New Haven: Yale University Press, 1971); Howard Wachtel, *Workers' Management and Workers' Wages in Yugoslavia* (Ithaca, N.Y.: Cornell University Press, 1973); and Harold Lydall, *Yugoslav Socialism: Theory and Practice* (Oxford, England: Clarendon Press, 1984).
3. Laura D'Andrea Tyson, "The Yugoslav Economy in the 1970s: A Survey of Recent Developments and Future Prospects," in U.S. Congress, Joint Economic Committee, *East European Economies Post Helsinki* (Washington, D.C.: Government Printing Office, 1977), p. 945.
4. Ellen Turkish Comisso, *Workers' Control Under Plan and Market* (New Haven: Yale University Press, 1979), p. 75.

5. An excellent survey of the 1970s can be found in Laura D'Andrea Tyson, *The Yugoslav Economic System and Its Performance in the 1970s* (Berkeley: Institute of International Studies, 1980); and Laura D'Andrea Tyson and Gabriel Eichler, "Continuity and Change in the Yugoslav Economy in the 1970s and the 1980s," in U.S. Congress, Joint Economic Committee, *East European Economic Assessment*, pt. 1 (Washington, D.C.: Government Printing Office, 1981), pp. 139–214.

6. For additional discussion of the role of enterprise directors in Yugoslavia, see David Granick, *Enterprise Guidance in Eastern Europe* (Princeton, N.J.: Princeton University Press, 1975), Chs. 11–13.

7. Dirlam and Plummer, *An Introduction to the Yugoslav Economy*, p. 57.

8. Ibid., p. 50.

9. Ibid.

10. In addition to Tyson, *op. cit.*, an excellent source is Janez Prasnikar and Jan Svejnar, "Economic Behavior of Yugoslav Enterprises," in Jones and Svejnar, eds., *Advances in the Economic Analysis of Participatory and Labor-Managed Firms*, Vol. 3 (Greenwich, Ct.: JAI Press, 1988).

11. Ibid.

12. See, for example, Comisso, *Workers' Control*, Ch. 6; Tyson, *The Yugoslav Economic System*, Ch. 2; Stephen Sacks, "Transfer Prices in Decentralized Self-Managed Enterprises," *Journal of Comparative Economics*, 1 (June 1977), 183–193; Prasnikar and Svejnar, *op. cit.*

13. Past investment procedures are discussed in John H. Moore, *Growth with Self-Management* (Stanford, Calif.: Hoover Institution Press, 1980), Ch. 8.

14. OECD, *Yugoslavia* (Paris: OECD, 1982), p. 34.

15. See Tyson, *The Yugoslav Economic System*, pp. 27–30.

16. See, for example, Moore, *Growth with Self-Management*; and John H. Moore, "Self-Management in Yugoslavia," in Joint Economic Committee, *East European Economic Assessment*, pt. 1, pp. 215–229.

17. A great deal has been written on these issues, especially on capital allocation. For a recent survey of developments and an introduction to basic issues, see Tyson and Eichler, "Continuity and Change in the Yugoslav Economy," pp. 156–164.

18. Ibid., p. 157.

19. World Bank, *World Bank Development Report 1987* (New York: Oxford University Press, 1987), Table 5.

20. Ibid., Table 4.

21. Ibid., p. 216.

22. See Laura D'Andrea Tyson, "A Permanent Income Hypothesis for the Yugoslav Firm," *Economica*, 44 (November 1977), 393–408.

23. See Tyson, *The Yugoslav Economic System*, pp. 39–51.

24. Wachtel, *Workers' Management and Workers' Wages in Yugoslavia*.

25. John R. Moroney, *Income Inequality Trends and International Comparisons* (Lexington, Mass.: Heath, 1979), p. 5.

26. Milenkovitch, *Plan and Market in Yugoslav Economic Thought*, pp. 57–58.

27. For an analysis and discussion of the issue of inflation and unemployment in Yugoslavia, see Laura D'Andrea Tyson, "The Yugoslav Inflation: Some Competing Hypotheses," *Journal of Comparative Economics*, 1 (June 1977), 113–146; and Michael L. Wyzan and Andrew M. Utter, "The Yugoslav Inflation," *Journal of Comparative Economics*, 6 (1982), 396–405.

28. Abram Bergson, "Entrepreneurship Under Labor Participation: The Yugoslav Case," in Joshua Rosen, ed., *Entrepreneurship* (Lexington, Mass.: Lexington Books, 1982), p. 199.

29. World Bank, *World Development Report 1987*, p. 233.

30. Between 1965 and 1980, exports of merchandise grew at an average annual rate of 5.6 percent, while imports grew at 6.6 percent. Comparable figures for the period 1980 to 1985 were 2.1 and –3.3 percent, respectively. See World Bank, *World Development Report 1987*, p. 221.

31. For a discussion of recent developments in the foreign sector, see Tyson and Eichler, "Continuity and Change in the Yugoslav Economy," pp. 174–211. This section is based on the discussion by Tyson and Eichler.

32. Ibid., p. 190.

33. For a discussion of these years, see Theodor Bergmann, *Farm Policies in Socialist Countries* (Lexington, Mass.: Lexington Books, 1975), pp. 129–152; and Robert F. Miller, "Group Farming Practices in Yugoslavia," in Peter Dorner, ed., *Cooperative and Commune* (Madison: The University of Wisconsin Press, 1977), pp. 163–197.
34. Gregor Lazarcik, "Comparative Growth, Structure, and Levels of Agricultural Output, Inputs, and Productivity in Eastern Europe, 1965–79," in Joint Economic Committee, *East European Economic Assessment*, pt. 2, p. 592.
35. Ibid., Table 2; World Bank, *World Development Report 1987*, p. 205.
36. Data here are from the World Bank, *World Development Report 1987*, text tables.
37. The Economist, Intelligence Unit, *Country Profile: Yugoslavia 1987–88* (London: The Economist, 1987), p. 9.
38. Kenneth Zapp, "Economic Reforms in Yugoslavia," paper presented at Midwest Economic Association Meeting, Chicago, IL, April 1988.

RECOMMENDED READINGS

General Works

Avner Ben-Ner and Egon Neuberger, "The Feasibility of Planned Market Systems: The Yugoslav Visible Hand and Negotiated Planning," *Journal of Comparative Economics*, 14 (December 1990), 768–790.

Abram Bergson, "Entrepreneurship Under Labor Participation: The Yugoslav Case," in Joshua Rosen, ed., *Entrepreneurship* (Lexington, Mass.: Lexington Books, 1982).

Ellen Turkish Comisso, *Workers' Control Under Plan and Market* (New Haven: Yale University Press, 1979).

———, "Yugoslavia in the 1970s: Self-Management and Bargaining," *Journal of Comparative Economics*, 4 (June 1980), 192–208.

Bogdan Denitch, *The Crisis of Yugoslav Socialism and State Socialist Systems: Limits and Possibilities* (Minneapolis: University of Minnesota Press, 1990).

Milojko Drulovic, *Self-Management on Trial* (Nottingham: Spokesman Books, 1978).

Vinod Dubey, ed., *Yugoslavia: Development with Decentralization* (Baltimore: The Johns Hopkins University Press, 1975).

Branko Horvat, "Yugoslav Economic Policy in the Post-War Period: Problems, Ideas, Institutional Developments," *American Economic Review*, 61 (June 1971), 70–169.

———, *The Yugoslav Economic System* (White Plains, N.Y.: M. E. Sharpe, 1976).

Derek C. Jones and Jan Svejnar, eds., *Advances in the Economic Analysis of participatory and Labor-Managed Firms*, Vols. 1–4 (Greenwich, Ct.: JAI Press, 1985).

Harold Lydall, *Yugoslav Socialism: Theory and Practice* (Oxford, England: Clarendon Press, 1984).

———, *Yugoslavia in Crisis* (Oxford, England: The Clarendon Press, 1989).

Deborah Milenkovitch, *Plan and Market in Yugoslav Economic Thought* (New Haven: Yale University Press, 1968).

John H. Moore, *Growth with Self-Management: Yugoslav Industrialization, 1952–1975* (Stanford, Calif.: Hoover Institution Press, 1980).

———, "Self-Management in Yugoslavia," in U.S. Congress, Joint Economic Committee, *East European Economic Assessment*, pt. 1 (Washington, D.C.: Government Printing Office, 1981), pp. 215–229.

V. Rus and R. Russell, eds., *International Handbook of Participation in Organizations* (New York: Oxford University Press, 1989).

Laura D'Andrea Tyson, *The Yugoslav Economic System and Its Performance in the 1970s* (Berkeley: Institute of International Studies, 1980).

———, "The Yugoslav Economy in the 1970s: A Survey of Recent Developments and Future Prospects," in U.S. Congress, Joint Economic Committee, *East European Economies Post Helsinki* (Washington, D.C.: Government Printing Office, 1977), pp. 941–998.

Laura D'Andrea Tyson and Gabriel Eichler, "Continuity and Change in the Yugoslav Economy in the 1970s and the 1980s," in U.S. Congress, Joint Economic Committee, *East European Economic Assessment*, pt. 1 (Washington, D.C.: Government Printing Office, 1981), pp. 139–214.

The Yugoslav Enterprise

Deborah A. Bateman, Mieko Nishimizu, and John M. Page, Jr., "Regional Productivity Differentials and Development Policy in Yugoslavia, 1965–1978," *Journal of Comparative Economics*, 12 (March 1988), 24–42.

Katrina V. Berman, "An Empirical Test of the Theory of the Labor-Managed Firm," *Journal of Comparative Economics*, 13 (June 1989), 281–300.

David Granick, *Enterprise Guidance in Eastern Europe* (Princeton, N.J.: Princeton University Press, 1975).

Norman J. Ireland and Peter J. Law, "Management Design Under Labor Management," *Journal of Comparative Economics*, 12 (March 1988), 1–23.

Derek C. Jones and Jan Svejnar, eds., *Advances in the Economic Analysis of Participatory and Labor-Managed Firms* (Greenwich, Ct.: JAI Press, 1985).

Janet Mitchell, "Credit Rationing, Budget Constraints, and Salaries in Yugoslav Firms," *Journal of Comparative Economics*, 13 (June 1989), 254–280.

Kathryn Nantz, "The Labor-Managed Firm Under Imperfect Monitoring: Employment and Work Effort Responses," *Journal of Comparative Economics*, 14 (March 1990), 33–50.

Hugh Neary, "The Comparative Statics of the Ward–Domar Labor-Managed Firm: A Profit-Function Approach," *Journal of Comparative Economics*, 12 (June 1988), 159–181.

Pavle Petrivic, "Price Distortion and Income Dispersion in a Labor-Managed Economy: Evidence From Yugoslavia," *Journal of Comparative Economics*, 12 (December 1988), 592–603.

Janez Prasnikar and Jan Svejnar, "Economic Behavior of Yugoslav Enterprises," in Jones and Svejnar, eds., *Advances in the Economic Analysis of Participatory and Labor-Managed Firms*, Vol. 3 (Greenwich, Ct.: JAI Press, 1988).

Stephen Sacks, "Divisionalization in Large Yugoslav Enterprises," *Journal of Comparative Economics*, 4 (June 1980), 290–325.

———, *Self-Management and Efficiency: Large Corporations in Yugoslavia* (Boston: Allen and Unwin, 1983).

Fernando B. Saldanha, "Fixprice Analysis of Labor-Managed Economies," *Journal of Comparative Economics*, 13 (June 1989), 227–253.

Laura D'Andrea Tyson, "Incentives, Income Sharing, and Institutional Innovation in The Yugoslav Self-Managed Firm," *Journal of Comparative Economics*, 3 (September 1979), 285–301.

Inflation

H. Flakierski, "Economic Reform and Income Distribution in Yugoslavia," *Comparative Economic Studies*, 31 (Spring 1989), 67–102.

Laura D'Andrea Tyson, "The Yugoslav Inflation: Some Competing Hypotheses," *Journal of Comparative Economics*, 1 (June 1977), 113–146.

Michael L. Wyzan and Andrew M. Utter, "Comment: The Yugoslav Inflation," *Journal of Comparative Economics*, 6 (1982), 396–405.

Agriculture

FAO, *The Development of Agriculture in Socialist Yugoslavia* (Rome: FAO, 1976).

Miles J. Lambert, "Yugoslav Agricultural Goals for 1976–85," *ACES Bulletin*, 20 (Fall–Winter 1978), 37–64.

Gregor Lazarcik, "Comparative Growth, Structure, and Levels of Agricultural Output, Inputs, and Productivity in Eastern Europe, 1965–79," in U.S. Congress, Joint Economic Committee, *East European Economic Assessment*, pt. 2 (Washington, D.C.: Government Printing Office, 1981), pp. 587–634.

OECD, *Agricultural Policy in Yugoslavia* (Paris: OECD, 1980).

Lung-Fai Wong and Vernon Ruttan, "A Comparative Analysis of Agricultural Productivity Trends in Centrally Planned Economies," in Kenneth R. Gray, ed., *Soviet Agriculture: Comparative Perspectives* (Ames: Iowa State University Press, 1990), 23–47.

Foreign Trade

Laura D'Andrea Tyson and Egon Neuberger, "The Impact of External Economic Disturbances on Yugoslavia: Theoretical and Empirical Explorations," *Journal of Comparative Economics*, 3 (December 1979), 346–374.

PART IV

INTERRELATIONSHIPS AND PERFORMANCE

14 Interrelationships Among Economic Systems: International Trade

Incredible changes, beginning at the very end of the 1980s, have altered the world economy in a fundamental way. Prior to this time, the flows of trade and capital between East and West were limited and were conducted according to fundamentally different arrangements. In the East, trade and capital flows were directed by a foreign trade monopoly rather than by the decisions of private firms. The foreign trade monopoly followed well-established rules and procedures that were familiar to both parties to the transaction. The East, moreover, did not observe the standard rules and procedures worked out by the various international organizations (the General Agreement on Trade and Tariffs, the World Bank, the International Monetary Fund) that govern trade in the West.

These vast differences in trading arrangements meant that the world could easily be divided into two distinct trading blocs — the East and the West. Differences in trading arrangements, along with factors distinctive to the planned socialist economy, kept East–West trade to a minimum. The planned socialist economy's aversion to private ownership of productive assets similarly limited the flow of capital from West to East. The lack of common "rules of the game" in international trade also acted as a brake on trade between the two blocs.

The radical economic and political reforms that began to sweep through the Soviet Union and Eastern Europe at the end of the 1980s have started to alter this uneventful equilibrium. Along with the decision to alter internal resource allocation processes, the countries of the Soviet Union and Eastern Europe have expressed their intention to change the way they conduct trade. In effect, the reform movements announced their intention to become full-fledged members of the world economic community — that is, to play by the same rules of the game as their Western trading partners.

Radical changes in trading arrangements do not take place overnight. The formerly planned economies of the East are in a period of transition, and whether they will effect changes successfully remains to be seen. Many of the traditional arrangements are still in place. Much dramatic change has already occurred in some countries of the East; in others, we have seen only declarations of intent to change the system.

In this chapter we emphasize the traditional planned-economy system of trade, a system based on strong state control exerted through a foreign trade monopoly and administrative currency controls. An understanding of the traditional system is vital in our effort to assess current prospects for change. We must understand why international trade was so limited by the traditional system, what obstacles that system places in the way of trade, and what resistance to opening up to the world economy should be expected. The chapter ends with a discussion of prospects for change in the traditional system.

THE FORCES INFLUENCING TRADE: COMPARATIVE ADVANTAGE VERSUS TRADE AVERSION

Capitalism and planned socialism take radically different approaches to international trade. The basic force explaining trade among capitalist nations is **comparative advantage**, described long ago by the classical economists. Participants in trade compare relative costs of foreign and home-produced goods. At existing exchange rates, the commodities that can be obtained abroad at lower prices will be imported; others will be produced at home. Free international trade benefits both trading partners by allowing each partner to specialize in commodities it can produce at lower relative costs. The respective trading partners exchange commodities at lower relative costs than would be possible in the absence of trade, thereby raising welfare in both countries.

The policy prescription of comparative advantage is that trade among countries should be free from government control, for free trade will maximize the welfare of both trading partners.

The traditional socialist approach to international trade has been called **trade aversion**.[1] International trade should supply the domestic economy with necessary imports called for by the economic plan. International trade is used to acquire *imports*; exports serve only as the means for acquiring them. This does not mean that the objective of socialist trade is to maximize imports. Rather the emphasis has been on averting trade and relying on the domestic economy to supply essential materials, using foreign imports as a "safety valve." The traditional socialist economy avoids heavy reliance on foreign suppliers, even when a product can be acquired more economically abroad.[2] In part, trade aversion stemmed from a view that the world market is subject to disturbances and fluctuations that planners cannot predict. Deliveries from other planned socialist economies could be irregular or late as a result of planning shortfalls and imbalances.

The comparative advantage doctrine suggests that foreign trade should be free of both external and internal restrictions and that decisions on what to buy and sell abroad should be made by private businesses. The decision rule for trade is simple: If one can purchase a product abroad more cheaply (at prevailing exchange rates) than the commodity can be made at home, it should be imported. When trade proceeds according to this rule, prices of traded goods equalize among trading partners. Instead of national prices, world prices will characterize world product markets.

The planned socialist economies have conducted foreign trade differently. Planners determine what imports will be purchased, and a foreign trade monopoly is charged with implementing import and export plans. No simple decision rule, such as trading according to comparative costs, is used. Instead, a series of criteria, both political and economic, determine imports and exports. The producers and users of the traded commodities have little to do with export and import decisions; rather a foreign trade monopoly makes such decisions.

The effectiveness with which a particular economic system conducts its trade affects economic outcomes. An economy that trades according to comparative advantage specializes its production in areas with relatively high productivity. An economy that underutilizes its trade potential denies itself the advantages of specialization and is forced to produce at home a wider range of products, some at low efficiency relative to world standards. Systemic underutilization of trade potential means a loss of output achievable from a given volume of factor inputs — that is, a loss of static efficiency.

A system's conduct of trade can affect economic performance in ways that are sometimes hard to predict. The decision to avoid heavy reliance on foreign suppliers and world markets may make the domestic economy less subject to external fluctuations (that is, more stable), and economic stability is one criterion by which economic performance is judged. Trade underutilization may also be justified on military grounds. Military self-sufficiency requires a diversified domestic economy even if this undermines comparative advantage. Moreover, there is the issue of economic and political independence. Does the economic dependence of one system on another ultimately lead to a loss of political independence?

CHARACTERISTICS OF TRADE IN EAST AND WEST

The most characteristic feature of Eastern trade in general and of East–West trade in particular has been its limited nature despite rapid growth in recent years. As shown in Figure 14.1, the developed capitalist nations (the West) accounted for 65 percent of world trade and 65 percent of world national income in the late 1980s. The socialist nations (including China) accounted for only 10 percent of world trade but for 20 percent of world national income.[3] The East conducts one-half as much international trade per dollar of national income as does the West. This marked underutilization of trade potential (trade aversion) by the socialist nations has been confirmed by econometric studies for the 1950s and 1960s, which found that if the socialist countries had participated in trade to the same degree as a capitalist country at the same stage of development, their trade ratios (trade as a percentage of GNP) would have been as much as 50 percent higher.[4]

One distinguishing feature of trade in the East is its limited magnitude relative to its potential as measured by capitalist economy standards. This remains true today despite the rapid expansion of the trade of the East between 1960 and the present. Between 1960 and 1990, Eastern trade (excluding the Asian communist countries) grew by a factor of 19, almost apace with Western trade,

Figure 14.1 Indicators of East–West Trade

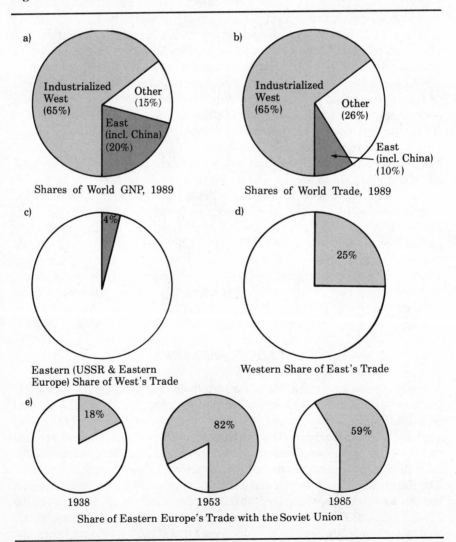

a) Shares of World GNP, 1989

- Industrialized West (65%)
- Other (15%)
- East (incl. China) (20%)

b) Shares of World Trade, 1989

- Industrialized West (65%)
- Other (26%)
- East (incl. China) (10%)

c) 4%
Eastern (USSR & Eastern Europe) Share of West's Trade

d) 25%
Western Share of East's Trade

e) 18%   82%   59%

1938   1953   1985

Share of Eastern Europe's Trade with the Soviet Union

Source: *Handbook of Economic Statistics 1990*, pp. 15, 150–151, 170.

which grew by a factor of 23.[5] Thus the Eastern share of world trade has continued to decline (although at a slower pace), starting from a low percentage of trade relative to national income in the immediate postwar period.

The volume of East–West trade is low, despite a 30-fold increase since 1960. According to Franklyn Holzman, writing in 1976, "East–West trade is not very important quantitatively and could be overlooked if it were not for its political implications."[6] In fact, East–West trade in the mid 1980s accounted for only 3 percent of world trade, down considerably from its pre-World War II rate of over 6 percent. As a proportion of world trade, the flow of goods and services between socialist and capitalist economic systems is relatively minor, though it is expanding. Because of low trade volumes in the East, East–West trade is proportionally more important to the East than to the West.[7] East–West trade accounts for only 4 percent of the trade of the West but for 25 percent of Eastern trade. In the East at least, East–West trade has assumed a position of some importance.

When discussing quantitative trends, one should also mention the major restructurings of Eastern European trade since the Second World War. In 1938 only 19 percent of Eastern Europe's imports came from Eastern Europe and the Soviet Union; by Stalin's death in 1953, this figure had risen to 82 percent. In 1982, imports from Eastern Europe and the Soviet Union accounted for 59 percent of the total for Eastern Europe and reflected a substantial shift toward the West since 1953.[8]

FOREIGN TRADE PLANNING UNDER PLANNED SOCIALISM

What lies behind trade aversion in the planned socialist economies? One key has been the method of foreign trade planning.[9] In the planned socialist states, foreign trade planning has been integrated into the overall planning process. A state planning commission establishes output targets for enterprises and compiles balances of important funded commodities. The foreign trade plan emerges from these targets and balances. Targeted imports are used to fill deficits in material balances; technology imports are employed to supply new planned technology; domestic enterprises are given supply and delivery plans for the foreign sector. A committee for material and technical supply typically deals with the actual allocation of important producers' goods and may have some barter dealings with other socialist countries. A committee on science and technology handles the acquisition of foreign technologies. The finance ministry and a foreign trade bank monitor the effect of foreign trade on the state budget.

Two types of organizations assist the planning organizations in constructing and implementing the foreign trade plan. They are the ministry of foreign trade (MFT) and the foreign trade organizations (FTO). Both are charged with working out the details of import and export plans, and both are responsible for making the actual contacts with domestic and foreign producers and determining the means of payment. The MFT, the state bank, and the foreign trade bank construct a balance-of-payments account to plan for the payment of international transactions. Figure 14.2 shows an organization chart for a typical foreign trade monopoly.

Figure 14.2 The Foreign Trade Monopoly

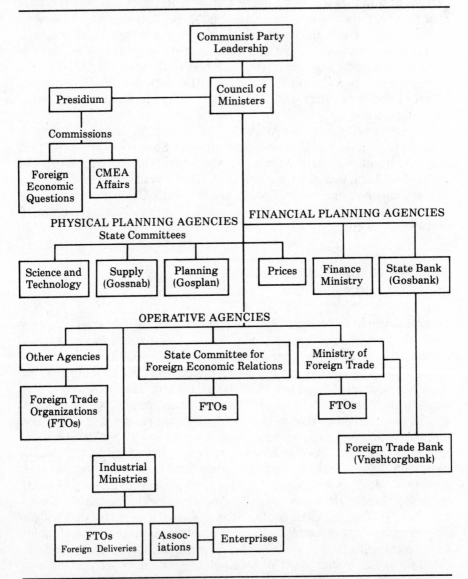

Source: H. Stephen Gardner, *Soviet Foreign Trade: The Decision Process* (Boston: Kluwer-Nijhoff, 1982), p. 2. Reprinted by permission of Kluwer Academic Publishers.

The state planning commission, the state bank, the foreign trade bank, the MFT, and the FTOs make up a **foreign trade monopoly**, which conducts the foreign trade of the socialist countries. There is little or no contact between domestic producer and foreign user or between foreign producer and domestic user; contacts proceed through the foreign trade monopoly. The domestic producer knows little about the requirements of the foreign user. The enterprise is simply told to deliver a certain portion of its planned output to a designated foreign trade organization, which is charged with making the sale abroad. The domestic enterprise receives the same proceeds from the sale abroad as from any other sale (the domestic wholesale price) and, unless special bonus arrangements are in effect, is no more interested in foreign sales than in domestic sales. In fact, domestic enterprises may avoid production for foreign customers because the FTO may be in a position to exercise more arbitrary authority over it in this case.[10]

In trade with Western countries, world market prices are used. In the case of trade among socialist countries, averages of past world market prices have generally been used. In a few instances current world market prices have been used. For the period 1971–1974, for example, 1965 to 1969 averages of world market prices were used. Because of increases in raw materials and other prices in the 1970s, it was agreed that prices would be based on an average of world market prices for the previous five years.[11] The use of world prices has been dictated by deficiencies in the domestic prices and the lack of meaningful exchange rates, which have prevented one price system from being accepted as a standard for East-bloc transactions. In the case of homogeneous products such as oil or coal, it is not difficult to determine world market prices. For heterogeneous products such as machinery, prices are often established through bilateral negotiations.

The system of foreign trade planning contributes to the underutilization of trade potential by the centrally planned economies. Rigid quantity-oriented systems are tempted to limit risks by minimizing dependence on outside suppliers. The same tendency toward trade aversion can be observed in centrally planned firms, which seek to make themselves as self-sufficient as possible. It can also be observed in international trade dealings. To include a foreign supplier of a commodity essential to the overall material balance makes plan success dependent on outside forces. To some extent, such pressures are less severe in the case of Western suppliers, for the capitalist market is viewed as sufficiently flexible to guarantee on-time deliveries.

Bilateralism and Inconvertibility[12]

No East-bloc currency has been freely convertible into a Western currency or into gold.[13] Nor are East-bloc currencies convertible into another East-bloc currency in any operational sense. Moreover, citizens in most Eastern countries have been prohibited from holding Western currencies, and the state trading monopoly possesses a monopoly over foreign exchange. One Eastern currency is not freely convertible into another at an established rate of exchange, and these currencies are not accepted as a means of payment for exchanged commodities. If a Bulgarian FTO arranges a sale to a Czech FTO, the Bulgarians cannot use the proceeds to buy freely the goods they desire from Czechoslovakia. If Czechoslovakia sells more to Bulgaria than it buys, the Czechs cannot select Bulgarian commodities to use up the surplus. It follows that it is not possible for the Bulgarians to use Czech currency to pay for imports from a third country, say, the Soviet Union.

Even if a third country were willing to make goods available, they would probably be so-called soft goods — that is, goods bartered at terms less favorable than the recipient country could obtain in the world market. Hard goods, such as raw materials, which can be readily sold in world markets, would not be made available on a currency basis.

Commodity inconvertibility characterizes the trade among the planned socialist economies. Even if one country has a trading surplus with another, it cannot buy goods freely from that country. If the surplus country could freely purchase goods on an unplanned basis, the domestic supply plan would be disrupted. The prices at which traded goods change hands are often out of line with opportunity costs. If surplus countries could freely select goods from a deficit country, they could opportunistically choose goods that exchange for irrationally low prices.

Commodity inconvertibility had a substantial impact on East-bloc trade. Between any pair of countries, sales are negotiated on a barter bases so that the values of commodities exchanged in both directions will balances. If Bulgaria wants to sell fruit to Czechoslovakia, a barter deal must be made whereby Bulgaria receives from Czechoslovakia commodities of an equivalent value. Only rarely are nonbalancing exchanges made (for credit). Arrangements between two countries according to negotiated exchanges of equivalent values are termed **bilateral** (as opposed to multilateral) agreements.

In the case of East–West transactions, barter arrangements involving equivalent values are desired by the Eastern trading partner, but they do not occur so frequently. Instead, East–West trade is generally cleared on a **multilateral** basis. Purchases and sales are cleared in a convertible Western currency (say, West German marks) or are financed by a credit arrangement (say, a German bank agreeing to finance a Bulgarian purchase). In the case of a sale to a Western country, the Eastern seller can use the hard-currency proceeds to purchase commodities from a second Western country.

Although the East-bloc countries have attempted in the past to establish some type of clearing arrangement within their bloc (for example, the International Bank for Economic Cooperation), such efforts have not succeeded, and most intrabloc trade has been conducted on a bilateral basis. The bilateralism of intrabloc trade is a major factor behind trade underutilization. Bilateralism means that it is impossible to achieve the optimal level of trade between two countries because of the necessity to balance the value of imports and exports. Accordingly, the Eastern countries do not always sell in the market where they could obtain the highest price, nor do they buy in the cheapest market. Bulgaria and Czechoslovakia must balance their sales to each other, even though a better arrangement might have called for an imbalance between them.

Balance-of-Payments Problems

On a formal level, the East-bloc countries did not suffer from a balance-of-payments problem. Exports and imports were planned by the state trade monopoly, and the foreign trade plan included a plan to balance international payments. If the projected receipts of foreign (convertible) currencies fall short of requirements, projected imports (or exports) are reduced (or increased) and a trade balance is thereby achieved. In the case of intrabloc trade, there is usually no balance-of-payments problem because exchanges of commodities are balanced via bilateral agreements. The balance-of-payments problem concerns supplies and demands for convertible currencies.

On a more substantive level, the balance-of-payments problem is related to the fact that (in the absence of credits) purchases from the West are limited to the value of sales to the West. Unlike the Western countries, the Eastern countries cannot pay for the excess of purchases over sales with their own currencies. But the East-bloc countries have been unable to compete in Western markets because of quality and service problems. The burgeoning demand for Western technology since 1960 has meant that the Eastern countries have had to purchase less from the West than they have desired.

The normalization of East–West trade relations in the 1970s, 1980s, and 1990s served to ease (but not solve) balance-of-payments problems. The West European countries have been willing to grant government-guaranteed credits to gain Eastern markets. Moreover, increases in the price of raw materials raised the Soviet Union's earnings of convertible currencies in the 1970s and early 1990s.[14] Eastern Europe's hard-currency debt grew by a factor of almost 3 between 1975 and 1980, spurred by détente and Western recessions. Much of this lending failed to yield hard-currency returns, resulting in severe debt service problems; moreover, the recessions of the late 1970s and early 1980s restricted international lending. These factors slowed Western lending to the East in the mid 1980s. Between 1980 and 1985, East European hard currency debt rose only by 4 percent.[15]

Several explanations have been advanced for the marketing difficulties experienced by the socialist economies, especially in the area of manufactured exports. The inflexibility of foreign trade planning and the lack of contact between the planned producer and the Western consumer explain much of the problem.[16] The reluctance of Eastern enterprises to produce for export and to produce spare parts can be cited as other factors. One point raised by the East-bloc countries themselves is that some Western governments have discriminated against socialist exports, and such discrimination is cited as a cause of hard-currency difficulties.[17]

Foreign Trade Criteria in Socialist Countries[18]

In deciding what commodities are to be imported and exported and from whom, foreign trade planners have relied on rules and agreements, many of which have little to do with comparative costs. Some decisions are based on political considerations. Others are based on long-term cooperative and trade agreements. Some decisions, however, can be based on economic criteria for making import and export decisions. These criteria apply the principle that imports and exports should be selected based on comparisons of domestic and foreign costs. In its simplest form, the standard index of foreign trade effectiveness of imports (E) is

$$E = \left(\frac{Pd}{Pf}\right)k \qquad (14.1)$$

where

Pd = the domestic cost of producing the product at home
Pf = the cost in foreign exchange of importing the commodity
k = the amount of foreign exchange earned from exports per unit of domestic costs of producing the exports

Let us say that East Germany could import steel from Poland at a price of 400 "valuta marks" per ton (Pf in our formula) and that the domestic cost of producing a ton of steel is 800 marks (Pd). Thus the ratio of the domestic price to the foreign exchange (valuta mark) price is 2 — a seemingly advantageous purchase. This price ratio must be adjusted however, by k, which measures the cost in domestic resources of exports to Poland to pay for this import. Clearly, the higher the domestic cost of paying for the import (the lower the k), the less desirable the purchase.

To calculate k, we determine the *average* ratio of the foreign exchange value of East German exports to Poland to the *average* cost in domestic prices of producing these exports. The careful reader will note the resemblance between k and the Western concept of an exchange rate, although the resemblance is remote. Let us assume that the k ratio is 1.2, which should be interpreted as meaning that 1.2 valuta marks of foreign exchange can be earned from 1 mark's worth of production (measured in domestic prices) from East German exports to Poland. The overall efficiency index therefore is 2 × 1.2 or 2.4.

We will use two examples to show how this formula can be applied to select imports and trading partners. Assume that East Germany must choose between importing coal from Poland and importing steel from Poland by determining which product yields the highest E index (that is, the highest ratio of the domestic to the imported price). Let us say that the domestic price of coal is twice the foreign exchange price ($E = 2$) but that the domestic price of steel is only one and one-half times the foreign exchange price ($E = 1.5$). If no other considerations are involved, coal rather than steel should be imported from Poland.

In the second example, East Germany must buy steel either from Poland or from Czechoslovakia. The valuta mark prices (Pf) are 400 marks for Poland

and 450 marks for Czechoslovakia, and the domestic prices (Pd) is again 800 marks. Whereas 1.2 valuta marks can be earned per mark of domestic production from exports to Poland (k), a higher value (say, 1.4) can be earned from exports to Czechoslovakia. The calculated E indexes are 2.4 for Polish steel and 2.49 for Czech steel, leading to the conclusion that, other things being equal, the steel import should come from Czechoslovakia.

Foreign trade criteria were used only in limited ways. Most trading decisions have been based on other considerations.[19] The rules are used primarily when planning exports and imports within narrow product groups.[20]

It is not hard to understand why the planned socialist economy has made limited use of foreign trade criteria. As long as domestic prices fail to reflect relative scarcity, mechanical efficiency formulas do not lead to optimal trade patterns. In fact, at the macro level, there is some evidence that administrative decisions have resulted in "rational" trading patterns.[21]

TRADE POLICY IN EAST AND WEST

We now turn to trade policy — in particular, to the formation of trading blocs and the gradual dismantling of barriers to trade — in the West and between the East and West after World War II. The specific issue treated in this section is the degree to which trade barriers have inhibited the growth of trade between East and West.

Postwar History: The West

The postwar period witnessed the rapid growth of world trade. In the West, this rapid growth was a consequence of both the high growth rates of the industrialized capitalist world and the dismantling of trade barriers that had been erected during the Great Depression. Moreover, the founding of customs unions in Western Europe — the European Economic Community (EEC) — in 1958 and the European Free Trade Association (EFTA) led to a marked integration of the West European economy and contributed to increased intra-European trade.

The industrialized capitalist countries entered the postwar era behind the high tariff walls of the 1930s but joined in 1947 into an organization committed to reducing those barriers — the General Agreement on Tariffs and Trade (GATT). Under the auspices of GATT, multilateral tariff reductions have been negotiated among participating countries, the most important being between the United States and the European Economic Community. In such tariff negotiations, the **most favored nation** (MFN) principle has been applied, whereby the participating parties agree to extend any negotiated reduction to all parties holding MFN status. MFN simplifies the negotiation of tariff reductions by eliminating the complicated task of negotiating tariff agreements with all affected parties.

The United States has participated in GATT tariff negotiations under periodic legislation. The Trade Expansion Act of 1962 gave the U.S. president authority to reduce U.S. tariffs by as much as 50 percent on articles accounting for some 80 percent of world trade. Negotiations were begun with the EEC on the basis of the Trade Expansion Act. These "Kennedy Round" and subsequent negotiations served to reduce substantially tariffs on commodities traded between the United States, Western Europe, and Japan. Later negotiations called the Tokyo Round were held in 1980. The 1984 Trade and Tariff Act authorized the president to enter into a new round of negotiations to reduce trade barriers (the Uruguay Round). The Uruguay Round negotiations tackled the difficult issues of agricultural protection of European and Japanese farmers and, as of late 1991, have failed to find a compromise solution. The success of the Western program of tariff reductions through multilateral negotiation remains a signal achievement. In 1932, the average tariff rate was 59 percent. After the Tokyo Round it had fallen to less than 7 percent (Figure 14.3).

Protectionist substitutes for tariffs have come to be widely used and have posed the most significant threat to free trade. Nontariff barriers such as quotas, import specifications, and the like are the major instruments in use today for the protection of domestic industries.

Figure 14.3 Average Import Duties, 1925–1990

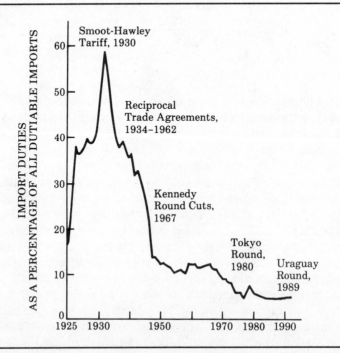

Source: *Historical Statistics of the United States; Statistical Abstracts of the United States,* 1987.

The basic framework for the postwar capitalist monetary system was created at the Bretton Woods Conference of 1944. The major capitalist countries agreed to establish a system of fixed rates of exchange among their currencies, with the U.S. dollar serving as the central currency. The International Monetary Fund (IMF) was established to oversee the system. Member countries agreed to peg their currencies around declared par values to the dollar by purchasing and selling their own currencies in foreign exchange markets. For its part, the United States pledged to convert dollars held by foreign governments into gold at a fixed rate of exchange. Credit arrangements were established to help member countries keep their currencies at par. Only in the case of a fundamental disequilibrium would members be allowed to change the values of their currencies vis-à-vis the dollar.

The notion behind this system of fixed exchange rates was that it would promote trade among countries by eliminating the risks of exchange rate fluctuations, and the postwar period did witness a remarkable expansion of trade. According to United Nations and IMF statistics, the trade turnover of the developed capitalist countries increased by a factor of 11 between 1948 and 1973 in a period of relatively mild inflation. Whether the Bretton Woods system can take credit for this expansion is not clear, but the system of orderly international monetary arrangements was probably conducive to expanded trade after the shocks of depression and world war.

The Bretton Woods system fell apart in August 1971 when the United States ceased converting dollars held by foreign governments into gold at a fixed rate of exchange. After attempts to return to a new fixed-exchange-rate parity system, by March of 1973 the major capitalist countries began to allow their currencies to fluctuate in value. A major factor behind the decision to abandon the fixed-exchange-rate system was the tendency for certain currencies to become over- or undervalued under the Bretton Woods system, thus placing pressure on the fixed-exchange-rate system. Even prior to the official abandonment of the fixed-exchange-rate system in 1973, there were several devaluations of "weak" currencies (the English pound) and "revaluations" of strong currencies (the German mark).

In 1976, at a conference in Kingston, Jamaica, the original IMF charter was amended to legalize the widespread system of floating currencies. Under the Jamaica Agreements, countries could adopt whatever exchange rate system they preferred (fixed or floating) but should avoid significant manipulation of their exchange rate. In 1979, the countries of the European Economic Community joined together in the European Currency Union (ECU). Member countries agreed to maintain their respective currencies at basically fixed rates relative to each other (joint floating rates).

A unified European market is scheduled to be achieved by 1992. "Europe 1992" calls for coordinated monetary and fiscal policies, a European central bank, and eventually a common European currency. When implemented, these policies will substantially reduce national sovereignty over economic policies in Europe.

Policies Toward the East[22]

One factor behind the limited East–West trade of the early postwar period was the effort, spearheaded by the United States, to limit the flow of strategic materials to the Soviet Union, Eastern Europe, and China. During this period, the United States used a series of measures to limit exports from the West to the East. Embargoes were placed on trade with mainland China and North Korea, and the U.S. Export Control Act of 1949 prohibited the export of a lengthy list of materials to the East. In 1947 the United States and Western Europe formed a coordinating committee, since called COCOM, to conduct a common embargo policy toward the communist countries. The Battle Act of 1951 called for the termination of aid to any country selling strategic materials to a communist country. The Trade Agreement Extension Act of 1951 denied MFN status to all Eastern countries except Yugoslavia. Therefore, trade with those countries was subject to the high tariff rates of the 1930s. Moreover, the major capitalist powers agreed not to extend long-term credits to communist nations — an effective limit on Eastern imports, given the weakness of Eastern sales to the West. (Poland was granted MFN status in 1960, Romania in 1975, Hungary in 1978, and China in 1980.)

After 1960, restrictions against East–West trade were eased, with the United States being one of the last countries to make trade concessions. The major changes came from Western European countries that were more dependent on trade than the United States, the countries that stood to lose the most from continued restrictions on East–West commerce. The threat of U.S. countermeasures was diminished after the termination of the Marshall Plan and the end of the European "dollar shortage." One by one, the Western European nations and Japan began to expand sales to Eastern Europe and the Soviet Union and to grant long-term credits to finance such sales. Moreover, most of the Western European countries granted MFN to their Eastern trading partners, leaving the United States as the major capitalist power that had failed to extend MFN to its communist trading partners. However, quantitative restrictions on Eastern imports remained an important deterrent in Western Europe.[23]

An apparent breakthrough in American trade relations with communist countries came, after extended negotiation, in October 1972, with the American–Soviet Trade Agreement. Having received concessions from the Soviet Union concerning repayment of a portion of Lend-Lease Aid, the American trade negotiators agreed to make Export-Import Bank credits available on a favorable basis and to grant MFN status to Soviet imports, subject to congressional approval. Soviet repayment of Lend-Lease debt was tied to congressional approval of MFN by 1975.

In December 1974, the Soviet Union annulled the American–Soviet Trade Agreement. Several reasons might be cited for this action. First, Congress openly tied the granting of MFN to freer emigration of Jewish citizens. Up to that point, such emigration had been promoted through quiet diplomacy. When this was turned into a formal condition for MFN, the Soviets interpreted the action as an excessive intrusion into their domestic political affairs. Second, Congress placed limitations on the amount of credits that could be granted under the agreement. These limitations would have prevented the Soviet Union from receiving the massive credits for major investment projects they desired from the United States; thus they made the agreement less attractive. Third, the increase in the world prices of raw materials, including gold and oil, dramatically improved the hard-currency earnings of the Soviet Union, rendering the granting of American credits less important. The situation deteriorated further as the United States imposed economic sanctions on the Soviet Union for their trials of dissidents in 1978, for the Soviet invasion of Afghanistan in late 1979, and for the imposition of martial law in Poland in late 1981.[24]

The dramatic economic and political changes that began in Eastern Europe and the Soviet Union in the late 1980s altered Western trade policy toward the East.[25] To assist the reform process, between September 1989 and May 1990 the industrialized West pledged to Poland and Hungary alone $11 billion in new credits, loan and investment guarantees, and food aid. A sum of $1 billion was created to stabilize the convertible Polish currency. The industrialized West also reached agreement to establish a European Bank for Reconstruction and Development, with an initial capitalization of $12 billion, to assist the reform efforts of Eastern Europe and the Soviet Union. In addition, the World Bank and the International Monetary Fund have approved substantial loans, earmarked primarily for Poland. The largest pledges of assistance have come from Germany, Japan, and France.

The new relationship between Washington and Moscow has led to substantial progress in normalizing trade relations between the two countries. The USSR has substantially eased restrictions on emigration, and the United States has agreed to grant MFN and to provide development assistance to the Soviet Union pending approval, by the Soviet parliament, of new emigration laws. In light of the Soviet Union's support of the United Nations resolution against the Iraqi invasion of Kuwait, the United States has agreed to waive a number of trade restrictions against the USSR. The Soviet President was invited as an observer to the summer 1991 Group of Seven economics conference in London at which time the USSR was granted junior membership in the IMF.

The European Community is on record as affirming that trade ties with Eastern Europe must be strengthened in order to promote political stability and economic reform in this region. The European Community has signed trade and cooperation agreements with Hungary, Poland, Czechoslovakia, Bulgaria, and East Germany. The economic and political unification of Germany automatically made the territory that used to be East Germany a full-fledged member of the European Community. Hungary, Poland, Czechoslovakia, Bulgaria, and Romania have become members of the World Bank and the IMF, and most have become members of GATT. The Soviet Union has applied to join these international organizations and has been granted observer status.

The position of the West on financial support of the East is that assistance should be provided to promote the transition to a market economy. The United

States, in particular, has been reluctant to provide major assistance without evidence that serious market reforms are indeed under way. For this reason, the West has been reluctant to provide assistance to Romania because of doubts about the seriousness of Romania's reform effort. Germany has spearheaded the effort to provide financial and technical assistance to the East.

It is difficult to assess the impact of Western restrictions on East–West trade. Some argue that the East chose trade aversion voluntarily and that quantitative restrictions and the failure of the United States to grant MFN have had a limited impact. The Eastern nations, however, emphasize these restrictions as the cause of limited East–West trade. Much attention has been devoted to the failure of the United States to grant MFN. Estimates of the effect of U.S. MFN vary substantially but suggest that its impact would vary widely. The effect would not be large in the case of the Soviet Union and Poland but would be substantial for the remainder of Eastern Europe, because tariff discrimination is greater on manufactured goods, which are more important in the exports of Czechoslovakia and Hungary. There have also been efforts to assess the impact of the various sanctions (grain embargoes and the like) imposed by the United States on the Soviet Union. The consensus is that their impact has been small.[26]

Postwar History: The East

The characteristic feature of postwar Western Europe has been the growing integration of its national economies. Postwar Eastern Europe, in contrast, experienced little economic integration. Instead, the emphasis was on the development of semi-independent national economies and on the avoidance of regional specialization. This is true even though the European countries formed their own international organization, the Council for Mutual Economic Assistance (CMEA), which was founded in 1949 for the purpose of promoting economic cooperation as the Soviet counterpart to the American Marshall Plan (see Figure 14.4).

The CMEA, unlike the European Economic Community, possessed no supranational authority over its members.[27] Instead, according to its charter of 1960, all nations had an equal vote, and any one nation could veto proposals involving supranational measures. At different times, the Soviet Union sought to give the CMEA supranational powers to promote economic integration and specialization, but such efforts were opposed by nations (principally, Romania and Hungary) that feared a loss of national independence. Despite various attempts to establish a CMEA currency (the "transferable" ruble) and despite the existence of a bank for multilateral clearing (the International Bank for Economic Cooperation), most negotiations on trade and technology transfers were carried out on a bilateral basis.

The CMEA adopted a number of programs designed to promote the economic integration of the CMEA countries.[28] The Comprehensive Program for Socialist Integration of 1971 consisted of a set of long-term proposals for bilateral economic and scientific cooperation and some voluntary joint planning.

The Agreed Plan for Multilateral Integration Measures, adopted in 1975 for the period 1976–1980, was a collection of ten large joint investment projects, eight of which were located in the Soviet Union. The Long-Term Special Purpose Program for Cooperation was signed in 1979 to cover the period from 1980 to

Figure 14.4 CMEA Organization Chart

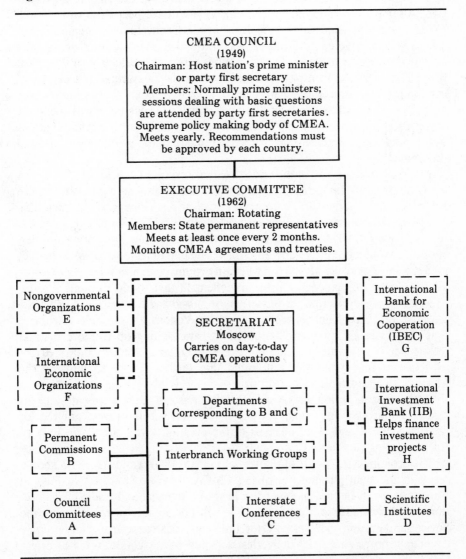

Source: Adapted from Paul Marer and John Michael Montias, "CMEA Integration: Theory and Practice," in U.S. Congress, Joint Economic Committee, *East European Economic Assessment*, Part 2 (Washington, D.C.: Government Printing Office, 1981), pp. 150–152.

1995. The cooperation agreements signed in the 1970s shifted the focus of economic integration in the direction of coordination of investment projects and were aimed at developing Soviet energy and raw material resources using Eastern European labor and capital equipment. These agreements did not result in a corresponding expansion of trade.[29]

There is controversy over whether the CMEA's presence increased economic specialization in Eastern Europe. One Western author thinks that the impact was considerable after 1964, but most authorities disagree. They find that the CMEA's impact on economic integration was limited, especially prior to 1970.[30] Even though thousands of products — primarily machinery, chemicals, and metals — were covered by CMEA specialization agreements, the share of total output involved in those industries remains minimal (perhaps 6 or 7 percent of CMEA machinery output). There is no single measure of the degree of economic integration or of changes in the degree of economic integration over time. The most serious study of this issue concluded that there was economic "disintegration" within CMEA, largely because the smaller CMEA nations began producing products that had been the monopoly of the larger planned economies.[31]

Much discussion has been devoted to answering the question, "Who was exploiting whom" in CMEA trade? If the Soviet Union sold goods that were traded in world markets to Eastern Europe at prices below world market, then the Soviet Union had in fact granted a hidden subsidy. The pricing formulas that governed CMEA trade certainly created an opportunity for subsidies, because raw material prices and other prices tended to lag behind world market prices. Subsidies could also occur when one country, such as the Soviet Union, allowed its trading partners to run up deficits in their trade accounts.[32]

Most experts agree that the Soviet Union subsidized Eastern Europe, particularly in the 1970s. Michael Marresse and Jan Vanous, for example, calculated that the Soviet Union sacrificed potential gains adding up to more than $5 billion per year in the period 1974 to 1978. Other estimates confirmed the existence of these subsidies but found that they were not so large as the Marresse–Vanous figures.[33]

If the Soviet Union chose to subsidize Eastern Europe, what were its motives? Marresse and Vanous argue that Soviet subsidies were granted for political reasons and represent part of the price of Soviet control in Eastern Europe during this period.

The economic and political reforms of the late 1980s and early 1990s should result in the final phasing out of the CMEA, as more countries of Eastern Europe gain full-fledged membership in world financial and trading organizations. In the meantime, Eastern Europe will not be able to retreat from the Soviet market, and vice versa. Over the years, Eastern Europe has become dependent on raw material deliveries from the Soviet Union, often at prices below the world market. The Soviet Union, on the other hand, has become dependent on Eastern Europe for machinery and equipment. It is likely that the Soviet Union will continue to serve as a market for Eastern European manufactures that do not find markets in the West. In this way, unemployment associated with the transition to a market economy can be held down in Eastern Europe. For its part, the Soviet Union will increasingly demand hard cash for its raw materials from Eastern Europe or will insist on the delivery of higher-quality East European food and consumer goods in return. Soviet–East European trade was converted to a hard-currency basis using world market prices in 1991.[34] The CMEA was abolished in mid 1991.

Joint Ventures[35]

While institutional barriers to East–West trade were falling and CMEA interest in Western imports was rising, the difficult issue of accommodating the transfer of technology through capital exports between different economic systems remained unresolved. Technology transfers among capitalist nations are financed through intergovernment loans, private loans, portfolio investment in equities, and direct investment. The last two were precluded in the East by virtue of prohibitions against private ownership. After considerable experimentation in the 1960s and 1970s, various forms of East–West industrial cooperation emerged. Industrial cooperation agreements played an important role in the expansion of East–West trade because of the East's interest in Western capital and technology. Such arrangements must go beyond traditional export and import operations; they call for a relationship between the supplier of the technology and the user that lasts for a number of years.

The early 1990s witnessed a remarkable liberalization of the mechanics of launching joint ventures in Soviet and East European legislation. In the 1970s and 1980s, restrictions on both private and foreign ownership required innovative (and typically ineffective) industrial cooperation. Deals had to be financed by countertrade arrangements (an example was financing Pepsi Cola's Soviet operations by selling Stolichnaya Vodka in the West) or by the sale of shares in future production. Only a limited number of such deals proved feasible. The Western investor did not have legitimate ownership rights, and the Western company was not allowed to manage the enterprise. For these reasons, the number of effective joint ventures established during the 1980s was limited.

The economic reforms of the 1990s have created new attitudes toward joint ventures, and new legislation is being developed. In most of the countries of Eastern Europe, equity ownership is allowed (up to 100 percent in some cases), and Western investment is protected by law against nationalization without adequate compensation. Moreover, new forms of industrial cooperation have opened up, including franchises and concessions.

In the long run, legislation should lead to meaningful cooperation between the East and West and should promote a significant flow of capital from West to East. Of course, how much capital and technology are transferred will depend on the ultimate success of the market reforms in this region. The major attractions of the East are the vast natural resources of the Soviet Union that require massive capital injections for development, the low labor costs of the region, and the unexploited consumer market of the East. In the short run, few success stories can be cited. In both the Soviet Union and Eastern Europe, there continue to be few working joint ventures, and those that do exist involve minimal capitalizations. Although there are more than 5000 registered joint ventures in the Soviet Union and Eastern Europe, the vast majority are small, with start-up costs of well below $1 million. In Eastern Europe, most joint ventures have been formed with Hungarian and Polish partners. The Western countries most active in East–West joint ventures are Germany and Austria. To date, American investment in the Soviet Union and Eastern Europe has been minimal.

East European Debt

The burgeoning hard-currency debt of Eastern Europe represents another obstacle to expanded East–West trade. This debt grew in the 1970s and 1980s as Western Europe and Japan pumped private and public loans into the region — particularly into Hungary, Poland, and what was then East Germany.

Eastern Europe's hard-currency debt rose from $6 billion in 1971 through $66 billion in 1980 to over $100 billion in 1990; Poland, Hungary, and East Germany accounted for 80 percent of the total. During the same period, the Soviet Union's hard-currency debt rose from less than $1 billion to $33 billion. With the economic and political reunification of Germany, East Germany's debt became the obligation of united Germany. Inasmuch as Soviet GNP is approximately 4 times that of Eastern Europe, Eastern Europe's $100 billion hard-currency debt looms large relative to the Soviet Union's $33 billion.[36]

If the loan proceeds had been used for productive investments that yielded hard-currency exports, the increase in Eastern Europe's indebtedness would not be particularly alarming. But such has not been the case. As Figure 14.5 reveals, the ability of Eastern Europe's two most prominent debtors, Poland and Hungary, to service their hard-currency debt is questionable. In both countries, hard-currency debt is about 5 times hard-currency export earnings. Moreover, with market interest rates reflecting the substantial risk of default, Poland and Hungary must apply virtually all their hard-currency earnings just to service their accumulated debt. The situation in the Soviet Union is less severe (largely because of the Soviet Union's ability to export raw materials for hard currency): The Soviet ratio of debt payments to hard-currency earnings is a more reasonable (but still alarming) 23 percent.[37]

The international banking community may have to write off a substantial portion of its loans to Eastern Europe as unrecoverable — just as they had to write off a substantial portion of their Latin American loans in the late 1980s. East European debt is currently being offered on world credit markets at a considerable discount.

The West continues to commit investment funds to Eastern Europe, despite the risk of default. However, private lending institutions are prepared to make loans to Eastern Europe only if the loans are guaranteed by a Western European government or by an international organization. Accordingly, many

Figure 14.5 Three Alternative Debt Burden Measures of the East European Countries, 1971, 1975, 1979, and 1989

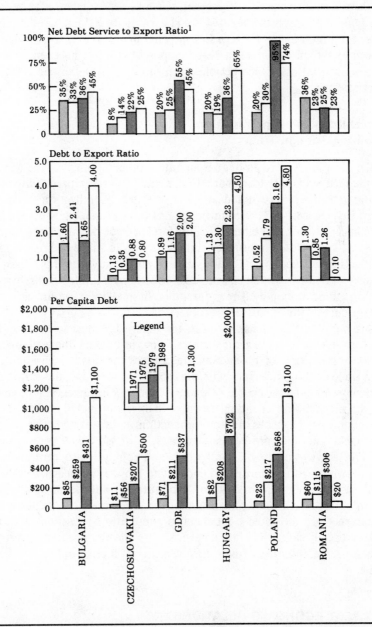

Source: Paul Marer, "Economic Performance and Prospects in Eastern Europe," copyright © 1980. Published in U.S. Congress, Joint Economic Committee, *East European Economic Assessment*, Part 1 (Washington, D.C.: Government Printing Office, 1981), p. 67; *Handbook of Economic Statistics 1989*, Table 19, Table 142; "Eastern Europe: Long Road Ahead to Economic Well-Being," A Paper by the Central Intelligence Agency Presented to the Subcommittee on Technology and National Security of the Joint Economic Committee, May 1990, Table C-1.

Eastern European loans are currently being granted for political rather than economic reasons. These loans are a way to help Eastern Europe make the difficult transition from plan to market, much as the Marshall Plan assistance of the United States in the late 1940s and early 1950s helped Western Europe recover from the war. As Eastern Europe's hard-currency reserves dwindled in response to the energy price increases imposed by Iraq's invasion of Kuwait, Western financial assistance became even more vital to the continuation of market reforms.

Socialist Economies in Transition: Liberalizing Foreign Trade

The liberalization of foreign trade is an important component of the transition from planned socialism to a market economy. The liberalized joint venture procedures that we have noted are a part of the liberalization packages in Eastern Europe. Most of the countries of Eastern Europe, including the Soviet Union, have declared that eliminating the foreign trade monopoly is a necessary step in the transition. Enterprises should be free to make their own foreign trade decisions. The Soviet Union, as a representative example, has given thousands of enterprises the right to deal directly with foreign firms, bypassing the foreign trade monopoly. The proliferation of small joint venture agreements is the product of this increased freedom.

For a number of reasons, however, the planned economies have found it difficult to liberalize trade arrangements. First, as long as domestic prices do not reflect true costs of production, enterprises may not make appropriate foreign trade decisions. Second, with the exception of Poland, the currencies of the region remain inconvertible. Without a convertible currency, foreign trade deals with the West must continue to be based on traditional financing methods: barter, countertrade, shares of future production, and so on. Often such innovative financing methods are beyond the capacity of individual enterprises and require the services of the old foreign trade monopoly. Third, central authorities have continued to control and coordinate limited hard-currency reserves. Enterprises that sell to the West for hard currency still do not gain control over this currency. As far as central authorities are concerned, the demands on hard currency are too intense for them to allow it to be distributed to those who have directly earned it. Until enterprises are allowed to enjoy the proceeds of their foreign initiatives, their involvement in foreign trade will not be effective.

EAST–WEST ECONOMIC RELATIONS WITH THE THIRD WORLD[38]

Up to this point, we have said little about international economics and the less developed countries (the LDCs). The LDCs tend to work as a bloc through the

United Nations Conference on Trade and Development (UNCTAD). Though all members of the United Nations can participate in UNCTAD, it has spoken primarily on behalf of the LDCs in matters of trade and development. The established international organizations such as GATT and the IMF are perceived by the LDCs as representing the interests of the industrialized countries, and UNCTAD provides the organizational framework through which the wishes and demands of the LDCs vis-à-vis the developed world are made known.

Although the trade of the industrialized capitalist countries and of the CMEA countries with the LDCs has not been a major element in world trade, Eastern and Western trade with the LDCs and aid to them are still of considerable import. Many LDCs have sought to remain uncommitted to either the Eastern or the Western bloc; their political importance in world affairs far exceeds their economic importance. Moreover, they tend to be the most unstable components of the world political order.

In some instances, the LDCs produce raw materials, such as petroleum, that are of considerable economic and strategic importance to the industrialized East and West. Some observers believe that Western and Eastern policy toward the LDCs is aimed at gaining control of their strategic raw materials. Moreover, the existence of a large and growing income gap between the rich and the poor nations is likely to contribute to political instability throughout the world. Recognition of this fact has focused attention on the development problems of the LDCs.

Capitalism and socialism have offered competing theories to the LDCs. The capitalist theory of development states that the LDCs must be content to exchange the products that they produce at a comparative advantage (raw materials, agricultural products). By doing so, they can obtain, at a minimum cost of their own resources, the imported materials required for their economic development. As their per capita income grows, the LDCs can gradually substitute domestic production for the machinery and manufactured goods they had previously imported. Capitalist development theory argues that the LDCs should maintain a basically capitalist economic system, albeit with stronger government controls, and should continued to produce traditional products until import substitution can be justified by sound profit-maximizing criteria.

The Marxist–Leninist theory of development has painted a quite different picture: Adherence to market economics and the comparative advantage will doom the LDCs to an indefinite period of subservience to the industrialized capitalist countries. This is the upshot of Lenin's famous theory of imperialism. The affluence of the industrialized capitalist countries is maintained by exploiting the labor and mineral resources of the LDCs, whose economic development is purposely retarded by the industrialized West. In order to develop, the LDCs must throw off their imperialist chains through wars of national liberation and join the ranks of the socialist countries. Then, they can begin the process of industrialization and the building of socialism.

There is considerable debate over the merits of the two analyses of LDC development strategy. The LDCs (through the forum of UNCTAD) have argued that they have been placed at a disadvantage in trade with the industrialized world for a variety of reasons and that it is the responsibility of the industrialized world to establish a "new international economic order." LDC dissatisfaction with the existing economic order centers on the fact that the LDCs have been relegated principally to the role of producing raw materials. Yet raw material prices fluctuate more erratically than the prices of manufactured goods (often because of the competitive nature of raw material markets). Moreover, the tariffs and quotas established by the industrialized countries discriminate against the raw material exports of the LDCs and keep their manufactured exports (such as textiles) out of the affluent countries. The LDCs argue, therefore, that the affluent countries should increase their aid, should admit LDC manufactured goods on a preferential basis, and should assist in stabilizing the prices of LDC raw materials at levels high enough to promote their economic development. Moreover, the LDCs note that they were particularly hard hit by the increase in energy prices and the world recessions of the 1970s and early 1980s. These developments have made it difficult for the LDCs to finance their growing external debt and to pay for imports necessary for economic development.

East-West Trade and Aid: The LDCs

Most world trade takes place among the industrialized capitalist countries and, to a much lesser degree, among the CMEA countries. East–West trade itself accounts for an insignificant share of world trade. The trade of the East and West with the LDCs is relatively limited. In 1985, LDC exports plus imports accounted for 7 percent of total East European trade turnover and 9 percent of Soviet trade turnover. In the mid-1980s, the LDC exports and imports of industrialized capitalist countries accounted for 14 percent of their total trade turnover, excluding the OPEC countries, and for 26 percent including the OPEC countries. In terms of volume, trade between the industrialized capitalist countries and the LDCs dwarfs that of the East. In 1982 the industrialized capitalist countries bought $323 billion worth of exports from the LDCs (including OPEC); the CMEA countries bought $14 billion worth. Eastern trade with the LDCs is small compared to that of the West both in relative terms (as a percentage of total Eastern trade) and in absolute dollar terms.

What has explained the limited trade of the East with the LDCs? One obvious explanation is that the East and the LDCs command only one-third of world GNP and, largely because of the East's limited participation in trade, less than one-fourth of world trade. Nevertheless, even these figures would predict larger trade volumes between the East and the LDCs than those actually observed. Another factor accounting for the low trade proportions is that the East is a relatively new entrant into LDC markets and lacks long-established trade relationships, which are often the consequence of past colonial rule.

One somewhat puzzling aspect of the limited amount of East–LDC trade is that there have been strong economic, as well as political, grounds for such trade. In the 1950s and 1960s, the Eastern European countries embarked on national programs of industrialization, de-emphasizing the production of raw materials and agricultural products. These efforts led to a shortage of raw materials in Eastern Europe. Thus its demand for the products typically exported by the LDCs was substantial. The LDCs, on the other hand, required machinery imports for their own industrialization, but as a result of the constant shortage of hard currency, they were not in a position to buy in the West. Accordingly, bilateral trade (raw materials for manufactures) appeared to represent a rational policy for both parties. If one examines the pattern of trade between the East and LDCs, the exchange of LDC raw materials and food products for Eastern manufactures and machinery does indeed predominate throughout the postwar era.

From the foregoing figures, it is apparent that the East is not in a position to exert much economic power over the LDCs. The East acts as a relatively minor buyer and seller in trade with the LDCs and does not wield the potential for economic control of the advanced capitalist nations. The same conclusion can be drawn about the disbursements of economic aid by East and West.

Between 1954 and 1985, the industrialized capitalist countries granted over $300 billion in economic assistance to the LDCs. Over the same period, the CMEA nations granted only $49 billion and mainland China $7 billion in economic aid. The CMEA loomed larger in the area of military assistance. Between 1954 and 1985, the CMEA nations provided military assistance of $28 billion. The striking feature of CMEA exports to the LDCs is the dominant role of military hardware sales. Moreover, CMEA arms exports and military aid tend to be concentrated among fewer client countries than is Western assistance. This is consistent with the general CMEA policy of concentrating both military and economic aid in countries where the expected political and economic benefits are highest. In this manner, the CMEA nations sought to compensate for their lower volume of assistance.

SUMMARY

1. This chapter deals with the economics of East–West trade and the trade of the East and West with the developing countries. The most important systemic factors affecting trade between East and West are the manner in which Eastern trade is planned by centralized authorities, the fact that Eastern prices fail to reveal the scarcity values of domestically produced commodities, and prohibitions against private ownership. These factors have led to a system of bilateral trade and to underutilization of trade potential on the part of the East, despite the rapid growth of East–West trade in recent years.
2. Institutional barriers to East–West trade took the form of quantitative restrictions in Western Europe and failure to grant MFN status to many Eastern countries by the United States. Institutional barriers have been

lowered substantially since the 1950s, and the remaining barriers combine systemic and institutional factors.

3. Although East–West trade in products and technology has been expanding rapidly over the past two decades, it remains small relative to trading potential. Arrangements have been developed that satisfy both the desire of Western firms for equity participation and the distaste of socialist countries for private ownership. The share of East–West trade in total Eastern trade has risen substantially since 1960, yet East–West trade is still inconsequential as a percentage of world trade and is likely to remain so for many years.

3. Commercial relations are affected by the ebb and flow of East–West political relations. The remaining barriers are for the most part inherent in the economic systems of capitalism and socialism. Capitalism, with its emphasis on profit maximization and decentralized decision making, promotes foreign trade and economic specialization, once barriers are removed. The planned socialist system has not proved to be well suited to the full utilization of trade potential. This is because of the inflexibility of the planning process, the absence of multilateralism and convertibility, the difficulty of making comparative cost evaluations, and the drive for national economic independence.

5. Most world trade is conducted among the industrialized countries; Eastern aid to and trade with the LDCs is small in both relative and absolute terms. The East is not in a position to exert much economic power over the LDCs.

NOTES

1. The standard discussions of the trade of the planned socialist economies are Frederic Pryor, *The Communist Foreign Trade System* (Cambridge, Mass.: M.I.T. Press, 1963); Franklyn Holzman, *International Trade Under Communism* (New York: Basic Books, 1976); Franklyn Holzman, *Foreign Trade Under Central Planning* (Cambridge, Mass.: Harvard University Press, 1979); P. J. D. Wiles, *Communist International Economics* (New York: Praeger, 1969); and the collection of studies in Alan Brown and Egon Neuberger, eds., *International Trade and Central Planning* (Berkeley: University of California Press, 1968).

2. For a more detailed discussion of this point, see Evsey Domar's discussion in Brown and Neuberger, *International Trade and Central Planning*, pp. 277–279.

3. These figures are from World Bank, *World Development Report 1982* (New York: Oxford University Press, 1982), pp. 110–111; U.S. Department of State, *The Planetary Product* (Special Report No. 58, October 1979), pp. 35–36; *Handbook of Economic Statistics, 1987.*

4. Accounts of these studies are found in Frederic Pryor's discussion in Brown and Neuberger, *International Trade and Central Planning*, pp. 159–165; and in Paul Gregory, *Socialist and Nonsocialist Industrialization Patterns* (New York: Praeger, 1970), p. 120. Also see Edward Hewett's study in Josef Brada, ed., *Quantitative Analytic Studies in East-West Economic Relations* (Bloomington, Ind.: Studies in East European and Soviet Planning and Development, 1976).

5. National Foreign Assessment Center, *Handbook of Economic Statistics 1990* (Washington, D.C.: Central Intelligence Agency, 1990), pp. 146, 165, and 170.

6. Holzman, *International Trade Under Communism*, p. 127.

7. Ibid., p. 128.

8. United Nations, *Monthly Bulletin of Statistics*, 37, 1983, pp. xxx–xxxiii.

9. For a discussion of foreign trade planning, see Herbert Levine, "The Effects of Foreign Trade on Soviet Planning Practices," in Brown and Neuberger, *International Trade and Central*

Planning, pp. 255–276; Lawrence Brainard, "Soviet Foreign Trade Planning," in U.S. Congress, Joint Economic Committee, *Soviet Economy in a New Perspective* (Washington, D.C.: Government Printing Office, 1976), pp. 695–708; and H. Stephen Gardner, *Soviet Foreign Trade: The Decision Process* (Boston: Kluwer-Nijhoff, 1983).

10. Gardner, *Soviet Foreign Trade*, Ch. 7.

11. Martin Kohn and Nicholas Lang, "The Intra-CMEA Foreign Trade System: Major Price Changes, Little Reform," in U.S. Congress, Joint Economic Committee, *East European Economies Post Helsinki* (Washington, D.C.: Government Printing Office, 1977), pp. 135–151; Marie Lavigne, "The Soviet Union Inside Comecon," *Soviet Studies*, 35 (April 1983), 135–153.

12. This discussion is based on Holzman, *International Trade Under Communism*, pp. 40–44.

13. As noted below, Poland achieved a convertible currency in 1990.

14. Jan Vanous, "Soviet and Eastern European Foreign Trade in the 1970s: A Quantitative Assessment," U.S. Congress, Joint Economic Committee, *East European Economic Assessment*, Part 2 (Washington, D.C.: Government Printing Office, 1981), pp. 698–704; Allen Lang and Hedija Kravalis, "An Analysis of Recent and Potential Soviet and Eastern European Exports to Fifteen Industrialized Western Countries," in Joint Economic Committee, *Eastern European Economies Post Helsinki*, pp. 1074–1075.

15. National Foreign Assessment Center, *Handbook of Economic Statistics 1990* (Washington, D.C.: Central Intelligence Agency, 1990), p. 48.

16. For a case study of Soviet-manufactured exports, see Paul Ericson, "Soviet Efforts to Increase Exports of Manufactured Products to the West," in Joint Economic Committee, *Soviet Economy in a New Perspective*, pp. 709–726.

17. Robert Campbell and John Hardt, eds., "The US–Soviet Agreement on Trade, Three Interpretations," *The ACES Bulletin*, 15 (Spring 1973), 108–113. Also see "Commercial Relations" (contributions by Jurew, Bresnick, and Pregelj), in Joint Economic Committee, *East European Economic Assessment*, Part 2, pp. 635–684.

18. The standard discussions of foreign trade criteria in socialist countries are Andrea Boltho, *Foreign Trade Criteria in Socialist Countries* (Cambridge, England: Cambridge University Press, 1971) and Edward Hewett, *Foreign Trade Prices in the Council for Mutual Economic Assistance* (London: Cambridge University Press, 1974). One should also consult the discussions in Brainard, "Soviet Foreign Trade Planning," pp. 701–704; and Holzman, *International Trade Under Communism*, pp. 33–36.

19. Brainard, "Soviet Foreign Trade Planning," p. 704.

20. Gardner, *Soviet Foreign Trade*, Ch. 7.

21. Steven Rosefielde, "Factor Proportions and Economic Rationality in Soviet International Trade," *American Economic Review*, 64 (September 1974), 670–681.

22. This discussion is based on Holzman, *International Trade Under Communism*, Ch. 4; Anton Malish, Jr., "An Analysis of Tariff Discrimination on Soviet and Eastern European Trade," *The ACES Bulletin*, 15 (Spring 1973), 43–56; and three essays in Joint Economic Committee, *East European Economies Post Helsinki*: Edward Hewett, "Recent Developments in East–West Economic Relations," pp. 174–198; Thomas Wolf, "East–West European Trade Relations," pp. 1042–1054; Karen Taylor, "Import Protection and East–West Trade," pp. 1132–1174; and Joint Economic Committee, *East European Economic Assessment*, Part 2, pp. 635–684.

23. T. A. Wolf, in "The Impact of Elimination of West German Quantitative Restrictions on Manufactures from Centrally Planned Economies," Band 112, *Weltwirtschaftliches Archiv* (Tübingen: J. C. B. Mohr, 1976), pp. 338–358, finds that the elimination of quantitative restrictions be West Germany between 1966 and 1976 had a significant effect on CMEA imports, especially machinery and equipment.

24. Jack Brougher, "1974–82: The United States Uses Trade to Penalize Soviet Aggression and Seeks to Reorder Western Policy," in U.S. Congress, Joint Economic Committee, *Soviet Economy in the 1980s: Problems and Prospects*, Part 2 (Washington, D.C.: Government Printing Office, 1983), pp. 419–453.

25. "Eastern Europe: Long Road Ahead to Economic Well-Being," A Paper Presented by the Central Intelligence Agency to the Subcommittee on Technology and National Security of the Joint Economic Committee of Congress, May 1990.

26. For an analysis of the effect of MFN on Polish–U.S. trade, see Thomas Wolf, "Effects of US Granting of Most Favored Nation Treatment to Imports from Eastern Europe: The Polish Experience," *The ACES Bulletin*, 15 (Spring 1973), 3–22. For a more general study, see Helen Raffel, Marc Rubin, and Robert Teal, "The MFN Impact on U.S. Imports from Eastern Europe," in Joint Economic Committee, *Eastern European Economies Post Helsinki*, p. 1427. For a view from the other side of the cost equation, see H. Stephen Gardner, "Assessing the Cost to the U.S. Economy of Trade Sanctions Against the USSR," Conference on East–West Trade, Technology Transfer, and U.S. Export Control Policy, University of South Carolina, March 1983.
27. Our discussion of CMEA is based largely on Holzman, *International Trade Under Communism*, Ch. 3; Hertha Heiss, "The Council for Mutual Economic Assistance – Developments Since the Mid-1960's," in U.S. Congress, Joint Economic Committee, *Economic Developments in Countries of Eastern Europe* (Washington, D.C.: Government Printing Office, 1970), pp. 528–542; Arthur Smith, "The Council for Mutual Economic Assistance in 1977: New Economic Power, New Political Perspectives, and Some Old and New Problems," in Joint Economic Committee, *East European Economies Post Helsinki*, pp. 152–173.
28. Lavigne, "The Soviet Union Inside Comecon," pp. 135–140.
29. James L. Ellis, "Eastern Europe: Changing Trade Patterns and Perspectives," U.S. Congress, Joint Economic Committee, *East European Economics: Slow Growth in the 1980's*, Vol. 2 (Washington, D.C.: Government Printing Office, 1986), p. 11.
30. For a discussion of this point, see Joseph Pelzman, "Trade Integration in the Council for Mutual Economic Assistance: Creation and Diversion, 1954–1970," *The ACES Bulletin*, 18 (Fall 1976), pp. 39–60; and Josef van Brabant, "Trade Creation and Trade Diversion in Eastern Europe: A Comment," *The ACES Bulletin*, 19 (Spring 1977), 79–98.
31. Paul Marer and John Michael Montias, "CMEA Integration: Theory and Practice," in Joint Economic Committee, *East European Economic Assessment*, Part 2, 177–179.
32. Lavigne, "The Soviet Union Inside Comecon," pp. 145–149.
33. Michael Marrese and Jan Vanous, *Soviet Subsidization of Trade with Eastern Europe – A Soviet Perspective*, Institute of International Studies (Berkeley: University of California Press, 1983). For a different, and lower, estimate, see Raimund Dietz, "Advantages and Disadvantages in Soviet Trade with Eastern Europe," U.S. Congress, Joint Economic Committee, *East European Economies: Slow Growth in the 1980s* (Washington, D.C.: Government Printing Office, 1986), pp. 263–301.
34. "Eastern Europe: Long Road Ahead to Economic Well-Being," pp. 30–33.
35. Our discussion of East–West industrial cooperation is based primarily on Carl H. McMillan, "Trends in East–West Industrial Cooperation," *Journal of International Business Studies* (Fall 1981), 53–67; Maureen Smith, "Industrial Cooperative Agreements: Soviet Experience and Practices," in Joint Economic Committee, *Soviet Economy in a New Perspective*, pp. 767–785; and Carl McMillan, "East–West Industrial Cooperation," in Joint Economic Committee, *East European Economies Post Helsinki*, pp. 1175–1224.
36. *Handbook of Economic Statistics 1990*, pp. 48 and 76.
37. Ibid., p. 76.
38. The next two sections are based primarily on Holzman, *International Trade Under Communism*, Ch. 5. The statistics are from Holzman; *Handbook of Economic Statistics*, various years; U.S. Department of State, *Soviet and East European Aid to the Third World, 1981* (February 1983).

RECOMMENDED READINGS

Guido Biessen, "Is the Impact of Central Planning on the Level of Foreign Trade Really Negative?" *Journal of Comparative Economics* 15 (March 1991), 22–44.
Andrea Boltho, *Foreign Trade Criteria in Socialist Countries* (Cambridge, England: Cambridge University Press, 1971).

Josef C. Brada, "The Political Economy of Communist Foreign Trade Institutions and Policies," *Journal of Comparative Economics* 15 (June 1991), 211–238.

Josef C. Brada, E. A. Hewett and Thomas A. Wolf, eds., *Economic Adjustment and Reform in Eastern Europe and the Soviet Union* (Durham, N.C.: Duke University Press, 1988).

Lawrence Brainard, "Soviet Foreign Trade Planning," in U.S. Congress, Joint Economic Committee, *Soviet Economy in a New Perspective* (Washington, D.C.: Government Printing Office, 1976), pp. 695–708.

Alan Brown and Egon Neuberger, eds., *International Trade and Central Planning* (Berkeley: University of California Press, 1968).

Benjamin Cohen, *Organizing the World's Money: The Political Economy of International Monetary Relations* (New York: Basic Books, 1977).

Renzo Daviddi and Efisio Espa, "The Economics of Ruble Convertibility: New Scenarios for the Soviet Monetary Economy," *Banca Nazionale del Iavoro Quarterly Review* 171 (December 1989).

H. Stephen Gardner, *Soviet Foreign Trade: The Decision Process* (Boston: Kluwer-Nijhoff, 1983).

Philip Hanson, *Trade and Technology in Soviet–Western Economic Relations* (New York: Columbia University Press, 1981).

Edward Hewett, *Foreign Trade Prices in the Council for Mutual Economic Assistance* (London: Cambridge University Press, 1974).

Franklyn Holzman, *Foreign Trade Under Central Planning* (Cambridge, Mass.: Harvard University Press, 1979).

——, *International Trade Under Communism* (New York: Basic Books, 1976).

Peter B. Kenen, "Transitional Arrangements for Trade and Payments Among the CMEA Countries" (Washington, D.C.: IMF Working Paper, January 1991).

Paul Marer and John M. Montias, eds., *East European Integration and East–West Trade* (Bloomington: Indiana University Press, 1980).

Peter Murrell, *The Nature of Socialist Economies: Lessons from Eastern European Foreign Trade* (Princeton, N.J.: Princeton University Press, 1990).

Egon Neuberger and Laura Tyson, eds., *The Impact of International Economic Disturbance on the Soviet Union and Eastern Europe* (New York: Pergamon, 1980).

Frederic Pryor, *The Communist Foreign Trade System* (Cambridge, Mass.: M.I.T. Press, 1963).

George Soros, *Opening the Soviet System* (London: Weinfeld and Nicolson, 1990).

U.S. Congress, Joint Economic Committee, *East European Economies Post Helsinki* (Washington, D.C.: Government Printing Office, 1977).

——, *East European Economic Assessment*, Part 2 (Washington, D.C.: Government Printing Office, 1981).

——, *East European Economies: Slow Growth in the 1980's* (Washington, D.C.: Government Printing Office, 1986).

Josef M. Van Brabant, *Socialist Economic Integration* (New York: Cambridge University Press, 1980).

——, *Adjustment, Structural Change, and Economic Efficiency: Aspects of Monetary Cooperation in Eastern Europe* (Cambridge, England: Cambridge University Press, 1987).

P. J. D. Wiles, *Communist International Economics* (New York: Praeger, 1969).

Thomas A. Wolf, *Foreign Trade in the Centrally Planned Economy* (London: Harwood, 1988).

15 Performance of Economic Systems

IN CHAPTER 3, WE DISCUSSED THE METHODOLOGY of comparing the performance of economic systems. Although certain objectives — a high standard of living, economic stability, growth, efficiency, good environmental quality — are desirable, the achievement of each goal extracts a price in terms of economic resources. Insofar as resources are limited, hard choices must be made among economic goals. Unless different economic systems place the same weight on each goal, it is difficult to evaluate the overall performance of the systems. The major long-term goal of planned socialism has been the "building of socialism." This goal required high rates of growth of industrial and military output, so the overriding objective was rapid economic growth. Other goals — efficiency, full employment, a "socialist" distribution of income — were also desired by the leadership, but lower priorities have been attached to their achievement.

The ranking of economic objectives among capitalist nations has been less uniform. Some countries emphasize economic stability; others, especially developing nations, stress economic growth. Others emphasize social goals. There is no one unifying goal that the capitalist nations have singled out as their principal objective. We would expect different economies to perform relatively well in achieving goals to which they attach high priority. To decide which economy has performed "better" would require a subjective judgment about which goals are more "important."

Evaluating performance is not easy even if we select only one criterion, such as economic growth. Some socialist countries have "out-grown" certain capitalist countries during certain time periods, and vice versa. The evaluation depends on *which* countries are included in the comparison and on the time period.

How do we select countries and time periods for comparison? One way would be to have a random selection to estimate the "true" capitalist and socialist growth rates. However, the number of countries and the historical perspective, especially on the socialist side, are too limited for random selection. Therefore, some selection criteria must be used. We wish to select countries most "representative" of their own systems, yet it is difficult to address the matter of representativeness. Should we compare only countries that are at about the same stage of economic development? Is it fair to compare the postwar rates of growth in Eastern Europe with the long-term historical growth of the capitalist nations?

For performance comparisons to be valid, the *ceteris paribus* assumption must hold. The economies compared should be alike *in all respects* except their economic systems. In the notation of Chapter 3, the *ceteris paribus* problem was described as follows: Outcomes (O) are a function of a variety of environmental factors ENV (for example, natural and human resource endowments and level of development), economic policy (POL), and the economic system (ES). Thus

$$O = f(\text{ENV, POL, ES}) \tag{15.1}$$

Because ENV and POL differ by country, one cannot make a statement about the impact of ES on outcomes without a clear understanding of the role of the ENV and POL factors.

Two examples illustrate these points. Labor productivity in the Soviet Union has been low relative to that in the United States and industrialized Western Europe.[1] The question, however, is whether this is a consequence of the *system* of planned socialism or a product of the other (ENV, POL) factors. The level of economic development of the Soviet Union lags behind that of the United States and Western Europe, and productivity is positively associated with economic development. Can the Soviet productivity gap be accounted for entirely by these other factors, or is the economic system itself to blame? *Long-term* economic growth in the Soviet Union may have outpaced that in the United States and Western Europe.[2] Is this a consequence of the economic system or of other factors?

Two related approaches can be used to deal with this problem. The first is to compare economies that are alike in all respects other than economic system. In terms of equation 15.1, this means making performance comparisons only in instances where ENV and POL are equal so that performance differences can be attributed to the system. The nearest (yet imperfect) example would be the comparison of previously unified countries that may belong to different economic blocs (East and West Germany or North and South Korea, for example), but such examples are rare.[3] Comparison of agricultural productivity in the Soviet Union and the United States in areas of similar land quality and climate would serve as a less-aggregated example. The basic drawback is that we cannot find real-world cases where all factors other than the economic system are constant.

The econometric approach to dealing with the *ceteris paribus* problem requires estimation of the impact of the ENV and POL factors on O. Once known, these factors can hypothetically be held constant, revealing the impact of the economic system on performance. This approach requires the investigation of *groups* of capitalist and socialist economies that differ according to ENV and POL characteristics, so that their impact can be isolated and held constant.[4]

Because economic systems are multidimensional, their attributes are difficult to measure, and we cannot formulate an *objective* and *quantitative* measure of ES that differentiates economies according to the degree of capitalism or planned or market socialism. We cannot determine whether the Soviet economy is more "planned socialist" than the East German economy was or whether the U.S. economy is more "capitalist" than the British economy. Therefore, we are forced to bunch real-world economies into political–economic groupings without being able to hold constant the effect of variations in ES *within* a particular group.

In this chapter, we group real-world economies into three categories used throughout this book: capitalism, planned socialism, and market socialism. This requires combining economies that differ in important respects, a process that further obscures the impact of the economic system on economic outcomes. In the comparisons that follow, intermediate- and low-income countries such as Greece, Spain, Turkey, and India are included in the "capitalist" group, despite their substantial differences from industrialized capitalist countries. Our own feeling is that there was much greater homogeneity within the planned socialist group that existed prior to the reforms of the late 1980s. Yet even they have differences (ownership and control arrangements in agriculture that affect agricultural performance), so the planned socialist economies are by no means uniform.[5]

Because real-world economies combine elements from different economic systems, one can speculate about how each economic system would have performed in its "pure" state (that is, perfectly competitive capitalism or centralized planning with perfect information and computation). Representatives of a particular economic system may not have performed "well" exactly because they deviate from the pure model; therefore, weaknesses should be attributed not to the economic system but to the deviations from it. If this line of argument is accepted, then performance must be evaluated in theoretical rather than empirical terms.

In our view, how well the representatives of economic systems have actually performed is the appropriate standard for evaluating the performance of economic systems. What counts is not how an economic system would conceivable perform under ideal circumstances but how well it performs in a real-world setting when confronted with powerful forces (imperfect competition, external effects, imperfect planning information, computational limitations) that prevent the ideal from being realized.

THE PERFORMANCE OF SYSTEMS

Recognizing the difficulties inherent in evaluating economic systems, we proceed to evaluation of the performance of capitalism and socialism. We take the most important performance indicators — economic growth, economic efficiency, the "fairness" of the distribution of income, and economic stability —

to determine how well selected representatives of capitalism and socialism have performed.

The Choice of Countries

The selection of representatives of capitalism and socialism is dictated by the availability of data. Data limitations dictate the principal emphasis on comparisons of the Soviet Union and East European (CMEA) nations with the industrialized and near-industrialized capitalist nations.[6] The data for the Asian communist countries (North Korea, Vietnam, Cambodia, and Mongolia) are too meager to support meaningful comparisons. Yugoslavia is included to capture the performance of market socialism, but it is difficult to generalize about the performance of market socialism from the Yugoslav experience alone. Comparisons of industrialized capitalism with planned socialism rest on firmer footing, for they are based on groups of capitalist and planned socialist countries.[7] Generalizations that emerge from these comparisons are more likely to be representative of the system, because average behavior is being observed.

How about the performance of China vis-à-vis its non-communist Asian counterparts? We do not know the degree to which China is representative of planned socialism in a large and backward economy. Chinese economic performance has been significantly affected by a series of political upheavals. We cannot establish whether these disruptions are endemic to the system at low levels of development. There is the further difficulty of finding appropriate counterparts against which to gauge China's economic performance. Should China be measured against Japan (an immediate Asian neighbor), against India[8] (another Asian neighbor, almost equally populous), or against the large and small non-communist Asian nations combined? If the yardstick is Japan, then Chinese performance will not be impressive; if Bangladesh, it will appear more impressive.

The number of former CMEA member states (excluding Mongolia, Vietnam, and Cuba for lack of data) is seven: Bulgaria, East Germany, Poland, Hungary, Romania, Czechoslovakia, and the Soviet Union. Our selection of industrialized and near-industrialized capitalist countries is based on three considerations: the availability of comparable data, the need to include some countries at levels of economic development comparable to that of the CMEA nations, and the desire to include the major capitalist countries (such as the United States, West Germany, and Japan).

Data: Concepts and Reliability

The data used in this chapter are Western recalculations of CMEA national aggregate statistics. Economic aggregates, such as GNP, industrial production, and per capita consumption, are not compiled uniformly by the national statistical agencies in Eastern and Western countries, although statistical practices are fairly uniform within the two blocs. The CMEA nations exclude from aggregate final output (net material product) "nonproductive" services, which do not directly support material production.[9] Thus personal transportation and communication services, government, and most professional services are excluded from net material product. Such "nonproductive" services are included in the United Nations system of national accounts used by the Western nations, so direct comparisons of Western GNP with CMEA net material product would be invalid. Also, socialist net material product includes some double-counting of outputs.

Pricing practices present another problem of statistical comparability. Aggregates are the sum of the products of prices times quantities. Substantial relative pricing differences can lead to further incomparabilities, especially if one system generates relatively high prices (large weights) for rapidly growing sectors such as industry and relatively low prices for slow-growing sectors such as agriculture. Differences in relative prices complicate the determination of relative levels of output (see the chapter appendix on index number relativity). In the planned economy, government intervention in price setting is more substantial than in the West, and substantial turnover taxes are applied to industrial products. This practice raises the relative weight of industry and accordingly the overall growth rate. Moreover, the CMEA nations do not include returns to capital or land in their prices, whereas such returns are automatically included in Western prices.

The aggregate figures cited in this chapter are recalculations that make the CMEA aggregates conform as closely as possible to standard Western national accounting practices.[10] The recalculated figures show considerably lower growth than that reported by the CMEA countries themselves. It should be emphasized that the Western recalculations have an unknown degree of reliability. Western authorities have access only to the published information released on a selective basis by the CMEA countries and must often make heroic assumptions.

Western recalculations of Soviet and East European national accounts make adjustments for omitted costs and for omitted product categories (such as services). They all use the "adjusted factor cost concept" pioneered by Abram Bergson.[11] As Bergson has pointed out, Western economists are not in a position to recalculate the output of planned socialist economies on the basis of utility values. If planners dictate the production of goods and services that do not raise welfare (such as excessively heavy reinforced concrete, inferior shoes, or the collected works of Leonid Brezhnev), we have no choice but to value these goods and services at the cost of supplying them. A market economy might reject these goods and services (by setting zero prices), but a planned socialist economy dictated by planners' preferences will continue to order their production.

The *Glasnost* movement that swept through the Soviet Union and Eastern Europe in the second half of the 1980s raised serious questions about the underlying reliability of CMEA statistical series.[12] For example, Romanian statistical authorities have subsequently revealed that Romanian statistics contained wild exaggerations of Romanian economic performance. Independent estimates by Soviet economists and journalists claim that official Soviet statistics overstated growth by a factor of more than 2.[13] Although the official statistical agencies of the Soviet Union and Eastern Europe have pledged to prepare revised growth statistics, they have not yet succeeded in doing so. Within Eastern Europe, the economic statistics of Hungary, Poland, and Yugoslavia appear to be the most reliable, those of Romania the least.

One condition of full membership in world international economic organizations is that the nation's statistical agencies compile reliable statistics that apply the statistical accounting procedures used by the rest of the world. For this reason, we should expect to see revised and improved statistical accounting procedures used in Eastern Europe in the next few years. In the meantime, we must make do with the available statistics.

An Economic Profile: Structural Characteristics of East and West

Table 15.1 provides an economic profile of the planned socialist countries, Yugoslavia, and selected capitalist countries. This profile shows what factors should be held constant in performance comparisons, and it provides insights into the socialist model of industrialization.[14] We focus on the mid-1980s as a period of relative "normalcy" in Eastern Europe prior to the dramatic changes of the late 1980s.

In terms of per capita income, the most widely used indicator of economic development, the Soviet Union and Eastern Europe were well behind the advanced capitalist countries in the mid 1980s. The per capita incomes in the more advanced planned socialist economies (Czechoslovakia, East Germany, the Soviet Union) were well below those in Japan and the United Kingdom and between those in Italy and Spain. Poland, Romania, and Hungary and the less-advanced Bulgaria were well below Italy and Spain but close to Greece. The CMEA countries as a group are less advanced than the industrialized Western countries with which they are most often compared.

Despite relatively low per capita income, the share of industry and construction in GNP in the CMEA countries was roughly equal to that of the capitalist countries in the mid 1980s. In fact, the CMEA industry share averaged 43 percent; the average of capitalist countries (United States to Italy) was 36 percent. One would have to conclude that, if per capita income were held constant, the planned socialist industry share has been high relative to capitalism. The CMEA shares of agriculture and services are even more different from their Western counterparts. Agriculture's share of both GNP and labor force has been quite high in the planned socialist countries once per capita income is held constant, but the share of the service sector is well below that of capitalist countries at similar levels of development. The data on investment rates do not yield a clear trend. The CMEA countries tend to have investment

Table 15.1 An Economic Profile of Socialist and Capitalist Countries in the 1980s

	(1) Per Capita GNP, 1985 (U.S. $)	(2) Population 1985 (Millions)	(3a) Share of Industry and Construction in GNP (1982)	(3b) Agriculture	(3c) Services	(4) Proportion of Labor in Agriculture (1985)	(5) Gross Investment as a Percentage of GNP (1982)
A. Planned Socialism							
East Germany	10,440	16.7	51	13	36	10	24
Czechoslovakia	8,750	15.5	49	15	36	13	25
Hungary	7,560	10.6	38	26	36	18	29
Soviet Union	7,400	278.9	42	19	39	19	30
Poland	6,470	37.2	37	27	36	29	27
Bulgaria	6,420	9.0	46	23	31	20	28
Romania	5,450	22.7	46	26	28	29	38
China	340	1,042.4	45	35	20	68	28
B. Market Socialism							
Yugoslavia	5,600	23.1	43	12	45	20	27

C. Capitalism

	(1) Per Capita GNP, 1985 (U.S. $)	(2) Population 1985 (Millions)	(3a) Share of Industry and Construction in GNP (1982)	(3b) Agriculture	(3c) Services	(4) Proportion of Labor in Agriculture (1985)	(5) Gross Investment as a Percentage of GNP (1982)
Norway	16,719	4.2	41	5	54	9	26
United States	16,710	238.6	34	3	63	3	19
Canada	16,538	25.4	32	4	64	5	25
Denmark	14,603	5.1	22	5	73	7	16
West Germany	14,432	61.0	53	3	44	6	23
France	13,755	55.0	41	4	55	9	21
Japan	13,312	120.7	40	5	55	10	31
Belgium	13,219	9.9	42	4	54	3	18
Netherlands	12,741	14.5	33	4	63	5	18
Austria	12,343	7.6	39	4	57	9	26
United Kingdom	12,042	56.4	33	2	65	3	17
Italy	10,928	57.1	41	6	53	13	21
Spain	9,008	39.1	34	6	60	18	20
Greece	6,854	10.0	31	17	52	31	25
Turkey	2,135	45,1	31	22	47	60	25
India	250	767.7	26	36	38	70	25

Sources: U.S. Department of Commerce, *Statistical Abstract of the United States, 1981* (Washington, D.C.: Government Printing Office, 1981), pp. 876–879; National Foreign Assessment Center, *Handbook of Economic Statistics 1986* (Washington, D.C.: Central Intelligence Agency, 1986); World Bank, *World Tables*, 3rd ed. (Baltimore: The Johns Hopkins University Press, 1984); OECD, *Historical Statistics, 1960–1985* (Paris, OECD, 1987); Thad Alton, "East European GNPs," Joint Economic Committee, *East European Economics: Slow Growth in the 1980s, Vol. 1* (Washington, D.C.: Government Printing Office, 1985), pp. 81–132. The East European investment rates are calculated by subtracting the rates of defense spending the GNP from Alton's residual expenditure category (p. 95).

rates in the high ranges of 24 to 38 percent, but one can find similarly high investment rates among the capitalist countries. The East German investment rate, on the other hand, was relatively low.

Other differences, not recorded in Table 15.1, can also be noted. If one breaks the industry sector down into heavy and light industry, the planned socialist shares of heavy industry are well *above* those of a capitalist country at a similar level of development. The shares of the urban population of the socialist countries are well *below* those of a capitalist country at a similar stage of economic development.

All of these features constitute the distinguishing characteristics of the socialist industrialization model. What was the logic behind the socialist model? It aimed at "building socialism" as quickly as possible. In order to do so, industrialization must be accorded priority. Activities that do not contribute to material production, such as services, should be limited, and, within industry, priority must be granted to heavy industry, which lays the foundation for socialism. Urbanization should be retarded to limit the flow of scarce investment resources into social overhead capital, a form of capital that does not lead immediately to expanded industrial capacity. Extra resources are devoted to agriculture to promote self-sufficiency, even if this works against comparative advantage. Resources are allocated away from consumption into investment in order to achieve a high investment rate.

The socialist industrialization model is important for two reasons. First, it represents a major alternative for the Third World countries. Second, the model underscores the point that the planned socialist economies have not been indifferent to *what* is being produced. Their objective has not been to maximize the growth rate of output per se, but to maximize the growth of particular branches. In the planned socialist countries, heavy industry has grown at an exceptionally rapid rate; services have not. Yet the measures we use in the following sections relate to the output and efficiency of production of *all* types of commodities, not merely those accorded high priority by the socialist industrialization model.

We must avoid generalizations concerning the one representative of market socialism in Table 15.1, Yugoslavia. Generalizations are difficult because Yugoslavia stands alone, and average tendencies cannot be contrasted. Table 15.1 clearly demonstrates, however, that Yugoslavia is a low-income country. Its per capita income places it between Turkey and Greece, and a very high proportion of its labor force is occupied in agriculture. It appears to have a high investment rate (33 percent) for a low-income country.

ECONOMIC GROWTH

Table 15.2 and Figure 15.1 supply data on GNP growth rates for the postwar period in socialist and capitalist countries. One should be cautious about attaching too much importance to small differences in growth rates both among countries and over time, for there is measurement error in such calculations. Moreover, the measured growth rate of economies experiencing substantial structural changes can be ambiguous — the problem of index number relativity.[15] Growth rates must be regarded as approximate and often ambiguous measures of the expansion of real goods and services. This is especially true of East–West comparisons, where substantial adjustments must be made to render the GNP data comparable.

In Table 15.2, we have assembled growth rates of real GNP and of real GNP per capita for the entire postwar period. In panel A we supply growth rates for the Soviet Union, Eastern Europe, and China. We also supply growth rates for Yugoslavia (panel B) and for a number of capitalist countries at various stages of economic development (panel C). We include comparative growth data for China and India, two poor and populous Asian giants, one a planned socialist economy, the other a basically capitalist economy.

Are there systemic differences in growth rates? Has economic growth been more rapid in the planned socialist economies? Table 15.2 examines postwar economic growth from the heady growth of the 1950s and 1960s to the generally slower growth of the mid-1970s and 1980s. It illustrates the dangers of using a pair of countries (such as the United States and the Soviet Union) to judge the growth performance of capitalism and socialism. One can find capitalist countries (such as Japan) that have grown much more rapidly than most socialist countries, and one can find socialist countries (such as Bulgaria, Romania, and China) that have grown more rapidly than most capitalist countries. Moreover, some countries grow rapidly in one period (Bulgaria in the 1950s and 1960s) and then grow slowly in another period (Bulgaria in the period 1975–1980).

It is difficult to reach firm conclusions about the growth performance of capitalism and socialism on the basis of these data. If one simply takes unweighted averages of the eight planned socialist and sixteen capitalist countries, the socialist group grew slightly more rapidly in the 1950s (5.7 percent per year versus 5.0 percent for the capitalist group). The capitalist group grew more rapidly in the 1960s (5.5 percent versus 4.4 percent in the first half and 5.5 percent versus 4.3 percent in the second half). The capitalist group experienced severe growth recessions in the mid-1970s (1974 and 1975), whereas the socialist group appears to have enjoyed a noticeable growth advantage for the first half of the 1970s (4.8 percent versus 3.9 percent). The growth of the capitalist group continued to lag during the second half of the 1970s (at 3.4 percent), but the slowdown of growth was even more severe in the socialist group (falling to below 3 percent). For the period 1980 to 1985, the average socialist growth rate exceeded the average capitalist rate. The marked slowdown of socialist growth in the second half of the 1980s (coupled with the recovery of capitalist growth rates) gives the clear advantage to the capitalist group. Trends in per capita GNP, given in parentheses in Table 15.2, mirror these GNP growth trends.

Table 15.2 Average Annual Growth of GNP and GNP Per Capita in Socialist and Capitalist Countries, 1950–1990 (Per Capita Figures in Parentheses)

	1950–1960	1960–1965	1965–1970	1970–1975	1975–1980	1980–1985	1985–1990[a]
A. Socialist Countries: Planned Socialism							
Czechoslovakia	4.8 (3.9)	2.3 (1.6)	3.4 (3.2)	3.4 (2.7)	2.2 (1.5)	1.5 (1.2)	1.2 (1.2)
East Germany	5.7 (6.7)	2.7 (3.0)	3.0 (3.1)	3.4 (3.8)	2.3 (2.5)	1.8 (1.9)	1.6 (1.6)
Soviet Union	5.7 (3.9)	5.0 (3.5)	5.2 (4.2)	3.7 (2.7)	2.7 (1.8)	2.0 (1.1)	1.8 (1.1)
Poland	4.6 (2.75)	4.4 (3.2)	4.1 (3.4)	6.4 (5.4)	.7 (0)	.7 (-1)	.2 (.2)
Hungary	4.6 (4.0)	4.2 (3.9)	3.0 (2.7)	3.4 (2.9)	2.0 (1.9)	1.7 (1.7)	
Romania	5.8 (4.55)	6.0 (5.3)	4.9 (3.7)	6.7 (5.8)	3.9 (3.0)	1.0 (.8)	.6 (.6)
Bulgaria	6.7 (5.9)	6.7 (5.7)	5.1 (4.2)	4.6 (4.2)	.9 (.9)	1.2 (1.0)	.4 (.4)
China	7.9 (5.6)	4.0 (2.5)	7.1 (4.0)	7.0 (4.5)	6.2 (4.6)	9.3 (8.0)	8.6 (7.2)
Unweighted average	5.7 (4.7)	4.4 (3.6)	4.3 (3.6)	4.8 (4.0)	2.6 (2.0)	2.4 (2.0)	.8 (.7)
Without China	5.4 (4.5)	4.5 (3.7)	4.1 (3.5)	4.5 (3.9)	2.1 (1.7)	1.4 (1.1)	1.8 (1.5)
B. Socialist Country: Market Socialism							
Yugoslavia	5.6 (4.4)	6.6 (5.4)	6.2 (5.2)	5.7 (4.5)	5.9 (4.4)	1.2 (.4)	.6 (.6)
C. Capitalist Countries							
United States	3.3 (1.5)	4.6 (3.2)	3.1 (2.1)	2.3 (1.6)	3.7 (2.6)	2.4 (1.4)	3.1 (2.1)
Canada	4.6 (1.3)	5.7 (3.8)	4.8 (3.0)	5.0 (3.6)	2.9 (1.9)	2.2 (.9)	3.3 (2.3)

	1950–1960	1960–1965	1965–1970	1970–1975	1975–1980	1980–1985	1985–1990[a]
West Germany	7.9 (6.3)	5.0 (3.5)	4.4 (3.9)	2.1 (1.7)	3.6 (3.7)	1.1 (1.4)	2.8 (2.4)
Denmark	3.6 (2.9)	5.1 (4.3)	4.5 (3.7)	2.8 (2.4)	2.7 (2.4)	2.3 (2.3)	
Norway	3.6 (2.5)	4.8 (4.3)	4.8 (3.9)	4.6 (4.0)	4.6 (4.2)	3.0 (2.8)	
Belgium	3.0 (2.5)	5.2 (4.5)	4.8 (4.4)	3.9 (3.5)	2.5 (2.3)	.4 (.4)	2.7 (2.7)
France	4.4 (3.8)	5.8 (4.5)	5.4 (4.5)	4.0 (3.2)	3.2 (2.9)	1.2 (.7)	2.7 (2.2)
Netherlands	5.0 (3.3)	4.8 (3.5)	5.5 (4.4)	3.2 (2.0)	2.6 (1.9)	.5 (.1)	2.1 (1.6)
Japan	7.9 (6.6)	10.0 (9.0)	12.2 (11.2)	5.0 (3.8)	5.1 (4.2)	3.9 (3.2)	3.8 (3.4)
Austria	5.6 (5.4)	4.3 (3.7)	5.1 (4.6)	3.9 (3.5)	4.0 (4.0)		
United Kingdom	3.3 (2.3)	3.1 (2.4)	2.5 (2.2)	2.0 (1.4)	1.6 (1.6)	1.7 (1.3)	3.1 (2.9)
Italy	5.6 (4.8)	5.2 (4.3)	6.2 (5.4)	2.4 (1.5)	3.9 (3.4)	.8 (.5)	2.9 (2.7)
Spain	6.2 (5.3)	8.5 (7.5)	6.2 (5.2)	5.5 (4.6)	2.3 (1.3)	1.4 (.8)	4.1 (3.7)
Greece	6.0 (5.0)	7.7 (7.2)	7.2 (6.6)	5.0 (4.5)	4.4 (3.2)	1.0 (.4)	
Turkey	6.4 (3.4)	4.8 (2.8)	6.6 (3.7)	7.5 (5.0)	3.1 (.6)	4.9 (2.7)	
India	3.8 (1.9)	4.0 (1.7)	5.0 (2.6)	3.0 (1.0)	3.4 (1.6)	4.1 (1.9)	6.0 (3.9)
Unweighted average	5.0 (3.7)	5.5 (4.4)	5.5 (4.5)	3.9 (2.95)	3.4 (2.6)	1.9 (1.3)	3.3 (2.7)

[a]1990 figures are preliminary.

Sources: Thad Alton, "Economic Structure and Growth in Eastern Europe," in U.S. Congress, Joint Economic Committee, *Economic Developments in Countries of Eastern Europe* (Washington, D.C.: Government Printing Office, 1970), p. 49; Thad Alton, "Comparative Structure and Growth of Economic Activity in Eastern Europe," in U.S. Congress, Joint Economic Committee, *East European Economies Post Helsinki* (Washington, D.C.: Government Printing Office, 1977), p. 237; Thad Alton, "Production and Resource Allocation in Eastern Europe: Performance, Problems, and Prospects," in U.S. Congress, Joint Economic Committee, *East European Economic Assessment*, Part 2 (Washington, D.C.: Government Printing Office, 1981), p. 381; U.S. Congress, Joint Economic Committee, *USSR Measures of Economic Growth and Development, 1950–1980* (Washington, D.C.: Government Printing Office, 1982), pp. 15–21; *Statistical Abstract of the United States, 1981*, pp. 878–879; Wilfred Malenbaum, "Modern Economic Growth in India and China: The Comparison Revisited, 1950–1980," *Economic Development and Cultural Change*, 31 (October 1982), 53; *Handbook of Economic Statistics 1990*; Thad Alton et al., Occasional Papers Nos. 75–79 of the Research Project on National Income in East Central Europe (New York, 1983), pp. 7–12, 25; Rush Greenslade, "The Real Gross National Product of the USSR, 1950–75," in U.S. Congress, Joint Economic Committee, *Soviet Economy in a New Perspective* (Washington, D.C.: Government Printing Office, 1975), p. 271; World Bank, *World Tables*, 3rd ed. (Baltimore: The Johns Hopkins University Press, 1983); OECD, *National Accounts, 1960–1985* (Paris: OECD, 1987); "Eastern Europe: Long Road to Economic Well-Being," Tables C-1 to C-21.

Because only eight planned socialist countries are included, the exceptionally fast or slow growth of any one has a strong effect on the averages of the group. As Table 15.2 shows, China's growth up to the mid-1970s was not so different from that of the other socialist countries. From 1975 onward, however, China's rapid growth stood in marked contrast to the slowing growth rates of the other socialist countries. If China is excluded from the socialist group, their average growth rate sinks well below that of the capitalist group from 1975 on. For example, for the period 1980 to 1985, the average socialist growth rate without

Figure 15.1 Average GNP Growth Rates, Planned Socialist and Capitalist Countries, 1950–1989 (Unweighted Annual Average Growth Rates)

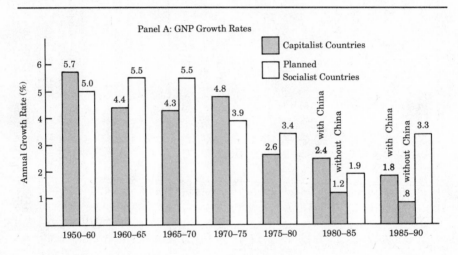

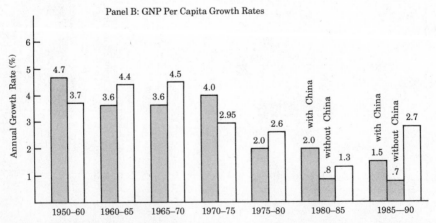

Source: Table 15.2.

China was a meager 1.2 percent per annum, versus the capitalist rate of 1.9 percent per annum. In fact, if one omits the soaring Chinese growth rates of the mid-1970s and 1980s, the decline in socialist growth rates is very pronounced: from above 4 percent per annum, through 2 percent in the late 1970s, to 1 percent in the 1980s. From 1985 to 1990, the collapse of socialist growth is so pronounced that Western growth outstrips socialist growth by a large factor whether China is included or not.

One contrast between capitalism and planned socialism that holds over the entire postwar period is the lesser variability of socialist country growth rates. From 1950 to 1960, for example, the gap between the lowest and highest socialist growth rate was the difference between 4.6 and 7.9 percent; for the capitalist group, the difference was between 3.0 and 7.9 percent. The capitalist averages conceal more variation among countries than do the socialist averages. This pattern has been altered somewhat by the marked contrast in growth rates between China and the other socialist countries after 1975, but it persists within the Soviet and East European group. The planned socialist economies have avoided the extreme differences among countries that characterize capitalist economic performance.

Direct comparisons of planned socialist and capitalist average growth rates did not reveal significant growth differences. However, if one makes a rule-of-thumb adjustment for differences in per capita income by including only the capitalist countries that fall within the approximate per capita income range of the socialist sample — say $6000 to $3000 — some striking findings emerge. The rationale for this adjustment is that growth rates in the postwar period have tended to vary inversely with the level of development. Countries with low per capita income have grown more rapidly as a group. Unfortunately for our purposes, there are few capitalist countries that fall within this income rate (four, to be exact: Spain, Greece, Italy, and Venezuela), but comparing their average growth rates with those of the Soviet Union and Eastern Europe is nevertheless informative. For the entire postwar period, the unweighted average annual growth rate of these four capitalist economies has been almost 6 percent (4.25 percent on a per capita basis). Even when China is included, the planned socialist average is around 4.5 percent per annum (3.8 percent on a per capita basis). Among countries at a similar stage of development, the planned socialist economies have experienced slower growth than their capitalist counterparts.[16]

Frederic Pryor has examined the comparative growth rates of capitalist and socialist economies for the period 1950 to 1979, using econometric methods to hold factors other than the economic system constant. Pryor finds that although the socialist-system effect is negative, the system coefficient is not statistically significant either for the growth of GNP or for the growth of GNP per capita.[17]

The pattern of decline of planned socialist growth rates goes a long way toward explaining the desire to convert from planned socialism to market resource allocation. Both East and West experienced relatively high rates of growth from 1950 through 1970. In the West, growth was well above long-term historical performance during this period. The growth rates of the planned socialist economies began their descent in the mid-1970s; lower growth rates were recorded in each successive half-decade. In the Soviet Union and Eastern Europe, economic growth had all but ceased by the latter half of the 1980s.

On the other hand, the West (after slow growth in the early 1980s) continued to grow at approximately its long-term historical rates. For the West, the first two decades after the war were periods of peak economic performance, after which it returned to its long-run historical pattern. The West, with two hundred years of recorded growth history, had demonstrated its ability to grow at reasonable rates over the long-run. The East, on the other hand, with a limited history of economic growth, feared that the planned socialist system had lost its ability to generate economic growth.

Yugoslavia, the one representative of market socialism, had higher average rates of growth than the capitalist and planned socialist countries until the 1980s, but Yugoslav growth was outdistanced by some other capitalist countries with low per capita income, such as Spain and Turkey. It is virtually impossible to generalize from the Yugoslav experience because of the diverse factors involved, but Yugoslavia does at least suggest the compatibility of market socialism with relatively high rates of growth over extended periods of time. One cannot know whether there is something unique about the Yugoslav case or whether it could be duplicated by other market socialist countries if they were to introduce the Yugoslav model.

The Chinese and Indian comparisons are included to shed light on the growth performance of capitalism and planned socialism in large and very poor countries. Although the Chinese data are fairly rough, most authorities agree that China has outperformed India in the areas of GNP growth and per capita GNP growth. It is likely that India and China entered the postwar era with similar levels of per capita income. China's current advantage in per capita income is the consequence of its more rapid growth.

The importance of China as a development model for poor, populous countries requires a further look at Chinese economic growth in an Asian context. Table 15.3 gives the annual growth rates of seven important Asian countries for the period 1960–1985. It shows that Chinese economic growth has indeed been rapid even compared to that of other rapidly growing Asian economies, such as Japan, South Korea, and Taiwan. Chinese economic performance looks even better when compared to that of poor, populous Asian countries. Chinese growth has been more than double that of India and Pakistan.[18]

There is no evidence that the planned socialist countries as a group have "out-grown" their capitalist counterparts. One would have to conclude, that the growth rates of capitalism and planned socialism were quite similar until the collapse of growth in the East after 1985. Thus the planned socialist growth experience as a group has been different from the long-term experience of the first planned socialist country, the Soviet Union, whose secular growth rate (from 1928 to 1990) is higher than the secular growth rates of the industrialized capitalist countries. If one were to contrast the postwar growth rates of the planned socialist countries with the century growth rates of the industrialized capitalist countries, the Soviet rate would appear to be relatively high. But the postwar period has been one of exceptionally high growth among capitalist countries, so the relevant yardstick against which to measure socialist growth performance is the postwar era, and this comparison fails to yield higher planned socialist growth.

The conclusion that economic growth has not been more rapid in the planned socialist economies is a strong one in view of the priority of growth in these countries and the low weight attached to economic growth by many of the capitalist countries. If one makes a crude *ceteris paribus* adjustment for differences in per capita income, capitalist growth even emerges as more rapid.

THE COSTS OF ECONOMIC GROWTH: EFFICIENCY AND CONSUMPTION

We turn now to the question of how efficiently and at what cost economic growth has been achieved. Extensive economic growth results from the expansion of the factors of production — land, labor, and capital inputs. Intensive growth is the consequence of increasing output per unit of factor input — that is, it is the product of increased efficiency. Economic growth is typically both extensive and intensive, for growth is normally the product of increases in both factor inputs and output per unit of factor input. At issue is which effect dominates.

Growth by means of the expansion of labor and capital inputs involves distinct economic costs. The expansion of labor inputs requires a sacrifice of leisure and time spent in household production activity; the expansion of the

Table 15.3 Annual GNP Growth Rates of Selected Asian Economies, 1960–1985

China	6.8
Taiwan	8.3
South Korea	8.0
Japan	6.2
Philippines	4.5
India	3.6
Pakistan	3.5

Source: National Foreign Assessment Center, *Handbook of Economic Statistics 1986* (Washington, D.C.: Central Intelligence Agency, 1986), Table 8 and Table 12.2.

capital stock requires a sacrifice of current consumption in order to accumulate capital. Extensive growth is a high-cost approach to economic expansion; intensive growth, though it requires some additional (nonquantifiable) inputs, such as better managerial methods and increased knowledge, is an essentially less costly means of achieving economic growth.

In the case of East–West comparisons, it is relevant to ask which economic system has done a better job in generating economic growth, where *better* is defined in terms of the relative weights of intensive growth versus extensive growth. Two such comparisons are relevant. The first, called **static efficiency**, involves taking a snapshot of planned socialist and capitalist countries at a particular point in time to determine how much output they are generating from a given amount of factor inputs. The second, called **dynamic efficiency**, probes the question of efficiency performance over time — that is, the extent to which output has been expanding more rapidly than inputs, the difference being the growth rate of factor productivity.[19]

It is not easy to contrast the static and dynamic efficiency of capitalism and planned socialism, for data are limited. Bits and pieces of evidence must be analyzed over limited periods of time, but from this scattered evidence we hope to draw some conclusions about the relative efficiency of capitalism and planned socialism.

Dynamic Efficiency

In Table 15.4, we supply information on the dynamic efficiency of the planned socialist and the industrialized capitalist countries. Specifically, we provide the annual growth rates of aggregate employment ($\hat{L}$) and reproducible capital ($\hat{K}$), which we then compare with the growth rate of aggregate output ($\hat{Q}$). By subtracting the growth rates of employment and capital, respectively, from the growth rate of output, we obtain the growth rates of labor productivity ($\hat{Q} - \hat{L}$) and capital productivity ($\hat{Q} - \hat{K}$), respectively.

Because the productivity of labor or capital is affected by substitutions between the two factors, it is desirable to have a comprehensive measure of the growth rate of combined labor and capital productivity. One must first calculate the growth rates of labor and capital combined ($\hat{L} + \hat{K}$), or total factor input. This is typically done by taking a weighted average of the growth rates of labor and capital, where the weights represent each factor's share of national income. Thus total factor productivity is defined as $\hat{Q} - (\hat{K} + \hat{L})$. Here

$$\hat{K} + \hat{L} = \hat{K}W_K + \hat{L}W_L$$

where

$$W_K = \text{capital's share of income}$$
$$W_L = \text{labor's share of income}$$

We use rates of growth of labor and capital combined ($\hat{L} + \hat{K}$), calculated in this manner. Inasmuch as a return to capital is typically not included in prices

Table 15.4 Annual Growth of Inputs and Output per Unit of Inputs in Socialist and Capitalist Countries

		(1) Employment (L̂)	(2) Fixed Capital (K̂)	(3) Labor & Capital (L̂+K̂)	(4) Output (Q̂)	(5) Labor Productivity (Q̂−L̂)	(6) Capital Productivity (Q̂−K̂)	(7) Total Factor Productivity Q̂−(L̂+K̂)
		A. Planned Socialist Countries						
Czechoslovakia	1950–60	.7	3.5	1.4	4.8	4.1	1.3	3.4
	1960–83	1.0	4.7	2.1	2.6	1.6	−2.1	.5
East Germany	1950–60	.0	2.0	.5	6.1	6.1	4.1	5.6
	1960–83	.3	4.0	1.4	2.8	2.5	−1.2	1.4
Soviet Union	1950–60	1.2	9.4	3.4	5.8	4.6	−3.6	2.4
	1960–85	1.3	7.3	2.8	3.6	2.3	−3.7	.8
Poland	1950–60	1.0	2.6	1.4	4.6	3.6	2.0	3.2
	1960–83	1.5	4.7	2.5	3.3	1.8	−1.4	.8
Hungary	1950–60	1.0	3.6	1.7	4.6	3.6	1.0	2.9
	1960–83	.3	5.0	1.7	2.9	2.6	−2.1	1.2
Romania	1950–60	1.1	—[a]	—	5.9	4.8	—	—
	1960–85	.4	—[a]	—	4.6	4.1	—	—
Bulgaria	1950–60	.2	—[a]	—	6.7	6.5	—	—
	1960–85	.5	—[a]	—	3.7	3.2	—	—
Unweighted average	1950–60	.8	4.2	1.7	5.5[b] (5.2)[c]	4.8	1.0	3.5
	1960–83(85)	.8	5.1	2.1	3.3[b] (3.0)[c]	2.5	−2.1	.9

Table 15.4 Annual Growth of Inputs and Output per Unit of Inputs in Socialist and Capitalist Countries (*Cont.*)

		(1) Employment ($\hat{L}$)	(2) Fixed Capital ($\hat{K}$)	(3) Labor & Capital ($\hat{L} + \hat{K}$)	(4) Output ($\hat{Q}$)	(5) Labor Productivity ($\hat{Q} - \hat{L}$)	(6) Capital Productivity ($\hat{Q} - \hat{K}$)	(7) Total Factor Productivity $\hat{Q} - (\hat{L} + \hat{K})$
				B. Capitalist Countries				
United States	1950–60	1.4	3.6	1.8	3.1	1.7	−.5	1.3
	1960–85	2.0	3.3	2.4	3.1	1.1	−.2	.7
Canada	1960–85	2.7	4.7	3.3	4.2	1.5	−.5	.9
Belgium	1950–62	.6	2.3	1.0	3.2	2.6	.6	2.2
Denmark	1950–62	.9	5.1	1.8	3.5	2.6	−1.6	1.7
	1950–60[d]	.1	4.2	1.0	4.9	4.8	.7	3.9
	1960–85	.7	4.8	1.8	3.9	3.1	−.9	2.1
West Germany	1950–60[d]	2.0	6.4	3.1	7.3	5.3	.9	4.2
	1960–85	.0	4.8	1.2	3.1	3.1	−1.7	1.9
Italy	1950–62	.6	3.5	1.3	6.0	5.4	2.5	4.7
Finland	1960–85	.7	4.6	1.9	3.9	3.2	−.5	2.0
Sweden	1962–83	.6	3.5	1.5	2.8	2.2	−.7	1.3
Netherlands	1950–62	1.1	4.7	1.9	4.7	3.6	.0	2.8
	1950–60[d]	.2	4.2	1.2	3.5	3.3	−.7	2.3
Norway	1960–85	.5	3.6	1.4	4.2	3.7	.6	2.8
United Kingdom	1950–60[d]	.7	3.4	1.2	2.3	1.6	−1.1	1.1
	1960–85	.5	3.2	1.1	2.3	1.8	−.9	1.2

	(1) Employment ($\hat{L}$)	(2) Fixed Capital ($\hat{K}$)	(3) Labor & Capital ($\hat{L} + \hat{K}$)	(4) Output ($\hat{Q}$)	(5) Labor Productivity ($\hat{Q} - \hat{L}$)	(6) Capital Productivity ($\hat{Q} - \hat{K}$)	(7) Total Factor Productivity $\hat{Q} - (\hat{L} + \hat{K})$
Japan 1953–70	1.7	9.8	3.8	10.0	8.3	.2	6.2
1970–85	.9	8.2	2.3	4.4	3.5	-3.8	2.1
Greece 1960–85	.4	5.8	2.0	5.1	4.7	-.7	3.1
Unweighted average[e] 1950–60	.9	4.7	1.8	4.8	3.9	.1	3.0
Unweighted average 1960–85	.9	4.7	1.9	3.7	2.8	-1.0	1.8

Note: All figures are annual growth rates.

$\hat{L}$ = growth rate of employment

$\hat{K}$ = growth rate of reproducible capital

$\hat{Q}$ = growth rate of output

$(\hat{L} + \hat{K})$ = growth rate of labor and capital combined

[a] The official Romanian and Bulgarian capital stock series are not cited because they are in current, not constant, prices.

[b] Average of all 7 countries.

[c] Average of first 5 countries.

[d] 1950–1962.

[e] Includes Japan, 1953–1970.

Sources: *Panel A: Employment:* Andrew Elias, "Magnitude and Distribution of the Labor Force in Eastern Europe," in U.S. Congress, Joint Economic Committee, *Economic Developments in Countries of Eastern Europe* (Washington, D.C.: Government Printing Office, 1970), pp. 208–214; Thad Alton, "Comparative Structure and Growth of Economic Activity in Eastern Europe," in U.S. Congress, Joint Economic Committee, *East European Economies Post Helsinki* (Washington, D.C.: Government Printing Office, 1977), p. 218; *Handbook of Economic Statistics 1980,* p. 47. *Capital Stock:* Official CMEA estimates of productive funds (*osnovnye fondy*) from *Statisticheski ezhegodnik stran-chlenov Soveta Ekonomicheskoi Vzaimopomoschi 1974* (Moscow: Statistika), p. 27; Alton, "Production and Resource Allocation in Eastern Europe," p. 372; *Handbook of Economic Statistics 1980,* p. 58; and Alton, "Comparative Structure and Growth," p. 223. *Output:* Table 10.1. *Panel B: Growth Rates of Employment, Reproducible Capital, and Output:* Edward Denison, *Why Growth Rates Differ* (Washington, D.C.: Brookings, 1967), pp. 42, 190, and Ch. 21; Edward Denison, *Accounting for United States Economic Growth, 1929–1969* (Washington, D.C.: Brookings, 1974), pp. 32, 58; Edward Denison and William Chung, *How Japan's Economy Grew So Fast* (Washington, D.C.: Brookings, 1976), pp. 19, 31; OECD, Department of Economics and Statistics, *Flows and Stocks of Fixed Capital, 1960–1985* (OECD: Paris, 1987); *Handbook of Economic Statistics 1986; World Table,* 3rd ed.

in the planned socialist countries, "synthetic" factor shares must be used to calculate their $\hat{L} + \hat{K}$ growth rates. We have chosen to use shares of .7 for labor and .3 for capital for the planned socialist countries; these shares are close to the average capitalist share.[20] Once the growth rate of combined factor inputs is calculated, it is then subtracted from the growth rate of output to obtain the growth rate of factor productivity $[\hat{Q} - (\hat{K} + \hat{L})]$. All of these figures are given in Table 15.4.

The approximate nature of these productivity calculations is worth emphasizing. Factors of production, especially labor, can expand in both quantitative and qualitative terms, yet our measure captures only its quantitative advance.[21] If comparable data were available, one could calculate a more comprehensive measure of labor's growth by adjusting for the growth in education, training, and composition of the labor force. However, data limitations do not allow such an adjustment of the planned socialist data, so we must restrict our analysis to quantitative factors. Because we use employment rather than actual hours, we are not even capturing the quantitative growth of labor accurately. Moreover, the capitalist data do not adjust for unemployment (which rose over this period). The productivity growth of labor actually employed would therefore be slightly higher than the rates given in column 5.

We are using the official capital stock estimates of the CMEA nations, except for the Soviet Union. We have no way of knowing whether they are comparable to Western data or how reliable these estimates are, although we do know that the figures for Romania and Bulgaria are inflated (they have not been included).[22] The official capital growth rates, however, appear to be in line with the Western figures; we doubt that they involve major distortions, though we have no proof.

What conclusions are to be drawn from Table 15.4 about the growth rates of factor inputs and factor productivity under planned socialism and advanced capitalism? The first is that through the mid 1980s, the growth rates of capital and labor inputs were similar for capitalism and socialism. The planned socialist and capitalist averages suggest roughly equivalent rates of growth of employment and, although the socialist growth rate of capital was probably slightly lower during the 1950s and higher thereafter, for the entire period capital grew at an average rate of roughly 5 percent in each economic system. The stereotype, fostered by the rapid growth of both labor and capital in the Soviet Union, that the planned socialist system generates a more rapid rate of growth of inputs is not supported. The rates of growth of labor and capital combined round to 2 percent per annum for both capitalism and planned socialism.

Unlike GNP growth, the variability of factor-input growth by country appears to be as great under planned socialism as under capitalism. Some planned socialist countries (East Germany, for example) experienced low growth of both labor and capital, while others (the Soviet Union and Poland) experienced rapid rates of input growth. One finds similar variability among the capitalist countries, with some (notably Japan) experiencing quite rapid growth of both labor and capital inputs relative to the other capitalist countries.

Both the socialist and the capitalist countries experienced a slowdown in productivity growth after the 1960s: The planned socialist growth rate of output declined after 1960 by about 40 percent; yet inputs, both labor and capital, grew more rapidly after 1960 (about one-quarter faster). Thus both labor and capital productivity and total factor productivity declined dramatically after 1960 in the planned socialist economies — labor productivity from an average of 4.8 to 2.5 percent, and total factor productivity from 3.5 to .9 percent. Efforts to stabilize the growth of output by raising the growth of inputs have not succeeded; rather than becoming more intensive, the growth of the planned socialist economies became more extensive after 1960.

The greater extensivity of socialist growth after 1960 is apparent when we compare the growth rates of total factor productivity with the growth rates of output. Taking those five socialist countries for which capital data are available, the average GNP growth rate was 5.2 percent per annum between 1950 and 1960, while the growth of efficiency (factor productivity) was 3.5 percent. Thus 3.5/5.2, or 67, percent of economic growth was accounted for by increasing output per unit of input. The corresponding figures for the 1960 to 1983 period are .9 percent and 3.0 percent. Thus from 1960 to 1983, only 30 percent of growth was accounted for by increasing inputs. The declining growth of productivity was felt by both labor and capital, but the decline in capital productivity from a positive rate to a rate of −2.1 percent per annum was especially prominent.

The capitalist group also experienced a slowdown in productivity growth after 1960. Average labor productivity growth fell from 3.9 to 2.8 percent; capital productivity growth fell from zero to −1.0 percent; and total factor productivity growth fell from 3.0 to 1.8 percent. In the 1950s, some 65 (3.0/4.8) percent of growth in the capitalist group was explained by the growth of efficiency; for the period 1960–1985, 49 (1.8/3.7) percent of growth was explained by efficiency gains. Falling rates of growth of productivity have characterized the cyclical downturns of capitalist countries over the years; it is unclear whether the more modest slowdown of capitalist productivity is the result of cyclical factors or has more deep-rooted causes.

Table 15.4 shows the planned socialist economies in a favorable light because it does not include the productivity collapse of the second half of the 1980s. During this period, all the planned socialist economies experienced negative productivity growth except the USSR, which experienced zero productivity growth.[23]

What are our overall conclusions concerning the growth of efficiency (factor productivity) under capitalism and planned socialism? As in the case of economic growth, there appears to be no evidence to suggest a more rapid rate of growth of productivity under planned socialism (see Figure 15.2). Since 1960, at least, it appears that the productivity performance of planned socialism has deteriorated seriously and that socialist growth has become much more extensive in character. We must emphasize that these conclusions are based on approximate data with little evidence on the qualitative growth of inputs. We believe, however, that they would hold up even if more exhaustive data were available.

Consumption Costs of Growth

One cost of economic growth is the sacrifice in current consumption required to add to the nation's stock of capital. Although growth rates in the East and West have been similar, it is not true that this growth was achieved with a similar allocation of resources between consumption and investment. Informa-

Figure 15.2 Productivity Growth in Socialist and Capitalist Countries, 1960–85

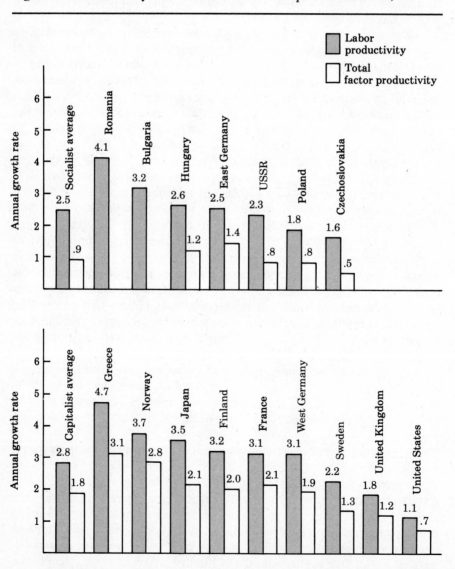

Source: Table 15.4.

tion on resource-allocation policies is summarized in Table 15.5.[24] Although the capitalist and socialist data cover slightly different time periods, they tell an interesting story. Again the GNP growth rates are quite similar, but personal consumption has fared relatively better than investment under capitalism. In fact, while personal consumption grew on the average at a more rapid rate in the capitalist sample (4.7 percent versus 3.6 percent), gross investment grew faster under planned socialism (6.4 percent versus 5.6 percent).

More interestingly, if one takes the ratio of the growth rate of consumption to the growth rate of investment as a measure of resource allocation, a distinct pattern emerges. Although there seems to be a positive relationship between this ratio and per capita income, the socialist consumption–investment ratios appear to be well below those of capitalist countries at a similar stage of development. The achievement of similar rates of growth in East and West has required a greater sacrifice of current consumption under planned socialism. In fact, the resource allocation pattern of the socialist countries is remarkably uniform (except in Czechoslovakia) and is closest to the patter of the less-industrialized capitalist countries (such as Turkey and Spain) and, surprisingly, of Japan and the United Kingdom.

Given the higher investment rates under planned socialism in the 1950s and 1960s, it follows that socialist per capita consumption will be lower for a given level of per capita national income *ceteris paribus*. This is the other side of the coin — namely, the cost of maintaining economic growth through expansion of capital inputs.[25] The absolute level of per capita consumption will depend on the economic potential of the country, and to argue that one country has outperformed the other simply because its standard of living is higher begs the question. The major issue is what standard of living is being supplied, given the economic resources at the nation's disposal. Such a comparison of capitalist and planned socialist living standards would show that the socialist living standards are low relative to per capita income. This reflects the decision of growth-oriented socialist planners to devote a relatively larger share of GNP to investment than under capitalism. However, the telling point is that this decision has not led to a notably higher rate of growth for the planned socialist nations. The planners' consumption policies have not paid off in terms of more rapid growth.

Static Efficiency

Static efficiency is an extremely difficult concept to measure. To do so correctly requires first a notion of an economy's productive potential, as defined by its total resources, and then a determination of how closely the economy comes to meeting that potential. This problem is explained in Figure 15.3. To show that the Soviet Union, for example, obtains half as much output as the United States from a given amount of conventional labor and capital inputs does not unambiguously prove the greater static efficiency of the American economy.

Table 15.5 Annual Rates of Growth of Personal Consumption, Investment, and GNP in Planned Socialist and Capitalist Countries

Country	(1) Personal Consumption	(2) Gross Investment	(3) GNP	(4) Consumption Growth as a Percentage of Investment Growth (1 ÷ 2)
A. Planned Socialist Countries				
Czechoslovakia (1950–67)	2.2	5.2	3.2	.42
East Germany (1960–75)	3.7	6.1	4.9	.61
Hungary (1950–67)	3.4	5.2	4.0	.65
Poland (1950–67)	4.2	7.9	5.1	.53
Soviet Union (1950–80)	<u>4.3</u>	<u>7.7</u>	<u>4.7</u>	<u>.56</u>
Unweighted average	3.6	6.4	4.4	.56
B. Capitalist Countries, 1950–1977				
United States	3.4	3.1	3.6	1.10
Canada	4.7	4.6	4.8	1.02
West Germany	4.7	5.0	4.8	.94
Denmark	3.5	4.9	3.8	.71
Norway	3.9	4.6	4.2	.85
Belgium	3.7	4.6	4.0	.81
France	5.0	6.1	5.0	.82
Netherlands	4.6	4.2	4.5	1.09
Japan	7.8	11.0	8.4	.71
Austria	5.4	5.1	4.9	1.06
United Kingdom	2.2	4.4	2.5	.50
Italy	4.6	5.0	4.8	.92
Greece	6.0	7.1	6.4	.85
Spain	5.2	6.7	5.6	.77
Turkey	<u>6.1</u>	<u>8.2</u>	<u>6.3</u>	<u>.74</u>
Unweighted average	4.7	5.6	4.9	.84

Sources: Thad Alton, "Economic Structure and Growth in Eastern Europe," in U.S. Congress, Joint Economic Committee, *Economic Developments in Countries of Eastern Europe* (Washington, D.C.: Government Printing Office, 1970), pp. 52–53; *Deutsches Institut fur Wirtschaftsforschung Wochenbericht*, 44 (June 1977), p. 199; Rush Greenslade, "The Real Gross National Product of the USSR, 1950–75," in U.S. Congress, Joint Economic Committee, *Soviet Economy in a New Perspective* (Washington, D.C.: Government Printing Office, 1975), p. 275; World Bank, *World Tables 1980* (Baltimore: The Johns Hopkins University Press, 1980), country tables; U.S. Congress, Joint Economic Committee, *USSR: Measures of Economic Growth and Development, 1950–80* (Washington, D.C.: Government Printing Office, 1982), pp. 65–67.

The measurement of conventional inputs may fail to capture the full range of resources (in both qualitative and quantitative terms) at the disposal of each economy.

One way to illustrate the static efficiency measurement problem is to note the strong positive relationship between the level of economic development and output per unit of input. Any evaluation of the static efficiency of capitalism and planned socialism must distinguish between "normal" differences caused by unequal economic development and differences due to the economic system. What is missing is information on what the economy should be able to produce at maximum efficiency from its resources.

Abram Bergson has made a careful study of comparative productivity under capitalism and socialism that sheds important light on the issue of relative

Figure 15.3 Why It Is Difficult to Evaluate Static Efficiency: Different Country Production Possibilities

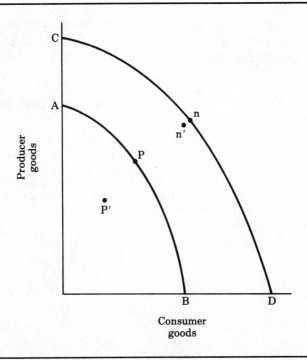

Explanation: CD represents the production possibilities frontier (PPF) of, say, the United States. AB is the PPF of, say, the Soviet Union. The U.S. PPF is to the northeast of the Soviet PPF because of greater resources and better technology. The relevant measure of static efficiency is how closely each economy comes to operating on its PPF. If, for example, the United States operates very close to n at n' and the Soviet Union operates at p', which is very far from p, the United States is statistically more efficient. In real-world measurement, all we observe is p' and n'. We have no way of knowing what p and n are.

productivity performance.[26] Bergson's data for 1975 are reproduced in Table 15.6. They give per capita outputs and labor (adjusted for quality differences), capital, and land inputs of various capitalist and socialist countries (where the socialist group includes Yugoslavia) as a percentage of the U.S. per capita figures. Bergson includes only "material sectors" in output and excludes services and housing that have a relatively low priority in the socialist countries. Table 15.6 shows, for example, that Italy had a per capita output 61 percent that of the United States, a per capita employment 75 percent that of the United States, and a per capita capital stock 62 percent that of the United States. The Soviet Union had a per capita output 60 percent that of the United States, a per capita employment 104 percent that of the United States, and a per capita capital stock 73 percent that of the United States.

The issue is whether the socialist countries systematically obtain less output from their available inputs than to the capitalist countries. In the data comparing Italy and the Soviet Union with the United States, Italy obtains more output from its available inputs. Italy and the Soviet Union have the same per capita output, yet the Soviet Union uses more labor and capital per capita to produce this output.

Bergson demonstrates that there is a systematic tendency for the output per worker (labor productivity) in socialist economies to fall short of output per worker in capitalist countries, when inputs are held constant. According to

Table 15.6 Per Capita Output, Employment, Capital and Land, 1975 (United States = 100)

Country	Output per Capita	Employment per Capita Adjusted for Labor Quality	Reproducible Capital per Capita	Farm Land per Capita
United States	100.0	100.0	100.0	100.0
West Germany	90.0	84.0	107.3	14.8
France	92.2	88.3	83.0	40.1
Italy	61.3	75.2	61.6	24.9
United Kingdom	67.2	89.6	77.2	14.5
Japan	82.8	129.0	95.2	5.4
Spain	64.6	95.4	47.7	67.0
Soviet Union	60.0	104.1	73.2	103.5
Hungary	61.1	115.6	70.9	59.8
Poland	54.8	122.7	51.6	50.4
Yugoslavia	41.5	98.8	35.9	45.6

Source: Abram Bergson, "Comparative Productivity: The USSR, Eastern Europe, and the West," *American Economic Review*, 77 (June 1987), 347.

Bergson's calculations, output per worker in the socialist group falls 25 to 34 percent short of output per worker in the capitalist group *ceteris paribus*.

Bergson's findings are important, though this sample is small. It will be a long time before a similar experiment on a larger number of countries can be performed. Meanwhile, we believe it is appropriate to conclude that socialist economies have relatively lower productivity, *ceteris paribus*, than industrialized capitalist countries.[27]

As we have shown, it is very difficult to assess the static efficiency of capitalist and socialist countries, because we are not able to determine how closely real-world economies operate to their production possibilities frontier. An important study seeks to provide some evidence on this subject for Soviet industry. Padma Desai and Ricardo Martin (following a line of inquiry opened by Judith Thornton) estimated production functions for various branches of Soviet industry. (A production function describes the technical relationships between inputs and outputs.)[28] Once the properties of these production functions are known, then it is possible to determine how closely Soviet industry approaches its production frontier. If capital and labor resources are not allocated so that marginal products are equalized across industries, less than maximum output is produced. Desai and Martin concluded that if resources were reallocated among branches to equalize marginal products, the output of Soviet industry would be raised from 3 percent to 10 percent. Moreover, they found that misallocation inefficiencies are growing over time.

What should we make of such estimates? First, we do not know the extent of resource misallocations in nonindustrial sectors. Are they greater or smaller than in Soviet industry? Second, these estimates do not capture fully other types of inefficiencies. Nevertheless, it is noteworthy that Desai and Martin are able to isolate significant inefficiencies. Western economists have been unable to locate significant inefficiencies in capitalist economies, particularly the inefficiencies associated with monopoly (the monopoly deadweight losses studied in Chapter 5). Yet in the Soviet case, we are able to find measurable efficiency losses.

What are our general conclusions about static efficiency under capitalism and planned socialism? We have no comprehensive measure of the productive potential of the various capitalist and planned socialist nations under investigation. All we have are rough measures of capital and labor inputs in strict quantitative terms; important qualitative variations are ignored, and other resources may be omitted. Yet our impression is one of lower output per worker under planned socialism after unsophisticated adjustments are made for differences in resource potential. The productivity collapse that took place in the Soviet Union and Eastern Europe after 1985 strengthens this conclusion.

INCOME DISTRIBUTION

Another measure of the merit of economic systems is the distribution of income among the members of society. What constitutes a good distribution of income must be a subjective matter, but there would be agreement that a distribution in which the top 5 percent of the population receives 95 percent of all income is "unfair" and that a completely equal distribution is "unfair" because those who contribute more to society are underrewarded. Marx himself rejected the notion of an equal distribution of income during the transition from socialism to communism, arguing instead for a distribution that reflected the individual's contribution to the well-being of society.[29]

Another reason why most people reject a perfectly equal distribution of income is that rewards must be offered for differential effort and for scarce resources; otherwise, incentives will diminish and the economy will not produce its potential output. The issue therefore is now to construct a distribution of income that both is "fair" and provides necessary incentives. Both socialism and capitalism must face this issue.

What differences would one expect in the distribution of incomes under capitalism and socialism? In capitalist societies, the two major sources of income inequality are the unequal distribution of property ownership (land and capital resources) and that of human capital. Both forms of capital yield income — the first in the form of property income from rent, interest, dividends, and capital gains, the second from wages and salaries.

Under both planned and market socialism, property other than consumer durables and housing is owned by the state, and the return from this state-owned property is at the state's disposal. Under capitalism, the bulk of property is owned privately, and property income accrues to private individuals.

The distribution of human capital depends, to some extent, on genetic factors, which should not vary systematically with the economic system. But it also depends on the manner in which schooling and on-the-job training are provided. Free or subsidized public schooling is available in both types of societies, although there is a greater tendency for the state to pay directly for higher education in socialist societies. Nevertheless, the differences between the two systems would not be expected to be great.

The major distinction is the virtual absence of private ownership of income-earning property under socialism. Unless offset by higher earnings differentials, the distribution of property plus labor income should be more nearly equal under socialism. The distribution of income after taxes will depend on the extent to which redistributive taxes and transfers are used by the state to equalize income distribution.

As to earnings differentials, planned socialist societies have recognized that labor cannot be allocated administratively and must be allowed relative freedom of choice of occupation. Therefore, the distribution of wage and salary income under socialism should follow roughly the same principles as under capitalism.

Arguments can be made, however, that the distribution of labor incomes will vary according to the economic system.[30] Some argue that labor income will be more equally distributed under socialism because of the more nearly equal distribution of education and training and because the government can control the power of strong labor groups. Moreover, socialist governments have a greater doctrinal commitment to equality.

Frederic Pryor made an extensive econometric study of the distribution of labor income among workers for the late 1950s and early 1960.[31] Pryor found that the distribution of labor income is *more nearly equal* under socialism, once per capita income and the size of the country are held constant. He also found that labor incomes are more unequal in the Soviet Union than in the other socialist countries; therefore, studies that generalize from the Soviet experience are likely to give a false impression.

More recent data on the distribution of earnings for full-time wage and salary earners confirm most of Pryor's findings for the 1950s and early 1960s. Persons in the top 10 percent of all U.S. earners (in the upper tenth percentile) averaged almost two times the earnings of the median earner in the late 1960s and early 1970s. In Yugoslavia, Poland, and the Soviet Union, the ratio was 1.75, whereas in Czechoslovakia and Hungary, earners in the upper tenth percentile earned only about 60 percent more than the median.[32] From these figures, we conclude that earnings are more nearly equally distributed in Eastern Europe, Yugoslavia, and the Soviet Union than in the United States. For the USSR, this appears to be a relatively new phenomenon, for as late as 1957, Soviet earnings were more unequal than those in the United States.[33]

We now turn from the distribution of *labor income* to the distribution of *total income*. Table 15.7 gives data on the distribution of per capita income after income taxes in a limited number of planned socialist and capitalist countries for which data are available.[34] There are certain weaknesses in these data. First, the socialist data generally exclude top income-earning families (party leaders, government officials, artists, and authors), including instead only families of workers and employees. These exclusions exaggerate the equality of the socialist distributions. Second, many activities considered legal in capitalist societies (the provision of private repair and medical services, for example) are provided on a sub rosa basis in planned socialist countries. These "second economy" activities often lead to substantial private incomes, which are not reported to the statistical authorities. Third, a relatively larger volume of resources (even excluding free educational and medical benefits) is provided in socialist societies on an extra-market basis — shopping privileges, official cars, vacations — and are not included in reported income. Benefits of this kind are also provided to executives, professionals, and government officials in capitalist societies. Company cars, subsidized executive lunchrooms, and stock options typically are not included in reported income. Finally, there is the matter of the distribution of economic power. In capitalist countries, economic power is distributed among government officials (both elected and appointed) and the owners of property resources. Major shareholders of large corporations possess considerable economic power over the distribution of society's resources. In planned socialist societies, the distribution of power has been concentrated in the hands of party and government officials, and it is likely (although not evident a priori) that economic power is more concentrated in planned socialist than in capitalist societies.

Table 15.7 shows that income is distributed more unequally in the capitalist countries in which the state plays a relatively minor redistributive role either

Table 15.7 Distribution of Per Capita Income Among Families After Income Taxes in Planned Socialist and Capitalist Countries

	U.K. 1969	U.S. 1968	Italy 1969	Canada 1971	Sweden 1971	Hungary 1964	Czecho-slovakia 1965	Bulgaria 1963–65	USSR 1966
Per capita income of individual in 95th percentile ÷ that of individual in 5th percentile	5.0	12.7	11.2	12.0	5.5	4.0	4.3	3.8	5.7
Per capita income of individual in 90th percentile ÷ that of individual in 10th percentile	3.4	6.7	5.9	6.0	3.5	3.0	3.1	2.7	3.5
Per capita income of individual in 75th percentile ÷ that of individual in 25th percentile	1.9	2.6	2.5	2.4	1.9	1.8	1.8	1.7	2.0

Source: P. J. D. Wiles, *Economic Institutions Compared* (New York: Halsted Press, 1977), p. 443. By permission of Basil Blackwell, Oxford.

through progressive taxation or through the distribution of social services (the United States, Italy, and Canada). Yet even where the state plays a major redistributive role (the United Kingdom and Sweden), the distribution of income appears to be slightly more unequal than in the planned socialist countries (Hungary, Czechoslovakia, and Bulgaria). The Soviet Union in 1966 appears to have had a less egalitarian distribution of income than its East European counterparts. The USSR distribution was scarcely to be distinguished from the British and Swedish distributions (it may even have been more unequal). The Soviet distribution appears to have become more nearly equal in recent years. Table 15.8 reveals that Soviet income distribution is more nearly equal than that in Australia, Canada, and the United States but not much different from that in Norway and the United Kingdom.

The Gini coefficient is a convenient summary measure of income inequality. The higher the Gini coefficient, the more unequal the distribution of income. A Gini coefficient of zero denotes perfect equality; a Gini coefficient of 1 denotes perfect inequality.

Gini coefficients for Great Britain and Sweden for the early 1970s are both around .25. The Czech, Hungarian, and Polish Gini coefficients for the same

Table 15.8 An International Comparison of Income Shares of Selected Percentile Groups, Distributions of Households by Per Capita Household Income, and GDP per Capita

Distribution, Country and Year	Percentage Income Share of			
	Lowest 10%	Lowest 20%	Highest 20%	Highest 10%
Nonfarm households (pretax) USSR, 1967	4.4	10.4	33.8	19.9
Urban households (post-tax) USSR, 1972–1974	3.4	8.7	38.5	24.1
All households (pretax) Australia, 1966–1967	3.5	8.3	41.0	25.6
Norway, 1970	3.5	8.2	39.0	23.5
U.K., 1973	3.5	8.3	39.9	23.9
France, 1970	2.0	5.8	47.2	31.8
Canada, 1969	2.2	6.2	43.6	27.8
U.S., 1972	1.8	5.5	44.4	28.6
All households (post-tax) Sweden, 1972	3.5	9.3	35.2	20.5

Source: Abram Bergson, "Income Inequality Under Soviet Socialism," *Journal of Economic Literature*, 22 (September 1984).

period are .21, .24, and .24, respectively — that is, very close to the British and Swedish coefficients. The Canadian and U.S. Gini coefficients, on the other hand, are .34 and .35, respectively, well above the socialist coefficients.[35]

Figure 15.4 provides Lorenz curves for Hungary, Sweden, West Germany, Spain, Mexico, and Yugoslavia. The reader will recall from Chapter 3 that the further the Lorenz curve departs from the line of perfect equality, the more unequal the distribution. These curves, which refer to the early 1970s, confirm the basic pattern shown in Table 15.7: Hungary is about the same as Sweden but is much more egalitarian than West Germany and Spain (two capitalist countries without considerable state income redistribution); Yugoslavia does not differ significantly from West Germany and Spain. However, there apparently was a narrowing of differentials in Yugoslavia between the early 1960s and early 1970s.

The Mexican Lorenz curve is included to make a general point about the Yugoslav (and Hungarian, Polish, Soviet, and Czech) distributions. As the Mexican curve shows, inequality tends to be negatively related to the level of development.[36] If one could adjust for lower per capita income, the socialist distributions would appear even more nearly equal than they do in direct comparisons.

In general, we conclude that the differences in distribution of income between the planned socialist economies and the capitalist welfare states are relatively minor. This is a surprising conclusion. One would have expected the absence of private ownership of property to make more of a difference. Nevertheless, differences are apparent when one contrasts the socialist distributions with those of the capitalist nations in which the state does not play a major redistributive role. In this instance, the expected contrast emerges, although we must re-emphasize the difficulty of interpreting the socialist distributions because of the omitted income categories.

ECONOMIC STABILITY

A final indicator of economic performance is economic stability. By economic stability we mean the absence of excessive movements in prices, unemployment, and output. Stability also refers to the absence of persistent (as opposed to cyclical) high unemployment rates or inflation rates.

The postwar era witnessed several recessions in the major capitalist countries, the most severe occurring in the mid-1970s and the start of the 1980s. Socialist countries experienced "growth recessions" — that is, periods when the growth rate declined but remained positive, but they largely avoided recessions before 1980. In the 1980s, however, the majority of the CMEA countries experienced periods of negative growth.

The literature recognizes that cyclical fluctuations are present in planned socialist economies, but it has been believed that socialist fluctuations are less pronounced. However, Frederic Pryor found (for a study covering the period 1950–1979) that socialist fluctuations in GNP, industrial output, and investment are not statistically distinguishable from capitalist fluctuations. Moreover, socialist fluctuations in agricultural output are more pronounced than those in capitalist agriculture.[37]

Figure 15.4 Lorenz Curves on the Distribution of Per Capita Income in Hungary, Sweden, West Germany, Spain, Yugoslavia, and Mexico[a,b]

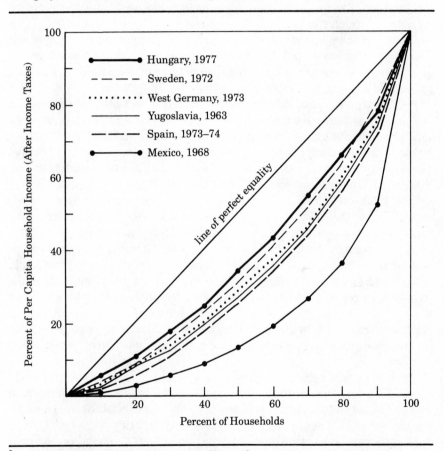

[a]For an explanation of the Lorenz curve see Chapter 2.
[b]Mexican data are prior to income taxes, but we doubt that their inclusion would move the Mexican Lorenz curve dramatically.

Sources: Malcolm Sawyer, *Income Distribution in OECD Countries* (Paris: OECD, 1976), p. 17; Jan Adams and Miloslav Nosal, "Earnings Differentials and Household-Income Differentials in Hungary – Policies and Practice," *Journal of Comparative Economics*, 6 (June 1982), 197; and Wouter van Ginneken, "Generating Internationally Comparable Income Distribution Data," *Review of Income and Wealth*, 28 (December 1982), 374.

The planned socialist economies have claimed that socialist planning "liquidated" unemployment. No society can eliminate unemployment entirely, for at any given time some people are in the process of changing jobs. It does appear that the planned socialist economies reduced the rate of unemployment to small proportions relative to capitalist economies.[38] This is a consequence of deliberate full-employment planning. Enterprises have been either unwilling or unable to release underemployed workers, creating such a problem that experiments have been attempted to encourage the laying off of redundant workers. Generally, however, enterprises have been given hiring quotas for new graduates, and the planning system served to provide employment for able-bodied individuals, whether in a necessary or an underemployed position.[39]

Moreover, the planned system has avoided unemployment problems by not allowing enterprises to fail. Enterprises have typically been rewarded on the basis of output rather than sales, and the existence of the enterprise has been guaranteed regardless of its performance.

If one examines price inflation under capitalism and planned socialism, a striking contrast emerges from the official statistics (see Table 15.9). Between 1960 and 1980, for example, the major capitalist countries experienced considerable inflation, which accelerated after 1970. According to official socialist indexes, on the other hand, consumer prices rose at a very modest pace over this period. The planned socialist economies' claims of virtual price stability for the 1960s and 1970s evoke skepticism about the official consumer price series.[40] First, the official price series ignore substantial price increases for "new" or "higher quality" products. Often an enterprise can obtain a higher price by claiming superficial or nonexistent quality improvements in its products. Second, the official series fail to capture the price increases of goods sold in legal and illegal free markets. Third, the official indexes to not include the costs of standing in line or of the bribes often required to obtain goods. When these circumstances prevail, demand exceeds supply at the established official price, and **repressed inflation** results. Supplies offered at established state prices are rationed out by standing in line, special shopping privileges, or ration coupons.

There is evidence that the official price series understate actual inflation in the CMEA countries. Recalculated price indexes (shown in parentheses in Table 15.9) suggest that prices rose more rapidly than official sources claim for the 1960 to 1980 period. In fact, the actual rate of inflation in Eastern Europe does not appear to be much different from that in West Germany, the industrialized Western nation with the most modest inflation rate. The relatively stable state retail prices conceal an unknown degree of repressed inflation, which has had a serious destabilizing effect in some planned socialist economies, such as Poland. For political and other reasons, authorities have been unwilling to raise official consumer prices to market-clearing levels. Price stability has been achieved only at the cost of serious shortages, redirection of purchasing power into collective farm markets and black markets, and growing discontent.

Table 15.9 Indexes of Consumer Prices in 1980 and 1989
(Recalculated Socialist Indexes in Parentheses)

	1980	*(1960 = 100)*	*1989*	*(1980 = 100)*
	A. Planned Socialist Countries			
Soviet Union	100	(140)	109	(–)
Bulgaria	130	(207)	113	(126)
Czechoslovakia	126	(173)	116	(115)
East Germany	98	(127)	110	(114)
Hungary	169	(210)	215	(220)
Poland	185	(254)	6515	(–)
Romania	120	(–)	130	(141)
	B. Market Socialist Country			
Yugoslavia	1449		246560	
	C. Capitalist Countries			
United States	280		150	
Canada	287		170	
Belgium	261		150	
France	382		178	
Italy	546		236	
Japan	420		119	
Netherlands	295		124	
United Kingdom	547		172	
West Germany	213		126	

Sources: *Statistical Abstract of the United States, 1981*, p. 881; *Economic Report of the President, 1981*, p. 355; Martin Kohn, "Consumer Price Developments in Eastern Europe," in U.S. Congress, Joint Economic Committee, *Eastern European Economic Assessment*, Part 2 (Washington, D.C.: Government Printing Office, 1981), p. 3330; Thad Alton et al., *Official Alternative Consumer Price Indexes in Eastern Europe, 1960–1980*, OP-68, Research Project on National Income in East Central Europe (New York, 1981); Directorate of Intelligence, CIA, *Soviet Gross National Product in Current Prices, 1960–80*, SOV 83-10037 (March 1983), pp. 6, 22; *Handbook of Economic Statistics 1990*, p. 45; "Eastern Europe: Long Road Ahead to Economic Well-Being," 1990, Tables C-2 to C-21; and *Narodnoe Khoziaistvo SSSR 1988*, p. 125.

The second column of Table 15.9 gives inflation rates for 1980 to 1989, a period that saw the partial liberalization of state price controls in the East. In the two countries that have converted most to market prices (Poland and Hungary), inflation well outpaced the West. Even in the Soviet Union, Bulgaria, and Romania, where prices remained state-controlled during this period (and where the official statistics probably understate inflation), inflation was about the same as in such low-inflation Western countries as Japan, Germany, and the Netherlands.

The rapid increase of prices in Poland and Hungary show the extent of repressed inflation on the eve of liberalization. The freeing of prices has led to very high rates of inflation. In Poland, the result was a 65-fold increase in prices in 1989 as price controls were removed, after which prices stabilized. The apparent price stability of earlier periods (as reflected in the official statistics) has concealed churning inflationary forces. In fact, the pent-up inflationary forces present a serious obstacle to economic reform. The conversion to a market economy requires releasing inflationary pressures. In Eastern Europe, both the governments and the public have a strong fear of inflation — of its effect on output and on the distribution of income. This fear of inflation reduces public support for market reform.

We refrain from drawing general conclusions about market socialism from the Yugoslav experience. As Table 15.9 attests, Yugoslavia has experienced a more rapid rate of inflation than any capitalist country in our sample. After 1980, Yugoslavia experienced hyperinflation. Moreover, the Yugoslav unemployment rate has been higher than that in the planned socialist countries.[41] Thus Yugoslavia does not appear to match the planned socialist record of stability but is more like a capitalist LDC in this regard. In fact, Yugoslav's rates approximate those of Portugal and Turkey.

The planned socialist countries have become increasingly subject to external disturbances such as energy shocks, shifting terms of trade, and excessive hard-currency debt problems. Moreover, the planned countries lack some of the means (such as currency devaluation and foreign equity participation) to correct external imbalances. The CMEA countries are threatened with increasing external instability in the future.

The ultimate test of the performance of an economic system is its long-run survivability. At this time in history, we are unsure about the viability and survivability of the planned socialist system. The inability of the system over the past decades, to generate growth, to achieve productivity advances, and to raise living standards has caused the leadership of the Soviet Union and Eastern Europe to search for alternatives to the planned system. Whether this search for a new economic system will be successful remains to be seen. It is quite possible that the planned socialist system will remain stubbornly in place, despite the leadership's best intentions to establish a new economic system. The defects of the planned socialist system — low productivity and poor quality — are well known to the leadership. The advantages of the industrialized capitalist system — high productivity, strong innovation, and high living standards — are equally well known. What is *not* known is how to make the transition from planned socialism to industrialized capitalism. It is also unclear whether the societies in question are prepared to bear the costs that the transition will inevitably entail.

SUMMARY

1. It is not possible to draw overall conclusions about the economic performance of socialism and capitalism without using subjective criteria. However, the performance of planned socialism and capitalism can be examined on the basis of how well each system measures up on a series of separate indicators of economic performance.

2. With per capita income held constant, industry shares are high under socialism relative to those under capitalism. Agriculture (in terms of its share of GNP and the labor force) and heavy industry are of greater importance under socialism than under capitalism; urbanization is underemphasized. Economic growth has *not* been more rapid under planned socialism, despite the high importance that socialist planners attached to the growth objective. Capitalist countries seem to have "out-grown" their planned socialist counterparts over the last twenty years and, if the level of economic development is held constant, perhaps over the entire postwar era. In any case, differences in growth rate have not been substantial over the long run.

3. The growth of factor inputs has been similar under capitalism and planned socialism over the postwar era, although after 1980 factor inputs probably grew more rapidly under planned socialism, despite the declining growth rate of output. During the early postwar era, the two systems were probably similar in productivity growth. During the 1950s, efficiency growth accounted for over 60 percent of planned socialist growth — a figure close to the capitalist performance — but after 1960, planned socialist growth became more extensive. Almost 80 percent of growth was accounted for by the expansion of inputs. In the 1960s and 1970s, socialist growth became quite expensive in terms of its reliance on increased factor inputs. This phenomenon is also apparent from the differential growth rates of consumption and investment, which suggest greater consumer sacrifices in the planned socialist economies. Holding other inputs constant, the planned socialist countries generally achieved less output per unit of labor input than did their capitalist counterparts.

4. Income is distributed more equitably under planned socialism than in those capitalist countries where the state does not play a major redistributive role. However, the differences between the distribution of income in so-called capitalist welfare states and in the planned socialist economies are surprisingly small.

5. Planned socialism has been more stable in terms of conventional measures such as unemployment and inflation. These measures, however, conceal some instabilities, such as shortages and black market activities, and a loss of economic efficiency has resulted.

NOTES

1. Abram Bergson, *Planning and Productivity Under Soviet Socialism* (New York: Columbia University Press, 1968).
2. Paul R. Gregory and Robert C. Stuart, *Soviet Economic Structure and Performance*, 4th ed. (New York: HarperCollins, 1990), Ch. 12.
3. See Joseph Chung, "The Economies of North and South Korea" (Annual Meeting of the American Economic Association, Atlantic City, N.J., September 1976) and Paul Gregory and Gert Leptin, "Similar Societies Under Differing Economic Systems: The Case of the Two Germanys," *Soviet Studies*, 24 (October 1977), 519–542. Also see the papers on the panel: "Different Strategies, Similar Countries: The Consequences of Growth and Equity" (Annual Meeting of the American Economic Association, New York, December 1982).
4. Gur Ofer, "Industrial Structure, Urbanization, and the Growth Strategy of Socialist Countries," *Quarterly Journal of Economics*, 90 (May 1976), 219–243; Gur Ofer, *The Service Sector in Soviet Economic Development* (Cambridge, Mass.: Harvard University Press, 1973); Paul Gregory, *Socialist and Nonsocialist Industrialization Patterns* (New York: Praeger, 1970); Frederic L. Pryor, *Public Expenditures in Communist and Capitalist Nations* (Bloomington: Indiana University Press, 1973); and Frederic L. Pryor, *Property and Industrial Organization in Communist and Capitalist Nations* (Bloomington: Indiana University Press, 1973). For a discussion of the pure methodology of econometric performance evaluation, see Edward Hewett, "Alternative Econometric Approaches for Studying the Link Between Economic Systems and Economic Outcomes," *Journal of Comparative Economics*, 4 (September 1980), 274–294. For a discussion of the methodology of growth comparisons, see Gur Ofer, "Soviet Economic Growth, 1928–1985," *Journal of Economic Literature*, 25 (December 1987), 1767–1833.
5. For example, Gregor Lazarcik has found that the centrally planned economies with more decentralized agriculture (such as Hungary and Poland) have performed better in terms of output and efficiency than those with centralized agriculture. On this, see Gregor Lazarcik, "Comparative Growth, Structure, and Levels of Agricultural Output, Inputs, and Productivity in Eastern Europe, 1965–79," in U.S. Congress, Joint Economic Committee, *East European Economic Assessment*, Part 2 (Washington, D.C.: Government Printing Office, 1981), pp. 587–634.
6. The major sources of data on the Soviet Union, Eastern Europe, and China are contained in various reports to the U.S. Congress prepared by the Joint Economic Committee. See, for example, *East European Economies: Slow Growth in the 1980s*, Vols. 1–3 (Washington, D.C.: Government Printing Office, 1986) and *Gorbachev's Economic Plans*, Vols. 1–2 (Washington, D.C.: Government Printing Office, 1987). Another useful statistical compendium is the Central Intelligence Agency, Directorate of Intelligence, *Handbook of Economic Statistics*. The most useful official East European source is the CMEA handbook: *Statisticheski ezhegodnik stran chlenov Sovet Ekonomicheskikh Vzaimopomoshichi*, various annual editions. For data on the Chinese economy, see U.S. Congress, Joint Economic Committee, *China: A Reassessment of the Economy* (Washington, D.C.: Government Printing Office, 1975); and Alexander Eckstein, ed., *Quantitative Measures of China's Economic Output* (Ann Arbor: University of Michigan Press, 1980).
7. Statistical comparisons of industrialized capitalism and planned socialism are Maurice Ernst, "Postwar Economic Growth in Eastern Europe," in U.S. Congress, Joint Economic Committee,

Economic Developments in Countries of Eastern Europe (Washington, D.C.: Government Printing Office, 1970), pp. 41–67; and Thad Alton, "East European GNPs," Joint Economic Committee, *East European Economies: Slow Growth in the 1980s*, Vol. 1, pp. 81–132. Also see Andrew Stollar and G. R. Thompson, "Sectoral Employment Shares: A Comparative Systems Context," *Journal of Comparative Economics*, 11 (March 1987), 62–80; and Thad Alton, "Production and Resource Allocation in Eastern Europe: Performance, Problems, and Prospects," in Joint Economic Committee, *East European Economic Assessment*, Part 2, pp. 348–408.

8. See, for example, Subramanian Swamy, "Economic Growth in China and India, 1952–1970: A Comparative Appraisal," *Economic Development and Cultural Change*, 21 (July 1973), 1–84; and Wilfred Malenbaum, "Modern Economic Growth in India and China: The Comparison Revisited," *Economic Development and Cultural Change*, 31 (October 1982), 45–84.

9. For a discussion of CMEA statistical practices, see Thad Alton, "Economic Structure and Growth in Eastern Europe," in Joint Economic Committee, *Economic Developments in Countries of Eastern Europe*, pp. 43–45; and Alton, "Production and Resource Allocation in Eastern Europe," pp. 384–408.

10. The pioneering work on reconstructing planned socialist national income accounts was for the Soviet Union and was carried out by Abram Bergson and his associates. For an account of these efforts, see Abram Bergson, "Introduction," *Real National Income of Soviet Russia Since 1928* (Cambridge, Mass.: Harvard University Press, 1961).

11. *The Real National Income of Soviet Russia Since 1928*, Chs. 2 and 3.

12. On this, see Directorate of Intelligence, *Measuring Soviet GNP: Problems and Solutions: A Conference Report*, SOV 90–10038, September 1990; "Eastern Europe: Long Road Ahead to Economic Well-Being," A Paper by the Central Intelligence Agency Presented to the Subcommittee on Technology and National Security of the Joint Economic Committee, May 1990; and Directorate of Intelligence, *Revisiting Soviet Economic Performance Under Glasnost: Implications for CIA Estimates*, SOV 88–10068, September 1988.

13. *Measuring Soviet GNP: Problems and Solutions*, p. 187.

14. For discussions of the socialist industrialization model, see Gregory, *Socialist and Nonsocialist Industrialization Patterns*; Ofer, "Industrial Structure, Urbanization, and the Growth of Socialist Countries" and *The Service Sector in Soviet Economic Development*; and Gregory and Stuart, *Soviet Economic Structure and Performance*, Ch. 12.

15. For a discussion of index number relativity, see Bergson, *Real National Income of Soviet Russia Since 1928*, Ch. 3.

16. This result was noted first by Abram Bergson in "Development Under Two Systems: Comparative Productivity Growth Since 1950," *World Politics*, 20 (July 1971), 579–617.

17. Frederic Pryor, *A Guidebook to the Comparative Study of Economic Systems* (Englewood Cliffs, N.J.: Prentice-Hall, 1985), p. 78.

18. See, for example, Swamy, "Economic Growth in China and India," pp. 81–83; and Malenbaum, "Modern Economic Growth in India and China," pp. 45–84.

19. For a discussion of the measurement of static and dynamic efficiency, see Bergson, *Planning and Productivity Under Soviet Socialism*.

20. Edward Denison and William Chung, *How Japan's Economy Grew So Fast* (Washington, D.C.: Brookings, 1976), p. 30.

21. The classic treatment of the measurement of factor productivity is Edward Denison, *Why Growth Rates Differ* (Washington, D.C.: Brookings, 1967).

22. Apparently the Romanian and Bulgarian capital stock figures are in current prices. On this, see Alton, "Comparative Structure and Growth of Economic Activity in Eastern Europe," p. 223.

23. "Eastern Europe: Long Road Ahead to Economic Well-Being," Tables C-1 to C-21.

24. A considerable amount of research has gone into the subject of the relative growth of investment and consumption in Eastern Europe. Unfortunately, studies that cover the 1970s have not succeeded in calculating directly the real growth of investment. For a discussion of this point, see Alton, "Production and Resource Allocation in Eastern Europe," pp. 314–367. Also see Alton, "East European GNPs," pp. 94–98.

25. See the following studies of per capita consumption in the USSR and Eastern and Western Europe: Terence Byrne, "Levels of Consumption in Eastern Europe," in Joint Economic Committee, *Economic Developments in Countries of Eastern Europe*, pp. 297–315; and U.S. Congress, Joint Economic Committee, *Consumption in the USSR: An International Comparison* (Washington, D.C.: Government Printing Office, 1981).

26. Abram Bergson, "Comparative Productivity: The USSR, Eastern Europe, and the West," *American Economic Review*, 77 (June 1987), 342–357. For Bergson's earlier work on this subject, see his discussion of relative Soviet output per unit in Abram Bergson, *The Economics of Soviet Planning* (New Haven: Yale University Press, 1964), Ch. 14. Also see Bergson, *Production and the Social System: The USSR and the West* (Cambridge, Mass.: Harvard University Press, 1978).

27. This view is shared by Pryor, *Property and Industrial Organization in Communist and Capitalist Nations*, p. 80.

28. Padma Desai and Ricardo Martin, "Efficiency Loss from Resource Misallocation in Soviet Industry," *Quarterly Journal of Economics*, 98 (August 1983), 441–456. Also see Judith Thornton, "Differential Capital Charges and Resource Allocation in Soviet Industry," *Journal of Political Economy*, 79 (May/June 1971), 545–561.

29. For comprehensive discussions of income distribution under capitalism and socialism, see P. J. D. Wiles, *Economic Institutions Compared* (New York: Halsted Press, 1977), Ch. 16; Martin Schnitzer, *Income Distribution: A Comparative Study of the United States, Sweden, West Germany, East Germany, the United Kingdom, and Japan* (New York: Praeger, 1974); and Abram Bergson, "Income Inequality Under Soviet Socialism," *Journal of Economic Literature*, 22 (September 1984).

30. See Pryor, *Property and Industrial Organization in Communist and Capitalist Nations*, pp. 74–75.

31. Ibid., pp. 74–89.

32. John R. Moroney, ed., *Income Inequality: Trends and International Compromise* (Lexington, Mass.: Heath, 1978), p. 5.

33. Janet Chapman, "Earnings Distribution in the USSR, 1968–1976," *Soviet Studies*, 35 (July 1983), 410–413.

34. See also a specialized study for the Soviet Union by Alastair McAuley, "The Distribution of Earnings and Income in the Soviet Union," *Soviet Studies*, 29 (April 1977), 214–237.

35. Harold Lydall, "Some Problems in Making International Comparisons of Income Inequality," in Moroney, *Income Inequality*, pp. 31–33.

36. Simon Kuznets, *Modern Economic Growth* (New Haven: Yale University Press, 1966).

37. For studies of socialist business and trade cycles, see C. W. Lawson, "An Empirical Analysis of the Structure and Stability of Communist Foreign Trade, 1960–68," *Soviet Studies*, 26 (April 1974), 224–238; G. J. Staller, "Patterns and Stability in Foreign Trade, OECD and COMECON," *American Economic Review* (September 1967); Josef Goldman, "Fluctuations and Trends in the Rate of Economic Growth in Some Socialist Countries," *Economics of Planning*, 4, no. 2 (1964), 89–98; Oldrich Kyn, Wolfram Schrette, and Jiri Slama, "Growth Cycles in Centrally Planned Economies: An Empirical Test," Osteuropa Institute, Munich, *Working Papers*, No. 7 (August 1975); Gerard Roland, "Investment Growth Fluctuations in the Soviet Union: An Econometric Analysis," *Journal of Comparative Economics*, 11 (June 1987), 192–206. Pryor's results are in Pryor, *A Guidebook*, pp. 114–118.

38. P. J. D. Wiles, "A Note on Soviet Unemployment in U.S. Definitions," *Soviet Studies*, 23 (April 1972), 619–628. David Granick, *Job Rights in the Soviet Union: Their Consequences* (Cambridge, England: Cambridge University Press, 1987).

39. Morris Bornstein, "Unemployment in Capitalist Regulated Market Economies and Socialist Centrally Planned Economies," *American Economic Review, Papers and Proceedings*, 68 (May 1978), pp. 38–43; and Paul Gregory and Irwin Collier, Jr., "Unemployment in the Soviet Union: Evidence from the Soviet Interview Project," *American Economic Review*, 78 (September 1988), 613–632.

40. Authoritative discussion of official socialist price indexes and repressed inflation are found in Richard Portes, "The Control of Inflation: Lessons from East European Experience," *Economica*, 44 (May 1977), 109–129. For some empirical estimates, see Richard Portes and David Winter, "The Demand for Money and Consumption Goods in Centrally Planned Economies," *Review of Economics and Statistics*, 60 (February 1978), 8–18; and Martin J. Kohn, "Consumer Price Developments in Eastern Europe," in Joint Economic Committee, *East European Economic Assessment*, Part 2, pp. 328–347.
41. World Bank, *World Tables 1976* (Baltimore: The Johns Hopkins University Press, 1976).

RECOMMENDED READINGS

Thad P. Alton and associates, *Economic Growth in Eastern Europe 1970 and 1975–1985*, Research Project on National Income in East Central Europe (New York: L. W. International Financial Research, Inc.), occasional paper no. 90.

Abram Bergson, "Comparative Productivity: The USSR, Eastern Europe, and the West," *American Economic Review*, 77 (June 1987), 342–357.

————, *Planning and Productivity Under Soviet Socialism* (New York: Columbia University Press, 1968).

————, *Productivity and the Social System: The USSR and the West* (Cambridge, Mass.: Harvard University Press, 1978).

————, "Productivity Under Two Systems: The USSR Versus the West," in Jan Tinbergen et al., eds., *Optimum Social Welfare and Productivity: A Comparative View* (New York: New York University Press, 1972).

————, "Income Inequality Under Soviet Socialism," *Journal of Economic Literature*, 22 (September 1984).

Trevor Buck, *Comparative Industrial Systems* (New York: St. Martin's, 1982).

Stanley Cohn, "The Soviet Path to Economic Growth: A Comparative Analysis," *Review of Income and Wealth* (March 1976), pp. 49–59.

Edward Denison, *Why Growth Rates Differ: Postwar Experiences in Nine Western Countries* (Washington, D.C.: Brookings, 1967).

Padma Desai and Ricardo Martin, "Efficiency Loss from Resource Misallocation in Soviet Industry," *Quarterly Journal of Economics*, 98 (August 1983), 441–456.

Irving B. Kravis, "Comparative Studies of National Incomes and Prices," *Journal of Economic Literature*, 22 (March 1984).

Irving B. Kravis, Allen Heston, and Robert Summers, "Real GDP per Capita for More Than One Hundred Countries," *Economic Journal*, 88 (June 1978).

————, *World Product and Income: International Comparisons of Real Gross Product* (Baltimore: The Johns Hopkins University Press for the World Bank, 1982).

Sima Lieberman, *The Growth of European Mixed Economies* (New York: Halsted Press, 1977).

Alastair McAuley, *Economic Welfare in the Soviet Union* (Madison: University of Wisconsin Press, 1979).

Angus Maddison, *Economic Growth in Japan and the USSR* (New York: Norton, 1969).

Wilfred Malenbaum, "Modern Economic Growth in India and China: The Comparison Revisited," *Economic Development and Cultural Change*, 31 (October 1982), 45–84.

Paul Marer, *Dollar GNPs of the USSR and Eastern Europe* (Baltimore: The Johns Hopkins University Press for the World Bank, 1985).

John Moroney, *Income Inequality: Trends and International Comparisons* (Lexington, Mass.: Heath, 1978).

Frederic Pryor, *Property and Industrial Organization in Communist and Capitalist Nations* (Bloomington: Indiana University Press, 1973).

———, *A Guidebook to the Comparative Study of Economic Systems* (Englewood Cliffs, N.J.: Prentice-Hall, 1985).

Martin Schnitzer, *Income Distribution: A Comparative Study of the United States, Sweden, West Germany, East Germany, the United Kingdom, and Japan* (New York: Praeger, 1974).

Subramanian Swamy, "The Economic Growth in China and India, 1952–1970: A Comparative Appraisal," *Economic Development and Cultural Change*, 21 (July 1973), 1–84.

U.S. Congress, Joint Economic Committee, *China: A Reassessment of the Economy* (Washington, D.C.: Government Printing Office, 1975).

———, *East European Economies: Slow Growth in the 1980s*, Vols. 1–3 (Washington, D.C.: Government Printing Office, 1985).

———, *Gorbachev's Economic Plans*, Vols. 1–2 (Washington, D.C.: Government Printing Office, 1987).

———, *USSR: Measures of Economic Growth and Development, 1952–1980* (Washington, D.C.: Government Printing Office, 1982).

P. J. D. Wiles, *Economic Institutions Compared* (New York: Halsted Press, 1977), Ch. 16.

———, *The Distribution of Income, East and West* (Amsterdam: North Holland, 1974).

Murray Yanowitch, *Social and Economic Inequality in the Soviet Union* (White Plains, N.Y.: M. E. Sharpe, 1977).

APPENDIX 15A:
THE INDEX NUMBER PROBLEM IN INTERNATIONAL COMPARISONS

In this chapter we cited a large number of statistics comparing the level of GNP, output per worker, and so on among capitalist and socialist countries.[1] For purposes of simplicity, we glossed over the fact that the price system that underlies the above valuations can have a substantial impact on the outcome. For example, for us to compare levels of GNP meaningfully, the GNPs of all countries being compared must be valued in some common currency (dollars, rubles, marks, pounds, whatever).

Let us take the case of comparing the levels of GNP of the Soviet Union and the United States in 1980. To simplify the illustration, let us say that both countries produce only two goods, wheat and lathes. In the USSR, wheat is expensive relative to lathes; in the United States, wheat is cheap relative to lathes (as judged by Soviet prices). Production and domestic prices of these two commodities in each country are given in Table 15A.1.

From this information, we can make two types of calculations: We can calculate the GNPs of both countries using U.S. prices or we can calculate the GNPs of both countries using Soviet prices.

In U.S. prices, we get

$$\text{Soviet GNP} = (\$2 \times 10) + (\$2 \times 20) \quad \text{or} \quad \$60$$
$$\text{U.S. GNP} = (\$2 \times 30) + (\$2 \times 40) \quad \text{or} \quad \$140$$

Result: In U.S. prices, Soviet GNP is 60/140 = 43 percent of U.S. GNP.

In Soviet prices, we get

$$\text{Soviet GNP} = (5R \times 10) + (1R \times 20) \quad \text{or} \quad 70R$$
$$\text{U.S. GNP} = (5R \times 30) + (1R \times 40) \quad \text{or} \quad 190R$$

Result: In Soviet prices, Soviet GNP is only 70/190 = 37 percent of U.S. GNP.

The comparison is more favorable when the prices of the other country are used than when the country's own prices are used. Why is this typically the case? It is an empirical fact that the relative prices of any country tend to be inversely related to the relative quantities produced by that country. Products that can be produced relatively cheaply (because of abundant domestic resources) tend to be produced in abundance, and products that can be produced relatively expensively tend to be limited in production. Insofar as relative prices differ among countries (as a result of differences in human capital and natural resources), we find that each country emphasizes the production of relatively cheap commodities. Therefore, when the GNP of one country is valued using the different relative prices of another country, its total output appears relatively large.

To take a real-world example of this index number phenomenon, we can cite studies of Soviet per capita consumption as a percentage of U.S. consumption. In 1976, Soviet and U.S. consumption per capita were 1,116R and 4,039R, respectively, when valued in rubles. In other words, the Soviet Union stood at 28 percent of the U.S. level. Valued in dollars, Soviet and U.S. per capita consumption were $2,395 and $5,598, respectively; that is, Soviet consumption per capita was 43 percent of the U.S. level. Which figure (28 percent or 43 percent) is the correct one? There is no "true" value in such comparisons. One comparison is as real as the other, for each system of relative prices yields a different answer.

It should be noted that in the comparisons used in this chapter, we consistently use dollar valuations. Dollar valuations make Soviet and East European values look more favorable than they would have if, say, ruble prices had been used.

Table 15A.1

	Output		Price	
	Wheat	*Lathes*	*Wheat*	*Lathes*
Soviet Union, 1980	10	20	5R	1R
United States, 1980	30	40	$2	$2

NOTE

1. U.S. Congress, Joint Economic Committee, *Consumption in the USSR: An International Comparison* (Washington, D.C.: Government Printing Office, 1981), p. 6.

REFERENCES

Trevor Buck, *Comparative Industrial Systems* (New York: St. Martin's, 1981), Ch. 5.

Irving B. Kravis et al., *A System of International Comparisons of Gross National Product and Purchasing Power* (Baltimore: The Johns Hopkins University Press, 1975).

Richard Moorsteen, "On Measuring Productive Potential and Relative Efficiency," *Quarterly Journal of Economics*, 75 (August 1981), 451–467.

PART V

SOCIALIST ECONOMIES IN TRANSITION

16 Perestroika: The Soviet Reform Experience

ANOTED OBSERVER OF THE SOVIET ECONOMY, Ed Hewett, characterizes economic reform in a simple and straightforward fashion as reforming "the institutional arrangements constituting the system by which resources are allocated." Put another way, changes in institutional arrangements (the economic system) affect the manner in which basic decisions about resource allocation are made, specifically to "alter the way those decisions are made in an effort to improve performance in areas of importance to political leaders."[1]

As Hewett emphasizes, economic reform is a process, not an event.[2] Accordingly, any reform program necessarily consists of a number of components and a sense of how the reform components are to be implemented over time. Not only must the end goals of the reform be agreed on, but also the components of the reform program must be consistent and the steps in their implementation must unfold in an appropriate sequence. Moreover, the reform program must have significant popular support if regime–population consensus is to be achieved and sustained, especially in the difficult transition period. Indeed, if a reform program is to be successfully implemented, effective transition policies must be formulated and administered to guide the economy through the transition process.

REFORM OF THE ADMINISTRATIVE COMMAND SYSTEM

As we noted in our discussion of economic reform in Chapter 4, no one really knows how to make the transition from the administrative command system to a "better" economic system. Both designing reform programs and implementing them have proved difficult. For a long time, the socialist economic systems have been largely isolated from the forces of change so familiar to market economies. Past planning arrangements and policies have created entrenched economic and bureaucratic structures that are unlikely to survive under an alternative system. Breathtaking structural and institutional changes must continue to take place before one can safely conclude that a new system has replaced the old administrative command system. Furthermore, resistance to change is inevitable. Indeed, one could argue that for radical economic reform to be implemented, past political arrangements must themselves be radically changed.

The interaction between political change and economic change has proven to be complex. In Eastern European cases, for example Poland, political change has been relatively swift, compete, and reasonably harmonious — resulting in a political environment in which economic reform could be implemented on a continuing basis. The Soviet case is much more complicated. While political change has in part facilitated economic reform, instability and uncertainty have undoubtedly limited the nature, scope, and pace of economic reform.

Prior to the coup of August 19, 1991, there was still a tendency, as we shall see in this chapter, to view the economic reform process as center directed. However, a major outcome of the coup was the decentralization of political and economic power from the center to local units, even though the formal arrangements for such changes remain to be developed. Even if the latter include some form of all-union arrangements, the nature of economic reform will change. What sort of changes might be expected?

First, it is obvious that the nature of new political arrangements will influence the nature of economic reform. In the new countries of Latvia, Lithuania, and Estonia, new programs must be defined, including the very critical issue of trading arrangements both with Soviet political units and with the West. For those sub-units remaining within some sort of new union, the nature of center/local arrangements will be critical.

Second, it is likely that any new set of arrangements will shift power to local levels. From an economic perspective, this will place new, important emphasis on the economic status of sub-units, for example the natural resource base, the extent of industrial and agricultural capacity, and the extent and quality of local infrastructure. Moreover, both the arrangements for, and terms of, inter-unit trade will take on new importance as central authorities no longer dictate resource shifts from one locale to another.

Third, it is likely that under significant decentralization, the nature and pace of economic reform will be uneven. While economic reform driven from below presents new challenges (as has been the case in China), it also presents barriers, especially for those regions less well off in terms of basic endowments and past attention to economic development. Thus, even if there remains a central reform plan (an issue we examine at the end of this chapter), local input and initiative are likely to be of increased importance under pending political arrangements.

Although there may be theoretical agreement on why the economic system must be changed, on prevailing policy imperatives, and on where the economy should ultimately be, the path from existing arrangements to the ideal of the reform model is still far from clear. In addition, the environmental conditions of the various socialist economies differ greatly, and the support of the population cannot be taken for granted. Decades of isolation from market resource allocation have in many cases left the population with little understanding of the costs and benefits associated with different systemic arrangements. Consequently, it is difficult to generate popular support for economic reform measures. The dismantling of the established order threatens substantial disruptions not only for the general population but also for economic administrators and enterprise managers, many of whom have learned to live with, and benefit from, the old system. Resistance to change can be expected.

The impending disruptions associated with any economic reform process might be characterized as a tradeoff between equity and efficiency. Although the introduction of market forces should improve economic efficiency, inflation and unemployment are also likely to result; neither is attractive to those accustomed to long-standing state guarantees of job rights and to stable retail prices. In all the administrative command economies, there is a general appreciation of the advantages of market resource allocation, but there is also doubt about whether the command order can be dismantled and replaced by a new system at a reasonable cost to the population and within a reasonable period of time. Moreover, in many cases (and especially in the Soviet Union), there is concern about the potential costs of a new economic order in terms of unemployment, inflation, and the like.

Perestroika as "Radical" Reform

In Chapter 4, we argued that although there have been a large number of reform attempts in socialist economic systems, until recently these attempts have tended to be unsuccessful and to be limited to changes within an existing system — the administrative command model. Even though Gorbachev himself characterized Perestroika as radical economic reform, we noted that this characterization has come to describe reform where all system components are being changed, and indeed where the magnitude of change is great. For example, in the case of Poland (which we examine in Chapter 18), the intention is a full transition from plan to market, along with associated systemic and policy changes. Judged from a Polish perspective, Perestroika of the 1980s might not be viewed as radical economic reform, though as we have noted, events of 1991 may change this posture. What is the nature of Soviet economic reform?

Economic reform in the Soviet Union has been associated with the Perestroika program initiated by Mikhail Gorbachev when he ascended to power in 1985, but Soviet economic reform — or possibly we should say reform attempts — actually began many years earlier in the late 1950s and early 1960s. These earlier reforms were limited in scope, they were designed to improve the existing economic system, and little or no serious effort was made to implement them. In this sense, the beginning of Perestroika did represent a major change in Soviet policy, and quite apart from the problems of implementation, it can be characterized as radical in character. But, in terms of both design and especially implementation, Soviet economic reform through 1991 has been much more limited than the major cases.

When Gorbachev first announced his intent to restructure the administrative command model, he was careful to label his reform radical reform in order to distinguish it from past, half-hearted attempts. From its very beginnings, Perestroika has been fundamentally different from past reform in another important dimension: It combines economic reform with social and political reform — with Glasnost and democratization. Perestroika, Glasnost, and democratization in fact represent major new initiatives in the Soviet Union. What were the forces driving these sorts of changes?

Why Perestroika?

The Soviet leadership of Mikhail Gorbachev embarked on a course of major social, political, and economic reform for a very simple reason: the deteriorating performance of the Soviet economy. The performance of the Soviet economy has long been a serious problem recognized at least in part by Soviet leaders. From its very beginnings, it has failed to provide adequate supplies of high-quality consumer goods and food products. But even more important, there has been a long-term decline in the performance of the Soviet economy, a decline that began in the immediate post-Khrushchev era and continued through the 1980s.[3] Rates of economic growth declined steadily from the 1960s on, and, most troubling, the growth of productivity plummeted. Many economies experience significant variations in rates of economic growth and certainly in productivity growth rates, but the persistence and magnitude of the Soviet decline have been alarming. Indeed, Gorbachev announced his reforms as a cure for the "period of stagnation" (period *zastoia*) that characterized the Brezhnev era (from the mid-1960s to the early 1980s), especially the latter years of this era. How serious were the performance problems, and what were the underlying causes?

Although a variety of different estimates of Soviet economic growth have been developed over the years, there has been surprising agreement on the existence of the slowdown, if not on its precise magnitude.[4]

In short, it became evident that the administrative command system could not, for a variety of reasons, sustain economic growth and, moreover, could not significantly improve the standard of living of the Soviet people. The evidence presented in Table 16.1 dramatically supports this point of view, and even these gloomy data may well understate the magnitude of the economic deterioration. During the era of Glasnost, attempts to reassess Soviet economic data have been made both inside and outside the Soviet Union. Ongoing reevaluations of the rates of change in the Soviet economy and the levels of economic development achieved may lead us to alter some traditional views of long-term Soviet economic performance.

The general decline of Soviet economic performance certainly spurred interest in economic reform, but we may in time discover more fundamental explanations. For example, we need to understand what drove a particular leader at a particular time to disavow the administrative command economy.

After all, economic malaise was not peculiar to the Gorbachev or the immediately pre-Gorbachev era, and earlier reforms had apparently failed. In addition, we must attempt to understand why the Soviet economy was apparently unable to adjust to new circumstances. Put another way, why was it apparently unable to move away from an extensive towards an intensive pattern of resource use?

From its inception, the Gorbachev reform was political as well as economic — a critical difference between Perestroika and earlier Soviet attempts at economic reform. The political side of the reform has already had monumental irreversible effects, both within the Soviet Union and in the countries of Eastern Europe. As we emphasized in Chapter 1, both 1990 and 1991 have been pivotal years. The Soviet empire dissolved, as one East European country after another underwent both political and economic change in an effort to break with the political and economic past. Indeed, the Soviet Union has itself undergone dramatic change as the former republics of Latvia, Lithuania, and Estonia achieve full independence, other republics declare intentions of sovereignty and efforts proceed to define a new union.

Finally, as compellingly as the evidence presented in Table 16.1 may support economic reform, it nevertheless leaves us unable to identify the root causes of failing economic performance. A careful reading of Chapter 15 and an understanding of the administrative command model can provide some general answers. The Soviet economy seems to have grown increasingly complex, until it could not be directed by a relatively simple planning mechanism. In addition, it proved ever more difficult to establish appropriate "rules of the game" capable of promoting rational resource allocation, at both microeconomic and macroeconomic levels, in a system where price and other information signals

Table 16.1 Soviet Economic Growth: The Background to Perestroika

	Average annual rate of growth				
	1966–70	1971–75	1976–80	1981–85	1986
Gross national product[a]	4.9	3.0	1.9	1.8	4.1
Per capita consumption[b]	4.9	3.0	1.8	n.a.	−0.1
Gross national product less agriculture & services	6.0	5.3	2.2	1.9	2.0
Factor productivity	.4	.3	−1.6	−1.1	−0.7
Manhours	2.5	3.0	.8	1.3	1.4
Capital	−1.3	−2.1	−3.7	−3.2	−2.6

[a]Measured by sector of origin at factor cost in 1982 prices.
[b]Measured in 1982 established prices.

Source: Directorate of Intelligence, *Handbook of Economic Statistics 1990* (Washington, D.C.: CIA, 1990), Tables 32, 36, and 39.

grew less and less appropriate. Moreover, as we have emphasized, the command model seemed unable to implement the technological change critical for sustaining economic growth. These are some of the basic forces underlying the slowdown in the growth of the Soviet economy.

Precedents to Perestroika

The process of economic reform in the Soviet Union did not begin with Perestroika, and in light of the failure of earlier reform attempts, it seems appropriate to examine them briefly.[5]

Economic reform in the Soviet Union really began in the late 1950s and early 1960s when suggestions for changes in the guidance of enterprises were promulgated by the Soviet economist Evsei Liberman.[6] At this early stage, the discussion of reform was limited and dealt with partial solutions. It focused on the rules governing enterprise operations in the context of a planned economy. The intent was to find fewer and better "success indicators" so that enterprises operating in the administrative command model would be able to improve their overall performance, meeting output targets, reducing costs, guaranteeing product mix, improving quality, and utilizing "hidden reserves."

The objective of early reform was to improve the way enterprises made decisions within the plan framework, but very little attention was paid to the environment in which enterprises operated and the variables used in making decisions, such as prices. Though managers were encouraged to make "better" decisions, scant attention was paid to fundamental matters such as property rights, market resource allocation, freedom of contract, and mechanisms of price formation, all of which are critical to the development of an appropriate decision-making framework.

The Liberman discussion of the late 1950s and early 1960s found official expression in the Kosygin reforms of 1965, a program named after Alexei Kosygin, prime minister of the Soviet Union during the early years of the Brezhnev regime. These reforms focused on simplifying the rules of guiding enterprises and on improving enterprise performance. The 1965 reform reduced the number of centrally set plan targets, gave enterprises limited authority to accumulate funds to be used for incentive purposes, and tried to improve product quality by emphasizing sales targets over production targets.

As with most early reforms of socialist systems, it was difficult to discover whether reform programs were in fact implemented. However, by the late 1960s, it had become evident to both Western and Soviet observers that the reform was "dead." In spite of formal announcements of the implementation of reform, precious little had changed. Moreover, many of the minor alterations of the planned system were reversed in the early 1970s.

Although the Kosygin reforms of 1965 did little to change the Soviet economic system, there were a number of announcements of reforms of the management and planning system in the years thereafter, especially in the late 1970s. Whereas the Liberman and Kosygin proposals had sought to deal, in a cautious way, with decentralization and management motivation, the reform proposals of the 1970s and early 1980s aimed at making planning more effective. Considerable attention was paid to computerization of planning, to standardization of quality, and to the elusive search for better success indicators for enterprise managers. The emphasis remained on adjustment in levels of decision making, on organizational change, and on changes in the nature of authority and responsibility vested in enterprise management. Price reform was discussed, but Soviet arrangements for price formation remained unchanged. The command system was retained, and once again, minimal attention was given to changing the character of decision-making tools.

THE PHASES OF PERESTROIKA

We have emphasized that prior to the onset of Perestroika in 1985, attempts to reform the Soviet economy had been partial in nature and were never combined with political and/or social change. Indeed, many of these reform programs were probably just not implemented. Thus even though the initial changes of the Perestroika era were far from radical in terms of their basic economic content, their combination with political and social change presented a new picture of Soviet economic reform. And yet, for the most part, the new ideas being espoused, as with earlier reform attempts, were resisted by those responsible for implementing reform, Soviet economic bureaucrats.[7] It is not surprising, then, that Gorbachev's strong rhetoric and the combination of economic reform with political change caught observers off guard. In the early phase of Perestroika, proposed changes seemed to be little more than extensions of previous flirtations with reform. In the beginning, Perestroika applied traditional and partial remedies, but as these remedies failed, more radical and comprehensive solutions were sought.

The Perestroika reform experience (to date) can be divided into four general phases.

The First Phase: Minor Tinkering

In phase 1, from 1985 to 1987, Gorbachev spoke of radical economic reform yet little was done. General reform principles were enunciated — decentralization of decision making, increased emphasis on the human factor, and a general speeding up (*uskorenie*) of the economy through democratization and the infusion of Western capital. An anti-alcohol campaign was initiated, changes were announced in the administrative hierarchy, and quality control was to be a major thrust in industry. Despite a growing consensus on the need to eliminate the administrative command system, critics during this early era could point to the absence of a comprehensive plan to change prevailing institutional mechanisms. In short, these early years were exciting from a political and social perspective, but there was no complete program of economic reform. There seemed to be no intention of changing the economic system let alone major components of the system.

The first phase of Perestroika seemed to be characterized by the naive belief that the problems of the administrative command system could be corrected easily. It was assumed that a reshuffling of investment priorities, improvements in human factors, and a loosening of central controls would lead to a resurgence of Soviet economic growth.

The Second Phase: Reform Legislation

Phase 2 of the Soviet reform experience seemed to answer the critics who pointed to the lack of a fundamental reform program. During this second phase, Soviet reformers began putting in place the legislative acts upon which the economic reform would be based. In June of 1987, the Central Committee of the Communist Party approved the basic decree (*osnovnoe polosheniia*) of the economic reform.[8] Thereafter, a series of decrees were passed to define what would ultimately be the essence of Perestroika. At the heart of these decrees was the Law on Enterprise approved in the summer of 1987.[9] The enterprise law and other laws pertaining to key areas such as foreign trade, joint ventures, and taxation were designed to lay the legislative foundations of Perestroika. Although one could argue that these decrees did not really constitute a comprehensive program, there was widespread agreement that at last Gorbachev was making serious proposals that addressed critical weaknesses in the Soviet economic system.

Under the 1987 enterprise law, Soviet enterprises were to become self-financing, semi-independent production units enjoying new autonomy but at the same time were to remain under a system of state guidance. Enterprises were to operate on a "full self-financing" basis (*polny khozrashchet*), which meant that enterprises that failed to cover their costs would go bankrupt and could no longer count on automatic state subsidies to enable them to continue operations. If implemented, this would be a major departure from past practices.

Officials in the planning commission and industrial ministries continued to have regulatory power over the enterprise in a number of dimensions, but state orders (*zakazy*) were to replace plan directives. The implication here was that the state would purchase goods and services from those enterprises that offered good quality and low cost, though the potential magnitude of state orders remained unclear. Moreover, wholesale markets were to be established for the purchase of inputs. Enterprises were to have increased authority to enter into direct contracts with suppliers and purchasers, bypassing the state supply agencies. Management was to be elected by a collective of workers, a reform that introduced democracy into the work place.

Although there was to be considerable autonomy in the disbursement of enterprise funds, the state retained a number of indirect controls, the most important being controls over prices and foreign economic relations. Previous reforms had failed to deal with the contradiction between administratively set prices and managerial autonomy, the latter implying that prices would be used in the managerial decision-making process.[10] The 1987 decrees envisioned a mix of administrative and market pricing. Price reform was to take place in two stages, beginning in 1988 and to be substantially complete by 1991. Some prices were to remain controlled, especially in cases where the supplier had monopoly power. Other prices were to be set by contracts according to market forces. However, the prices that would result would be far from market prices.[11] As we shall see, significant price reform remained a major stumbling block in the implementation of Perestroika in this and in later stages.

Enterprise guidance is a critical aspect of any economic system. This is the reason that so much attention is given to this issue in the Soviet context. However, while these new enterprise regulations are major departures from past Soviet practices, they nevertheless represent far less than the changes being implemented in Poland and Hungary. This is why Perestroika, from an economic point of view, is less than radical in character. Moreover, as we will note later, it remains to be understood the way in which these past components of Perestroika might be translated into new reform measures in local political units of the post-coup era. One could argue that the directions of change will be sustained, though in many cases the speed of change is likely to be more rapid and possibly more uneven among various regions.

Wage reform was also to be a basic component of Perestroika.[12] There were to be both systemic and policy changes. In essence, Gorbachev argued that after many years of leveling, wage differentials should be increased, especially differentials in base rates. According to the original legislation, wage increases would be limited by the growth of productivity, the latter being intended to grow more rapidly than the former. Wage differentiation would come about through greater enterprise autonomy in the establishment of wage rates, but the emphasis was to be on generating wage funds from enterprise revenues, not through grants from the state budget. New emphasis was to be placed on strengthening institutions concerned with displaced workers. Wage flexibility was seen as fundamental to the "human factor," and Gorbachev emphasized the need for significant increases in labor productivity. These changes would also represent a major departure from past practices.

There were to be changes in the sphere of capital investment, but more from a policy perspective than in terms of systemic changes. As Perestroika unfolded, it became evident that Gorbachev was willing to change long-standing capital allocation priorities and to place greater emphasis on the consumer sector at the expense of the military and of heavy industry. At the same time, he emphasized the modernization of existing but outmoded industrial capacity rather than the traditional Soviet practice of expanding capacity by building new plants and acquiring new equipment.

A great deal of attention has been paid to the enterprise law — and rightly so. It is a fundamental document that addresses the most important aspects of socialist economic reform: the nature of enterprise guidance and the relationships between enterprises and the myriad of organizations they must deal with.

In June of 1990, a new enterprise law was passed, to take effect in January of 1991. This law spells out many basic details of enterprise existence, but it also limits their size, in terms of numbers of employees, by type of economic activity. This aspect of the legislation, along with other decrees on de-monopolization, is designed to address the issue of industrial structure in the post-command Soviet economy.

Finally, the enterprise law of 1990 provided guarantees to enterprises regardless of their particular form of property, an important consideration in light of the new property law discussed below.

Beyond the basic changes contained in the enterprise law, additional decrees focused on a number of other important areas of the economy. In late 1986, the Law on Cooperatives legalized a variety of private activities that had previously been part of the underground second economy. The Law on Cooperatives opened the way for significant expansion of local initiative under the rubric of the cooperative form of organization. The Law on Cooperatives sought to promote the formation of small, service-oriented companies. Cooperatives were to be kept small by restrictions on hired labor, and the workers in the cooperative had to be members of the cooperative, not hired employees. These size limitations, it was felt, would limit the exodus of workers from state enterprises where pay and working conditions were less attractive than those in cooperatives. Although there has been some retrenchment in the powers given to the cooperative sector, these essentially private enterprises contribute a small but increasing share of output. Again, we can expect variations at the local level.

In March of 1990, new legislation on ownership was passed. This legislation, though likely to vary at the republic level, provides for a variety of different ownership arrangements, including public and individual ownership, though the latter is circumscribed and does not include, for example, land. This legislation will undoubtedly be modified over time as new political realities are expressed in legislation, but it has provided the underpinnings for a variety of new organizational forms in the Soviet economy, such as collective ownership, joint stock ownership, and ownership through a workers' collective. The law also envisages reduction of state ownership as a form of property associated with the command economy. This reduction is to take place slowly through decentralization of control, a process described in Soviet literature as de-statification as opposed to de-nationalization.[13]

As we emphasized in Chapters 2 and 3, ownership arrangements or property rights are a critical component of any economic system. Soviet attitudes towards new ownership arrangements, at least as represented by the views of Mikhail Gorbachev and legislation of the early Gorbachev years, have been quite conservative, especially when compared to the nature and pace of privatization taking place in Poland and Hungary. Through the 1980s, the critical relationship between private property, markets, and market signals such as prices does not seem to have been appreciated in the Soviet reform setting. Here again, we find a major reason to emphasize that from an economic perspective and when compared to reform programs in the advanced East

European cases, Perestroika of the 1980s was less than radical economic reform.

To the extent that new political realities lead to the decentralization of political and economic power, these changes along with possible attitude changes at the central leadership level may lead to more innovative developments in property arrangements at the local level. We might also expect greater regional variation in both the nature and the pace of change.

In 1986 and thereafter, a number of decrees were passed to change the organizational arrangements and policies of the foreign trade sector. The new foreign trade regulations addressed many of the impediments to foreign trade that we noted in our discussion of the administrative command system in Chapter 12. First, the foreign trade hierarchy was simplified and the monopoly of the Ministry of Foreign Trade was ended. In 1986 the role of the Ministry of Foreign Trade had been reduced and largely replaced by the State Committee for Foreign Economic Relations. A new organization, the State Foreign Economic Commission, was created, and the Bank for Foreign Trade became the new Bank for Foreign Economic Affairs. Specifically, enterprises were granted the right to enter directly into foreign trade with foreign firms. Foreign trade banking arrangements were liberalized to facilitate trade with the West. Firms that earned foreign exchange were to be allowed to retain part of their earnings to self-finance their foreign operations independently of the state foreign trade monopoly. In 1988 the Ministry of Foreign Trade was abolished, and its functions were taken over by the USSR Ministry of Foreign Economic Relations.

In addition to changes in the foreign trade arrangements, new legislation facilitated joint ventures between Soviet enterprises and foreign enterprises. Although the new joint venture laws at first restricted foreign ownership rights, the distribution of profits, and the like, subsequent legislation substantially liberalized many of the initial provisions.[14] By the late 1980s, joint venture laws permitted majority Western ownership and in some cases complete Western ownership. A major problem limiting the potential for joint ventures — and an issue remaining to be discussed in subsequent transition programs — was the thorny issue of ruble convertibility.[15] Under new post-coup arrangements, it is likely that these directions of change will continue, at least under any sort of new, even loose, union arrangements.

The Perestroika program also addressed one of the weakest points of the Soviet administrative command system, agriculture. Early reform proposals in agriculture were significant in scope but ultimately were limited in application and benefit, at least for the remainder of the 1980s. Just as in the past, initial reform in the agricultural sector seemed to focus on organizational change and the level of decision making. Gorbachev sought to improve the integration of the Soviet food complex by creating in 1985 a "super-ministry" for agriculture: the State Committee of the Agro-Industrial Complex, or Gosagroprom. The creation of Gosagroprom represented a continuation of past Soviet reform tendencies to try to resolve fundamental economic problems by means of organizational changes, especially those contained in the "Food Program" of 1982. Gosagroprom was created to serve as an overall supervisor of the agricultural sector and, in particular, to solve problems of coordination at the local level through the earlier-created RAPOs (raion agricultural production organizations). These organizations did not function effectively and were phased out in 1989, to be replaced by other organizational arrangements such as the *agrokombinat*, the agro-firm, and the agro-association.[16]

Like earlier attempts to solve problems through organizational reshuffling, the Gosagroprom experiment was a failure. The agricultural "superministry" was abolished at the union level in 1989 and replaced by the State Commission for Food and Procurement.

A second major reform of agriculture has been the largely unsuccessful attempt to introduce lease contracting. Begun with the collective contract brigade in the early Gorbachev years, the concept of leasing was formalized in legislation introduced toward the end of the 1980s.[17] The essence of this type of change was a fundamental reorientation of the relationship between peasant and superior, especially with regard to systems of rewards. Specifically, the objective has been to link effort and reward more closely, first with a contractual arrangement and then with a lease arrangement. The fundamental idea was to allow farm members to lease farm assets for a rental charge. The land leases could be long-term (50 years), and the lease could be passed on in the form of inheritance. Although various types of contractual arrangements are apparently quite widely used, the same cannot be said for lease arrangements.

In early 1990, important new land legislation was passed. This legislation does not resolve the issue of private ownership as such, though it does permit a variety of new organizational arrangements in the countryside. This legislation, which also permits local variation, will undoubtedly be modified over time and will result in significant regional variations. These variations will be of special importance insofar as power is shifted to local levels.

Though it was of limited application in the early 1990s, the concept of leasing, in conjunction with the new land legislation, may prove important in the future. Leasing circumvents ideological restrictions on the private ownership of land but can also be a close substitute for private ownership, particularly when combined with the right of inheritance. Unfortunately, the initial impact of leasing was minimal. Leasing rules were complex, and few knew how the terms of a lease should be established. Moreover, traditional problems emerged, such as the absence of markets for the purchase of inputs to be used on the leased land, mistrust of the arrangements on the part of peasants, and limited interest in new initiatives that would have to be undertaken by an aging rural population accustomed to income security in state and collective farms.

The potential benefits of leasing arrangements remain to be achieved in the Soviet case. However, for a variety of understandable reasons, leasing has not become widespread. Much of the responsibility for leasing is local, yet local officials lack the skills necessary to develop and implement local arrangements. Even with such skills, the practical appeal of leasing might be limited in a setting of continuing political uncertainty facing a rural population not accustomed to local initiative. New power sharing arrangements may reduce elements of uncertainty, though regional differences in the application of leasing arrangements will be important, that is assuming that a far more radical transformation to private ownerships arrangements is not envisioned.

A major and long-standing problem in Soviet agriculture has been the system of product distribution. Gorbachev has emphasized the need to improve processing equipment and distribution arrangements in agriculture, especially transport, storage, processing, and packaging. There is no evidence, however, that the distribution system has improved. A possible exception is the apparent use of military facilities to manufacture agricultural processing equipment, which has presumably given that effort a high priority and the advantage of a technologically more advanced sector. A number of functions of the ministry governing food processing have been transferred to the defense sector, and additional deliveries of food processing equipment have been promised. Since the summer of 1991, distribution issues have moved to center stage. With the demise of the command economy but an absence of new distribution mechanisms and arrangements, there is a widespread perception that distribution, especially for food products, has become less reliable and more uneven. This has become an issue in discussions of U.S. aid.

We have spoken of several organizational changes; there have been important policy changes as well. At the forefront of policy changes is a new emphasis on "intensive technology," especially the use of more and better off-farm inputs such as chemical fertilizers; increased financial discipline for farms; and price reforms to reduce the role of subsidies in the agricultural sector.

In spite of these and related reform proposals, agricultural performance remains mixed, and problems such as distribution bring daily attention to the sorry state of Soviet agriculture.

The Third Phase: Creating Rules of Implementation

Despite continuing discussion and the development of several variants of reform plans (which we examine below), Perestroika did not enter the third phase prior to the coup attempt of August 1991. As we have emphasized, changed political realities are likely approaches to economic reform, though movement towards the market is likely to be sustained along with the development of appropriate transition policies. Indeed as we shall see, the latter are essential if more serious economic consequences (greater declines in output, more rapid price increases, more serious unemployment and the like) are to be avoided.

Market allocation cannot be superimposed on an existing administrative command economy. It requires appropriate "rules of the game," such as contract enforcement, well-defined ownership rights, freedom of price setting, and the like. Market allocation requires "modern" economic institutions, such as a modern tax system and a commercial banking system regulated by a central bank.[18] The enterprise law, the joint venture law, and other laws of Perestroika can be effective only when the market "rules of the game" are understood and uniformly applied in commercial dealings.

The Fourth Phase: Economic Reform In the Post-Coup Era

As we have already emphasized, the events of August 1991 have dramatically changed both the political and the economic setting. While it is unlikely that future economic reform will begin from first principles, nevertheless political realities, even with the existence of a central government and some sort of all-union arrangements, will dictate the existence of substantial decision making authority and responsibility at local levels. What could such arrangements mean for the future of economic reform?

Assuming reasonable political stability and a loose federation of some type, it is likely that reform will continue, though with substantial differentials from one region to another as local legislation reflects local preferences and possibilities. Although we might view this as delayed implementation of the third stage of Perestroika (creating the rules of implementation), it is better viewed as a new stage. Clearly there will not be a simple continuation of past reforms, though to understand future directions, it is useful to examine the essence of reform discussion prior to the coup attempt of August 1991. Thereafter, we examine the current state of the Soviet economy and discuss likely future reform scenarios.

Put another way, it is one thing to develop a reform program that relies on market-type scarcity prices and quite another to spell out the means by which these prices will be established. The rules that will make this transition possible must be developed and implemented.

Although Soviet reformers have paid lip service to the need to create market institutions, promises of implementation have been vague, and timetables have not been set. Implementation requires the Soviet leadership to address the most fundamental issues that define the nature of the economic and political system — property rights, civil law, and the separation of economic and political functions: broadly speaking, the issue of privatization. The defining of property rights is the most sensitive issue of all. It determines the distribution of wealth and power in society and, in the Soviet context, fundamentally alters one of the cornerstones of the Soviet economic system.

THE TRANSITION PLAN: SHOCK THERAPY VERSUS GRADUALISM

Although there appears to have been a reasonable consensus on the long-term objectives of Perestroika, agreement on the strategy of the transition from plan to market has proved elusive.[19] All sides in the debate appear to take advantage of the benefits of market allocation and the unleashing of private initiative. All sides also envisioned, in the name of efficiency, a reduction in the amount of state intervention in the affairs of enterprises. And yet, resistance to change has been persistent.

In examining the discussion of Soviet economic reform, it is useful to think of participants as representing a spectrum of ideas on implementation, ranging from the gradualists (implement reform slowly) through the shock therapists (implement comprehensive reforms quickly). The gradualists, as represented by the Soviet economic bureaucracy entrenched in state committees, in ministries, and in the party, have argued for a gradual transition. These arguments appeared in the official reforms proposals put forward by the Council of Ministers, headed by Nikolai Ryzhkov, who was prime minister from 1985 until early 1991. A gradual transition, it has been argued, would limit the transition costs in the form of unemployment, income redistribution, and inflation.

Specifically, a comprehensive state "industrial policy" would be required to guide the economy through the transition. Subsidies should be withdrawn gradually from retail prices and from unprofitable enterprises; credit should be granted on the basis of administrative decisions rather than anticipated rates of return; the state should attempt to create a more competitive economy before abandoning it to the forces of market allocation. The state should continue to control strategic industries through output and supply planning, and privatization would proceed slowly.

The gradualists argue that considerable preparation is required before allocation can be turned over to the market. In particular, macro-imbalances must be corrected before markets can work. The state budget deficit must be brought under control, and the excess purchasing power of the population has to be dissipated. Thus, in addition to bringing about reform, the policies of the transition period must be carefully developed and implemented to limit the costs of the transition.

The "shock therapy" advocates, such as Boris Yeltsin, maintain that gradualism will yield the worst of both worlds. The failure to create new market institutions and the continuation of traditional administrative methods will send inappropriate signals to system participants and will probably result in economic chaos. An economy cannot be half planned and half market; it must be either fish or fowl. Until resources are allocated primarily in response to market forces, those who favor administrative methods will be in a position to impede further progress.

The "shock therapy" advocates point to the apparent successes of the Polish experiment, wherein Poland moved swiftly to a market economy. Lines have disappeared, unemployment has risen but not disastrously, inflation increased but was brought under control, and the power of the administrative bureaucracy has been decimated. Of course, as we noted in Chapter 4 and will reemphasize in Chapter 18, the environment for economic reform in Poland is very different from that prevailing in the Soviet Union.[20]

Perestroika: What Has Happened?

We have argued that it has always been difficult to measure to what degree economic reform has been formally implemented in the Soviet Union, let alone to assess the impact of that reform on the general performance of the economy. The case with Perestroika is no different, though its combination with Glasnost at least enables us to hear the frequent complaints of the Soviet consumer. Although there has certainly been change in the economy, the results thus far have been unsatisfactory from the perspective of performance.

The growth of output and productivity have continued to fall (Table 16.2), though there have been considerable year-to-year fluctuations. Lines for buying goods have continued to grow. Widespread rationing has had to be initiated. Leasing arrangements have not expanded significantly in agriculture, and although private economic activity has expanded, the cooperative sector remains limited and is viewed by many with skepticism.[21] Rather than focusing on production, cooperatives have turned to intermediation and speculation, often diverting low-priced goods from state channels for sale at high prices in the cooperative sector. Viewed with disdain by the Soviet population, such practices undermine popular support for market-type reforms.[22]

The ultimate rejection of economic reform by bureaucratic forces found expression in the coup attempt of August 19, 1991. However, there are a variety of fundamental reasons for the limited effectiveness of Perestroika as it developed through the 1980s.

As we have emphasized throughout our discussion of economic reform, the process of reform is far more difficult than most imagine. The Soviet experience clearly supports this view.

Table 16.2 The Soviet Economy Under Perestroika

	Average annual rate of growth				
	1986	1987	1988	1989	1990
Gross national product[a]	4.1	.3	2.2	1.4	−2.0
Per capita consumption[b]	−2.1	0.4	3.0	3.2	
Consumer price index: (1980 = 100)	111.0	116.0	119.0	122.0	139.0
Soviet exports[c]	97.0	107.7	110.7	109.3	104.1
Soviet imports[c]	88.9	96.0	107.3	114.7	120.9
Net hard-currency debt[d]	20.9	26.4	26.8	36.1	45.4

[a] GNP is measured by sector of origin at factor cost in 1982 prices.
[b] 1982 established prices.
[c] Includes all trade, in billions of current U.S. dollars.
[d] Gross debt minus assets in Western banks, in billions of current U.S. dollars.

Source: Directorate of Intelligence, *Handbook of Economic Statistics 1990* (Washington, D.C.: CIA, 1990), and *Beyond Perestroika: The Soviet Economy in Crisis* (Washington, D.C.: CIA, 1991).

First, it is quite clear that after political change has taken place, political stability is a necessary condition for successful economic reform.[23] The political system in the Soviet Union, just as elsewhere in socialist countries, has been in a state of continuing flux. The critical issues of republic–federal relations were unresolved prior to the coup attempt and remain fundamentally unresolved. Clearly the nature of any federation and the nature of shared power among remaining republics (excluding Latvia, Lithuania, and Estonia) is critical. The very makeup of the Soviet Union remains uncertain. Will the USSR break up into independent units? Will secession beyond the Baltics be allowed? It is difficult to define the process of reform before answering these basic political questions. Moreover, in a period of political uncertainty, it is important to relate possible political configurations to the varying reform scenarios in an effort to discover in what ways, and to what degree, political and economic harmony can be achieved and sustained. However we may ultimately assess the Polish experiment, differences between the Polish and Soviet cases argue strongly against the "shock therapy" approach in the Soviet Union, at least as the Soviet Union has been defined in the past.

Second, although many have argued that the original legislation designed to represent Perestroika constituted a reasonably comprehensive economic reform program, major and critical components of the original plan were not implemented, even in cases where additional and modifying legislation had been introduced. For example, price reform has been postponed, and much more important, the most likely basis of price formation in a market context — the issue of private property — remains unresolved (legislation in 1990 did broaden the scope of private economic activity). The promised liberalization of foreign trade has yet to materialize, because centralized controls on foreign exchange earnings have been reimposed. The freedom of enterprises to set contractual prices has been challenged. These issues are only complicated by the political uncertainty.

Third, the sequencing of reform has proved difficult. Enterprise decision making cannot be decentralized, because there is virtually no market structure in which enterprises can function. Market mechanisms are largely absent. Foreign businesses have been very slow to enter into joint ventures with the Soviet Union, and those that have done so proceeded slowly and achieved limited results. Again, sequencing and implementation may be a problem. Although the ruble has been devalued, changes designed to effect convertibility of the ruble have not been made, and the lack of ruble convertibility is a critical problem in spite of forward-looking legislation in the area of joint ventures. (Here, Soviet experience is quite different from that in Eastern Europe.) Numerous examples of non-harmonious sequencing and implementation exist. Agricultural reform and the improvement of food supplies (a frequent target of reforms) have been largely absent, resulting in a steady worsening of shortages in the Soviet Union and especially in Soviet cities. For the average Soviet citizen, Perestroika has resulted in a steady reduction in standard of living.

Fourth, the pace of economic reform may well have been inappropriate, and the fundamental difficulties of reform less than fully recognized. Again, key areas of change (price reform, for example) have been delayed. In other areas, such as privatization, there has been no substantive plan to proceed toward fundamental changes in ownership arrangements, let alone to ponder the contours of any market that might result from privatization. Frequently it is difficult to pinpoint the reasons for delay, but no doubt they include political instability, lack of clarity in the specification of reform alternatives, and generalized fear of change.

Fifth, although it is difficult to assess the extent to which Soviet leaders in fact remain committed to radical reform, the difficulties and delays of the first five years should give us pause. It is quite clear that from an equity point of view, the marketization of a previously socialist command economy is destined to alter distributional arrangements in fundamental ways. It is not clear whether Soviet leaders (let alone Soviet citizens) are fully committed to such changes. Most would seem to want to have the efficiency the market offers without jeopardizing the equity of socialist policies, although Mikhail Gorbachev may have changed his views on the latter since the summer of 1991. Soviet consumer hostility to high prices in the private sector does not bode will for future, more general price changes. In an economy where much in the consumer sector is subsidized, the issues are far wider than the well-known cases of retail food prices alone.

Finally, all sides in the reform debate have recognized that marketization will fundamentally alter power relationships. The close link between power and control of resources is evident in the skirmishes that have taken place on a daily basis in the Soviet Union over control of building permits, oil export licenses, prices, and so on. Under the administrative command system, the power of the Communist party derived, to a great extent, from its ability to control resources and the benefits resulting from the use of those resources. If resources are allocated as the impersonal forces of the market dictate, entrenched bureaucratic power will disappear. Those who have held power and benefited from it are not likely to relinquish that power quickly, nor will they be willing to shift it to others under new rules of the game. Reform discussions of the latter part of 1990 and early 1991 demonstrated that wide variations of opinion and belief persist in the Soviet Union.

Perestroika: The Reform Options of the 1990s

In the early years of Perestroika, Soviet economic performance seemed to rebound somewhat. Moreover, as the legislative content of Perestroika unfolded, there was widespread agreement that the reform program would take time to implement. In his early speeches, Gorbachev envisioned slower economic growth in the early stages of Perestroika, to be replaced by faster growth in the 1990s. Economic growth in 1986 was good, and though there were significant declines in 1987 and 1988, optimism about performance in the remainder of the decade prevailed. However, this optimism proved unwarranted. By 1989 it was clear that the economy was in deep trouble. In addition to growing ethnic and regional discontent sapping labor productivity, shortages of consumer goods worsened, unemployment increased, and inflation continued to rise in the face of growing budget deficits. Although available data on many of these issues may not be wholly accurate, Western estimates of the late 1980s suggested a rising inflation rate (though it was under 5 percent annually) and a growing budget deficit estimated at roughly 10 percent of GNP, some five times that of the United States in percentage terms.

Many argued that the Soviet economy was on a downhill course for one major reason: The administrative command system of earlier years was gradually but surely being eroded, but nothing was taking its place. In effect, the Soviet economy was rapidly becoming a system without guidance. Surveys from the late 1980s reveal that there has indeed been a substantial increase in enterprise autonomy — in all areas except price formation and foreign economic relations. And there was a parallel decline in the central authority of the industrial ministries and state committees.[24]

Soviet enterprises gained autonomy before market institutions have been created to impose a new form of discipline on them. The result has been chaos. Enterprises refused to fulfill state orders or carry out supply plans. The cement that held the traditional system together — command and discipline — eroded. The cement of the new system — profit motivation, flexible prices, and contract enforcement — was not put in place.

Throughout 1989, a series of policy steps were taken in an effort to stabilize the economy. A basic strategy was established to cut state expenditures in traditional areas such as defense and to shift spending to the consumer sector. With shortages of consumer goods persisting, rationing was introduced in 1990, especially in large cities. The Soviet ruble was devalued for tourist expenditures.

In a drastic step, the new government of Prime Minister Pavlov (the former finance minister) announced in early 1991 a monetary reform that withdrew 50- and 100-ruble notes from circulation, thereby further undermining faith in the ruble. This monetary reform was designed to punish speculators who had accumulated large denominations of rubles, but it introduced chaos into the already confused Soviet banking system. Moreover, many outraged Soviet citizens complained that such policies eliminated personal savings accumulated over long periods of time.

In 1990, as we have emphasized, there was a great deal of new legislation passed. In addition to the land law we discussed, there were new tax laws and a new set of banking arrangements, including the creation of an independent central bank.

It is clear that as the decade of the 1980s came to an end, Perestroika as it had been defined was not working. But the attempt at stabilization through policy imperatives did not bring the discussion to an end.

The Two Plans: Transition Proposals

In the spring of 1990, major new legislation pertaining to property rights seemed to bring state dominance to an end. In addition, a transition plan was submitted to the Supreme Soviet by Soviet Prime Minister Nikolai Ryzhkov.

Moreover, amid continuing discussion and debate, two prominent reform economists, Nikolai Petrakov and Stanislav Shatalin, joined the Gorbachev team, possible signaling a more aggressive movement toward the market, a strategy very different from that advocated by Ryzkov. The task of the Shatalin group was to combine the Ryzkov plan with a plan announced by Boris Yeltsin and to come up with a new plan to present to the Supreme Soviet in the fall of 1990.

By the fall of 1990, two major plans surfaced.[25] The Shatalin plan (a document similar to an earlier Yeltsin 500-day plan) was produced by the team of Gorbachev advisors under the leadership of Stanislav Shatalin. A second plan, the Ryzkov plan, was presented essentially as a slower variant of the Shatalin plan. Both were designed to move the Soviet economy toward a market system, but at different rates and in somewhat different ways. In October of 1990, Gorbachev presented the Soviet Parliament with a "presidential plan" that was basically a variant of the Shatalin plan modified by Abel Aganbegian, a well-known Soviet economist. This plan was similar to the Shatalin plan but was much more limited in scope and lacked the timetable for implementation. This document, along with special powers granted to Gorbachev to implement the transition, became the operational basis for decision making as 1990 drew to an end.

These plans quickly came to represent what appeared to have been absent: a framework for transition. They also included changes not fully addressed in early Perestroika legislation, and in this sense they represented progress in the third stage of Perestroika. It is important, therefore, to put these plans in perspective, bearing in mind that the Shatalin plan, substantially modified, became the presidential plan ultimately adopted in October of 1990 to become operative on November 1 of that year.

Both the Shatalin and the Ryzkov plans envisioned a transition to markets based on private property — that is, privatization. However, although market-determined, flexible prices are emphasized, both plans allow exceptions (in areas such as raw materials, for example). The two plans differed considerably in their views of implementation. In the Shatalin plan, a strict and phased schedule was established, whereas in the Ryzkov plan, the period of transition was much more vague. Though both plans acknowledged macro-management and stabilization as functions of the central government, they differed in the details. Both agreed on the general objectives of economic growth, stability, and regional equality. Possibly the most important difference between the two plans was in the fundamental issue of center–periphery relations, ironic in light of subsequent developments. Both supported a division of powers and responsibilities, but Ryzkov envisioned greater central authority and Shatalin, much greater decentralization.[26]

What were the prospects for implementing the presidential (revised Shatalin) plan? Unfortunately, the political issues of center–periphery relations and the accompanying ethnic strife sapped Gorbachev's power to engineer change. Continuing pre-emancipation difficulties in the Baltic, combined with the resignations of key Gorbachev advisors, also weakened Gorbachev's power to implement radical reform. In December of 1990, Edward A. Shevardnadze, the widely respected Soviet foreign minister, resigned, expressing regret about the growing centralization of power in the Soviet Union. Later, in the summer of 1991, he would lead a new reform party in opposition to the Communist party. Thereafter, in January of 1991, Gorbachev called for suspension of laws providing freedom of press, and Stanislav Shatalin, author of the 500-day economic reform plan, along with others, resigned from the Gorbachev advisory sphere (they continue to speak out on the critical issues involved in the transition).

Finally, it is worth emphasizing that although the original Shatalin plan was simplified and modified in important ways, some of the basics remained. Thus the presidential plan specified three stages for the transition.[27] In the first stage (100 days), a voluntary economic union would be created, with a single unified currency, macroeconomic control from the center, but gradual introduction of markets at the local level. A reserve banking system would be established, and state assets would be gradually sold as an initial step toward privatization. Foreign exchange control would be decentralized, but central access to some foreign exchange would be sustained.

In stage 2 (days 100–250), prices would be increased and a fall in output would be expected. Price reform would include consumer protection through minimum wages, indexation of incomes, and the like. There would also be a move to make the ruble convertible.

Finally, in stage 3 (days 250–500), more price reform would be implemented, and expected increases in unemployment would be handled via increased benefits such as severance pay and unemployment insurance. In the final days of this stage, a turnaround in the output of the economy was expected to make possible a substantial reduction in subsidies.

Although change continued in the Soviet Union the issue of developing a reform plan remained fully active in 1991.

THE SOVIET ECONOMY IN THE 1990s

Through the end of the 1980s and into the 1990s, traditional components of the command economy, for example the authority and mechanisms of central planning, were gradually dismantled. At the same time, a plethora of legislative acts defined the contours of new arrangements and policies, yet fell short of committing the Soviet Union to a transition process, as taking place in Eastern Europe. At the same time, concern for failing economic performance often found expression in the reimplementation of controls such that from the perspective of economic reform, a mixed and generally unsatisfactory picture emerged. We have described this picture as the failure to commit to a full transition program. However, as the discussion of reform alternatives continued, the failed coup of August 19 dramatically interrupted the course of events, placing political issues at the forefront of our attention. How will these events impact upon the nature of economic reform?

From an economic perspective, there are three major issues to be considered as we examine possible directions of change in the reform process. First, what is the nature of contemporary Soviet economic performance and how pressing is the need for immediate action? Second, what are the new political realities, to which we have made reference in this chapter? Finally, how will the latter impact upon the former and what will be the resulting nature of the economic reform process?

Performance Issues

Although we have stressed the importance of ongoing reexaminations of Soviet economic data, the evidence of economic decline remains quite strong. In 1989 Soviet gross national product grew by 1.4 percent over 1988.[28] In 1990 GNP declined by 2 percent, and for the first quarter of 1991, the decline was reported to be 8 percent. At the same time, retail prices increased by 14 percent in 1990 and by 24 percent in the first quarter of 1991. Shortages persisted, regional disparities grew wider, and the budget deficit increased. For both 1989 and 1990, aggregate imports exceeded aggregate exports, and with a hard-currency deficit on current account for both years, the Soviet net hard-currency debt increased by roughly $10 billion. In the fall of 1991, Gorbachev made it clear that if the Soviet population was to be adequately fed, large amounts of food aid would be necessary. Most of the developments through 1991 reinforced the need for a comprehensive reform program, a serious and full commitment to that program and possibly most important, transition policies appropriate for both short- and long-term difficulties.

Along with declining economic performance, however, these years have seen continuing systemic and policy changes. As we have already noted, Gorbachev asked for and was granted emergency powers in the fall of 1990. These powers pertain largely to matters of economic stabilization and led to controls on enterprise behavior, new rules for the distribution of food, and the like. In addition, an anti-crisis program was developed in 1991 designed primarily to reinstitute controls in such areas as central–local relations, the limiting of potential strikes, and the provision of benefits such as credits to agriculture. A number of controls were also implemented to limit the growth of budgetary expenditures, while at the same time expanding safety-net measures.

As these measures were implemented, Gorbachev again wrestled with the need for a basic reform plan. In the summer of 1991, amid rumors that he might soon abandon the Communist party, he indicated that he would try to merge two new plans. A radical plan similar to transition plans being implemented in Eastern Europe was proposed by Grigory A. Yavlinsky, a Gorbachev advisor, with assistance from economists in the United States. This plan was to be merged with a much more conservative plan proposed by Soviet Prime Minister Valentin S. Pavlov. In a sense, the Soviet leader, in the summer of 1991, again found himself developing a reform program and seeking a meaningful political base from which to implement it. At the same time, he seemed unwilling to break decisively with the past, seeking instead a middle way. The events of August 1991 could change this posture, possibly resulting in more decisive changes.

The Failed Coup of August 1991:
New Political Realities

On August 19, 1991 a group of hard-line communists staged a coup to replace the leadership of Mikhail Gorbachev and, presumably, to alter and reverse the path of democratization and economic reform in the Soviet Union.[29] However, by August 21 the coup had failed, Gorbachev was returned to power and Boris Yeltsin emerged substantially enhanced in stature as a result of his resistance to coup events. Although only time and careful analysis will allow an in-depth assessment of the impact of these events, it seems likely that the setting for Perestroika will remain fundamentally changed.

On August 25, Gorbachev resigned as head of the Communist party, effectively ending the role of the Communist party in Soviet political and economic affairs.

In early September, The Congress of Peoples Deputies approved the introduction of new government organs bringing the Congress to an end and replacing it with organs whose main constituents would be the republics. Officially a set of interim arrangements, the highest government body became the State Council headed by Gorbachev and composed of the heads of the union republics to deal with foreign affairs, military matters, and law and order.

The highest legislative body became the Supreme Soviet with a Council of the Union and Council of the Republics. In addition, an interrepublic economic committee was created to be responsible for economic reform. Ivan Silayev, the Premier of the Russian Republic, was named to head the committee. Grigory A. Yavlinsky, the author of a plan emphasizing a radical transformation of the Soviet economy towards market forces, was included in the committee.

By the end of August, more than half of the Soviet republics had declared their independence from Moscow. This pattern continued with all republics, except the Russian Republic, seeking some form of autonomy. With Gorbachev struggling to redefine the union, the events of early September effectively shifted major powers to the republic level. The new political arrangements noted above were created and shortly thereafter the new State Council approved independence for Latvia, Lithuania, and Estonia. With the infolding of these dramatic events and the shape of any future union undecided, what might remain of Perestroika?

Economic Reform in the 1990s: The Post-Coup Era

We have emphasized that the setting for economic reform in the Soviet Union has changed in significant ways. Thus, while it is not possible to know the specific contours of reforms which may unfold in future years, it is possible to appreciate the new setting and to do so under the important assumption that some form of union sustains, even with substantially increased powers at the local levels.

First, important forces limiting the nature and the pace of economic reform have been lessened or eliminated. Although one does not remove the results of many years of Communist party domination with a simple legislative act, nevertheless the influence of party forces has been formally removed and informally lessened. At the same time, it is apparent that Gorbachev is now more committed to significant reform, and indeed those in charge of planning such changes are of a similar mind.

Second, to the extent that the forces noted above facilitate the development of a real transition program, regional forces (however they may ultimately be defined in a new union) will be of much greater importance. We have emphasized that decentralization may facilitate the transition process, permitting local variations of both substance and speed. In any new setting, the nature of center-local relations, especially economic relations, will be of great importance.

Third, to the extent that the reform process is decentralized to a substantial degree, important new issues emerge. From the perspective of Soviet Union republics as they are presently defined, vast differences of resource endowment and economic development exist. These differences and the resulting regional income differentials increase the likelihood of conflict over real differences in levels of living. At the same time, regional differentials necessitate careful attention to the rapid development of internal markets. For these markets, both the rules of the game and the infrastructure appropriate for markets must be defined.

Fourth, while the new regional emphasis of reform is being understood, the need for macroeconomic transition policies becomes more pressing. But again, for issues such as the growing budget deficit, transition policies will work only if their formulation and execution take place reasonably quickly and within the context of some agreed upon form of union. These tasks are complex and significant.

In a sense, the Soviet Union has a window of opportunity. Although new challenges have arisen, at the same time, many past obstacles to reform have been removed or weakened. In this context, there is room for optimism.

SUMMARY

1. Like many other planned socialist economic systems, the Soviet Union has attempted economic reform on numerous occasions. However, the advent of Perestroika in the mid-1980s under the leadership of Mikhail Gorbachev signaled more serious, radical economic reform. Not only were the provisions of Perestroika broader and deeper than those of earlier reform attempts, but also Perestroika was to be combined with political and social change under Glasnost.

2. Perestroika, like earlier reform attempts, was motivated by poor economic performance. In the initial years of the Perestroika era, there was no comprehensive program to guide change. However, beginning in 1987 and continuing to the present, there has been a continuing series of important legislative decrees dealing with almost all aspects of the Soviet economic system. In spite of this large body of legislation, the pace and depth of economic reform under Perestroika remained limited through the end of the 1980s.

3. The traditional mechanisms of the Soviet administrative command system have been gradually weakened. But as the old system has eroded, no new system has taken its place. Thus, in the absence of a *comprehensive* reform program to define a new system (including transition policies and a firm commitment to fundamental systemic change), past political instability has limited the impact of partial efforts, and modest stabilization policies and anti-crisis measures have failed to control the excesses of budgetary spending, wage increases, and the like. Moreover, as with earlier reform attempts, there has been a tendency for the partial relaxation of constraints to be followed by the reimposition of controls and regulations.

4. In the early 1990s, there was some improvement in relations between the center and some republics. But Mikhail Gorbachev continued to discuss the formulation of a serious reform (transition) plan while the performance of the economy slipped. In a sense, a race was set in motion: There are limits to the willingness of the Soviet population to tolerate further declines in the standard of living. Stabilization policies must be used to bring macroeconomic variables under control, and serious economic reform must be executed such that adjustment costs can be borne and the recovery of the economy set in motion.

5. Since the dramatic events of August 1991, the setting of economic reform has changed. The Communist party has been effectively eliminated as a political and economic force and new state organs have been established giving substantially increased power to the republics. In this setting, discussion continues on a new union and the issues of economic reform. With market advocates in positions of power and past barriers (especially the Communist party) lessened or eliminated, the potential for radical reform exists, though it is likely to have much greater regional variability than in the past.

NOTES

1. Ed. A. Hewett, *Reforming the Soviet Economy* (Washington, D.C.: Brookings, 1988), p. 12.
2. Ibid., p. 20.
3. For more detail on long-term Soviet economic performance, see Paul R. Gregory and Robert C. Stuart, *Soviet Economic Structure and Performance*, 4th ed. (New York: HarperCollins, 1990), Ch. 12.
4. Directorate of Intelligence, "Revisiting Soviet Economic Performance Under Glasnost: Implications for CIA Estimates," SOV 88-10068, September 1988.
5. *Soviet Economic Structure and Performance*, Ch. 12.

6. There is an extensive literature on economic reform in the Soviet Union, especially on the nature of reform in the 1960s and 1970s. For a discussion of this reform and references to the specialized literature, see *Soviet Economic Structure and Performance*, Part 4.

7. Paul Gregory, *Restructuring the Soviet Economic Bureaucracy* (Cambridge, England: Cambridge University Press, 1989).

8. *Reforming the Soviet Economy*, p. 325.

9. For an excellent discussion of the enterprise law, see Richard E. Ericson, "The New Enterprise Law," The Harriman Institute *Forum*, 1 (February 1988).

10. For a discussion of the complex issue of price reform, see Morris Bornstein, "Problems of Price Reform in the U.S.S.R.," in NATO, Directorate of Economic Affairs, *Soviet Economic Reforms: Implementation Under Way* (Brussels: NATO, 1989), pp. 130–144.

11. Soviet reformers have emphasized the dangers of market pricing in an economy characterized by monopoly power. For an analysis of this thinking, see Heidi Kroll, "Reform and Monopoly in the Soviet Economy," Center for Foreign Policy Development, Brown University, 1990.

12. For a discussion of wage and income issues, see Janet G. Chapman, "Income Distribution and Social Justice in the Soviet Union," *Comparative Economic Studies*, 31 (Spring 1989), 14–45; and Janet G. Chapman, "Gorbachev's Wage Reform," *Soviet Economy*, 4 (1988), 338–365.

13. For a brief summary of new ownership arrangements in the Soviet Union, see Nicoletta Amodio, "Forms of Ownership in the USSR," *Most*, 1 (1991), 114–117.

14. For a discussion of recent developments, see Carl H. McMillan, "Strategy or Tactics? Recent Initiatives in Soviet Foreign Economic Policy," NATO, Directorate of Economic Affairs, *Soviet Economic Reforms: Implementation Under Way* (Brussels: NATO, 1989), 145–156; and Daniel Thorniley, "Reforming the Soviet Foreign Trade Structure and Adapting to Change," in *Soviet Economic Reforms*, 157–84. For a discussion including Eastern Europe, see Peter B. Kenen, "Transitional Arrangements for Trade and Payments Among the CMEA Countries" (Washington, D.C.: IMF Working Paper, January 1991).

15. For a discussion of this issue, see Steven Rosefielde and R. W. Pfouts, "Ruble Convertibility: Demand-Responsive Exchange Rates in a Goal-Directed Economy," *European Economic Review*, 34 (November 1990), 1377–1397; for background, see Thomas A. Wolf, "Market-Oriented Reform of Foreign Trade in Planned Economies," in Oleg T. Bogomolov, ed., *Market Forces in Planned Economies* (Basingstoke, England: Macmillan Academic and Professional Ltd., 1990), pp. 199–216.

16. For a discussion of changing organizational arrangements, see Jim Butterfield, "Devolution of Decision Making and Organizational Change in Soviet Agriculture," *Comparative Economic Studies*, 32 (Summer 1990), 29–64.

17. For a discussion, see Karen Brooks, "Lease Contracting in Soviet Agriculture in 1989," *Comparative Economic Studies*, 32 (Summer 1990), 85–108.

18. Reform of financial institutions is a critical and complicated aspect of economic reform in socialist systems. For a discussion, see V. Sundararajan, "Financial Sector Reform and Central Banking in Centrally Planned Economies," unpublished manuscript, IMF working paper 1p/90/120 (Washington, D.C.: IMF, 1990).

19. The issue of transition has been important in the East European reforms. We discuss these reforms in Chapter 18.

20. For a discussion of the Polish case, see Jan Winiecki, "Post-Soviet-Type Economies in Transition: What Have We Learned from the Polish Transition Programme in its First Year?" *Weltwirtschaftliches Archiv*, Band 126 (1990), 765–790.

21. For a discussion of recent activity in the private sector, see Karin Plokker, "The Development of Individual and Cooperative Labour Activity in the Soviet Union," *Soviet Studies*, 2 (July 1990), 403–428.

22. The issue of Soviet popular opinion on markets has been addressed in recent survey evidence. See Robert J. Shiller, Maxim Boycko, and Vladimir Korobov, "Popular Attitudes Toward Free Markets: The Soviet Union and the United States Compared," *American Economic Review*, 81 (June 1991), 385–400.

23. For a useful discussion of contemporary political developments, see, for example, Stephen White, Alex Pravda, and Zvi Gitelman, eds., *Developments in Soviet Politics* (Durham, N.C.: Duke University Press, 1990).

24. Paul Gregory, "The Impact of Perestroika on the Soviet Planned Economy: Results of a Survey of Moscow Officials," *Soviet Studies*, 43, 5 (1991).

25. For a detailed comparison of these plans, see Padma Desai, "Soviet Economic Reform: A Tale of Two Plans," The Harriman Institute *Forum* (December 1990). For a general discussion of the events of 1990 pertaining to these two plans, see Ed. A. Hewett, "The New Soviet Plan," *Foreign Affairs*, 69 (Winter 1990–1991), 146–166.

26. For details of these differences, see Desai, *Soviet Economic Reform*.

27. This discussion is based on Ed. A. Hewett, "The New Soviet Plan."

28. Data here are from CIA and DIA, *Beyond Perestroika: The Soviet Economy In Crisis* (Washington, D.C.: CIA, 1991).

29. The interested reader can follow the development of events in the excellent coverage provided by the *New York Times*.

RECOMMENDED READINGS

General Works

Anders Aslund, *Gorbachev's Struggle for Economic Reform* (Ithaca, N.Y.: Cornell University Press, 1989).

U.S. Congress, Joint Economic Committee, *Gorbachev's Economic Plan*, Vols. 1 & 2 (Washington, D.C.: U.S. Government Printing Office, 1987).

Padma Desai, *Perestroika in Perspective*, revised paperback edition (Princeton, N.J.: Princeton University Press, 1990).

——, "Soviet Economic Reform: A Tale of Two Plans," The Harriman Institute *Forum* (December 1990).

——, "Perestroika, Prices, and the Ruble Problem," The Harriman Institute *Forum* (November 1989).

David Dyker, ed., *The Soviet Economy Under Gorbachev: The Prospects for Reform* (London: Croom Helm, 1987).

Paul R. Gregory and Robert C. Stuart, *Soviet Economic Structure and Performance*, 4th ed. (New York: HarperCollins, 1990).

Ed. Hewett, *Reforming the Soviet Economy* (Washington, D.C.: Brookings, 1988).

John E. Tedstrom, ed., *Socialism, Perestroika, and the Dilemmas of Soviet Economic Reform* (Boulder, Colo.: Westview Press, 1990).

Peter Wiles, ed., *The Soviet Economy on the Brink of Reform* (Boston: Unwin Hyman, 1988).

The Enterprise and Administration

Richard E. Ericson, "The New Enterprise Law," The Harriman Institute *Forum*, 1 (February 1988).

Paul R. Gregory, *Restructuring the Soviet Economic Bureaucracy* (Cambridge, England: Cambridge University Press, 1990).

Foreign Trade

Renzo Daviddi, "Ruble Convertibility: A Realistic Target?" in NATO, *Soviet Economic Reforms: Implementation Underway* (Brussels: NATO, 1989), pp. 193–212.

Carl H. McMillan, "Strategy or Tactics? Recent Initiatives in Soviet Foreign Economic Policy," in NATO, *Soviet Economic Reforms: Implementation Underway* (Brussels: NATO, 1989), pp. 145–156.

Steven Rosefielde and R. W. Pfouts, "Ruble Convertibility: Demand-Responsive Exchange Rates in a Goal-Directed Economy," *European Economic Review*, 34 (November 1990), 1377–1397.

Daniel Thorniley, "Reforming the Soviet Foreign Trade Structure and Adapting to Change," in NATO, *Soviet Economic Reforms: Implementation Underway* (Brussels: NATO, 1989), pp. 157–184.

Thomas A. Wolf, "Market-Oriented Reform of Foreign Trade in Planned Economies," in Oleg T. Bogomolov, ed., *Market Forces in Planned Economies* (Basingstoke, England: Macmillan Academic and Professional Ltd., 1990), pp. 199–216.

Agriculture

Ken Gray, *Soviet Agriculture: Comparative Perspectives* (Ames: Iowa State University Press, 1990).

William Moskoff, *Perestroika in the Countryside* (Armonk, N.Y.: M. E. Sharpe, 1990).

Works by Soviet Authors

Agan Aganbegyan, *The Economic Challenge of Perestroika* (Bloomington: Indiana University Press, 1988).

——, *Inside Perestroika* (New York: HarperCollins, 1990).

Mikhail Gorbachev, *Perestroika: New Thinking for Our Country and the World* (New York: Harper-Collins, 1987).

Nikolai Shmelyev and Vladimir Popov, *The Turning Point: Revitalizing the Soviet Economy*, with a preface by Richard E. Ericson, translated by Michele A. Berdy (New York: Doubleday, 1989).

Special Topics

Josef C. Brada and Ronald L. Groves, "The Slowdown in Soviet Defense Expenditures," *Southern Economic Journal* (April 1988), 969–983.

Directorate of Intelligence, *Measuring Soviet GNP: Problems and Solutions* (Washington, D.C.: National Technical Information Service, 1990).

H. Rowen and C. Wolfe, *The Impoverished Superpower: Perestroika and the Burden of Soviet Military Spending* (San Francisco: Institute for Contemporary Studies, 1990).

Michael Ryan, *Contemporary Soviet Society: A Statistical Handbook* (Brookfield, Vt.: Edward Elgar Publishing Company, 1990).

The Economy of the USSR: Summary and Recommendations. IMF, The World Bank, Organization for Economic Cooperation and Development and European Bank for Reconstruction and Development (Washington, D.C.: 1990).

Transition to the Market, Parts I and II (Moscow: Cultural Initiative Foundation, 1990).

17 China: Socialism, Planning, and Development

CHINA HAS FASCINATED THE WEST FOR CENTURIES. Western economists are interested in modern China for three principal reasons. First, the characteristics of Chinese industrialization distinguish it from other cases that we have examined. After the Chinese Communist party came to power in 1949, a period of socialist industrialization began. The Chinese applied the Soviet model, with alterations, in a highly underdeveloped setting.[1] Second, the easing of Chinese-American hostilities in the early 1970s sharply expanded communication between the two countries.[2] This era has provided Americans a long-denied opportunity to examine the Chinese system on a firsthand basis. This opportunity was enriched in the late 1970s and early 1980s when the Chinese began to release a substantially increased volume of information about their economy.[3] In spite of a difficult political situation in China in the late 1980s, interaction with the West has largely been sustained. The result has been a sharply expanded and productive dialogue, considerably enhancing our knowledge of the Chinese economy. Third, the post-Mao era has seen major changes in the Chinese economic system. These changes are of great interest to the comparative economist, not only for their impact on Chinese development, but also for the enrichment they provide to our understanding of the traditional Soviet model of development.

There is much more to the Chinese economy than reform, although changes of the late 1970s through the 1980s clearly dominate current interest. In light of developments in the Soviet Union and Eastern Europe, economic reform in China is a subject of major importance.

The Setting

First, China is a very large country by any definition. It is sobering to compare China with Canada, another large country. Canada, with a population of approximately 25 million, has a land area of 3.8 million square miles. China, with a population of slightly more than one billion, has a land area of just over 3.6 million square miles. Indeed, if the Chinese population should continue to

441

increase at the average annual rate of 2.1 percent of the past two decades, a new Canada, in terms of population, would arise in China roughly every fifteen months![4] Both land and population are resources that can contribute to economic development, but people must eat, and considerable portions of China's land are inappropriate for increasing the food supply, at least in the absence of capital investment.

Second, China is a resource-rich country, but, once again, its resources must be exploited to support the objective of economic development. Although coal is a major source of energy, only recently has China undertaken a major effort to utilize its oil riches. In addition, sharp variations in climate and fertility, along with large areas of rough terrain, make the application of large amounts of capital essential to raise agricultural output, despite China's vast land area.

Third, China is a poor country. Substantial economic progress has been made since the industrialization drive began in the early 1950s, but China in 1989 had a per capita income of about $400.[5] China's per capita income, though above that of its immediate neighbors India and Pakistan, ranks well below that of Taiwan, South Korea, and Malaysia. From the standpoint of the economy, then, the major goals are still industrialization and economic development, even though we should interpret such data and comparisons with caution.

Finally, a nonsystemic feature is the unique Chinese historical experience. China is the oldest existing civilization in the world, a source of great pride to the Chinese people. While there are numerous ethnic minorities in China (primarily in the western part of the country), the dominant nationality group is the *han* nationality. The Chinese language comprises many varying dialects; the Mandarin dialect is dominant. The rich heritage of the Chinese people is an important if unmeasurable influence on their attitudes toward and participation in the modernization process.

China and the Soviet Model

The economic, social, and cultural differences between China and the other socialist countries are striking. To the extent that we wish to make comparisons between China, with its low income, and, say, the United States, with its high income, great caution must be taken. Comparisons of China with India, or even contemporary China with the Soviet Union of the 1930s, make more sense. Even in this latter comparison it is important to note that China in 1949 was probably much more backward than Russia in 1917.

In looking back on the problems that must have faced Chinese leaders and planners in adapting the Soviet model, we encounter several key questions: How could the Chinese economy, in the absence of the advantages enjoyed by Russian leaders in 1917 (a basic industrial capacity, a transportation network, and so on), institute a planned socialist economic system in a large and very poor peasant economy? In developing such a planned socialist economy, what modifications of the Soviet model would have to be made to account for the very large Chinese population, its relative poverty, and its primarily rural character? To what extent would the Chinese natural resource base support industrial development, especially in view of sharp regional disparities and the likelihood that foreign trade would play a relatively small role? Could the Soviet model of rapid industrialization, used twenty years earlier under rather different circumstances, be transplanted in whole or in part to the Chinese case?

China at the time of the 1949 revolution was a classic LDC: low per capita income, significant population pressure on arable land and other resources, and an absence of institutions appropriate for economic development. China, with a land mass slightly larger than that of the United States and about half that of the Soviet Union, and with a population roughly four times that of the United States and about three and one-half times that of the Soviet Union, began in 1949 to implement to Soviet model, with important and interesting modifications. The result has been substantial economic growth and development that has, however, been interrupted when ideological and political factors have gained supremacy over economic factors.

In looking at different economic systems in action, we have varied the format from case to case in order to highlight the system's salient features. Chinese economic development can best be understood in terms of its historical evolution since 1949 and, in particular, as a modification of the Soviet model of economic development. What we wish to learn from the Chinese experience is, above all, the extent to which a system of planned socialism is a suitable vehicle for economic development in a large country of extreme poverty. Moreover, as we will observe later, the matter of economic reform in such a system is also of great interest.

THE HISTORY OF PLANNING IN CHINA

The Beginnings of Industrialization: The 1950s

The Chinese People's Republic was proclaimed by Mao Zedong in 1949. Between 1949 and 1952 a period of consolidation ensued. Two main goals were sought. First, the redistribution of land to individual households was implemented in preparation for ultimate collectivization. The latter, however, was to be pursued without undue haste. Second, nationalization and consolidation of the holdings in the industrial sector took place in preparation for the development of national economic planning. Other steps were taken — financial reform, educational reform, and other changes deemed necessary to stabilize the economy in preparation for the beginning of the first five-year plan in 1953. However, the basic steps were toward changing the ownership base and the means of guiding the economy. In this respect, China's first steps were much like those of the Soviet Union in the aftermath of the revolution.

Inevitably, the Chinese experience with change in the rural sector is compared to the Soviet experience of the late 1920s and early 1930s, especially

inasmuch as Soviet collectivization brought with it a number of important negative consequences.[6] Did the Chinese leadership modify the Soviet approach? On
the surface, both countries utilized initial land reform and similar experimental
forms of organization — the elimination of class differences at a rapid pace, the
distribution of machinery and equipment through centralized facilities, and
pressure to hold down rural food consumption levels. At the same time, there
were differences. Possibly the most important achievement was the avoidance
of substantial destruction (of cattle, facilities, and so on) in China.[7] This factor
alone has led most observers to believe that the extremes of the Soviet model
were avoided. Possibly the Chinese countryside was better prepared in terms of
ideological and organizational factors, though certainly not in terms of machinery and equipment. Also, the state farm a key feature of the Soviet experience,
was not introduced until later in China.

In sum, the Chinese adopted the basic Soviet model of land reform and
subsequent collectivization; the differences, however, were sufficient to preclude
the extreme negative consequences experienced in the Soviet Union. However,
the success of Chinese collectivization in transferring resources to the needs of
industrialization remains an open question, just as it remains an open issue in
the Soviet Union.

The Planning Apparatus

The second important policy of the early years was the nationalization of
industry and the development of a system of national economic planning.
During the early 1950s there was a gradual transition from private industry
toward socialist industry — certainly more gradual than in the Soviet Union
after 1928, but probably less gradual if one includes the Soviet periods of war
communism and the New Economic Policy. The shift from private to socialist
industry in China was targeted to be slow, though toward the latter part of the
first five-year plan it proved to be rapid. The pattern of change was from
private ownership to elementary state capitalism, then to advanced state capitalism, and finally to socialist industry.[8] However, by 1955, 68 percent of the
gross value of output was accounted for by state industry and only 16 percent
by joint state–private enterprises.[9] Indeed, even handicraft production was
brought under state control in moves reminiscent of the excessive nationalization of Soviet war communism. Thus, although the plans for the socialist
transformation in both agriculture and industry called for a relatively gradual
pace, the experience in 1955–1956 demonstrated that ideology and political
considerations could accelerate the rate of change.

Soviet leaders learned from their experiences between 1917 and 1928 that
if the market is to be abolished, a substitute mechanism must be developed for
economic activity to continue in a coordinated fashion. The Chinese planning
structure, put in place in the early 1950s and subsequently modified, was ini-

tially similar to the Soviet model.[10] The basic unit of production activity was the enterprise. As in the Soviet Union, a dual party–state administrative structure drew up and implemented (and often interrupted) five-year plans for both agriculture and industry. Chinese plans are formulated largely by the State Planning Commission, which like Gosplan in the Soviet Union, operated through an industrial ministry system communicating with regional and enterprise officials and ultimately assembling a plan. Once it is approved by the State Council, that plan becomes law for all enterprises.

Output targets are expressed in value and physical terms. A material balance is worked out in a time sequence utilizing both central directive and local information. Control figures are established. After they are assembled and "balanced" at the national level, those figures become plan targets. Inevitably, this system produced problems similar to those found in the Soviet case — imbalance and shortages, poor quality, late plans, and deviation of results from targets. Chinese thinking on reforming this system began to surface in the mid-1950s, but it was overshadowed by the political and ideological upheavals of the late 1950s.

The early 1950s was a period of unrest. Then, after the liberal Hundred Flowers Campaign (1956–1957), during which there was open discussion and criticism of the system, the Great Leap Forward was launched (1958–1960).[11] The Great Leap was a massive resurgence of ideology, which replaced rationality. Campaigns were instigated with revolutionary fervor to emphasize a new role for the peasantry, especially through small-scale industry in the countryside and the introduction of communes. Development of water resources was also stressed.

For a variety of economic, political, and ideological reasons, the Great Leap was abandoned by 1960, but the commune system, introduced in 1958, remained, with modifications.[12] The Rural Peoples Communes were initially set up as very large units combining a number of collectives (advanced cooperatives) to produce agricultural and handicraft products and to serve as local units of government. The original communes (roughly 26,000 in number and averaging about 4,600 households each) faced difficulties. Basically, agricultural units encompassing some 50,000 households were too difficult to coordinate, and individual incentives were overshadowed by the size of the collective. Subsequent modifications improved the commune system.

The First Ten Years

How can we appraise the first ten years of the Chinese industrialization experience? As one observer has noted: "In general, it can be said that during 1953–57, the Chinese followed the broad outlines of the Stalinist strategy of selective growth under conditions of austerity with three important qualifications."[13] First, less pressure was placed on the agricultural sector, possibly in recognition of the important underlying element of the Chinese case: a large, rural, poor population. Presumably the Chinese leaders had learned from the Soviet experience with rapid collectivization, for despite many similarities between the two cases, the extreme costs of the Soviet case were avoided in China.

Second, unlike the Soviet case, where state resources were directed toward the agricultural sector through state farms, Machine Tractor Stations, and so on, agriculture in the early years of the new Chinese regime was largely self-financed. This may have reflected the much lower level of economic development in China in 1949 than in the Soviet Union in, say, 1928.[14]

Third, the Chinese relied heavily on the state enterprise as a revenue source from which state investment funds would be derived. In 1953, for example, revenue from state enterprises accounted for roughly 35 percent of total budgetary revenue; this figure rose to 46 percent by 1957. In comparison, by far the most important source of budgetary revenue in the early years of Soviet industrialization was the turnover tax, and revenues from enterprises played a minor role. The decision not to rely on taxes forced from the peasants represented the planners' realization that such a policy could not be applied to a subsistence agriculture.

During the 1950s, the Chinese generally followed the Soviet "industry first" strategy. Between 1953 and 1957, heavy industry in China absorbed an average of 85 percent of industrial investment. At the same time, only 8 percent of state investment was devoted to agriculture, while aggregate investment accounted for roughly 20 to 25 percent of the national product.[15] These figures suggest a relatively high rate of accumulation for a poor country (though not nearly so high as the comparable rate for the Soviet Union in the early 1930s), with emphasis on industry in general and heavy industry in particular.

China's economic performance during the 1950s was generally strong, though uneven. There was an impressive doubling of GNP per capita, a ninefold increase in industrial production, a modest increase in agricultural production. Overall, the early years were ones of consolidation. The first five-year plan witnessed substantial growth of production; the latter part of the 1950s saw a mixture of progress and retrogression in both industry and agriculture.

The striking feature of Chinese economic performance in the 1950s was the impact of ideological disruptions. According to Subramanian Swamy's calculations, Chinese GNP grew at an annual rate of 6 percent from 1952 to 1956.[16] The 1958 level of GNP, however, was not regained until 1963. Thus the Great Leap caused an enormous setback in Chinese growth.

The Great Leap Forward was abandoned in the late 1950s at a time when relations between China and the Soviet Union were deteriorating rapidly. The ideological (and economic) break between the two countries was almost complete by 1960. Although the role of outside aid in the Chinese development experience was minimal, the Soviet contribution was important in the early years, especially in the area of technical assistance. The break would prove to be a sobering experience for Chinese leaders and planners.

The 1960s: Development and Disruption

Like the earlier decade, the 1960s can be conveniently divided into two very different periods: moderation in the early 1960s and upheaval in the late 1960s.

The early 1960s was a period of relative calm in which there was a tendency to look toward balance in economic development, modernization in the agricultural sector, and recovery from the aftermath of the Great Leap. In industry, the 1960s was a period of rather substantial reform — a movement away from the overwhelming importance of gross output (the major success indicator of the 1950s) toward quality in production and the elimination of major deficiencies in the planning system.

In a sense, both central control and local initiative were variables to be changed. The center tried to put pressure on enterprises to improve quality, to be concerned with efficiency, and to enhance the role of technical expertise in the decision-making process. At the same time, there was a tendency to shift many decisions, especially minor ones, to the local level. For example, local industrial establishments were set up to serve local (especially rural) needs. Although the emphasis on enterprise efficiency and profitability came under sharp attack during the Cultural Revolution of the late 1960s, evidence suggests that in the 1960s the Chinese industrial structure was modified to suit peculiar Chinese conditions, and the modifications for the most part withstood later upheavals.

During the early 1960s, new emphasis was placed on agriculture's role in the economy and on the need for mechanization and reorganization in that sector. The communes underwent substantial change. Because communes were found to be too large, the intermediate (brigade) and lower-level (team) units assumed new importance. Emphasis on nonmaterial rewards, a hallmark of the earlier commune system, was changed in favor of material incentives and the reintroduction of private plots. Although the number of communes was reduced during the 1960s, their role in the social, cultural, and political affairs of the countryside remained intact through the 1970s.

In addition to organizational changes and policy shifts, the 1960s witnessed a widespread educational campaign among the Chinese people. There was an effort to re-educate the population in the ways of Mao. This campaign laid the foundations for the Cultural Revolution.

If the early 1960s was a period of rationality — reform and change along a well-defined continuum — the opposite could be said of the Cultural Revolution of 1966–1969. The Cultural Revolution, difficult for the Western observer to fully comprehend, was an upheaval of ideas, an abandonment of much that had preceded it. Emanating from a Communist party struggle, the Cultural Revolution was not a debate over economic ideas. In fact, its disastrous disruption of economic activity became apparent only later. However, although economic activity was substantially disturbed, the basic organizational arrangements in industry and in agriculture do not seem to have been altered in significant ways.

Like the Great Leap, the Cultural Revolution had a devastating effect on output. Disruption was so great that meaningful GNP estimates during the Cultural Revolution are not available. Swamy's estimates show that GNP failed to increase between 1965 and 1970, a loss of output equal to or more severe than that of the Great Leap.[17]

China After the Cultural Revolution

Ironically, examination of events related to the Chinese economy since the 1970s reveals a pattern of twists and turns and an intermix of ideology and economics reminiscent of earlier years. Notwithstanding the rapprochement between China and the United States and a sharply increased flow of information about the Chinese economy, it remains difficult to assess with any certainty the impact of programs and policies developed during these years.

The early 1970s was a period of recovery from the Cultural Revolution.[18] Western scholars have generally argued that the Cultural Revolution was a major setback to Chinese economic development and modernization. Furthermore, the attempted return to normalcy of the early 1970s was interrupted. Zhou Enlai, a long-term advocate of a moderate path of industrialization, died in January 1976. The following September, Mao Zedong, the father of the revolution and the advocate of a continuation of the revolutionary mentality, died. Shortly thereafter, in October 1976, the "Gang of Four," representing the revolutionary left and espousing continuation of the Stalinist mode of industrialization, were arrested amid great ideological fervor.[19] These events paved the way for what would turn out to be fundamental changes in Chinese economic policy. The resurgence of conservative elements, however, meant an immediate resumption of the drive toward industrialization and modernization.

In 1978 a ten-year plan for China's modernization was announced by Hua Guofeng. This plan, covering the period 1975–1985, was to pursue the "Four Modernizations" — industry, agriculture, science and technology, and defense. The initial plan was grandiose. The average annual rate of growth of industrial output was to be 10 percent, of agricultural output, 4–5 percent. The stress would be traditional: industry at the forefront, heavy industry in particular. By the end of 1978, however, imbalances in the economy led to important shifts. Hua Guofeng announced a major program of economic reform and effectively scrapped the ten-year plan. In effect, one-year plans replaced the defunct ten-year plan. In 1982 a five-year plan was announced for 1981–1985, though this plan actually covered the period from 1983 to 1985. What were the imbalances, and what steps were taken to reform the system?

Fundamentally, the problems that plagued the Chinese economy in the 1970s and 1980s derived from China's unyielding pursuit of the Stalinist model of industrialization. Material incentives were weakened by the continuing emphasis on accumulation. Moreover, the lion's share of that accumulation was devoted to heavy industry. As a result, there were growing problems in the areas of energy, transportation, and consumer goods.

Although the Chinese have tended to modify their working arrangements without a formal and specific reform program, the program announced at the end of 1978 and subsequently subsumed under the "eight-point program" really amounted to a major modification and consolidation of the system. Reforms were directed at a number of problems.

First, priorities were changed. Light industry, agriculture, and infrastructure were to receive new attention. For example, the share of investment devoted to heavy industry fell from 54.7 percent in 1978 to 40.3 percent in 1981.[20]

Second, there was to be a substantial attempt to decentralize decision making in industrial enterprises. Industrial enterprises were to become responsible for their own operations. They were given greater authority and more responsibility for, among other things, the distribution of enterprise revenues. Increasingly, enterprise profits could be retained for enterprise investment, worker bonuses, and so forth.

Third, substantial changes were to be implemented in agriculture. These reforms focused on changes in the mechanism of payment and in the importance of material incentives.

CHINA: THE RURAL ECONOMY

In our examination of different economic systems, we have not always paid special attention to the rural economy. By most definitions, however, agriculture (broadly defined to include rural economic activity in general) is the dominant sector of the Chinese economy. Moreover, the **commune** is an interesting and important organizational unit that is worthy of considerable attention.

Prior to 1978, the commune was the best-known unit of organization in rural China.[21] The conduct of basic economic activity was in the hands of the **production team**, a combination of a number of households; within a village, production teams would combine to form a brigade; brigades would combine to form a commune. Above the commune, the county has been the state unit responsible for directing agricultural activity. It has played a major role in implementing the national economic plan administered by the Ministry of Agriculture and Forestry.[22]

The commune had a reward system not unlike that used prior to 1966 in Soviet collective farms. Individuals would accumulate points for work done on a daily basis. Their remuneration would then be based on the residual income of the commune, which consisted of revenues less expenses (the latter including investment in the commune).

Rural reform in China since the late 1970s has fundamentally changed the nature of the rural economy. It stands in marked contrast to the "industry first" reform scenario in the Soviet Union.

The initial focus of rural reform in China in the late 1970s was the implementation of different kinds of contracting and elimination of the production team, a sub-unit of the commune.[23] By the early 1980s, contracting had become so widespread that individual households were the dominant farm unit; this effectively brought collectivization to an end.

Just as important changes were made in the means of determining output, important changes also occurred on the input side. Under the new arrangements, households became able to contract for land use, and the terms of land use have become increasingly liberal. Other inputs are generally purchased, though in some cases (such as equipment), group arrangements are usually made.

Beyond changes in the arrangements of the agricultural economy per se, there have also been important changes in the growth of small-scale rural-based industry.[24] Small-scale rural industry has grown in importance. Most significantly, new, noncooperative forms of enterprise have arisen that exhibit a variety of different organizational forms. In a real sense, marketization has come to China through the rural sector of the economy.

CHINA: PERFORMANCE AND REFORM IN THE 1990s

In many respects, contemporary Chinese economic performance has been very good, especially in agriculture in the years following the introduction of the **household contract responsibility system**. However, as the decade of the 1980s came to an end, there was a significant reversal in Chinese economic fortunes. It is important that we examine both the good and the bad sides of contemporary Chinese economic performance and try to understand the impact of the latter on the continuation of economic reform.

In 1988, China had a per capita gross national product equivalent to approximately 330 U.S. dollars.[25] Although this represents a relatively low level of economic achievement, it nevertheless reflects significant growth and represents a pattern of structural change that is rather typical of an economy going through the early stages of industrialization.

Between 1965 and 1980, Chinese gross domestic product grew at an average annual rate of 6.4 percent, whereas for the period 1980–1988, the rate of growth increased to 10.3 percent; judged by international standards, both are exceedingly good rates of growth. The improvement in the rate of growth of agricultural output has been especially notable. It increased from an average annual rate of 2.8 percent for the period 1965–1980 to 6.8 percent in the period 1980–1988. For the same two periods, industrial output grew at average annual rates of 10.0 and 12.4 percent, respectively.

Not surprisingly, there were important sectoral changes in the Chinese economy during these periods. For example, the product share of agriculture declined from 44 percent in 1965 to 32 percent in 1988, while for the same years, the industry share in total output increased from 39 percent to 46 percent.

Although the distribution of income became more uneven in the 1980s, the consumer shared in the gains made by the Chinese economy. Again for the period 1980–1988, consumption grew at an average annual rate of 7.4 percent, though for the same period, government consumption grew at an even faster rate of 9.4 percent. Between 1965 and 1988, the share of consumption in gross domestic product fell from 61 to 56 percent; at the same time, the shares of both savings and investment increased.

The foreign sector has been an important area of Chinese economic development. Between 1965 and 1980, Chinese exports grew at an average annual rate of 5.5 percent; for the same period, imports grew at the rather faster rate of 7.9 percent. However, comparable figures for the period 1980–1988 were 11.9 and 13.1 percent for export and imports, respectively. During these years, the commodity composition of Chinese foreign trade changed quite significantly. On the import side, the relative importance of food and related imports declined, while the relative importance of machinery and related imports increased. Manufactured goods became increasingly important exports, while exports of primary products became less important. China has accumulated a significant hard-currency debt, but the expense of servicing debt was estimated in 1988 to be a rather modest 1 percent of gross domestic product.

Although the economic record we have just summarized is a very positive record in most respects, careful examination of the second half of the 1980s reveals a more complicated picture. Specifically, from the mid-1980s to the end of the decade, China experienced economic difficulties that, in combination with growing state intervention, seemed to suggest a reversal of earlier positive reforms.

From the year 1987 through the end of the decade, serious inflation developed; it apparently approached 30 percent on an average annual basis by 1989.[26] This inflation reflected excess aggregate demand in an environment where a mix of controls and enterprise autonomy in a monopolistic setting and inappropriate basic prices led to increasing distortions. At the same time, weakened performance in the industrial sector limited the growth of government revenues and led to a budget deficit that grew sharply in the second half of the 1980s.

The Chinese leadership responded to these economic difficulties late in 1988 by imposing an austerity program. This program consisted largely of state controls in a variety of areas. Although the problem of inflation was brought under control, unemployment increased and, most important, there was a sharp decline in the rate of growth of output of the economy. Thus the problem for the 1990s quickly became the need to sustain economic growth without permitting the return of unacceptable rates of inflation.

In the 1990s, there is a more fundamental issue at hand. Will it be possible to sustain economic growth while sustaining the progress of economic reform? Indeed, it is not clear that the latter is a very high priority for the present Chinese leadership.

The posture of Chinese economic reform in the 1990s is complex and unpredictable. In the early 1980s, the Chinese economy performed well. However, Chinese leaders' efforts to control unacceptable outcomes during the late 1980s suggested a willingness to limit the extent of economic reform. In some sectors, such as foreign trade, there was a major retrenchment via the implementation of new economic controls. In the long term, however, the Chinese must come to grips with the problem of center–periphery relations both political and financial, because marketization of the local economy seems to proceed, however unevenly, quite apart from what the Chinese leaders may wish.

SUMMARY

1. China is an interesting case. Here a modified Soviet model of centrally planned socialism has been implemented in a very large but poor country characterized by substantial regional diversity and rich natural resources. Since the beginnings of Chinese socialism in 1949, economic and political theorists have been fascinated by issues of economic development there and especially by China's ideological modifications of the traditional Soviet model. However, since the late 1970s, our attention has focused primarily on the nature of economic reform in China, a setting very different from that of other formerly planned socialist systems. Economic reform in China represents a major reform attempt, in a very large but substantially underdeveloped economy, via modified Soviet-type planning and administrative arrangements.
2. In addition to differences in the setting of reform in China, the strategy of Chinese reform has differed from that in other cases: It emphasized agricultural reform in the initial stages. However, just as elsewhere, political factors have often limited the pace of reform and retarded the move toward greater reliance on market forces.

NOTES

1. Although cross-country comparison of GNP must be interpreted with caution, a per capita gross national product of $131 (measured in 1980 dollars) must rank China as a very poor country on the eve of the socialist industrialization drive. For a useful long-term comparison of basic economic and developmental indicators, see Arthur G. Ashbrook, Jr., "China: Economic Modernization and Long-Term Performance," in U.S. Congress, Joint Economic Committee, *China Under the Four Modernizations*, Part 2, Section V (Washington, D.C.: Government Printing Office, 1982), pp. 151–368.
2. For a detailed discussion of the path of Sino-American normalization, see Joint Economic Committee, *China Under the Four Modernizations*, Part 1, pp. 171–223.
3. For a discussion, see K. Chao, "The China-Watchers Tested," *The China Quarterly*, 81 (1980), 97–104; Erik Dirksen, "Chinese Industrial Productivity in an International Context," *World Development*, 11 (April 1983), 381–387. Since 1982, China has published an annual statistical handbook.
4. For recent population estimates from the Chinese census, see "Chinese Population Census — 1982," *Communist Affairs — Documents and Analysis*, 2 (July 1983), 319–321; for greater detail, see John S. Aird, "Recent Demographic Data from China: Problems and Prospects," in Joint Economic Committee, *China Under the Four Modernizations*, Part 1, pp. 171–223. For an

update, see Kaun-I Chen, "China's Food Policy and Population," *Current History*, 86 (September 1981), 257–260, 274–276. The population of China in 1989 was estimated to be 1,102.4 million with an annual growth rate of 1.4 percent. See *Handbook of Economic Statistics 1990* (Washington, D.C.: CIA, 1990), Table 3.

5. *Handbook of Economic Statistics*, Table 3.

6. Although collectivization may have been a factor in the consolidation of Soviet power in the countryside, recent evidence suggests that collectivization had little influence on the magnitude of the surplus shifted into the industrialization effort. For evidence, see James R. Millar, "Mass Collectivization and the Contribution of Soviet Agriculture to the First Five-Year Plan: A Review Article," *Slavic Review*, 33 (December 1974), 750–766.

7. There was some unrest and disruption in China, but markedly less than that which occurred in the Soviet Union. For a comparison, see Jan S. Prybyla, *The Political Economy of Communist China* (Scranton, Pa.: International Textbook, 1970), Ch. 5.

8. For a discussion of the transitional phases, see Prybyla, *The Political Economy of Communist China*.

9. Ibid., p. 175.

10. For a useful outline of the basic features of the Chinese administrative structure and changes through time, see Thomas G. Rawski, "China's Industrial System." in U.S. Congress, Joint Economic Committee, *China: A Reassessment of the Economy* (Washington, D.C.: Government Printing Office, 1975), pp. 175–198. For a recent comparison of the Chinese experience and the Soviet experience, see Robert F. Dernberger, "The Chinese Search for the Path of Self-Sustained Growth in the 1980s: An Assessment," in Joint Economic Committee, *China Under the Four Modernizations*, Part 1, pp. 19–76.

11. For a discussion of this period, see Roderick MacFarquhar, *The Hundred Flowers Campaign and the Chinese Intellectuals* (New York: Praeger, 1960).

12. For a discussion of the early commune, see Kenneth R. Walker, "Organization of Agricultural Production," in Alexander Eckstein, Walter Galenson, and Ta-Chung Liu, eds., *Economic Trends in Communist China* (Chicago: Aldine, 1968), pp. 440–452. For a study of the private sector, see Kenneth R. Walker, *Planning in Chinese Agriculture: Socialization and the Private Sector, 1956–1962* (Chicago: Aldine, 1965). For an update of organizational changes into the 1970s, see Frederick W. Crook, "The Commune System in the People's Republic of China, 1963–74," in Joint Economic Committee, *China: A Reassessment of the Economy*, pp. 366–410; a useful recent source is Frederic M. Surls and Francis C. Tuan, "China's Agriculture in the Eighties," in Joint Economic Committee, *China Under the Four Modernizations*, Part 1, pp. 419–448.

13. Prybyla, *The Political Economy of Communist China*, pp. 144–145.

14. For example, in terms of agricultural performance, we might make the following crude comparison. In China in 1949, grain production was 0.20 metric ton per capita; in the Soviet Union in 1928–1929, grain production was 0.47 metric ton per capita. Chinese data are from Ashbrook, "China: Economic Modernization and Long-Term Performance," p. 104; Paul R. Gregory and Robert C. Stuart, *Soviet Economic Structure and Performance*, 3rd ed. (New York: Harper & Row, 1986), p. 244; and TsSU (Central Statistical Administration), *Naselenie SSSR 1973* (Moscow: Statistika, 1975), p. 7.

15. These data are from Prybyla, *The Political Economy of Communist China*, pp. 135 ff.

16. Subramanian Swamy, "Economic Growth in China and India 1952–1970: A Comparative Appraisal," *Economic Development and Cultural Change*, 21 (July 1973), 62.

17. Ibid.

18. An excellent survey of these years can be found in Dernberger, "The Chinese Search for the Path of Self-Sustained Growth," pp. 19–76.

19. For a discussion of the revolutionary left in the economic context, see Robert F. Dernberger and David Fasenfest, "China's Post-Mao Economic Future," in U.S. Congress, Joint Economic Committee, *Chinese Economy Post-Mao* (Washington, D.C.: Government Printing Office, 1978), pp. 3–47.

20. Chu-yuan Cheng, "China's Industrialization and Economic Development," *Current History*, 82 (September 1983), 266.
21. A useful source on the communes is Frederick W. Crook, "The Commune System in the People's Republic of China, 1963–1974," in U.S. Congress, Joint Economic Committee, *China, A Reassessment of the Economy* (Washington, D.C.: Government Printing Office, 1975), p. 411–437.
22. For a discussion of prereform arrangements, see, for example, Henry J. Groen and James A. Kilpatrick, "China's Agricultural Production," in U.S. Congress, Joint Economic Committee, *Chinese Economy Post-Mao*, Vol. I (Washington, D.C.: Government Printing Office, 1978), pp. 607–652.
23. For a discussion of changes in the rural economy, see for example Kuan-I Chen, "China's Changing Agricultural System," *Current History*, 82 (September 1983), 259–263, 277–278; Kuan-I Chen, "China's Food Policy and Population," 257–260, 274–276; Yak-Yeow Kueh, "China's New Agricultural-Policy Program: Major Economic Consequences, 1979–1983," *Journal of Comparative Economics*, 8 (December 1984), 353–375; Nicholas R. Lardy, *Agriculture in China's Modern Economic Development* (Cambridge, England: Cambridge University Press, 1983); Dwight Perkins and Shahid Yusuf, *Rural Development in China* (Baltimore: The Johns Hopkins University Press, 1984); Kenneth R. Walker, "Chinese Agriculture During the Period of Readjustment, 1978–83," *China Quarterly*, 100 (December 1984), 783–812; Kenneth R. Walker, *Food Grain Procurement and Consumption in China* (Cambridge, England: Cambridge University Press, 1984); Peter Nolan and Dong Fureng, eds., *Market Forces in China* (London: Zed Books Ltd., 1990); Anthony Y. C. Koo, "The Contract Responsibility System: Transition from a Planned to a Market Economy," *Economic Development and Cultural Change*, 38 (July 1990), 797–820.
24. For a discussion of rural industry, see for example William A. Byrd and Lin Qingsong, eds., *China's Rural Industry* (New York: Oxford University Press, 1991); and Victor Nee and Frank W. Young, "Peasant Entrepreneurs in China's 'Second Economy': An Institutional Analysis," *Economic Development and Cultural Change*, 37 (January 1991), 293–310.
25. The data used here and in the following sections are from the World Bank, *World Development Report 1990* (Washington, D.C.: The World Bank, 1990). For those interested in agricultural data, the various publications of the U.S. Department of Agriculture, such as *China Situation and Outlook Report* and *CPE Agriculture Report*, are especially useful.
26. For a discussion of recent developments, see for example Directorate of Intelligence, *The Chinese Economy in 1989 and 1990: Trying to Revive Growth While Maintaining Social Stability* (Washington, D.C.: CIA, 1990).

RECOMMENDED READINGS

General Works

Richard Baum, ed., *China's Four Modernizations: The New Technological Revolution* (Boulder, Colo.: Westview Press, 1980).
Chu-yuan Cheng, *China's Economic Development: Growth and Structural Change* (Boulder, Colo.: Westview Press, 1982).
Gregory Chow, *The Chinese Economy* (New York: Harper & Row, 1984).
Robert F. Dernberger, ed., *China's Development Experience in Comparative Perspective* (Cambridge, Mass.: Harvard University Press, 1980).
Audrey Donnithorne, *China's Economic System* (New York: Praeger, 1967).
Alexander Eckstein, *China's Economic Development: The Interplay of Scarcity and Ideology* (Ann Arbor: University of Michigan Press, 1975).
———, *China's Economic Revolution* (New York: Cambridge University Press, 1977).
———, *Communist China's Economic Growth and Foreign Trade* (New York: McGraw-Hill, 1969).

Alexander Eckstein, Walter Galenson, and Ta-Chung Liu, eds., *Economic Trends in Communist China* (Chicago: Aldine, 1968).

Christopher Howe, *China's Economy: A Basic Guide* (New York: Basic Books, 1978).

Gary H. Jefferson and Wenyi Yu, "The Impact of Reform on Socialist Enterprises in Transition: Structure, Conduct, and Performance in Chinese Industry," *Journal of Comparative Economics*, 15 (January 1991), 45–54.

Thomas P. Lyons, *Economic Integration and Planning in Maoist China* (New York: Columbia University Press, 1987).

Nicholas Lardy, *Economic Growth and Distribution in China* (New York: Cambridge University Press, 1979).

Jan S. Prybyla, *The Chinese Economy: Problems and Policies*, 2nd ed. (Columbia: University of South Carolina Press, 1981).

——, *The Political Economy of Communist China* (Scranton, Pa.: International Textbook, 1970).

Carl Riskin, *China's Political Economy* (New York: Oxford University Press, 1987).

Kai Yuen Tsui, "China's Regional Inequality, 1952–1985," *Journal of Comparative Economics*, 15 (March 1991), 1–21.

U.S. Congress, Joint Economic Committee, *China: A Reassessment of the Economy* (Washington, D.C.: Government Printing Office, 1975).

——, *China Under the Four Modernizations* (Washington, D.C.: Government Printing Office, 1982).

——, *Chinese Economy Post-Mao* (Washington, D.C.: Government Printing Office, 1978).

——, *An Economic Profile of Mainland China*, Vols. I and 11 (Washington, D.C.: Government Printing Office, 1967).

——, *China's Economic Dilemmas in the 1990s: The Problems of Reforms, Modernization, and Interdependence*, Vols. 1 and 2 (Washington, D.C.: Government Printing Office, 1991).

The Rural Economy

William A. Byrd and Lin Qingsong, eds., *China's Rural Industry* (New York: Oxford University Press, 1991).

Kang Chao, *Man and Land in Chinese History: An Economic Analysis* (Stanford: Stanford University Press, 1987).

Kuan-I Chen, "China's Food Policy and Population," *Current History*, 86 (September 1987), 257–260, 274–276.

Yak-Yeow Kueh, "China's New Agricultural-Policy Program: Major Economic Consequences, 1979–1983," *Journal of Comparative Economics*, 8 (December 1984), 353–375.

Nicholas R. Lardy, *Agriculture in China's Modern Economic Development* (Cambridge, England: Cambridge University Press, 1983).

Victor Nee and Frank W. Young, "Peasant Entrepreneurs in China's 'Second Economy': An Institutional Analysis," *Economic Development and Cultural Change*, 37 (January 1991), 293–310.

Dwight H. Perkins, *Agricultural Development in China, 1368–1968* (Chicago: University of Chicago Press, 1969).

——, ed., *Rural Small-Scale Industry in the People's Republic of China* (Berkeley: University of California Press, 1977).

Economic Reform

Anthony Y. C. Koo, "The Contract Responsibility System: Transition from a Planned to a Market Economy," *Economic Development and Cultural Change*, 38 (July 1990), 797–820.

Deepak Lah, "The Failure of the Three Envelopes: The Analytics and Political Economy of the Reform of Chinese State-Owned Enterprises," *European Economic Review*, 34 (September 1990), 1213–1231.

Elizabeth J. Perry and Christine Wong, *The Political Economy of Reform in Post-Mao China* (Cambridge, Mass.: Harvard University Press, 1987).

Lim Wei and Arnold Chao, eds., *China's Economic Reforms* (Philadelphia: University of Pennsylvania Press, 1983).

Gordon White, "The Politics of Economic Reform in Chinese Industry: The Introduction of the Labour Contract System," *The China Quarterly*, 11 (September 1987), 365–389.

Christine P. W. Wong, "The Economics of Shortage and Problems of Reform in Chinese Industry," *Journal of Comparative Economics*, 10 (December 1986), 363–387.

Yaun-Li Wu, *The Economy of Communist China: An Introduction* (New York: Praeger, 1965).

Special Topics

William Byrd, *China's Financial System: The Changing Role of Banks* (Boulder, Colo.: Westview Press, 1983).

Alfred K. Ho, *Joint Ventures in the People's Republic of China* (New York: Praeger, 1990).

Thomas P. Lyons, "Interprovincial Disparities in China: Output and Consumption, 1952–1987," *Economic Development and Cultural Change*, 39 (April 1991), 471–506.

Feng-hwa Mah, *The Foreign Trade of Mainland China* (Chicago: Aldine, 1971).

Andrew G. Walder, *Communist Neo-Traditionalism: Work and Authority in Chinese Industry* (Berkeley: University of California Press, 1986).

——, "Wage Reform and the Web of Factory Interests," *The China Quarterly*, 109 (March 1987), 22–41.

——, *Wage Patterns and Wage Policy in Modern China, 1919–1972* (Cambridge, England: Cambridge University Press, 1973).

18 | Eastern Europe: Socialism in Transition

IN CHAPTER 4 WE DISCUSSED THE BASIC PRINCIPLES of economic reform, which pertain to both market capitalist and planned socialist economic systems. We want to reemphasize here that economic reform implies changes in the four major system components: the level of decision making, the use of plan or market, property rights, and incentive arrangements. Although the patterns of economic reform in different socialist systems have been broadly similar, there are also important differences from one case to another. Moreover, reform in Eastern Europe has been different in many dimensions from that proposed and/or occurring in the Soviet Union. Before we turn to closer examination of selected instances of reform in Eastern Europe, we should give a brief overview of the general setting in which East European reform unfolds and the impact of this setting on the process of reform and on its results.

THE EAST EUROPEAN SETTING

Prior to the era of Glasnost and Perestroika, the Soviet Union had not been a leader among planned socialist systems in the sphere of economic reform. However, a comparison of various past reform attempts in Eastern Europe with reform attempts in the Soviet Union reveals similarities, including failure (for the most part) of implementation.[1] Most would argue, though, that the era of Glasnost and Perestroika introduced by Soviet leader Mikhail Gorbachev in the mid-1980s opened the door for major changes, both political and economic, in Eastern Europe. At the same time, differences between the East European setting and that of the Soviet Union have been important, and in the 1990s, economic reform in Eastern Europe — at least in a number of important cases — has been much more aggressive than that in the Soviet Union. Let us examine some of the reasons for this.

First, the economic history of Eastern Europe is in most respects quite different from that of the Soviet Union. In most East European countries, the prevailing political and economic arrangements were imposed from outside in the years immediately following World War II. Though there have been exceptions (for example, the early abandonment of command planning in Yugoslavia and the mixed implementation of collectivization in some cases), most political and economic arrangements in these countries followed Soviet arrangements very closely. Thus a Communist party determined basic economic priorities, and resource allocation was directed through a system of centralized (balance) planning. The means of production were usually nationalized ai.d agriculture collectivized. Incentive arrangements came to resemble those of a planned socialist system, the emphasis falling on a more egalitarian distribution of income and an increased reliance on social rewards. In sum, these systems closely resembled the model of the planned socialist system outlined in Chapter 2.

However, it is important to remember that the East European systems, as set up in the late 1940s and early 1950s, had functioned by the mid-1980s for only about 35 years. In the Soviet Union, by contrast, planning and collectivization were introduced in 1928 — roughly 60 years ago and some 10 years after the Bolshevik revolution. In short, when major changes began in the mid-1980s, the command economy had had a much shorter time to take hold in Eastern Europe, so people's experience with and memory of market forces were much more recent than in the Soviet Union.

Second, although there was considerable discussion and debate in the Soviet Union of the 1920s about the level of economic development and the appropriateness of various alternative development strategies, there was no such discussion and debate in the East European cases.[2] The planned socialist economic systems of Eastern Europe (with the exception of Yugoslavia) were imposed by the Soviet Union after the establishment of totalitarian political (communist) regimes. However, these economic systems were imposed in countries that had already experienced economic growth and economic development under very different market systems.

Third, the East European countries have always differed significantly from the Soviet Union in terms of the environment in which an economic system must function. Most East European countries are relatively small, are poor in terms of resource endowment, and thus rely heavily on foreign trade. One might argue that this latter factor has been responsible for keeping the East European development patterns closer to what one might expect to find in a market scenario. In the contemporary period, as the East European countries attempt to move from plan to market, the similarity of East European industrial structures to market-influenced patterns is an important factor facilitating economic reform. Put another way, if market forces are to be introduced, less structural change will be necessary for those cases where world market forces influenced resource allocation under planning. Moreover, one might expect the technological level of industry in these relatively open economies to be higher than in those countries where trade aversion was strong.

Fourth, as we have emphasized, there have been over the years significant differences in the degree to which the Soviet model *could* be imposed in the different East European countries. These differences help to explain contemporary variations in reform implementation. For example, we might contrast the extreme case of Albania, until recently a strict Stalinist command economy, with that of Yugoslavia, a country that broke with the Soviet empire years ago in spite of sustained political power centered in a communist party. Even without looking to these extremes, however, we can discern important differences between lower-income countries such as Bulgaria, where reform has been limited, and middle-income countries such as Hungary, which have long sustained a reform effort. At the same time, Czechoslovakia, a country that has little experience in reform and has been subjected to considerable political repression, currently pursues economic reform with vigor.

Fifth, the countries of Eastern Europe differ significantly from the Soviet Union in yet another important dimension: their cultural background and religious and ethnic composition. We have emphasized that economic reform requires change but that, paradoxically, political stability may be a prerequisite to economic (systemic) change. The Soviet Union is, of course, a federation of fundamentally diverse peoples who differ in culture, religion, and ethnic heritage. In many respects, these differences and the difficulty of forging new political arrangements have overshadowed Mikhail Gorbachev's attempts to promote economic reform.

In the East European cases, with the major exceptions of Yugoslavia and (to a lesser degree) Czechoslovakia, there is a much greater degree of cultural, religious, and ethnic uniformity. In these circumstances, it is easier to develop a sustained political consensus capable of implementing new social and economic initiatives. Such a consensus is essential to a successful transition to a market economy, because the costs (such as unemployment) are immediate and many of the benefits (such as more and better consumer goods) are delayed.

As we examine economic reform in Eastern Europe, it is important to keep in mind these environmental factors. All influence the reform process and help account for the fact that different outcomes occur in different cases.

Economic Reform in Eastern Europe: The Background

The background of economic reform in Eastern Europe is not unlike that in the Soviet Union, even though, as we have emphasized, the setting is rather different. The brief political thaw following the death of Stalin in the early 1950s did permit a freer discussion of ideas, which, along with growing problems of economic performance, led to limited attempts to develop and implement economic reform. Initially, these changes were modest in scope, and they typically followed the Soviet reform pattern: Try to improve decision making while preserving socialist objectives and the essence of the planning system. This was the focus of the New Economic System in the GDR (see Chapter 10) and of the New Economic Mechanism introduced in Hungary in 1968 (discussed later in this chapter). The potential for genuine economic reform was certainly limited by Soviet influence. Indeed in some cases (such as Czechoslovakia in 1968), reform was abruptly forestalled by Soviet intervention. In other cases, such as Hungary, reform attempts dating from the late 1960s were sustained on a limited basis, to become the background for more serious reform in the present era. There were, then, numerous attempts at reform in Eastern Europe. What were the major forces promoting these efforts?

First, as was the case in the Soviet Union, rates of economic growth in Eastern Europe have undergone a long-term secular decline. The magnitude of this decline (see Table 18.1) has varied from case to case, but overall it has been pervasive. Moreover, these countries had taken pride in being high-growth economies, even if the costs, such as little growth of consumer well-being, were also high. At the same time, growth in productivity slackened, especially in the late 1970s and 1980s. And inflation quickened, though it was most serious in Poland and Yugoslavia. Repressed inflation, though difficult to measure, grew in importance in the 1980s.

Second, East European countries relied heavily on foreign trade as a means of stimulating economic growth in the 1970s. Their strategy was to promote exports in Western markets so that the imports required both to stimulate technological change in industry and to enhance consumer well-being could be obtained without the growth of hard-currency debt. Unfortunately, this strategy was not successful. The energy crisis led to a significant slackening of Western markets at the very time when East European nations were becoming more aggressive in these markets. East European imports were sustained, but largely by means of building a substantial hard-currency debt. The magnitude of debt repayment subsequently led to considerable internal belt-tightening for these countries in the 1980s — precisely the opposite of what had been intended.

Third, one could argue that in Eastern Europe, the possibilities for economic growth through extensive means had initially been less promising than in the Soviet case and had been exhausted more quickly. In light of the level

Table 18.1 Economic Growth and Performance in Eastern Europe: The Background to Reform

| | *Average annual rate of growth: real per capita GNP* | | | | |
	1961–70	*1971–80*	*1981–85*	*1985*	*1986*
Eastern Europe	3.4	2.4	1.0	.2	2.2
Bulgaria	5.0	2.3	.1	−3.2	4.7
Czechoslovakia	2.4	2.3	1.0	.4	1.9
East Germany	3.2	3.5	1.7	3.3	1.6
Hungary	3.1	2.5	.6	−2.3	2.4
Poland	3.3	3.0	1.0	.2	2.1
Romania	4.2	3.5	−.6	−1.4	3.1

Source: Directorate of Intelligence, *Handbook of Economic Statistics 1990* (Washington, D.C.: CIA, 1990), Table 10.

of economic development in Eastern Europe compared to that in the Soviet Union, it is not surprising that the imperative for reform was strong and that developments of the Gorbachev era quickly spilled over into Eastern Europe. In the absence of Soviet backing, interest in the administrative command model faded fast.

East European Reform Programs: Similarities and Differences

In this chapter we pay special attention to Poland and Hungary. We do so because these countries are both examples of aggressive reform but have employed different strategies. However, before we consider these cases in greater detail, it is useful to summarize the East European reform experience, noting important similarities and differences among the various cases. To do so will entail some repetition of basic themes.

First, economic reform in Eastern Europe (at least in Poland, Hungary, and Czechoslovakia) is generally described as a *transition* in that these countries seek to replace the planned economy with a market economy rather than attempting merely to modify the former.

Second, transition programs have varied in speed and intensity. Some countries have pursued reform on a "gradual" basis, whereas others, like Poland, have pursued what is often termed a "big bang," or rapid, approach to reform. However, we must remember that even in those countries not pursuing a "big bang" or "shock therapy" approach, the process of transition in Eastern Europe has been relatively rapid, especially when compared to reforms of the past — and notably so when compared to the recent Soviet record, which we examined in detail in Chapter 16. It is important, therefore, to be aware of the basic issues associated with transition and of the extent to which the attempted *speed* of transition alters the overall reform experience.

Third, although it is possible to examine and understand the basic elements of economic reform and even of transition from one system to another, we really do not have a general theory of change in economic systems. In some cases — for example, during such a period of rapid change as the 1990s — it is difficult even to develop a way to classify the issues involved in transition.

Fourth, important differences exist from one country to another. Our view of the socialist transition process is heavily influenced by our image of the best-known and most advanced reforms, such as those of Poland, Hungary, and Czechoslovakia. We know much less about, and tend to pay less attention to, developments where reforms are proceeding at a slower pace, as in Romania and Bulgaria.

The General Transition Process

Following the advent of Perestroika and Glasnost in the Soviet Union in the mid-1980s, a period of political relaxation and (ultimately) major change unfolded in Eastern Europe. Fundamental political changes occurred rapidly in countries like Poland and Hungary, much less so in Bulgaria and Romania. Figure 18.1 offers a simple, stylized view of contemporary political and economic reform (transition) in Eastern Europe.

In the aftermath of political change, economic reform programs were debated and developed. Although the programs differ from one case to another, the process of reform is similar in most cases (possible exceptions are the former German Democratic Republic, Yugoslavia, Romania, Bulgaria, and Albania).

After political change had been effected, countries such as Poland, Hungary, and Czechoslovakia envisioned a set of transition policies that were to be followed by, or associated with, privatization and the replacement of the centrally planned economic system with a market economic system. Of course the programs differed somewhat, but all would lead to major changes if judged in terms of the criteria developed in Chapter 2. Decision making would be decentralized, the market would replace the plan, private ownership would replace public (or state) ownership, and wage incentives would be typical of those found in market economic systems. Privatization would necessarily be fundamental to the creation of *markets*, though the contours of the latter remain the subject of both theoretical and practical controversy.

The transition policies focused on both microeconomic and macroeconomic issues, though transition policies per se belong largely in the latter category. From a microeconomic perspective, the reform scenarios included the elimination of the planning mechanism and the decentralization of decision making to the firm level, along with strict financial discipline for the firm — a "hard budget constraint," to use Kornai's expression. The implication here is that

Figure 18.1 Reform in Eastern Europe

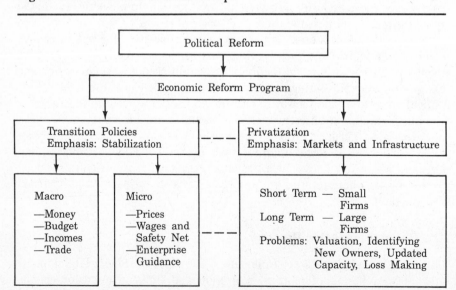

production decisions would increasingly derive from the market and that the allocation of inputs would also be based on market forces. Most important, firms, under a changing price regime, would be required to cover their own costs rather than seeking budgetary support. Changing tax arrangements would require that enterprises become contributors to the state budget. Finally, in the foreign trade sphere, firms would be encouraged to seek foreign markets.

In the macroeconomic context, transition policies focused on the creation of monetary stability (at most, limited inflation) through controls on the expansion of the money supply, limits on state spending and especially on the bailing out of nonprofitable firms, and limits on the expansion of wage payments. In addition, emphasis was placed on a reorientation of foreign trade based on a gradual movement toward a convertible currency — first on an internal and limited basis, subsequently on a full external basis.

There is no doubt that, compared to past economic reforms in planned socialist economic systems, contemporary reforms in most East European countries are indeed fundamental: They can aptly be classified as marking the transition from one economic system to another. What is to be expected for this transition?

It is important to understand that on the eve of reform (transition), these economies are in disequilibrium, and by this we mean far more than simply imbalances in particular markets. These are countries with distorted industrial structures, inappropriate patterns of foreign trade, and fundamental disequilibrium in consumer goods markets. To put it another way, they do not "look like" market systems, the latter having developed for many years under different systemic and policy arrangements. Under these conditions, one might well expect a rocky transition.

In most cases, shrinkage of the economy (that is, a reduction of output in absolute terms) has been anticipated, though the period over which such a reduction might occur is less clear. Several factors account for this output reduction. Some enterprises may fail simply because they are inefficient and unable to function under new financial and other rules. The potential magnitude of the bankruptcy problem is difficult to estimate in advance. In many instances, there has been a tendency to continue subsidizing loss-making enterprises, especially the large, dominant state enterprises. In addition, the disruption of enterprise activities (for example, through the lack of availability of intermediate inputs until market arrangements can be put in place) may lead to the downfall of the enterprise.

Fundamentally, the goal of transition policies is *stabilization* of the economy while basic systemic changes can be made that will make it possible to sustain production and ultimately foster economic growth. The focus is short-term at first, though longer-term issues must be considered.

As we noted in our discussion of reform in Chapter 4, the most critical issue is privatization, because privatization is the means through which a market (the new mechanism for resource allocation) and related market mechanisms (the infrastructure) can be created. But for at least five major reasons, privatization has proved difficult to achieve.

First (though this is more typical of the Soviet Union than of Eastern Europe), transition to market may be taking place in countries where there is little immediate experience with markets. Second, most socialist transition cases present unique problems such that the practical development of markets — indeed, the very *nature* of markets — proves very difficult to define. Third, beyond the basic mechanisms of decentralized exchange that are characteristic of markets, most socialist economic systems lack the *infrastructure* necessary for developing such arrangements. The absence of a modern banking system is a striking case in point. Fourth, issues of both timing and sequencing are important and complex. Are there advantages to rapid implementation such as has been attempted in Poland, or is a gradualist approach better in some cases? In what order should the steps of reform be taken — for example, the freeing of prices, the development of banking arrangements, and the introduction of financial markets?

These issues have dominated the general discussion of transition, and their importance will be evident as we proceed to examine Poland and Hungary in the next section.

Fifth, and most fundamentally, how privatization is resolved determines the long-term distribution of wealth. Accordingly, one would expect a long-term process of soul-searching prior to full-scale privatization. Some of the assets to be privatized (natural resources, hotels, some manufacturing facilities) will be quite valuable. Other assets (assets of antiquated manufacturing facilities) will have little income-producing potential in a market environment. Who will get the valuable assets? Will assets be transferred only to immediate employees? Employee participation would be good for incentives and productivity, but how about the unlucky individuals who happen to be employed in enterprises with worthless assets? If a society's productive assets are divided fairly equally, incentives to use these assets efficiently will be less, but the outcome would be more "fair."

The appropriate way to privatize a society's assets is not at all obvious. A political and social consensus must first emerge before an acceptable solution can be found.

In studying these cases, we emphasize economic reform. However, as we have argued in our examination of other countries, it is necessary to understand the background of each country and the economic systems that have been in place there in recent history. It is against this background that we will consider reform and the contemporary transition experience.

POLAND: FROM PLAN TO MARKET VIA SHOCK THERAPY

Until Solidarity won the parliamentary elections in Poland in the summer of 1989, the Polish economy had been, since the end of World War II, a rather typical planned socialist economic system.[3] State ownership predominated, and though economic reform was attempted in varying degrees at different times, little real systemic change had taken place. Moreover, as Table 18.1 shows, the rate of economic growth continued to decline, and the period saw recurring shortages, increasing inflation, and an understandably declining work ethic.

Beginning in 1990, Poland took decisive steps toward a market economy. This "shock therapy" approach was to be sudden, and in this it differed significantly from the gradualist approach being discussed in other socialist systems. In addition to freeing prices, Poland implemented monetary controls, the zloty was made convertible into hard currencies, and steps were taken to control wage increases.

As we shall see, the "shock therapy" approach has not been without critics. Moreover, although the Polish case quickly attracted the interest of those who study the problems of socialist transition, it was viewed as unique. Thus it was argued that, for a variety of reasons that were discussed earlier, reform was much more likely to succeed in Poland than in a case like the Soviet Union. But before we examine the Polish reform experience in greater detail, we must review what brought the Polish economy to the reform phase and how, at that point, it might be different from other socialist countries.

We begin our discussion of Poland with a brief examination of the setting. Then we discuss the Polish command system, considering the extent to which this system led to distortions in the Polish economic structure. Finally, we turn to the issue of transition and examine the mechanisms utilized and the results achieved thus far.

Poland: The Setting

By European standards, Poland is a relatively large country. With a land area of just over 300,000 square kilometers, it is just over half the size of France. Moreover, with a population that approached 38 million in 1990, Poland is some 68 percent of the size of France in terms of population.

We noted in Chapter 16 that Poland is frequently viewed as having a homogeneous society, a factor that facilitates economic reform. Although social homogeneity is difficult to measure and may well be overstated in the Polish case and in other cases (for example, there are regional differentials, urban–rural differentials, and the like), the basic statistical evidence is strong. In terms of religion, 95 percent of the Polish population is Roman Catholic. From an ethnic standpoint, 98.7 percent of the population is Polish, and only a few minority groups occur.

Urbanization and industrialization have changed the nature of Polish life and customs, but the church, family, and folk ties that have sustained Poland for a long time remain strong. Thus, although Poland must deal with problems of modernization, it also has valued traditions and a clear identity. These qualities make implementing change more manageable here than in many other countries.

In terms of natural resources, Poland is a country of considerable regional diversity, though major portions of the land area are not especially fertile.

Poland's main energy resource is coal; basic minerals and some deposits of oil and natural gas also exist.

As we have emphasized throughout this book, both basic data and methods of computing economic aggregates of socialist systems are currently under scrutiny. New evidence that will make it possible to do different kinds of computations may well lead to important adjustments. With these reservations in mind, however, we note that Poland was reported to have a per capita gross national product of approximately $4500 measured in 1989 U.S. dollars.[4] This figure places it between the high-income countries of the region (Hungary and Czechoslovakia) and the low-income countries (Bulgaria, Romania, Yugoslavia) and at one-quarter that of the United States. Prior to the onset of major economic reform, the bulk of Polish industry was state-owned and planned. Agriculture (representing roughly one-fifth of total Polish output) was a mixed system wherein the private sector produced about three-quarters of the total agricultural product. Foreign trade turnover — that is, exports plus imports — represents roughly one-third of Polish product, again using U.S. dollar measures.

Poland: The Command Economy

The organizational arrangements of the Polish command economy were established immediately after World War II and closely resembled those prevailing in the Soviet Union. There was widespread nationalization of property, central planning mechanisms were established, and agriculture was socialized. In addition to organizational arrangements, Polish economic policies of the era, such as those on investment, sectoral development, and the like, closely mirrored the Soviet model.

Although Poland attempted modification of the command system as early as 1956 when collectivization was abandoned, little actually changed. Over time, private agriculture was neglected by the state, and continuing political protests, especially in the early 1970s, signaled both political and economic difficulties.

The 1970s was a difficult decade for many countries, especially those that rely on imported oil. The Polish strategy in the 1970s and later was to stimulate the domestic economy through the importation of foreign technology. This was not an unreasonable strategy in theory, but Western economies were themselves in the midst of the energy crisis and the recession it caused. Poland's effort to expand exports failed, hard-currency debt accumulated, and the projected impact of Western technology on the Polish economy was minimal. As the 1970s came to an end, it was evident that domestic retrenchment would be essential — a difficult path in light of the continuing unrest among Polish workers. The 1980s began with roughly three years of martial law and an attempt to achieve economic stabilization.

After half-hearted economic reforms in the early 1980s, the rise of Solidarity (which had been outlawed in 1982) proved that major systemic and structural reform was necessary. Even so, and despite the fact that Polish economic performance was deteriorating badly, serious economic reform did not begin until the late 1980s.

The Polish Transition: The "Big Bang" in Practice

The Polish transition from plan to market has been watched closely by a variety of interested observers. Although many of the policy and systemic changes introduced in Poland are familiar hallmarks of the general reform scene, the speed of implementation in the Polish case is unique.

There had been attempts to decentralize decision making in large state-owned Polish enterprises in the 1980s, but these reforms failed to change outcomes (a possible exception is their contribution to the wage explosion that took place toward the end of the decade). Moreover, on the eve of reform in Poland (the reform program began officially on January 1, 1990), macroeconomic conditions there were in a state of severe disequilibrium. Although the exact nature of monetary overhang in Poland (as elsewhere) has been the subject of debate, there was a significant budget deficit, wage increases were out of control, and hyperinflation had resulted. Poland's hard-currency debt position was better than that of Hungary, but the debt that had been accumulated did little to stimulate the Polish economy, the zloty was overvalued, and no debt relief from external sources was in sight.

In the fall of 1989, most price controls were lifted (on both producer and consumer goods), public spending was reduced, and the zloty was devalued. In the second stage of major reform, begun in 1990, the budget deficit was sharply cut, largely through a reduction of subsidies to state enterprises. A positive real rate of interest was to be implemented, and the market was to be used to signal changes in the value of the zloty. The latter was a critical measure, because foreign trade and the impact of this trade on the Polish industrial structure was to be a key component of the overall reform strategy. In January of 1990, the government set the exchange rate of the zloty at 9500 to the dollar (this represented a devaluation from 1989), a rate roughly approximating its value on the black market, and it established convertibility of the zloty for international trade. Many trade restrictions were eliminated, and internal exchanges were set up to handle the buying and selling of hard currencies. Although these changes resulted in domestic inflation, the initial increases proved to be short-term and the exchange rate of the zloty has proved to be realistic.

Finally, wage increases were to be controlled partly through wage indexation and partly through a new tax on wage increases that exceeded established guidelines.

Privatization is a major element of the Polish strategy of transition. In 1990 the Polish government passed a law creating a Ministry of Ownership Change, a mechanism to supervise the process of privatization.[6] Privatization has proceeded rapidly, though it has been achieved mainly for small enterprises in the trade and service sectors. Industrial output in the private sector grew by 8.5

percent in 1990 and is reported to represent roughly 17 percent of total Polish industrial output.[7]

Though privatization has been very successful for small-scale enterprises, the picture for large state enterprises is quite different. For reasons we noted earlier, privatization of these enterprises has proceeded very slowly. In addition, the economic position of these enterprises worsened as the state took decisive measures to introduce a hard-budget constraint. In addition to price changes and wage limitations, subsidies have been ended and protection from foreign competition has been sharply reduced. This new setting has encouraged enterprise managers to reduce costs by restricting unnecessary output and reducing the labor force. However, the strong commitment to rapid privatization was reinforced in June of 1991, when it was announced that a major portion of state industry would be privatized through creation of stock funds, with the population receiving vouchers.

Beyond these changes in the state sector, new guidelines have been introduced to monitor enterprise performance. Furthermore, a new Industrial Restructuring Agency will consider how remaining state enterprises should be handled, to what extent privatization is possible, and what restructuring should take place for those enterprises that are not viable in the new setting. These new arrangements are designed to ensure a rapid transformation of the Polish industrial structure, to make it similar to and competitive with market economic systems, and to achieve this result quickly and as openly as possible.

Note that these comprehensive reforms in Poland cover all the critical areas discussed in Chapter 4 and earlier in this chapter. Moreover, beginning from very precarious economic circumstance in 1989, these changes were introduced simultaneously and rapidly. We will now do our best to assess the early results.

The Polish Economy in the 1990s

It is clear that economic reform in Poland has been radical and has moved sharply and swiftly away from the plan toward the market. In addition to the expanded influence of market mechanisms, decision making has been decentralized, private property introduced, and incentive arrangements changed. By most standards, the initial results have been encouraging.

First, stabilization measures cut the rate of inflation sharply from a reported 40–50 percent per month at the end of 1989 to roughly 4–5 percent per month in 1990.[8] At the same time output fell, though supplies of consumer goods in stores increased. Employment in industry declined by 20 percent during 1989 and 1990, although it is reported that only a relatively small portion of this reduction in the labor force was caused by forced layoffs. The unemployment rate was reported to be 6.5 percent at the end of 1990.

Another major positive facet of the Polish reform experience has been the foreign trade sector. There has been a significant expansion of exports, especially to hard-currency markets. This expansion resulted in part from the devaluation of the zloty to market-clearing levels and in part from the reorientation of trade away from the Soviet Union and other East European trading partners. At the same time, as a result of restrictive policy measures and the higher domestic cost of these imports, import demand declined.

A third qualified success has been privatization. Although the initial pace of privatization was rapid, this early privatization was largely that of small-scale enterprises in the area of trade and services. Although Polish reformers take seriously the need to pursue privatization of major state enterprises, bringing this about will remain a critical task for the next several years.

Can these achievements be sustained in the coming years? We discuss this issue more generally in the next section, but the Polish case deserves specific comment. Quite clearly, the continued success of the Polish transition will depend on the continuing implementation of appropriate stabilization measures. Although this may seem relatively straightforward, it requires cohesion and commitment among policy makers and a willingness among the populace to pay the costs of the transition. Pressures for wage increases must be resisted, and the process of privatization must proceed. To the extent that the latter can be achieved, the contours of new market arrangements can be defined. Finally, although uncertainty in foreign markets remains, relief of hard-currency debt will unquestionably add a measure of flexibility.

Another issue is the extent to which the Polish "success" (if we can call it that) was promoted by Western assistance. In light of the Polish leadership's commitment to rapid transition, the West has provided considerable assistance in the form of exchange-rate stabilization funds, debt restructuring, and government guarantees.

HUNGARY: THE NEW ECONOMIC MECHANISM AND PRIVATIZATION

Early works in comparative economic systems devoted little attention to the Hungarian economy. Over the last twenty years, however, Western economists have begun to pay more attention to Hungary.

As one prominent observer of Hungary and other East European systems has noted, "The Hungarian reform experience says as much about central planning as it does about Hungary, and therefore an understanding of that experience is important for those interested in the prospects for reform in all of Eastern Europe, and indeed, in the Soviet Union."[9] In other words, Hungary is a prototype of economic reform for the former planned socialist economic systems of Eastern Europe, and presumably elsewhere. These thoughts, expressed some ten years ago, remain relevant in the 1990s as Hungary, like other socialist systems, pursues a transition to the market. However, the background of reform in Hungary is important to a proper analysis of contemporary problems and prospects.

Prior to 1968, Hungary applied the Soviet model of centrally planned socialism in a typical fashion. But then, in 1968, Hungary began to introduce by far the most radical economic reform attempted in Eastern Europe (with the exception of Yugoslavia). In the words of one early observer of this reform, "It clearly represents the most radical postwar change, in the economic system of any Comecon country, which has been maintained over a period of years and gives promise of continuity."[10]

Although the reform program in Hungary met with only partial success, the problems that have arisen (conflicts of objectives, for example, and difficulty in persuading participants to change their ways) are fundamental to the reform experience of planned socialist systems.

Hungary shares many features with other Eastern and Southeastern European countries, such as Yugoslavia. It provides a refreshing contrast to the Soviet Union, which in some important respects is atypical. Hungary is a small country heavily dependent on foreign trade. The Hungarian experience with reforming foreign trade, and in particular its efforts to become integrated into the world economy both East and West, is prototypical. The difficulties of reforming the foreign trade mechanism are crucial to the Hungarian economy as well as to the economies of many other systems of Eastern Europe.

Hungary: The Setting

Hungary is located in central Europe. Its land area of approximately 36,000 square miles makes it roughly the same size as the state of Indiana. Its population of about 11 million is comparable to that of the population of Illinois. Although Hungary is not self-sufficient in energy, it does have supplies of coal, oil, and a number of minerals, including important bauxite deposits.

Although it has some rolling hills and low mountains, Hungary is basically a flat country with good agricultural land and a favorable climate. As in other East European countries, the period since World War II has seen the population flow from rural to urban areas and a changing balance of industrial and agricultural activity. Today, approximately half the population lives in urban areas.

Hungary is not particularly prosperous. Most estimates of its gross national product or per capita gross national product place Hungary in the middle of the East European countries.[11] It is generally wealthier than Bulgaria and Yugoslavia and certainly wealthier than Albania; it ranks behind East Germany and Czechoslovakia. Hungary's per capita income appears to be close to that of Greece. In this sense, economic development remains a key issue in Hungary. By the standards of Western Europe, Hungary remains relatively poor; by the standards of the Third World, Hungary ranks among the more affluent countries.

The Hungarian Economy: Prereform

The postwar reconstruction of the Hungarian economy began quite modestly in 1945.[12] Before the implementation of a three-year plan in 1947 (1947–1949), the main policies included stabilization of the currency, changes in the nature of rural landholdings, and the beginnings of nationalization. The first three-year plan was designed primarily to bring the economy up to prewar levels of economic activity. During this time, a planning mechanism was created and the share of national income going to investment increased sharply. The changes were not radical, however, and balanced development was envisioned.

The era of balanced development came to an end with the introduction of a five-year plan in 1950. The share of national income devoted to investment was increased substantially, and the bulk of new investment was directed toward heavy industry. This policy was partially reversed toward the end of the plan period, but it was reaffirmed in 1955–1956.

A number of economic trouble spots cried out for attention. There was an observed need to improve industrial labor productivity, especially through the development of a better incentive system to offset the declining supply of labor from rural areas. Supply–demand imbalances were growing increasingly severe. Waste and imbalance in the material–technical supply system created the need for a substantially modified coordinating mechanism among enterprises.[13]

In addition, excess demand for investment led to substantial amounts of unfinished new construction and to the neglect of old facilities. Some mechanisms for the more rational allocation of capital investment had to be found. The adoption and diffusion of technological advances were seen as inadequate. Technological improvement was considered crucial for continued development of the economy.

This background seems familiar: a small country, the Soviet (Stalinist) model of industrialization, overcentralization, emphasis on extensive growth, rigidities of the plan mechanism, incentive problems, and the resulting difficulties. Against this background, the New Economic Mechanism first promulgated in a party resolution in 1966 was put into practice in 1968. Over twenty years later, it remains one of the most important reform programs of planned socialist systems.

Intent of the New Economic Mechanism

There is disagreement about the importance and effect of the Hungarian reform program. The New Economic Mechanism (NEM) has generally been interpreted as leaving the power to control the main lines of economic activity (volume and direction of investment, consumption shares) with the central authorities, while relying on the market to execute the routine activities of the system.[14] The NEM called for substantial decentralization of decision-making authority and responsibility from upper-level administrative agencies to the enterprise level. In a general way, NEM bears a close resemblance to the Lange model. Let us consider the original blueprint of NEM.

The objective of NEM was to combine the central manipulation of key variables with local responsibility for the remaining decisions. The first change was a significant reduction in the number and complexity of the directives emanating from the central planners. Although annual and five-year targets remained in force and determined the overall directions of change, individual enterprises were allowed to respond to the largely uncontrolled forces of supply and demand. The market was to assume a new role in determining both the input mix and the output mix and in coordinating inter-enterprise activities. In most cases, enterprises were to be freed from compulsory output targets. The plans became considerably less detailed; greater emphasis was to be placed on five-year plans, less on one-year plans.

Second, an elaborate array of financial mechanisms was developed. The prevailing theme was less control from above, the use of profits as an indicator of success, and, above all, the utilization of profits by the enterprise. Profits were to be used in an incentive system for both managers and workers and also for financing decentralized investment. The latter was to become an important share of total investment in the economy under NEM.

In general, the decreasing emphasis on administrative controls would be replaced by what Istvan Friss termed the "economic regulators."[15] These economic regulators would include a price policy, enterprise wage policy, investment policy, credit policy, trade policy, and fiscal and budget policy. The use of such regulators would facilitate enterprise autonomy, while keeping enterprise activities within bounds acceptable to state planners.[16] For example, price flexibility would prevail, but within the limits of tolerable inflation. Wage policy would also be flexible, but within the policy goal of full employment. Decentralized investment at the enterprise level would be encouraged, but investment through the state budget would exert state influence over the general direction of economic activity.

Foreign trade reform was a major component of NEM. In general, NEM called for less detailed planning in the foreign trade sector; in particular, a new role was envisioned for producing enterprises vis-à-vis the Foreign Trade Corporations. Individual enterprises would be encouraged to engage directly in foreign trade. To facilitate this shift, price flexibility was introduced so that some domestic prices could respond to changes in foreign currency prices. As one observer of the reform noted, even with the maintenance of various types of controls in the foreign trade sector, this program was of major importance, for it implied a genuine economic (as opposed to accounting) function for the exchange rate in a socialist planned economy.[17]

The potential appeal of the Hungarian economic reform is evident. As one analyst has noted, its development represents a clear-cut alternative to the East German reform.[18] Hungary has attempted by far the most radical reform of all the planned socialist systems. Although NEM has not been without problems, it has remained in effect for two decades — long enough for us to assess its effectiveness.

From a theoretical point of view, the Hungarian reform represents a significant departure from the Soviet model and a real attempt to combine decision making at the center and the periphery as suggested by the Lange model. The center retained responsibility for certain important decisions, but lesser decisions were left to individual producing and consuming units. In particular, market influences were to determine prices, though in many cases — especially for products deemed important by planners — central price controls were maintained and limits on the magnitude of most price changes were instituted.

Problems of Implementation: The Early Years

The Hungarian reformers have encountered three main types of difficulties.[19]

First, political constraints, notably Soviet concern and vested domestic interests, have limited the extent to which central control over key variables could be replaced by decentralized decision making. The political constraint also affected foreign trade. The political setting necessarily circumscribed what could be attempted and achieved. (Hungary witnessed the abortive attempt at economic reform in Czechoslovakia suppressed by the Soviets in the late 1960s.)

Second, it was quite evident that the structure of the Hungarian economy, like other planned socialist systems, would be molded by the priorities of the Soviet model. No reform program, regardless of political flexibility, could expect to avoid serious problems during the transition period. Indeed, the fundamental problem of effectively combining market and plan mechanisms in a manner consistent with central priorities would have to be resolved through considerable experimentation.

Third, planned socialist systems typically operate under different policy objectives from market capitalist systems. We have examined the problem of comparing economic systems when both objectives and constraints differ. In the Hungarian case, there were important constraints on the achievements of the reform program. David Granick, in his analysis of the Hungarian reform, identifies a number of them — limited tolerance of unemployment and inflation and a lack of desire for sharply expanded mobility of the labor force.[20] These constraints, though important, were not sufficiently severe to lead to abandonment of the reform scheme, although they have led to various modifications of its original goals.

For example, the market mechanism was intended to generate prices to which the industrial enterprises would respond, but intolerance of inflation led to the subsequent imposition of rather severe price controls. Fear of inflation also led to controls on wages, a measure that doubtless helped to control inflation but also damaged the incentive structure.

The reform was implemented with the existing industrial structure. Hungarian industrial enterprises, after the amalgamation of the early 1960s, were large; unlike other socialist countries, Hungary had not developed intermediate-level industrial authorities. Thus by 1970, there were only 812 industrial enterprises in Hungary; they averaged seven plants each and were relatively concentrated geographically. As Granick notes, this spelled an oligopolistic industrial structure in which planners could talk to enterprises rather easily without going through intermediate agencies.[21] In this framework, it is unclear to what extent

NEM actually improved information flow, nor is it clear what impact the oligopolistic structure had on the rationality of decentralized price setting.

The sharp changes in world oil prices in the early 1970s made it necessary to connect external and internal prices on a permanent basis. Staged adjustments of internal prices (both producer and consumer prices) and revaluation of the Hungarian currency to keep internal price increases below external price increases offered a reasonable means for accomplishing these goals, in the view of Bela Csikos-Nagy.[22]

To summarize, in the early years of NEM (that is, into the early 1970s), Hungarian economic performance, especially growth performance, was good. By the mid-1970s, however, it was harder to achieve domestic policy objectives (in particular, the growth of consumption and the growth of exports) in the face of an increasingly unattractive world economic situation. Hungary responded by reversing NEM to a degree. During this period, the use of market-type mechanisms (such as prices) declined, while state intervention in the economy increased.[23] For example, domestic prices became less meaningful as taxes and subsidies were introduced to shelter the domestic Hungarian economy from troubling world market forces. Controls over enterprise financial behavior were strengthened. The result was a slowdown of economic performance, the accumulation of foreign debt, and a less positive outcome for NEM.

NEM in the Seventies and Eighties

World economic conditions of the 1970s inhibited the progress of economic reform. At the same time, however, the reform programs were significantly limited by problems typical of the centrally planned socialist systems. As Edward Hewett observes, though it is true that economic decision making is far more decentralized in Hungary today than it was two decades ago (and more decentralized than it is in any of the other CMEA countries), Hungary's economy is still more centralized than would have been anticipated in 1968.[24]

Although Hungary was able to translate past economic performance into enhanced standards of living for the population, performance slipped in the 1970s. According to official statistics, the average annual rate of growth of net material product in industry was 7.6 percent for the period 1970–1975, 5.7 percent for the period 1975–1978, and 2.8 percent in 1979. From 1980 to 1982, economic growth averaged about 1 percent per year.[25] In addition, according to United Nations calculations, the domestic consumer price index was increasing during the 1970s at just under 6 percent on an average annual basis. This was an astronomical inflation rate by the standards of the pre-1968 period.[26]

Most important, the terms of trade with both the West and COMECON countries turned sharply against Hungary in the mid-to-late 1970s.[27] The inevitable result was a growing annual external deficit and an accumulating external hard-currency debt for a country that relied on imports and was less than competitive in world export markets.

As Hewett has noted, Hungary faced two major problems as a result of the economic events of the 1970s.[28] First, to restrain inflationary pressures, there was a need for demand management, which had to take place primarily within the enterprise sector; it could not act on aggregate consumption, as is typical in Western economies. Second, there was a need to improve the organization of supply at the microeconomic level, a system closely but uncontrollably tied to the foreign sector.

Faced with these difficulties, Hungarian leaders altered their economic policies to address the basic economic problems in the system. The changes of the late 1970s and early 1980s seemed once again to move the economy closer to the original goals of NEM. However, as with earlier reform efforts, bureaucratic inertia and the inherent difficulty of implementing new procedures stood as obstacles to success.

Hungarian economic policy of the late 1970s and early 1980s was directed toward the achievement of two broad objectives.[29] First, an effort was made to maintain the achieved standard of living of the Hungarian people, despite an inevitable slowdown. Second, to bring the trade imbalance under control, a set of procedures was instituted to keep the advancement of the domestic economy within the realistic limits of its trade potential.

Specifically, a stabilization program was introduced, and familiar measures were enacted to bring debt under control. Steps were taken to improve Hungarian access to credit (Hungary joined the IMF and the World Bank in the early 1980s), and limits were placed on domestic demand so that import growth could be constrained and export growth expanded. Curbs on the growth of domestic demand limited the growth of both consumption and investment. Investment could be controlled through changes in the state budget, and consumption through the state's ability to limit wages.

Total gross domestic investment declined from an index of 100 in 1978 to 68.5 in 1984.[30] Real earnings of wage earners and employees declined from an index of 100 in 1978 to 97.2 in 1982, although real consumption grew in the same period as a result of slippage in the private sector. During these years, a variety of measures were taken to improve the convertible currency trade balance. The objective in the 1980s was a gradual but continuing reduction in the convertible currency debt. The average annual rate of growth of gross domestic product slipped from 5.5 percent for the period 1965–1980 to 1.8 percent for the period 1980–1985, a combination of improvement in agriculture with sharp declines in industrial and service growth rates.[31]

The NEM proposed to use economic regulators (prices, investment rules, credit arrangements, and so forth) to improve the efficiency of industrial enterprises. As both Hungarian and Western observers have emphasized, however, Hungarian industrial enterprises have been protected by a myriad of regulations (implemented by the planners, the banking system, state agencies, and others) and protective policies such as subsidies.[32] This support system, kept largely intact in the 1970s and 1980s, had a number of negative consequences.

First, the investment component of aggregate demand was largely out of control and grew rapidly.[33] The drive by individual enterprises to expand investment in order to achieve plan targets and the willingness of the state to support this behavior led to overexpansion of investment. Second, there was excess demand for investment goods. Furthermore, with imports playing a major role in Hungarian industrial inputs, and with little effective control over enterprise purchases of inputs from the foreign sector, inefficiencies were bound to arise. Third, Hungarian industrial enterprises, protected in the domestic market and from world markets, had little incentive to develop effective exports or, for that matter, substitutes for imports.

In light of these developments, government policy began to emphasize equilibrium in the domestic economy and control of the foreign trade imbalance. In the late 1970s and early 1980s, some controls were expanded — for example, direct controls over certain types of enterprise investment. At the same time, emphasis was placed on enterprise self-financing of investment, a policy designed to flush the industrial enterprise from its protective cover. Finally, substantial price adjustments were made in the early 1980s.

Because the use of the price mechanism as an economic lever is of fundamental importance, the matter of prices warrants further consideration. One of the basic goals of NEM was an expanded role for prices as regulators in the system. In other words, prices were to be gradually adjusted so that they would come, more or less, to reflect relative scarcities in the system. This adjustment was to come about by using world market prices as a guide. These pricing goals have not been accomplished.

After many years of isolation from market forces, domestic Hungarian prices at the time of the reform bore little relation to world market prices and even less to relative scarcities. Fundamental adjustments in relative prices were required if Hungarian prices were to reflect relative scarcities. The various programs of price controls and price freezes precluded these changes, and dramatic shifts in the world economy (rising energy prices in the 1970s) exacerbated the Hungarian adjustment problem.[34] Nevertheless, pricing policies of the late 1970s and 1980s once again moved in the general direction of adjusting Hungarian prices toward world market prices.[35]

Further adjustment of prices was to take place in two general steps. First, prices of Hungarian producer goods were to be gradually adjusted to reflect world market prices. Second, Hungarian consumer foods prices were to be adjusted to cover domestic producer goods prices. Some subsidies and taxes (a major source of past distortions) were to cushion the initial impact. Ideally, these changes should force enterprises to face economic reality rather than rely on subsidies. In addition, where highly profitable enterprises have been a major source of government revenue, new revenue sources will have to be found. In the 1980s, price increases have been implemented. The prices of many consumer goods have risen.

The adjustment of prices in the foreign trade sector is equally complex. A major, though largely unachieved, aim of NEM was to move enterprises out of their protective cover and place them in an aggressive posture vis-à-vis the world economy. Achievement of this goal was retarded by a number of factors. First, protective subsidies remained in effect for many enterprises engaging in foreign trade. Second, fundamental adjustments in domestic and foreign trade prices were slow in coming. Third, means had to be found to coordinate the NEM system of trade with that of its planned socialist trading partners.

Hungarian enterprises cannot make rational decisions as long as meaningful comparisons of domestic and foreign prices are impossible. Initial steps have been taken to bring the forint (the domestic Hungarian currency) into line with world currencies in order to set a meaningful, though controlled, exchange rate that would reflect the purchasing power of the forint.[36] Multiple exchange rates, long typical of the Hungarian foreign exchange system, were abandoned in 1982. By these means, Hungary sought to strengthen the rationality of enterprise decision making by making it possible to compare domestic costs and prices with foreign costs and prices.

Many economic systems had to respond to external market shocks in the 1970s and 1980s, but in Hungary's case, the common East European problem of hard-currency debt was a major driving force. At the same time, although some traditional macroeconomic tools were used in the adjustment process, interest in reform continued in Hungary.

Hungary: A Gradual Approach to Reform

The elements of economic reform and transition in Hungary are similar to the general East European patterns that we have already discussed.[37] In the case of Hungary, it is difficult to identify a particular date on which the transition process began. The beginning of 1990 is a convenient date for purposes of analysis, though as we shall see, important legislation was introduced before this.

Contemporary policies are based on a major reform program introduced in the spring of 1991 to guide the Hungarian economy for the next four years. This program is designed to sustain existing transition measures, but it also focuses on speeding up the transition. The directions of change are familiar.

First, the issue of privatization dominates the reform discussion. Hungary attempted to decentralize enterprise management in the 1980s largely through the introduction of worker participation in management. These changes, along with new laws on privatization introduced in the late 1980s, led to some privatization, especially by existing management in small firms. This initial privatization was the subject of considerable controversy; especially sensitive was the issue of appropriate valuation and the potential rights of past (precommunist) owners.

In 1990, a state property agency was created to oversee the privatization process and especially to implement a policy of reducing significantly the size of the state sector. In spite of these steps and despite very liberal laws on foreign involvement, privatization in Hungary has occurred predominantly in small firms; for large state-owned firms, the traditional problems remain. Valuation is difficult, especially in loss-making enterprises. Moreover, it is hard to find buyers for these types of enterprises, let alone to arbitrate the potential rights of past owners. And just as elsewhere, privatization in Hungary is likely to become slower and more difficult as the focus shifts to the less attractive, large enterprises.

In addition to privatization per se, Hungary has addressed the creation of infrastructure (for example, a stock market) and new rules designed to change the guidance of enterprises. Accounting procedures have been refined and bankruptcy laws strengthened so that state subsidies can be curtailed and hard budgets introduced into large state-owned enterprises.

Hungary has also pursued a variety of stabilization measures and has liberalized policies in the sphere of foreign trade, though to a lesser degree and certainly more gradually than Poland. Domestic price controls have been substantially removed, and enterprises are permitted to enter into and benefit from foreign trade transactions. Although there are limits on the holding of foreign exchange, the Hungarian forint is substantially convertible for business purposes. However, the Bank of Hungary has maintained controls such that it has access to foreign exchange earnings to serve as repayment of the Hungarian hard-currency debt. (Hungary has a per capita hard-currency debt roughly twice that of Poland.[38]) Hungary has followed a tight monetary policy designed to create a balanced budget and also to exert financial pressure on enterprises.

Hungary has very liberal laws regarding foreign investment, including the possibility of full foreign ownership with permission. Moreover, repatriation laws are liberal. Not surprisingly, Hungary has been considered a leader in the quest to attract foreign investment, though the magnitude of this investment and its overall impact on the Hungarian economy probably remain modest.

The initial results of the transition process in Hungary have generally been positive when judged against the sorts of expectations that we discussed earlier. At the same time, it is proving difficult to sustain popular support as the inevitable costs of the transition process take their toll.

The Hungarian Economy in the 1990s

In spite of a tendency to compare the processes of economic reform in Poland and Hungary, there are important differences between the two systems, and especially in the degree to which prior reform had taken place. Although some would argue that the New Economic Mechanism was quite limited compared to contemporary reforms, nevertheless the reform process has a significant history in Hungary. The differences between the Hungarian and Polish cases are important.

Inflation has been much less serious in Hungary than in Poland. The annual rate of inflation for 1989 has been estimated at roughly 17 percent. Although the inflation rate increased to about 29 percent in 1990, this performance has been viewed as positive. In addition, wage increases have generally been controlled.

Largely because of a shift away from trade with former CMEA trading partners, the volume of Hungarian trade has declined. At the same time, the Hungarians have experienced growth in exports to Western markets and a generally weak domestic demand for imports — both important developments for the overall trade balance. The good news on the exports side, however, tends to be sector-specific. Hard-currency debt remains a serious problem, and the movement toward a convertible currency has been much slower than in the Polish case. Finally, the Hungarian budget deficit has increased.

The Hungarian economy was projected to shrink by approximately 3 percent in 1991, and associated declines in consumption and investment were anticipated. The state property agency is moving ahead with privatization. The overall relatively slow pace of reform in Hungary may well dictate less sharp downturns and less severe fluctuations during the periods of downturn but, at the same time, rather slower recoveries and a longer time in which to achieve normalization. As with Poland, the effectiveness of the macroeconomic policies being implemented, world market conditions (such as the price of oil), and domestic structural change through privatization will all affect both short-term and longer-term outcomes.

EASTERN EUROPE: THE REFORM SCENE

The transition from plan to market in Eastern Europe is important, not only for those who live with and implement the transition, but also for those interested in the subject of comparative economic systems. For a variety of reasons, if the transition cannot succeed in countries such as Poland and Hungary, it is unlikely to succeed elsewhere.

Obviously, it is too early to render any definitive judgment on these cases, let alone on the more general issues of transition. Indeed, it is difficult to chart even basic day-to-day changes in these countries. That having been said, let us try to assess the outcomes that have occurred so far.

Judged in terms of our earlier discussion of economic reform and projected outcomes in the early stages of transition from plan to market, there is room for guarded optimism as we examine the early results in Hungary and Poland. At the same time, there remain a number of basic forces that will heavily influence future economic trends.

First, although initial political transformations are substantially complete in Eastern Europe (with important exceptions such as Yugoslavia), there are cases (such as Romania) where political instability and a lack of cohesion (derived in part from the political legacy of the communist era) make agreement on reform very difficult. Clearly, in these cases, the path of reform will be slower and much more difficult than in the leading cases that we have examined.

Second, the initial results of the transition have been generally as expected. In Table 18.2 we summarize a number of useful indicators. As anticipated, in all cases there has been a downturn in output — occasionally a downturn of

Table 18.2 Political and Economic Developments in Eastern Europe: A Summary

Status of	Country						
	Poland	Hungary	Czech and Slovak Federal Republic	Bulgaria	Romania	Albania	Yugoslavia
Post Economic Reform	Limited efforts in the 1980s	Important: New Economic Mechanism since 1968	Limited: ended by Soviet intervention 1968	Limited	None	None	Important: Worker management and market socialism
Per Capita GNP – 1989, in U.S. $	4607	6303	7922	3610	3154	n.a.	3409
Percent Change in GNP: 1989–90	–8.9	–3.6	–3.2	–3.6	–11.3	n.a.	–6.9
Official Consumer Price Index in 1989, 1980 = 100	3387	276	120	363	186	n.a.	761175
Real per Capita Disposable Income in 1989, 1980 = 100	116	115	115	126	121	n.a.	114
Current Economic Reform	Aggressive pursuit of transition, privatization continues	Ambitious transition plan in progress: stabilization, privatization, and attention to trade	Transition pursued with caution; initial results not as good as in Poland but positive	Reform began in 1991; price flexibility, privatization, and trade reform	Modest reforms from 1991; price adjustment, some privatization, and foreign investment	1990–91: Limited first steps; decentralization, some privatization, and restructuring	Political turmoil and an economy largely without guidance

Source: Compiled from "Eastern Europe: Coming Around the First Turn" (Washington, D.C.: CIA, 1991).

significant magnitude. Inflation has been very uneven and in some cases (such as Yugoslavia and pre-reform Poland) very rapid. However, post-reform inflation rates generally leave some room for optimism, especially in those cases where stabilization policies have been developed and applied.

Third, we have noted that initial privatization usually proceeded rather quickly but that, after the privatization of small firms (especially in the service sphere), the pace of change decreased significantly. This latter development reflects the onset of major difficulties: the private sector must now absorb large, state-owned, loss-making, and often technologically backward enterprises. The privatization of these firms presents serious problems, as does a setting where valuation is fraught with difficulties, buyers are hard to find, claims from the past must be handled, and contemporary management skills are wanting.

Fourth, although inflation and unemployment have necessitated a growing concern for safety-net measures of various types, there is also a sense that the availability of consumer goods and services has improved.

All of these considerations seem to support a measure of optimism about the eventual outcome of the transition process. At the same time, there are important dimensions where change must be sustained if the transition is to be successful. Stabilization policies must be maintained — a tall order in those cases where consumer patience is lacking. Privatization must proceed, and it must increasingly reflect the contours of new market arrangements, including the infrastructure required for markets to function effectively. These changes must be sustained even in the face of political dissension, consumer dissatisfaction, and an uncertain international economic environment. These restraining forces will in large part dictate the pace and ultimate success or failure of the transition process.

SUMMARY

1. In this chapter we have examined the process of economic reform — that is, the transition to a market economy — in Eastern Europe, focusing on Poland and Hungary. Although important differences distinguish one reform scenario from another, there are nevertheless many similarities among them. Thus, in most cases, initial political reform was followed by the development of a program of economic reform, a program generally committed to the creation of a market economy. This commitment is quite firm, but numerous difficulties inevitably arise in implementing reform. Experience has yielded hard-won insight into the nature of appropriate microeconomic and macroeconomic policies for the transition period — policies designed to ensure reasonable stability as the underlying economic mechanisms are changed. These changes include both privatization and the creation of an appropriate infrastructure to support market arrangements and decentralized decision making.

2. Our examination of Poland and Hungary emphasized both differences and similarities. Poland has been of great interest as a result of its policy of rapid change in a setting where only limited reform had taken place before, but where worker acceptance of change could be judged as a positive contributing factor. Hungary on the other hand, is a country with a history of significant past economic reform, though its greater isolation from external markets has meant a slower path to integration.

NOTES

1. Though they occurred in widely different settings, most pre-Gorbachev reforms in socialist economic systems were aimed at making planning work better, generally through changes in enterprise guidance arrangements.
2. For a discussion of the early Soviet experience, see Paul R. Gregory and Robert C. Stuart, *Soviet Economic Structure and Performance*, 4th ed. (New York: HarperCollins, 1990), Part I.
3. There is a large body of literature on the Polish economic experience under socialist planning. A good reference for the early years is John Michael Montias, *Central Planning in Poland* (New Haven: Yale University Press, 1962). Tracing developments over time can be done through the U.S. Congress, Joint Economic Committee Series, especially *East European Economies Post-Helsinki* (Washington, D.C.: Government Printing Office, 1977); *East European Economic Assessment* (Washington, D.C.: Government Printing Office, 1981); and *East European Economies: Slow Growth in the 1980s* (Washington, D.C.: Government Printing Office, 1985).
4. We have emphasized that care should be taken when interpreting these data. For example, a recent *PlanEcon* report estimates the current Polish national product to be $3410 per capita on the basis of purchasing power parity and $2350 on the basis of the current (market) exchange rate for the zloty. See "How Big are the Soviet and East European Economies?" *PlanEcon*, 6 (December 28, 1990), 15.
5. Although the beginning of the Polish "big bang" is usually dated from January 1, 1990, significant policy changes were introduced earlier.
6. I. Grosfeld and P. Hare, "Privatization in Hungary, Poland and Czechoslovakia," *European Economy*, forthcoming.
7. "Eastern Europe: Coming Around the First Turn" (Washington, D.C.: CIA, 1991), p. 4.
8. Jeffrey D. Sachs, "Poland's Big Bang: A First Report Card," *The International Economy* (January/February 1991), 41.
9. Edward A. Hewett, "The Hungarian Economy: Lessons of the 1970s and Prospects for the 1980s," in U.S. Congress, Joint Economic Committee, *East European Economic Assessment*, Part 1 (Washington, D.C.: Government Printing Office, 1981), p. 522.
10. David Granick, "The Hungarian Economic Reform," in Morris Bornstein, ed., *Comparative Economic Systems: Models and Cases*, 3rd ed. (Homewood, Ill.: Irwin, 1974), p. 219.
11. See, for example, Paul Marer, "Economic Performance and Prospects in Eastern Europe: Analytical Summary and Interpretation of Findings," in U.S. Congress, Joint Economic Committee, *East European Economic Assessment*, Part 2 (Washington, D.C.: Government Printing Office, 1981), pp. 19–95.
12. For background information on these years, see Bela A. Balassa, *The Hungarian Experience in Economic Planning* (New Haven: Yale University Press, 1959).
13. A classic work on the problems of overcentralization in the Soviet-type economy is J. Kornai, *Overcentralization in Economic Administration* (London: Oxford University Press, 1959).
14. Much has been written about the Hungarian economic reform. Works devoted to the initial reform movement include Granick, "The Hungarian Economic Reform"; Richard Portes, "Hungary: Economic Performance, Policy, and Prospects," in U.S. Congress, Joint Economic

Committee, *East European Economies Post Helsinki* (Washington, D.C.: Government Printing Office, 1977), pp. 766–815; I. Friss, ed., *Reform of the Economic Mechanism in Hungary* (Budapest: Akademai Kiado, 1969); P. G. Hare, "Industrial Prices in Hungary, Part I," *Soviet Studies*, 28 (April 1976), 189–196; P. G. Hare, "Industrial Prices in Hungary, Part II," *Soviet Studies* 28 (July 1976), 362–390; Bela A. Balassa, "The Firm in the New Economic Mechanism in Hungary," in Morris Bornstein, ed., *Plan and Market: Economic Reform in Eastern Europe* (New Haven: Yale University Press, 1973), pp. 347–372; and William F. Robinson, *The Pattern of Reform in Hungary: A Political, Economic and Cultural Analysis* (New York: Praeger, 1973). For more recent developments, see Hewett, "The Hungarian Economy"; P. G. Hare, H. K. Radice, and N. Swain, eds., *Hungary: A Decade of Economic Reform* (London: Allen and Unwin, 1981); and Paul Marer, "Exchange Rates and Convertibility," in Joint Economic Committee, *East European Assessment*, Part 1, pp. 525–548.

15. Friss, *Reform of the Economic Mechanism in Hungary*, pp. 18–21.

16. For a discussion of constraints, see David Granick, *Enterprise Guidance in Eastern Europe* (Princeton, N.J.: Princeton University Press, 1975), pp. 245–254.

17. Thomas A. Wolf, "Exchange Rate Adjustments in Small Market and Centrally Planned Economies," *Journal of Comparative Economics*, 2 (September 1978), 226–245.

18. Granick, "The Hungarian Economic Reform," p. 232.

19. Portes, "Hungary."

20. Granick, "The Hungarian Economic Reform," p. 221.

21. Ibid., p. 224.

22. Bela Csikos-Nagy, "The Hungarian Economic Reform After Ten Years," *Soviet Studies*, 30 (October 1978), 540–546.

23. Bela Balassa, "The Hungarian Economic Reform, 1968–82," *Banca Nazionale Del Lavori Quarterly Review*, 145 (June 1983), 163–184.

24. Hewett, "The Hungarian Economy," p. 38.

25. Marer, "Economic Performance," p. 38.

26. The Economist Intelligence Unit Ltd., *Quarterly Economic Review of Hungary: Annual Supplement, 1982* (London: The Economist, 1982), p. 15; Thad Alton et al., *Occasional Paper*, no. 75.

27. Hewett has computed that the net barter terms of trade for Hungary (that is, the export price index divided by the import price index) declined between 1970 and 1978 (with most of the decline coming after 1974) by roughly 20 percent for trade with CMEA countries. See Hewett, "The Hungarian Economy," p. 496.

28. Ibid., pp. 500 ff.

29. F. Havasi, "The Sixth Five-Year Plan of the Hungarian National Economy (1981–1985)," *Acta Oeconomica*, 26 (1982), 1–16.

30. Paul Marer, "Hungary's Balance of Payments Crisis and Response, 1978–84," in U.S. Congress, Joint Economic Committee, *East European Economies: Slow Growth in the 1980s*, Vol. 3 (Washington, D.C.: Government Printing Office, 1986), p. 313.

31. World Bank, *World Development Report 1987* (New York: Oxford University Press, 1987), pp. 195–283.

32. See, for example, Hewett, "The Hungarian Economy"; M. Tardos, "Options in Hungary's Foreign Trade," *Acta Oeconomica*, 26 (1981), 29–49.

33. According to computations made by Ed. Hewett, the ratio of investment to gross domestic product grew from just over 20 percent in the early 1960s to just over 30 percent in the late 1970s, while the ratio of consumption to gross domestic product declined from just over 65 percent to just over 55 percent. See Hewett, "The Hungarian Economy," p. 495.

34. For example, if domestic prices for food products in Hungary were to reflect world market prices, generally subsidies would have to be removed and prices would in many cases increase significantly. Such a result, though appealing on efficiency grounds, might run counter to the East European distaste for inflation.

35. Price increases (competitive wholesale) for industry were introduced in January 1980. Consumer goods prices have been increased on a regular basis. In 1982, the prices of basics such as housing (rent) and rail transit were increased.

36. Traditionally, the issue of the convertibility of the forint has been complex. For an excellent summary of basic issues, see Paul Marer, "Exchange Mechanisms," in Joint Economic Committee, *East European Economic Assessment*, Part 1 (Washington, D.C.: Government Printing Office, 1981), pp. 525–548; and Paul Marer, "Hungary's Balance of Payments Crisis."

37. A considerable number of sources discuss recent developments in Hungary. See, for example, Richard Portes, "Introduction to Economic Transformation in Hungary and Poland," *European Economy*, 43 (March 1990); A. L. Hillman, "Macroeconomic Policy in Hungary and Its Microeconomic Implications," *European Economy*, 43 (March 1990), 55–66; David M. Newberry, "Tax Reform, Trade Liberalization and Industrial Restructuring in Hungary," *European Economy*, 43 (March 1990), 67–96; I. Szekely, "Reform of the Hungarian Financial System," *European Economy*, 43 (March 1990), 107–24; J. Kornai, *The Road to a Free Economy* (New York: Norton, 1990); and Blue Ribbon Commission, *Hungary in Transformation to Freedom and Prosperity* (Indianapolis: The Hudson Institute, 1990).

38. See, for example, the country debt data in Directorate of Intelligence, *Handbook of Economic Statistics 1990* (Washington, D.C.: CIA, 1990), Table 19.

RECOMMENDED READINGS

General

Robert W. Campbell, *The Socialist Economies in Transition: A Primer on Semi-Reformed Systems* (Bloomington: Indiana University Press, 1991).

"Eastern Europe: Coming Around the First Turn" (Washington, D.C.: CIA, May 1991).

Sabastian Edwards, "The Sequencing of Economic Reform: Analytical Issues and Lessons from Latin American Experience, *World Economy*, 1 (1990).

Hans Genberg, "On the Sequencing of Economic Reforms in Eastern Europe" (Washington, D.C.: IMF Working Paper, 1991).

Robert Holzmann, "Budgetary Subsidies in Centrally Planned Economies in Transition" (Washington, D.C.: IMF Working Paper, 1991).

B. W. Ickes, "A Macroeconomic Model for Centrally Planned Economies," *Journal of Macroeconomics*, 12 (1990), 23–45.

Barbara Lee and John Nellis, "Enterprise Reform and Privatization in Socialist Economies" (Washington, D.C.: The World Bank, Discussion Paper #104, 1990).

Peter Murrell, " 'Big Bang' versus Evolution: East European Economic Reforms in the Light of Recent Economic History," *PlanEcon* (July 26, 1990).

———, "Public Choice and Socialism," *Journal of Comparative Economics*, 14 (June 1991).

Richard Portes, "Introduction to Economic Transformation in Hungary and Poland," *European Economy*, 43 (March 1990).

Martin Schrenk, "Whither Comecon?" *Finance and Development*, 27 (December 1990).

V. Sundararajan, "Financial Sector Reform and Central Banking in Centrally Planned Economies" (Washington, D.C.: IMF Working Paper, 1990).

Poland

Irena Grosfeld, "Prospects for Privatization in Poland," *European Economy*, 43 (March 1990), 139–158.

David Lipton and Jeffrey Sachs, "Creating a Market Economy in Poland," *Brookings Papers on Economic Activity*, 1 (1990).

Leon Podkaminer, "Estimates of Disequilibria in Poland's Consumer Markets 1965–1978," *Review of Economics and Statistics*, 62 (August 1982), 423–432.

D. M. Nuti, "Internal and International Aspects of Monetary Disequilibrium in Poland," *European Economy*, 43 (March 1990), 169–182.

Jeffrey Sachs and David Lipton, "Poland's Economic Reform," *Foreign Affairs*, 69 (Summer 1990), 47–66.

Jeffrey D. Sachs, "Poland's Big Bang: A First Report Card," *The International Economy* (January/ February 1991), 40–43.

Mark Schaeffer, "State Owned Enterprises in Poland: Taxation, Subsidization and Competition Policies," *European Economy*, 43 (March 1990).

Richard Portes, "Introduction to Economic Transformation in Hungary and Poland," *European Economy*, 43 (March 1990).

Hungary

Jan Adam, "Work-Teams: A New Phenomenon in Income Distribution in Hungary," *Comparative Economic Studies*, 31 (Spring 1989), 46–65.

Blue Ribbon Commission, *Hungary in Transformation to Freedom and Prosperity* (Indianapolis: The Hudson Institute, 1990).

A. L. Hillman, "Macroeconomic Policy in Hungary and its Microeconomic Implications," *European Economy*, 43 (March 1990), 55–66.

Peter B. Kenen, "Transitional Arrangements for Trade and Payments Among CMEA Countries," (Washington, D.C.: IMF Working Paper, 1991).

Janos Kornai, *The Road to a Free Economy* (New York: Norton, 1990).

D. M. Newberry, "Tax Reform, Trade Liberalization and Industrial Restructuring in Hungary," *European Economy*, 43 (March 1990), 67–96.

I. Szekely, "The Reform of the Hungarian Financial System," *European Economy*, 43 (March 1990), 107–124.

PART VI

PROSPECTS

19 | Comparing Economic Systems: Trends and Prospects

Ⅰn THE FIRST CHAPTER OF THIS BOOK, we emphasized a theme that would remain important throughout: The reforms introduced in the mid-1980s in the Soviet Union by Mikhail Gorbachev had, by the end of the decade, changed much of the socialist world and, indeed, had altered how we look at that world. The typical contrast between a planned socialist economic system and a market capitalist economic system had to be modified, as many of the planned socialist systems entered an era of significant political and economic change and moved toward substantially greater reliance on market forces.

Although the economic reforms in the Soviet Union through the 1980s may have been more modest than those in many East European countries, nevertheless the mechanics of transition (that is, of moving from one set of systemic arrangements to another) are of central importance for the 1990s. The issues that arise during such a transition — and especially in the course of privatization — are very different from those that planned socialist systems faced in the 1970s and 1980s, when energy shocks and lagging economic performance in the absence of serious economic reform captured our attention.

We also emphasized that the 1990s will be a decade in which the world order will grapple with economic, political, and social problems both old and new. For many nations, poverty and the need for economic growth remain a focal point. For many of these nations, it is not clear that planning and socialism should be quickly abandoned. After all, many have looked to the earlier growth experience of the socialist countries as a model for rapid structural change. Moreover, the contemporary transition experiences in socialist systems will be a major new test for market economic principles.

Beyond the issue of standard of living, the matter of pollution is receiving a great deal of attention, especially as we learn more about general environmental neglect in Eastern Europe. But, even if communication on such issues improves among nations, the resources for handling them may not be available, especially in those countries that face a very difficult systemic transition.

Finally, quite apart from changes in the socialist order, forces beyond these countries' borders — whether they be changes in international objectives or changes in trading arrangements — will be critical through the 1990s. Europe 1992 poses a challenge for the United States and its local ties with Canada and Mexico. And it poses an even greater challenge for the former socialist nations of Eastern Europe and the various Soviet republics in a new setting, all of whom must seek and develop new trading arrangements based on rules very different from those of the past. Such changes will necessitate important adjustments for all these countries.

A SUMMARY OF THEMES

No two economic systems are identical, despite similarities of structure and performance. The difficulty of making comparisons does not make it any less important to try to do so, nor does it decrease the need to understand capitalism and socialism.

We have tried to systematize comparative economic systems to provide an understanding of how the economic system influences economic outcomes. The subject is much too broad and diverse for a simple summary. Moreover, the field is undergoing such change that any summary might well be dated within a short period. We shall focus on several themes, which place our deliberations in perspective.

Three closely related questions have been asked in this book. First, what is an economic system? How can it be characterized and how can its real-world variants be isolated and identified? Second, what is the relationship between an economic system and economic outcomes? More specifically, can we identify certain system characteristics or mechanisms with specific outcomes such that the economic system itself may be considered variable and hence capable of being manipulated to alter future outcomes? Third, how do outcomes differ among economic systems?

To examine these issues, we chose a framework of system models and compared these models with real-world systems, looking for similarities and differences. We then compared the performance of different systems by using a variety of performance indicators. Name tags of economic systems are significant only because most people think in terms of the well-known systems of capitalism and socialism. The **system mechanisms** used to manipulate resource allocation are more important.

System mechanisms are organizational arrangements (plan or market), the level of decision making, property-holding arrangements, and the motivation system. Certain system characteristics affect economic outcomes in generally observable ways. Consider one example. Most observers of economic systems would agree that the level at which decisions are made has an important effect on resource allocation and, furthermore, that the more centralized the decision-making arrangements, the greater the degree of *control* that can be exercised over economic outcomes. We found evidence to support this viewpoint in the Soviet case, where a centralized planning apparatus permitted the planners to favor rapid economic growth in the early stages of economic development at a pace that market forces probably would not tolerate. The ability to manipulate resource allocation can also be found (though to a lesser degree) where the plan is used in quite different settings, such as France. Within the framework of this popular classification scheme (capitalism and socialism), we must deal with system characteristics from which we can derive expectations about economic outcomes.

Note that even when we can relate an observed outcome to a system element, our assessment may still be largely subjective. For example, let us assume that past Soviet high growth rates have at least in part been achieved via high investment ratios and that these high investment ratios have been achieved in large part through **central control** of investment decisions. Soviet planners would argue that such a mechanism is justified because a higher saving rate imposed on one generation will substantially benefit later generations. Such an observation may be technically correct, but who is to decide which generation is to benefit and which generation is to pay? We would argue that such a decision should be made by the population at large, not by a central planner.

Finally, the analysis of economic systems has focused on identifying and isolating the differences among them and relating these differences, where possible, to differing economic outcomes. This type of comparison is difficult, so we have worked with readily identifiable systems (such as central planning) and system components (such as socialist policies for the distribution of rewards). In the past, *change* in the planned socialist systems has not been viewed as fundamental.

In the contemporary era, these systems and policies are still recognizable, but real-world variants have changed and continue to do so. In Chapter 4, we emphasized that all systems undergo change. But whereas we tend to view change in market capitalist systems as ongoing and as initiated on a relatively decentralized basis, we have viewed reform in the planned socialist systems as centrally directed and rather more sporadic through time. In the contemporary era, however, there have been reform programs designed to identify a new set of system components and policy imperatives to replace the traditional arrangements. Given the degree of change proposed and the speed with which change is generally intended to take place, these reforms are widely viewed not as simply a reshuffling of existing arrangements, but rather as a *transition* to a new system based on market forces rather than planning. The emphasis, therefore, has been on the nature of the transition process. Negotiating this period successfully will require devising a plan for new system arrangements and policies and — of equal importance — policies appropriate to the transition period. Finally, unlike previous reforms in socialist systems, where organizational change was paramount, contemporary reforms focus on changing the major mechanism of resource allocation. The establishment of a market mechanism to replace the plan calls for *privatization*. As we have noted, implementing the system of private ownership on which market relationships will be based has proved difficult.

BEYOND THE ECONOMIC SYSTEM: POLICY, IDEOLOGY, AND NATURAL ENVIRONMENT

The economist must move beyond the narrow confines of assuming that economic outcomes are a function only of the conventional economic inputs of land, labor, and capital brought together in the immediate production process. Specifically, we have argued that the economic *system* must be entered into this relationship so that we can observe *its* impact on economic outcomes. In fact, we devoted Chapter 3 to assessing the system's impact on performance. The economic system has an enormous impact on economic outcomes. Economic life in the Soviet Union and in the United States are obviously different because of the differing economic systems. Noneconomic forces sometimes closely related to the economic system also affect economic outcomes. The list of noneconomic forces that can influence economic outcomes is quite long; it includes differences in policy, ideology, environment, past development experience, and so on. The impact of these sorts of forces is important in two special dimensions. First, in our analysis of the traditional administrative command model, they influence outcomes. Second, environmental and other factors are important to our understanding of the reform process, especially the transition to a market-type economy. Let us examine some specific examples.

Traditionally, Soviet leaders argued that unemployment (an important outcome) had been eradicated in the Soviet system and that it remained only in market capitalist systems. Moreover, full employment of labor was viewed as a characteristic feature of socialism. Western economists point out that this past Soviet claim was in part statistical myth and in part the result of an overstaffing policy by enterprises. They argue that there was frictional unemployment in the Soviet Union, though few reliable records are available,[1] while lagging productivity results from institutional arrangements that encourage Soviet enterprises to retain unnecessary employees.

Was the achievement of full employment in the Soviet Union an element of the economic system? Was it a matter of economic policy that the system could change if it desired? Was it a matter of basic ideology? Past Soviet leaders would probably argue that full employment is an ideological factor and that unemployment under socialism will necessarily (by definition?) be eradicated. Yet Yugoslavia, which has been identified as a socialist economic system, has a continuing and substantial unemployment problem. In Hungary, under the New Economic Mechanism and current transition policies, the issue is how much unemployment was tolerated as a matter of economic policy as it moves towards a market system.

The Soviet system had a centralized economic system in which a particular policy objective (in this case, full employment) could be achieved at the expense of efficiency. The United States has a similar policy objective (note the Full Employment Act of 1946). With the limited mechanisms in its control, the U.S. government has not been able to achieve this objective, largely because it cannot force decentralized economic units (enterprises) to accept the resulting inefficiency. In the U.S. system, the full employment objective would have to be achieved by some incentive system, such as offering enterprises subsidies to hire people they don't need. We have in effect chosen efficiency over full employment, whereas historically the Soviet Union has chosen full employment over efficiency. Policymakers may be forced to substitute one policy objective for another (in this case, greater efficiency at the cost of tolerating some unemployment).

There is a tendency to identify system elements according to things that can be measured. Because ideology is difficult to measure or even to describe, it is unlikely to be identified as an element of the economic system. On the other hand, a system of beliefs can be a powerful driving mechanism for goal achievement. Witness the past economic disruptions in China, motivated by ideological considerations.[2]

Economic systems are embedded in a natural environment, and that environment affects economic outcomes. In this context, the Cuban economy (which we have not discussed) is particularly interesting. One historical characteristic of planned socialist systems has been a substantial degree of autarky in foreign trade. Planned socialist systems have historically engaged in trade at rates below what one would find for capitalist market economic systems at similar levels of economic development.

Although the Cuban economic system exhibits many components of the Soviet model, one would not expect Cuba to pursue a strict trade aversion strategy, given its very small size and its geography.[3] Certainly if it were possible to compare Cuba with market economies that are *similar* except for their economic system, we might find that Cuba still fits the trade aversion model. However, compared to other planned socialist countries, one would not expect trade aversion to be a major component of Cuban trade policy.

Recently, a great deal of attention has been paid to the impact of both system and nonsystem features on economic reform, especially where reform implies a transition to a market system. Indeed, our discussion of Perestroika in the Soviet Union and our characterization of reform processes in the countries of Eastern Europe has revealed important differences in the ability to implement reform and in the speed at which reform has taken place. Unfortunately, no simple relationship has emerged between system and nonsystem features and reform success. Even so, some generalizations can be made. For example, it is apparent that countries at a higher *level* of economic development find reform easier than those at a lower level of development. Thus we might expect reform to proceed more smoothly in, say, Poland than in Bulgaria. Similar characterizations might be made with respect to natural resource endowment, extent of past participation in foreign trade, degree of past structural change, and so on. In addition to the importance of systemic features in the contemporary reform and transition settings, it is likely that longer-term research will lead to modifications in our picture of the administrative command model.

In sum, it is likely that a number of forces — policy, ideology, and natural environment — will necessarily modify a particular form of economic system under differing applications. We may still wish to classify all such cases as representing a single economic system, but we must recognize the importance of these "nonsystem" (or "system-related") elements. In addition to the traditional inputs to the production process, a myriad of forces influence economic outcomes. In the countries we have examined, especially those with similar economic systems, some differences in outcomes can be traced to nonsystem forces. For example, economic performance in Japan and Germany has probably been affected by a strong, nonquantifiable work ethic and discipline. Performance in China has been subject to ideological disruptions (the Great Leap Forward, the Cultural Revolution). The Yugoslav economy has been strongly affected by regional and ethnic factionalism. Unfortunately, because these other forces are not readily measured, they tend to be ignored by economists and left to the attention of other social scientists.

ECONOMIC SYSTEMS: DEVELOPMENT AND CONVERGENCE

Let us turn briefly to a different theme: how economic systems change through time. Our analysis of economic systems and their impact on outcomes has been cast in static terms except for Chapter 4 on the reform of institutions. Both economic systems and outcomes change over time. A basic feature of Marxist thought is that systems and outcomes change inexorably (and predictably) over time (see Chapter 6). The realization that systems are not immutable has led many observers to suggest that we should examine not economic systems themselves but the process of economic development. Economic development, even in cases where the economic systems differ, may introduce unifying characteristics. Even where the development process is initially carried out through widely varying institutional arrangements, the process of convergence guarantees similar outcomes in the long run. In this section, we examine briefly the nature of economic development, its relationship to economic systems, and the concept of convergence. Although contemporary change would seem to establish a new set of rules for rapid transition towards market-type systems, the background of the convergence idea is more complex.

A truly dynamic analysis of economic systems would have to include an explanation of the mechanisms of change. The literature of economic development has devoted much more attention to this question than has the field of comparative economic systems. Indeed, the appeal of the Marxian idea stems, in large part, from its inclusion of inevitable stages of social and economic development. Unlike other stage theories, such as that proposed by W. W. Rostow,[4] it offers an explanation of how and why society proceeds from one stage to another. Indeed, beyond the stage theories, the development literature contains numerous other attempts to explain economic progress.

Most explanations are made without reference to the economic system. The mainstream explanation of development proceeds in terms of the dynamics of supply and demand and technological change, which cause a structural transformation from a primarily agricultural to a primarily industrial (urban) society. This literature also focuses on the mechanics of bringing inputs into the production process, ensuring accumulation, and ultimately increasing per capita incomes. Why such change comes about in the first instance (and why it has been limited to a minority of the world's population) is largely unexplained, except in very general terms — for example, the "relative backwardness" explanation proposed by Alexander Gerschenkron[5] and the even more general explanation of Simon Kuznets that development is caused by the systematic application of scientific knowledge to economic activities.[6] **Development economics**, for the most part, tends to downplay the potential role of institutional (organizational) characteristics in the development process, though most development economists would argue that economic development cannot take place without the simultaneous creation of an appropriate institutional infrastructure. Few general economists have given explicit consideration to the socialist development alternative in this developmental framework.[7]

If we believe that differences among systems have an important impact on economic outcomes, why do we not examine the process of economic development under differing economic systems? This we can do, though not with the regularity or the sorts of controls that one would like. The principal difficulty is that the experience with economic development under planned socialism is limited to sixty-five years of Soviet growth, the postwar history of Eastern Europe, and the emerging record of China. On the other side, we have more than a century of recorded statistical history on capitalist development.

From the work of Hollis Chenery, Simon Kuznets, and others, it is quite evident that one can observe regularities in the pattern of economic development over a wide range of economic systems, both capitalist and socialist.[8] At the early levels of economic development, labor is concentrated in, and output generated primarily by, the agricultural sector. As development proceeds, the industrial sector gradually begins to dominate the agricultural sector. The share of the labor force in the service sector rises, and the "heavy industry" share of industrial output rises. Furthermore, regularities in other variables — the sources of capital formation (foreign versus domestic), the dynamics of population change, the role of foreign trade in development — can be observed.

Can we, in observing such regularities, control for the economic system as a variable in the development process? John M. Montias, Frederic Pryor, Paul Gregory, Gur Ofer, and others have observed regularities in the socialist development process that can be contrasted with observed regularities in the capitalist development process.[9]

Some general observations can be made about comparative industrialization patterns. The planned socialist economic systems (compared to capitalist systems at *similar* levels of development) stress capital-intensive heavy industry, downplay service-oriented activities, devote more substantial labor resources to agriculture, and maintain relatively low foreign trade proportions. The rate of consumption is depressed; proportionally more consumption needs are met by communal consumption supplied directly by the state; and investment ratios are high and are concentrated in heavy industrial activities. High employment levels are maintained, and income distribution is more even than in comparable capitalist countries. A demographic transition from high birthrates and high death rates to low birthrates and low death rates occurs.

In almost all instances, the socialist model of economic development is *directionally* consistent with the capitalist pattern. The typical changes in sector share occur under conditions of socialist economic development. The decline (or rise) in the consumption (or investment) share also occurs during capitalist development, as does the decline in trade proportions and the growing equality of the income distribution. What distinguishes the socialist from the capitalist development experience is the speed and magnitude of shifts in resource allocation patterns. Viewed over time, changes that require fifty to a hundred years in capitalist societies are compressed into a decade or two in socialist societies. Viewed in a cross-sectional context, planned socialist societies tend to attain resource allocation patterns typical of capitalist countries at a much higher level of economic development.

Given the speed and direction of change that we observe in contemporary socialist systems, it might be useful to compare these systems not to capitalist systems in general but to contemporary high-growth capitalist systems. Such a comparison would in part control for the fact that the socialist systems we examine are of necessity "late developers" and thus have access to technology, for example, that is not readily available to earlier developers.

These sorts of patterns are observed when planned socialist and market capitalist systems are compared. However, there are problems with this sort of analysis that necessitate caution in interpreting the results. Although we have argued that the name tags attached to differing systems are important as a mechanism for classification and hence understanding, we have nevertheless emphasized that system *mechanisms* are capable of being transplanted from one setting to another. Rather than compare economies typically labeled market capitalist and planned socialist, it might be as appropriate to compare economies that use and that do not use national economic planning or that vary according to the equality of income distribution or the degree of public ownership. It is evident that there is a wide variety of dimensions for comparing industrialization patterns, many of which have not been empirically investigated.[10]

A second aspect of capitalist–socialist developmental comparisons involves the time element. Most such comparisons have been made in a limited historical time horizon, because they have been restricted by problems of classification and the availability and comparability of data. Once sufficient historical perspective is gained, comparisons of capitalist and socialist industrialization patterns through time will enable us to consider some fundamental and interesting questions. We have noted that the planned socialist economies have accelerated the process of structural change that accompanies (characterizes) economic development. Their economic structure is generally more "advanced" than their level of economic development. This pattern of resource allocation was selected because the socialist planners thought it would lead to a higher rate of growth of output than could have been achieved by "normal" capitalist resource allocation patterns. In the future, two alternatives are possible. One is that these structural differences will persist; if so, it will be apparent that they are permanent features of the economic system. The other alternative is that socialist and capitalist structural features — and hence resource allocation patterns — will become more similar.

The second alternative has tended to lend support to one interpretation of what is popularly termed the **convergence hypothesis**.[11] Economists and others examining the process of economic development and modernization have observed regularities, even where different systems have prevailed. The basic notion of the convergence hypothesis is that as development proceeds, social systems, their component economic systems, and even the system elements or mechanisms become increasingly similar over time. The fundamental source of such change is the alleged similarity of basic forces facing even widely differing systems, such as modernization, the development of interest groups, factory work, urban living, the complexity of production, and pluralization. The basic convergence case is as follows: Though economic systems may differ in how they allocate resources at any particular time, the differences will tend to lessen, as time passes, in response to unifying basic forces of economic development.

What are the merits of this hypothesis? How does one observe whether convergence is taking place? As we have stressed throughout this book, we can take the ideal case of comparing differing system *models*, one with another, or we can compare real-world economic systems. Unfortunately, this dictum is often ignored, and investigators tend to compare the reality of one system with the model of the other. For example, the inefficiencies of Soviet planning are often contrasted with the model of perfectly competitive capitalism. And in Soviet texts, descriptions of "perfect" Soviet planning are presented as though they represent the reality of Soviet planning.

A more fruitful approach would be to compare the extent to which reality differs from model, to determine whether such divergences are greater in the capitalist or the socialist mode, and to consider how such differences vary through time. Furthermore, the paradigm of the planned socialist economic system is less well developed than that of the capitalist economic system. Therefore, changes in capitalist economic systems are largely couched in terms of changing *outcomes*, whereas changes in the planned socialist system are typically described as *economic reform*.

If we were to compare either models or real-world systems, it would be necessary to compare them at one point in time and then again after change (or reform, as we describe it) has occurred. Only then could we make a case for or against the convergence of systems (or system models) through time.

There are two fundamental problems in the measurement of convergence. First, whether we look at convergence in terms of system mechanisms or in terms of outcomes, how do we select the list of variables in terms of which convergence or change will be measured and evaluated? Such a list would inevitably reflect personal value judgments. Second, even if we could agree on a list of variables, how would we aggregate them to observe change through time?

Would each variable be assigned the same weight, or would some be considered more important than others? In either case, how would the weights be selected? It is difficult to specify a model of the convergence process that is subject to unequivocally acceptable empirical verification.

Most studies of convergence select variables arbitrarily and focus on the change in these variables over time. For example, it has been argued that economic reform in the socialist planned economies of the Soviet Union and Eastern Europe has consisted primarily of the introduction of market forces and the application of profit as a managerial success criterion. At the same time, the introduction of national economic planning or, at a minimum, an expanded role for the government in the allocation of resources has been suggested as the trend in some Western market capitalist systems. Thus it is argued that the mechanisms utilized for resource allocation are growing more alike, over time, in these two cases. Measurement problems aside, one can find some evidence to support the existence of both phenomena — an expanded role for the government in the major capitalist economies and an expanded role for the market in the Soviet Union and Eastern Europe. However, it is difficult to evaluate the significance of these isolated events or jump from them to a general theory of economic convergence.

The convergence literature has also attempted to extend the notion of convergence into noneconomic spheres such as political and social convergence. This approach suffers from the same methodological problems: How are we to establish (measure) the convergence of multidimensional political and social phenomena and, given the multidimensionality of economic systems, make general judgments about the direction of movement of whole economic systems?

There is yet another interpretation of the convergence hypothesis, which is related to the observation of structural change.[12] If, in the Soviet case, capital-intensive heavy industry is emphasized (and the service sector depressed) at an early stage of economic development, will the shares of these sectors "converge" to some "normal" share (as determined by shares in developed capitalist countries) at a later and more mature stage of economic development? Cross-sectional examination of socialist and capitalist systems has found that when levels of development are held constant, socialist systems seem to be under-urbanized compared to capitalist systems. Will this difference persist, or will socialist urbanization patterns ultimately move toward capitalist patterns of urbanization? According to this convergence concept, change in the underlying system can be observed through changes in the observed pattern of resource allocation. Although the notion of structural convergence is appealing, for it appears to be more quantifiable than other convergence concepts, the matter remains largely open for future investigation.

ECONOMIC SYSTEMS: THE FUTURE

After many years of relative stasis, the field of comparative economic systems is enjoying a resurgence and a renewal, both of which will lead to the development and the introduction of new ideas and new ways of thinking. However, many of the basic precepts of the field will remain.

Economic systems have always differed and will continue to differ. If we could relate those differences to differences in outcomes, then we could think in terms of an optimal regime, always allowing for differences in nonsystem elements. In this sense, comparing different systems will remain a cornerstone of the field of comparative economic systems.

Moreover, even though it may be difficult to generalize about systems and outcomes, the study and analysis of system components will continue to be an important focus of the field. For example, it will be difficult to convince the leaders of the many underdeveloped nations that economic planning has nothing to offer them.[13] Most will be prepared to cite the dramatic changes brought about by Soviet planning and will have substantially less interest in the niceties of converting from extensive to intensive growth patterns.

Of course, the field of comparative economic systems is much more than a study of system models and the components of those models. It is the analysis of real-world economic systems and of how these systems can adjust to real-world problems, whether they use the tools of economic policy to do so or need to make more basic, systemic change. Unquestionably, different real-world systems will respond to their various problems in different ways.

The industrialized market capitalist systems must face the perennial problems of inflation, unemployment, and balance-of-payments difficulties. Moreover, they must do so in a new world setting where priorities have changed and the simplistic arrangements of the market mechanism's past may not suffice for an effective future. After the energy shocks of the 1970s and the productivity problems of the 1970s and 1980s, few can take comfort in the fact that socialist systems seek radical reform.

Much of the world remains in poverty. Any meaningful new world order must confront this fact. To what extent can the issue of underdevelopment be addressed from the vantage point of economic systems? Have we learned lessons about the role of government intervention, the nature of reward systems, and how such systemic and policy characteristics might be modified over time? Can a better understanding of different economic systems and system components contribute to a better life for many in the less-developed world?

Although most peoples seek a better standard of living, this goal has been elusive for those living in the systems that embraced centrally planned socialism (or had it thrust upon them). In the 1990s, these systems face many of the problems faced by other, dissimilar systems, but they also face more serious challenges.

Fundamentally, the former socialist systems seek economic efficiency through the transition from planned socialist arrangements toward market capitalist arrangements. We have emphasized that this transition requires a blueprint, but it requires much more. Specifically, effective transition policies are essential to guide a changing economic system through largely uncharted waters. Moreover, while the transition is in progress, political leaders must be able to convince their populations that an appropriate new social contract can in fact be established, that the long-term benefits will outweigh the short-term costs, and that these changes can be implemented within a reasonable number of years.

It is evident from our discussion that these sorts of changes will be more difficult and more time-consuming than is generally realized. Moreover, the trajectory will be different in each case, depending on a variety of important conditions and influences, such as the level of economic development, the extent of past structural distortions, the past and potential role of foreign trade, and the natural resource base.

Although the simplistic models of the past may seem archaic in the future, our interest will remain focused on different systems, system components, and nonsystem factors and on the extent to which new arrangements of these forces can in fact result in improved economic performance.

NOTES

1. For attempts to calculate unemployment in the Soviet Union, see P. J. D. Wiles, "A Note on Soviet Unemployment in US Definitions," *Soviet Studies*, 23 (April 1972), 619–628; David Granick, *Job Rights in the Soviet Economy* (New York: Cambridge University Press, 1987); Paul Gregory and Irwin Collier, "Soviet Unemployment: Evidence From the Soviet Interview Project," *The American Economic Review*, 78 (September 1988), 613–632; S. Rapawy, "Labor Force and Employment in the USSR," in U.S. Congress, Joint Economic Committee, *Gorbachev's Economic Plans*, Vol. I (Washington, D.C.: Government Printing Office, 1987), pp. 187–212.

2. For a discussion of ideology in the context of economic systems, see Alexander Gerschenkron, "Ideology as a System Determinant," in Alexander Eckstein, ed., *Comparison of Economic Systems* (Berkeley: University of California Press, 1971), pp. 269–299.

3. For an analysis of planning in Cuba, see C. Mesa-Lago and Luc Sepherin, "Central Planning in Cuba," in Morris Bornstein, ed., *Comparative Economic Systems: Models and Cases*, 3rd ed. (Homewood, Ill.: Irwin, 1974), pp. 367–392. For a recent view, see Andrew Zimbalist, ed., "Cuba's Socialist Economy Toward the 1990s," *World Development*, 15 (January 1987).

4. Walt W. Rostow, *The Stages of Economic Growth*, 2nd ed. (New York: Cambridge University Press, 1971). See also Walt R. Rostow, *The World Economy: History and Prospect* (Austin: University of Texas Press, 1978). For a summary of different approaches to economic development, see Charles P. Kindleberger and Bruce Herrick, *Economic Development*, 3rd ed. (New York: McGraw-Hill, 1977), Ch. 2; see also Malcolm Gillis, Dwight H. Perkins, Michael Roemer, and Donald R. Snodgrass, *Economics of Development*, 2nd ed. (New York: Norton, 1987).

5. Alexander Gerschenkron, *Economic Backwardness in Historical Perspective* (Cambridge, Mass.: Harvard University Press, 1962).

6. Simon Kuznets, *Modern Economic Growth* (New Haven: Yale University Press, 1966), Ch. 1.

7. Lloyd G. Reynolds, *Image and Reality in Economic Development* (New Haven: Yale University Press, 1977).

8. See, for example, Simon Kuznets, *Economic Growth and Structure* (New York: Norton, 1965); Simon Kuznets, *Economic Growth of Nations: Total Output and Production Structure* (Cambridge, Mass.: Harvard University Press, 1971); and Hollis Chenery and Moises Syrquin, *Patterns of Development, 1950–1970* (New York: Oxford University Press, 1975).

9. See John Michael Montias, *The Structure of Economic Systems* (New Haven: Yale University Press, 1976); Frederic L. Pryor, *Public Expenditures in Communist and Capitalist Nations* (London: Allen and Unwin, 1968); Frederic L. Pryor, *Property and Industrial Organization in Communist and Capitalist Nations* (Bloomington: Indiana University Press, 1973); Paul Gregory, *Socialist and Nonsocialist Industrialization Patterns* (New York: Praeger, 1970); Gur Ofer, *The Service Sector in Soviet Economic Growth* (Cambridge, Mass.: Harvard University Press, 1973);

and Paul Gregory, "Fertility and Labor Force Participation in the Soviet Union and Eastern Europe," *Review of Economics and Statistics*, 64 (February 1982), 18–31; for a recent analysis see Jan Winiecki, *The Distorted World of Soviet-Type Economies* (Pittsburgh: University of Pittsburgh Press, 1988).

10. Pryor has done some pioneering work on the impact of system elements on economic outcomes. See Frederick L. Pryor, "Property Institutions and Economic Development: Some Empirical Tests," *Economic Development and Cultural Change*, 20 (April 1974), 406–437; and Frederic L. Pryor, "The Impact of Social and Economic Institutions on the Size Distributions of Income and Wealth," *American Economic Review*, 57 (March 1973), 50–73. Advances in both methods and data availability now permit more sophisticated analysis of socialist–capitalist comparisons. See, for example, John P. Burkett, "Systemic Influences on the Physical Quality of Life: A Bayesian Analysis of Cross-Sectional Data," *Journal of Comparative Economics* (June 1985), 145–163; John P. Burkett, "PQLI as a Measure of Comparative Performance: Comment," *Comparative Economic Studies*, 28 (Summer 1986), 59–68; and Edward F. Stuart, "The PQLI as a Measure of Comparative Economic Performance," *ACES Bulletin*, 26 (Winter 1984), 25–43.

11. There is a substantial body of literature on the convergence hypothesis. For a useful early survey, see James R. Millar, "On the Theory and Measurement of Economic Convergence," in Bornstein, *Comparative Economic Systems*, pp. 481–492.

12. See Robert C. Stuart and Paul R. Gregory, "The Convergence of Economic Systems: An Analysis of Structural and Institutional Characteristics," in *Jahrbuch der Wirtschaft Osteuropas* [Yearbook of East European Economics], Band 2 (Munich: Gunther Olzog Verlag, 1971), pp. 425–442.

13. For a discussion of reform in a development context, see Sabastian Edwards, "The Sequencing of Economic Reform: Analytical Issues and Lessons from Latin American Experiences," *World Economy*, 1 (1990).

RECOMMENDED READINGS

W. Brus and K. Laski, *From Marx to the Market* (Oxford, England: Clarendon Press, 1989).
Janos Kornai, *The Road To a Free Economy* (New York: Norton, 1990).

Index